ADVANCES IN CORPORATE FINANCE AND ASSET PRICING

ADVANCES IN CORPORATE FINANCE AND ASSET PRICING

EDITED BY

L. RENNEBOOG

Department of Finance and CentER, Tilburg University, The Netherlands
TILEC (Tilburg Law and Economics Center)
ECGI (European Corporate Governance Institute)

ELSEVIER

Amsterdam – Boston – Heidelberg – London – New York – Oxford
Paris – San Diego – San Francisco – Singapore – Sydney – Tokyo

ELSEVIER B.V.
Radarweg 29
P.O. Box 211, 1000 AE
Amsterdam, The Netherlands

ELSEVIER Inc.
525 B Street, Suite 1900
San Diego, CA 92101-4495
USA

ELSEVIER Ltd
The Boulevard, Langford Lane
Kidlington, Oxford OX5 1GB
UK

ELSEVIER Ltd
84 Theobalds Road
London WC1X 8RR
UK

First edition 2006

Library of Congress Cataloging in Publication Data
A catalog record is available from the Library of Congress.

British Library Cataloguing in Publication Data
A catalogue record is available from the British Library.

ISBN-10: 0-444-52723-0
ISBN-13: 978-0-444-52723-3

∞ The paper used in this publication meets the requirements of ANSI/NISO Z39.48-1992 (Permanence of Paper).
Printed in The Netherlands.

This book is in the honour of Professor Dr. Piet Duffhues.

Piet Duffhues has built out his entire career at Tilburg University. His impact on financial economics in the Netherlands cannot be underestimated. For four decades, he introduced modern financial economic theories in corporate finance and asset pricing in his numerous publications and leading Dutch textbooks. He is an all-round academic focusing on the practical relevance and implementability of financial theories. As stimulating lecturer, he shaped the economic insights of many thousands of students.

With Piet Duffhues' retirement, the academic profession in the Netherlands loses an outstanding lecturer, a prolific researcher and a fine colleague.

Contents

Part 2 Corporate Governance

Part 3 Capital Structure and Valuation

Part 4 Asset Pricing and Monetary Economics

Contributors

Peter-Paul Angenendt is Treasurer Middle Office at Wolters Kluwer NV in Amsterdam. He graduated from Tilburg University with degrees in International Economics & Finance (BA and MSc) and International Business (MSc). His research interests are corporate finance, venture capital financing and initial public offerings and mergers & acquisitions.

Arnoud Boot is a professor of Corporate Finance and Financial Markets at the University of Amsterdam and director of the Amsterdam Center for Law & Economics (ACLE). He is a member of the Dutch Social Economic Council (SER) and advisor to the Riksbank (Central Bank of Sweden). He is also a research fellow at the Centre for Economic Policy Research (CEPR) in London and at the Davidson Institute of the University of Michigan. His research focuses on corporate finance and financial institutions, and has appeared in major academic journals, such as the *Journal of Finance*, *American Economic Review* and *Review of Financial Studies*. In addition to his academic activities, Professor Boot is consultant to several financial institutions and corporations. His consultancy activities concern the regulation and strategic positioning of financial institutions, corporate finance, governance and antitrust issues. For these activities, he has also established the Amsterdam Center for Corporate Finance, a think tank designed to improve the interaction between theory and practice.

Kees Cools is executive advisor at The Boston Consulting Group, located in the Amsterdam office. He is one of the experts within BCG's Corporate Finance and Strategy Practice and head of the world-wide marketing and research activities within that practice. He is a professor of Corporate Finance at the University of Groningen in the Netherlands. In both his client work and his academic research Kees focuses on issues of corporate strategy, corporate finance, corporate governance and performance management. He obtained a PhD in finance, masters in economics and bachelor in philosophy from Tilburg University and is a chartered accountant.

Peter de Goeij is an assistant professor of Finance at Tilburg University. He graduated from Tilburg University with a master degree in econometrics. At the Catholic University of Leuven he obtained a master degree in economics and a PhD in economics with a specialization in financial econometrics. He has published in the *Journal of Banking and Finance*, *Journal of Financial Econometrics* and *Finance Research Letters*. His research interests cover various fields such as multivariate GARCH models, term structure modelling, financial econometrics and asset pricing. Peter is also active as a researcher at CentER Applied Research of Tilburg University.

Abe de Jong is an associate professor in Corporate Finance at RSM Erasmus University in the Netherlands. He obtained his PhD at the Department of Finance of Tilburg University. Abe's research interests are in the area of empirical corporate finance and include capital structure choice, risk management and corporate governance. As a PhD student in Tilburg, Abe has been Piet Duffhues' teaching assistant for a course on treasury management. Especially, Abe's work in the area of corporate risk management has benefited from the creative and original work of Piet Duffhues in this field.

Frans de Roon graduated in Business Administration (Finance) in 1993 at Tilburg University. He received his PhD in 1997 in Tilburg and was rewarded with the SNS Bank best-thesis award. Currently, Frans holds a chair in Investments at Tilburg where he is also dean of Academic Affairs at Tias Business School, head of the Finance division of CentER Applied Research and a member of the management team of Tilburg Center of Finance. He is also an associated scholar of the European Institute of Advanced Studies in Management (EIASM). From 1996 to 2000 he was an associate professor at the Erasmus School of Economics in Rotterdam where he was also the director of the Rotterdam Institute of Financial Management. Frans' research is on financial markets (portfolio problems, empirical finance, performance measurement, alternative investments, emerging markets and futures markets). He published in the *Journal of Finance*, *Journal of Financial Economics*, *Journal of Empirical Finance* and *Journal of Financial and Quantitative Analysis*.

Hans Degryse is a professor of Financial Intermediation and Markets at Tilburg University, holder of the AFM Chair on Financial Regulation, and a research fellow at the CESIfo. He obtained his PhD in Economics at the Catholic University of Leuven. He held appointments at the University of Leuven and the University of Lausanne, and was a short-term visitor of CSEF-Salerno. He has published in the *Journal of Finance*, *Economic Journal*, *Journal of Financial Intermediation*, *Financial Management*, *Review of Finance*, *Journal of Industrial Economics*, *European Economic Review*, *Journal of Banking and Finance* and others. His research interests are financial intermediation, banking, financial markets and market icrostructure.

Douglas DeJong is the Murray professor of Accounting at the Tippie College of Business, University of Iowa. He received his BBA and MBA from the University of Iowa and his PhD from the University of Michigan. He is past director of the McGladrey Institute of Accounting Research and director of the Doctoral Program in Accounting. Doug has held a Research Professorship at Tilburg University. Doug's research interests are in corporate governance and economic theory and its application to strategic settings in markets and organizations. He has published in the leading journals in accounting, economics and finance. Doug served on the editorial boards of the *Accounting Review*, *Journal of Contemporary Accounting Research* and *Research in Accounting Regulation*. Doug also worked for the operational audit and management review staffs of the Department of Defense and the U.S. Army, and in the audit and management advisor groups of PricewaterhouseCoopers in

Chicago. He has served as an expert witness on issues connected with anti-trust and as an advisor on international corporate governance issues.

Marc Goergen holds a degree in economics from the Free University of Brussels, an MBA from Solvay Business School and a DPhil from Oxford University. He has held appointments at Manchester Business School and the ISMA Centre (University of Reading). He currently holds a chair in finance at the University of Sheffield Management School. Marc's research interests are in corporate ownership and control, corporate governance, mergers & acquisitions, dividend policy, corporate investment models, insider trading and initial public offerings. Marc has widely published in academic journals such as *European Financial Management, Journal of Business Finance & Accounting, Journal of Corporate Finance, Journal of Finance* and *Journal of Law & Economics*. He has also written two books on corporate governance (published by Edward Elgar and Oxford University Press). Marc is a Research Associate of the European Corporate Governance Institute and a fellow of the International Institute for Corporate Governance & Accountability.

Jos Grazell is a senior lecturer in Corporate Finance at the Department of Finance at Tilburg University. He received a master degree in Economics (Macro Economics) and in Business Administration (Financial Management) from Tilburg University. He published several papers on the subject of ownership structure, corporate governance and performance of the firm. His main research interests are of institutional economics, finance and law, capital formation, company control and asset restructuring.

Vasso Ioannidou is an assistant professor in the Finance Department at Tilburg University, and a research fellow at the CentER for Economic Research. Her research interests include bank regulation and supervision, monetary policy, credit availability and credit risk transfer. She has published in the *Journal of Financial Intermediation*. She received a BA degree in Economics from the University of Cyprus and a PhD degree in Economics from Boston College.

Rezaul Kabir holds the chair in Finance at the University of Stirling, Scotland, the United Kingdom. He received his PhD degree in Finance from University of Maastricht and Master degrees in Business Administration and Economics from University of Leuven. He was an associate professor of Finance at University of Tilburg, and a guest professor of Empirical Corporate Finance at University of Antwerp. He was also a visiting professor at University of Liege, New York University and Central University of Finance and Economics (Beijing). His research is primarily multi-disciplinary, empirical and policy-oriented, and spans a variety of issues on corporate finance, corporate governance, managerial compensation, business groups, insider trading, trading suspensions, stock-market crash and derivatives. Articles authored by him have appeared in several books as well as economics, finance and management journals including *Applied Financial Economics* (1994), *Journal of Multinational Financial Management* (1993), *European Economic Review* (1996), *Strategic Management Journal* (1997, 2006), *Journal of Economics and Business* (2002), *Journal of Corporate Finance* (2003) and *Journal of Business, Finance & Accounting* (2006).

Arman Khachaturyan is a restructuring director of the Armenia Telephone Company and research fellow at the Centre for European Policy Studies. His areas of expertise include: company law, corporate governance, takeovers, disclosure, comparative corporate law, and finance.

Igor Loncarski is a PhD student at the Finance department at Tilburg University in the Netherlands since 2003. He obtained the MSc degree in Financial Management at Faculty of Economics at Ljubljana University in Slovenia in 2002, where he also worked as a teaching and research assistant. Igor has taught various Corporate Finance and Financial Management courses, both at the university level and those for specialized degrees at the Slovenian Institute of Auditors. His research interests are in the area of corporate finance, in particular on the issues related to capital structure and security issuance. In the past, he participated in several applied research projects for Slovenian companies and governmental institutions. His current research is focused on the motivation of companies to use convertible debt in their capital structures and on determinants of market reactions to the announcements of convertible debt issues.

Marina Martynova is a PhD candidate in Financial Economics at Tilburg University, and a research fellow of the European research program 'New Forms of Governance' coordinated by the European University Institute in Florence. She graduated from the Center for Economic Research and Graduate Education of Charles University (CERGE-EI) with an MA degree in economics and from St. Petersburg State Engineering-Economic Academy with an MSc in economics and management. Marina is a member of Tilburg Law and Economics Center (TILEC). Her research interests are corporate governance regulation, mergers & acquisitions, corporate finance, dividend policy and managerial remuneration. Marina's current research is dedicated to the empirical analysis of regulatory environments and other determinants of mergers and acquisition patterns in Europe.

Joseph McCahery is a professor of Corporate Governance and Business Innovation at the University of Amsterdam, Faculty of Economics and Econometrics. He is also Goldschmidt visiting professor of Corporate Governance at the Solvay Business School at the University of Brussels, and professor of International Business Law at Tilburg University, Faculty of Law. He obtained his PhD from Warwick University. He has contributed to the literature on banking and securities law, corporate law, corporate governance, the political economy of federalism and taxation and has published in a wide range of top academic journals. He is an editor of the European Business Organization Law Review, and an associate editor of Economics Bulletin. He has served as an expert on corporate governance for the OECD and Center for European Policy Studies (CEPS).

Gerard Mertens is a professor of Financial Analysis at RSM Erasmus University and fellow of ERIM. He holds a PhD in accounting from Maastricht University. Until 2004 he was director at NIB Capital Bank. Prior to his appointment at Erasmus, he was a professor of Financial Accounting at Nijenrode University, projectmanager and staff member of the Limperg Institute, visiting professor at the University of Leuven and associate professor and

CentER research fellow at Tilburg University. His research and publications focus on corporate governance, (quality of) financial reporting and disclosure.

Theo Nijman is the F. van Lanschot professor of Investment Analysis at Tilburg University. Theo published extensively in many top-level academic journals, including the *Journal of Finance*, *Econometrica* and the *Journal of Financial and Quantitiave Analysis*. His publications cover many topics in empirical finance and financial econometrics and range from performance measurement to emerging markets and from temporal aggregation and volatility modelling to market micro-structure and long-term investment decisions. Theo was Scientific Director of CentER (2000–2004), the internationally renowned research institute of Tilburg University. Currently he is the scientific director of Netspar and of the Tilburg Center of Finance (TCF). Netspar is a network for studies on pensions, ageing and retirement in which many universities, pension funds and insurance companies participate. TCF is set-up to disseminate academic research in Finance to 15 Dutch institutional parties. Theo Nijman is also an academic advisor of Inquire Europe, the European meeting platform for academics and asset managers.

Steven Ongena is currently a professor in empirical banking at CentER — Tilburg University in the Netherlands and a CEPR research fellow in financial economics. Previously he taught at the Norwegian School of Management (BI). His doctorate is from the University of Oregon. He also studied at the Universities of Alberta and Leuven. His research interests include firm-bank relationships, bank mergers and acquisitions and financial systems. He has published in the *Journal of Finance*, *Journal of Financial Economics*, *Journal of Financial Intermediation*, *Financial Management*, *Oxford Review of Economic Policy*, *Journal of Banking and Finance* and other journals.

Maria Fabiana Penas is an assistant professor at the department of Finance at Tilburg University, and a research fellow at the CentER for Economic Research. She got her bachelor degree from the University of Buenos Aires, and graduated from the Center for Macroeconomic Studies of Argentina with a Master in Economics and from the University of Maryland with a PhD in Economics. She held positions as Economist at the Central Bank of Argentina and at the Field Office of the World Bank in Buenos Aires. She also held an appointment at the Free University in Amsterdam. She has published in the *Journal of Financial Economics*. Her current research interests include: relationship banking, financial regulation, bailout policy and corporate finance.

Yiannos Pierides is an assistant professor in the Department of Public and Business Administration at the University of Cyprus. In the past, he worked in the capital markets groups of the Chemical Bank in New York and he has been a consultant in the corporate finance practice of McKinsey & Co. in New York. His research interests include the structuring, pricing and hedging of derivatives, especially second generation or exotic derivatives, the use of derivatives for speculation, especially in emerging markets with arbitrage opportunities, the influence of psychological factors on the determination of stock market prices and the design of investment strategies to benefit from them. He has published in the *Journal of Economic Dynamics and Control, Journal of the Futures and Options*

Association and *Journal of Portfolio Management.* He received a BA degree in Economics from the University of Cambridge, an MBA and a PhD degree in Finance from the Massachusetts Institute of Technology.

Luc Renneboog is a professor of Corporate Finance at Tilburg University, and a research fellow at the Tilburg Law and Economics Center (TILEC) and the European Corporate Governance Institute (ECGI). He graduated from the Catholic University of Leuven with degrees in management engineering (MSc) and in philosophy (BA), from the University of Chicago with an MBA and from the London Business School with a PhD in financial economics. He held appointments at the University of Leuven and Oxford University, and visiting appointments at London Business School, European University Institute (Florence), HEC (Paris), Venice University and CUNEF (Madrid). He has published in the *Journal of Finance, Journal of Financial Intermediation, Journal of Law and Economics, Journal of Corporate Finance, Journal of Banking and Finance, Journal of Law, Economics & Organization, Cambridge Journal of Economics, European Financial Management, Oxford Review of Economic Policy*, and others. He has co-authored and edited several books on corporate governance, dividend policy, and venture capital for Oxford University Press. His research interests are corporate finance, corporate governance, dividend policy, insider trading, law and economics and the economics of art.

Juan Carlos Rodriguez got his PhD in Economics from the University of Maryland with a thesis on equilibrium models of asset pricing. He was a postdoctoral fellow at Eurandom, in the Netherlands, where he worked on multivariate extreme value theory. Currently he is assistant professor at the Department of Finance at Tilburg University, and a research fellow at the CentER for Economic Research. He also held appointments at the Universidad de San Andres and the Universidad del CEMA, both in Buenos Aires, Argentina. His current research interests include: asset pricing models with incomplete information, the effects of the predictability of stock returns on strategic asset allocation and the use of copulas in the modelling of contagion of financial crises. He has presented his research at the Western Finance Association and the American Finance Association meetings.

Ailsa Röell's connection with Piet Duffhues dates from her arrival a decade ago at Tilburg University, where she much appreciated his generous, wise and stimulating contributions to the intellectual life of the Finance Department. She is a professor of Finance and Public Policy in the School of International and Public Affairs at Columbia University in New York, retaining a part-time link with Tilburg University. She obtained her PhD in Political Economy from Johns Hopkins University, and previously worked at the London School of Economics, Université Libre de Bruxelles and Princeton University. She has published extensively in stock market microstructure; her current research includes a survey of corporate governance and empirical work on U.S. securities class action litigation, as well as joint research with Abe de Jong on the evolution of financing and control in the Netherlands over the 20th century, exemplified by the contribution to this volume.

Peter Roosenboom is an assistant professor of Corporate Finance at RSM Erasmus University and member of ERIM. He holds a PhD in finance from Tilburg University. His research interests include corporate governance, venture capital and Initial Public Offerings. His work has been published in the *Journal of Corporate Finance, European Financial Management Journal, International Review of Financial Analysis, International Journal of Accounting* and the *Journal of Management & Governance*.

Anjolein Schmeits holds a PhD from the University of Amsterdam. She is affiliated with the Stern School of Business at New York University. Previously, she was an assistant professor of Finance at the Olin School of Business at Washington University in St. Louis. She has taught advanced corporate finance courses in Olin's undergraduate, MBA and Executive MBA programs, and received several teaching awards. Her research focuses on the interaction between financial intermediation and corporate finance. In particular, she examines the economic role of banks and credit rating agencies, and analyzes how the organization and competitive structure of the financial sector affect contract design and firms' financing choices. Her research has been published in the *Review of Financial Studies*, the *Journal of Financial Intermediation*, and other journals. She has also participated in several consulting projects on the functioning of capital markets in the Netherlands and the financing of the Dutch corporate sector.

Jacques Sijben is professor (emeritus) in Monetary Economics at Tilburg University (1984–2004) and is still at Tias-Business School. He graduated (cum laude) in economics at Tilburg University (1966) and with a PhD in economics in 1974. In 1966 he became an assistant professor in Monetary Economics at Tilburg University and held an appointment at the Flemish Economic High School in Brussels and was guest lecturer at the Prague School of Economics, the University of Sienna, Bocconi University (Milan), the Universities of Valencia, Namur and Bochum and at the Vlerick-Leuven-Gent Management School. Since 1986 he is a guest lecturer at the University of the Dutch Antilles (Curacao). He published several books and published in *Kredit und Kapital, De Economist, Jahrbücher für National-ökonomie und Statistik, The Journal of Financial Services Research, Australian Economic Papers* and the *Journal of International Banking Regulation*. His research interests are Monetary Theory and Policy, Money, Banking and International Financial Markets. He was a director of Studies of the post-graduate course Financial Economic Management of the Tias Business School (1986–2004) and a member of the Social Economic Council in the Netherlands (1992–2000).

Luc Soenen is a professor of Finance at California Polytechnic University in San Luis Obispo and holds a joint appointment with Tias Business School (Tilburg University). He has a D.B.A. in Finance from Harvard University, an MBA from Cornell University and a BBA from Leuven University. His research and teaching interests focus on corporate finance and international financial management. He has published three books and over 100 articles in academic journals including the *Journal of Portfolio Management, Journal of Business Finance and Accounting, Journal of Business Research, Journal of Futures Markets, Journal of Cash Management, Journal of Economics & Business, Columbia Journal of World Business, The Engineering Economist, Journal of Investing, Managerial Finance, Multinational Business Review, European Management Journal, Management International Review, Long Range Planning, Global Finance Journal, Journal of Asian*

Business, *Asia Pacific Journal of Finance, Emerging Markets Review, Financial Analysts Journal, Journal of Multinational Financial Management* and *Journal of Financial Research*.

Jenke ter Horst is an associate professor in Finance at Tilburg University. His research interests cover financial econometrics, mutual fund and hedge fund behavior, and behavioral finance. In particular, he has published papers on behavioral preferences for individual securities, return-based style analysis, survivorship biases in mutual fund performance, persistence in performance of mutual funds and hedge funds. These papers are published in the *Journal of Financial and Quantitative Analysis, Review of Economics and Statistics* and *Journal of Empirical Finance*. Currently, he is working on the effects of conditioning biases in evaluating the performance of hedge funds, the performance of ethical mutual funds and behavioral factors in the pricing of financial products. Jenke obtained his PhD in 1998 on longitudinal analysis of mutual fund performance. He taught various finance courses at both undergraduate and graduate level, and he is also active in executive teaching. Since 2002, Jenke is also a senior researcher at CentER Applied Research of Tilburg University.

Tjalling van der Goot is an associate professor at the University of Amsterdam, where he teaches Financial Accounting and Financial Statement Analysis. He received his MBA from the Erasmus University Rotterdam and his PhD degree from the University of Amsterdam. In the setting of IPOs, his research focuses on corporate governance mechanisms, financial statement analysis and valuation. His studies have been published in international academic journals, such as the *International Review of Law and Economics, The International Journal of Accounting* and *International Review of Financial Analysis*. He has been Guest Editor of a special issue on IPOs of the *Journal of the European Financial Management Association*. Furthermore, he is the author of various books. In 2004 he received the award for outstanding Empirical Research from the Southern Finance Association. He is member of the board of the Vereniging van Effectenbezitters and advisor of Euronext N.V.

Mindel van de Laar is an analyst at The Boston Consulting Group (BCG), working for the worldwide Corporate Finance and Strategy Practice. She has a PhD in economics on Foreign Direct Investment to Central and Eastern Europe and Central Asia and masters in international economics, both from Maastricht University in the Netherlands. Prior to joining BCG, Mindel worked as a researcher at the Maastricht Graduate School of Governance and as consultant for the World Bank and other institutions.

Ger van Roij studied economics at Tilburg University and is an associate professor of money and banking at the Faculty of Economics and Business Administration of this university. His PhD dissertation (Tilburg University) was on The Monetary Impact of the Eurodollar Market. For many years, he has also lectured in the finance, money and banking programs at TIAS Business School. He published several books and a number of papers on international monetary and financial relations and on international financial markets.

Alessandro Sbuelz (BSc in Economics, Bocconi, 1994; MSc in Economics, Bocconi, 1995; PhD in Finance, London Business School, 1999) is tenured assistant professor in Finance at the University of Verona since 2005. He was previously assistant professor in Finance at Tilburg University since 2000. His expertise is Continuous-Time Finance with publications on American Options, and Barrier Derivatives, and Equity-Based Credit Risk (Economic Notes, Finance Letters, *International Journal of Theoretical and Applied Finance*, Risk Letters) and with current research on Asset Pricing under Uncertainty Aversion and Strategic Asset Allocation.

Chris Veld is an associate professor of Finance at Simon Fraser University (SFU) in Vancouver. He received his PhD in 1992 from Tilburg University for a thesis that was supervised by Piet Duffhues and Piet Moerland. Before joining SFU he was affiliated with Tilburg University until July 2004. He has published a large number of papers in academic journals such as *The Journal of Finance*, *Journal of Financial and Quantitative Analysis* and *Journal of Banking and Finance*. He also published a number of articles in Dutch, including several with Piet Duffhues. His current research interests include risk preferences of individual investors, motives for the issuance of convertible bond loans, behavioral finance and corporate spin-offs. He is associate editor of European Financial Management and Review of Futures Markets. Currently Chris also serves as the PhD director of the Faculty of Business Administration at SFU.

Yulia Veld-Merkoulova has received her PhD in 2003 from Erasmus University Rotterdam and her Master's in Finance in 1999 from Tilburg University. Later she worked for the Department of Financial Management, Rotterdam School of Management. Her research interests include microstructure of futures markets, hedging strategies, corporate spin-offs, risk attitudes, and experimental finance. She has published her work in *Journal of Banking and Finance*, *Journal of Futures Markets* and *International Review of Financial Analysis*.

Charles Wasley is an associate professor of Accounting at the Simon School of Business at the University of Rochester (Rochester, New York, USA). He holds BS and MS degrees in Accounting from The State University of New York at Binghamton, USA and a PhD in Accounting from the University of Iowa USA. Prior to is appointment at the Simon School, he held appointments at the Olin School of Business at Washington University in St. Louis, USA and the University of Iowa, USA. His research has been published in the *Journal of Accounting and Economics*, *Journal of Accounting Research*, *The Accounting Review*, *Journal of Financial Economics*, *Journal of Finance*, *Journal of Corporate Finance*, *Journal of Accounting, Auditing and Finance* and *Journal of Portfolio Management*. Charles' research interests are the role of accounting information in capital markets, voluntary corporate disclosure, security market microstructure, market efficiency and methodological issues in accounting research.

Bas Werker is a professor of Finance and Econometrics at Tilburg University. His research interests cover various fields in asset pricing and asymptotic statistics. He has published his work in journals as the *Annals of Statistics*, *Journal of Econometrics* and *Journal of Finance*. Bas holds a PhD (1995) from Tilburg University and has been involved in the supervision of several PhD projects. In the past he has been affiliated to Université de Sciences Sociales in Toulouse and, from 1997to 2000 the Université Libre de Bruxelles (Institut de Statistique and ECARES). At Tilburg, Bas has taught courses in econometrics, investment analysis and statistics at all levels (undergraduate, graduate and PhD). Currently, Bas is the chairman of the Department of Finance, board member of the Tilburg Center of Finance and senior researcher at the CentER for Applied Research and Netspar.

List of Figures

Chapter 3: The Performance of Acquisitive Companies

Chapter 6: Consolidation of the European Banking Sector: Impact on Innovation

**Chapter 9: Shareholder Lock-in Contracts: Share Price and Trading Volume
Effects at the Lock-in Expiry**

List of Tables

Chapter 20: A Risk Measure for Retail Investment Products

Chapter 1

Introduction: Corporate Restructuring and Governance, Valuation and Asset Pricing

Luc Renneboog

1.1. Introduction

From a financial perspective, the 1990s were a remarkable decade. It is characterized by an unprecedented number of corporate restructurings in terms of mergers and acquisitions (M&As), initial public offerings (IPOs), public-to-private transactions, spin-offs and divestitures, and recapitalizations. The first part of this book focuses on reorganizations from different perspectives: restructurings in Europe versus the USA, short- versus long-term wealth effects of M&As, the international evidence of spin-offs and corporate focus strategies, and the consolidation in the banking world. In recent years, there have also been many changes in corporate governance regulation, triggered by a host of corporate scandals. Part 2 of this book will cover these issues on the international and domestic levels. It also deals with the effectiveness of specific corporate governance devices like shareholder's lock-in agreements and managerial stock options. In Part 3, the focus is on the changes in and the determinants of capital structure. In particular, the authors discuss convertible debt issues, give a historical perspective of the evolution of the capital structure and also give an explanation for the importance of the interbank loan market. Asset pricing and monetary economics is the topic of the last part of the book. Here, models to improve portfolio theories and interest-rate structures are proposed, momentum in stock prices is analysed and the reasons for the changes in the monetary policy of the central banks over the past three decades are examined.

1.2. Corporate Restructuring

In Chapter 2, the aim of Martynova and Renneboog is twofold: they provide a comprehensive overview of the European takeover market in the 1990s and investigate the determinants of the value that the M&As are expected to create. The European-takeover market

Advances in Corporate Finance and Asset Pricing
Edited by L. Renneboog
© 2006 Elsevier B.V. All rights reserved.
ISBN: 0-444-52723-0

rivals its US counterpart in number of deals, in average deal value and in the degree of hostility. The primary reasons for the surge in takeovers are the equity markets boom, deregulation (e.g. in the financial sector) and privatizations (both in Western Europe, like in France, and in Central Europe), technological innovations (e.g. the Internet applications and the dynamics of the telecommunication sector) and the process of globalization of markets (including the further homogenization of the Continental European markets resulting from the introduction of the Euro). Martynova and Renneboog calculate the cumulative average abnormal returns (CAARs) at the announcement of the takeover and over the price runup period: these CAARs amount to more than 21%, but most of these returns are generated prior to the first public announcement. It seems that information leakages, trading on rumours or insider trading are responsible for the large price runup. As documented in the M&A literature of previous takeover waves, the target shareholders are able to capture most of the expected value creation because the CAARs of the bidders are less than 1%. A more detailed analysis of the bidders' CAARs reveals that the bidders' shareholders react positively to a friendly M&A but frown on a hostile bid or a tender offer. The authors show evidence that the announcement returns vary substantially by the means of payment whereby all-cash bids trigger higher target returns and all-equity bids depress the bidder returns. There is also a remarkable difference in target returns between domestic deals in the UK and Continental Europe. This difference is also visible in the cross-border acquisitions. The reason brought forward in Chapter 2 relates to differences in corporate governance between the (Anglo)-American governance regime and the block-holder-based system of Continental Europe. The former is characterized by better accounting standards, a better developed capital market, a higher degree of transparency and better shareholder's protection mechanisms. There is also evidence that the announcement of a focus strategy generates significantly higher abnormal returns than the announcement of diversification into an unrelated business segment. Finally, Martynova and Renneboog demonstrate that takeovers occurring at a later stage of the takeover wave trigger lower gains to shareholders than M&As at the beginning of the wave. For both bidding and target firms, the lowest 6-month CAARs are realized in M&As that occur at the end of the wave (2000–2001) and many M&A deals undertaken in the late 1990s destroy bidder shareholders' value. Unprofitable takeovers at the later stages of the wave result from limited information processing, hubris and managerial self-interest.

Whereas Chapter 2 focuses on the expectations about the synergetic value at the announcement of the deal, Cools and van de Laar take a different perspective in Chapter 3. They study the long-term value creation of US firms with an active acquisition strategy. They contrast this to the strategies of firms that grow via frequent acquisitions and through organic growth. They demonstrate that the growth rate of highly acquisitive companies is almost twice as high as that of organic growers but — logically — only creates shareholders' value if the operating returns are above the cost of capital. Unsurprisingly, frequent bidders grow twice as fast as organically growing firms. However, the long-term stock performance of acquisitive companies only slightly surpasses that of companies with organic or mixed growth strategies. The authors explain this finding by the fact that the bidding firms pay high premiums of usually 20–30% for the target firms, which undermines the long-term value creation of the merged firm. Consistent with finance theory, Cools and van de Laar report that only companies that grow acquisitively at operating returns above the cost of capital generate superior stock returns. An important question in the context of Chapter 3 is whether the performance of the acquirers results from their acquisition strategies or whether it is the other way around (only successful firms with high performance undertake acquisitions). While the operating returns of the frequent bidders equal, at best, those of other firms, the (slightly) superior market performance of the frequent bidders may be due to the growth through acquisitions. Finally, there is also some evidence that frequent bidders learn from undertaking multiple acquisitions.

Chapter 4 complements the conclusions from the two previous chapters as it examines the reverse process, namely *spin-offs*. There is strong evidence that divestitures are expected to create value for the shareholders (as the abnormal returns on the announcement of a divestitures are significantly positive). This positive effect is not limited to the expectations of the short run but excess returns are also visible up to 3 years following the restructuring. A spin-off is a special case of a divestiture whereby the shareholders receive a *pro rata* distribution related to part of the company or a subsidiary and hold subsequent to the transaction shares in two companies (the mother company and the subsidiary). Veld and Veld-Merkoulova investigate both the short-run and long-term performance of 156 European spin-offs over the 1990s. Like in the USA, European spin-offs are positively received by the stock market: the CAAR immediately around the event day amounts to 2.6%, but differs significantly between firms enhancing the corporate focus by means of a spin-off and firms retaining a diversified strategy. The former have CAARs of 3.6%, whereas the latter trigger abnormal returns of merely 0.8%. The difference in focus/diversification strategy seems to be the only reason to explain the difference as short-run returns as neither the level of information asymmetry at the time of the spin-off nor the corporate governance regime of the firm is able to explain the difference in the market reaction at a spin-off announcement. One does not expect to see any effect of the spin-off in the long run because according to the efficient market hypothesis, the positive effects of the spin-off should be incorporated in the announcement date returns. Veld and Veld-Merkoulova calculate long-run excess returns by taking the difference between a company's return and that of a matched firm. They find that the differences in return between the parents, subsidiaries and pro-forma combined firms and a matched portfolio, are neither economically nor statistically insignificant. Hence, they conclude that European capital markets react efficiently to the information released at the spin-off announcements.

The sector which has experienced the most dramatic changes due to the liberalization and deregulation is the financial sector. Interbank competition has increased substantially and the difference between traditional financial institutions and non-banking financial institutions (like mutual funds, insurance companies) has become more blurred. Furthermore, even commercial companies have entered the credit card business and financial market innovations challenge the banks' traditional lending products. Many product innovations and securitization (zero-coupon bonds, collateralized mortgage obligations, Eurodollars, warrants, callable bonds and all kinds of derivatives) have struck root, frequently aided by the revolution in information technology. In this context of rapid change, Boot and Schmeits ask in Chapter 5 the question whether or not the traditional relationship-banking will survive given the current focus on transaction-oriented financial markets. Their answer is affirmative: they argue that the fundamentals of banking have *not* changed and that a deviation from relationship-banking has undermined the competitive position of banks. Subsequently, they think about how modern banking will evolve, what its optimal scale is and which activities ought to be combined to create an optimal scope. In other words, they are evaluating the use of bank alliances, joint ventures and M&As in banking. It is generally believed that in a fiercely competitive environment, banks can quickly and significantly increase efficiency by merging. This process is thought to lead to efficiency gains resulting from cost-savings and economies of scale. However, Boot and Schmeits dismiss these popular explanations and point out that the empirical evidence on scale and scope economies in banking is far from conclusive. They doubt whether the anticipated economies resulting from bank M&A activity are large enough to justify consolidation and scope expansion. The authors believe that relationship-banking offers distinct benefits, and see it as the banks' *raison d'être*.

In Chapter 6, Degryse, Ongena and Penas also focus on the banking sector but take a different perspective. They are contemplating the consequences of the far-reaching changes in the financial sector on corporate growth and innovation in Europe. Can the Lisbon Agenda to make Europe by 2010 "the most competitive and dynamic knowledge-based economy in the world, capable of sustainable economic growth with more and better jobs and greater social cohesion" be realized in a world with rapid financial innovations? This question is answered negatively as they show that financial integration resulting from escalating competition and consolidation in the European banking sector may jeopardize the funding of start-ups and other small and young firms. Fiercer interbank competition may undermine vital risk-sharing between banks and innovators, while banking consolidation may make banks unwilling or unable to handle small firm loan applications, as existing information in bank–firm relationships may evaporate. However, the authors believe that these problems are transitory. Weighing the current evidence, Degryse, Ongena and Penas argue that competition and relationship-finance are not necessarily inimical and that other existing or *de novo* banks may accommodate the denied loan applicants. In addition, the rapidly deepening venture capital markets in Europe will play a key role in the "filling up the potential financing gap".

1.3. Corporate Governance

McCahery and Khachaturyan give an overview of the current transatlantic corporate governance debate in Chapter 7. They state that recent financial scandals at Enron and Parmalat involved questionable dealings that took on a global dimension. The Sarbanes-Oxley Act (SOXA) of 2002 was designed to improve the governance and accountability of boards, managers and gatekeepers by inducing increased oversight and monitoring of US-listed companies and reputational intermediaries. As SOXA also applies to non-US firms that are listed on a US exchange and obliges European Union (EU) audit firms to register with the US Public Accounting Oversight Board, this extraterritorial application has triggered widespread criticism in Europe. EU policy-makers quickly responded to the US scandals by accelerating their own company law modernization and corporate governance reform program that was earlier instituted by the Commission through the High-Level Working Group. In order to establish a new framework for corporate governance, the EU launched its Action Plan in May 2003. The Action Plan is intended to give a fresh and ambitious impetus to EU company-law harmonization and is meant to meet three challenges in the area of corporate governance: (i) improving the integrity and accountability of board members, (ii) restoring the auditors' credibility and (iii) promoting fair presentation of the company through sound and reliable accounting and, hence, restoring investor confidence and fostering efficiency and competitiveness of businesses in the EU.

In Chapter 8, de Jong, DeJong, Mertens and Wasley study the unique corporate governance system of the Netherlands and assess the effectiveness of the self-regulation initiative in the Netherlands as outlined by the Committee on Corporate Governance in 1997. A key element of the report was its reliance on self-enforcement, through market forces, to implement and enforce its recommendations. When domestic Dutch firms reach a certain size, they are legally required to organize as a *structured regime*, which removes numerous powers from shareholders. For example, the supervisory board elects the members of the management board as well as its *own* members. Consequently, de Jong et al. expect that this extreme form of separation of ownership from control has a negative relation with firm value. Indeed, they demonstrate that firms under the legally required structured regime exhibit a significantly lower Tobin's Q. Furthermore, contrary to the role of outside monitoring, they find that outside and industrial shareholders have a negative influence on firm value in the Netherlands. This implies that outside institutions do not play a significant monitoring role. de Jong et al. conclude that self-regulation, which relies on monitoring without enforcement by either exchanges or governments, or where there is limited or no outside monitoring, is unlikely to be successful. They cast considerable doubt on the success of other (similar) self-regulation initiatives undertaken by EU countries.

In the following two chapters, the focus is on various corporate governance devices, which are designed to reduce asymmetric information between the market and the insiders, namely lock-in contracts (Chapter 9), and pay-for-performance managerial remuneration contracts (Chapter 10). During the late 1990s, many Western European countries saw the emergence of stock market segments attracting high-growth and high-technology firms (e.g. the Euro New Markets, Easdaq). Their initial success was followed by a painful downfall in 2000 along with the severe stock market decline. Several markets were even closed down or restructured (e.g. the *Neuer Markt*). Angenendt, Goergen and Renneboog focus in Chapter 9 on IPOs on the French *Nouveau Marché*. In young, high-technology firms there is usually a high degree of asymmetric information between the existing shareholders, the underwriter and the public. One way to mitigate such asymmetric information is the use of shareholder's lock-in contracts. These contracts comprehend the prohibition for the locked-in shareholders to sell a certain percentage of their shares for a specified period after the IPO. The duration of the lock-in agreement and the percentage of shares locked in may signal the commitment of the pre-IPO shareholders who hold on to (part of) their shares at the IPO. In most Continental European countries (and contrary to the USA), specific types of shareholders (usually insiders, directors and founders) are subject to mandatory lock-in contracts. However, Angenendt et al. observe that most firms apply voluntary lock-in contracts (which may differ across shareholder types) and contracts which are more stringent than the minimum requirement. The authors study the price and volume effects at the expiry of the lock-in agreements and find that the abnormal returns and the trading volume increase at the lock-in. These effects are especially pronounced at the expiry dates of insider lock-in contracts. Angenendt et al. do not find significant abnormal returns at the expiries of the lock-in contracts with venture capitalists, even though trading volume increases at their lock-in expiry. The authors argue that if lock-in contracts and the degree of under-pricing are substitute signals of firm quality, a positive relation is expected between under-pricing and the abnormal returns at expiry. However, there is no evidence of that relation for them to conclude that the two signalling devices are complementary.

van der Goot, Mertens and Roosenboom explain in Chapter 10 that the agency problems which arise at the flotation of a firm can be reduced by mean of stock options. This way, managers bear the wealth consequences of their decisions and may, hence, be incentivized to act in the interest of outside shareholders. While this sounds theoretically plausible, the reality is different. In numerous recent academic studies, it is shown that the granting of stock options does not lead to value maximization. Indeed, option grants to top management are largely related to accounting performance. van der Goot et al. study option grants and exercises for a sample of Dutch IPOs. At the IPO, there is substantial dilution of the managerial ownership (from 52% prior to the IPO to 35% after the IPO). While stock option grants may mitigate the negative effects of managerial ownership dilution, at the end of the second fiscal year — after the year of IPO — 86% of the stock option grants at the IPO have already been exercised. Therefore, the authors conclude that the incentives from stock options are short lived. They also show that stock option grants are positively related to a firm's accounting and stock market performance and its growth opportunities. When they turn to the exercise of stock options, they report that the holders of the stock options are more ready not to exercise their options when their firm experiences a strong stock price performance. Early exercise usually occurs in periods of active trading in the firm's stock and when the firm's dividend payout ratio is high.

Grazell concludes the corporate governance part of this book in Chapter 11. He describes the origins of the changes in corporate governance regimes, which we have witnessed over the past decade and a half. The main stimuli were accounting scandals, minority shareholder expropriation, corporate mismanagement and excessive managerial remuneration policies. Grazell subsequently comes up with a taxonomy of the relation between institutions and corporate governance based on theories of institutional economics. He also subsequently turns to the modern law and finance theories, which related corporate governance to legal origin and the degree of protection of the various stakeholders. He concludes with a concise overview of some key aspects of corporate governance codes and discusses the relation between institutions, corporate governance and firm performance.

1.4. Capital Structure and Valuation

In Part 3 of this book, we first focus on capital structure decisions, like the issue of convertible bonds (Chapter 12), the financial structure of Dutch-listed firms (Chapter 14) and how the financial structure has evolved over time (Chapter 13). This part also includes two chapters on the capital structure of banks: Chapter 15 is on the market of syndicated loans and Chapter 16 explains theoretically why interbank loans exist. This part concludes with a chapter that relates corporate growth to share price performance (Chapter 17).

Loncarski, ter Horst and Veld argue in Chapter 12 that the evidence on the motives for the issuance of convertible debt is far from conclusive. As convertible debt is a source of financing in between debt and equity, the stock market reacts negatively on the announce-ment of a convertible debt issue. The firm can model convertible debt in different ways: it can either be more debt-like or be more equity-like. The market response to the issue of equity-like convertible debt is similar to the market reaction to equity issues, which is con-sistent with the Myers-Majluf adverse selection model. Loncarski et al. argue that convert-ible debt is generally regarded as a delayed-equity instrument. In contrast, little support is found for the usage of convertible debt to shift corporate risk. The interesting reasons for a convertible issue have not been investigated thoroughly (e.g the tax motivation). To the authors' surprise, surveys reveal that managers still find a lower coupon rate of convertible debt as an important argument for its issuance: given that convertibles include a conversion feature, the view that convertibles are a cheaper source of financing than straight debt is deceptive. They conclude that there is a large discrepancy between the theoretical and prac-tical reasons of why companies issue convertible bonds. Analysis of surveys shows that practitioners adhere to irrational motives to issue convertibles whereas the theoretical liter-ature presents a number of rational motives. These rational motives are confirmed in some of the cross-sectional studies. The authors reconcile these contradictory findings by argu-ing that *managers act smarter than they speak* (they follow rational motives without being aware of this). The second explanation is that the proxies to measure abstract concepts such as informational asymmetry in the cross-sectional studies are weak.

In Chapter 13, de Jong and Röell show that the financial markets and institutions in the Netherlands have been historically shaped by a unique mix of influences: a stock exchange culture dating back to the Dutch golden age of sea-borne-trading dominance, a legal sys-tem handed down from a brief period of French occupation, and strong influences from neighbouring Germany as well as from the Anglo-American countries. In order to capture the evolution in the financing of Dutch-listed firms in the twentieth century, the authors examine capital structure in three different time periods: 1923, 1958 and 1993. In the early part of the twentieth century, liquidity was the keyword: firms aim to optimize liquid assets and the risk of a liquidity crisis is avoided at the expense of excessive liquidity. de Jong and Röell then jump to 1958, when the consensus view on financial structure is that the maturities of debt ought to be matched with those of the assets — short debt is used for current assets, while long-debt finances fixed assets. By 1993, modern (initially Anglo-American) theories on capital structure had already been introduced for some time (e.g. some Modigliani and Miller's irrelevance theorems, costs and benefits of debt and equity financing): the optimal debt ratio minimizes the cost of the capital.

In Chapter 14, Kabir connects to the previous chapter as he studies the capital structure of modern-listed Dutch firms. He hereby focuses on security offerings and intends to answer the two core-financing decisions: "How much profit should be ploughed back into the business rather than paid out as dividends?" and "What proportion of the deficit should be financed by borrowing rather than by an issue of equity?" The internal source of financ-ing is retaining earnings while the external ones consist of private sources like bank loans and private placements, or public sources like the issue of new securities in domestic and foreign capital markets. As long as the total cash flow generated by the assets of the firm remains unchanged, financing decisions do not change the overall firm value. Kabir shows that these assumptions have been relaxed one by one in the academic literature. Capital structure decisions attempt to reduce taxes and bankruptcy costs, and/or are used as signalling, bonding or control devices. The empirical evidence demonstrates that there is a decline in the share price at the announcement of common stock and convertible bond offerings, and an insignificant stock price movement at the announcement of straight debt. Kabir shows that most Dutch companies have a preference for internal funds, as have most firms in Western economies. This source of funds is the cheapest (there is the finance-pecking order) but also entails that management is not subjected to the disciplining from the banks or the capital market. In line with previous research, Kabir shows that there is a significant decline in shareholders' wealth when companies announce rights issues in the Netherlands. This reflects the fact that the choice of an equity issue is regarded as an important signal to the markets. Kabir also shows that companies issue shares when these are overvalued. Finally, he discusses the shareholders' wealth effect of debt financing, e.g. the issue of convertible debt and the issue of warrants by Dutch corporations do not trigger a significant change in the share prices.

van Roij defines syndicated loans in Chapter 15 as loans granted by a syndicate of banks and based on a joint loan agreements. This credit instrument originated in the 1970s of last century and it quickly developed as the most attractive and important international financing instrument in the early 1980s. While the market faded as of the second half of the 1980s, it strongly re-emerged as an important global funding instrument since the early 1990s. van Roij explains the main characteristics of syndicated loans. Given that the secondary market is liquid, the interest of non-bank financial institutions in syndicated loans as an investment outlet has increased. This secondary market has stimulated the integration of bank loan markets and bond markets, and has contributed to the role of non-bank financial institutions as investors in syndicated loan participations. As a consequence, more opportunities have arisen for risk diversification, market integration and market liquidity.

The capital structure of banks is analysed by Ioannidou and Pierides in Chapter 16. The authors show that financial institutions have been selling loans to other banks for over a century and that this market has recently expanded more rapidly. These loans sales are either a cheaper source of finance or a way to diversify a bank's portfolio as it is a cheaper source of finance than issuing equity or raising deposits. Loan sales provide a funding source that is not subject to deposit insurance premiums or reserve requirements, which reduces its cost. Also, by shrinking the balance sheet, loan sales allow a bank to reduce its capital requirements. Furthermore, sales with recourse or backed by standby letters of credit could still be cheaper than risky debt, since they have payoff characteristics similar to secured debt. Whereas past research only examines the expected value of loan sales, Ioannidou and Pierides show that loans sales are a cheaper source of finance by examining how the correlation structure of loan returns affects the bank's choice of financing. Their theoretical model suggest that if the bank's loans are not all positively correlated, the bank prefers to sell loans in the secondary market instead of issuing equity. In contrast, when all loans are positively correlated, there is no strategy that results in a gain for the bank's existing shareholders.

Soenen concentrates in Chapter 17 on the relentless search for growth. He gives a few examples of firms for which this quest for growth has turned into a disaster. He argues that the search for growth is not new but symptomatic for many companies with disappointing consequences for the shareholders. While the fastest way to grow is through takeovers, this is significantly different for organic growth strategies. According to Soenen, real growth depends on innovations. Indeed, while some companies focus on the top line of the income statement, they erroneously ignore the bottom line. Soenen shows that although the corporate profitability measures generally rise with earnings and sales growth, an optimal point exists beyond which further growth destroys shareholder's value. As an investor you would receive the highest risk-adjusted returns by buying the stock of firms that persistently produced moderate sales and earnings growth rates. Had this investor focused on the high-fliers, the risk-adjusted returns would have been negative. He concludes that investing in the fastest growing firms is a very risky proposition, which will most likely lead to shareholder's value destruction.

1.5. Asset Pricing and Monetary Economics

In Chapter 18, de Goeij makes a case for the importance of fixed-income securities in the investment portfolios of individuals, pension funds, insurance companies and mortgage banks. The author intends to provide a better understanding of the types of fixed-income-related risks. In addition, he deals with the price determination of assets, which are combinations of fixed-income securities and derivatives (bond options, interest rate swaps, interest swaptions, caps and floors). One of the primary aims of this chapter is to demonstrate the state of the art in interest rate and term-structure modelling. This chapter starts with a general asset-pricing framework and incorporates a model for the term structure including the time-series behaviour of the stochastic discount factor. In addition, the most important topics in the term-structure literature are highlighted. These include the expectations hypothesis, the modelling of short interest rates and affine yields models. Finally, de Goeij relates the financial and macroeconomic term-structure literature.

ter Horst, de Roon and Werker state in Chapter 19 that the parameter values to compute efficient portfolios have to be estimated using the available data, which may lead to sub-optimal portfolios. While the early literature has attempted to improve on the sample average by means of shrinkage or Stein estimators, or capital asset pricing model (CAPM) estimators, the disadvantage of these methods is that they hinge on strong priors on expected returns. For example, they assume that there is a common value for the means or the expected returns can be fully explained by their market beta. ter Horst et al. take an alternative view and propose an adjustment in mean-variance efficient portfolio weights that incorporate this uncertainty or estimation risk. They show that investors can easily incorporate uncertainty in the mean returns by basing their mean-variance efficient portfolio on pseudo risk aversion rather than on their actual risk aversion. The pseudo risk aversion is always higher than the actual risk aversion and the difference between the two depends on the number of assets under consideration, the sample size and the efficient set constants. This adjustment factor is different from the adjustment obtained in a Bayesian approach, in that it also takes into account the curvature of the mean-variance frontier. This signifies that it captures the intuition that estimation risk is more serious a problem when errors in the expected returns are very costly in terms of volatility. The authors apply the adjustment in mean-variance efficient portfolio weights to international portfolios, and show that the adjustments are non-trivial for the G5 country portfolios and that they are even more important when emerging markets are included and short sales are excluded.

They also demonstrate that, in case of time-varying expected country returns, the adjustment induces a significantly smaller variability in portfolio weights.

In Chapter 20, Nijman and Werker highlight some recent important developments in the market for retail investments. Retail investors can now invest in a wide gamut of investment funds as well as structured products including complicated derivatives. Retail investors are not always sophisticated investors, but simple and reliable information about the cost-loading and expected return of these products is scarce. Moreover, the so-called savings products (insurance, mortgage and retirement products) often contain an element of investment choice such that they have become, in fact, speculative investments. The authors also claim that many investors do not take well-informed investment decisions. To reduce complexity and help investors to make more informed decisions, Nijman and Werker develop a risk measure for retail investment products, which is based on the expected payoff of the financial product in bad scenarios. As of January 2006 most retail products with an investment component offered in the Netherlands will have to report their risk classification in the *Financiële Bijsluiter* or the financial information leaflet. Their risk measure, called *Guise*, is based on some simplifying assumptions and, hence, has its limitations (e.g. it does not address portfolio risk). Still, the authors argue that the risk measure may be very informative for retail investors and the Dutch regulator intends to make such a risk indicator mandatory.

The following topic on persistence in share price returns is addressed by Rodriguez and Sbuelz in Chapter 21. They study the autocorrelation in returns or momentum, which has often been translated into simple though successful trading rules: for example, "buy winners and sell losers" to profit from momentum, or contrarian strategies to profit from mean reversion. The authors develop a theoretical framework, which captures an investor's trading strategy based on momentum in a continuous-time asset-allocation setting. Rodriguez and Sbuelz assume that investors with a momentum-trading strategy compare the latest levels of stock returns to a target or long-run level. In addition, their model allows investors to compare current returns to the past performance of returns and introduce positive autocorrelation of holding-period returns. The authors isolate three effects of momentum on strategic asset allocation: the speculative effect, the conditional-hedge effect and the unconditional-hedge effect. By introducing observable (current and past) returns as the benchmark, momentum is introduced in a realistic and practical way.

The final chapter (Chapter 22) of this book is on monetary policy. Sijben first concentrates on the dichotomy of monetary rules versus discretion in monetary policy. It is clear that a consistent and transparent anti-inflation policy yields a better macroeconomic outcome than a time-inconsistent and discretionary policy. Over the past two decades, the central banks' monetary policy-regime consists of the pre-announcement of an anti-inflation strategy and the priority to monetary stability by anchoring low and stable inflationary expectations (flexible inflation-targeting).

While reaching low inflation and monetary stability has been successful, financial instability has increased. Indeed, globalization of financial markets, a sharpening of international competitiveness between financial institutions, a blurring of these institutions and an increase of both of liquidity and the availability of credit has changed the financial landscape dramatically. Sijben argues that it is possible that due to central banks' success and gained reputation in fighting inflation, inflationary pressures first show up in asset-price inflation and increase the vulnerability of financial systems. He also concentrates on how central banks should deal with financial imbalances and boom–bust cycles in asset prices within the low-inflation environment and how central banks should reconcile monetary and financial stability. Sijben also takes part in the academic debate about an *ex ante* versus an *ex post* intervention of the central bank in order to mitigate an asset-bubble and emphasizes the crucial role of an early warning system in the monetary policy framework with regard to building up financial imbalances.

Acknowledgement

We are grateful to Sandra de Brouwer and to Theo Jurrius for their excellent assistance in editing this book.

PART 1

CORPORATE RESTRUCTURING

Chapter 2

Mergers and Acquisitions in Europe

Marina Martynova and Luc Renneboog

2.1. Introduction

It is now a well-known fact that mergers and acquisitions (M&As) come in waves. Golbe and White (1993) were among the first to observe empirically the cyclical pattern of M&A activity. Thus far, five waves have been examined in the literature: those of the early 1900s, the 1920s, the 1960s, the 1980s and the 1990s. Of these, the most recent wave was particularly remarkable in terms of size and geographical dispersion. For the first time, Continental European firms were as eager to participate as their US and UK counterparts, and M&A activity in Europe hit levels similar to those experienced in the USA. It is widely believed that the introduction of the Euro, the globalization process, technological innovation, deregulation and privatization, as well as the financial markets boom spurred European companies to take part in M&As during the 1990s.

This chapter provides a comprehensive overview of the European takeover market. We characterize the main features of the domestic and cross-border corporate takeovers involving European companies in the period 1993–2001 and contrast them to those of takeovers in the second takeover wave of 1984–1989. We provide detailed information on the size and dynamics of takeover activity in 28 Continental European countries and the UK and Ireland. In addition, we investigate the shareholder short-term wealth effects of a large sample of European M&As. We examine how the estimated shareholder wealth effects vary depending on the different types of takeovers (merger or tender offer), bid attitude (friendly or hostile), payment method (all-cash, all-equity, or mixed), legal status of the target firm (public or private), takeover strategy (focus or diversification) and the legal origin of bidder and target. As all these bid-specific characteristics reflect the bidders' motives (shareholder value-maximization objective, managers' personal utility or managerial hubris), we expect them to explain a significant part of variation in the shareholder wealth effects across the takeover deals.

The bulk of previous research on M&A activity is confined to the USA and UK. We believe that a European-wide study contributes to this literature, as it allows us to evaluate

Advances in Corporate Finance and Asset Pricing
Edited by L. Renneboog
© 2006 Elsevier B.V. All rights reserved.
ISBN: 0-444-52723-0

the impact of a wide range of institutional settings, and legal and regulatory rules on the pattern of M&A activity. In comparison to the USA and UK, Continental European companies are characterized by weaker investor protection and less developed capital markets (La Porta, Lopez-de-Silanes, Shleifer, & Vishny, 1998), and by more concentrated ownership structure (Faccio & Lang, 2002). The analysis presented in this chapter emphasizes the potential differences in Anglo-American markets for corporate control and Continental European ones.

The rest of this chapter is outlined as follows. In Section 2.2, we provide a detailed overview of the European market for corporate control in 1984–2001. Section 2.3 reviews the main findings from previous studies on M&As. Section 2.4 describes the data sources, sample statistics and methodology used to compute cumulative average abnormal returns (CAARs). Section 2.5 investigates the short-term wealth effects for target and bidder firms realized in intra-European M&As in the 1990s. We relate the announcement effect to the various characteristics of target and bidding firms and of the bid itself. Section 2.6 concludes.

2.2. The Fifth Takeover Wave in Europe

The most recent (the fifth) wave of M&As was particularly remarkable compared to its predecessors. For the first time, Continental European firms were as eager to participate in takeovers as their US and UK counterparts, and M&A activity in Europe hit levels similar to those experienced in the USA. While the main engine of takeover activity in Europe during the 1990s was still the UK, M&As in Continental Europe have risen substantially both in number of deals and total transaction value compared to the previous decades. According to the Thomson Financial Securities Data, 87,804 M&A deals were recorded for Europe (including the UK) during 1993–2001. In contrast, there were only 9958 such transactions during the fourth European merger wave (1983–1989). The fifth wave in Europe is impressive in monetary terms as well, since its total value adds up to US$ 5.6 trillion (see Figure 2.1), more than eight times the combined total of the fourth wave.

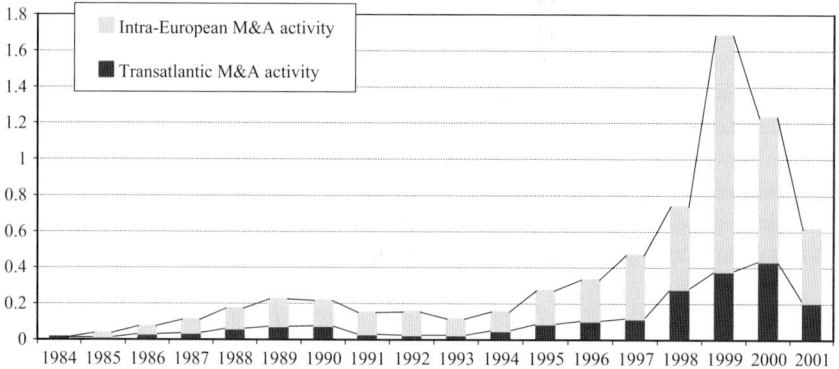

Figure 2.1: European takeover activity: total value of deals (in US$ trillion).
Source: Thomson Financial Securities Data.

As depicted in Figures 2.1 and 2.2, there was a pattern of strong growth in the European M&A market over the last 20 years. From being almost negligible in the beginning of the 1980s, the takeover market reached a level of 4000 annual transactions by the end of the fourth takeover wave. Furthermore, it started with 7000 M&As at the beginning of the fifth wave in 1993, and more than doubled by 2000.

The growing M&A activity in the late 1980s was mainly due to a significant increase in the number of transatlantic deals (whereby US firms were most active as acquirers). The opposite is true for the market for corporate control in the 1990s: the surge can be largely explained by the increase in intra-European transactions while the number of transatlantic M&As remained relatively stable (on an average of 2500 per annum). Much of the change in focus towards intra-European deals can be attributed to the challenges brought about by the development of the single European market and the introduction of the Euro in the 1990s. Fragmented and mostly domestically oriented European companies resorted to takeover deals as a means to survive the tougher regional competition created by the new market. The introduction of the Euro has put additional pressure on firms, as it eliminated all currency risks within the Eurozone and reduced the home bias of investors. Cross-border acquisitions are expected to yield cost advantages and are to enable firms to expand their business more rapidly abroad. Moreover, takeover activity was fuelled by the creation of a liquid European capital market which provides companies with new sources of financing (such as Euro-denominated bonds). As a result of such economic and structural changes on the Continent, the market for corporate control in Europe peaked at US$ 1.2 trillion in 1999, a marked contrast with the peak of the fourth merger wave which amounted to merely US$ 0.15 trillion.

2.2.1. Cross-Border versus Domestic Acquisitions

Of the intra-European M&As of the period 1993–2001, one-third were cross-border deals. Figure 2.3 illustrates that the value of the international transactions account for nearly half of the total investment in M&As by the end of 1999, up from 22% in 1995. The figures

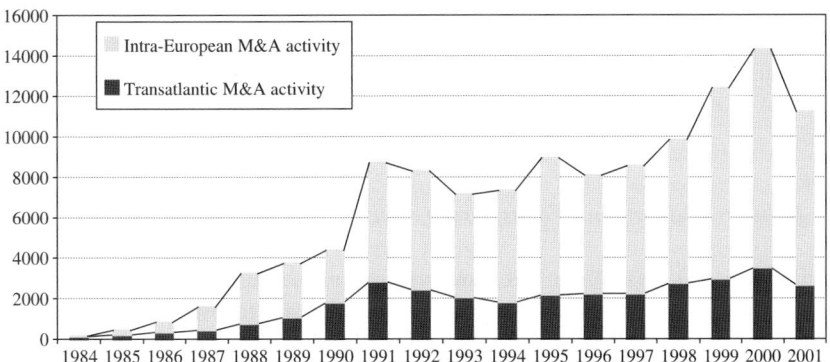

Figure 2.2: European takeover activity: the total number of deals.
Source: Thomson Financial Securities Data.

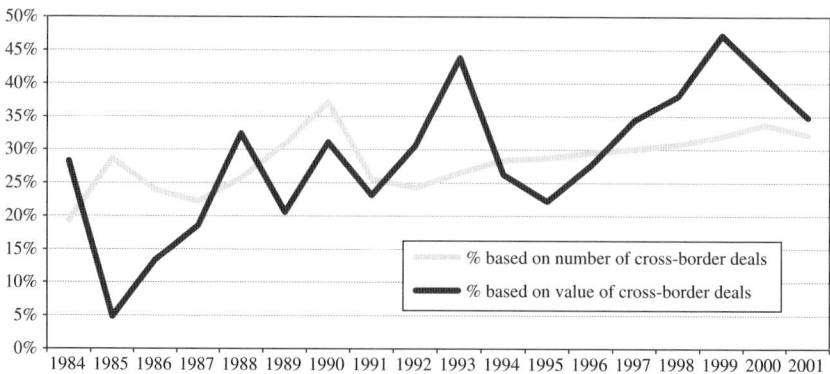

Figure 2.3: Cross-border acquisitions as a percentage of all intra-European deals.
Source: Thomson Financial Securities Data.

also reflect the impact of some unprecedented mega-deals such as the acquisition of Mannesmann by Vodafone in 1999 (for US$ 202 billion).

Figure 2.4 shows that the most active participants in the intra-European cross-border market as acquirers were British, German and French firms, which paid together more than US$ 1 trillion to takeover foreign firms. These deals represented 70% of the total amount spent on intra-European cross-border M&As over the period 1993–2001. Firms from the UK, Germany and France were also most frequently the targets of cross-border acquisitions; they were sold for a total of US$ 0.9 trillion during the fifth takeover wave, amounting to about 60% of the overall value of cross-border M&As. The UK and France were the biggest net acquirers in cross-border takeovers, whereas Germany was a net receiver in the intra-European cross-border market. Figure 2.5 sketches a similar picture based on the number of cross-border acquisitions. The number of cross-border deals surpassed the number of domestic ones in the Benelux countries, Austria and Ireland. Another interesting observation relates to the Eastern European countries that joined the European Union (EU) in 2004. In these countries, many firms were acquired by West-European bidders, predominantly from neighbouring countries (Scandinavia, Austria and Germany). Likewise, Italian, Spanish and Portuguese firms were more fre-quently involved in M&As as targets (of German, British and French bidders) than as bidders.

2.2.2. Industry Clusters and Focus versus a Diversification Strategies

The differences in cross-border M&A patterns across the European countries partly result from restructuring needs in the major national industries. Processes like deregulation and privatization have led to cross-border consolidations in, amongst others, the financial sec-tor and the utilities, by allowing former state-owned companies to acquire firms abroad and to have foreign investors participate in their equity capital. Also, the increasing R&D expenditures gave another boost to international M&As in the high-technology industries

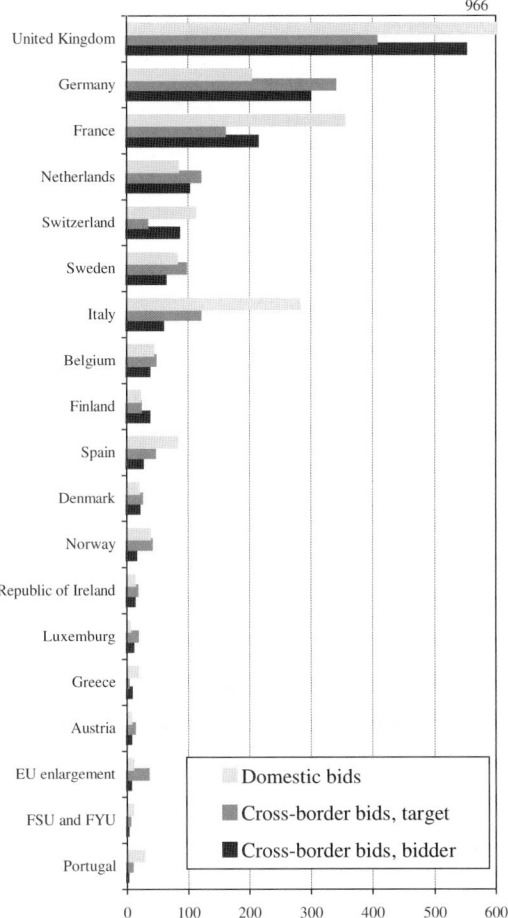

Figure 2.4: Total value of M&As during 1993–2001 by country of bidding and target firms (US$ million). *Source*: Thomson Financial Securities Data.

including biochemistry and pharmaceuticals (see Figure 2.6). Figure 2.7 illustrates the amounts invested through cross-border acquisitions by industry. Although small in terms of the number of deals, the takeovers in the telecommunication sector represented a total value of US$ 470 billion over the period 1993–2001. This accounts for a one-third of the total value of cross-border acquisitions. Another 30% of such foreign investments went to the banking, natural resources and utilities sectors (for a not insignificant extent through the reorganization of former state-owned firms). Figure 2.8 shows similar patterns for the domestic M&A markets.

Table 2.1 discloses that many cross-border M&As made in the 1990s were between firms from the same or related industries. This confirms that international business expansion was

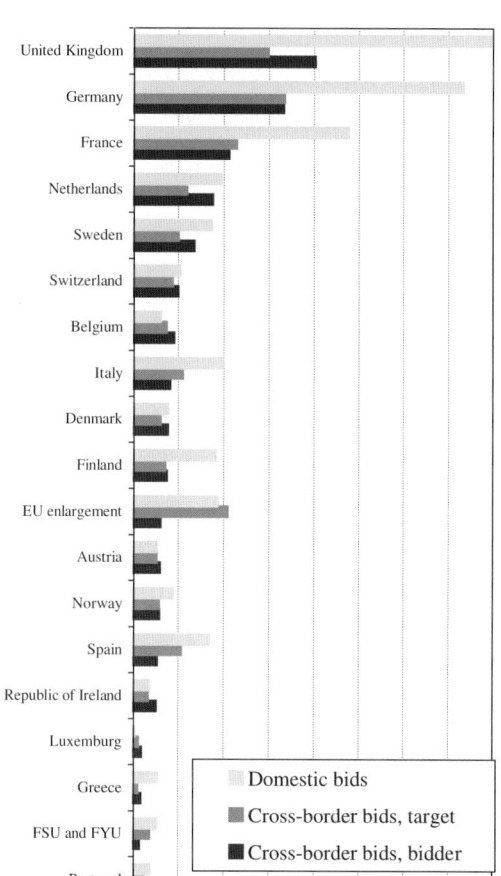

Figure 2.5: Total number of M&As during 1993–2001 by country of bidding and target firms. *Source*: Thomson Financial Securities Data.

one of the goals inciting firms to participate in European cross-border M&As in the 1990s. The smaller percentage of deals within the telecommunication sector can be explained by the fact that the telecommunications mainly engaged in vertical integration with high-technology firms. Such takeovers accounted for about 30% of the deals involving telecommunication acquirers. The fact that most of the domestic and cross-border deals (both horizontal and vertical ones) involved firms in related industries, consolidates the trend to focus on core business which started in the 1980s. Figure 2.9 depicts that the percentage of total M&A related to divestitures increased (both in terms of number of deals and of takeover value) until 1993 but this effect clearly decreased over the fifth takeover wave. Thus, the steady decline in the relative number of divestitures is in line with the fact that the main incentive for European firms in the 1990s boiled down to business expansion in order to address the challenges of the new European market.

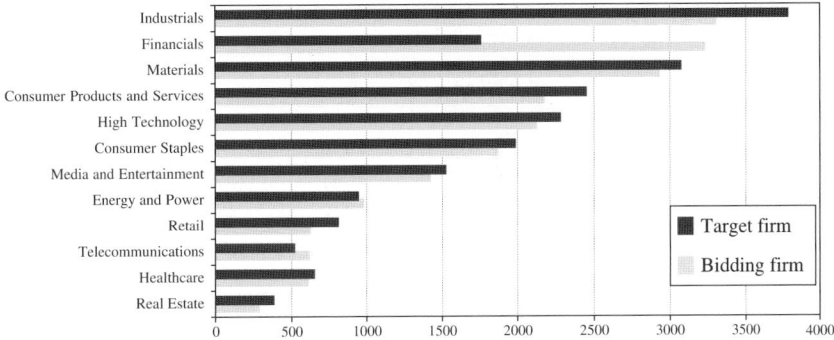

Figure 2.6: Total number of cross-border M&As during 1993–2001 by primary industry. *Source*: Thomson Financial Securities Data.

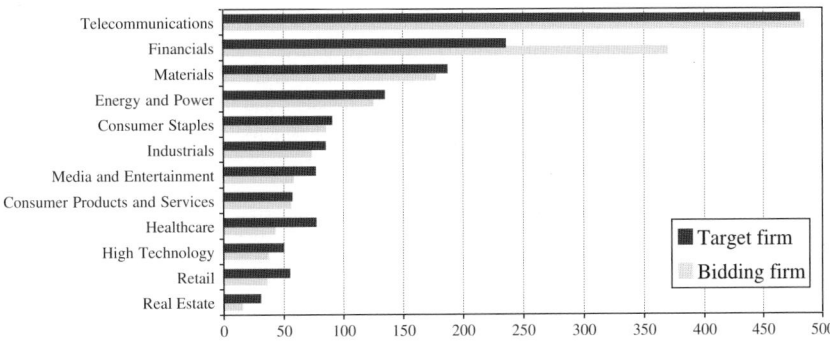

Figure 2.7: Total value of cross-border M&As during 1993–2001 by primary industry.

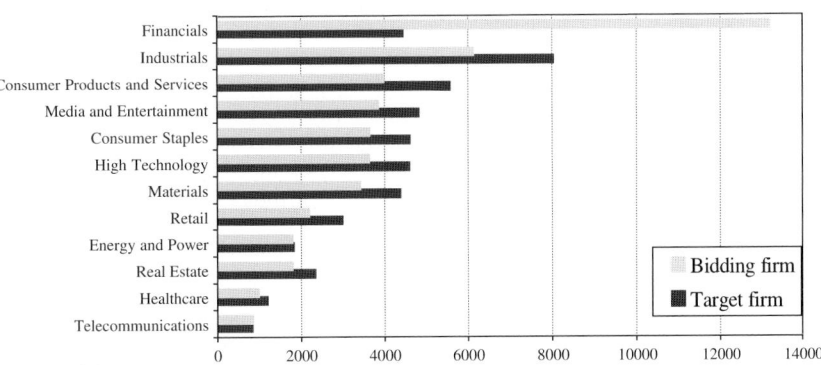

Figure 2.8: Total number of domestic M&As during 1993–2001 by primary industry. *Source*: Thomson Financial Securities Data.

Table 2.1: Intra-industry takeovers as a percentage of total number of cross-border and domestic European M&As.

	Cross-border bids (%)	Domestic bids (%)
Media and entertainment	79.4	78.9
Consumer staples	76.6	76.5
High technology	72.4	71.9
Real estate	72.4	75.0
Industrials	70.6	68.2
Materials	69.3	63.2
Healthcare	67.7	70.2
Retail	66.3	71.4
Energy and power	65.0	65.0
Consumer products and services	62.0	62.5
Telecommunications	48.0	41.3
Financials	45.9	27.7

Note: This table shows the percentage of intra-industry M&As based on the total number of all European takeover announcements within each industry during 1993–2001. An acquisition is classified as an intra-industry takeover if both bidding and target firms operate in the same industry (bidder's and target's 2-digit SIC codes are the same). The sample is partitioned into domestic and cross-border acquisitions.

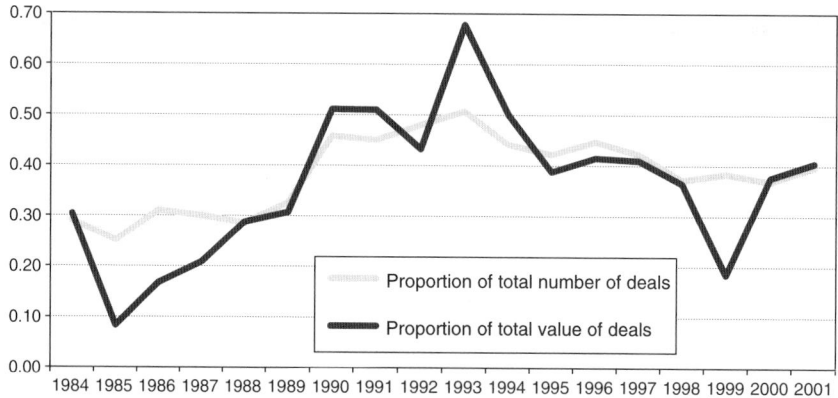

Figure 2.9: Proportion of divestitures in total M&A activity.
Source: Thomson Financial Securities Data.

2.2.3. Means of Payment

Corporate growth via takeovers, often taking the form of mega-deals, requires considerable financial resources which forces cash-constrained firms to finance the acquisitions with equity or a combination of equity and debt. The boom of the stock market in the second half of the 1990s increased the attractiveness of equity as a means of payment for acquisitions. At the same time, the European market for corporate bonds grew rapidly and provided another accessible source of funds. In addition, a European junk-bond market emerged. Low interest rates and a bank attitude more receptive to risky loans also facilitated M&A activity. Consequently, we observe a switch from cash towards equity and debt in the financial composition of the takeover bids.

Figure 2.10 exhibits that the proportion of the total value of acquisitions paid in cash averaged about 67% in the 1980s, but declined to 40% over the 1990s. A similar pattern is perceived in the proportion of the number of pure cash deals, which fell by half in the last decade compared to the 1980s (see Figure 2.11). Whereas the proportion of common equity used in acquisitions augmented to a high 39% of the total value of all acquisitions (in 1998), the relative number of all-equity bids in the 1990s was still rather small. As depicted in Figure 2.11, the combination of equity, debt and cash became the most popular

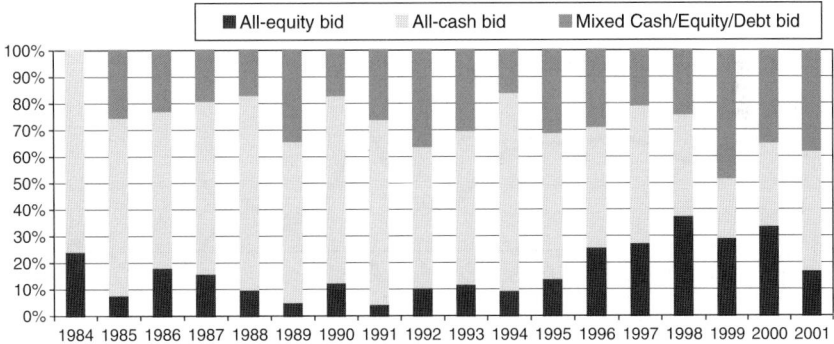

Figure 2.10: Percentage of all-cash, all-equity and mixed bids (based on total value of European M&A activity). *Source*: Thomson Financial Securities Data.

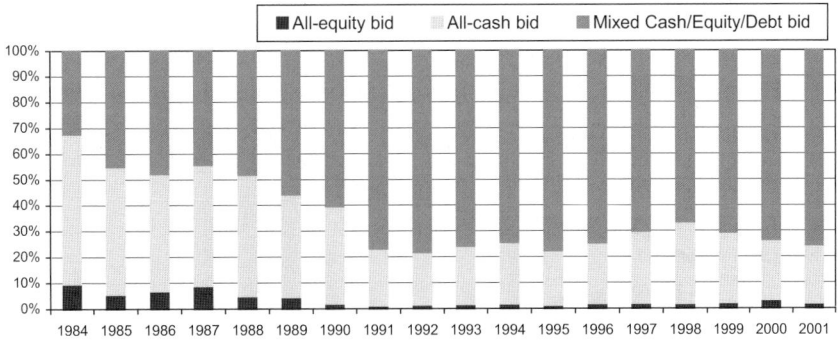

Figure 2.11: Percentage of all-cash, all-equity and mixed bids (based on total number of European M&As). *Source*: Thomson Financial Securities Data.

method of payments for European M&As during 1991–2001, accounting for about 75% of all deals.

It is commonly believed that the bull market of the 1990s caused a switch from cash to equity financing in M&A deals: the overvaluation of equity provides bidders with a cheap currency to pay for their acquisitions. Figure 2.12 provides some supporting evidence: whereas the relative number of all-cash transactions is inversely related to the changes in the market index, the trend in all-equity bids is positively correlated to the market. Moreover, there is a clear relation between the choice of the payment method and the size of a takeover (see Figure 2.13). Firms with insufficient cash resources to finance large acquisitions have increasingly resorted to a combination of equity and debt, but the very large transactions are fully financed with equity. Figure 2.13 also confirms that the average value of the M&As, especially of the all-equity bids, augments in line with the market index over the 1990s.

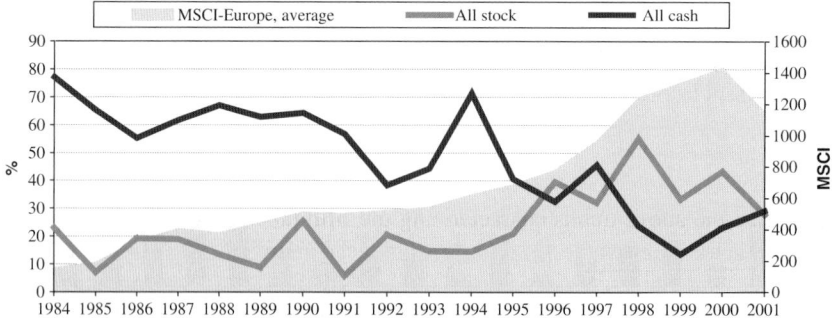

Figure 2.12: Percentage of all-cash and all-equity bids (based on total value of M&As).
Source: Thomson Financial Securities Data and DataStream.

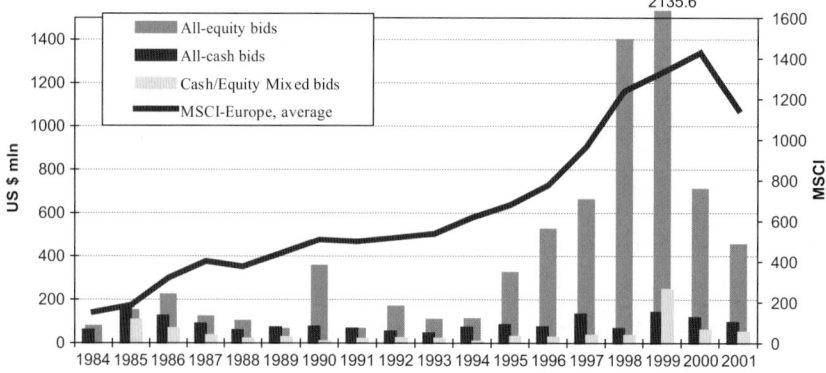

Figure 2.13: Average value of all-cash, all-equity and mixed bids initiated by listed bidders.
Source: Thomson Financial Securities Data and DataStream.

2.2.4. Hostile Takeovers

Paying too high a price for a target firm is more likely to occur when takeover activity is peaking because the bids become more aggressive and trigger more frequently opposition by the target firm. Figures 2.13 and 2.14 show that in 1999, at the peak of the fifth European wave, the average value of deals and the number of hostile bids are both standing out. In that year, an unprecedented number of hostile deals with a total worth of US$ 501 billion (about half the total value of all M&As in 1999) occurred.

Theoretically, fewer hostile takeovers are expected when the stock market is climbing, as target shareholders prefer to sell their shares when they are likely to be overpriced. Figure 2.14 depicts that this is indeed the case for the UK domestic takeovers. In this country, the number of hostile bids in the past decade significantly fell compared to the 1980s. In contrast, the domestic bids in Continental Europe and the cross-border bids increased in both number and value compared to the previous wave. Moreover, hostile takeover activity in Europe during the 1990s emerged even in countries in which there was none before. Many hostile bids, which would have been opposed by the political and financial establishment in the 1980s, were welcomed in the 1990s. This last observation is predominantly valid for domestic takeovers, as in the case of cross-border bids, governments still tend to protect national champions and erect barriers for foreign raiders.[1]

2.2.5. Summary

To summarize the above trends characterizing the fifth takeover wave in Europe, we first note that the market for corporate control experienced significant growth in the 1990s partially caused by a significant increase in the number of intra-European acquisitions, of which one-third was cross-border transactions. British, German and French firms were the most active acquirers, but also the most popular targets in the cross-border M&A market. Central European firms were frequently targets in the international market for corporate control. The largest number of cross-border M&As has occurred in the industrial sector,

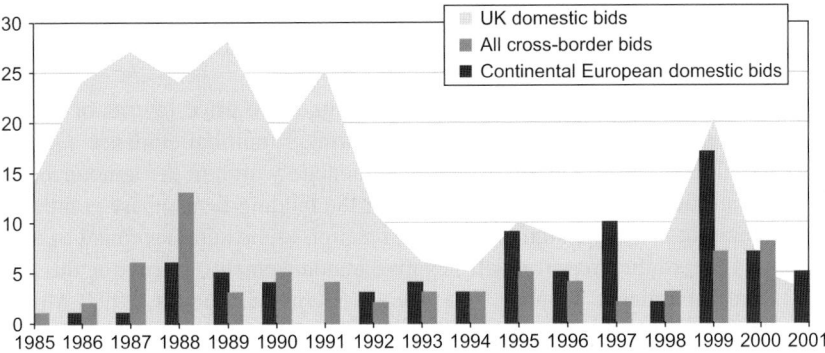

Figure 2.14: The number of European hostile takeovers.
Source: Thomson Financial Securities Data.

while in terms of total money spent on international M&As the telecommunication sector sticks out. In the domestic takeover market, the financial sector has experienced strong takeover activity. Overall, the number of M&As in related industries significantly surpasses the number of diversifying takeovers.

The financial structure of takeover bids in the 1990s switched from a dominance of cash to a combination of equity, debt and cash, and — specifically for the largest transactions — to all-equity. The peak of the fifth merger wave in Europe is characterized by an increase in the number of hostile M&As, largely due to the fact that Continental Europe experienced growth in both domestic and cross-border unsolicited bids. The UK domestic market attenuates this trend as here we observe a fall in the number of hostile transactions compared to the 1980s wave.

2.3. Literature Overview

2.3.1. Market Reaction to Takeover Announcement

The empirical literature is unanimous in its conclusion that takeovers create value for the target and bidder shareholders combined, with the majority of the gains accruing to the target shareholders. Shareholders of target firms invariably receive large premiums (on average 10–30%) relative to the pre-announcement share price. Jarrell and Poulsen (1989), Servaes (1991), Kaplan and Weisbach (1992), Mulherin and Boone (2000), for instance, report average US target abnormal returns of 29% (for 1963–1986), 24% (for 1972–1987), 27% for (1971–1982), and 21% (for 1990–1999), respectively. Similarly to their US counterparts, UK and Continental European targets gain average announcement returns of 24% during the period 1955–1985 (Franks & Harris, 1989), 19% in 1966–1991 (Danbolt, 2004), and 13% in 1990–2001 (Goergen & Renneboog, 2004). Schwert (1996) emphasizes that the share price reactions of target shareholders are not limited to the announcement day but commence already 42 days prior to the initial public announcement of the bid. Numerous studies report that the price run-up is substantial and often even exceeds the announcement effect itself: the run-up is between 13% and 22% over a period of 2 months prior to the bid (Asquith, Bruner, & Mullins, 1983; Dennis & McConnell, 1986; Goergen & Renneboog, 2004). These returns imply that the bids are anticipated, and result from rumours, information leakages, or insider trading.

There is a considerable contrast between the large share price returns of target firms and the frequently negligible returns of bidding firms. Empirical evidence suggests that bidder shareholders realize abnormal returns immediately around the announcement day which are insignificantly different from zero. For the bidding firms, there is little consensus in the literature about the sign of the price reaction to the announcement of an M&A. About half of the studies report small negative announcement returns for the acquirers (see e.g. Franks, Harris, & Titman, 1991; Healy, Palepu, & Ruback, 1992; Mulherin & Boone, 2000; Andrade, Mitchell, & Stafford, 2001), whereas the other half finds zero or small positive announcement abnormal returns (see e.g. Asquith, Bruner, & Mullins, 1983; Loderer & Martin, 1990; Schwert, 2000; Moeller & Schlingemann, 2005). The share price run-up prior to a takeover announcement over a 1-month period is positive, but mostly insignificant for bidder shareholders (Dennis & McConnell, 1986; Smith & Kim, 1994; Schwert, 1996).

As the target shareholders earn large positive abnormal returns and the bidder shareholders do not lose on average, takeovers are expected to increase the combined market value of the merging firms' assets. The empirical literature unanimously documents significant positive announcement effect for the combined firm, although the size of the total effect varies across studies. Bradley, Desai, and Kim (1988), Lang, Stulz, and Walkling (1989), and Healy, Palepu, and Ruback (1992) compute average abnormal returns for the combined firm of 7% for 1963–1984, 11% for 1968–1986, and 9% for 1979–1984, respectively. Franks, Harris, and Titman (1991), Kaplan and Weisbach (1992), and Mulherin and Boone (2000) report total takeover announcement gains of 4% for different sub-periods between 1971 and 1999, whereas Andrade, Mitchell, and Stafford (2001) state that the combined announcement effect for the period 1973–1998 is 1.8% in the USA.

2.3.2. Determinants of Share Price Reactions

The M&A literature has shown that a variety of attributes affect the value of bidding and target firms at the announcement of corporate takeovers.[2] First, the announcements of tender offers and of hostile acquisitions generate higher target returns than the announcement of friendly M&As. In contrast, bidder returns on the announcement day are significantly lower in hostile bids than in friendly M&As (see e.g. Servaes, 1991; Franks & Mayer, 1996; Gregory, 1997; Goergen & Renneboog, 2004).

Second, when the bidding management owns large equity stakes, the share price reactions of bidding firms are higher (see e.g. Agrawal & Mandelker, 1987; Healy, Palepu, & Ruback, 1997). This suggests that, when managers do not own equity, the fact that agency problems in the firm are higher is discounted in the share prices. The bidder shareholders may therefore believe that managers with low share participation give priority to growth strategies (including value-destroying mergers), rather than focus on shareholder's value maximization.

Third, all-cash bids generate higher target and bidder returns than all-equity acquisitions (see e.g. Franks, Harris, & Titman, 1991; Andrade, Mitchell, & Stafford, 2001; Moeller, Schlingemann, & Stulz, 2004). The announcement that an equity bid is made may signal that the bidding managers believe that their firms' shares are overpriced so that investors adjust the bidders' share prices downwards. This is in line with the fact that managers attempt to time equity issues to coincide with surging stock markets or even at the peak of the stock market cycle.

Fourth, acquiring firms with excess cash destroy value by overbidding. Several papers have shown evidence that free cash flow is frequently used for managerial empire building (see e.g. Jensen, 1986; Lang, Stulz, & Walkling, 1991; Servaes, 1991).

Fifth, corporate diversification strategies destroy value (Morck, Shleifer, & Vishny, 1990; Berger & Ofek, 1995; Hubbard & Palia, 1999; Doukas, Holmen, & Travlos, 2002). This confirms that companies should not attempt to do what investors can do better than themselves (i.e. creating a diversified portfolio).

Sixth, the acquisition of value companies leads to higher bidder and target returns. Rau and Vermaelen (1998) show that the acquisition of firms with low market-to-book ratios generates high abnormal returns for the shareholders of the bidding firm whereas the takeover of firms with high market-to-book ratios yields substantial negative abnormal returns.

Finally, target firms in cross-border acquisitions tend to pocket larger abnormal returns than their counterparts in domestic bids (Wansley, Lane, & Yang, 1983; Dewenter, 1995; Danbolt, 2004). It follows that the share price of bidders acquiring foreign firms significantly underperforms that of bidders participating in domestic takeovers (Conn, Cosh, Guest, & Hughes, 2005). The market anticipates that regulatory and national cultural differences between the bidders' and targets' countries may lead to difficulties in managing the post-merger process (Baldwin & Caves, 1991; Schoenberg, 1999).

2.3.3. Motives for Takeovers

The literature offers several alternatives as to what motivates companies to participate in corporate takeovers. The key explanations are synergies and the correction of managerial failure. Typically, takeovers (are expected to) create operating and financial synergies. Operating synergies arise through the realization of economies of scale and scope, the elimination of duplicate activities, vertical integration, the transfer of knowledge or skills by the bidder's management team, and a reduction in agency costs by bringing organization-specific assets under common ownership (Ravenscraft & Scherer, 1987; 1989). The creation of operating synergies reduces production and/or distribution costs, yielding an incremental cash flow accruing to the firm's post-merger shareholders. Operating synergies tend to arise mainly when the merging firms are in the same or related industries (Comment & Jarrell, 1995). Further, operating synergies may include acquisition of technology or intangible assets, such as acquisition of knowledge of new markets in cross-border takeovers.

Diversifying takeovers are expected to benefit from financial synergies. Financial synergies may include improved cash flow stability, lower bankruptcy probability (Lewellen, 1971; Higgins & Schall, 1975), cheaper access to capital, an internal capital market (Bhide, 1990), the use of underutilized tax shields, as well as contracting efficiencies created by a reduction in managers' employment risk (Amihud & Lev, 1981).

The role of hostile acquisitions as a disciplinary force to correct managerial failure is also often cited as a motive. In this scenario, hostile takeovers target poorly performing firms and replace underperforming management. Until recently, this disciplinary market for corporate control existed mostly in the USA (Morck, Shleifer, & Vishny, 1988; Bhide, 1989; Martin & McConnell, 1991). Hasbrouck (1985), Palepu (1986), Morck, Shleifer, and Vishny (1989), and Mitchell and Lehn (1990) provide evidence that, prior to the acquisition, US target firms in hostile takeovers significantly underperform their peers in friendly M&As. However, Franks and Mayer (1996) cast doubt on the role of the M&A market as a disciplinary device in the UK. Also, a growing number of recent empirical studies report that the disciplining function of hostile takeovers is not the primary motive for the target firms' managers to oppose takeover attempts (Ravenscraft & Scherer, 1987; Martin & McConnell, 1991; Schwert, 2000). Hostility may also result from a bargaining strategy to extract a higher premium for the target shareholders (Schwert, 2000) or from the target directors' viewpoint that the proposed takeover is incompatible with the target's long-term strategy.

Domestically oriented companies frequently resort to cross-border takeovers as a means to survive the tough international competition in global markets. Expansion abroad also enables companies to exploit differences in tax systems and to capture rents resulting from market inefficiencies such as national controls over labour markets (Scholes & Wolfson, 1990; Servaes & Zenner, 1994). In addition, imperfect capital markets allow firms to exploit favourable exchange rate movements by moving operations to other countries or by acquiring foreign firms (Froot & Stein, 1991; Cebenoyan, Papaioannou, & Travlos, 1992; Kang, 1993).

In this chapter, we investigate the short-term returns for a large sample of intra-European domestic and cross-border M&As. We analyse whether the type of offer has an important impact on the premium paid for the target's shares. Furthermore, we look at the possible impact of different means of payment (all-cash, all-equity, or combinations of cash, equity and loan notes) on the bid premium. Given that the level of stock market development and corporate governance regulation differ substantially between the UK and Continental Europe, we investigate whether the abnormal returns for targets and bidders of these regions are significantly different. We also examine the announcement effect of unsuccessful bids to check whether the market already accounts for this ultimate effect at the moment of the first-bid announcement. We also study the impact of the stock market bubble by controlling for the impact of year-of-bid effects.

2.4. Data Sources, Descriptive Statistics and Methodology

2.4.1. Sample Selection

We select our sample of European acquisitions launched between 1993 and 2001 — during the fifth takeover wave — from the M&As Database of the Securities Data Company (SDC), which contains detailed historical data on M&As dating back to 1984. We only select domestic and cross-border intra-European takeovers; both the acquirer and the target are from countries within Continental Europe and the UK. The deals also involve firms from Central and Eastern Europe as well as the European former Soviet countries. Further, we retain only the transactions involving a change in control and thus exclude deals intending to buy a mere minority participation. It should be noted that our sample includes not only firms that were successfully taken over but also takeover attempts. The resulting list comprised 25,240 M&A announcements.

In order to reduce endogeneity problems and enhance the comparability of the deals, we focus only on transactions between independent companies. That is, we exclude bids if the bidding party is the management or the employees, or if the target is a subsidiary. In addition, we avoid dealing with the special regulatory environment and accounting issues related to financial institutions: we exclude banks, savings banks, unit trusts, mutual funds and pension funds. These filters reduce the dataset to 13,312 takeover announcements.

We also only retain the takeover deals in which at least one of the participants is a publicly traded company on a European stock exchange in order to ensure the availability of sufficient publicly disclosed information about the parties involved and about the bid. This reduces the sample to 5278 takeover announcements. In one-fifth of the sample (1124 announcements), both bidder and target are listed. The sample includes 4671 (88.5%) acquisitions made by bidders listed on a stock exchange. This figure can be further divided into 1124 (21.3%) and 3547 (67.2%) bids for public and private targets, respectively. The remaining 607 (11.5%) of the sample constitute bids on publicly traded targets by unlisted bidders.

We also exclude the bids made by the same bidder if these bids occur within less than 300 trading days since the previous announcement of a bid. The reason is that we want to avoid biases in the estimation of the parameters we need in order to calculate the abnormal returns, because we use an estimation period of 240 days ending 60 days before the event and an event window spanning 60 days before and 60 days after the event day. In addition, if two bids on separate firms by the same acquirer are announced within an interval smaller than 2 months, we eliminate both deals as their event windows would overlap. The remaining sample includes 3216 bid announcements.

We verified the quality of the SDC data by comparing the information on the announcement date, the companies' countries of origin, the transaction value, payment structure, share of control acquired, bid completion status and the target's attitude towards the bid with the information from LexisNexis, the Financial Times and Factiva as the SDC records do frequently not coincide with those of the other sources, corrections were necessary in 36.2% of the deals.

Market and share price returns are gathered from DataStream. We only consider the prices of shares with voting rights, defined as ordinary shares or Class A shares for the companies issuing dual-class shares. Our final sample consists of 2419 deals involving firms from 28 European countries. This sample is representative for the European merger activity during the 1990s for non-financial companies.

2.4.2. Sample Statistics

During the 1990s, about 70% of the intra-European takeover bids targeted a domestic firm (Table 2.2). However, at the peak of the fifth takeover wave (1998–2000), cross-border bids accounted for more than half of all takeovers. In 60% of the takeovers, the deals related to a merger or the acquisition of the full equity of the target firm; while in the remainder the bidder acquires absolute control (more than 50% of the voting rights).

We consider an acquisition as hostile if the board of directors of the target firm rejects the offer for whatever reason. Hostility may, for instance, also result from a bargaining strategy to extract a higher premium for the target shareholders (Schwert, 2000) or from the target directors' viewpoint that the proposed strategic plan underlying the acquisition is incompatible with the target firm's own strategy. We also consider all acquisitions with competing bidders as hostile.[3] Within the unopposed takeovers, we also identify the tender offers.[4] Our sample counts 162 (7%) hostile bids, 2257 (93%) friendly M&As, of which 473 are tender offers.

The sample consists of 1941 (80%) successfully completed M&As, 207 (9%) failed bids as a consequence of successful opposition against the bid or a collapse of the friendly takeover negotiations, and 271 (11%) pending negotiations. According to SDC, a transaction is classified as pending if it has been announced but has not been completed or withdrawn.[5] While the total number of M&As surged, the annual number of withdrawn

Table 2.2: Sample composition (number of bids).

	1993	1994	1995	1996	1997	1998	1999	2000	2001	1993–2001	%
Total sample	171	229	228	229	229	292	411	408	222	2419	100.0
Domestic bid	131	171	159	168	160	193	280	269	150	1681	69.5
Cross-border bid	40	58	69	61	69	99	131	139	72	738	30.5
Merger/acquisition of 100%	95	124	138	144	138	110	153	170	88	1451	60.0
Acquisition of voting majority	76	105	90	85	91	182	258	238	134	968	40.0
Hostile bid	13	13	23	12	17	18	32	27	7	162	6.7
Friendly M&A	158	216	205	217	212	274	379	381	215	2257	93.3
Of which: tender offers	23	31	43	39	56	68	97	76	40	473	19.6
Completed bid	129	177	186	189	191	251	344	312	162	1941	80.2
Pending bid	21	27	19	27	11	20	37	68	41	271	11.2
Withdrawn bid	21	25	23	13	27	21	30	28	19	207	8.6
Private target	118	160	143	167	142	181	224	256	139	1530	63.2
Listed target	53	69	85	62	87	111	187	152	83	889	36.8
Diversification	59	99	83	98	76	85	132	147	82	861	35.6
Industry focus	112	130	145	131	153	207	279	261	140	1558	64.4
All-cash bid	48	74	84	91	100	112	177	165	87	938	38.8
All-equity bid	33	36	31	26	41	30	60	61	31	349	14.4
Mixed bid	45	37	45	53	32	52	68	60	42	434	17.9
Undisclosed payment	45	82	68	59	56	98	106	122	62	698	28.9

Note: Table shows the number of all the takeover announcements in our sample and partitions this sample in several ways: (i) domestic and cross-border deals; (ii) acquisition of 100% control and acquisition of majority interest; (iii) friendly M&As (excluding tender offers), unopposed tender offers and hostile bids; (iv) completed, pending and withdrawn bids; (v) private and public target firm legal status; (vi) diversification and focus acquisition strategy; and (vii) all-cash, all-equity, or mixed cash, equity and debt payment structure in takeovers.

Table 2.4: Sample composition by countries of bidding and target firms.

	Domestic deals					Cross-border deals									
						Classification by bidder country					Classification by target country				
	All	% by country	Friendly M&A	Tender offer	Hostile bid	All	% by country	Friendly M&A	Tender offer	Hostile bid	All	% by country	Friendly M&A	Tender offer	Hostile bid
1 Austria	11	0.7%	11	0	0	31	4.2%	30	1	0	20	2.7%	16	1	3
2 Belgium	23	1.4%	22	1	0	34	4.6%	28	5	1	14	1.9%	11	3	0
3 Bulgaria	0	0.0%	0	0	0	0	0.0%	0	0	0	2	0.3%	2	0	0
4 Croatia	0	0.0%	0	0	0	1	0.1%	1	0	0	6	0.8%	6	0	0
5 Cyprus	3	0.2%	3	0	0	2	0.3%	1	1	0	0	0.0%	0	0	0
6 Czech Republic	9	0.5%	8	1	0	1	0.1%	1	0	0	25	3.4%	25	0	0
7 Denmark	30	1.8%	21	3	6	32	4.3%	25	6	1	21	2.8%	16	4	1
8 Estonia	0	0.0%	0	0	0	0	0.0%	0	0	0	13	1.8%	13	0	0
9 Finland	53	3.2%	52	0	1	32	4.3%	29	2	1	20	2.7%	19	0	1
10 France	219	13.0%	176	30	13	111	15.0%	92	10	9	89	12.0%	81	7	1
11 Germany	175	10.4%	165	8	2	89	12.0%	71	14	4	94	12.7%	91	2	1
13 Hungary	4	0.2%	4	0	0	5	0.7%	5	0	0	3	0.4%	3	0	0
14 Ireland	11	0.7%	6	4	1	27	3.6%	18	7	2	16	2.2%	10	5	1

15 Italy	39	2.3%	32	4	3	28	3.8%	24	3	1	44	5.9%	43	0	1
16 Latvia	0	0.0%	0	0	0	1	0.1%	1	0	0	4	0.5%	4	0	0
17 Lithuania	1	0.1%	1	0	0	0	0.0%	0	0	0	6	0.8%	5	1	0
18 Luxemburg	0	0.0%	0	0	0	7	0.9%	6	1	0	5	0.7%	4	1	0
19 The Netherlands	2	0.1%	1	1	0	27	3.6%	16	10	1	45	6.1%	37	7	1
20 Norway	58	3.5%	44	9	5	32	4.3%	29	1	2	37	5.0%	23	7	7
21 Poland	22	1.3%	22	0	0	0	0.0%	0	0	0	37	5.0%	34	3	0
22 Portugal	1	0.1%	1	0	0	1	0.1%	1	0	0	11	1.5%	10	1	0
23 Romania	2	0.1%	2	0	0	0	0.0%	0	0	0	11	1.5%	11	0	0
24 Russia	10	0.6%	10	0	0	3	0.4%	3	0	0	10	1.4%	9	1	0
25 Slovenia	0	0.0%	0	0	0	0	0.0%	0	0	0	4	0.5%	2	2	0
26 Spain	46	2.7%	33	6	7	9	1.2%	4	5	0	33	4.5%	30	3	0
27 Sweden	102	6.1%	62	29	11	69	9.3%	59	7	3	48	6.5%	38	10	0
28 Switzerland	22	1.3%	19	1	2	39	5.3%	26	10	3	28	3.8%	22	4	2
29 UK	838	49.9%	485	274	79	159	21.5%	136	19	4	94	12.7%	41	40	13
Total	1681	100.0%	1180	371	130	740	100.0%	606	102	32	740	100.0%	606	102	32

Note: Table shows the number of all the takeover announcements in our sample by country and partitions this sample in several ways: (i) by domestic and cross-border deals; (ii) by friendly M&As (excluding tender offers), unopposed tender offers and hostile bids; and (iii) by target and by bidder country.

M&A market. The Scandinavian M&A market is also sizeable: Scandinavian acquirers conduct 14.6% of all domestic and 22.2% of all cross-border deals in Europe. Relative to the other major economies in Europe, the takeover activity in Italy is remarkably low. The countries that became member states of the EU in 2004 account for 15% of all the targets in cross-border M&As. In contrast, domestic acquisitions and cross-border bids made by companies from these countries are almost non-existent and merely constitute 2.5% and 1.4% of total domestic and cross-border M&A activity, respectively.

2.4.3. Methodology

We measure the share price reaction to takeover announcements by computing the abnormal returns around the announcement day. Abnormal returns (ARs) are defined as the difference between the realized return (R) and a benchmark return (BR), which is the expected return in case would not have been a M&A announcement:

$$AR_{i,t} = R_{i,t} - BR_{i,t}, \tag{2.1}$$

where i and t denote the security and the day, respectively.

To calculate the realized dividend-adjusted daily returns, we use the DataStream return index (RI), the daily share prices (P) and the dividends (D):

$$RI_{i,t} = RI_{i,t-1} \times \frac{P_{i,t}}{P_{i,t-1}}, \tag{2.2}$$

except when t is ex-date of the dividend payment then:

$$RI_{i,t} = RI_{i,t-1} \times \frac{P_{i,t} + D_{i,t}}{P_{i,t-1}}. \tag{2.3}$$

Given the above index (which is also corrected for stock splits, we compute dividend-adjusted daily returns as follows:

$$R_{i,t} = \frac{RI_{i,t} - RI_{i,t-1}}{RI_{i,t-1}}. \tag{2.4}$$

The existing literature on event studies introduces a variety of methodologies to estimate BRs. Most of the studies implicitly assume that the pre-merger strategies of the bidder and target firms persist. Under this assumption, asset-pricing models such as the market-adjusted model, the market model, or the Fama–French three-factor model are used to predict the BRs based on the company's pre-merger performance. Consistent with the previous studies we also adopt the persistency assumption and estimate the market model.[9]

The market model BRs are given by:

$$BR_{i,t} = \hat{\alpha}_i + \hat{\beta}_i R_{m,t}, \tag{2.5}$$

where $R_{m,t}$ is actual market return on day t. The market model captures the differences in the risk-free rate across countries in $\hat{\alpha}_i$ and the risk of a security with respect to the market portfolio in $\hat{\beta}_i$. To insure the robustness of our results, we apply four techniques to estimate the parameters. First, we estimate Equation (2.5) using ordinary least square (OLS) regressions. Second, as described in Blume (1979), we adjust the estimated beta for mean-reversion using expression (2.6): β_i^A. Third, we control for non-synchronous trading which may cause a downward bias on $\hat{\beta}_i$ (Dimson, 1979; Dimson & Marsh, 1983). To calculate a Dimson-beta, β_i^D, we run the regression (2.7) and sum the 6 beta-coefficients as in Equation (2.8). Fourth, we correct the Dimson-beta for reversion to the mean by applying Blume (1979):

$$\beta_i^A = 0.34 + 0.67 \cdot \hat{\beta}_i \tag{2.6}$$

$$R_{i,t} = \alpha_i + \beta_{i,t-3}R_{m,t-3} + \beta_{i,t-2}R_{m,t-2} + \beta_{i,t-1}R_{m,t-1} + \beta_{i,t}R_{m,t}$$
$$+ \beta_{i,t+1}R_{m,t+1} + \beta_{i,t+2}R_{m,t+2} + \varepsilon_{i,t} \tag{2.7}$$

$$\beta_i^D = \hat{\beta}_{i,t-3} + \hat{\beta}_{i,t-2} + \hat{\beta}_{i,t-1} + \hat{\beta}_{i,t} + \hat{\beta}_{i,t+1} + \hat{\beta}_{i,t+2}, \tag{2.8}$$

where $R_{m,t+k}$ for $k \in \{-3, -2, -1, 0, 1, 2\}$ are daily lagged and leading market returns, and $\hat{\beta}_{i,t+1}$ for $k \in \{-3, -2, -1, 0, 1, 2\}$ are the corresponding parameter estimates.

The market model parameters are estimated over a period of 240 trading days (from 300 to 60 days prior to the event day 0). The event day is either the day of the announcement or the first trading day following the announcement in case the announcement is made on a non-trading day.

We employ two different indices (in separate regressions) as proxies for the market. First, since the study concerns the European market for corporate control in which cross-border acquisitions constitute one-third of all transactions, we opt for a European-wide index including companies from the Eurozone, Scandinavia and the UK (assuming that the indices of Western Europe are also capturing the evolution in Central Europe). As this index ought to consist of large and madcap firms, we choose the MSCI-Europe index and the Standard & Poor (S&P) Europe 350. Second, in order to capture the specifics of corporate governance regulation in each country and their impact on corporate financial performance, we also estimate the abnormal returns using local market indices. For each country, we take the all-share index of the main national stock exchange. These indices are obtained from DataStream.

We calculate the CAARs for N securities over different event windows (from day t_1 to day t_2) as follows:

$$\text{CAAR}_\tau = \frac{1}{N}\sum_{i=1}^{N}\text{CAR}_{i\tau} = \frac{1}{N}\sum_{i=1}^{N}\sum_{t=t_1}^{t=t_2}\text{AR}_{i,t}, \tag{2.9}$$

where τ denotes an event window (t_1, t_2), for $-60 \leq t_1 < t_2 \leq +60$.

To tests the significance of the CAARS, we compute the standard parametric test statistics as discussed in detail by Brown and Warner (1985), and one non-parametric rank statistics developed by Corrado (1989).[10] The portfolio test statistic assumes that the ARs are larger for securities with higher variance. Hence, equal weights are given to the returns of individual securities. The statistic follows a Student-t distribution, and is approximately standard normal under the null hypothesis. The portfolio test statistics is calculated as:

$$t_p = \frac{CAAR_\tau}{\hat{\sigma}(CAAR_\tau)}, \qquad (2.10)$$

where $\hat{\sigma}(CAAR_\tau)$ is the cross-sectional sample standard deviation of CAARs over the event window τ for the sample of N securities:

$$\hat{\sigma}(CAR_\tau) = \sqrt{\frac{1}{N^2} \sum_{i=1}^{N} \sum_{t=t_1}^{t_2} \hat{\sigma}_i^2}, \qquad (2.11)$$

where $\hat{\sigma}_i$ is an estimator for the standard deviation of the ARs for security i computed over the estimation window (T_{0i}, T_{1i}):

$$\hat{\sigma}_i = \sqrt{\frac{1}{L_i - 2} \sum_{t=T_{0i}}^{T_{1i}} (R_{i,t} - \hat{\alpha}_i - \hat{\beta}_i R_{m,t})^2}, \qquad (2.12)$$

where L_i is the number of observations for security i in the estimation window (T_{0i}, T_{1i}) and equals 240 ($T_{0i} = -300$ and $T_{1i} = -60$). The standard deviation of the cumulative abnormal returns (CARs) in Equation (2.11) is based on the assumption that ARs of different securities are uncorrelated. This is generally the case when there is no overlap in the event windows of individual securities. If the assumption were not valid, then the portfolio statistic would be biased.

Our second parametric tests statistic, the standardized test statistic, assumes that the true ARs are constant across securities. This statistic gives more weight to the securities with lower variance of the ARs. A correct specification requires cross-sectional independence of ARs. Under the null hypothesis, the distribution of this test statistic is Student-t, which converges to the standard normal distribution as the number of securities increases. The statistic is calculated as:

$$t_{st} = \sqrt{\frac{N(L_i - 4)}{L_i - 2}} \, \frac{1}{N} \sum_{i=1}^{N} \frac{CAR_{i\tau}}{\hat{\sigma}(CAR_{i\tau})}, \qquad (2.13)$$

where $\hat{\sigma}(CAR_{i\tau})$ denotes the sample standard deviation of the CARs of the individual securities referring to the event window τ:

$$\hat{\sigma}(CAR_{i\tau}) = \sqrt{\sum_{t=t_1}^{t_2} \hat{\sigma}_i^2}, \qquad (2.14)$$

with $\hat{\sigma}_i$ defined as in Equation (2.12).

The Corrado test statistic is non-parametric and hence free of any specific assumptions on the return distribution. Moreover, this test statistic does not require the returns to be symmetrically distributed as is necessary for a correct specification of the non-parametric tests.[11] The test can also handle the problem of cross-sectional dependence of ARs. The

Corrado test ranks each security's time series of ARs and then aggregates these individual security's ranks into a time series of mean portfolio ranks. Under the null hypothesis of zero abnormal performance on the event day (window), the distribution of the rank statistic converges to the standard normal distribution. The statistic is specified as follows:

$$t_{\text{rank}} = \frac{1}{N} \sum_{i=1}^{N} \frac{K_{i,Ho} - 0.5(L + 1)}{\hat{\sigma}(K)}. \tag{2.15}$$

The standard deviation $\hat{\sigma}(K)$ is estimated using the entire sample of securities and their time series of ARs:

$$\hat{\sigma}(K) = \sqrt{\frac{1}{L} \sum_{\{j\}} \left(\frac{1}{N} \sum_{i=1}^{N} (K_{ij} - 0.5(L + 1)) \right)^2}, \tag{2.16}$$

where K_{ij} denotes the rank of ARs (or CARs) in security i's time series in the estimation and event periods combined:

$$K_{ij} = \text{rank}(AR_{ij}), \tag{2.17}$$

where j stands for the order in the time sequence of ARs over the analysed period. Thus, if daily ARs are considered, then $j = -300, \ldots, +60$. When multiple-day CARs are considered, j is the order of windows of τ-day length composing the period $(-300, +60)$. We denote $K_{i,Ho}$ the rank of the abnormal returns (CARs) of security i on the event day (window) for which we hypothesize and test that the returns are insignificant. L denotes the number of observations (ARs or CARs) comprising the time series for each security, such that L equals $360/\tau$ for daily ARs and L equals $360/\tau$ for CARs over the window of τ days. The rank test uses the fact that the expected rank under the null hypothesis is $0.5(L + 1)$.

Campbell and Wasley (1996) show that, compared to parametric test statistics, the rank test is consistently best specified and the most powerful test statistic across numerous event conditions, such as multi-day event periods, clustered event days and increases in variance on the event day.

2.5. Results

In this section, we focus on univariate analyses of CAARs for target and bidding firms realized in intra-European M&As. We relate the CAARs to the various characteristics of target and bidding firms and of the bid itself: these include the location of the target (domestic versus cross-border M&As), the type of the takeover (hostile bid, tender offer, merger, friendly acquisition), the nationality and legal origin of the bidding and target firms, the means of payment (all-cash, all-equity or mixed offer), the success or failure of the negotiations (successfully completed, pending or withdrawn), the sub-period of the takeover wave in which the bid was announced (the run-up, the peak and the decline of the wave), the legal status of the target firm (listed versus privately held), the corporate strategy (focus versus diversification strategy), and the form of the takeover (a full acquisition versus a partial control acquisition).

2.5.1. Target versus Bidding Firms

As a bidding firm is expected to create significant additional corporate value when it acquires a target firm, the target shareholders will only be enticed to sell their share stakes if they are offered a substantial premium. This premium (the future synergetic value) should be immediately reflected in the target firms' share prices. Figure 2.15 depicts that the announcement of a takeover bid causes substantial positive abnormal returns for the target shareholders: on the event day, an abnormal return of 9% is realized. In addition, there is a significant increase in target share prices over the period of 2 months (about 40 trading days) prior to the initial public announcement. On average, investors owning shares in the target firm for a period starting 2 months prior to the event day and selling their shares at the end of the event day would earn a return of 21% (Table 2.5). After about 25 trading days subsequent to the event day, the CAAR decreases by 2% due to the fact that some bids are withdrawn as a consequence of successful opposition by the target's board of directors or that delays in takeover negotiations raise investors' concerns about the ultimate success of the bid.

In comparison to the target CAARs, the price reactions for the bidding firms are modest. Figure 2.16 shows a small (though statistically significant at the 1% level) abnormal return of 0.5%. Over a 10-day window centred around the event day, the statistically significant CAAR amounts to 0.8%. Strikingly, the CAARs of the bidding firm generated over a 3-month period (−3%) subsequent to the bid are significantly negative. This negative return includes the effects of all revisions in expectations and in the offer price and

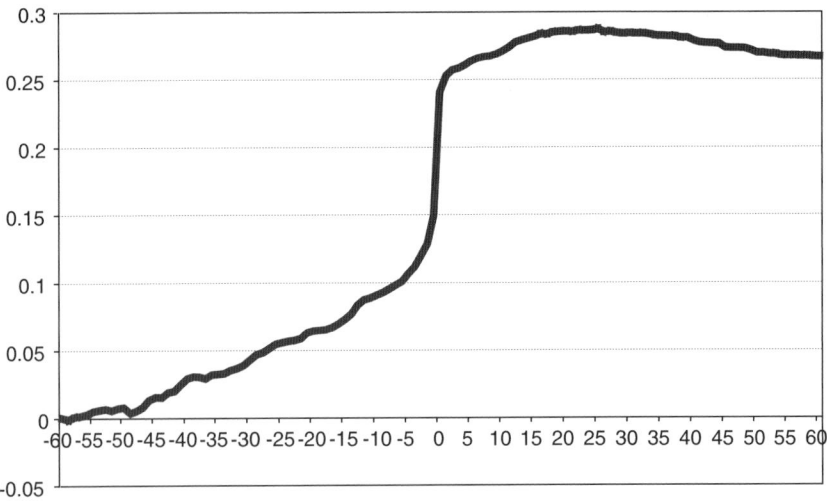

Figure 2.15: Target CAARs around the M&A announcement. *Note*: This figure shows the market reaction to the announcement of M&A transactions for target firms as well as the CAARs before and after the event (day 0). The benchmark used in the market model is the MSCI-Europe index returns; the model parameters are estimated over 240 days starting 300 days prior to the acquisition announcement.

Mergers and Acquisitions in Europe   **41**

Table 2.5: CAARs for target and bidding firms.

Event window	Bidding firms					Target firms				
	[−40, −1]	[T = 0]	[−1, +1]	[−5, +5]	[−60, +60]	[−40, +1]	[T = 0]	[−1, +1]	[−5, +5]	[−60, +60]
CAAR (%) Whole sample	0.39	0.53	0.72	0.79	−2.83	11.49	9.13	12.47	15.83	26.70
t_{rank}	0.76	4.90[a]	4.28[a]	3.19[a]	−2.48[b]	4.54[a]	15.41[a]	16.94[a]	12.36[a]	6.67[a]
t_p	0.83	7.19[a]	5.63[a]	3.21[a]	−3.18[a]	3.28[a]	9.97[a]	7.53[a]	6.10[a]	12.44[a]
t_{st}	1.27	12.33[a]	14.37[a]	6.26[a]	1.96[b]	28.93[a]	150.01[a]	115.05[a]	78.68[a]	62.57[a]
% Positive	48	50	50	51	50	69	70	78	79	76
Number of observations	2109					760				

Note: Table reports average values of CAARs for bidding and target firms for five different event windows. $T = 0$ stands for the day of the bid announcement. Abnormal returns are computed as the difference between realized and market model benchmark returns. For each firm we calculate daily benchmark returns using MSCI-Europe index returns and the market model parameters are estimated over 240 days starting 300 days prior to the acquisition announcement and ending 60 days prior to the announcement. Two parametric tests (Brown & Warner, 1985) and one non-parametric test (Corrado, 1989) are used to assess the significance of the CAARs. The definitions of the t-tests are given in Section 2.4.3. '% *Positive*' is a percentage of takeover announcements with a positive CAR in our sample. Statistical significance level at: a: 1% and b: 5%, respectively.

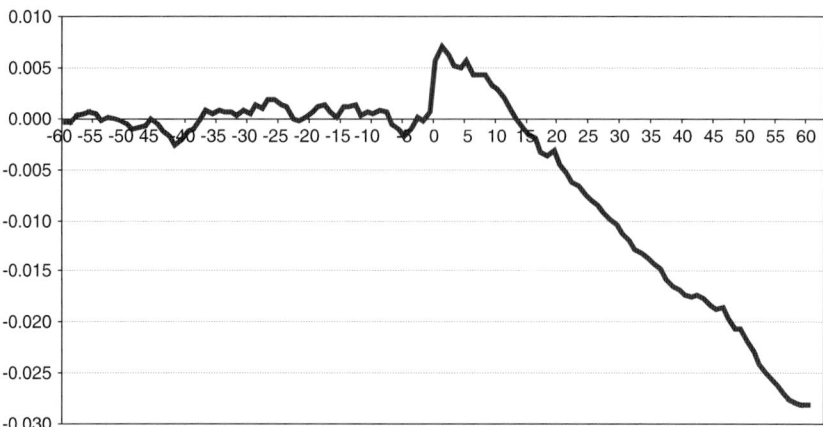

Figure 2.16: Bidder CAARs around the M&A announcement. Note: This figure shows the market reaction to the announcement of M&A transactions for bidding firms as well as the CAARs before and after the event (day 0). The benchmark used in the market model is the MSCI-Europe index returns; the model parameters are estimated over 240 days starting 300 days prior to the acquisition announcement.

may therefore be a more complete measure of the takeover wealth effect for the shareholders of the bidding firm. In the next subsections, we show that the negative pattern of the post-announcement abnormal returns is affected by various characteristics of the transaction, such as opposition by the board of the target firm against the bid, the payment method and the expected (or realized) outcome of the M&A negotiations.

2.5.2. Hostile Bids versus Friendly M&As

To analyse the market reactions to the different types of takeovers, we partition all bids into three groups based on the target firm's attitude towards the bid (hostile versus friendly) and by the form of the bid (tender offer versus negotiated M&A). For all of these types, there is a strong positive increase (statistically significant at the 1% level) in the target share prices at the bid announcement, as shown by Figure 2.17. Expectedly, hostile bids generate the largest abnormal returns (15%) to the target shareholders on the announcement day. The returns of hostile takeover bids are significantly higher than the ones for friendly M&As and unopposed tender offers: the announcement effect is only 3% for friendly M&As and 12% for unopposed tender offers. We do not consider unopposed tender offers as hostile, as (by definition) they are not opposed by the board of directors of the target firm. However, as the bidder bypasses the board of directors of the target firm with a tender offer and addresses the target shareholders directly, a tender offer, even unopposed, is somewhere between a friendly bid and a hostile one. Therefore, we expect unopposed tender offers to trigger large share price increases for the target firms. When a hostile bid is made, the share price of the target immediately reflects the expectation that opposition will lead to upward revisions of the offer price. Likewise, an offer made directly to the shareholders by means

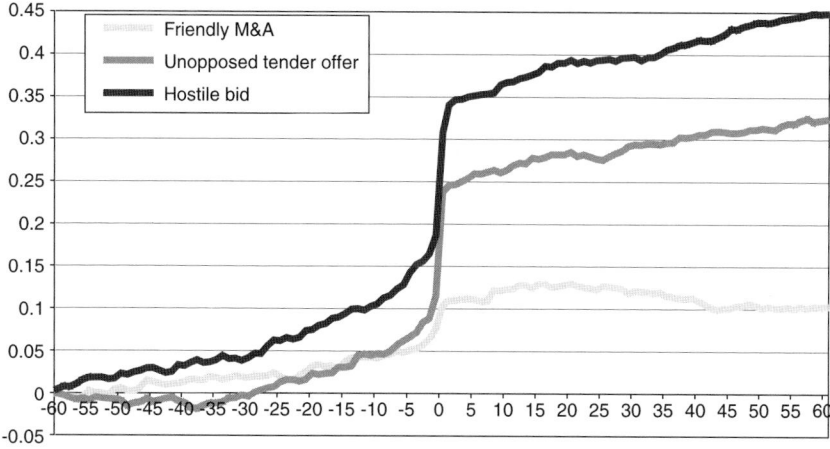

Figure 2.17: Target CAARs by bid attitude (friendly versus hostile) and by form of the bid (tender offer versus negotiated M&As). *Note*: This figure shows the evolution of the market reaction to the announcement of M&A transactions for target firms by bid attitude and by form of the bid. The sample of hostile acquisitions includes deals in which the target firm's board opposes the takeover and deals in which a competing bidder was present. The day of the bid announcement is day 0. Abnormal returns are computed as the difference between realized and market model benchmark returns. For each firm we calculate daily benchmark returns using MSCI-Europe index returns and market model parameters are estimated over 240 days starting 300 days prior to the acquisition announcement.

of a tender offer is also usually occurring at a substantial premium above the pre-announcement market price. Figure 2.17 also unveils that there are large differences in the share price run-ups between friendly and hostile takeover bids. A hostile acquisition generates a CAAR of more than 30% over a 2-month period preceding and including the announcement day. In contrast, the target share prices of friendly M&As (excluding unopposed tender offers) significantly underperform those of hostile bids and tender offers both before and after the deal announcement. Over the holding period of 6 months centred on the event day, friendly M&As trigger a CAARs of only 10%, whereas the wealth effects amount to 32% for unopposed tender offers and 44% for hostile bids.

Figure 2.18 reports the CAARs for the bidding firms by attitude and by type of takeover. The bidding firms' shareholders clearly react differently to the announcements of friendly M&As, unopposed tender offers or hostile bids. In the 2-month period prior to the bid, the CAARs of the bidding firms decrease slightly in the case of friendly M&As, whereas those for bids which will later be publicly announced as tender offers or hostile bids are significantly positive at 2.9% and 1.6%, respectively. It seems that a takeover via a tender offer or hostile bid is anticipated by the market and evaluated positively. On the event day, the share price endures a small negative price correction. The reason is that the shareholders of the bidding firms fear that their firm will offer too high a premium in case

Figure 2.18: Bidder CAARs by bid attitude (friendly versus hostile) and by form of the bid (tender offer versus negotiated M&As). *Note*: This figure shows the evolution of the market reaction to the announcement of M&A transactions for bidding firms by bid attitude and by form of the bid. The sample of hostile acquisitions includes deals in which the target firm's board opposes the takeover and deals in which a competing bidder was present. The day of the bid announcement is day 0. Abnormal returns are computed as the difference between realized and market model benchmark returns. For each firm we calculate daily benchmark returns using MSCI-Europe index returns and market model parameters are estimated over 240 days starting 300 days prior to the acquisition announcement.

of bid opposition or in case of a direct offer to the target shareholders as upward price revisions erode the synergy value accruing to the bidder. The announcement of a friendly M&A is greeted favourably by the market as the ARs are significantly positive (0.8%).

Irrespective of the takeover type, all bidders realize significant decreases in market value over the 3-month post-event period. It seems that the market price reactions to the announcements (and prior to the event) are overoptimistic and that the bidders' shareholders have second thoughts about the transaction. The abnormal returns for the bidding firms accumulated starting 3 months prior through 3 months after the bid announcement are virtually zero (0.02%) in unopposed tender offers, but significantly negative in hostile bids and friendly M&As (−1.6% and −4.4%, respectively).

2.5.3. Means of Payment in Takeover Bids

The means of payment is generally considered to be an important signal of the quality of the target firm (or the potential synergy value). If the offer consists of cash, the bidding firm signals that it wants to pay off the target shareholders in order to not share future value increases of the merged firms. In contrast, an all-equity offer signals that the bidders' shareholders intend to keep the target shareholders involved in the merged company and share its risk. Hence, the target shareholders believe that their firm is peach when the bidder makes a cash offer while their firm may be less valuable when an all-equity bid is made. Asymmetric information between the bidder's management and outside investors may influence the choice of the means of payment in an acquisition and the consequent market reaction to the announcement of the payment method. We report strong evidence in Figure 2.19 that the target's share price reaction is indeed sensitive to the means of payment in a takeover bid. All-cash offers as well as bids combining cash, equity and loan notes trigger substantially higher abnormal returns (12% and 10%, respectively, at the announcement) than all-equity bids (7%). Figure 2.19 also shows that the announcement effect combined with the price run-up (over 2 months prior to the event day) yields CAARs almost 26% and 24% for all-cash bids and combined offers, respectively. The corresponding return for all-equity bids is merely 15%. Regardless of the event window, the CAARs of cash-financed bids are significantly higher than those of equity-financed bids at the 1% significance level. Strikingly, acquisitions with undisclosed payment method hardly lead to a price change at the announcement (at 0.5% which is insignificantly different from zero). The lack of information on such bids is even penalized by the market as the share price decreases by 4% over 3-month period subsequent to the event day.

If the managers of a bidding firm are convinced that the true value of their firm's shares is worth more than the current share price, they will prefer not to issue equity (to

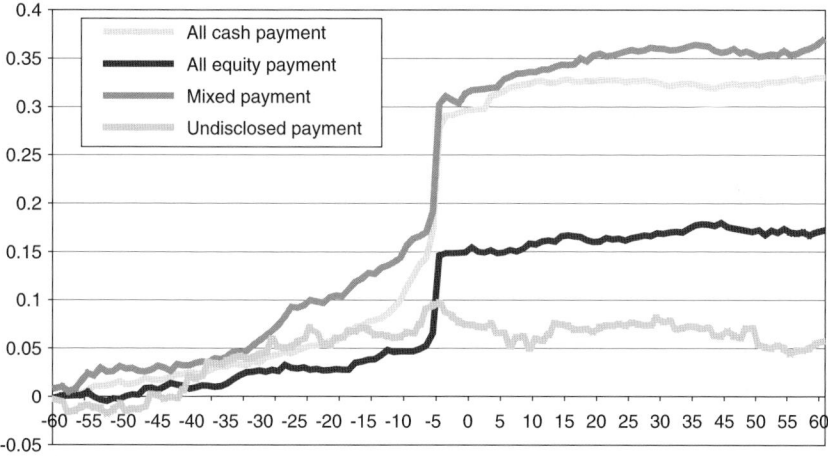

Figure 2.19: Target CAARs by means of payment. *Note*: This figure shows the market reaction to the announcement of M&A transactions for target firms by means of payment employed in the transaction: all-cash, all-equity, and mixed cash, equity, or offers of which the payment was not disclosed (and remains unknown to date). The day of the announcement is day 0. Abnormal returns are computed as the difference between the realized and market model benchmark returns. For each firm we calculate the daily benchmark returns using MSCI-Europe index returns and the market model parameters are estimated over 240 days starting 300 days prior to the acquisition announcement.

finance an all-equity bid or a mixed offer) but to finance the acquisition with cash. Hence, the market may interpret the financing choice as a signal about firm's under- or overvaluation, and revise the share price of the firm offering cash (equity) upwards (downwards). Thus, a negative price correction is expected for all-equity bids and a positive one for all-cash bids. Figure 2.20 confirms this: the bidder's shareholders greet offers involving cash payments more favourably (0.6% for all-cash and 0.9% for mixed bids) than all-equity offers (of which the abnormal returns are indistinguishable from zero). In the period following the bid announcement, the bidders' share prices all decline but bids involving equity payments decline substantially more than all-cash offers. The CAARs over a 6-month period of all-cash bids are not significantly different from zero (at –0.9%), whereas those of all-equity bids and mixed offers are significantly negative (–2.2% and –2.8%, respectively). This negative price reaction to bids involving equity confirms that the market believes that equity payments transmit a signal that the bidding firm is overvalued.

2.5.4. Domestic versus Cross-Border Acquisitions

As pointed out above, 70% of the intra-European M&As are domestic deals. Figure 2.21 depicts that the announcement effect of domestic and cross-border targets amounts to 10%

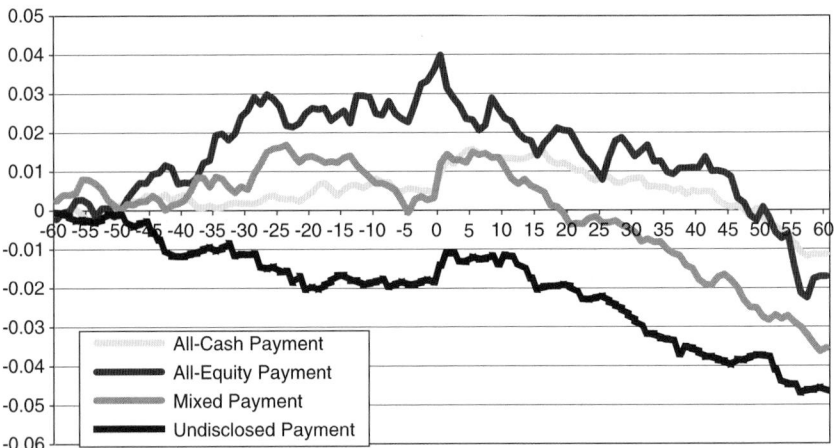

Figure 2.20: Bidder CAARs by means of payment. *Note*: This figure shows the market reaction to the announcement of M&A transactions for bidding firms by means of payment employed in the transaction: all-cash, all-equity, and mixed cash, equity, or offers of which the payment was not disclosed (and remains unknown to date). The day of the announcement is day 0. Abnormal returns are computed as the difference between the realized and market model benchmark returns. For each firm we calculate daily benchmark returns using MSCI-Europe index returns and the market model parameters are estimated over 240 days starting 300 days prior to the acquisition announcement.

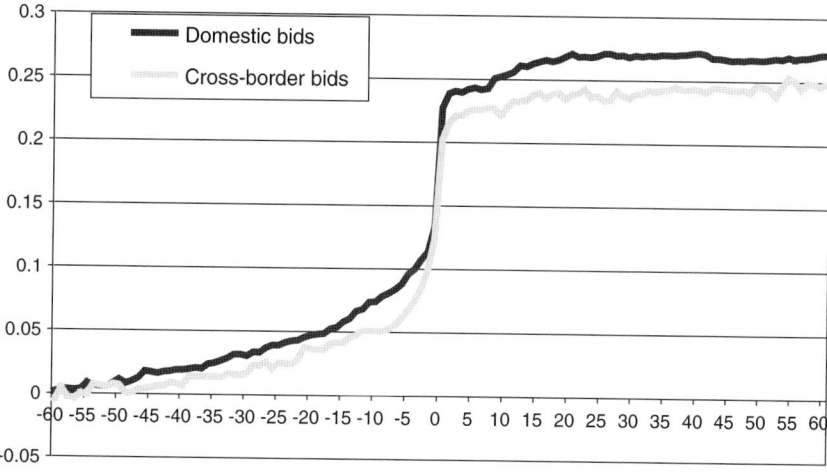

Figure 2.21: Target CAARs in domestic and cross-border bids. *Note*: This figure shows the market reaction to the announcement of domestic and cross-border M&A transactions for target firms. The day of the bid announcement is day 0. Abnormal returns are computed as the difference between the realized and market model benchmark returns. For each firm we calculate daily benchmark returns using MSCI-Europe index returns and the market model parameters are estimated over 240 days starting 300 days prior to the acquisition announcement.

and 8%, respectively. This difference is statistically significant. When we add the price run-up (from 40 trading days prior to the event), the difference of nearly 3% remains significant. One reason why premiums are on average higher for domestic targets than for cross-border targets is that the sample of domestic M&As includes a higher proportion of UK targets (50% versus only 13% in the cross-border takeover sample). Furthermore, we have shown above that hostile acquisitions occur more frequently in the UK than in Continental Europe and trigger larger price reactions. Furthermore, the sample composition may give another reason for the difference in premiums: 15% of the cross-border targets are companies from countries that joined the EU in 2004 or are expected to join in 2007. The CAARs of target firms from these countries in the domestic takeover sample amounts to merely 2.5%. The share prices of these Central European cross-border targets are virtually unaffected by the announcement of a takeover bid and even sharply decline after the event day.

Figure 2.22 also reveals that bidding firms engaging in cross-border bids experience lower announcement effects than those undertaking domestic acquisitions (0.4% versus 0.6%, respectively), the difference of which is statistically significant. Subsequent to the event day, the negative price correction for bidding firms is larger for cross-border bids than for domestic ones (−3.6% versus −2.5%). Some of the reasons for these effects are presented in the subsequent two subsections.

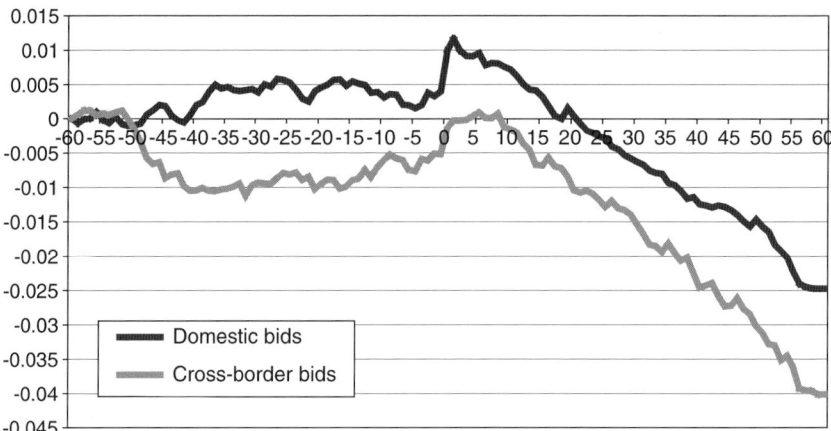

Figure 2.22: Bidder CAARs in domestic and cross-border bids. *Note*: This figure shows the market reaction to the announcement of domestic and cross-border M&A transactions for bidding firms. The day of the bid announcement is day 0. Abnormal returns are computed as the difference between the realized and market model benchmark returns. For each firm we calculate daily benchmark returns using MSCI-Europe index returns and the market model parameters estimated over 240 days starting 300 days prior to the acquisition announcement.

2.5.5. UK versus Continental European Bids

As 85% of the companies listed on the London Stock Exchange are widely held, they are continually up for auction (Goergen & Renneboog, 2004). Thus, an active market for corporate control takes place in the UK. In contrast, the number of listed firms in Continental Europe is much lower and most listed firms (around 85–90% in Germany and France) have concentrated ownership or control (for a detailed overview of ownership and control in Europe, see Barca & Becht, 2001; Faccio & Lang, 2002). Hence, unsurprisingly, about half of the sample of target and bidding firms listed on a stock exchange are located in the UK or Ireland, and hostile acquisitions are more rare in Continental Europe. As there is a high degree of disclosure in the UK, a liquid and well-developed equity market (McCahery & Renneboog, 2002) and a higher degree of shareholder protection (La Porta, Lopez-de-Silanes, Shleifer, & Vishny, 1998), we expect higher premiums in takeover bids involving UK firms.

We do indeed confirm this conjecture: the announcement effect is substantially larger for the UK target firms in domestic bids (13.7%) than for Continental European targets (4.5%). This significant difference even augments over the period including the event day and the price run-up over 2 months prior to the event: the premiums amount to 28% and 12% for UK and European targets, respectively (Figure 2.23). The Continental European bidders' CAARs over the same period are similar to those of the UK bidders (they amount to about 1%). Still, Figure 2.24 shows that the negative price correction that takes place

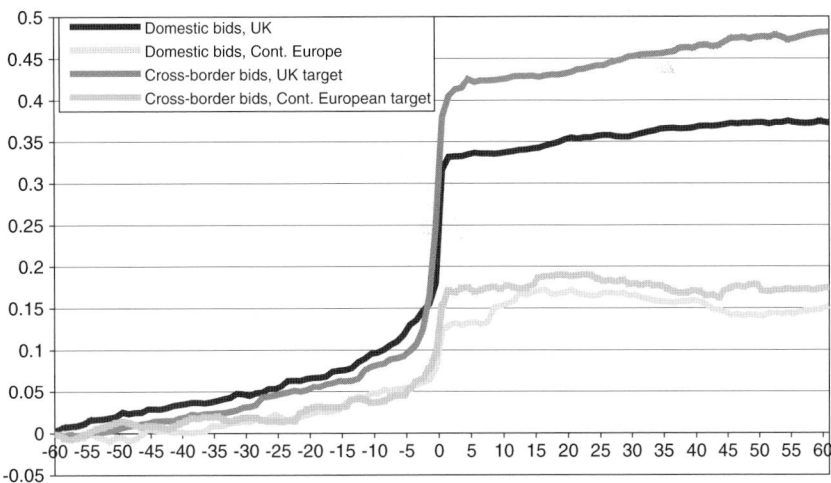

Figure 2.23: Target CAARs (UK versus Continental European targets). *Note*: This figure shows the market reaction to the announcement of domestic and cross-border M&A trans-actions for UK and Continental European target firms. The day of the bid announcement is day 0. Abnormal returns are computed as the difference between the realized and mar-ket model benchmark returns. For each firm we calculate daily benchmark returns using MSCI-Europe index returns and the market model parameters are estimated over 240 days starting 300 days prior to the acquisition announcement.

over the 3 months subsequent to the bid announcement is substantially larger for acquirers from Continental Europe.[12]

When we examine the short-term wealth effects in cross-border acquisitions from the perspective of the location of the target (UK versus Continental Europe), we find the fol-lowing. When UK firms are acquired, the premium offered towers above that of Continental European target firms: 13.8% versus 5.9% at the announcement (Figure 2.23). When we add the price run-up period, the numbers increase to 37% versus 14%, respec-tively. Over a 6-month period around the event day, UK target firms' short-term wealth effects amount to 48.1% while their Continental European counterparts' share prices rise to 17.3%, on an average. This difference in premiums may reflect a more strict takeover legislation in the UK than in the Continental European countries, which protects the target shareholders from expropriation by the bidder and gives the target shareholders more power to extract higher premiums in takeover negotiations (Goergen, Martynova, & Renneboog, 2005).

The short-term wealth effects of foreign firms bidding on UK targets is not significantly different from zero, whereas that of foreign firms attempting to acquire firms in Continental Europe is 0.5% which is statistically significantly different from zero (Figure 2.24). The reason a bid on a Continental target is hailed more positively than a bid on a UK target may lie in the fact that the premiums paid for Continental targets are substan-tially lower (see above).

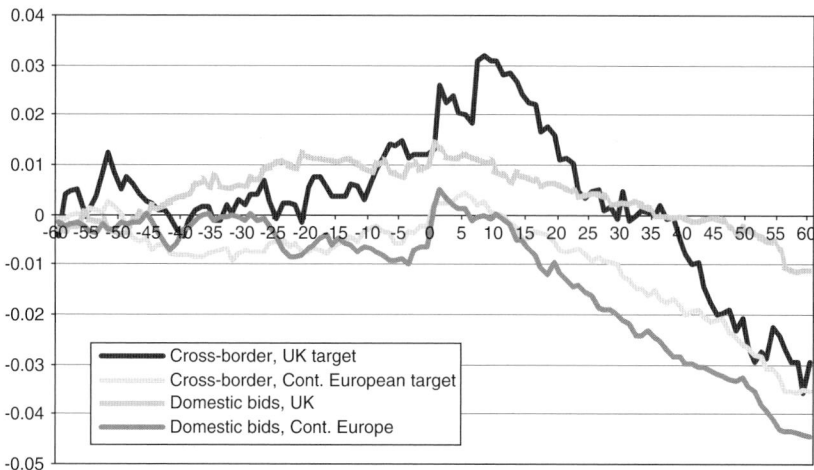

Figure 2.24: Bidder CAARs (UK versus Continental European targets). *Note*: This figure shows the market reaction to the announcement of domestic and cross-border M&A transactions for UK and Continental European bidding firms. The day of the bid announcement is day 0. Abnormal returns are computed as the difference between the realized and market model benchmark returns. For each firm we calculate daily benchmark returns using MSCI-Europe index returns and the market model parameters are estimated over 240 days starting 300 days prior to the acquisition announcement.

When we focus on the location of the bidding firm (UK versus Continental Europe), we arrive at the following results. There is little difference between the CAARs over the event day and the price run-up period for target firms approached by a UK or a Continental European bidder (21.5% versus 20.5%, respectively). The shareholders of Continental European bidding firms react more positively to cross-border bids than the shareholders of UK bidding firms, as the announcement effect for bidders are 0.5% and 0.2%, respectively.

2.5.6. Legal Origin of the Bidding and Target Firms

Although the difference in CAARs between Continental Europe and the UK is remarkable, there is also some variation in the market reaction to takeovers across the Continental European countries. Differences in the laws and their enforcement may explain a part of this variation. Rossi and Volpin (2004) show that the legal environment and takeover regulation are important determinants of the takeover gains. They report that takeover premiums are higher in countries with higher shareholder protection and in countries where the mandatory bid requirement is enforced by law. To control for the impact of the legal environment on takeover premiums, we classify all acquisitions into five groups according to the legal origin of the bidding (and target) firms, following La Porta, Lopez-de-Silanes, Shleifer, and Vishny (1998). Countries from the former communist block are classified according to their (staged) accession to the EU, as this event has had an important impact on their regulatory environment.

Figure 2.25 exhibits the marked differences in target share price reactions at the announcement, over the price run-up period and over the post-announcement period for domestic bids by legal origin. As also documented above, the target firms of English legal origin experience very large wealth effects over all windows (around, before and after the event day). Importantly, target firms in Scandinavian countries, which have a corporate governance legislation and institutional financial environment close to that of the UK (La Porta, Lopez-de-Silanes, Shleifer, & Vishny, 1998), also exhibit strongly positive CAARs (of 21% over the event day and the price run-up period). While the target firms in countries of the recent (2004) and the upcoming (2007–2009) EU enlargement have the lowest

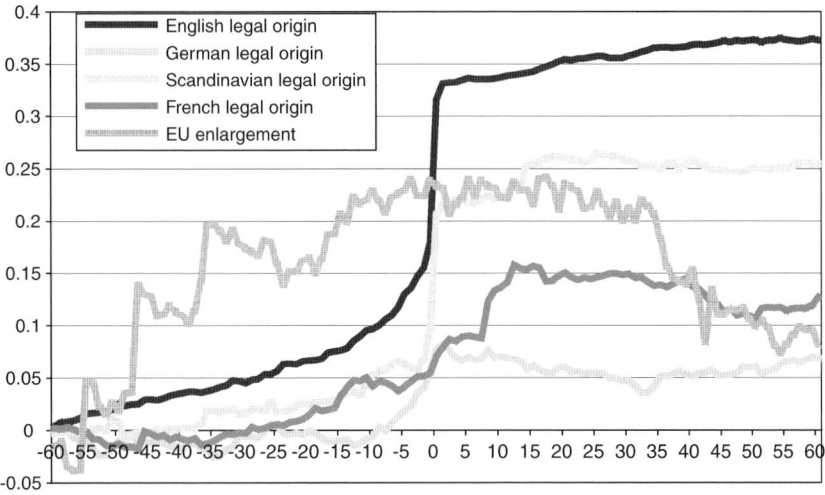

Figure 2.25: Target CAARs in domestic bids by legal origin. *Note*: This figure shows the market reaction to the announcement of domestic M&A transactions for target firms by legal origin. Countries are grouped according to their legal origin following the classification by La Porta, Lopez-de-Silanes, Shleifer, and Vishny (1998) and according to the EU enlargement process. Countries are grouped as follows: English legal origin (Ireland and the UK); German legal origin (Austria, Germany, Switzerland); French legal origin (Belgium, France, Greece, Italy, Luxemburg, the Netherlands, Portugal, Spain); Scandinavian legal origin (Denmark, Iceland, Finland, Norway, Sweden); 2004 EU Accession (Czech Republic, Cyprus, Estonia, Hungary, Latvia, Lithuania, Poland, Slovak Republic, Slovenia); 2007–2009 likely EU Accession (Bulgaria, Croatia, Romania). The day of the bid announcement is day 0. Abnormal returns are computed as the difference between the realized and market model benchmark returns. For each firm we calculate the daily benchmark returns using MSCI-Europe index returns and the market model parameters are estimated over 240 days starting 300 days prior to the acquisition announcement.

announcement effect (–0.5%), that of target firms of French and German legal origin is also particularly low (with CAARs of 1.7% and 2.3%, respectively).

Figure 2.26 documents that the legal origin of the bidding firm also has a clear impact on the bidders' abnormal returns in domestic bids. Takeovers by bidding firms of English, German and Scandinavian legal origin generate significantly positive announcement effects whereas those by bidders of French legal origin and of the EU enlargement are not different from zero. Overtime windows of 6 months symmetrically around the event date, we find that the bidders in domestic takeovers face negative share price movements (for firms in countries of the recent EU enlargement and of countries of German legal original) or abnormal returns indistinguishable from zero (for firms of French, UK and Scandinavian legal origin).

Turning to cross-border acquisitions, we show in Figure 2.27 that the CAARs spanning the 2-month price run-up period as well as the announcement effect is highest for targets

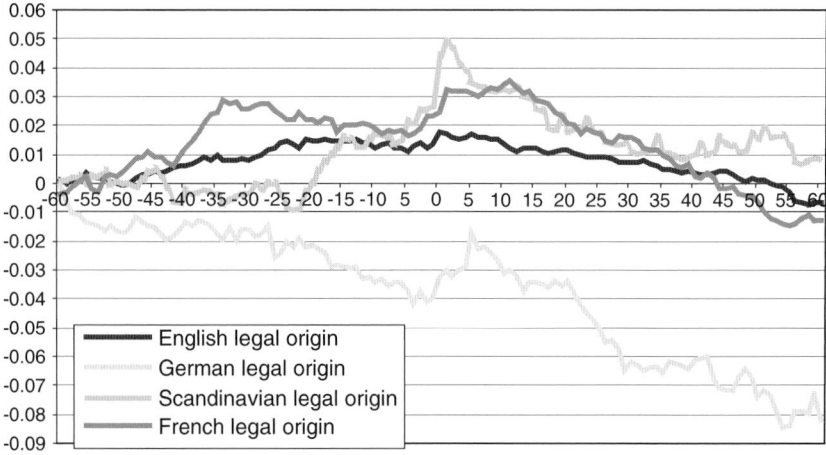

Figure 2.26: Bidder CAARs in domestic acquisitions by legal origin. *Note*: This figure shows the market reaction to the announcement of domestic M&A transactions for bidding firms by legal origin. Countries are grouped according to their legal origin following the classification by La Porta, Lopez-de-Silanes, Shleifer, and Vishny (1998) and according to the EU enlargement process. Countries are grouped as follows: English legal origin (Ireland and the UK); German legal origin (Austria, Germany, Switzerland); French legal origin (Belgium, France, Greece, Italy, Luxemburg, the Netherlands, Portugal, Spain); Scandinavian legal origin (Denmark, Iceland, Finland, Norway, Sweden); 2004 EU Accession (Czech Republic, Cyprus, Estonia, Hungary, Latvia, Lithuania, Poland, Slovak Republic, Slovenia); 2007–2009 likely EU Accession (Bulgaria, Croatia, Romania). The day of the bid announcement is day 0. Abnormal returns are computed as the difference between the realized and market model benchmark returns. For each firm we calculate the daily benchmark returns using MSCI-Europe index returns and the market model parameters are estimated over 240 days starting 300 days prior to the acquisition announcement.

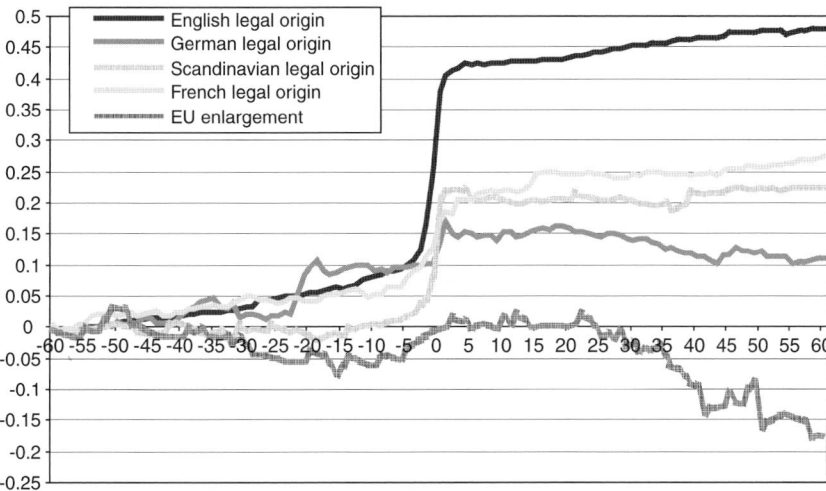

Figure 2.27: Target CAARs in cross-border bids by target legal origin. *Note*: This figure shows the market reaction to the announcement of cross-border M&A transactions for target firms by legal origin. Countries are grouped according to their legal origin following the classification by La Porta, Lopez-de-Silanes, Shleifer, and Vishny (1998) and according to the EU enlargement process. Countries are grouped as follows: English legal origin (Ireland and the UK); German legal origin (Austria, Germany, Switzerland); French legal origin (Belgium, France, Greece, Italy, Luxemburg, the Netherlands, Portugal, Spain); Scandinavian legal origin (Denmark, Iceland, Finland, Norway, Sweden); 2004 EU Accession (Czech Republic, Cyprus, Estonia, Hungary, Latvia, Lithuania, Poland, Slovak Republic, Slovenia); 2007–2009 likely EU Accession (Bulgaria, Croatia, Romania). The day of the bid announcement is day 0. Abnormal returns are computed as the difference between the realized and market model benchmark returns. For each firm we calculate the daily benchmark returns using MSCI-Europe index returns and the market model parameters are estimated over 240 days starting 300 days prior to the acquisition announcement.

of English legal origin (37%), followed by the effect for those of Scandinavian legal origin (30%), of French legal origin (14%), and of German legal origin (13%). The corresponding effect for targets from the Central European countries is indistinguishable from zero (Figure 2.28).

Given that the corporate governance regime of the acquiring firm is imposed on the target firm,[13] it is important to consider the wealth effect after classifying the cross-border takeover bids based on the legal origin of the acquirer. Figure 2.29 discloses that the differences between the target share price reactions by legal origin of the bidder are less heterogeneous than those classified by legal origin of the target. As usual, we find that the announcement market reaction when bidders are of English legal origin is larger than those when bidders of the other legal origins. Figure 2.30 shows that the bidders' share prices are close to zero at the announcement.

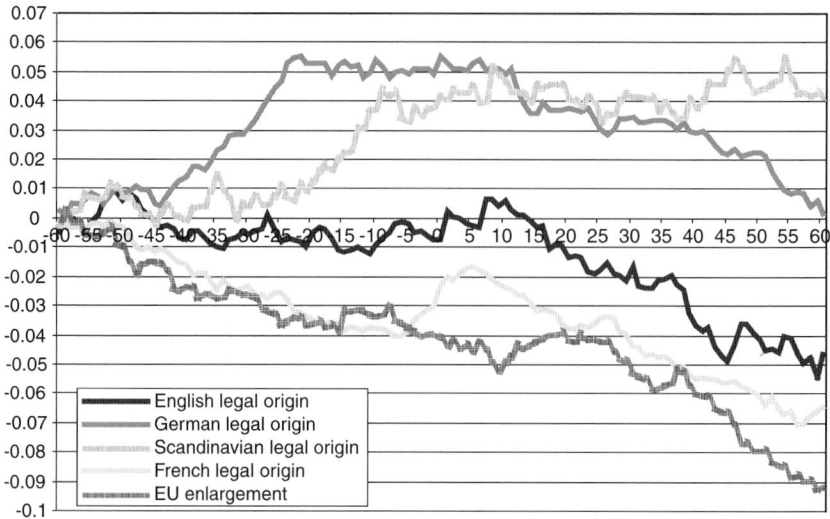

Figure 2.28: Bidder CAARs in cross-border bids by target legal origin. *Note*: This figure shows the market reaction to the announcement of cross-border M&A transactions for bidding firms by legal origin. Countries are grouped according to their legal origin following the classification by La Porta, Lopez-de-Silanes, Shleifer, and Vishny (1998) and according to the EU enlargement process. Countries are grouped as follows: English legal origin (Ireland and the UK); German legal origin (Austria, Germany, Switzerland); French legal origin (Belgium, France, Greece, Italy, Luxemburg, the Netherlands, Portugal, Spain); Scandinavian legal origin (Denmark, Iceland, Finland, Norway, Sweden); 2004 EU Accession (Czech Republic, Cyprus, Estonia, Hungary, Latvia, Lithuania, Poland, Slovak Republic, Slovenia); 2007–2009 likely EU Accession (Bulgaria, Croatia, Romania). The day of the bid announcement is day 0. Abnormal returns are computed as the difference between the realized and market model benchmark returns. For each firm we calculate the daily benchmark returns using MSCI-Europe index returns and the market model parameters are estimated over 240 days starting 300 days prior to the acquisition announcement.

2.5.7. Bid Completion Status

In this section, we address the question as to whether the markets are able to anticipate the ultimate success or failure of the M&A negotiations. The negotiations are assumed to be ultimately successful if the acquired number of shares is sufficient for the bidder to exercise control, or if the required majority of the target shareholders accept the bid. Out of the 2419 announcements in our sample 207 ultimately failed, and 271 resulted in prolonged negotiations between the bidder and the target's shareholders (pending bids). Irrespective of the ultimate success or failure of the bid, we find significantly positive announcement effects for the target firms (Figure 2.31). The event-day effect is significantly larger (by

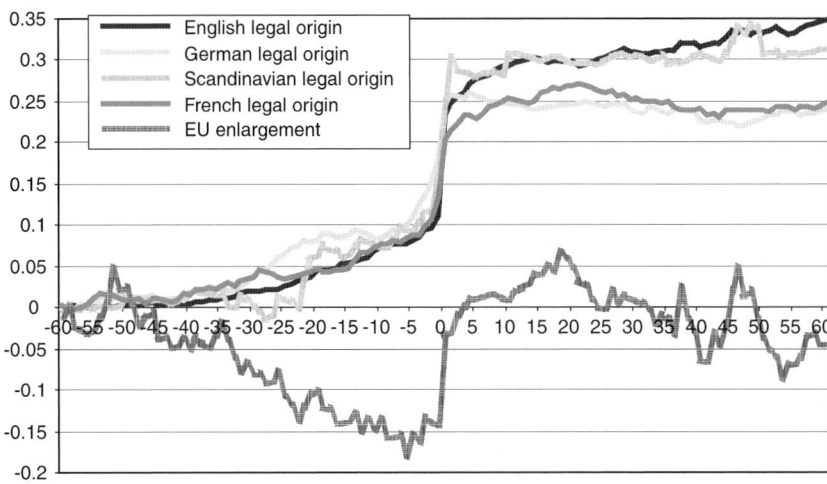

Figure 2.29: Target CAARs in cross-border bids by bidder legal origin. *Note*: This figure shows the market reaction to the announcement of cross-border M&A transactions for target firms by bidder legal origin. Countries are grouped according to their legal origin following the classification by La Porta, Lopez-de-Silanes, Shleifer, and Vishny (1998) and according to the EU enlargement process. Countries are grouped as follows: English legal origin (Ireland and the UK); German legal origin (Austria, Germany, Switzerland); French legal origin (Belgium, France, Greece, Italy, Luxemburg, the Netherlands, Portugal, Spain); Scandinavian legal origin (Denmark, Iceland, Finland, Norway, Sweden); 2004 EU Accession (Czech Republic, Cyprus, Estonia, Hungary, Latvia, Lithuania, Poland, Slovak Republic, Slovenia); 2007–2009 likely EU Accession (Bulgaria, Croatia, Romania). The day of the bid announcement is day 0. Abnormal returns are computed as the difference between the realized and market model benchmark returns. For each firm we calculate the daily benchmark returns using MSCI-Europe index returns and the market model parameters are estimated over 240 days starting 300 days prior to the acquisition announcement.

1–2%) for the successful bids than for the failures and pending deals. However, over the 2-month window prior to and including the event day, there is no difference in the CAARs between failed and successful bids (21.8% versus 21.5%). For the same period, pending acquisitions underperform successful and withdrawn bids by 3–5%.

Figure 2.31 shows that whereas the CAARs for the target firms in successful bids are not significantly different from zero subsequent to the announcement, the abnormal returns for the failed bids rise (by about 10%) over the 3 months post-event window. This may result from the fact that the market is relieved that the bid is withdrawn and anticipates other bids in the near future. In contrast, the CAARs for targets in pending acquisitions fall (by about 5%) over the 40 days after the initial announcement, most likely as a reaction to the ongoing uncertainty.

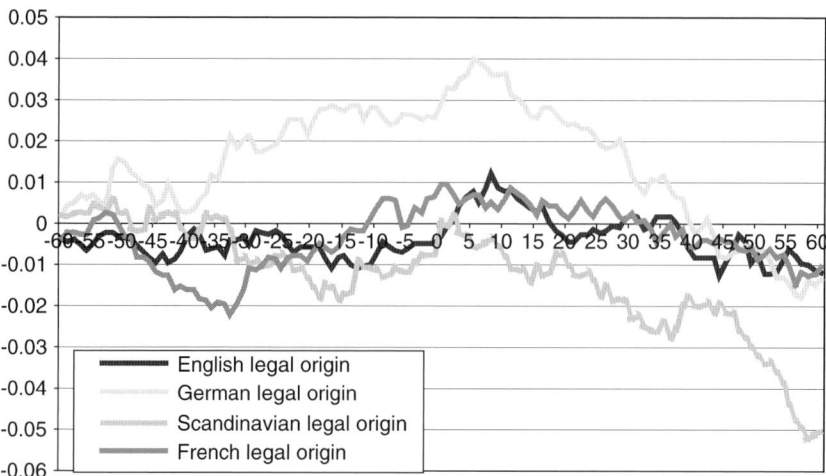

Figure 2.30: Bidder CAARs in cross-border acquisitions by bidder legal origin. *Note*: This figure shows the market reaction to the announcement of cross-border M&A transactions for bidding firms by legal origin. Countries are grouped according to their legal origin following the classification by La Porta, Lopez-de-Silanes, Shleifer, and Vishny (1998) and according to the EU enlargement process. Countries are grouped as follows: English legal origin (Ireland and the UK); German legal origin (Austria, Germany, Switzerland); French legal origin (Belgium, France, Greece, Italy, Luxemburg, the Netherlands, Portugal, Spain); Scandinavian legal origin (Denmark, Iceland, Finland, Norway, Sweden); 2004 EU Accession (Czech Republic, Cyprus, Estonia, Hungary, Latvia, Lithuania, Poland, Slovak Republic, Slovenia); 2007–2009 likely EU Accession (Bulgaria, Croatia, Romania). The day of the bid announcement is day 0. Abnormal returns are computed as the difference between the realized and market model benchmark returns. For each firm we calculate the daily benchmark returns using MSCI-Europe index returns and the market model parameters are estimated over 240 days starting 300 days prior to the acquisition announcement.

The announcement effect for unsuccessful bidders is negative (–0.6%), but not statistically significant from zero (Figure 2.32). The total wealth effects (over a 6-month time span) of completed, pending and withdrawn takeovers range between –6% and –3%, with most losses occurring to the bidding firms facing difficulties to complete the takeover negotiations.

2.5.8. Focus versus Diversification Strategies

Although conglomerate acquisitions are expected to create operational and/or financial synergies, the creation of diversified firms is associated with a number of disadvantages such as rent-seeking behaviour by divisional managers (Scharfstein & Stein, 2000),

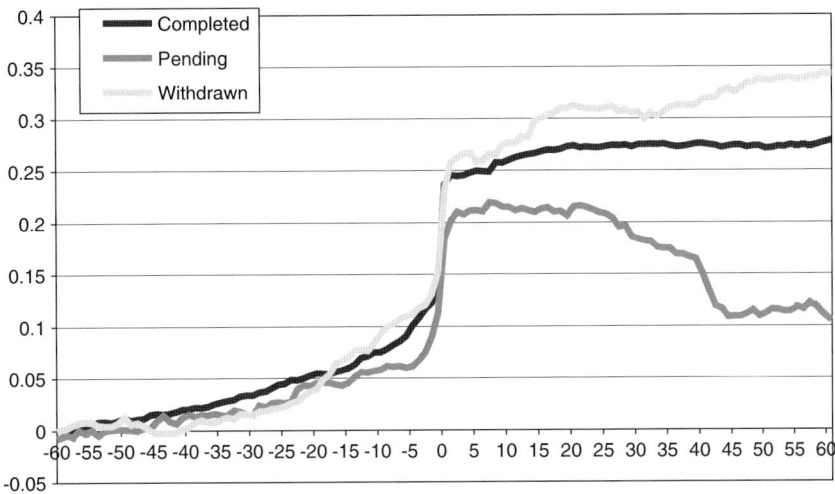

Figure 2.31: Target CAARs by bid completion status. *Note*: This figure shows the market reaction to the announcement of M&A transactions for target firms by bid completion status. A takeover is considered to be completed if the bidder has successfully acquired control over the target company; it is withdrawn if the bidder failed to acquire control over company; and pending if the acquisition of control has been announced but has not been completed or withdrawn afterwards. The day of the bid announcement is day 0. Abnormal returns are computed as the difference between the realized and market model benchmark returns. For each firm we calculate daily benchmark returns using MSCI-Europe index returns and the market model parameters are estimated over 240 days starting 300 days prior to the acquisition announcement.

bargaining problems within the firm (Rajan, Servaes, & Zingales, 2000), or bureaucratic rigidity (Shin & Stulz, 1998). These disadvantages of diversification may outweigh the alleged synergies and result in wealth destruction for the shareholders of both the bidding and target firms.

Our sample of 2419 takeover announcements includes 861 conglomerate takeovers in which bidder and target operate in unrelated industries. Figure 2.33 compares the CAARs of the target firms in diversifying takeovers with those of M&As in industry-related or focus-oriented M&As. Irrespective of the corporate strategy, shareholders of the target firm can pocket significantly positive abnormal returns at the announcement day. However, these returns are significantly larger (by 2.4%) for unrelated takeovers. Over the period including the announcement day and the price run-up period, the targets of diversifying takeovers enjoy a CAAR of about 24% whereas the ones of takeovers with a focus strategy experience a CAAR of about 19%. Regardless of the length of the window, diversifying takeovers beat M&As with a focus strategy in the short-run. The difference is likely to be a result of more aggressive bids in diversifying takeovers and greater willingness of bidders to overpay for the unrelated target firms. This is because diversifying acquisitions are more likely

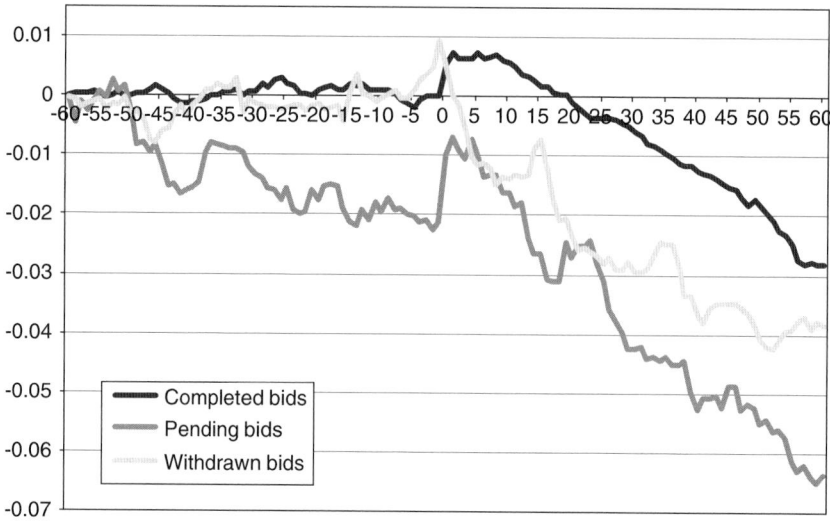

Figure 2.32: Bidder CAARs by bid completion status. *Note*: This figure shows the market reaction to the announcement of M&A transactions for bidding firms by bid completion status. A takeover is considered to be completed if the bidder has successfully acquired control over the target company; it is withdrawn if the bidder failed to acquire control over company; and pending if the acquisition of control has been announced but has not been completed or withdrawn afterwards. The day of the bid announcement is day 0. Abnormal returns are computed as the difference between the realized and market model benchmark returns. For each firm we calculate daily benchmark returns using MSCI-Europe index returns and the market model parameters are estimated over 240 days starting 300 days prior to the acquisition announcement.

to occur when bidding firms suffer from agency conflicts and free cash flow problems. In the literature, there is evidence that the management of such firms often acquires unrelated business for personal reasons (e.g. for 'empire building' purposes) at the expense of shareholder value or that managerial hubris leads bidding firms to pay too high premiums.

These conjectures are consistent with our results for bidding companies: diversification destroys value on average and is largely driven by the personal objectives of managers. Figure 2.34 show that bidding firms have significantly higher short-run wealth effects around the announcement of a business expansion within the core industry in comparison to the abnormal returns around the announcement of business diversification (0.63% versus 0.36%). Also, it appears that the market anticipates the focus strategy of the bidder, because there is a statistically significant run-up in the bidder's share price over the 2-month period prior to the event day. While the share price augments to 1.4% preceding the intra-industry bid announcement, it declines by the same percentage preceding the announcement of a conglomerate takeover.

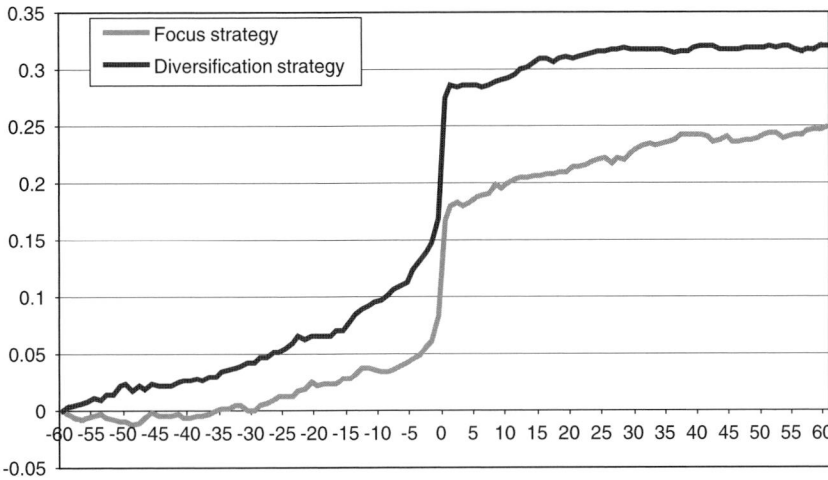

Figure 2.33: Target CAARs by corporate strategy (focus versus diversification). *Note*: This figure shows the market reaction to the announcement of M&A transactions for target firms by takeover strategy (focus versus diversification). A takeover strategy is considered to be focus-oriented if the 2-digit SIC codes of the bidding and target firms coincide and to be diversification-oriented if this is not the case. The day of the bid announcement is day 0. Abnormal returns are computed as the difference between the realized and market model benchmark returns. For each firm we calculate the daily benchmark returns using MSCI-Europe index returns and the market model parameters are estimated over 240 days starting 300 days prior to the acquisition announcement.

2.5.9. Public versus Private Target Firms

Acquisitions of privately held companies account for the majority of the intra-European acquisitions, namely more than 60%. The theoretical and empirical literature suggests that bids for such firms may lead to bidder returns that exceed those obtained in the bids for public firms (Chang, 1998; Faccio, McConnell, & Stolin, 2004; Moeller, Schlingemann, & Stulz, 2004). The fact that the shares of privately held firms are by definition illiquid, may create a price discount. Also, privately held firms are frequently controlled by one investor or investor group with which negotiations may have a better chance to succeed than when a public tender offer has to be launched. However, the acquisition of a private firm may entail considerably more risk for the acquirer due to the fact that less reliable information about the true value and growth potential of the firm is available. Figure 2.35 exhibits that the announcement of an acquisition of a private firm causes significantly positive abnormal returns of 0.8% to the bidder's shareholders, whereas the announcement of a bid for a public firm results in an (insignificantly) negative return of –0.1%. Moeller, Schlingemann, and Stulz (2004) and Faccio, McConnell, and Stolin (2004) confirm that a

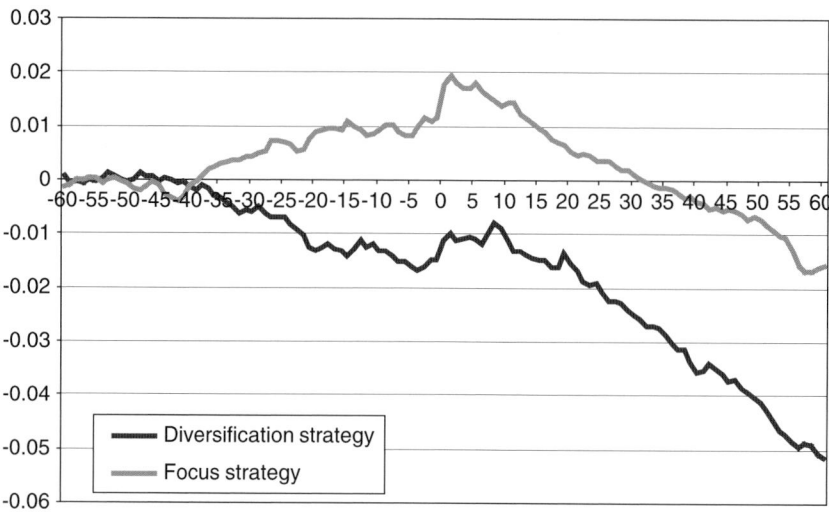

Figure 2.34: Bidder CAARs by corporate strategy (focus versus diversification). *Note*: This figure shows the market reaction to the announcement of M&A transactions for bidding firms by takeover strategy (focus versus diversification). A takeover strategy is considered to be focus-oriented if the 2-digit SIC codes of the bidding and target firms coincide, and to be diversification-oriented if this is not the case. The day of the bid announcement is day 0. Abnormal returns are computed as the difference between the realized and market model benchmark returns. For each firm we calculate the daily benchmark returns using MSCI-Europe index returns and the market model parameters are estimated over 240 days starting 300 days prior to the acquisition announcement.

bid on a private target results in substantially higher announcement CAARs to the bidders than a bid on a public firm.

In contrast, the post-announcement returns over longer time windows decline to almost –3% when a private firm is acquired and to –1.3% when a listed firm is taken over (both percentages are significant at the 1% level). This result is in line with Bradley and Sundaram (2004) who report that the 2-year post-announcement returns in takeovers of a public target are insignificant from zero, whereas these returns are significantly negative when the target is private.

2.5.10. Full versus Partial Acquisitions

Figure 2.36 depicts that when a firm announces its intention to acquire full control of a target firm by bidding on the entire equity capital, the abnormal returns to the target firm's shareholders are significantly higher than when a firm merely intends to acquire majority

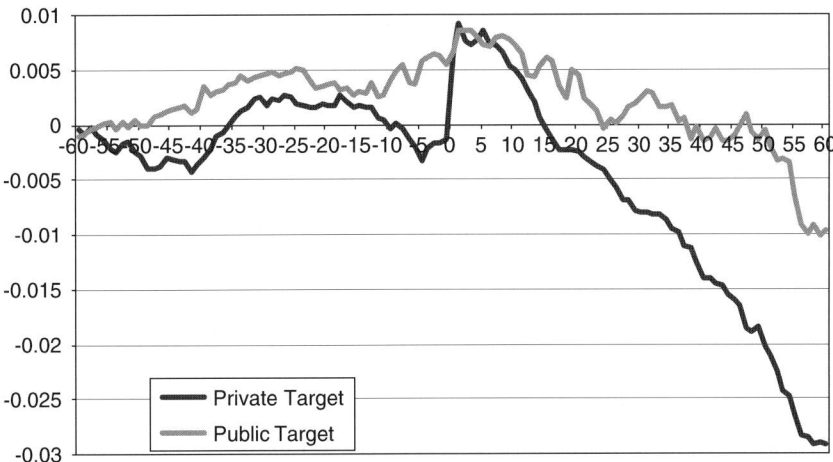

Figure 2.35: Bidder CAARs by target legal status (private versus public). *Note*: This figure shows the market reaction to the announcement of M&A transactions for bidding firms by legal status of target firms (public versus private). A target firm is considered to be private if it is a stand-alone firm not listed on any stock exchange. The day of the bid announcement is day 0. Abnormal returns are computed as the difference between realized and market model benchmark returns. For each firm we calculate the daily benchmark returns using MSCI-Europe index returns and the market model parameters are estimated over 240 days starting 300 days prior to the acquisition announcement.

control. At the announcement day, the share price of the target subject to a full acquisition rises by 12%, an increase which is more than five times larger than the abnormal return of a target subject to the partial-control acquisition. Investors purchasing equity of the target firm 3 months prior to a full takeover and selling the shares at the end of 3 months subsequent to the announcement earn a CAAR of 31%. In contrast, only 14% can be pocketed over the same period in case of a partial acquisition. The lower returns for partial-control acquisitions may reflect the concern that a control transfer may load to expropriation of the rights of the remaining minority shareholders.

However, Figure 2.37 exhibits that bidder's shareholders also dislike partial acquisitions. Although the announcement effect of partial acquisitions is significantly positive (0.4%), it is notably lower than the announcement effect of the full takeover (0.6%). Also, the acquisition of a majority interest is associated with significant negative abnormal returns both prior and after the transaction announcement whereas a full acquisition is preceded by a significant increase in the equity value of the bidding firm. In sum, investors holding shares of the bidding firm over the 6-month period centred around the event day accumulate significant losses of –5% in case of a partial acquisition, whereas those holding shares in full takeovers obtain returns insignificantly different from zero.

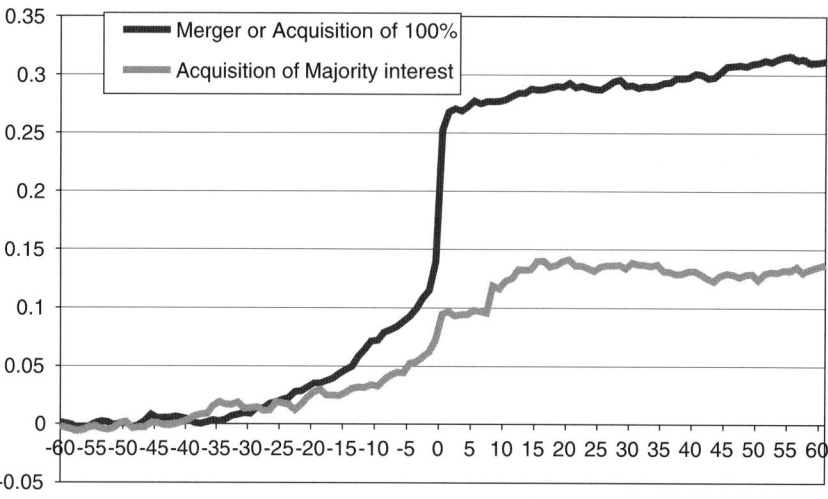

Figure 2.36: Target CAARs by the form of takeover. *Note*: This figure shows the market reaction to the announcement of M&A transactions for target firms by form of takeover (a merger or acquisition of 100% of the equity versus and acquisition of a majority stake). An acquisition of a majority stake occurs if the total shareholding of the bidder after the deal completion is less than 100%. The day of the bid announcement is day 0. Abnormal returns are computed as the difference between the realized and market model benchmark returns. For each firm we calculate the daily benchmark returns using MSCI-Europe index returns and the market model parameters are estimated over 240 days starting 300 days prior to the acquisition announcement.

2.5.11. The Good, the Bad and the Ugly (Takeovers at the Start, the Peak and the Decline of the Fifth Takeover Wave)

M&A activity during the 1990s was characterized by continual increases in the number of takeovers and in the average bid value. The increase in value of intra-European takeovers grew by more than 280% over the period of 1996–1999. The year 1999 was not only remarkable in terms of the total bid value (US$ 1.3 million), but also in terms of the number of hostile acquisitions: there were 44 hostile offers compared to an average of 19 in previous years. Shelton (2000) reports that bidder gains decline during takeover peaks which suggests that bidders then tend to bid more aggressively. They also show that bidders display a greater tendency to overpay and to undertake more risky M&As. Harford (2003) confirms that takeovers occurring at a later stage of the wave trigger lower abnormal returns to the bidder's shareholders than those at the beginning of the wave. They interpret this finding as resulting from more limited information processing, managerial hubris and managerial self-interest. A similar decline in takeover profitability over the 1990s wave is documented in Moeller, Schlingemann, and Stulz (2005). They argue that their evidence supports Jensen (2004): high valuations increase managerial discretion,

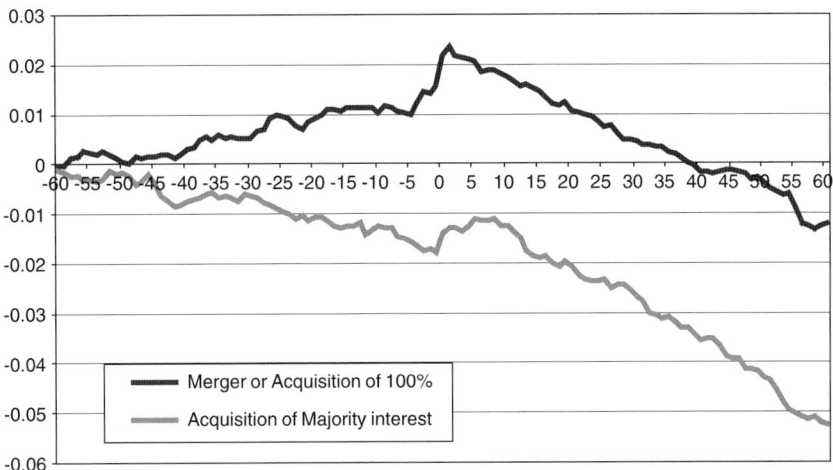

Figure 2.37: Bidder CAARs by the form of takeover. *Note*: This figure shows the market reaction to the announcement of M&A transactions for bidding firms by form of takeover (a merger or acquisition of 100% of the equity versus and acquisition of a majority stake). An acquisition of a majority stake occurs if the total shareholding of the bidder after the deal completion is less than 100%. The day of the bid announcement is day 0. Abnormal returns are computed as the difference between the realized and market model benchmark returns. For each firm we calculate the daily benchmark returns using MSCI-Europe index returns and the market model parameters are estimated over 240 days starting 300 days prior to the acquisition announcement.

making it possible for executives to make poor acquisitions when they have run out of good ones.

Our sample includes 857 (35%) bids that occur in the beginning of the fifth wave (1993–1996), 931 (38%) bids in the middle of the wave (1997–1999), and 630 (27%) bids in the period when the M&A activity slows down (2000–2001). Figure 2.38 shows significant differences in terms of the price reaction to bids of the three sub-periods of the takeover wave. At the announcement day, the target firms gain an average premium of 8% prior to 1997, 10% in 1997–1999 and 9% in 2000–2001. The differences between the three figures are statistically significant at the 1% level. The second stage of the takeover wave is also standing out in terms of the price run-up for target firms: it amounts to 13% (up from 8% observed in 1993–1996). Over longer time windows, for instance, over a 6-month window symmetrically around the event day, the post-1999 bids yield lower CAARs (21%) than those in 1997–1999 (31%) and those of the pre-1997 bids (25%). From Figure 2.38, it is clear that the target shareholders gain most at the peak of the takeover wave, but at whose expense? Clearly, Figure 2.39 shows that the bidders' shareholders do not seem to realize yet that their firm may be overpaying at the peak of the takeover wave. The sum of the price run-ups and the announcement effects for takeover bids at the beginning, peak and decline of the wave are 0.19%, 1.47% and 1.12%, respectively. However, when we

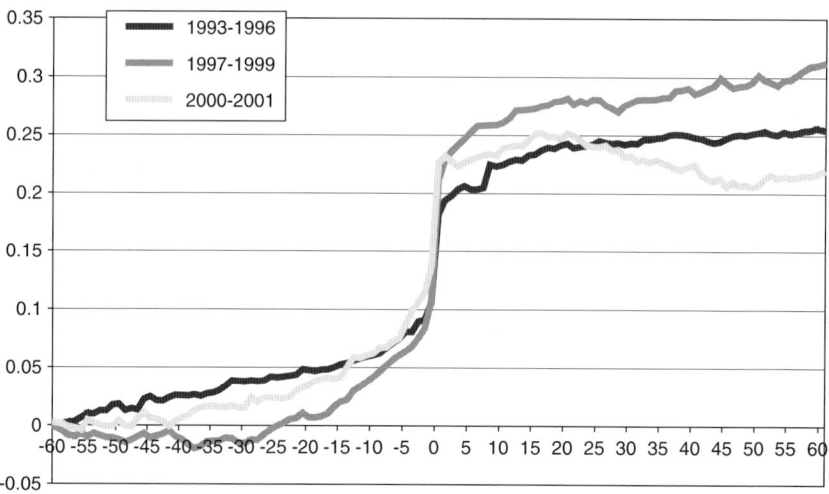

Figure 2.38: Target CAARs by sub-periods of the fifth takeover wave. *Note*: This figure shows the market reaction to the announcement of M&A transactions for target firms by sub-periods of the fifth takeover wave: bids announced in the beginning of the wave (1993–1996), at the peak of the wave (1997–1999), and subsequent to the peak (2000–2001). The day of the bid announcement is day 0. Abnormal returns are computed as the difference between the realized and market model benchmark returns. For each firm we calculate the daily benchmark returns using MSCI-Europe index returns and the market model parameters are estimated over 240 days starting 300 days prior to the acquisition announcement.

calculate CAARs over longer time windows (e.g. 6 months), it seems that the bidder share-holders realize that the bids may have been excessive at the peak and at the decline over the takeover wave: the CAARs amount to 0.52% (1993–1996), −1.30% (1997–1999) and −9.87% (2000–2001).[14] It should be noted that the substantial decline subsequent to the M&A peak is already corrected for the strong downward equity market movement. From the middle of 2000, the M&A climate has turned bleak and the stock market decline has made bidder shareholders very pessimistic about future synergies of the takeovers. Thus, our evidence shows that from a bidder's perspective, good M&As have turned bad (and even ugly) due to the reasons given above (e.g. managerial hubris and self-interest, herding).

2.6. Conclusions

This chapter provides a comprehensive overview of the European takeover market. We examine the main features of the domestic and cross-border corporate takeovers facing European companies in 1990–2001 and contrast them to those of the takeovers of the

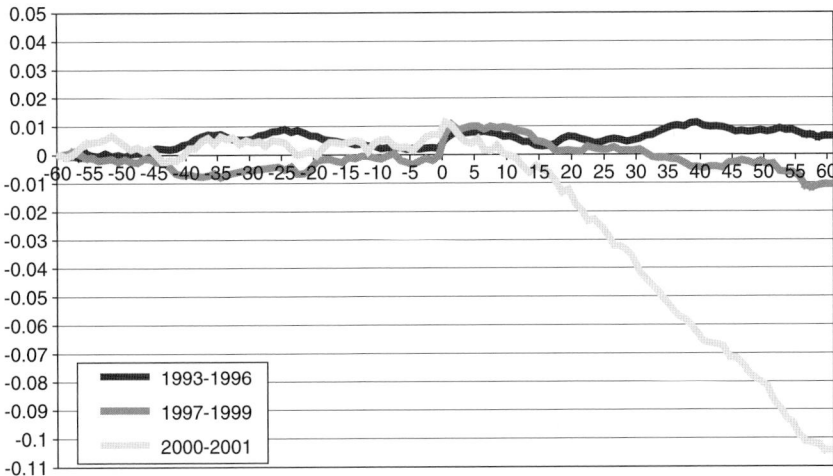

Figure 2.39: Bidder CAARs by sub-periods of the fifth takeover wave. *Note*: This figure shows the market reaction to the announcement of M&A transactions for bidding firms by sub-periods of the fifth takeover wave: bids announced in the beginning of the wave (1993–1996), at the peak of the wave (1997–1999), and subsequent to the peak (2000–2001). The day of the bid announcement is day 0. Abnormal returns are computed as the difference between the realized and market model benchmark returns. For each firm we calculate the daily benchmark returns using MSCI-Europe index returns and the market model parameters are estimated over 240 days starting 300 days prior to the acquisition announcement.

fourth takeover wave (1984–1989). Our analysis reveals that: (i) a substantial proportion of intra-European M&As in the 1990s were cross-border transactions; (ii) both cross-border and domestic M&A activity tended to occur between firms in related industries; (iii) the financial structure of takeover bids in the 1990s switched from a dominance of cash to a combination of equity, debt and cash, and — specifically for the largest transactions — to all-equity; and (iv) the number of hostile bids in Continental Europe increased over the 1990s, whereas the number of hostile transactions in the UK domestic market has decreased compared to the 1980s wave. These characteristics of the M&A sample suggest that takeovers in the 1990s mainly occurred for reasons of cost cutting, expanding into new markets, or exploiting the mispricing premium.

The bulk of European M&As of the 1990s was expected to improve efficiency as they triggered substantial share price increases at the announcement, most of which were captured by the target-firm shareholders. We find large announcement effects (of 9%) for the target firms compared to a statistically significant announcement effect of merely 0.5% for the bidders. Including the price run-up, the share price reaction amounts to 21% for the targets and 0.9% for the bidders. However, we show that market expectations about takeover profitability depend on the different attributes of the bids. For instance, the type of takeover bid is an important determinant: hostile takeovers trigger substantially larger price reactions to the target shareholders (15.5% on the event day) than friendly M&As (3%). This stands in marked contrast with the share price reaction of bidding firms: a hostile acquisition triggers a negative abnormal return of –0.4% whereas that of a merger or friendly acquisition generates a positive abnormal return of 0.8%.

There is also strong evidence that the means of payment has a large impact on the share prices of bidder and target. All-cash offers trigger abnormal returns of almost 12% upon announcement which is significantly higher than the average returns (of 7%) in all-equity offers. All-equity bids are more frequent in large transactions and in friendly M&As. In the 3-month period subsequent the bid announcements, deals involving equity payments are associated with substantially larger declines in bidders' share price than all-cash offers.

Domestic mergers or acquisitions trigger higher wealth effects to the target shareholders than cross-border operations. However, the premiums paid depend on the location of the target. When a UK target is involved, the abnormal returns are higher than those of bids involving a Continental European target. Further, when we partition our sample based on the legal origin of target and bidding firms, we find that target firms of French, German and EU Accession legal origins earn the lowest abnormal return upon the bid announcement, whereas UK and Scandinavian targets earn most. The evidence suggests that the differences in level of stock market development and corporate governance regulation across countries of different legal origins have a large impact on premiums paid in takeovers.

We also show that the announcement effect for the target shareholders is significantly larger in diversifying bids than in intra-industry or focus-oriented bids. The opposite is observed for the bidding firm: the announcement of a focus strategy generates significantly higher abnormal returns than the announcement of a diversification into an unrelated business segment. This evidence suggests that bidders tend to bid more aggressively in unrelated acquisitions and hence to overpay and that diversifying acquisitions are driven by motives other than shareholder profit maximization. Acquisitions of private target firms are associated with significant positive abnormal returns to the bidders (0.8% at day 0). In contrast, acquisitions of public companies trigger negative average abnormal returns to the bidders which are insignificantly different from zero.

Finally, we demonstrate that takeovers occurring at a later stage of the takeover wave trigger lower gains to shareholders than M&As at the beginning of the wave. For both bidding and target firms, the lowest 6-month CAARs are realized in M&As that occur at the end of the wave (2000–2001) and many M&A deals undertaken in the late 1990s destroyed bidders' value. The result is similar to findings reported in recent empirical literature for US M&As (e.g. Moeller, Schlingemann, & Stulz, 2005) and indicates that takeover waves tend to pass their optimal stopping point. Unprofitable takeovers at the later stages of the wave result from limited information processing, hubris and managerial self-interest.

Acknowledgements

We are grateful to Rolf Visser for allowing us to use the databases of Deloitte Corporate Finance and to Marc Goergen, Philippe Rogier, Peter Szilagyi and Grzegorz Trojanowski for valuable comments. Luc Renneboog thanks the Netherlands Organization for Scientific Research for a replacement subsidy of the programme 'Shifts in Governance'; the authors also gratefully acknowledge support from the European Commission via the 'New Modes of Governance'-project (NEWGOV) led by the European University Institute in Florence; contract number CIT1-CT-2004-506392.

Endnotes

1. It is believed that the French and Italian Governments are rather successful in protecting their national champi-ons. In these countries, hostile cross-border acquisitions hardly ever succeeded in the 1990s. The French and Italian Governments encouraged (often inefficient) mergers between national firms to create large national cor-porations and hence made these firms immune against acquisitions by foreign firms. Examples are the acquisi-tion of Telecom Italia by Olivetti (although it was a hostile bid, its success was largely due to do support by Italian Government that blocked the bid for Telecom Italia by Deutsche Telecom) or the merger between the French supermarket chains Carrefour and Promodes preventing their acquisition by the American chain Wal-Mart.
2. For an overview of the evidence on the wealth effects of M&A activity and the motives for takeovers, see Jensen and Ruback (1983), Jarrell, Brickley, and Netter (1988), Agrawal and Jaffe (2000), Bruner (2003), and Martynova and Renneboog (2005).
3. We do not consider white knight acquisitions as hostile. The reasons are: (1) in the acquisition by a white knight target shareholders usually get lower prices than the price offered by the competing (hostile) bidder, and (2) white knight bidder do not meet opposition from the target firm. There are very few bids with white knights; classifying these bids as hostile would not materially affect the results.
4. A friendly tender offer is a public offer to the target shareholders asking them to sell their shares for cash and/or equity at a pre-specified price or equity-exchange ratio, while the target board of directors does not oppose the bid. An acquisition is considered to be successful if a sufficient number of shares are tendered such that the bidder gains control over the target. In friendly M&As the shareholders of each firm approve the deal. Generally, a majority of 2/3 or more of shareholder votes is required for the merger or acquisition to succeed (the required percentage may vary by country).
5. We have checked the status of all bids which were labelled as 'pending' in the SDC database. To do so, we used LexisNexis and Factiva and have changed the completion status when pending bids were ultimately completed or withdrawn. For a number of bids, no further information was released in the financial press such that we retained the pending status for these bids. It should be noted that many of the pending bids are the ones in which the bidder its intention to acquire control over the target firm, but the acquisition will include several parts. That is, at the announcement, the bidder acquires a large stake in the target of, say, 20% and it also promises to acquire full control (the remaining 30–70%) in a near future.
6. We define 'companies in related industries' as firms for which the primary 2-digit SIC codes coincide. Changing this definition to the 3-digit SIC classification, does not materially change the results in the remainder of this chapter.
7. The sample also includes 698 bids (29%) that lack information about the method of payment. The number of undisclosed payment structures partially results from low disclosure requirements in the countries where these bids occurred. The highest proportion of M&As with undisclosed payment method is observed in Austria (68% of all bids in the country), Germany (67%), and Switzerland (57%).
8. The largest acquisitions by year are: the US\$ 1.5 billion bid by Lagardere Group for Matra-Hachette (both are located in France); the US\$ 2.5 billion bid in 1994 by Enterprise Oil for Lasmo (both are UK firms); the US\$ 5.5 billion bid in 1995 by Granada Group for Forte (both are UK firms); the US\$ 30 billion bid in 1996 by Ciba-Geigy for Sandoz (both are located in Switzerland); the US\$ 3.5 billion bid in 1997 by Rallye for Casino Guichard Perrachon (both are French firms); the US\$ 35 billion bid in 1998 by Britain's Zeneca Group for Sweden's Astra; the US\$ 202 billion bid in 1999 by Vodafone on Mannesmann; the US\$ 14 bil-lion bid in 2000 by Vodafone for Spain's Airtel; and the US\$ 7 billion bid in 2001 by Germany's E.ON (for-merly Veba/Viag) for Britain's Powergen.
9. We exclude market-adjusted model as it assumes that the impact of the market is similar across securities. Furthermore, there is a significant variation in the risk-free interest rate across countries: for example, on February 4, 2004 the 3-month government interest rate was 2.5% in Eurozone, 4.13% in UK, 0.24% in Switzerland, 12.68% in Hungary, 5.47% in Poland.

10. The parametric statistics differ with regard to their assumptions about whether or not abnormal returns are constant across securities or increase with the variance. Both parametric test statistics are based on the assumption of joint normality of the abnormal returns.
11. The requirement of symmetry is often violated when daily data are considered. According to Brown and Warner (1985), and Campbell, Lo, and MacKinlay (1997), it is likely that the cross-sectional distribution of daily abnormal returns is skewed to the right.
12. Appendices 2A and 2B show the CAARs of the bidding and target firms by country of origin.
13. According to international law, when a foreign firm acquires 100% of a domestic firm, the nationality of the latter changes. Hence, the target firm usually adopts the accounting standards, disclosure practices, and governance structures of the acquiring firm (Bris & Cabolis, 2004; Rossi & Volpin, 2004).
14. This result is unlikely to be driven by outliers, as the median value of CARs over window (–60, +60) for takeovers in 2000–2001 equals –5.4% (Q25 = –24% and Q75 = 21%).

References

Agrawal, A., & Jaffe, J. (2000). The post-merger performance puzzle. In: A. Gregory, & C. Cooper (Ed.), *Advances in Mergers and Acquisitions* (pp. 7–41). Amsterdam: JAI Press.

Agrawal, A., & Mandelker, G. (1987). Managerial incentives and corporate investment and financing decisions. *Journal of Finance, 42,* 823–837.

Amihud, Y., & Lev, B. (1981). Risk reduction as a managerial motive for conglomerate mergers. *Bell Journal of Economics, 12,* 605–617.

Andrade, G., Mitchell, M.L., & Stafford, E. (2001). New evidence and perspectives on mergers. *Journal of Economic Perspectives, 15,* 103–120.

Asquith, P., Bruner, R., & Mullins, D. (1983). The gains to bidding firms from merger. *Journal of Financial Economics, 11,* 121–139.

Baldwin, J.R., & Caves, R.E. (1991). Foreign multinational enterprises and merger activity in Canada. In: L. Waverman (Ed.), *Corporate globalization through mergers and acquisitions* (pp. 89–122). Calgary: University of Calgary Press.

Barca, F., & Becht, M. (2001). (Eds) *The Control of Corporate Europe.* Oxford: Oxford University Press.

Berger, P.G., & Ofek, E. (1995). Diversification's effect on firm value. *Journal of Financial Economics, 37,* 39–65.

Bhide, A. (1989). The causes and consequences of hostile takeovers. *Journal of Applied Corporate Finance, 2,* 36–59.

Bhide, A. (1990). Reversing corporate diversification. *Journal of Applied Corporate Finance, 3,* 70–81.

Blume, M. (1979). Betas and their regression tendencies: some further evidence. *Journal of Finance, 34,* 265–267.

Bradley, M., Desai, A., & Kim, E.H. (1988). Synergistic gains from corporate acquisitions and their division between the stockholders of target and acquiring firms. *Journal of Financial Economics, 21,* 3–40.

Bradley, M., & Sundaram, A. (2004). Do acquisitions drive performance or does performance drive acquisitions? Working paper, Duke University.

Bris, A., & Cabolis, C. (2004). The value of investor protection: firm evidence from cross-border mergers, Yale ICF Working paper no. 02-32.

Brown, S.J., & Warner, J.B. (1985). Using daily stock returns: the case of event studies. *Journal of Financial Economics, 14,* 3–31.

Bruner, R.F. (2003). Does M&A pay? In: R.F. Bruner (Ed.), Applied mergers and acquisitions (Chapter 3), New York: Wiley Finance.

Campbell, C.J., & Wasley, C.E. (1996). Measuring abnormal daily trading volume for samples of NYSE/ASE and NASDAQ securities using parametric and nonparametric test statistics. *Review of Quantitative Finance and Accounting, 6*, 309–326.

Campbell, J.Y., Lo, A.W., & MacKinlay, A.C. (1997). *The econometrics of financial markets.* Princeton: Princeton University Press.

Cebenoyan, A., Papaioannou, G., & Travlos, N. (1992). Foreign takeover activity in the US and wealth effects for target firm shareholders. *Financial Management, 21*, 58–68.

Chang, S. (1998). Takeovers of privately held targets, methods of payment, and bidder returns. *Journal of Finance, 53*, 773–784.

Comment, R., & Jarrell, G. (1995). Corporate focus and stock returns. *Journal of Financial Economics, 37*, 67–88.

Conn, R., Cosh, A.D., Guest, P.M., & Hughes, A. (2005). The impact on U.K. acquirers of domestic, cross-border, public and private acquisitions. *Journal of Business Finance and Accounting,* forthcoming.

Corrado, C.J. (1989). A nonparametric test for abnormal security-price performance in event studies. *Journal of Financial Economics, 23*, 385–395.

Danbolt, J. (2004). Target company cross-border effects in acquisitions into the UK. *European Financial Management, 10*, 83–108.

Dennis, D.K., & McConnell, J.J. (1986). Corporate mergers and security returns. *Journal of Financial Economics, 16*, 143–187.

Dewenter, K. (1995). Does the market react differently to domestic and foreign takeover announcements? Evidence from the US chemical and retail industries. *Journal of Financial Economics, 37*, 421–441.

Dimson, E. (1979). Risk measurement when shares are subject to infrequent trading. *Journal of Financial Economics, 7*, 197–226.

Dimson, E., & Marsh, P. (1983). The stability of UK risk measures and the problem of thin trading. *Journal of Finance, 38*, 753–783.

Doukas, J., Holmen, M., & Travlos, N. (2002). Diversification, ownership and control of Swedish Corporations. *European Financial Management, 8*, 281–314.

Faccio, M., & Lang, L. (2002). The ultimate ownership of Western European Corporations. *Journal of Financial Economics, 65*, 365–395.

Faccio, M., McConnell, J., & Stolin, D. (2004). Returns to acquirers of listed and unlisted targets. *Journal of Financial and Quantitative Analysis,* forthcoming.

Franks, J., & Harris, R. (1989). Shareholder wealth effects of corporate takeovers: the U.K. experience 1955–1985. *Journal of Financial Economics, 23*, 225–249.

Franks, J., Harris, R., & Titman, S. (1991). The postmerger share-price performance of acquiring firms. *Journal of Financial Economics, 29*, 81–96.

Franks, J., & Mayer, C. (1996). Hostile takeovers and the correction of managerial failure. *Journal of Financial Economics, 40*, 163–181.

Froot, K., & Stein, J. (1991). Exchange rates and foreign direct investments: an imperfect capital markets approach. *Quarterly Journal of Economics, 106*, 1191–1271.

Goergen, M., Martynova, M., & Renneboog, L. (2005). Corporate governance convergence: evidence from takeover regulation reforms. *Oxford Review of Economic Policy, 21*, 243–268.

Goergen, M., & Renneboog, L. (2004). Shareholder wealth effects of European domestic and cross border takeover bids. *European Financial Management, 10*, 9–45.

Golbe, D.L., & White, L.J. (1993). Catch a wave: the time series behaviour of mergers. *Review of Economics and Statistics, 75*, 493–497.

Gregory, A. (1997). An examination of the long run performance of UK acquiring firms. *Journal of Business Finance and Accounting, 24*, 971–1002.

Harford, J. (2003). Efficient and distortional components to industry merger waves. Unpublished paper presented at AFA 2004 San Diego Meetings.

Hasbrouck, J. (1985). The characteristics of takeover targets: Q and other measures. *Journal of Banking and Finance, 9*, 351–362.

Healy, P., Palepu, K.G., & Ruback, R.S. (1997). Which takeovers are profitable: strategic or financial? *Sloan Management Review, 38*, 45–57.

Healy, P.M., Palepu, K.G., & Ruback, R.S. (1992). Does corporate performance improve after mergers? *Journal of Financial Economics, 31*, 135–175.

Higgins, R., & Schall, L. (1975). Corporate bankruptcy and conglomerate merger. *Journal of Finance, 30*, 93–113.

Hubbard, R.G., & Palia, D. (1999). A reexamination of the conglomerate merger wave in the 1960s: an internal capital markets view. *Journal of Finance, 54*, 1131–1152.

Jarrell, G., Brickley, J., & Netter, J. (1988). The market for corporate control: the empirical evidence since 1980. *Journal of Economic Perspectives, 2*, 49–68.

Jarrell, G., & Poulsen, A. (1989). The returns to acquiring firms in tender offers: evidence from three decades. *Financial Management, 18*, 12–19.

Jensen, M. (1986). Agency costs of free cash flow, corporate finance, and takeovers. *American Economic Review, 76*, 323–329.

Jensen, M. (2004). Agency costs of overvalued equity. Harvard NOM Working paper no. 04-26; ECGI – Finance Working paper no. 39/2004.

Jensen, M., & Ruback, R. (1983). The market for corporate control: the scientific evidence. *Journal of Financial Economics, 11*, 5–50.

Kang, J. (1993). The international market for corporate control — Mergers and acquisitions of US firms by Japanese firms. *Journal of Financial Economics, 11*, 345–371.

Kaplan, S., & Weisbach, M. (1992). The success of acquisitions: evidence from divestitures. *Journal of Finance, 47*, 107–138.

La Porta, R., Lopez-de-Silanes, F., Shleifer, A., & Vishny, R. (1998). Law and finance. *Journal of Political Economy, 106*, 1113–1155.

Lang, L., Stulz, R., & Walkling, R. (1989). Managerial performance, Tobin's Q, and the gains from successful tender offers. *Journal of Financial Economics, 24*, 137–154.

Lang, L., Stulz, R., & Walkling, R. (1991). A test of the free cash flow hypothesis: the case of bidder returns. *Journal of Financial Economics, 29*, 315–335.

Lewellen, W. (1971). A pure financial rationale for the conglomerate merger. *Journal of Finance, 26*, 521–545.

Loderer, C., & Martin, K. (1990). Corporate acquisitions by listed firms: the experience of a comprehensive sample. *Financial Management, 19*, 17–33.

Martin, K., & McConnell, J. (1991). Corporate performance, corporate takeovers, and management turnover. *Journal of Finance, 46*, 671–687.

Martynova, M., & Renneboog, L. (2005). Takeover waves: the triggers, performance and motives. Working paper, European Corporate Governance Institute.

McCahery, J., & Renneboog, L. (2002). Recent developments in corporate governance. In: J. McCahery, P. Moerland, T. Raaijmakers, & L. Renneboog (Eds), *Convergence and diversity of corporate governance regimes and capital markets*. Oxford: Oxford University Press.

Mitchell, M.L., & Lehn, K. (1990). Do bad bidders become good targets? *Journal of Political Economy, 98*, 372–398.

Moeller, S., & Schlingemann, F. (2005). Global diversification and bidder gains: a comparison between cross-border and domestic acquisitions. *Journal of Banking and Finance, 29*, 533–564.

Moeller, S., Schlingemann, F., & Stulz, R. (2004). Firm size and the gains from acquisitions. *Journal of Financial Economics, 73*, 201–228.

Moeller, S., Schlingemann, F., & Stulz, R. (2005). Wealth destruction on a massive scale? A study of acquiring-firm returns in the recent merger wave. *Journal of Finance, 60*, 757–782.

Morck, R., Shleifer, A., & Vishny, R. (1988). Characteristics of targets of hostile and friendly takeovers. In: A. Auerbach (Ed), *Corporate takeovers: causes and consequences.* Chicago: National Bureau of Economic Research.

Morck, R., Shleifer, A., & Vishny, R. (1989). Alternative mechanisms for corporate control. *American Economic Review, 89*, 842–852.

Morck, R., Shleifer, A., & Vishny, R. (1990). Do managerial objectives drive bad acquisitions? *Journal of Finance, 45*, 31–48.

Mulherin, J.H., & Boone, A.L. (2000). Comparing acquisitions and divestitures. *Journal of Corporate Finance, 6*, 117–139.

Palepu, K.G. (1986). Predicting takeover targets: a methodological and empirical analysis. *Journal of Accounting and Economics, 8*, 3–35.

Rajan, R., Servaes, H., & Zingales, L. (2000). The cost of diversity: the diversification discount and inefficient investment. *Journal of Finance, 55*, 2537–2564.

Rau, P.R., & Vermaelen, T. (1998). Glamour, value and the post-acquisition performance of acquiring firms. *Journal of Financial Economics, 49*, 223–253.

Ravenscraft, D.J., & Scherer, F.M. (1987). Mergers, sell-offs and economic efficiency. Washington, DC: The Brookings Press.

Ravenscraft, D.J., & Scherer, F.M. (1989). The profitability of mergers. *International Journal of Industrial Organization, 7*, 101–116.

Rossi, S., & Volpin, P. (2004). Cross-country determinants of mergers and acquisitions. *Journal of Financial Economics, 74*, 277–304.

Scharfstein, D., & Stein, J. (2000). The dark side of internal capital markets: divisional rent-seeking and inefficient investment. *Journal of Finance, 55*, 2537–2564.

Schoenberg, R. (1999). Cultural compatibility in international acquisitions. In: F. Burton, M. Chapman, & A. Cross (Eds), *International business organization: subsidiary management, entry strategies and emerging markets* (pp. 294–306). New York: St. Martin's Press; London: Macmillan Press.

Scholes, M., & Wolfson, M. (1990). The effects of changes in tax laws on corporate reorganization activity. *Journal of Business, 63*, 141–164.

Schwert, G.W. (1996). Markup pricing in mergers and acquisitions. *Journal of Financial Economics, 41*, 153–162.

Schwert, G.W. (2000). Hostility in takeovers: in the eyes of the beholder? *Journal of Finance, 55*, 2599–2640.

Servaes, H. (1991). Tobin's Q and the gains from takeovers. *Journal of Finance, 46*, 409–419.

Servaes, H., & Zenner, M. (1994). Taxes and the returns to foreign acquisitions in the United States. *Financial Management, 23*, 42–56.

Shelton, L.M. (2000). Merger market dynamics: insights into behaviour of target and bidder firms. *Journal of Economic Behavior and Organization, 41*, 363–383.

Shin, H., & Stulz, R. (1998). Are internal capital markets efficient? *Quarterly Journal of Economics, 113*, 531–552.

Smith, R.L., & Kim, J.H. (1994). The combined effects of free cash flow and financial slack on bidder and target stock returns. *Journal of Business, 67*, 281–310.

Wansley, J., Lane, W., & Yang, H. (1983). Shareholder returns to US acquired firms and domestic acquisitions. *Journal of Business Finance and Accounting, 10*, 647–656.

Appendix 2.A: Cumulative Abnormal Returns for Target Firms by Country of Their Incorporation.

	ALL	AUS	BEL	DEN	FIN	FRA	GER	IRE	ITA	NL	NOR	ESP	SWE	SWZ	UK	OTH*
CAAR % [−40, −1]	8.92	2.75	−0.66	5.15	0.29	3.43	8.57	18.61	13.30	19.00	8.29	16.37	10.91	8.18	15.59	4.55
t_{rank}	3.27[a]	0.32	−0.11	1.37	0.03	1.40	3.17[a]	1.72	2.30[b]	2.57[b]	2.56[b]	2.86[b]	3.12[a]	2.44[b]	11.13[a]	0.38
t_p	2.49[b]	0.49	−0.07	1.05	0.04	1.32	3.35[a]	2.44[c]	3.31[a]	4.00[a]	2.72[a]	2.18[b]	4.17[a]	2.29[b]	18.68[a]	0.70
t_{st}	26.53[a]	−0.76	0.79	1.87[c]	−0.55	2.74[a]	4.63[a]	2.70[b]	5.04[a]	3.28[a]	2.33[b]	6.16[a]	4.11[a]	2.25[b]	28.01[a]	0.74
% Positive	69	64	60	69	25	61	70	100	71	77	65	71	70	79	72	51
CAAR % [T = 0]	9.01	0.29	5.52	4.28	4.36	0.82	2.00	0.50	1.04	11.47	10.77	6.39	11.52	7.87	13.90	−0.40
t_{rank}	14.37[a]	0.30	1.45	1.56	2.06	1.99[b]	2.44[b]	1.17	0.80	2.79[b]	3.14[a]	2.81[b]	5.71[a]	2.84[a]	13.38[a]	−0.19
t_p	9.54[a]	0.32	3.53[a]	5.52[a]	36.80[a]	1.94[c]	4.87[a]	0.41	1.59	14.95[a]	21.95[a]	5.35[a]	27.60[a]	13.83[a]	104.62[a]	−0.03
t_{st}	147.15[a]	4.10[a]	4.43[a]	6.23[a]	48.97[a]	3.61[a]	6.17[a]	0.73	3.12[a]	22.93[a]	26.81[a]	12.41[a]	31.90[a]	17.92[a]	169.37[a]	−0.11
% Positive	70	64	80	69	100	44	61	50	42	85	63	76	76	86	81	57
CAAR % [−1, +1]	12.28	2.88	3.48	5.42	5.74	1.84	4.44	2.88	2.44	19.44	15.67	9.65	15.07	11.77	18.18	0.33
t_{rank}	16.82[a]	0.90	0.69	1.49	3.36[b]	2.29[b]	3.25[a]	0.78	1.80[c]	3.55[a]	4.33[a]	3.96[a]	6.62[a]	4.28[a]	15.81[a]	−0.35
t_p	7.51[a]	1.86[c]	1.28	4.03[a]	27.32[a]	2.69[a]	6.29[a]	2.35[c]	2.16[b]	14.74[a]	18.45[a]	4.67[a]	21.04[a]	11.93[a]	79.01[a]	0.65
t_{st}	114.15[a]	6.72[a]	3.08[b]	5.53[a]	34.10[a]	5.94[a]	8.00[a]	4.24[a]	2.97[a]	18.88[a]	21.96[a]	11.27[a]	24.73[a]	13.67[a]	125.97[a]	0.45
% Positive	78	55	90	85	100	55	63	67	58	85	79	88	93	86	86	48

CAAR % [−5, +5]	14.73	6.33	2.80	3.83	6.87	5.30	3.96	6.73	6.55	23.59	16.19	9.42	17.13	11.71	22.93	−1.24
t_{rank}	10.50[a]	0.95	0.30	0.79	4.17[b]	3.10[a]	1.40	2.25[c]	2.66[b]	4.42[a]	4.01[a]	3.24[a]	6.71[a]	3.28[a]	17.80[a]	−0.79
t_p	4.70[a]	2.14[b]	0.54	1.50	15.58[a]	4.07[a]	2.97[a]	1.65	3.04[a]	13.39[a]	10.05[a]	2.39[b]	12.55[a]	6.26[a]	52.32[a]	0.32
t_{st}	76.96[a]	11.80[a]	2.45[b]	6.20[a]	19.03[a]	7.82[a]	5.22[a]	2.92[b]	3.55[a]	15.67[a]	11.78[a]	5.99[a]	14.40[a]	7.18[a]	83.19[a]	0.31
% Positive	79	64	70	77	100	64	66	100	71	92	72	82	85	79	89	45
CAAR % [−60, +60]	18.01	4.81	2.58	20.01	4.79	14.62	6.67	37.63	3.17	37.72	27.29	35.52	22.29	18.00	38.59	−2.34
t_{rank}	2.03[b]	0.54	0.11	3.98[a]	3.10[b]	1.93[c]	1.46	2.15[c]	0.31	3.79[a]	4.36[a]	2.86[b]	3.33[a]	2.76[b]	16.79[a]	−6.61[a]
t_p	1.73[c]	0.49	0.15	2.35[b]	3.39[b]	3.24[a]	1.50	2.83[b]	0.45	5.73[a]	5.12[a]	2.75[b]	4.91[a]	2.91[b]	26.60[a]	−0.27
t_{st}	38.17[a]	0.49	2.52[b]	6.15[a]	3.45[b]	6.29[a]	1.69[c]	4.07[a]	1.60	5.31[a]	6.06[a]	7.05[a]	5.18[a]	3.09[a]	41.23[a]	−0.11
% Positive	76	64	60	92	100	65	55	67	63	77	70	76	72	79	87	45
Number of observations	760	11	10	13	4	105	56	6	24	13	43	17	54	14	357	27

AUS: Austria; BEL: Belgium; DEN: Denmark; FIN: Finland; FRA: France; GER: Germany; IRE: Ireland; ITA: Italy; NL: The Netherlands; NOR: Norway; ESP: Spain; SWE: Sweden; SWZ: Switzerland; UK: United Kingdom.

OTH*: Bulgaria, Croatia, Czech Republic, Cyprus, Estonia, Hungary, Latvia, Lithuania, Romania, Slovakia.

Statistical significance levels at: a: 1%, b: 5% and c: 10%, respectively.

The definitions of the t-tests are given in Section 2.4.3.

Appendix 2.B: Cumulative Abnormal Returns for Bidding Firms by Country of Incorporation.

	ALL	AUS	BEL	DEN	FIN	FRA	GER	IRE	ITA	LUX	NL	NOR	POR	ESP	SWE	SWZ	UK	OTH*
CAAR % [-40, -1]	0.88	3.53	1.15	-3.04	0.12	0.51	-2.72	6.33	4.549	14.49	4.17	4.44	12.92	4.21	2.56	2.32	0.37	-11.06
t_{rank}	1.59	1.19	0.70	-1.57	1.12	-0.52	-1.29	2.18[b]	2.39[b]	2.06	1.05	1.75[c]	0.52	1.30	1.99[b]	0.93	0.96	-0.30
t_p	1.65[c]	1.97[c]	0.69	-1.22	1.45	-0.46	-1.21	2.62[b]	2.44[b]	1.77	1.09	2.10[b]	1.16	2.30[b]	2.59[a]	1.28	1.34	-0.34
t_{st}	3.87[a]	1.40	2.05[b]	-1.76[c]	1.17	-1.09	-0.70	4.38[a]	3.27[a]	1.79	1.63	1.78[c]	0.36	-0.20	2.46[b]	2.60[b]	4.16[a]	-3.00[a]
% Positive	50	43	57	42	49	45	44	67	67	100	57	61	50	63	54	56	49	40
CAAR % [T = 0]	0.51	1.28	0.23	0.75	2.51	0.02	0.75	-0.14	0.70	1.70	-0.68	0.77	0.44	0.60	1.06	-0.11	0.37	1.07
t_{rank}	4.79[a]	1.23	0.80	2.23[b]	2.78[a]	0.07	2.52[b]	-0.61	1.19	1.29	-1.07	1.14	0.29	1.42	1.91[c]	-0.19	2.33[b]	0.00
t_p	6.12[a]	3.35[a]	0.52	2.56[b]	7.97[a]	0.05	3.40[a]	-0.32	1.96[c]	1.19	-1.36	2.02[b]	0.24	1.84	4.48[a]	-0.36	4.10[a]	0.30
t_{st}	12.55[a]	1.82[c]	0.55	2.98[a]	8.93[a]	1.15	5.47[a]	-0.59	1.32	1.17	-0.86	2.37[b]	-0.11	2.41	3.83[a]	2.09[b]	8.31[a]	0.37
% Positive	50	55	49	54	62	47	56	56	47	67	48	57	50	51	49	53	48	53
CAAR % [-1, +1]	0.74	0.96	1.11	0.90	3.78	0.60	0.73	3.16	1.38	-0.02	0.19	0.58	1.50	0.80	1.18	0.44	0.39	-1.78
t_{rank}	4.51[a]	0.83	1.31	1.58	2.60[b]	1.41	1.80[b]	1.58	2.13[b]	-0.03	0.19	0.71	2.82	0.79	1.84[c]	0.62	1.53	-0.32
t_p	5.16[a]	1.45	1.45	1.77[c]	6.93[a]	0.97	1.92[c]	4.26[a]	2.24[b]	-0.01	0.22	0.88	0.48	1.41	2.88[a]	0.86	2.46[b]	-0.14
t_{st}	15.04[a]	0.12	1.27	2.69[a]	8.27[a]	3.47[a]	2.97[a]	3.00[a]	2.37[b]	-0.02	0.81	-0.33	0.52	1.50	2.74[a]	2.60[b]	6.49[a]	-1.10
% Positive	51	45	51	54	58	48	55	56	55	67	52	43	50	53	53	47	50	47

CAAR % [−5, +5]	0.74	4.83	3.03	0.10	2.16	0.42	0.13	5.58	0.55	9.55	2.22	1.40	−0.84	0.49	1.52	0.59	0.52	−4.91
t_{rank}	2.84[a]	2.14[b]	1.97[c]	0.12	1.34	0.45	0.20	1.74	0.52	3.60	1.14	1.17	−0.36	0.31	1.84[c]	0.62	1.41	−0.82
t_p	2.67[a]	3.82[a]	2.06[b]	0.10	2.07[b]	0.36	0.18	3.92[a]	0.47	2.01	1.34	1.11	−0.14	0.45	1.95[c]	0.60	1.73[c]	−0.57
t_{st}	6.74[a]	2.77[a]	2.63[b]	−0.04	2.62[a]	−1.40	1.63	3.55[a]	0.58	2.10	2.14[b]	0.82	−0.38	0.35	1.73[c]	1.68[c]	4.76[a]	−1.30
% Positive	51	58	62	46	54	54	51	67	45	100	48	49	50	55	57	47	49	38
CAAR % [−60, +60]	−2.94	3.96	2.80	−2.16	2.64	−8.27	−7.79	1.77	5.04	30.56	8.81	−1.23	22.23	10.13	−2.39	−5.83	−0.97	−18.64
t_{rank}	−2.45[b]	0.58	0.42	−0.64	0.46	−2.03[b]	−2.29[b]	0.29	1.14	1.14	1.01	−0.23	0.44	2.15[b]	−0.62	−0.99	−0.55	−0.95
t_p	−3.21[a]	0.94	0.57	−0.67	0.76	−2.10[b]	−3.20[a]	0.38	1.29	1.94	1.60	−0.29	1.12	2.82[a]	−0.92	−1.78[c]	−0.97	−1.68[c]
t_{st}	2.42[b]	0.31	2.05[b]	−1.54	1.18	−2.64[a]	−0.50	0.28	2.06[b]	1.88	2.41[b]	−0.65	0.15	2.85[a]	0.32	−0.51	−4.15[a]	−1.00
% Positive	50	50	68	44	48	48	49	50	53	67	57	50	50	63	48	44	50	34
Number of observations	2194	40	47	50	84	305	243	36	49	3	21	76	2	49	157	55	917	60

AUS: Austria; BEL: Belgium; DEN: Denmark; FIN: Finland; FRA: France; GER: Germany; IRE: Ireland; ITA: Italy; LUX: Luxemburg; NL: The Netherlands; NOR: Norway; POR: Portugal; ESP: Spain; SWE: Sweden; SWZ: Switzerland; UK: United Kingdom.

OTH[*]: Bulgaria, Croatia, Czech Republic, Cyprus, Estonia, Hungary, Latvia, Lithuania, Romania, Slovakia.

Statistical significance levels at: a: 1%, b: 5% and c: 10%, respectively.

The definitions of the t-tests are given in Section 2.4.3.

Chapter 3

The Performance of Acquisitive Companies

Kees Cools and Mindel van de Laar

3.1. Introduction

Mergers and acquisitions (M&As) are as much a part of corporate life as doing business itself. During 1985–2004 more than 300,000 deals were completed globally, spread increasingly, evenly across the three main regions: the Americas, Europe, and Asia Pacific.[1] The late 1990s saw the largest M&A wave in history. After the decline in 2000–2003, the number of M&A deals has started to grow again (see Figure 3.1). In 2004 alone, 21,620 acquisitions were completed globally, with a combined value of more than 1.500 billion USD. Moreover, many of the companies frequently engaged in M&A activity, reflected in the fact that 60% of the companies that made an acquisition in 2004 had made an acquisition before.[2]

Given the large number of M&As and the large sums of money involved, it is not surprising that this field has been the focus of a significant amount of research. Most of these research have consisted of event studies that look at pre- and post-performance around the announcement of deals, but there have also been various accounting studies, as well as surveys of executives (see Bruner, 2004, for a recent survey of the literature). Initially, most of the event studies only looked at short-term stock returns at the time the M&A was announced. Typically these studies found (statistically significant) negative returns for the bidders, although zero and positive returns were also reported. Event studies that looked at medium-term (2–5 year) returns predominantly reported negative bidder returns, suggesting "second thoughts" by the bidders' shareholders (e.g. Moeller, Schlingemann, & Stulz, forthcoming). The accounting studies analyzed the acquirers' financial results before and after acquisitions, and overall the results for the acquirers are mixed.

For the target firms, the findings are much clearer. Target shareholders enjoy both economically and statistically significant positive returns, both in the short and medium term, in the 20–30% range. In sum, acquisitions seem to create value, but the gains end up in the pockets of the targets' shareholders.

In addition to general wealth effects, many studies have also looked at the underlying drivers of value effects of acquisitions. Determinants that positively affect bidders' returns

Advances in Corporate Finance and Asset Pricing
Edited by L. Renneboog
© 2006 Elsevier B.V. All rights reserved.
ISBN: 0-444-52723-0

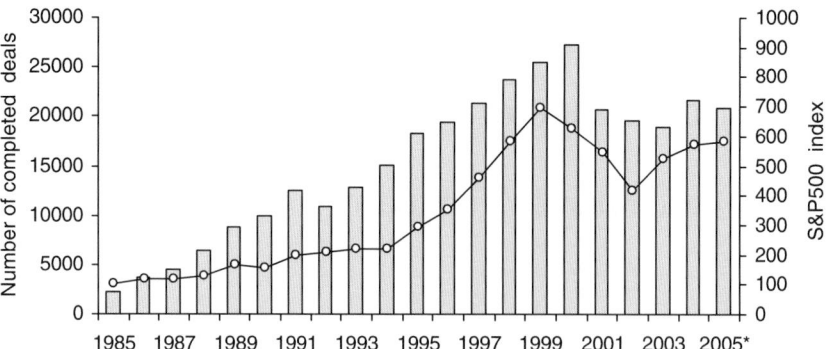

Figure 3.1: Number of M&As completed in 1985–2005 compared to the S&P index. *Notes*: (1) The number of deals for 2005 are projected based on the number of deals completed in January–August 2005, added with estimations for the number of deals in September–December, based on the January 2005 data multiplied by an average month index created using the data for 2003 and 2004. (2) The numbers displayed in the table are the number of completed deals per calendar year, for which the effective data was available. (3) The S&P 500 data are indexed, with 1985 as the base year (=100). All indices are taken end-prices. For 2005 the end-price is defined as September 30. *Source*: Thomson Financial M&A database.

are focused (non-diversifying) deals (e.g. Berger & Ofek, 1995), tender offers (e.g. Rau & Vermaelen, 1998), the managements' stake in the company (e.g. Healey, Palepu, & Ruback, 1997) and the announcement of an acquisitive strategy (e.g. Asquith, Bruner, & Mullins, 1983; Schipper & Thompson, 1983; Gregory, 1997). Characteristics that negatively affect acquirers' returns are mergers that are paid in stock instead of cash (Huang & Walkling, 1987; Yook, 2000) cross-border acquisitions (Moeller & Schlingemann, forthcoming), and acquisitions by "glamor stocks" (Rau & Vermaelen, 1998). "Learning effects" also have an impact: the performance of acquisitions improves as companies learn from successive deals (e.g. Very & Schweiger, 2001; Leshchinskii & Zollo, 2004).

The study described in this chapter adds to the existing literature by analyzing the long-term performance of firms with highly acquisitive strategies versus firms that grow organically or by a mixture of organic and M&A growth. To the best of our knowledge, this type of analysis has not been carried out before.

The study is based on a balanced panel of 705 US firms, and studies the relationship between their different growth strategies and stock performance over a 10-year period (1993–2002). It reveals that firms growing through acquisitions outperform companies with an organic or mixed growth strategy, on average, but the differences are not statistically significant. Furthermore, our study demonstrates that the growth rate of highly acquisitive companies is almost twice as high as that of organic growers but only creates shareholder value if the operating returns are above the cost of capital. We also come to the conclusion that acquisitions drive performance, not the other way around.

The rest of this chapter covers the following issues: Section 3.2 describes long-run global and regional M&A behavior in Europe, Asia, the Americas, and the USA; Section 3.3 discusses the study data methodology, as well as previous research; Section 3.4 provides the empirical results; Section 3.5 discusses the findings; and Section 3.6 concludes.

3.2. Long-Term Global M&A Trends

When analyzing long-term returns of M&A activity it is important to understand global merger trends. We report acquisition activity for the three main global regions: the Americas, Europe, and Asia Pacific. Since we use a US sample for our analysis of acquisitive strategies, we describe how merger activities in the USA relate to the regional and global trends.

The data are taken from the Thompson Financial M&A database. The Thomson database includes 309,438 deals carried out by 132,355 firms over the period 1985–2005.

Figure 3.2 presents an overall picture of merger activity since 1897. It shows that mergers come in waves and that in the late 1990s we experienced the fifth and largest merger wave in history. Figure 3.1 zooms in on the last 20 years and describes how the global number of completed deals has developed between 1985 and 2005. The number of completed acquisitions has rocketed from 2232 deals in 1985 to 27,197 deals in 2000, an increase of more than 1100%. After the height of the last merger wave in 2000 the number of deals sharply declined. In 2003 the number of deals was back at the level of the mid-1990s again. The first signs of an upswing were apparent in 2004, when the number of completed deals increased by 6% compared to 2003.

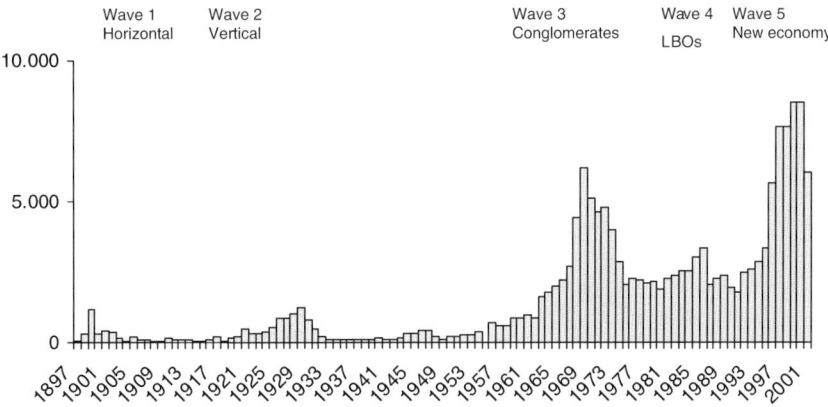

Figure 3.2: Merger waves since 1897. *Source*: 1897–1904, Gaughan, Mergers, Acquisitions, and Corporate Restructurings; 1904–1954, Nelson, Merger Movements in American Industry, 1895–1956; 1955–1962, Historical Statistics of the US – Colonial Times to 1970; 1963–1997, Dollar Value, Mergerstat Review, 1998, Value Creators Report 2002.

We also looked at the monthly trends for 2003, 2004, and the first three-quarters of 2005. Except for June, all monthly deal numbers for 2004 and 2005 are higher than in 2003. This suggests that M&A activity is recovering globally.

When we zoom in on the underlying regions, different patterns emerge (see Figure 3.3). Most strikingly, Asia Pacific's wave pattern differs from Europe's and the Americas'. Since 1985, the number of completed deals by Asian acquirers has continuously increased, with only two small exceptions in 1992 and 2001, rising from 62 new deals in 1985 to 5177 deals in 2004, nearly as high as Europe. The yearly rise in number of deals in Asia for the last 20 years was over 30% per year on average, starting from a 140% increase in 1986 to 11% rise in 2004.

The US and European patterns are very similar to each other and drive the global trend. One striking difference between these two regions is that the (height of) US merger wave preceded the one in Europe by 2 years, peaking in 1998, compared to 2000 in Europe. The US recovery also started earlier than Europe's and the rest of the Americas: the US decline stopped in 2001, with a strong upswing in 2004. In the other parts of the Americas the decline continued until 2003, when the number of merger deals rose again. It should be noted, however, that the US acquiring firms constituted the lion's share of all merger deals in the Americas, accounting for more than 90% of all the Americas' successful merger bids. In Europe, there is no sign of recovery yet. The number of deals in Europe in 2004 was at the 1995 level of around 6000, and by 2005, based on data for the first three-quarters, M&A activity still had not picked up in this region. In other words, the global upswing in 2004 and 2005 that we mentioned earlier is totally driven by the USA and Asia Pacific.

One interesting observation is that there is a strong relationship between the volume of successful M&A bids and the Standard & Poors 500 (S&P 500) index, as Figure 3.1

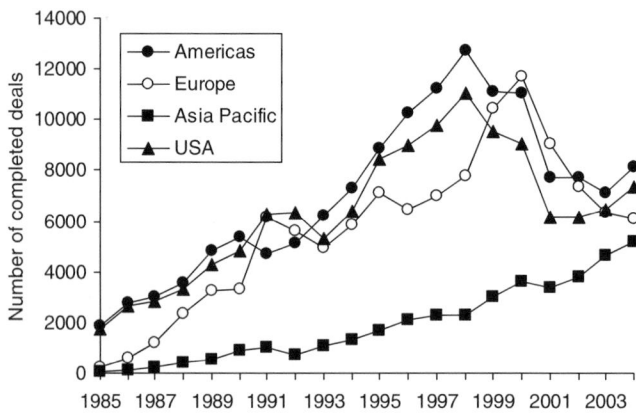

Figure 3.3: Number of acquisition deals by region of the acquiring firm (1985–2004). *Notes*: (1) The numbers included are the new deals completed that year. (2) Americas includes North and South America; Europe includes Western and Eastern Europe, and Asia Pacific includes Central and South-East Asia, Australia, and New Zealand. *Source*: Thomson Financial M&A database.

illustrates. During the downturn in 1999–2000 and the upswing in 2002–2003, merger activity seems to lag behind the development of the stock market. However, when considering the number of deals done by companies from the USA only, we find that the wave structure of the number of deals clearly exceeds the S&P 500 wave structure by 1 year, instead of lagging 1 year. We will discuss the relationship between (rising) stock prices and M&A activity in more detail in Section 3.5 (see Figure 3.4).

The regional trends for the *target* firms are similar to the patterns of the acquiring companies (see Figure 3.5). Again, the number of US target firms is already recovering by 2002, 2 years before the global recovery set in. A recovery is not yet visible for European targets. The numbers for the Asia Pacific show that this region is not only becoming more important as an acquirer region but also as target region, steadily increasing, and almost reaching European levels.

These different trends can be partly explained by the preference of local acquirers to invest abroad or within their own nation: 25% of all deals between 1985 and 2005 are cross-border deals, either within or across regions. In the 1980s, cross-border deals across the acquirers' own regions were predominant (65% of all cross-border deals were across regions), but over time a shift to deals within regions became visible. In 2004 cross-border deals within and between regions were equally popular (see Figure 3.6). Compared to the Americas and Asia, European acquirers more often look for cross-border targets, with a stable 30% of all deals being done outside their own region. In Asia Pacific the trend is clearly inward, both in absolute and relative terms. In 2004, 85% of all Asian deals were done within their own nation, 10% in their own region, and only 5% of the takeover targets were companies from other regions. Twenty years earlier, in 1985, 67% of all deals by Asian acquirers were cross-border deals in other regions. Although the absolute numbers were much smaller at the time, this might explain the persistent rise in the number of acquisitions by both Asian acquirers and

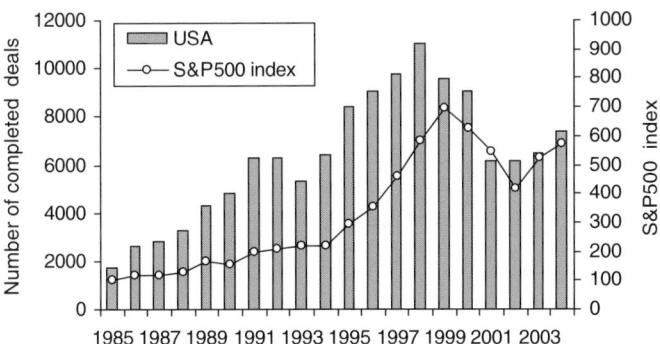

Figure 3.4: Number of M&As completed in 1985–2005 in the USA compared to the S&P index. *Notes*: (1) The numbers displayed in the table are the number of completed deals per calendar year, for which the effective data was available. (2) The S&P 500 data are indexed, with 1985 as the base year (=100). All indices are taken end-prices. For 2005 the end-price is defined as September 30. *Source*: Thomson Financial M&A database.

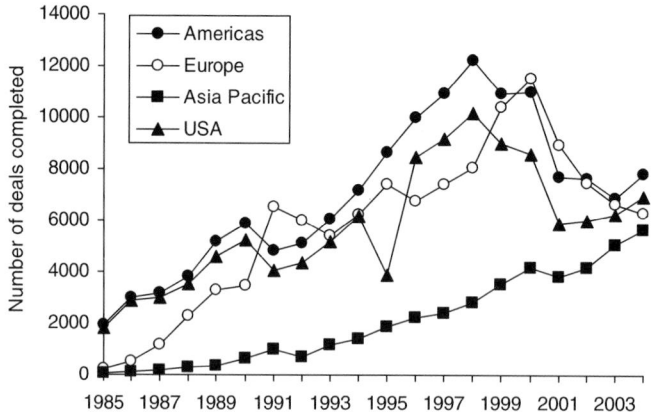

Figure 3.5: Number of acquisition deals by region of the target firm. *Notes*: (1) The numbers included are the new deals completed that year. (2) Americas includes North and South America; Europe includes Western and Eastern Europe and Asia Pacific includes Central and South East Asia, Australia, and New Zealand. *Source*: Thomson Financial M&A database.

Asian targets. With the Asian acquirers increasing in absolute numbers, and with the majority of the Asian acquirers investing in a target of their nation or region, it is clear that the number of Asian targets is increasing as well. In the Americas, the reverse is true. In 1985, 12% of the American acquisitions were cross border, whereas in 2004 that number was 20%, of which 60% were done in different regions.

Overall, regional trends of acquisitions over the last 20 years show very different patterns. Globally, the fourth and fifth waves took place in the last two decades and in the USA and Asia Pacific we might even be on the verge of the sixth wave. While M&A activity was at an all-time high in the Americas and Europe in 1998 and 2000, respectively, the number of Asian Pacific acquisitions has been rising relatively steadily since 1985.

Our analysis in the rest of this chapter focuses on US firms for the period 1993–2002. This period covers the fourth and fifth US M&A wave, but excludes the recovery that set in after 2003. The remainder of this chapter examines whether M&A activity in the USA over this period created value for shareholders and the driving forces behind it.

3.3. Methodology and Sample

3.3.1. Our Different Methodology Explained

In our study, we look at the results of companies over a period of 10 years, from 1993 until 2002. We divide the companies into three groups, based on whether their growth strategy is organic, mixed, or highly acquisitive. Unlike other M&A studies, we analyze

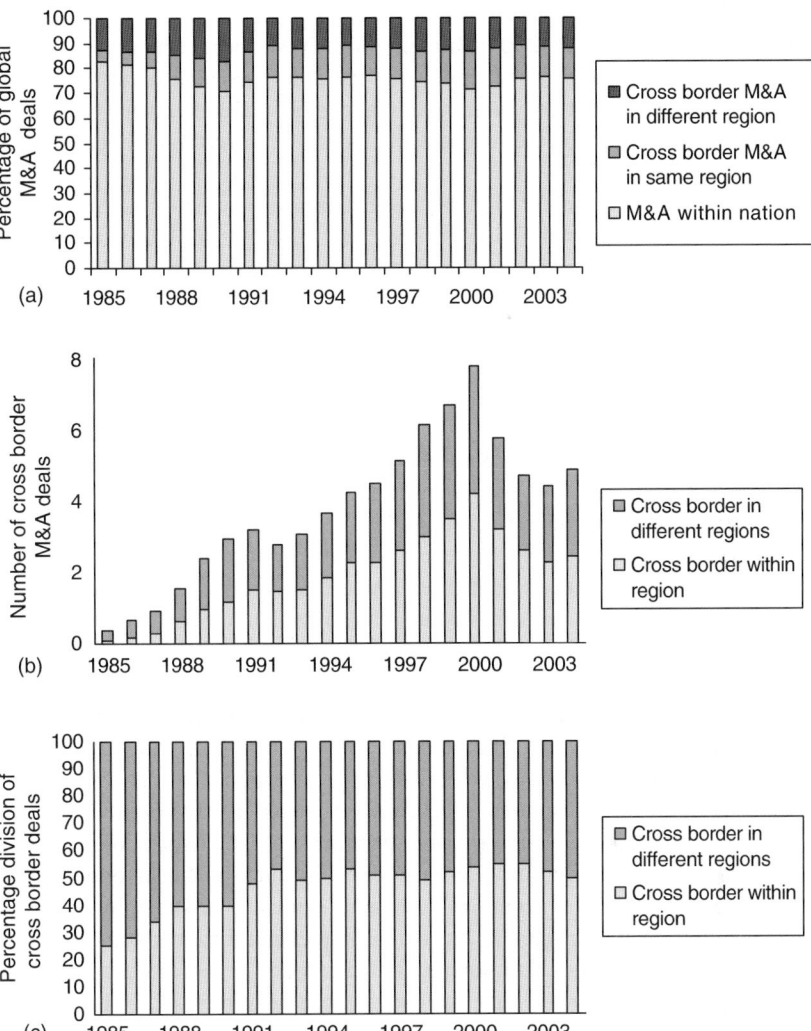

Figure 3.6: Cross-border deal development over time. (a) Global cross-border deals as percentage of all merger deals over time. (b) Number of cross-border deals within and between regions over time. (c) Percentage division of cross-border deals within and between regions. *Note* (3.6 a): The percentages are based on the division of the number of global completed deals each year. (3.6 b and c): The numbers included are the new deals completed that year. *Source*: Thomson Financial M&A database.

the companies' long-term market returns, as well as other characteristics of companies, finding patterns of different strategic behavior depending on the growth strategies. In the following section, we give a short overview of M&A literature to-date and argue why we opted for our different methodology.

Numerous studies have examined *short-term* announcement returns of acquisitions (see Andrade, Mitchell, & Stafford, 2001; Bruner, 2002; 2004, for recent surveys of the literature). Generally, these studies have found that the announcement returns to bidders are often negative, although zero and positive announcement price effects have also been documented. The shareholders of the *target* firms, however, have typically enjoyed positive returns in the 20–30% range.

Specific deal conditions affect bidders' stock returns around the time of the announcement. In terms of how the transaction is financed, cash deals have a better-than-average performance than stock deals. Buyer-shareholder returns are zero to significantly positive for cash deals, whereas deals paid in stock result in negative returns for the bidder (Asquith, Bruner, & Mullins, 1987; Huang & Walkling, 1987; Yook, 2000; Heron & Lie, 2002). Rau and Vermaelen (1998) conclude that "value-oriented buyers" — those buying companies with low book-to-market values — were more successful at creating value than the so-called "glamor buyers" (targets with a high book-to-market value and high P/E multiple). In addition, acquisitions aimed at cost effectiveness are more successful than acquisitions to expand market power (Mueller, 1985; Ravenscraft & Scherer, 1987; Eckbo, 1992; Houston, James, & Ryngaert, 2001). Fuller, Netter, and Stegemoller (2002) find that acquisitions of smaller firms, which are more likely to be non-public or privately held firms and to be cash financed, create more value than successful bids for larger firms. Lastly, frequent acquirers or acquisitions done by firms that announce they will follow an acquisitive strategy have better returns than infrequent acquirers (Asquith, Bruner, & Mullins, 1983; Schipper & Thompson, 1983; Gregory, 1997; Bradley & Sundaram, 2004).

There are a number of reasons why the short-term event studies may have failed to explain reactions to M&As. First, the market's initial reaction does not always fully and "correctly" anticipate the long-run effects of an acquisition deal. The short-run effect measured through the announcement effect may be biased or may not incorporate the full range of factors that ultimately influence the share price of the merged company (Gregory, 1997; Andrade, Mitchell, & Stafford, 2001). Second, in studying the announcement effects of a sample of deals, instead of groups of companies with similar strategies, acquirers, and infrequent acquirers were included in the same sample. But different strategies entail different company characteristics and potentially differences in performance. For example, Leshchinskii and Zollo (2004) report that experienced acquirers build M&A capabilities that improve their long-term performance. Such (experience) factors are not considered in the large majority of studies that examine deal-specific results.

Third, various methodological and empirical problems of event studies have recently been identified. Mitchell, Pulvino, and Stafford (2004), for example, show that half of the negative announcement price reactions of acquisitions are short lived since they are caused by merger arbitrage short selling and that consequently "the common conclusion that mergers destroy value is not convincing".

Fewer event studies have analyzed the medium- or long-run performance of acquiring firms, with medium or long run defined as a period of 2–5 years. Although the evidence is mixed, the majority of these studies indicate that companies suffer wealth losses from acquisitive activities. Asquith, Bruner, and Mullins (1983), Agarwal, Jaffe, and Mandelker (1992), Gregory (1997), Loughran and Vijh (1997), Moeller, Schlingemann, and Stulz (2003), and Bouwman, Fuller, and Nain (2003) find that stockholders of acquiring firms experience a statistically significant wealth loss. This underperformance, as the one recorded in the short term, is largely driven by the negative response to acquisitions paid in stock. Firms that paid for the deal in cash or used mixed payments performed better. In contrast, Franks, Harris, and Titman (1991) find no evidence of abnormal post-acquisition performance.

Bradley and Sundaram (2004) study the impact of serial acquisitions and find that the aggregate result of both pre- and post-announcement returns of a portfolio of acquiring firms performs better than two composed benchmark portfolios. Their conclusions, however, are driven by the pre-deal returns (we will come back to that in Section 3.5). Their overall conclusion seems consistent with a number of studies that report statistically significant positive stock returns when firms announce that they will follow an acquisitive strategy (e.g. Asquith, Bruner, & Mullins, 1983; Schipper & Thompson, 1983; Gregory, 1997).

Recent articles have also identified various methodological problems in studies of long-run abnormalities. Bouwman, Fuller, and Nain (2003) provide a literature survey on why long-run announcement effects are criticized frequently. One of the main arguments is that test statistics based on the abnormal returns used for the reference portfolios are misspecified or biased (Barber, Lyon, & Tsai, 1996). Also the bootstrapping methodology used in some studies to calculate abnormal returns is inappropriate (Mitchell & Stafford, 1999). In addition, the definition of the announcement window is problematic (Gregory, 1997; Andrade, Mitchell, & Stafford, 2001; Bouwman, Fuller, & Nain, 2003).

A common denominator of both short- and long-term studies is that they focus on the characteristics of the deals instead of the characteristics of the companies. In particular, the acquisitiveness of companies is seldom taken into account. Due to the various problems associated with both short- and long-term event studies, and as we want to study the effect of acquisitive strategies of companies, in comparison with organic and mixed strategies, we have taken a different approach. We measure the acquisitiveness of individual companies by the number and total value of all deals during a 10-year period and then analyze the average 10-year stock returns for highly acquisitive and non-highly acquisitive companies.

3.3.2. Sample

In order to analyze the long-term relationship between acquisitiveness, growth, and shareholder returns, we constructed a sample of US firms for the period 1993–2002. All companies included fulfilled the following conditions:

1. Included in the S&P 1500 in 2002.
2. Listed for the full 10 years of the period analyzed.
3. Had a 2002 market value of more than 500 million USD.
4. Supported by deal information and financial data for the full 10-year period.

This produced a sample of 705 US companies.[3]

Financial data and M&A deal data were taken from S&P Compustat database. The M&A data were spot checked against two other databases: the Bloomberg corporate actions database and Securities Data Corp (SDC) transaction database. The S&P Compustat data are primarily annual financial data, but contain dummy variables from the annual reports indicating if certain specific activities such as mergers occurred. We used five variables to determine whether or not mergers occurred and to assess the size of these mergers: (a) occurrence of merger, (b) revenue contribution from mergers, (c) net income contribution from mergers, (d) capital expenditures on acquisitions (cash deals), and (e) any significant change in the number of shares (equity deals). Based on these five variables, we generated dummy variables, called "merger years", indicating whether a firm engaged in acquisitions in each year of the period. If there were no deals, the "merger years" variable is zero. If the firm engaged in one or more deals, the variable has a value of one, irrespective of how many deals were done in each year. In addition, for each firm we calculated the total value of all deals, and generated a variable called "relative deal value": this is the ratio of the total deal value over the market value of the acquiring company in 2002.[4]

Our sample period, 1993–2002, includes most of the stock market boom and bust years in the late 1990s and early 2000s. The S&P 500 index at the end of our sample period, December 31, 2002, after the decline of the fifth wave, was equal to the S&P 500 index in June 1997, when the market was booming.[5] By including the extraordinary "boom and bust" periods, our findings are less vulnerable for over-reaction to mergers in the late 1990s compared to recent studies that only studied the bull market period.

To determine the acquisitiveness of companies we analyzed three categories of companies: organic growth companies, highly acquisitive growth companies, and companies with a mixed growth strategy. Organic growers are firms with no more than 1 year with M&A deals in the 10-year sample period, and with a total deal value of not more than 5% of their 2002 market value. In total, 108 firms were classified as organic growth firms. Firms are classified as highly acquisitive growers if they are engaged in M&A deals in 5 or more years of the 10 sample years, and if the total deal value of all deals exceeds 70% of their market value in 2002; 148 firms in the sample fulfill these conditions; the remaining 449 are categorized as mixed growers.

Table 3.1 provides summary statistics of the 705 sample firms. The data show that the majority of the sample firms are mainly active in industrial goods, consumer goods, or technology and communication. There is no significant difference of industry division among firms when looking at the subgroups by growth strategy.[6]

The average market value of the sample companies over the sample period is 9159 million USD. However, some outliers drive the average market value strongly upward. The median market value is substantially lower (2228 million USD), with about 80% of all firms having an average market value below the group average. This weighting of below-average firms is similar for each of the three growth categories, indicating that large firms are equally divided over the three subgroups we created.

3.4. Results

3.4.1. Main Findings on the Performance of Acquisitive Strategies

In this section, we examine how the market values different styles of long-term growth. We compare the median yearly total shareholder returns (TSR) over the 10-year sample period for acquisitive, mixed, and highly acquisitive companies.[7] We use median instead of average yearly TSR in order to control for outliers. The median annual TSR for the entire sample is 10%. Figure 3.7 compares the TSR for the three different growth strategies. The figure shows both the median TSR for each group (indicated by the large dot) and

Table 3.1: Summary statistics for the sample firms.

Industry Division		
	Number of firms	Percentage division
– Industrial goods	212	30%
– Consumer goods	156	22%
– Technology and Communication	155	22%
– Energy	108	15%
– Health care	55	8%
– Financial Services	13	2%
– Business Services	6	1%

Size		
Average Market Value in million USD (Standard Deviation)	9159 (25384)	
Median Market value in million USD (Standard Deviation)	2228 (25384)	
Market value size categories	Number of firms	Cumulative percentage division
– ≤ 1000 million USD	176	25%
– 1001–2500 million USD	200	53%
– 2501–5000 million USD	111	69%
– 5001–7500 million USD	58	77%
– 7501–10000 million USD	38	83%
– ≥ 10001 million USD	122	100%

Total Shareholder Return	
Average TSR (Standard Deviation)	11.1 % (9.91)
Median TSR (Standard Deviation)	10.0 % (9.91)

Growth Strategy	
Organic Growth	108 firms
Mixed growth	449 firms
Highly Acquisitive growth	148 firms

Note: Organic growers have no or maximum one year with acquisitions activities in the ten sample years, and the total deal value of those deals does not exceed 5 percent of their 2002 market value. Highly acquisitive firms have engaged in M&A deals in at least 5 out of the ten sample years, and the total deal value of all deals exceeds 70 percent of their 2002 market value. The remaining firms have a mixed growth strategy.

the range of average annual stock returns for the middle 3 quintiles (indicated by the shaded bars).

As the exhibit demonstrates, the median TSR for the highly acquisitive segment (10.8%) is more than a full percentage point greater than that for companies pursuing an

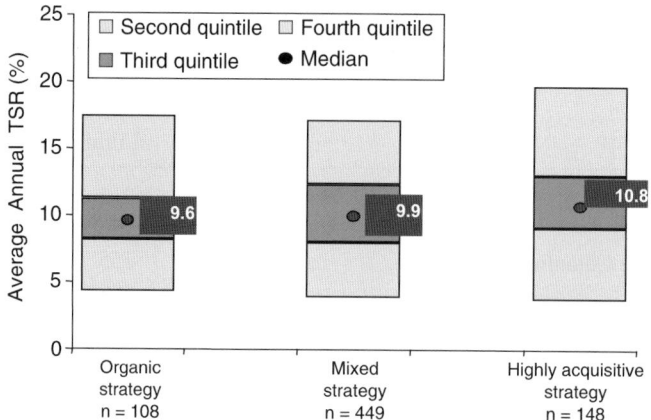

Figure 3.7: The impact of growth strategy on stock-market performance (1993–2002). *Note*: Median TSRs are included per strategy. They are based on the 10-year averages per company. Top and bottom quintiles excluded from the graph because of extreme values. *Sources*: Compustat; BCG analysis.

organic strategy (9.6%) and nearly 1% point more than companies with mixed strategies (9.9%). Over the total 10-year sample period, the acquisitive companies have outperformed the organic growth companies by 29% points. These results seem consistent with Bradley and Sundaram (2004), who find that frequent acquirers outperform infrequent acquirers. However, contrary to their results, the differences we find between the median TSR of each group are not statistically different from zero.[8,9]

Ordinary least square (OLS) regression analyses, using the 10-year TSR as the dependent variable, confirm these results (see Table 3.3). In all regressions we included a dummy for acquisitive companies. As control variables, we added the firm's size (measured in average 10-year log market-capitalization), industry sector dummies for consumer goods, energy, industrial goods, and technology and communication and risk (measured by *beta*). Models 1 and 2 include a dummy for companies with a mixed growth strategy and in Model 1 also dividend yield is added. In Models 3 and 4, the dummy for companies with a mixed strategy is excluded and Model 3 included dividend yield whereas in Model 4 that variable is taken out.

Size, measured by market capitalization, is always positive and significant, consistent with recent studies (Rouwenhorst, 1999; Chan, Karceski, & Lakonishok, 2000; Cools & Van Praag, 2005) that examine the same period, but not with Fama and French (1992; 1998) who have studied earlier years. Apparently, the well-documented "small firm effect" was absent in the 1990s and even opposite was true; "big was beautiful" in those years. An interesting finding is that dividend yield has a negative and is highly significant, indicating that high dividend payments were correlated with high stock returns. We expect the dummy for highly acquisitive strategy to be positive but insignificant, consistent with the results presented earlier. The results indeed show that the dummy for highly acquisitiveness is insignificant in all models. Only in Model 4, where both dividend yield and a dummy for mixed strategy are absent, acquisitiveness is positively related to stock returns, consistent with the results reported above. Apparently, dividend yield and acquisitiveness are negatively correlated, which we will further discuss in Section 4.2.

In order to test the robustness of our results, and, in particular, the impact on our findings of our definition of acquisitiveness, we performed a number of analyses using different definitions and different thresholds to define "high acquisitiveness". In Table 3.2, we report 10-year median TSRs for the acquisitiveness of companies, defined by only the number of deal years, as well as by only the total deal value criterion. Irrespective of the definition of acquisitiveness our findings are confirmed; in all cases highly acquisitive firms generate the highest TSR.

In addition to using different variables to define acquisitiveness, we also raised the threshold of high acquisitiveness for all three definitions described above. We increased the threshold by increasing the number of deal years, as well as by increasing the total deal value as a percentage of the 2002 market value of the acquirer.[10] When augmenting the number of deal years, the 10-year median TSR of the firms in the highly acquisitive segment further increases.[11] However, the differences with the other two segments

Table 3.2: Regression Results.

	Model 1	Model 2	Model 3	Model 4
Dummy highly acquisitive	−2.13	−1.25	−0.80	0.14
	(1.18)*	(1.23)	(0.85)	(0.89)
Dummy mixed growth	−1.62	−1.71		
	(1.00)	(1.05)		
Dividend yield	−2.14		−2.14	
	(0.25)**		(0.25)**	
(ln) Market capitalization	1.70	1.50	1.67	1.46
	(0.24)**	(0.25)**	(0.24)**	(0.25)**
Consumer goods	−0.34	0.53	−0.14	0.74
	(1.09)	(1.14)	(1.09)	(1.14)
Energy	2.37*	−1.30	2.63	−1.03
	(1.23)	(1.21)	(1.22)**	(1.20)
Industrial Goods	0.25	−0.60	0.40	−0.44
	(1.02)	(1.06)	(1.01)	(1.06)
Technology and communication	1.18	2.52**	1.13	2.48
	(1.01)	(1.05)	(1.01)	(1.05)**
Industry beta	−0.52	2.73	−0.54	2.71
	(1.02)	(1.00)**	(1.02)	(1.00)**
Constant	2.71	−2.03	1.59	−3.22
	(2.28)	(2.32)	(2.17)	(2.21)
Adjusted *R*-squared	0.17	0.08	0.17	0.08

Note: N=701
Standard deviation values are given in brackets
* significant at 10% level
**significant at 5 % level

remain statistically insignificant.[12] When we increase the total deal value from 70% of the 2002 market value to 80%, 90%, and even 100%, keeping the number of deal-years threshold at five, we again find that the median TSR for the most acquisitive firms further increases.

The median TSR for companies with a total deal value that exceeds their 2002 market value is lower than the TSR for companies that did acquisitions in each of the 10 sample years with a total deal value exceeding 70% of their 2002 market value. Apparently, the absolute value of a deal has less impact on performance than the sheer number of deals (see Tables 3.3(a)–3.3(c)). These results indicate that increasing the threshold for acquisitiveness, irrespective of the definition used, results in a higher average TSR performance.

These results confirm that long-term stock returns of acquisitive strategies are somewhat higher compared to organic and mixed strategies, but the differences are not statistically significant. In other words, contrary to conventional wisdom, there is no inherent disadvantage to growth by acquisition. If anything, it is likely to be more advantageous to grow through M&As.

Figure 3.7 also illustrates that there is a wide variation of returns within each group. The larger relative size of the quintile bands for companies pursuing a highly acquisitive strategy reflects a moderately higher variance of returns, consistent with the inherent risks associated with acquisitions.

To understand the drivers of the different growth strategies, we segmented each category into "fast growers" (above the median rate of revenue growth for the category) and "slow growers" (below the median for the category). Figure 3.8 shows that, on average, the high-growth companies in each category perform better, irrespective of the type of growth strategy. Across the three growth strategies in our study, the fast growers outperform the slow growers by roughly 6–7%, on average. This finding provides additional support for the conclusion that the market rewards long-term acquisitive growth strategies. Another finding in Figure 3.8 is that in order to produce roughly the same shareholder return, the fast-growing acquisitive companies need to grow nearly twice as fast as the fast-growing organic companies (an average annual growth rate of 29.7% as opposed to 17.3%). This is consistent with the well-documented fact that a significant part of the value creation resulting from acquisitions will be captured by the selling shareholders in the form of a 20–30% takeover premium (*cf.* Jensen & Ruback, 1983; Datta, Pinches, & Narayanan, 1992).

3.4.2. Does Performance Drive Acquisitions or Do Acquisitions Drive Performance?

Although the stock returns of frequent acquirers are higher than those of less frequent acquirers, this finding does not answer the causality question: "Do acquisitions drive performance or does performance drive acquisitions?" In order to shed some light on this question we analyzed the characteristics of the 74 companies in the highly acquisitive high-growth segment. This indicated that the superior performance was indeed due to the acquisitions they were making and not to other factors. Three pieces of evidence support this conclusion. First, there is no industry bias in this segment. In other words, these companies are not clustered in high-growth industries and simply benefitting from riding a wave of rapid industry expansion.

Table 3.3(a): Firm performance by different growth strategies, and different definitions of acquisitiveness.

	Organic	Mixed	Highly acquisitive
Median TSR based on years with deals and deal value criteria (1)	9.6 (*N* = 108)	9.9 (*N* = 449)	10.6 (*N* = 148)
Median TSR based on years with deals only (1)	9.8 (*N* = 133)	10.1 (*N* = 207)	10.1 (*N* = 365)
Median TSR based on only deal value criteria (2)	9.9 (*N* = 523)		10.4 (*N* = 182)

Notes:
(1) Organic growth firms had mergers or acquisitions in 0 or 1 year of the 10 years, highly acquisitive firms in 5 or more years of the 10 years, and mixed-strategy firms in 2, 3, or 4 year of 10 years.
(2) Highly acquisitive firms are those firms of which total deal value of all deals exceeds 70% of their 2002 market value.

Table 3.3(b): Firm performance by different growth strategies, and different definitions of acquisitiveness and increasing thresholds of acquisitiveness using years with deals.

	Organic	Mixed	Highly acquisitive
Threshold at 5 years and deal value >70	9.6 (*N* = 108)	9.9 (*N* = 449)	10.6 (*N* = 148)
Threshold at 7 years and deal value >70	9.6 (*N* = 108)	10.0 (*N* = 492)	10.8 (*N* = 105)
Threshold at 10 years and deal value >70	9.6 (*N* = 108)	10.0 (*N* = 550)	12.4 (*N* = 47)

Table 3.3(c): Firm performance by different growth strategies, and different definitions of acquisitiveness and increasing thresholds of acquisitiveness using deal value.

Deal value as percentage of 2002 market value	Acquisitive based on deal value exceeding 70% of 2002 market value		Acquisitive based on deal value exceeding 80% of 2002 market value		Acquisitive based on deal value exceeding 90% of 2002 market value		Acquisitive based on deal value exceeding 100% of 2002 market value	
	O&M	H	O&M	H	O&M	H	O& M	H
Median TSR	9.9 (*N*=523)	10.4 (*N*=182)	9.9 (*N*=547)	10.4 (*N*=158)	9.8 (*N*=569)	11.4 (*N*=136)	9.6 (*N*=583)	11.6 (*N*=122)

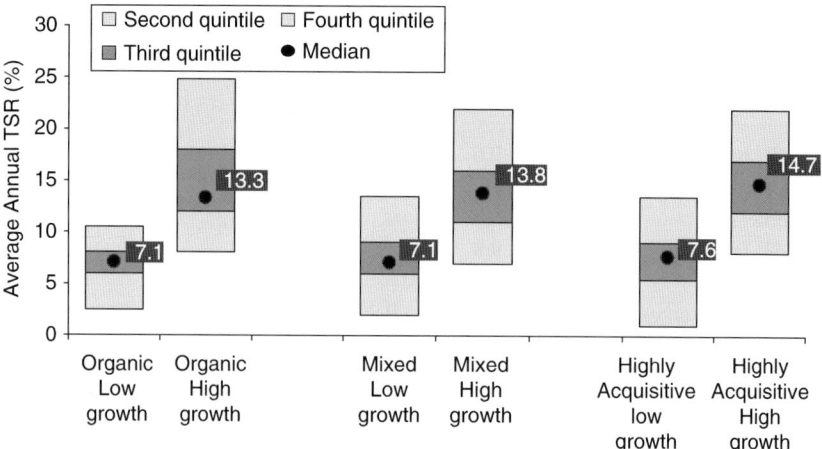

Figure 3.8: The impact of growth strategy and growth rate on stock-market performance (1993–2002). *Note*: Median TSRs are included per strategy. They are based on the 10-year averages per company. Top and bottom quintiles excluded from the graph because of extreme values. *Sources*: Compustat; BCG analysis.

Second, the profitability of these companies (measured by cash flow return on investment, or CFROI, above the weighted-average cost of capital) was about equal to that of the rest of the companies in the sample. In addition, the median CFROI over the 10-year period for the companies in the highly acquisitive segment were even lower than that of the other two groups, although these differences are not statistically significant.[13] Moreover, while the CFROI of the highly acquisitive firms increased over our 10-year sample, the operating returns of their counterparts decreased. Apparently, the 74 highly acquisitive high-growth companies managed to increase their profitability by acquiring and successfully integrating the target companies. This strongly indicates that it was not high profitability or excess cash that drove these companies' acquisitions or generated their above-average TSR. Therefore, it is most likely that their above-average TSR was indeed a product of their above-average growth, which was primarily fueled by their acquisitive strategy.

But if these companies had only average profitability, how did they fund their acquisitions? Through a combination of below-average dividends and above-average debt (see Figure 3.9).

The dividend yield of the highly acquisitive firms was 0.4 versus an average dividend yield of 1.8 for the organic and mixed growers. As was indicated by the regression analyses in Section 4.1, acquisitiveness and dividend yield are negatively correlated. In addition, the median leverage of the highly acquisitive high-growth companies was 5% higher, on average, than the other companies in all the years, with an average leverage of 36.2% versus 31.5% for the other firms. Typically, low dividends and high leverage decrease a company's stock-market returns (e.g. Naranjo, Nimalendran, & Ryngaert, 1998). For these high-growth, highly acquisitive companies, however, this turns out not to have been the

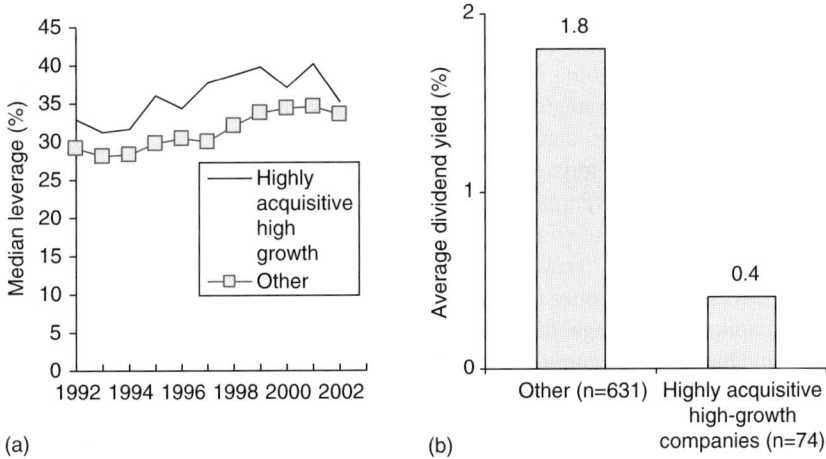

Figure 3.9: Comparative (a) median leverage % and (b) average dividend yield %. *Notes*: Leverage is defined as (total debt + pref. equity)/(total capital employed + short-term borrowing – total intangibles). For the leverage chart, there are 54 highly acquisitive high-growth companies included, for which the full 1993–2002 data were available. There are 421 other companies included. *Sources*: Compustat; BCG analysis.

case. As Figure 3.9 shows, the median TSR of these companies is above average for the sample as a whole and equivalent to that of the fast-growing companies pursuing organic or mixed growth strategies. Apparently, the disadvantages of low dividends and high leverage are outweighed by the value created through acquisitive growth itself. What is more, the fact that their median *beta* is only slightly greater than that of the sample as a whole (0.97 versus 0.90) suggests that these companies are especially good at managing the extra risk that growth by acquisitions typically involves.

Third, these highly acquisitive high-growth companies do relatively better in individual deals. We analyzed the announcement effects for all the deals in our sample with a relative size of more than 5% of the acquiring company's market capitalization at the time of the transaction. Our results confirm the common finding that acquisitions of public targets have slightly negative announcement effects, on average. However, when we compare the performance of the highly acquisitive high-growth companies to high-growth companies pursuing a mixed strategy, we find that the acquisitive companies do better.[14] Although the announcement effect for the acquisitions of public targets remains negative, it is substantially less than that of the mixed-strategy companies. For public targets, the 3-day price effect at announcement is –1.72% for frequent bidders versus –2.46% for the other two categories. The difference between both averages is statistically significant at the 5% level. The average 3-day announcement effects for private acquisitions of the two groups are roughly the same (2.45% versus 2.11%, not a statistically significant difference). These findings provide additional evidence that investors seem to distinguish between deals conducted by experienced acquirers and those done by less experienced acquirers.

3.4.3. The Operating Drivers of Acquisitive Strategies

Our research also reveals some interesting patterns in the way these companies pursued their acquisitive growth strategies. Figure 3.10 charts the relationship between CFROI (plotted on the vertical axis) and growth in the asset base (measured by change in gross investment, plotted on the horizontal axis) for 56 highly acquisitive high-growth companies that produced above-average TSR during the 10 years studied.[15] As the left-hand figure demonstrates, 26 of these companies started the decade with CFROI below the cost of capital. Instead of trying to "grow out of their problems", they spent the early years of the decade improving CFROI, only turning to growth once returns had reached or exceeded the cost of capital. On average, these companies grew by 300% over the 10-year period of our study, and their median cumulative TSR was 15% greater than the market average. The 30 companies that began the decade with CFROI above the cost of capital generated shareholder returns almost entirely through growth (see the right-hand figure). During the period of our study, they grew by 800%, on average, and their cumulative TSR was 58% greater than the market average.

Thirteen companies in the highly acquisitive high-growth segment did *not* generate above-average TSR. Why? As the left-hand figure in Figure 3.11 shows, two of these companies tried to grow when profitability was below the cost of capital. Although they initially seemed to be able to grow successfully, eventually this growth proved unsustainable. Their profitability not only declined over the full period of the study, they also "hit a wall" in the later years and had to shrink their asset base. As a result, their cumulative TSR was a 65% *below* the market average.

Eleven other companies (portrayed in the right-hand figure of Figure 3.11) were reasonably profitable at the beginning of the period, but their profitability also declined over

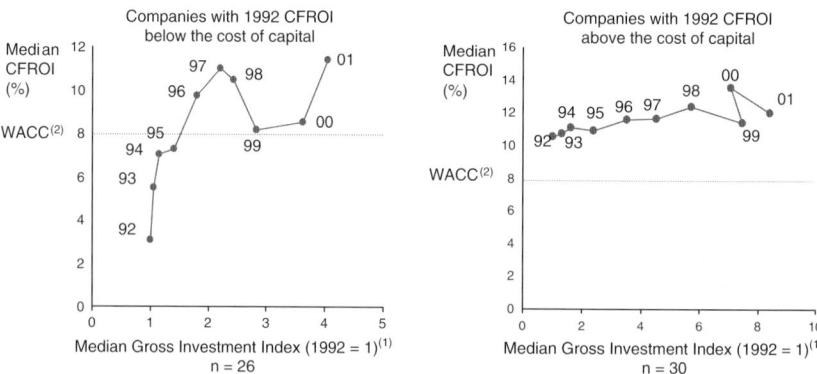

Figure 3.10: Profitability and asset growth of highly acquisitive high-growth companies. *Notes*: (1) Graphs begin in 1992 to capture change in gross investment for 1993 and end in 2001 because of unavailability of 2002 gross-investment data for many companies. (2) Weighted average cost of capital, 1992 (estimated). *Sources*: Compustat; Datastream; BCG analysis.

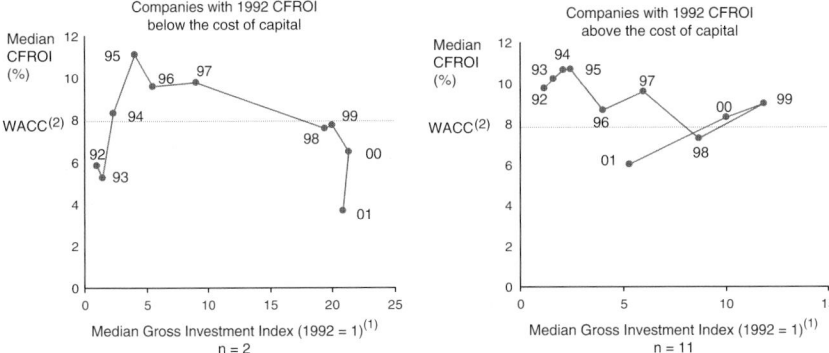

Figure 3.11: Profitability and asset growth of highly acquisitive high-growth companies. *Notes*: (1) Graphs begin in 1992 to capture change in gross investment for 1993 and end in 2001 because of unavailability of 2002 gross-investment data for many companies. (2) Weighted average cost of capital, 1992 (estimated). *Sources*: Compustat; Datastream; BCG analysis.

time. Their growth too was unsustainable, since it came at the expense of declining returns. By the end of the period, they had to divest large parts of their portfolio. It is likely that they overpaid for the companies they bought and were unable to realize the synergies necessary to justify the acquisitions. Their median cumulative TSR was 31% below the market average.

The performance of the highly acquisitive high-growth companies in our sample is fully in keeping with what one would expect from the principles of value management. In fact, the best performers in our complete sample combined high growth with high levels of CFROI, no matter what growth strategy they pursued. Figure 3.12 segments our full sample according to each company's level of revenue growth and CFROI: low, medium, and high.[16] It dramatically illustrates that as CFROI increases so too does TSR. And those companies that combine high CFROI with high growth generate the highest returns.

The main implication of our analysis is that the key to above-average stock-market performance is to focus on opportunities for growth that yield the highest returns on capital, no matter how that growth is achieved. True, simply bulking up on acquisitions does shareholders no good, unless these acquisitions are based on a sound acquisitive strategy and effective M&A capabilities. But the equivalent is true for companies pursuing a growth strategy driven by organic investments of capital. Although faster growers on average outperform slower growers, independent of the kind of growth, the return on investment is the ultimate differentiator between above- and below-average growth strategies.

3.5. Discussion

The topic of multiple acquirers has been largely overlooked in the literature and the few studies that do exist have primarily looked at stock price behavior around the announcement

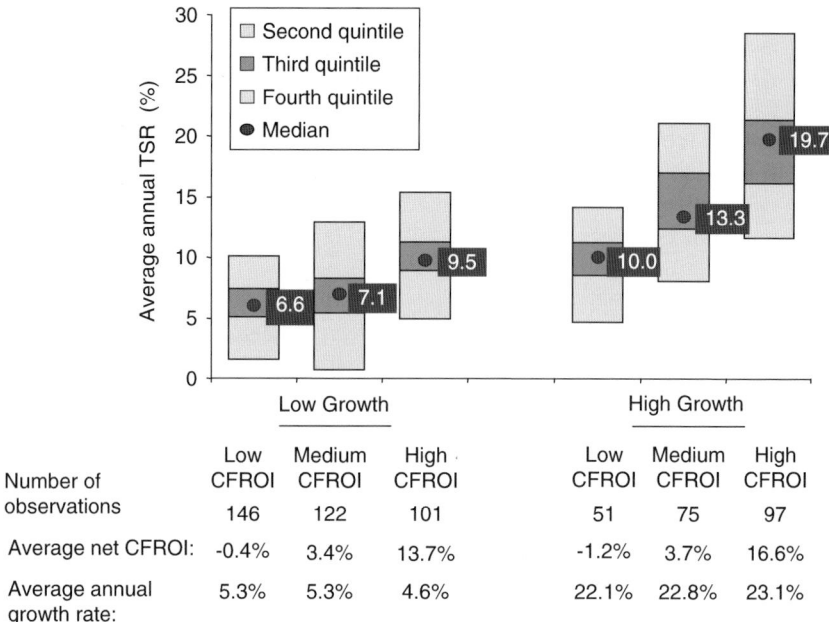

Figure 3.12: The impact of CFROI and growth on stock-market performance. *Note*: Top and bottom quintiles excluded from the graph because of extreme values. *Sources*: Compustat; BCG analysis.

of the deal. Schipper and Thompson (1983) analyzed 55 companies and found 13% abnormal return in the 12 months previous and including the announcement of the acquisition program. For subsequent merger announcements they find very little price reaction, unlike Asquith, Bruner, and Mullins (1983) who present evidence that bidder returns remain positive through the fourth bid. Interestingly, based on the Schipper and Thompson data, Malatesta and Thompson (1985) report that announcement effects are positive, even for deals that are part of an acquisition program that has been announced earlier. Gregory (1997), in his study to the long-run acquisition effects of 420 deals done by UK firms, finds that over a 2-year period the returns of acquiring firms are negative. However, the returns for regular acquirers are significantly better than the results of "one-off" acquirers (–5.18% versus –11.17%, respectively). Twenty years later Bradley and Sundaram (2004) resume the thread of empirical research on multiple bidders for the USA and find for a sample of the 1990s that acquisitive companies outperform non-acquisitive ones.[17] That result is based on the 1- and 2-year *pre*-announcement returns plus the 1- and 2-year *post*-announcement returns. The superior pre-announcement returns are primarily driven by those deals where the bidder offers stock, not cash.

The fact that, contrary to Bradley and Sundaram (2004) we do not find a significant out-performance of frequent bidders, is likely to be caused by the different period studied and by the different methodology used. The conclusion of Bradley and Sundaram that acquisitions by frequent bidders create shareholder value is exclusively caused by the extraordinary 1- and 2-year *pre*-announcement run-up of the stock price, which is largely driven by deals paid in stock, and not cash. The subsequent post-announcement price effect was on average negative, but not nearly sufficient to wipe out the prior gains. The 1- and 2-year pre-announcement stock price run-up, however, was inherent to the extraordinary period in US history that was studied by Bradley and Sundaram. Their 10-year sample period ends in 1999, at the very top of the longest and strongest bull market in US history. The massive overvaluation in the 1990s (Jensen, 2005) fueled the largest M&A wave in history through the "rational response of managers to less-than-rational markets" (Shleifer & Vishny, 2003) to acquire companies paid in stock on a very large scale. The results of Bradley and Sundaram that frequent bidders outperformed the market seems therefore a direct consequence of the bull market, given the fact the out-performance is measured by *pre*-announcement returns. It is also consistent with the model developed by Shleifer and Vishny (2003) which predicts that bidders in stock acquisitions earn high *prior* returns. Indeed, it is not unlikely that for acquirers during the bull market of the 1990s that used their overvalued stock as a means of payment, "performance" drove acquisitions, not the other way around.

There are at least two reasons why our study is less sensitive to the effects of the massive overvaluation in the late 1990s and the consequent merger wave. First, our sample period ends at the end of 2002, when stock prices had returned to their 1997 level. Second, we measure stock performance over the entire sample period.

There is one other factor that explains the differences between Bradley and Sundaram's findings and the findings of both the US studies from the 1980s and our results. Similar to the announcement price effects that we reported in Section 3.4, Bradley and Sundaram also find that the post-announcement price effect of frequent bidders is negative, consistent with a negative signaling effect when acquisitions are paid in stock, that the stock is overvalued. These negative announcement effects differ from the positive announcement effects that were found by Asquith, Bruner, and Mullins (1983), and Malatesta and Thompson (1985) on frequent bidders. A possible explanation is that the merger wave of the late 1990s was much different from the mergers in the 1970s and the "hostile" takeover wave of the 1980s (Shleifer & Vishny, 2003). While in the late 1990s mergers were fuelled by the fast-rising stock prices and often paid in stock, in the 1970s and 1980s the medium of payment was cash rather then stock and the rationale was eliminating inefficiencies by restructuring or break-up rather than realizing synergies. In other words, the acquisitions in the 1980s generated positive price reactions since they were geared towards eliminating operating inefficiencies, thereby enhancing value, whereas the negative price reactions in the 1990s can just be viewed as a result and signal of massive overvaluation in the late 1990s. In addition, Mitchell, Pulvino, and Stafford (2004) have shown that half of the negative price effects of stock-financed mergers in the period 1994–2000 (which fully overlaps with the period that was studied by Bradley and Sundaram) were caused by merger arbitrage short selling, consistent with the notion that short-run demand curves for stocks are not perfectly elastic.

Do acquisitions drive performance, not the other way around? The early studies on frequent bidders from the 1980s base that conclusion on the results of post-announcement event studies of both acquisition programs and individual acquisitions. Especially for the announcement of an acquisition *program* the causality is clear: the price effect is not the cause but the effect on shareholder value of the acquisition (program). For subsequent acquisitions it is much less clear since, in an efficient market, the benefits of the program are capitalized in the announcement of the program itself and the announcements of subsequent announcements of individual deals should be neutral, unless they deviate from the acquisition plan as it was initially announced. Consequently, even in a perfectly efficient market a value-creating acquisition can cause a negative announcement effect. When the value-creating potential of the deal is positive, but less so than anticipated at the time the acquisition program was announced, then the share price will drop at announcement.

Our argument about the causality issue is different but straightforward: as we found that operating returns of frequent bidders are the same or even slightly lower compared to other companies, superior growth (above the cost of capital) has to be the driver of superior stock returns. Since the extraordinary growth of frequent bidders is entirely driven by acquisitions, it is the acquisitions that must drive superior performance, not the inverse.

All in all, our study and the existing literature show that frequent acquirers outperform or at least match other companies, whereas in general acquisitions often destroy value. One of the most likely explanations for this is that there is a strong learning effect in doing M&As. Bernardo and Chowdhry (2002) point out that learning is fundamentally at the heart of a firm's behavior, both at an organizational and individual level. This also applies to carrying out acquisitions successfully, which is a complex and difficult task that requires specific capabilities, experience, and skills. Frequently engaging in mergers enhances learning, not only for doing a specific deal but also for mastering the entire acquisition processes (Very & Schweiger, 2001). This would explain why frequent bidders outperform other companies, since they gradually build M&A capabilities that enable them to better prepare, negotiate, and execute future deals and learn how to master the important post-merger integration process. This is supported by Leshchinskii and Zollo (2004) who examine how learning from previous acquisition experience affects the long-term performance, based on 564 acquisitions done by 47 US banks between 1977 and 1998. They find that the degree to which frequent acquirers articulate and codify their experience in *ad hoc* tools significantly affects the long-term performance and that also a high level of integration of the target within the acquirer's organization improves the long-term performance. A similar learning effect in a different context is documented by van de Laar (2004) in a study on Dutch foreign investment behavior.[18] For firms with multiple investments van de Laar (2004) finds that the later deals of experienced firms tend to be more successful than their earlier deals.

A different organizational learning aspect of acquisitions is put forward by Vermeulen and Barkema (2001) as well as Barkema and Vermeulen (2001). In a study of 25 Dutch corporations over nearly 30 years (1966–1994), they find that firms that grow only organically become more rigid over time, whereas firms engaging in acquisitive growth stay more flexible and alert. In addition, engaging in acquisitions enhances survival chances. Vermeulen (2005) adds that relatively smaller acquisitions on a regular basis can help managers revitalize their organizations continuously, before rigidity and complacency set in. Acquisitions can trigger a process that he refers to as *hybrid vigor*, which introduces variety to organizations, and introduces managers to new things they may not have realized they needed. Once managers are aware of this effect, some elect to undertake acquisitions specifically for this reason.

A personal, not organizational, element of learning is analyzed by Aktas, De Bodt, and Roll (2005). Building on the hubris hypothesis of Roll (1986), they argue that for CEO's affected by hubris, the learning process when doing multiple acquisitions allows them to progressively correct over-optimism and overconfidence. They become more aggressive in deal bidding and the premium rises when their experience in estimating synergies and selecting targets grows. This may result in lower immediate abnormal returns for successive acquisitions, consistent with the findings of Bradley and Sundaram (2004) and Conn, Cosh, Guest, and Hughes (2004).

It is not just event studies that have limitations; our approach of analyzing the long-term effects of acquisitive *strategies* also has its limitations. First, our definition of acquisitiveness is arbitrary. By using different hurdles for both the number of years with deals of acquisitive companies and the total deal value (relative to the market value of the bidder), we were able to mitigate that issue. Another approach would have been to endogenously determine the cut-off rates for acquisitive, mixed, and organic strategies. Second, since the three strategies are defined over the entire 10-year period, there is not immediate matching between the time of each deal and the exact movements of the stock price. Third, the disadvantage of using a balanced panel is the possibility of survivorship bias. Fourth, differences in risk amongst both companies and the various growth strategies are not taken into account. Fifth, our sample included only US-listed companies, US-specific characteristics, and regional differences are not considered.

Taken these limitations into consideration, future research could try to match deals and stock price movements better by analyzing the short- and long-term performance of (portfolios of) companies that do a certain number (e.g. 5–10) of acquisitions within a shorter period of time (e.g. 2 years). Another improvement would be to analyze the performance of companies that went bankrupt or were taken private, to account for a potential survivorship bias. Another future avenue of research would be to gather company-specific time series data on the development of M&A processes, capabilities, and tools, which can then be (cor)related to the firm's performance and acquisition patterns. Yet another important extension would be to replicate such a study for Europe and Asia, and to relate the differences to the M&A trends of the different regions that were reported in Section 3.2. And lastly, multivariate analyses in addition to mainly bivariate analyses would add to the robustness of the analysis.

3.6. Conclusion

We find that the long-term stock performance of acquisitive companies matches or even surpasses that of companies with organic or mixed growth strategies. This conclusion is consistent with the few existing studies (e.g. Schipper & Thompson, 1983; Bradley & Sundaram, 2004) on frequent bidders. Although the stock performance of frequent bidders is only slightly higher than the other two categories, their growth rate is almost twice as high. The acquisition premiums of usually 20–30% are the most likely explanation for the bidders' relatively modest value creation of acquisitive growth. Consistent with finance theory, we also reported that only companies that grow acquisitively at operating returns above the cost of capital generate superior stock returns.

On the important issue of causality, our results strongly suggest that acquisitions drive performance, not the other way around. Since the operating returns of the frequent bidders equal, at best, those of other firms, the (slightly) superior market performance must be due to the high growth rate, which is almost entirely generated through M&A activity. Our standpoint on the causality issue is consistent with the findings of the event studies on frequent bidders from the 1980s. The reverse conclusion of Bradley and Sundaram (2004) is driven by the pre-announcement run-up of the stock price and massive overvaluation in the late 1990s, which clearly generated many acquisitions, paid in stock.

Finally, there is a range of learning arguments that underpin the positive effect of frequent bidders on shareholder value. The existence of a learning curve for M&A capabilities is the most obvious one. Another organizational learning argument, taken from the management literature, is that acquisitions enable companies to avoid rigidity and inertia, and to acquire new complementary capabilities and skills from other companies. Finally, it is not just the organization that learns from frequent M&As; it also helps the CEO to understand how to assess synergies and select targets, avoiding the risk of overpaying.

Acknowledgments

We gratefully acknowledge the research assistance of Hans le Grand and Brett Schiedermayer, in particular for the analysis described in Section 3.4.

Endnotes

1. This number is based on the total number of deals effectively closed mentioned in the Thomson Financial M&A database. The analysis in Section 3.4 is in part based on Cools et al (2004).
2. This percentage is based on the acquirer name used in the Thomson Financial M&A database. The total deal value displayed in the Thomson Financial M&A database for 2004 was 1549.602 million USD, but the deal value was available for only about 50% of all deals.
3. The financial data and deal information data are collected by the BCG Value Science Center.
4. For the calculation of the total deal value per firm, we used the deals and deal values mentioned in the Thomson financial M&A database.
5. On December 12, 2002 the S&P index was 880, similar to the S&P index on June 12, 1997.
6. A Pearson χ^2 test using BCG classification for industries, showed Pearson $\chi^2(6) = 9.1804$, with a $P = 0.164$.
7. TSR is defined as the [(yearly capital gain + dividends paid)/stock price on the first trading day of the year] − 1.
8. The median test, assuming a non-parametric distribution, shows that highly acquisitive companies versus organic and mixed-strategy firms, both come from sub-samples with the same median. There is thus no evidence that the median of highly acquisitive firms is significantly higher than that of the other subgroups. The median test gives a Pearson $\chi^2(1) = 1.5517$ with a $P = 0.213$.
9. When assuming a normal distribution of TSR, we find no significant difference in TSR of the highly acquisitive companies versus the other companies. The average TSR for the combined organic and mixed growing firms is 10.9. The average TSR for highly acquisitive firms is 11.5. The difference is insignificant, with $t = 0.6238$ and $P < t = 0.2665$ (assuming unequal variances). Also additional tests between subgroups organic and highly acquisitive, and mixed and highly acquisitive the difference is insignificant. Additional tests, the Kwallis test ($\chi^2 = 0.657$ with two d.f. $P = 0.7198$) and the Wilcoxon Rank sum test ($z = -0.802$, $P > |z| = 0.4226$) confirm that there is no significant difference in TSRs between the three subgroups.
10. Highly acquisitiveness was defined as companies with at least 5 years of deals and a total deal value exceeding 70% of the 2002 market value. We increased these criteria to 6, 7, 8, 9, and 10 years with deals in turn,

jointly with a total deal value of at least 70% of the 2002 market value. In addition, we kept 5 years with deals stable, and increased the total deal value to be 80, 90, and 100% of the 2002 market value. We did not change the definition of organic growth and all firms that previously were highly acquisitive but are not under the new definition, become mixed growers.

11. We use the median TSR instead of the average TSR, to exclude the influence of the outliers with extreme TSR values.

12. $t = -1.0208$, $P < t = 0.1559$.

13. The one-way test testing whether the average CFROI of the organic and mixed growers (on average 15.2) was significantly larger than the CFROI of highly acquisitive growers (on average 9.8) had a $t = 0.5398$ with $P > t = 0.2948$.

14. We have eliminated the high-growth organic segment from this analysis because of the very few acquisitions in this segment.

15. Figures 3.10 and 3.11 include only those companies with available financial data for the full 1993–2002 period.

16. Due to limitations in the data, we could estimate average CFROI (net of cost of capital) for only 592 companies in our sample.

17. Fuller, Netter, and Stegemoller (2002) study deals by companies that have done five acquisitions or more, but they compare the performance of deals with different characteristics (e.g. stock versus cash offers, public versus private targets and size of the deal). Fuller, Netter, and Stegemoller (2002) do not compare the performance of frequent bidders with the performance of less frequent bidders or organic growth.

18. Greenfield investments, M&As.

References

Agarwal, A., Jaffe, J., & Mandelker, G. (1992). The postmerger performance of acquiring firms: A re-examination of an anomaly. *Journal of Finance*, *47*, 1605–1621.

Aktas, N., De Bodt, E., & Roll, R. (2005). *Hubris, learning and M&A decisions*. Working paper. http://ssrn.com/abstract=721882.

Andrade, G., Mitchell, M., & Stafford, E. (2001). New evidence and perspectives on mergers. *The Journal of Economic Perspectives*, *15*, 103–120.

Asquith, P., Bruner, R., & Mullins, D. (1983). The gains to bidding firms from merger. *Journal of Financial Economics*, *11*, 121–139.

Asquith, P., Bruner, R., & Mullins, D. (1987). Merger returns and the form of financing. *Proceedings of the Seminar on the Analysis of Security Prices*, *34*, 115–146.

Barber, B.M., Lyon, R., & Tsai, C.-L. (1996). *Holding size while improving power in tests of long-run abnormal stock returns*. Working paper, University of California.

Barkema, H., & Vermeulen, F. (2001). International expansion through start-up or acquisition: A learning perspective. *Academy of Management Journal*, *41*, 7–26.

Berger, P.G., & Ofek, E. (1995). Diversification's effect on firm value. *Journal of Financial Economics*, *37*, 39–65.

Bernardo, A.E., & Chowdhry, B. (2002). Resources, real options, and corporate strategy. *Journal of Financial Economics*, *63*, 211–234.

Bouwman, C., Fuller, K., & Nain, A. (2003). *The performance of stock-price driven acquisitions*. Working paper, University of Michigan Business School.

Bradley, M., & Sundaram, A. (2004). *Do acquisitions drive performance or does performance drive acquisitions*. Working paper, Duke University.

Bruner, R.F. (2002). Does M&A pay? A survey of evidence for the decision-maker. *Journal of Applied Finance*, *Spring–Summer*, 48–68.

Bruner, R.F. (2004). *Applied mergers and acquisitions*. Hoboken: John Wiley & Sons, Inc.

Chan, L.K.C., Karceski, J., & Lakonishok, J. (2000). New paradigm or same old hype in equity investing? *Financial Analyst Journal*, *56*, 3–36.

Conn, R.C., Cosh, A., Guest, P.M., & Hughes, A. (2004). *Why must all good things come to an end? The performance of multiple acquirers*. Working paper, Cambridge University.

Cools, K., King, K., Neenan, C., & Tsusaka, M. (2004). *Growing through acquisitions; The successful value creation record of acquisitive growth strategies*. The Boston Consulting Group, Boston, USA

Cools, K., & Van Praag, M. (2005). *The value relevance of voluntarily disclosing a single corporate performance target: An empirical analysis*. Working paper.

Datta, D., Pinches, G., & Narayanan, V. (1992). Factors influencing wealth creation from mergers and acquisitions: A meta-analysis. *Strategic Management Journal*, 13, 67–86.

Eckbo, B.E. (1992). Mergers and the value of antitrust deterrence. *Journal of Finance*, 47, 1005–1030.

Fama, E., & French, K. (1992). The cross-section of expected stock returns. *Journal of Finance*, 47, 427–465.

Fama, E., & French, K. (1998). Value versus growth: The international evidence. *Journal of Finance*, 53, 1975–1999.

Franks, J., Harris, R., & Titman, S. (1991). The post merger share price performance of acquiring firms. *Journal of Financial Economics*, 29, 81–96.

Fuller, K., Netter, J., & Stegemoller, M. (2002). What do returns to acquiring firms tell us? Evidence from firms that make many acquisitions. *The Journal of Finance*, 57, 1763–1793.

Gregory, A. (1997). An examination of the long run performance of U.K acquiring firms. *Journal of Business Finance and Accounting*, 24, 971–1002.

Healey, P., Palepu, K., & Ruback, R. (1997). Which takeovers are profitable: Strategic or financial? *Sloan Management Review*, 38, 45–57.

Heron, R., & Lie, E. (2002). Operating performance and the method of payment in takeovers. *Journal of Financial and Quantitative Analysis*, 27, 137–155.

Houston, J., James, C., & Ryngaert, M. (2001). Where do merger gains come from: Bank mergers from the perspective of insiders and outsiders. *Journal of Financial Economics*, 60, 285–331.

Huang, Y., & Walkling, R.A. (1987). Abnormal returns associated with acquisition announcements: Payment, acquisition form and managerial resistance. *Journal of Financial Economics*, 19, 329–350.

Jensen, M. (2005). The agency cost of overvalued equity. *Financial Management*, 34, 5–19.

Jensen, M., & Ruback, R. (1983). The market for corporate control: The scientific evidence. *Journal of Financial Economics*, 11, 5–50.

Leshchinskii, D., & Zollo, M. (2004). *Can firms learn to acquire? The impact of post-acquisition decisions and learning on long-term abnormal returns*. Working paper, INSEAD.

Loughran, T., & Vijh, A. (1997). Do long-term shareholders benefit from corporate acquisition? *Journal of Finance*, 52, 1765–1790.

Malatesta, P., & Thompson, R. (1985). Partially anticipated events: A model of stock price reactions with an application to corporate acquisitions. *Journal of Financial Economics*, 14, 237–250.

Mitchell, M.L., Pulvino, T.C., & Stafford, E. (2000). *Limited arbitrage in equity markets*. Working paper no. 01-069, Harvard Business School.

Mitchell, M.L., Pulvino, T.C., & Stafford, E. (2004). Price pressure around mergers. *Journal of Finance*, 59, 31–63.

Mitchell, M.L., & Stafford, E.(1999). *Managerial decisions and long-term stock price performance*. CRSP Working paper no. 453. http://ssrn.com.abstract=94137

Moeller, S.B., & Schlingemann, F.P. (forthcoming). Are cross-border acquisitions different from domestic acquisitions? Evidence on stock and operating performance for U.S. acquirers. *Journal of Banking and Finance*.

Moeller, S.B., Schlingemann, F.P., & Stulz, R.M. (2003). Firm size and the gains from acquisitions. *Journal of Financial Economics*, 73, 201-228.

Moeller, S.B., Schlingemann, F.P., & Stulz, R.M (forthcoming). Wealth destruction on a massive scale: A study of acquiring firm returns in the merger wave of the late 1990's. *Journal of Finance*.

Mueller, D. (1985). Mergers and market share. *Review of Economics and Statistics, 67,* 259–267.

Naranjo, A.M., Nimalendran, M., & Ryngaert, M. (1998). Stock returns, dividend yields and taxes. *Journal of Finance, 53,* 2029–2057.

Rau, P.R., & Vermaelen, T. (1998). Glamour, value and the post-acquisition performance of acquiring firms. *Journal of Financial economics, 49,* 223–253.

Ravenscraft, D.J., & Scherer, F.M. (1987). Merger, sell-offs and economic efficiency. Washington, DC: Brooklings Institution.

Roll, R. (1986). The hubris hypothesis of corporate takeovers. *Journal of Business, 59,* 197–216.

Rouwenhorst, K. (1999). Local return factors and turnover in emerging stock markets. *Journal of Finance, 54,* 1439–1464.

Schipper, K., & Thompson, R. (1983). Evidence on the capitalized value of merger activity for acquiring firms. *Journal of Financial Economics, 11,* 437–467.

Shleifer, A., & Vishny, R.W. (2003). Stock market driven acquisitions. *Journal of Financial Economics, 70,* 295–311.

van de Laar, M. (2004). *Dutch direct investment in Central and Eastern Europe and Central Asia.* Unpublished dissertation, Maastricht University.

Vermeulen, F. (2005). How acquisitions can revitalize companies. *MIT Sloan Management Review, 46,* 45–51.

Vermeulen, F., & Barkema, H. (2001). Learning through acquisitions. *Academy of Management Journal, 44,* 457–476.

Very, P., & Schweiger, D.M. (2001). The acquisition process as a learning process: Evidence from a study of critical problems and solutions in domestic and cross border deals. *Journal of World Business, 36,* 11–31.

Yook, K.C. (2000). *Larger return to cash acquisitions: Signalling effect or leverage effect?* Working paper, Baltimore, MD, John Hopkins.

Chapter 4

The Announcement Effects and Long-run Stock Market Performance of Corporate Spin-offs: International Evidence

Chris Veld and Yulia Veld-Merkoulova

4.1. Introduction

There is a broad consensus in both the academic and the popular literatures that spin-offs tend to create value for shareholders. This consensus is based on evidence from a number of studies indicating that, on average, the announcement of a spin-off by a US firm is associated with a positive abnormal stock return. Moreover, shares of firms completing spin-offs appear to exhibit excess returns over periods of up to 3 years following the restructuring. During the last decade, spin-offs have become more popular in Europe, perhaps due to the documented positive wealth effects in the USA. The large number of European spin-offs completed in recent years provide us with an opportunity to examine whether the conclusion that spin-offs tend to create value only applies to US firms or whether it is more broadly applicable.

A spin-off is a pro-rata distribution of the shares of a firm's subsidiary to the shareholders of the company. No cash transaction takes place. After the spin-off, the shareholders of the parent company hold shares in both the parent company and the subsidiary. Announcements of spin-offs by US firms are associated with strongly significant abnormal returns that range from 1.32% to 5.56%.[1] Spin-offs of companies that increase their industrial focus by divesting a division in a different branch than the parent company are associated with higher abnormal returns than spin-offs of companies that do not increase their industrial focus (see e.g., Daley, Mehrotra, & Sivakumar, 1997; Desai & Jain, 1999). In addition, Krishnaswami and Subramaniam (1999) also find that firms with higher levels of information asymmetry exhibit higher abnormal returns in the announcement period. These results show that the market efficiently responds to the spin-off announcements by incorporating expected future benefits into the current stock price.

Advances in Corporate Finance and Asset Pricing
Edited by L. Renneboog
© 2006 Elsevier B.V. All rights reserved.
ISBN: 0-444-52723-0

A number of US studies also find long-run superior performance of spun-off firms and their parents. Cusatis, Miles, and Woolridge (1993), Desai and Jain (1999) and McConnell, Ozbilgin, and Wahal (2001) find that parents and subsidiaries, involved in a spin-off, out-perform matching firms. Contrary to the results for the announcement period, the finding for the long-run excess returns is remarkable. According to the efficient market hypothesis, the positive effects of the spin-off should be incorporated in the announcement date returns. An interesting question is then whether spin-offs are really associated with positive long-run excess returns or whether the US results were a consequence of chance. Fama (1998) argues that studies finding significant long-run returns receive more attention in the academic and in the popular literature because they are more interesting. For this reason, Fama (1998) and Lyon, Barber, and Tsai (1999) argue that it is useful to study such anomalies out-of-sample. In case of spin-offs it makes sense to study spin-offs outside the USA. This gives us out-of-sample results on the long-run performance of companies involved in spin-offs.

In this chapter we study European spin-offs.[2] Spin-offs have only become popular in Europe during the second-half of the 1990s. In the period from 1987 to 1994, only 62 spin-offs took place. From 1995 onwards the volume of spin-offs rapidly increased. The period from January 1995 to September 2000 witnessed no less than 170 European spin-offs. Different results between the USA and Europe can *a priori* be expected due to corporate governance differences. Differences in corporate governance between countries can be measured by means of the index of La Porta, Lopez-de-Silanes, Shleifer, and Vishny (1998). According to this index, shareholders of companies in continental Europe are less protected than shareholders in Anglo-Saxon countries.

The most important results from this study can be summarized as follows. In total, 156 spin-offs that were announced by European companies over the period from January 1987 to September 2000 are analysed. The cumulative average abnormal return is 2.62% over the 3-day event window. This number increases to 2.66% for the subsequently completed spin-offs. The cumulative average abnormal return is 3.57% for completed spin-offs by companies that increase their industrial focus and only 0.76% for non-focus-increasing companies. The difference between these two sub-samples is significantly different from 0. This result is in line with previous studies for the USA. The divestiture of relatively large subsidiaries is also associated with larger abnormal returns. Contrary to Krishnaswami and Subramaniam (1999), we do not find any relation between the level of information asymmetry and the size of the abnormal return. However, introducing information asymmetry in the regression weakens the industrial focus effect. Therefore, the evidence on the industrial focus effect is not conclusive. The short-run results are not different between countries with different corporate governance systems.

Long-run excess returns, defined as the difference between the company return and the return on a matching firm, are mostly insignificant. The long-run excess returns in our study are higher for countries with *lower* levels of shareholder protection. Therefore, it cannot be concluded that the difference between our results and previously published results for the USA can be attributed to differences in corporate governance systems. If that were the case, the long-run excess returns in our study would have been higher for countries with higher levels of shareholder protection. The results in this chapter support the efficient market hypothesis. We conclude that, on average, spin-offs really create value, as they are associated with positive abnormal returns on the announcement date. However, unlike US studies, we do not find evidence that spin-offs, on average, exhibit positive long-run excess returns.

The rest of this chapter is organized as follows. In Section 4.2 we discuss the factors that can explain the wealth effects from spin-offs. The data description and the methodology are included in Section 4.3. The empirical results are included in Section 4.4. The chapter is concluded in Section 4.5 with summary and conclusions.

4.2. Factors That Can Explain the Wealth Effects from Spin-offs

4.2.1. Improvement of Industrial Focus

The motive that is most frequently mentioned in literature for conducting a spin-off is the intention of the firm to concentrate on its core business. Daley, Mehrotra, and Sivakumar (1997), Krishnaswami and Subramaniam (1999) and Desai and Jain (1999) find that the abnormal returns for the focus-increasing spin-offs are larger than for the non-focus-increasing spin-offs. Focus-increasing spin-offs are generally defined as spin-offs in which the parent company has a different two-digit Standard Industry Classification (SIC) code than the subsidiary. Desai and Jain (1999) also study the long-run performance of spin-offs after the announcement date. This leads to the interesting result that the superior performance of the focus-increasing spin-offs persists in the post-spin-off period. We test the hypothesis that spin-offs of firms that increase their industrial focus are associated with higher abnormal returns than spin-offs of firms that do not increase their industrial focus.

4.2.2. Information Asymmetry

Krishnaswami and Subramaniam (1999) argue that firms may engage in a spin-off because there is information asymmetry between the management of the firm and the external capital market. This information asymmetry may result in undervaluation of the firm. After the spin-off, information asymmetry, and hence undervaluation, is likely to decrease. Krishnaswami and Subramaniam (1999) find that firms with higher levels of information asymmetry exhibit higher abnormal returns adjusted for the probability of a spin-off upon the announcements of spin-offs.

Habib, Johnsen, and Naik (1997) also presents an information-based explanation for spin-offs. They derive a model in which a firm can increase its value by spinning off a subsidiary. The spin-off will lead to an increase of the number of securities that is traded on the market. This makes the price system more informative and, hence, leads to a decrease of information asymmetry. This decrease of information asymmetry will lead to an increase of the total value of the firm and its spin-off subsidiaries.

Krishnaswami's and Subramaniam's (1999) article suggests the testable hypothesis that spin-offs of firms with large information asymmetries are associated with higher abnormal returns than spin-offs of firms with low information asymmetries. Habib, Johnsen, and Naik's (1997) article leads to the hypothesis that firms, which show a decrease in information asymmetry after the spin-off, experience positive long-run excess returns.

4.2.3. Corporate Governance

It is often argued that managers in Anglo-Saxon countries are more focussed on share-holder value creation, and that managers in continental European countries are more likely to take the interests of all the firm's stakeholders into account (see e.g., Moerland, 1995). According to La Porta, Lopez-de-Silanes, Shleifer, and Vishny (2000), their index of "shareholder rights", which stems from La Porta, Lopez-de-Silanes, Shleifer, and Vishny (1998), is a suitable measure for corporate governance differences between countries. This index ranges from 0 to 7. A high value of the index means that shareholders are better protected against the adverse behavior of managers. We analyse whether spin-offs in countries with lower shareholder protection are associated with lower abnormal returns than spin-offs in countries with higher shareholder protection.

4.2.4. Geographical Focus

Companies can increase their geographical focus by spinning off a foreign division. Based on the literature on relationship between geographical diversification and firm value, it is possible to expect either a positive or a negative relationship between spin-off announce-ment returns and an increase in geographical focus.[3] The first reason for an increase in geo-graphical focus to reduce firm value is that the spin-off of a foreign division may lead to reduced economies of scale in production. The second reason is that the spin-off may sig-nal that the firm previously may have made a poor decision of expanding to the foreign market. The third reason is that the firm may be at a relative disadvantage to competitors who operate internationally. Other theories state that an increase in geographical focus may lead to an *increase* in firm value. First, the reduced complexity of the firm may lower monitoring and coordinating costs. Second, the managers might have chosen to globally diversify in order to decrease their own risks even if it results in lower shareholder value. Third, the possibility of cross-subsidization of less efficient divisions is reduced.

Given the arguments presented above, an increase in geographical focus may either be associated with higher or with lower abnormal returns. The outcome depends on the strength of the arguments in favour of a decrease in geographical focus versus the argu-ments in favour of an increase of geographical focus. The geographical focus dummy cor-responding to an increase in geographical focus is designed to measure its total effect on shareholder value in our sample.

4.2.5. Other Variables

4.2.5.1. Taxes   In the USA some spin-offs are taxable.[4] Empirical research by Copeland, Lemgruber, and Mayers (1987) and Krishnaswami and Subramaniam (1999) shows that taxable spin-offs are associated with lower positive abnormal returns than non-taxable spin-offs. Spin-offs in European countries generally do not create tax problems, because it is possible to defer tax payments (see Appendix 4A for details). Exceptions apply to Germany, France and the Netherlands (before 1998). In Germany spin-offs can be arranged in a tax-neutral way. However, if more than 20% of the shareholders transfer their shares within 5 years after the spin-off, the spin-off will still be taxed (Zaman, 1998). In

France the problem is that it is not possible for the company to ask for approval from the tax authorities before the transaction is carried out. In both Germany and France it is not known at the announcement date whether the spin-off will be taxed. The decision on the taxation in France will only be taken after the spin-off date. In Germany it will depend on the transfer of shares in the period after the spin-off. For this reason we do not include a variable on taxation in our analysis.

4.2.5.2. Regulation   Schipper and Smith (1983) and Krishnaswami and Subramaniam (1999) have studied whether regulatory motives play a role for American companies to engage in a spin-off. Both studies show that the abnormal returns are not affected by the regulatory status of the spin-off. In Appendix 4A, we discuss the regulatory consequences of European spin-offs. From this appendix it can be concluded that regulation does not cause an obstacle for spin-offs to be carried out in European countries. An analysis of the literature on the regulation of spin-offs in Europe also has not led to a motive that makes spin-offs particularly attractive for regulatory purposes.

4.2.5.3. Wealth transfers   Another potential explanation for the positive stock market reaction to spin-off announcements is the possibility to transfer wealth from bondholders to shareholders.[5] The measurement of this effect requires the use of bond data. However, since most European companies use non-tradable bank debt instead of bonds, we cannot measure this effect for the firms in our sample.

4.2.5.4. Size of spin-off   A number of studies find that the wealth effects are larger when the portion of assets that is divested is larger (see e.g., Hite & Owers, 1983; Miles & Rosenfeld, 1983; Krishnaswami & Subramaniam, 1999). In our study we control for this by using the market value of equity of the divested subsidiary relative to the sum of the equity capitalizations of the parent and the subsidiary. This is computed on the day of the completion of the spin-off.

4.3. Data Description and Methodology

4.3.1. Data Description

We analyse a sample of European spin-offs. A European spin-off is defined as a spin-off in which a European parent spins-off a subsidiary. This subsidiary can be either from the same or from a different country. All European countries are taken into account with the exception of the Eastern European, formerly Socialist, countries.

The sample covers the period from January 1987 to September 2000. The announcement dates are obtained from the Securities Data Company (SDC) Mergers and Acquisitions Database. Data on stock prices, market values of equity and market indices are derived from Datastream. Primary SIC codes are from the Compustat (where available) and SDC databases. The original sample consisted of 230 European spin-offs. Table 4.1 reports the annual distribution of the announcements to spin-off a part of the company.

Table 4.1: Observations by announcement year.

Year	UK	GER	FRA	ITA	SWE	NOR	DEN	FIN	NL	B	CH	SP	AUS	IRE	GRE	Total
1987	2	1														3
1988	2		2			1										5
1989	7		1			1										9
1990	6						1		1							8
1991	6	1			1	5			2							15
1992	2	1			2	1		1								7
1993	4				1	1								2		8
1994	3			1	1			1	1							7
1995	11	1		1				1	1				1			16
1996	10		3	1	9						2	1				26
1997	11	1		1	3						1					17
1998	13	5		1	7	2			3							31
1999	10	4	1	5	4		2			1	3	3		1		34
2000	15	4	1	4	2	2		3		1	3	3	2		4	44

	UK	GER	FRA	ITA	SWE	NOR	DEN	FIN	NL	B	CH	SP	AUS	IRE	GRE	Total
Total number of observations	102	18	7	14	30	18	3	6	7	2	9	4	3	3	4	230
-/- multiple announcements	8	1	2			1	1	2							1	16
-/- no stock prices in Datastream or contaminating information	17	4		3	6	7	1	2	3	2	3	2			1	51
-/- multiple parents	7															7
Total sample	70	13	5	11	24	10	1	2	4	0	6	2	3	3	2	156
Completed	51	4	2	8	22	8	1	2	2	0	2	1	3	2	0	108

Notes: Distribution of European companies that announced a spin-off in the period from January 1987 to September 2000 by announcement year and country of the parent company. The spin-off announcements are identified from the SDC Mergers and Acquisitions Database. Spin-offs are eliminated for the following reasons:
1. double records of companies that announce the spin-off of two or more subsidiaries on the same dates,
2. spin-offs by multiple parents, and
3. spin-offs for which no Datastream price data are available and/or for which the announcement was contaminated by other important news on the company. Countries are denoted as follows: UK for United Kingdom, GER for Germany, FRA for France, ITA for Italy, SWE for Sweden, NOR for Norway, DEN for Denmark, FIN for Finland, NL for the Netherlands, B for Belgium, CH for Switzerland, SP for Spain, AUS for Austria, IRE for Ireland and GRE for Greece.

The row with the total number of observations shows that with 44% the UK is heavily represented in the total sample (102 out of 230 observations). Other countries that are relatively well represented include Sweden with 30 observations (13%), Germany with 18 observations (8%), Norway with 18 observations (8%) and Italy with 14 observations (6%). The remaining 10 countries take up 21% of the sample (48 observations). The last column of Table 4.1 shows that the distribution in time is also disproportionate. Most announcements, 168 (73%), were made in the period from January 1995 to September 2000. The period from 1987 up to and including 1994 only counted for 62 (27%) observations.

A number of spin-offs had to be eliminated from the original sample. The first reason is that a parent company sometimes announced spin-offs of two or more subsidiaries simultaneously. We checked these double records and eliminated 16 double counts. We also eliminated announcements where one subsidiary was spun-off by multiple parents. The only case where this applied was with the English utility National Grid. This led to the elimination of seven announcements. The third reason is that for a large number of companies no stock prices were available in Datastream and/or the announcement was contaminated with other important financial news on the company. This led to the elimination of 51 observations. The final sample consists of 156 observations. This final sample still shows a large representation of the UK with 70 observations (45%), Sweden with 24 observations (15%), Germany with 14 observations (9%) and Italy with 11 observations (7%). Out of these 156 spin-off announcements, 108 were completed at the moment this research was finalized (April 2002), 31 were still pending and 17 were withdrawn.

4.3.2. Proxies

The variables that are used in the analysis are related to the hypotheses described in Section 4.2:

- *Industrial focus*: An improvement in industrial focus is measured using a dummy variable. This variable is 1 if the two-digit SIC code of the subsidiary is different from the two-digit SIC code of the parent (spin-off of an unrelated division) and 0 if the two-digit SIC codes are the same.[6]
- *Information asymmetry*: The information variable that is used, the normalized standard deviation of forecasts, is derived from the Institute of Brokerage for Investment Services (IBES). This variable is measured as the standard deviation of all earnings forecasts made in the last month of the fiscal year preceding the spin-off announcement year. The idea behind this variable is that disagreement between analysts is an indication of information asymmetry. We normalize the standard deviation by dividing it by the stock price of the firm in the middle of the month in which the standard deviation of forecasts is measured. We have also made calculations for a second variable (i.e., the earnings forecast error) measured before the announcement of the spin-off, from now on to be referred to as the forecast error.[7] Both variables are positively and significantly (at the 1%-level) correlated. They also generally give the same results. For this reason we only report results for the normalized standard deviation of forecasts.[8]

- **Shareholder rights:** Shareholder rights are measured using the index put forward by La Porta, Lopez-de-Silanes, Shleifer, and Vishny (1998). The index ranges from 0 (very low shareholder protection) to 7 (very high shareholder protection). Not surprisingly, the value of the index is lower for countries in continental Europe than for Anglo-Saxon countries.[9]
- **Geographical focus:** Like industrial focus, an increase in geographical focus is measured using a dummy variable. This variable is 1 if a foreign division is spun-off and 0 if a domestic division is spun-off.
- **Relative size:** Relative size is measured as the market value of equity of the divested subsidiary relative to the sum of the equity capitalizations of the parent and the subsidiary. This is computed on the day of the completion of the spin-off (see also Krishnaswami & Subramaniam, 1999). The mean market value of the parents after the spin-off is 5642 million US dollars with a median of 921 million US dollars. This is much higher than the market value of the parents in studies on US spin-offs. For example, Desai and Jain (1999) report an average post-spin-off market value of 1123 million US dollars with a median of 268 million US dollars. Krishnaswami and Subramaniam (1999) report statistics that are close to the ones reported by Desai and Jain (1999). The mean relative size in our sample is 33.51% with a median of 29.62%. A comparison with the US studies shows that the relative size of the subsidiaries is also larger than in the USA. For example, Desai and Jain (1999) find a mean relative size of 21.5% and a median of 13.8%.

4.3.3. Methodology

4.3.3.1. Event study methodology The announcement effects of the spin-offs are measured using an event study methodology as described in, for example, Mikkelson and Partch (1986) and Hite and Owers (1983). Daily abnormal returns are measured using the market model:

$$AR_{i,t} = R_{i,t} - \alpha_{0,i} - \alpha_{1,i} R_t^M,$$

where $AR_{i,t}$ is the abnormal return for firm i at day t, $R_{i,t}$ denotes the return on security i at day t, defined as $\ln(P_{i,t}) - \ln(P_{i,t-1})$, and R_t^M is the return on the market index, that is measured in a similar way as $R_{i,t}$. The market index chosen is the Datastream total return index for the individual European countries.[10] The parameters α_0 and α_1 are estimated over the estimation period by running an ordinary least squares regression of the stock returns on a constant and the return of the market index. Denoting the announcement date, reported by SDC, as day 0, this estimation period ranges from day -220 to day -21. The event window ranges from day -1 to day $+1$.

Average abnormal returns on event day t are calculated as:

$$AAR_t = \frac{\sum_{i=1}^{N} AR_{i,t}}{N},$$

where N is the sample size.

Cumulative average abnormal returns for the whole event window are equal to,

$$CAR(-1,+1) = \frac{\sum_{i=1}^{N} \sum_{t=-1}^{+1} AR_{i,t}}{N}.$$

The statistical significance of the average and cumulative average abnormal returns is based on the average of standardized abnormal returns $SAR_{i,t}$, calculated for each company.
Each individual standardized abnormal return is found as:

$$SAR_{i,t} = \sqrt{\frac{AR_{i,t}}{s_i^{2}*\left(1+\dfrac{1}{200}+\dfrac{(R_{i,t}^{M}-AR^{M})^2}{\sum_{j=-220}^{-21}(R_{i,j}^{M}-AR^{M})^2}\right)}},$$

where s_i^2 is the residual variance from the company i market model estimation, and AR^M is the mean market return during the estimation period.
The test statistic for the average abnormal returns is equal to,

$$Z_t = \frac{\sum_{i=1}^{N} SAR_{i,t}}{\sqrt{N}}.$$

This test statistic is asymptotically unit normally distributed under the assumption that the average abnormal return is 0.

Consequently, the test statistic for the cumulative average abnormal returns over the 3-day event window can be calculated as:

$$Z(-1,+1) = \frac{\sum_{i=1}^{N} \sum_{t=-1}^{+1} SAR_{i,t}}{\sqrt{N*3}}.$$

This statistic has a unit normal distribution under the hypothesis that the cumulative average abnormal return over the event period is 0 (assuming that returns are independent).

4.3.3.2. Methodology for the calculation of the long-run excess returns   There is a large amount of literature on the calculation of long-run excess returns. In this literature a number of methods are proposed, most of which suffer from statistical problems.[11] We use one of the commonly accepted methodologies, that is, the matching-firm approach of Barber and Lyon (1997).[12] Within this matching-firm approach we look in each country for a matching firm based on the size of a company and on its market-to-book ratio. More specifically, in the first month after the spin-off for which we have data in Compustat we divide all the companies in a certain market (country) into deciles based on the size of the company. Size is defined as the market value of equity. In the decile that includes the sample firm we look for the five companies that are closest to our sample firm in terms of the market-to-book ratio. The closest matching firm is designated as the first matching firm; the second closest matching firm is designated as the second matching firm and so on to the fifth matching firm. The stock return on the sample firm is then compared to the return on the matching firm. If the first matching firm disappears for whatever reason, we use the second matching firm from there on. If this firm also disappears, we continue with the third matching firm and so on. If the sample firm disappears, it is assumed that the proceeds are invested in its matching firm from that moment onwards. The application of this method only allows for the use of ordinary t-statistics for events that occur at random. Brav (2000) argue that a problem occurs if the events are not uncorrelated across firms as might be the case with spin-offs. Lyon, Barber, and Tsai (1999) recognize this and they present a method to adjust t-statistics for overlapping samples. We use this methodology in our analysis. Following Lyon, Barber, and Tsai (1999), we estimate the elements of the variance–covariance matrix Σ for the overlapping long-run returns of firms i and j as:

$$\sigma_{ij} = \frac{1}{\tau - a} \sum_{t=s+a}^{s+\tau} (\mathrm{AR}_{i,t} - \overline{\mathrm{AR}}_i)(\mathrm{AR}_{j,t} - \overline{\mathrm{AR}}_j),$$

where firm i's excess return is calculated from period s to $s + \tau$, firm j's excess return is calculated from period $s + a$ to $s + a + \tau$, and $0 \leq a < \tau$. $\mathrm{AR}_{i,t}$ and $\mathrm{AR}_{j,t}$ are the monthly excess returns for firms i and j, respectively, and $\overline{\mathrm{AR}}_i$ and $\overline{\mathrm{AR}}_j$ are their means calculated over the $\tau - a$ overlap period. Lyon, Barber, and Tsai (1999) show that this method reduces the misspecification due to the overlap of the long-run returns.[13]

The long-run returns on the combined firm reflect the total impact of a spin-off on the wealth of an investor holding the stock of the parent company prior to the reorganization. These returns are calculated as a weighted average of excess returns on the parent and subsidiary stock, where the relative market values of equity on the spin-off date (or on the first date after the spin-off that they are available) are used as weights.

4.4. Results

4.4.1. Announcement Date Results

The event study results for the whole sample are included in Table 4.2.

The results for all countries show a cumulative average abnormal return of 2.62% for the event window from day −1 to day +1. This abnormal return is significant at the 1% level. The abnormal returns for smaller event windows, that is, day 0 and day −1 to day 0, are also significantly positive at the 1%-level. These results are confirmed in the non-parametric sign

Table 4.2: Abnormal returns on the announcement date.

Interval	Cumulative average abnormal returns			
	Mean (%)	z-statistic	Median	Percentage positive
All Europe (*N*=156)				
−10 to −1	0.77	3.50***	0.49	53.21
−1 to 0	1.74	8.99***	0.61***	58.97**
0	1.19	8.30***	0.27***	62.82***
−1 to +1	2.62	10.23***	0.89***	62.82***
+1 to +10	−0.33	−0.27	−0.03	49.36
Including:				
UK (*N*=70)				
−10 to −1	1.18	2.79***	0.61	60.00*
−1 to 0	2.19	7.72***	0.95***	61.43*
0	1.88	8.91***	0.62***	67.14***
−1 to +1	2.54	7.39***	0.50***	60.00*
+1 to +10	−1.68	−0.87	−0.27	47.14
Sweden (*N*=24)				
−10 to −1	1.12	1.96**	1.64	54.17
−1 to 0	0.66	1.17	0.00	50.00
0	0.57	0.88	0.04	58.33
−1 to +1	0.82	0.87	0.11	58.33
+1 to +10	2.24	0.22	−0.38	41.67
Germany (*N*=13)				
−10 to −1	4.42	1.94*	2.26*	61.54
−1 to 0	2.49	2.89***	0.24	53.85
0	0.69	1.28	0.12	53.85
−1 to +1	2.56	2.08**	0.04	53.85
+1 to +10	1.14	0.68	2.03	69.23
Italy (*N*=11)				
−10 to −1	−1.11	−0.38	−2.17	36.36
−1 to 0	3.62	5.75***	2.43*	72.73
0	1.51	3.84***	1.03	72.73
−1 to +1	7.97	8.28***	4.16**	81.82*
+1 to +10	2.89	1.62	0.64	54.55

Notes: Cumulative average abnormal returns for the whole sample of 156 spin-off announcements by European companies from January 1987 to September 2000. The spin-off announcements are identified from the SDC Mergers and Acquisitions Database. Abnormal returns are based on the market model, estimated over a 200-day period for each company (from day −220 to day −21). The significance of the medians is tested by means of the Wilcoxon signed rank test. The sign test is used to test the significance of the percentage of firms with positive abnormal returns. The null-hypothesis for the sign test is that the proportion of positive cumulative average abnormal returns is equal to 50%.
Significance level: * (10% level), ** (5% level) and *** (1% level).

test that tests for the number of positive observations. The results for Europe are in line with the American studies that were discussed in the introduction.

Separate results are presented for countries for which we have more than 10 observations. The cumulative average abnormal return for the UK is 2.54% for the event window from day −1 to day +1. This return is also significant at the 1%-level. Similar results are found for the windows from day −1 to day 0 and for day 0. Our results for the event window day −1 to day 0 are in line with Murray (2000). However, he found an insignificant cumulative average abnormal return for the event window day −1 to day +1, where we find a strongly significant cumulative average abnormal return.

For Italy we find a significantly positive cumulative average abnormal return of 7.97% for the event window from day −1 to day +1. Sweden is the only exception with a cumulative average abnormal return of 0.82%, which is not significantly different from 0.[14] In the case of Germany we find a significantly positive cumulative average abnormal return of 2.56% for day −1 to day +1 event window. This might indicate that German investors are not very afraid of being taxed in a later stage. The major shareholders of the company might have agreed that they would hold on to their shares for the 5-year period mentioned in the fiscal law.

Not all spin-offs that were announced in our sample period were completed as well. At the time of the completion of our analysis (April 2002), 108 spin-offs were completed. The other 48 spin-offs were withdrawn or, as in most cases, are still pending. Since we are primarily interested in the question whether spin-offs create value, we also calculated mean cumulative abnormal returns for the sub-sample of completed spin-offs. The results are presented in Table 4.3.

In this table we see that the cumulative average abnormal return is 2.66% for the event window from day −1 to day +1. This abnormal return is significant at the 1%-level. It can be concluded that the returns for the whole sample and the returns for the completed sample are very close to each other. Given our focus on the question whether spin-offs create value, we continue our analysis with the completed spin-offs.[15]

In Table 4.4 the event study results are presented for different sub-samples.

In Panel A the event study results are compared for companies that increase industrial focus and for firms that do not increase industrial focus. In total, 73 companies increase their industrial focus by carrying out a spin-off. The mean abnormal return for these companies is 3.57%. The mean abnormal return for the 35 companies in the non-industrial focus sub-sample is only 0.76%. The difference between the two samples is 2.80%. This difference is significant on the 5%-level. The difference in the medians of the two samples is 1.82%, which is significant on the 10%-level. This is similar to the earlier reported results for the USA by Daley, Mehrotra, and Sivakumar (1997), Krishnaswami and Subramaniam (1999) and Desai and Jain (1999). They find that the abnormal returns are larger for the focus-increasing-spin-offs than for the non-focus-increasing spin-offs.

In Panel B we compare abnormal returns between companies with a high information asymmetry and companies with a low information asymmetry. The high information asymmetry sub-sample is associated with a mean cumulative average abnormal return of 1.44% and the low information asymmetry sub-sample exhibits a cumulative average abnormal return of 3.45%. We hypothesized the inverse relationship. However, both the mean and the median differences are not significantly different from 0.

Table 4.3: Abnormal returns on the announcement date: completed spin-offs.

Interval	Cumulative average abnormal returns			
	Mean (%)	z-statistic	Median	Percentage positive
All Europe (*N*=108)				
−10 to −1	0.62	2.57**	0.58	54.63
−1 to 0	1.75	7.20***	0.69***	60.19**
0	1.25	6.98***	0.17**	60.19**
−1 to +1	2.66	8.06***	0.90***	61.11**
+1 to +10	−0.35	−0.80	−0.28	46.30
Including:				
UK (*N*=51)				
−10 to −1	1.39	2.19**	0.87	64.71**
−1 to 0	2.33	6.80***	1.04***	60.78
0	1.93	7.83***	0.69***	66.67**
−1 to +1	2.41	5.38***	0.39**	60.78
+1 to +10	−2.07	−1.96*	−0.60	41.18
Sweden (*N*=22)				
−10 to −1	0.81	1.92*	1.64	54.55
−1 to 0	0.71	1.19	0.00	50.00
0	0.57	0.81	0.03	54.55
−1 to +1	0.87	0.88	0.06	54.55
+1 to +10	−0.52	−0.97	−0.38	40.91
Germany (*N*=4)				
−10 to −1	4.78	0.72	4.77	50.00
−1 to 0	2.04	1.09	1.75	75.00
0	−0.67	−0.33	−1.23	25.00
−1 to +1	3.42	1.42	2.82	50.00
+1 to +10	0.44	−0.09	2.15	50.00
Italy (*N*=8)				
−10 to −1	−2.67	−1.28	−2.43	25.00
−1 to 0	2.20	3.31***	1.29	75.00
0	1.61	3.58***	0.69	75.00
−1 to +1	7.87	6.83***	3.18**	75.00
+1 to +10	7.14	3.37***	4.40**	75.00

Notes: Cumulative average abnormal returns for the sub-sample of 108 announcements of spin-offs by European companies from January 1987 to September 2000 that were subsequently completed. The spin-off announcements are identified from the SDC Mergers and Acquisitions Database. Abnormal returns are based on the market model, estimated over a 200-day period for each company (from day −220 to day −21). The significance of the medians is tested by means of the Wilcoxon signed rank test. The sign test is used to test the significance of the percentage of firms with positive abnormal returns. The null-hypothesis for the sign test is that the proportion of positive cumulative average abnormal returns is equal to 50%.
Significance level: * (10% level), ** (5% level) and *** (1% level).

Table 4.4: Announcement period abnormal returns of the completed spin-offs by sub-sample.

Panel A: Cumulative average abnormal returns (−1, +1) for sub-samples based on industrial focus

	Increase industrial focus			Do not increase industrial focus			Difference	
	Mean	Median	N	Mean	Median	N	Mean	Median
CAR	3.57	1.74	73	0.76	0.26	35	2.80	1.48
Test statistics	4.00***	4.04***		1.36	1.07		2.08**	1.82*

Panel B: Cumulative average abnormal returns (−1, +1) for sub-samples based on information asymmetry (normalized standard deviation of forecast)

	High information asymmetry			Low information asymmetry			Difference	
	Mean	Median	N	Mean	Median	N	Mean	Median
CAR	1.44	0.23	46	3.45	1.44	45	−2.01	−1.21
Test statistics	2.01*	1.72*		2.78***	2.80***		1.41	1.14

Panel C: Cumulative average abnormal returns (−1, +1) for sub-samples based on the level of shareholders' protection

	High shareholders' protection			Low shareholders' protection			Difference	
	Mean	Median	N	Mean	Median	N	Mean	Median
CAR	2.17	0.39	61	3.30	1.95	47	−1.13	−1.56
Test statistics	2.84***	2.32**		3.02***	3.37***		0.87	1.07

Table 4.4: Continued.

Panel D: Cumulative average abnormal returns (-1, $+1$) for sub-samples based on geographical focus

	Increase geographical focus			Do not increase geographical focus			Difference	
	Mean	Median	N	Mean	Median	N	Mean	Median
CAR	2.81	1.53	8	2.65	0.89	100	0.17	0.64
Test statistics	1.70	1.33		3.89***	3.77***		0.07	0.36

Notes: Three-day cumulative average abnormal returns for sub-samples of 108 announcements of spin-offs by European companies from January 1987 to September 2000 that were subsequently completed. The spin-off announcements are identified from the SDC Mergers and Acquisitions Database. Abnormal returns are based on the market model, estimated over a 200-day period for each company (from day -220 to day -21). Industrial-focus-increasing spin-offs are defined as spin-offs of subsidiaries that have a two-digit SIC code that is different from the parent company. High (Low) level of information asymmetry is defined as being above (below) the medium asymmetry value. High level of shareholders' protection includes countries with anti-director rights index equal to 4 or 5. Low level of shareholders' protection includes countries with anti-director rights index equal to 0, 1, 2 and 3. Geographical focus-increasing spin-offs are defined as spin-offs of subsidiaries from a different country than the parent firm. The significance of the means is tested using a *t*-statistic. The significance of the medians is tested by means of the Wilcoxon signed rank test. The difference in means is tested using a *t*-statistic. The difference in medians is tested using the Mann–Whitney statistic. Significance level: * (10% level), ** (5% level) and *** (1% level).

In Panel C we compare the high and low shareholder protection sub-samples. They show mean cumulative average abnormal returns of 2.17% and 3.30%, respectively. The means and medians are not significantly different for the two sub-samples.

Finally, in Panel D the results are compared for companies that spun-off a foreign division and for companies that spun-off a domestic division. The mean cumulative average abnormal return for the companies that spun-off a foreign division is 2.81%. The mean cumulative average return for the companies that spun-off a domestic division is 2.65%. The difference is a positive 0.17%. However, this difference is not statistically significant.

In Table 4.5, the regression results are presented for the cumulative average abnormal returns of the subsequently completed spin-offs over the 3-day interval.

Although the total number of completed spin-offs is 108, the maximum number of observations in Table 4.5 is 84. This is caused by the inclusion of a control variable that

Table 4.5: Regression of abnormal returns for completed spin-offs.

Variable	(1)	(2)	(3)	(4)	(5)
Intercept	−2.075	−1.917	1.138	−2.122	2.298
	(−1.378)	(−0.996)	(0.563)	(−1.418)	(1.125)
Industrial focus	2.666**	1.865	2.213*	2.669**	1.092
	(2.337)	(1.452)	(1.831)	(2.336)	(0.809)
Relative size	10.162**	11.805*	11.124**	10.180**	13.081**
	(2.147)	(1.910)	(2.156)	(2.152)	(2.132)
Normalized standard		−14.512			−23.493
deviation of forecasts		(−0.453)			(−0.773)
Shareholder rights			−0.844		−1.114
			(−1.199)		(−1.556)
Geographical focus				0.549	1.699
				(0.299)	(0.621)
Number of observations	84	72	84	84	72
R^2	0.160	0.161	0.188	0.160	0.211
Adjusted R^2	0.139	0.124	0.157	0.129	0.151

Notes: Regression coefficients for the 3-day cumulative average abnormal returns for the completed announcements of 84 spin-offs by European companies from January 1987 to September 2000. Only includes the results for those completed spin-offs for which the relative size of the spin-off is known. The spin-off announcements are identified from the SDC Mergers and Acquisitions Database. Industrial focus is a dummy variable equal to 1 if the first two digits of the primary SIC code of a subsidiary to be spun-off are different from the first two digits of the primary SIC code of the parent company, and 0 otherwise. The normalized standard deviation of forecasts is measured as the standard deviation of the analyst earnings forecasts in the last months of the fiscal year preceding the spin-off announcement, divided by the stock price. The "shareholder rights" index is a summary measure of shareholder protection. This index ranges from 0 to 7. The source of these data is La Porta, Lopez-de-Silanes, Shleifer, and Vishny (1998). Geographical focus is a dummy variable equal to 1 in the case of a spin-off of a foreign subsidiary, and equal to 0 if the spin-off is domestic. The relative size is equal to the ratio of the market value of the spun-off subsidiary equity to the sum of the market values of the equity of the parent and the subsidiary on the day of the spin-off.
Significance level: * (10% level) and ** (5% level), based on White heteroscedasticity-adjusted standard errors, *t*-statistics are in parentheses.

measures the size of the spun-off subsidiary relative to the size of the parent company. This variable is referred to as relative size. Unfortunately, this variable is only available for a limited number of companies. The reason for this is that this variable is only available if Datastream reports both the market value of equity of the parent and the market value of equity of the subsidiary. In a number of cases the subsidiary is not traded on a major stock exchange and, therefore, we do not have reliable data on the market value of equity of the subsidiary. In a few cases, the subsidiary is traded, but its market value is not reported in Datastream. These two factors explain the reduction of the sample size from 108 to 84 companies.

The first regression in Table 4.5 shows that industrial focus has a positive and significant coefficient. This confirms the earlier reported results from Table 4.4. In regression (2) we include both industrial focus and the normalized standard deviation of forecasts. The last mentioned coefficient has a very small *t*-statistic. This is in line with the results in Table 4.4. Therefore, we conclude that, contrary to Krishnaswami and Subramaniam (1999), we do not find any relationship between the announcement returns and the level of asymmetric information. The inclusion of the normalized standard deviation of forecasts leads to a disappearance of the significance of the industrial focus variable. In regression (3) we include a measure for shareholder protection (the shareholder rights). This variable does not show the expected positive sign; it shows a negative sign instead. However, this coefficient is not significant. This can be explained by the fact that spin-offs are considered to be value creating in countries with different levels of shareholder protection.[16] In this regression, the sign for industrial focus becomes significant again. In regression (4) we include both industrial and geographical focus. The geographical focus variable is not significant. This is probably caused by the fact that the positive effects on the increase of geographical focus are canceled out by the negative effects. As in the previous regression, the variable on industrial focus is significant. Finally, in regression (5) we include all four variables. In this regression the variable for industrial focus is no longer significant. This leaves us with some mixed evidence on this variable. We conclude that industrial focus does play a role, but its importance is limited. The coefficient for size is significantly different from 0 in all regressions. This confirms earlier results from, for example, Hite and Owers (1983) and Miles and Rosenfeld (1983) that large spin-offs are associated with higher abnormal returns.

4.4.2. Long-run Performance

In Table 4.6, the annualized long-run excess returns of the parent companies, the subsidiaries and the pro-forma combined firms in the period after the spin-off are included.

There is a discussion in the literature on the use of equal-weighted versus value-weighted returns. Loughran and Ritter (2000) argue that equal-weighted returns are more relevant from the point of view of an investor who wants to predict the abnormal returns associated with a random event. Fama (1998), on the other hand, argues that value-weighted returns should be studied, because they more accurately capture the total wealth effects that are experienced by investors. The implications for market efficiency can be completely different. This point is very well illustrated by Brav, Geczy, and Gompers (2000). They present a scenario in which a sample contains 1000 firms, 999 of which have

Table 4.6: Long-run returns in excess of the matching-firm return.

	Number of observations	Equal –weighted		Value weighted		Percentage positive
		Mean	t-statistic	Mean	t-statistic	
Panel A: All parent firms						
t_{sp} to t_{sp} + 6	106	3.88	0.27	1.32	0.18	48.11
t_{sp} to t_{sp} + 12	105	−0.65	−0.12	4.43	1.44	49.52
t_{sp} to t_{sp} + 24	86	6.49	1.50	14.28***	5.31	59.30
t_{sp} to t_{sp} + 36	68	−0.41	−0.10	−3.96	−1.37	48.53
Panel B: All subsidiaries						
t_{sp} to t_{sp} + 6	70	11.96	0.66	−24.45**	−2.17	50.00
t_{sp} to t_{sp} + 12	70	12.58	0.83	−15.75	−1.17	52.86
t_{sp} to t_{sp} + 24	60	13.72	1.03	−22.04*	−1.69	65.00
t_{sp} to t_{sp} + 36	53	15.15	0.97	4.62	0.30	67.92
Panel C: All pro-forma combined firms						
t_{sp} to t_{sp} + 6	61	−2.23	−0.25	0.80	0.12	44.26
t_{sp} tot_{sp} + 12	61	−2.33	−0.45	−0.89	−0.18	49.18
t_{sp} to t_{sp} + 24	51	4.24	1.00	8.49*	1.79	60.78
t_{sp} to t_{sp} + 36	45	2.01	0.43	1.61	0.48	53.33

Notes: Annualized returns defined as company stock return minus matching-firm stock return for spin-offs by European companies from January 1987 to September 2000. The spin-offs are identified from the SDC Mergers and Acquisitions Database. The pro-forma combined firm is created by weighing the return of the parent and that of the subsidiary by the market value of equity at the spin-off date. The equal-weighted returns are calculated as the average excess returns for the whole sample. The value-weighted excess returns are calculated as the average excess returns weighted by the market values of equity at the spin-off dates. The significance of the means is tested using a *t*-statistic, corrected for the cross-correlation of long-run returns. t_{sp} is the spin-off ex-date. t_{sp} + 6 (12, 24, 36) is the period from the spin-off date to 6 (12, 24 and 36) months after the spin-off date. Significance level: * (10% level), ** (5% level) and *** (1% level).

a 1 million US dollar market capitalization (the small firms) and one firm that has a 1001 million US dollars market capitalization (the large firm). If it is assumed that the small firms have all underperformed by an equal percentage of 50%, while the large firm has overperformed by 50%, it can be seen that an equal-weighted measure will indicate a severe mispricing (−50%), while a value weighting will lead to the conclusion that the sample performance is virtually 0. From our perspective we prefer the analysis of equal-weighted returns. The reason for this is that we want to test whether a random spin-off will be associated with long-run superior performance. Therefore, our focus will be on the equal-weighted returns. However, in order to capture the value effects for the market as a whole, we present value-weighted returns as well.

In Table 4.6, the excess returns are calculated as the difference between the company returns and the returns on a matching firm. This matching procedure is described in Section 4.3.3. With regard to Table 4.6 it has to be pointed out that the number of observations goes down with the study horizon because there are shorter time series available for the more recent announcements. This is caused by the fact that our last announcement was from September 2000. First the equal-weighted returns will be discussed.

In Panel A, the results for the parent companies are presented. The mean annualized returns are positive for the periods of 6 months and 2 years after the spin-off and are negative for the periods of 1 and 3 years after the spin-off. However, all returns are insignificant. Our results differ from previous results that were published for the USA. For example, Cusatis, Miles, and Woolridge (1993) and Desai and Jain (1999) find that parents of spin-offs perform significantly better than similar firms in the 3-year period after the spin-off.

In Panel B, we present the results for the subsidiaries. This sample only shows insignificant mean excess returns. This result is also different from earlier results for the USA. Desai and Jain (1999) find significantly positive excess returns for their sample of subsidiaries.

A spin-off involves a pro-rata distribution of shares of the subsidiary. This enables us to create a pro-forma combined firm in the period following the spin-off. Following Desai and Jain (1999), we create this "firm" by weighing the return of the parent and that of the subsidiary by the market value of equity at the spin-off date.[17] This gives us the return an investor would have earned if he had held on to the shares of both the parent and the subsidiary after the spin-off. In Panel C of Table 4.6, we see that the pro-forma combined firms are associated with non-significant negative mean excess returns in the 6-month and the 1-year periods after the spin-offs. The mean excess returns in the 2- and 3-year periods after the event are positive, but also insignificant.

A close look at the equal-weighted returns in Table 4.6 reveals that there is definitely no significant long-run effect for spin-offs. Although the number of observations in Panel A is fairly high (between 68 and 106), all *t*-statistics are very small (between −0.12 and 1.50). This result is also found for the subsidiaries (Panel B) and for the pro-forma combined firms (Panel C).

Table 4.6 also includes value-weighted returns. Panel A shows insignificant mean excess returns for the 6-month and the 1-year periods after the spin-off. The period of 2 years after the spin-off shows a significantly positive excess return. However, it turns into a non-significant mean excess return in the 3-year post-spin-off period. We study whether this decline is created by a reversal of a company for which both data on the 2- and the 3-year periods are available, or whether it is caused by a company for which no 3-year data are available. We find that the Swiss company Novartis mainly causes the decline. In the 2-year period this company, that has a weight of 21.31% in the sample, shows an excess return of 45.90%. This excess return drops to 1.79% over the 3-year period after the spin-off. The subsidiaries in Panel B show significantly negative mean excess returns in the 6-month and 2-year periods after the spin-off. However, the 1- and 3-year periods show non-significant returns. The pro-forma combined firms in Panel C mostly have insignificant returns. The significantly positive return for the 2-year period in Panel C is caused by the same outlier as in Panel A.

Brav, Geczy, and Gompers (2000) and Loughran and Ritter (2000) argue that researchers should be careful with drawing conclusions for market efficiency from studies on long-run excess returns. This warning is based on the fact that, for example, equal- and value-weighted returns can lead to different conclusions. If we review our results it can be concluded that the value-weighted returns, and even more so the equal-weighted returns, indicate that the European markets are efficient. This gives some support for the idea of Fama (1998) that the long-run effects following US spin-offs are rather a result of chance than of causality. However, given the warnings of Brav, Geczy, and Gompers (2000) and Loughran and Ritter (2000) it should be noticed that more research on different capital markets is necessary before a definite conclusion can be drawn.

In Table 4.7, the relation between the long-run excess returns of the parent firms and their underlying variables is studied.

We focus on the 1- and the 2-year excess returns. The reason for this is that we want to study a relatively long period after the completion of the spin-off. Therefore, we leave out the 6-month excess returns. As we only have a limited number of observations for the 3-year period, we also leave out these results. In regression (1) we present the results for the 1-year excess returns; regression (2) shows the results for the 2-year horizon. The coefficient for the relative size of spin-off is insignificant in both the regressions.

Table 4.7: Regression of long-run excess return: parent firms.

Variable	1-year excess return	2-year excess return
Intercept	6.978 (0.355)	30.413* (1.893)
Industrial focus	−2.141 (−0.189)	−0.811 (−0.066)
Geographical focus	−40.971** (−2.167)	−24.237* (−1.942)
Relative size	−0.582 (−0.027)	26.809 (1.375)
Normalized standard deviation of forecasts	−241.083 (−0.531)	−620.783 (−1.545)
Change in normalized standard deviation of forecasts	−850.904* (−1.746)	−57.401 (−0.131)
Shareholder rights	−1.953 (−0.513)	−7.090** (−2.254)
Number of observations	62	52
R^2	0.205	0.215
Adjusted R^2	0.118	0.110

Notes: Regression coefficients for the 1- and 2-year returns in excess of the matching portfolio return for the European companies that performed a spin-off. The spin-off dates are identified from the SDC Mergers and Acquisitions Database. Industrial focus is a dummy variable equal to 1 if the first two-digits of the primary SIC code of a subsidiary to be spun-off are different from the first two digits of the primary SIC code of the parent company, and 0 otherwise. Geographical focus is a dummy variable equal to 1 in the case of a spin-off of a foreign subsidiary, and equal to 0 if the spin-off is domestic. The normalized standard deviation of forecasts is measured as the standard deviation of the analyst earnings forecasts in the last months of the fiscal year preceding the spin-off announcement, divided by the stock price. Changes in the normalized standard deviation of forecasts are measured from the end of fiscal year preceding the spin-off announcement to the end of the fiscal year in which the spin-off is completed. The "shareholder rights" index is a summary measure of shareholder protection. This index ranges from 0 to 7. The source of these data is La Porta, Lopez-de-Silanes, Shleifer, and Vishny (1998). The relative size is equal to the ratio of the market value of the spun-off subsidiary equity to the sum of the market values of the equity of the parent and the subsidiary on the day of the spin-off.
Significance level: * (10% level) and ** (5% level), based on White heteroscedasticity-adjusted standard errors; *t*-statistics are in parentheses.

The industrial focus variable has very low *t*-statistics in both the regressions. The results for this variable are different from the result of Desai and Jain (1999), who find that the US firms that increase their industrial focus with a spin-off exhibit higher long-run excess returns than firms that do not increase their industrial focus.

The geographical focus variable is significantly negative in both regressions. We study whether this result is caused by negative earnings surprises for these companies. Earnings forecast data are available for five of the six companies in Table 4.7 that spin off a foreign division. For three of them negative earnings surprises in the first post-spin-off year are followed by negative abnormal returns. For another firm, a small positive earnings surprise of less than 5% is followed by negative long-run performance. In only one case we find that a positive earnings surprise is followed by a positive abnormal return. Overall, these companies experience an average earnings surprise of -242.47% of the expected earnings in the first post-spin-off year, with a median of -28.99%. Therefore, we conclude that the high negative coefficient for geographical focus improvement is explained by negative earnings surprises. These negative earnings surprises may be caused by the negative consequences of increasing geographical focus that were mentioned in Section 4.2.4. It may, for example, be possible that the increase in geographical focus has led to reduced economies of scale in production or the firm has put itself at a disadvantage relative to competitors who operate internationally.

The pre-spin-off level of information asymmetry is not significant in both regressions. Therefore, we do not find any support for the hypothesis that firm with higher information asymmetry before the spin-off display better long-run performance. We also test the model of Habib, Johnsen, and Naik (1997) by measuring the impact of the changes in the information asymmetry on the long-run performance of spin-off parents. The change in the normalized standard deviation of forecasts exhibits the expected negative sign in both regressions. However, this sign is only significant in the first regression. Therefore, we conclude that there is some, albeit weak, evidence for the model of Habib, Johnsen, and Naik (1997).

The coefficient for the shareholder rights shows a negative sign in both regressions. Moreover, in one of the regressions this coefficient is statistically significant. This is remarkable since it means that a higher level of shareholder protection is associated with lower long-run excess returns. It is unlikely that this finding can be explained by the more or less shareholder-friendly treatment of spin-offs in different countries, since we saw in Tables 4.3–4.5 that the announcement returns were very similar in countries with different shareholder protection. This result can possibly be explained by the fact that firms that undertake spin-offs also continue to maintain their shareholder-oriented policy in the long run.

Our methodology controls for the financial characteristics of the matching firms in the sense that we look for firms with similar size and book-to-market value. However, it is possible that in countries with less shareholder protection, the "average firm" that is used as a match is more likely to undertake actions that benefit other stakeholders rather than the shareholders, while the firms that perform spin-offs are more focussed on shareholder value maximization. It is possible that this creates a long-run difference in the stock price performance between the sample and the matching firms. On the other hand, in countries with a good shareholder protection, such as the UK, other firms are more forced to act in the interests of shareholders than in a country like Belgium. This may explain the significantly negative sign for the shareholder rights variable in our regression in Table 4.7.

Table 4.8: Regression of long-run excess return on the abnormal returns on announcement date.

	6 months		1 year		2 years		3 years	
Constant	−6.628	−3.902	−7.959	−3.318	4.715	3.707	1.314	0.227
	(−0.703)	(−0.391)	(−1.441)	(−0.581)	(0.822)	(0.691)	(0.293)	(0.055)
Day 0 abnormal return	4.434**		3.287*		−0.307		1.248	
	(2.013)		(1.715)		(−0.170)		(0.846)	
Day −1 to day +1 abnormal return		0.041		−0.839		0.598		1.401
		(0.036)		(−1.536)		(0.350)		(1.227)
Number of observations	54	54	54	54	45	45	39	39
Adjusted R^2	0.01	−0.02	0.03	0.01	−0.02	−0.02	−0.01	0.03

Notes: Regression coefficients for the 6-month to 3-year returns on a pro-forma combined firm for the European companies that performed a spin-off. The spin-off dates are identified from the SDC Mergers and Acquisitions Database. Day 0 and day −1 to day +1 abnormal returns are based on the market model, estimated over a 200-day period for each company (from day −220 to day −21). The 6 months to 3 years annualized excess returns are defined as company stock price return minus matching-firm return. The pro-forma combined firm is created by weighing the return of the parent and that of the subsidiary by the market value of equity at the spin-off date. Significance level: * (10% level) and ** (5% level), based on White heteroscedasticity-adjusted standard errors; *t*-statistics are in parentheses.

From a market efficiency point of view it is interesting to study whether the announcement period returns and the long-run excess returns are related. This analysis is included in Table 4.8.

We find that for the 6-month and 1-year post-spin-off periods, the day 0 abnormal returns are positively related to the long-run excess returns. This would indicate that the market underreacts to the spin-off announcement. However, the coefficient is insignificantly negative for the 2-year post-spin-off period and insignificantly negative for the 3-year period. The finding of a possible underreaction is also not confirmed for the 3-day announcement period abnormal returns since the coefficients for all four regressions are insignificant. Furthermore, it can be remarked that the explanatory power of all regressions is extremely small. The adjusted R^2 varies between -0.02 and 0.03. Therefore, it can be concluded that there is not much evidence for underreaction at the announcement.

4.5. Summary and Conclusions

We study the wealth effects and the efficiency of the European capital market for the case of corporate spin-offs. Announcements of spin-offs may be associated with a wealth increase for the shareholders by means of positive abnormal returns. Such a wealth increase can be accomplished if the spin-off leads to an increase in industrial focus or if the spin-off leads to a decrease of the information asymmetry between the management of the firm and its shareholders. The efficient market hypothesis implies that there is no long-run effect. Possible wealth effects will be incorporated in the stock price at the moment the spin-off is announced.

We study announcement effects and long-run performance for a sample of 156 European spin-offs announced from January 1987 to September 2000. We find that the announcement of a subsequently completed spin-off is associated with a positive abnormal return of 2.66% over a 3-day window. We find some evidence that the abnormal returns are positively related to an increase in the industrial focus. There does not seem to be a relationship between the abnormal returns and the level of information asymmetry at the time of the spin-off. The corporate governance system does not make a difference for the market reaction to a spin-off announcement. In line with the efficient market hypothesis we do not find any significant long-run excess return in the period after the spin-off. If the return on the parents, subsidiaries and the pro-forma combined firms is compared to the return on a matching portfolio, we find that the excess returns are both economically and statistically insignificant. This leads us to conclude that the capital markets in Europe efficiently react to the information contained in the spin-off announcements.

Acknowledgement

This is a revised version of the chapter that earlier appeared in the *Journal of Banking and Finance* under the title: Do spin-offs really create value? The European case (2004), *28*, 1111–1135. (Reprinted with permission from Elsevier).

Endnotes

1. See, for example, Rosenfeld (1984), Copeland, Lemgruber, and Mayers (1987), Slovin, Sushka, and Ferraro (1995), Johnson, Klein, and Thibodeaux (1996), Daley, Mehrotra, and Sivakumar (1997), Desai and Jain (1999), Krishnaswami and Subramaniam (1999), Mulherin and Boone (2000) and Maxwell and Rao (2003).

2. Other empirical research on announcements of non-US spin-offs was carried out by Janssens de Vroom and Van Frederikslust (2000), Murray (2000) and Koh, Koh, and Koh (2004). Janssens de Vroom and Van Frederikslust (2000) find positive abnormal returns for their "English Legal Origin sample" of 176 observations (that mostly includes the US and the UK) and insignificant abnormal returns for their "Other Legal Origin sample" of 34 observations. Murray (2000) finds positive abnormal returns for UK companies. Koh, Koh, and Koh (2004) find positive abnormal returns for a sample of divestitures in Singapore. All three studies only look at announcement date returns and not at long-run excess returns.

3. See, for example, Bodnar, Tang, and Weintrop (2000) and Denis, Denis, and Yost (2002) for an overview of these competing theories.

4. See Schipper and Smith (1983), Copeland, Lemgruber, and Mayers (1987, pp. 136) and Krishnaswami and Subramaniam (1999) for a discussion on the tax consequences of US spin-offs.

5. Hite and Owers (1983), Schipper and Smith (1983), Dittmar (2004) and Veld and Veld-Merkoulova (2005) find that the announcement period *bond* returns are either positive or not significantly different from zero. Schipper and Smith (1983) and Dittmar (2004) find that only a small number of companies decline in bond ratings after the spin-off. On the other hand, Maxwell and Rao (2003) do find evidence that bondholders on average suffer a significantly negative abnormal return in the month of the spin-off announcement. Another study that finds such a wealth transfer is Parrino (1997). In a case study of the Marriott spin-off, he shows that the restructuring not only reduced the collateral on Marriott's existing debt, but also reduced the bondholder claims on cash flows from the business.

6. Ideally, we would also like to use data on the number of segments and on the segment sales. However, the data for these variables are not available in Compustat for European companies. This is probably caused by the fact that in most European countries there is no legal obligation to report data on segment sales.

7. The average earnings forecast in the last month of the year preceding the spin-off announcement is defined as the predicted earnings. The forecast error is defined as the ratio of the absolute difference between the predicted earnings and the actual earnings per share to the stock price in the middle of the forecast month. Firms with more information asymmetry are expected to have higher forecast errors.

8. Results for the forecast error are available from the authors on request.

9. The index has the following values for the countries in our study: UK (5), Germany (1), France (3), Italy (1), Sweden (3), Norway (4), Denmark (2), Finland (3), the Netherlands (2), Belgium (0), Switzerland (2), Spain (4), Austria (2), Ireland (4) and Greece (2).

10. A disadvantage of using single country indexes is that some European markets are fairly small and their indexes are largely dominated by a few large companies. An alternative would be to use a single European index for the whole sample. However, only a relatively limited number of observations in our sample are from small markets. Besides that, the use of a European index also has some disadvantages, since European capital markets are not fully integrated. Therefore, the use of a single European index will introduce noise. For these reasons, we have chosen single country indexes.

11. See, for example, Barber and Lyon (1997), Fama (1998), Lyon, Barber, and Tsai (1999), Brav (2000), Brav, Geczy, and Gompers (2000) and Loughran and Ritter (2000) for a discussion of the various methods.

12. This methodology was also used in recent studies by Desai and Jain (1999) on spin-offs, and by Eckbo, Masulis, and Norli (2000) on seasoned equity offerings.

13. A similar method of correcting for cross-correlation of long-run excess returns was used by Mitchell and Stafford (2000). They assumed that correlations between overlapping returns are linearly decreasing in the overlapping period, and they based their estimates on the sub-sample of firms with complete overlap. Unlike their method, the correction used by us does not require us to make an assumption about the correlation structure.

14. The results for Sweden are partly driven by announcements of Swedish banks that spun-off big property divisions that they were forced to acquire during the loan crisis of the early 1990s. These announcements were generally associated with negative abnormal returns.

15. A disadvantage of this approach is that we introduce a look-ahead bias by assuming that investors know which spin-offs will actually be carried out and which ones will not. However, a comparison of Tables 4.3 and 4.4 shows that the results are very much alike. Detailed results for the whole sample are available on request from the authors.
16. It should also be noticed that the shareholder rights index does not control for the rights of bondholders and other stakeholders such as employees. This may also distort the coefficient estimates in this regression and in following regressions that include the shareholder rights variable.
17. Desai and Jain (1999) use the market value of equity at the end of the month of the spin-off.
18. During our sample period, the following countries were member states of the European Union. From 1951: Belgium, France, Germany, Italy, Luxembourg and the Netherlands. From 1973: Denmark, Ireland and the UK. From 1981: Greece. From 1986: Spain and Portugal. From 1995: Austria, Finland and Sweden.
19. Note that countries are not obliged to incorporate the directive.
20. See Raedler (1994).
21. See Poetgens and Jakobsen (1999) and Van Olffen, Buijn and Simonis (1998).
22. The market value of KPN and TNT Post Groep after the spin-off was 17.9 billion US dollars and 11.6 billion US dollars, respectively, making it one of the largest spin-offs in Europe.

References

Barber, B.M., & Lyon, J.D. (1997). Detecting long-run abnormal stock returns: The empirical power and specification of test statistics. *Journal of Financial Economics, 43*, 341–372.

Bodnar, G.M., Tang, C., & Weintrop, J. (2000). *Both sides of corporate diversification: The value impacts of geographic and industrial diversification.* Working paper of Johns Hopkins University.

Brav, A. (2000). Inference in long-horizon event studies: A Bayesian approach with application to initial public offerings. *The Journal of Finance, 55*, 1979–2016.

Brav, A., Geczy, C., & Gompers, P.A. (2000). Is the abnormal return following equity issuances anomalous? *Journal of Financial Economics, 56*, 209–249.

Copeland, T.E., Lemgruber, E.F., & Mayers, D. (1987). Corporate spinoffs: Multiple announcement and ex-date abnormal performance. In: T.E. Copeland (Ed.), *Modern finance and industrial economics: Papers in honor of J. Fred Weston* (pp. 114–137). NY: Basil Blackwell Inc.

Cusatis, P.J., Miles, J.A., & Woolridge, J.R. (1993). Restructuring through spinoffs: The stock market evidence. *Journal of Financial Economics, 33*, 293–311.

Daley, L., Mehrotra, V., & Sivakumar, R. (1997). Corporate focus and value creation: Evidence from spinoffs. *Journal of Financial Economics, 45*, 257–281.

Denis, D.J., Denis, D.K., & Yost, K. (2002). Global diversification, industrial diversification, and firm value. *The Journal of Finance, 57*, 1951–1980.

Desai, H., & Jain, P.C. (1999). Firm performance and focus: Long-run stock market performance following spinoffs. *Journal of Financial Economics, 54*, 75–101.

Dittmar, A. (2004). Capital structure in corporate spin-offs. *Journal of Business, 77*, 9–44.

Eckbo, B.E., Masulis, R.W., & Norli, O. (2000). Seasoned public offerings: Resolution of the 'new issues puzzle'. *Journal of Financial Economics, 56*, 251–291.

Fama, E.F. (1998). Market efficiency, long-term returns, and behavioral finance. *Journal of Financial Economics, 49*, 283–306.

Gibbs, P. (1999). *Quarterly focus: European spin-off market.* Morgan Guaranty Trust Company, Mergers & Acquisitions Research, London.

Habib, M.A., Johnsen, B.D., & Naik, N.Y. (1997). Spinoffs and information. *Journal of Financial Intermediation, 6*, 153–176.

Hite, G.L., & Owers, J.E. (1983). Security price reactions around corporate spin-off announcements. *Journal of Financial Economics, 12*, 409–436.

Janssens de Vroom, H., & Van Frederikslust, R. (2000). *Shareholder wealth effects of corporate spinoffs*. Working Paper of Erasmus University, Rotterdam.

Johnson, S.A., Klein, D.P., & Thibodeaux, V.L. (1996). The effects of spin-offs on corporate investment and performance. *The Journal of Financial Research, 19*, 293–307.

Koh, F.C.C., Koh, W.T.H., & Koh, B.S.K. (2004). *Corporate divestitures and spinoffs in Singapore*. Working Paper of Singapore Management University.

Krishnaswami, S., & Subramaniam, V. (1999). Information asymmetry, valuation, and the corporate spin-off decision. *Journal of Financial Economics, 53*, 73–112.

La Porta, R., Lopez-de-Silanes, F., Shleifer, A., & Vishny, R. (1998). Law and finance. *Journal of Political Economy, 106*, 1113–1155.

La Porta, R., Lopez-de-Silanes, F., Shleifer, A., & Vishny, R. (2000). Investor protection and corporate governance. *Journal of Financial Economics, 58*, 3–28.

Loughran, T., & Ritter, J.R. (2000). Uniformly least powerful tests of market efficiency. *Journal of Financial Economics, 55*, 361–389.

Lyon, J.D., Barber, B.M., & Tsai, C.L. (1999). Improved methods for tests of long-run abnormal stock returns. *The Journal of Finance, 54*, 165–201.

Maxwell, W.F., & Rao, R.P. (2003). Do spin-offs expropriate wealth from bondholders? *The Journal of Finance, 58*, 2087–2108.

McConnell, J.J., Ozbilgin, M., & Wahal, S. (2001). Spin-offs, ex ante. *Journal of Business, 74*, 245–280.

Mikkelson, W.H., & Partch, M.M. (1986). Valuation effects of security offerings and the issuance process. *Journal of Financial Economics, 15*, 31–60.

Miles, J.A., & Rosenfeld, J.D. (1983). The effect of voluntary spin-off announcements on shareholder wealth. *The Journal of Finance, 38*, 1597–1606.

Mitchell, M.L., & Stafford, E. (2000). Managerial decisions and long-term stock price performance. *Journal of Business, 73*, 287–329.

Moerland, P.W. (1995). Alternative disciplinary mechanisms in different corporate systems. *Journal of Economic Behavior and Organization, 26*, 17–34.

Mulherin, J.H., & Boone, A.L. (2000). Comparing acquisitions and divestitures. *Journal of Corporate Finance, 6*, 117–139.

Murray, L. (2000). *An assessment of the wealth effects of spin-offs on the London Stock Exchange*. Working Paper of University College Dublin.

Parrino, R. (1997). Spin-offs and wealth transfers: The Marriott case. *Journal of Financial Economics, 43*, 241–274.

Poetgens, F.P.G., & Jakobsen, M. (1999). Netherlands: Tax-neutral division of companies. *European Taxation*, 81–88.

Raedler, A.J. (1994). *General report on the conference on national and international tax consequences of demergers*. International Fiscal Association, Toronto.

Rosenfeld, J.D. (1984). Additional evidence on the relation between divestiture announcements and shareholder wealth. *The Journal of Finance, 39*, 1437–1448.

Schipper, K., & Smith, A. (1983). Effects of recontracting on shareholder wealth: The case of voluntary spin-offs. *Journal of Financial Economics, 12*, 437–467.

Slovin, M.B., Sushka, M.E., & Ferraro, S.R. (1995). A comparison of the information conveyed by equity carve-outs, spin-offs and asset sell-offs. *Journal of Financial Economics, 37*, 89–104.

Van Olffen, M., Buijn, F.K., & Simonis, P.H.M. (1998). *Splitsing van ondernemingen* (translated Split-ups of companies). Deventer: Boom Juridische Uitgevers.

Veld, C., & Veld-Merkoulova, Y.V. (2005). *An empirical analysis of the stockholder-bondholder conflict in corporate spin-offs*. Working paper of Simon Fraser University and Erasmus University Rotterdam.

Zaman, D.F.M.M. (1998). *Splitsing: Juridisch en fiscaal* (translated Split-up: Legal and fiscal). Deventer: Kluwer Juridische Uitgevers.

Appendix 4A: The Regulatory and Fiscal Environment for European Spin-offs.

Spin-offs are legally possible in all European countries. For members of the European Union, the sixth EC-directive on corporation law is important.[18] This directive, that defines the legal terms for split-ups, stems from December 17, 1982. Member states were advised to incorporate it in their laws by January 1, 1986.[19] However, in some countries it took longer to incorporate this directive in the national law. For example, in Belgium corporate law did not cover split-ups until June 29, 1993 (Zaman, 1998). This does not mean that split-ups were illegal. They were permitted and they were generally legally arranged using the framework that was set in the fiscal law. In Europe, the legal frameworks for spin-offs are generally based on the laws for split-ups. However, in some cases it took some time before a special framework for spin-offs was set up. For example, until February 1998, Dutch companies that wanted to spin-off one or more divisions had to go through a large range of complicated procedures. This ended on February 1, 1998 with the adoption of a law in which matters were significantly simplified (see Van Olffen, Buijn, & Simonis, 1998).

In principle, spin-offs may cause an income tax problem, because they can be seen as a distribution of income or capital and be taxed accordingly. On July 23, 1990 the European Union adopted the so-called "Merger Directive". According to this directive, the capital gains taxation on a spin-off is deferred. In other words, the tax authorities consider a spin-off as the re-arrangement of investments that the investor already owns, and as a result, levy no taxes. This directive applies to intra-community spin-offs. The ultimate intention for this directive is its application in all countries within the European Union.[20] According to Gibbs (1999), tax deferral does not cause major problems in most European countries. Like in the USA, it is important that the spin-offs are carried out for business reasons. In some countries, spin-offs are associated with potential fiscal problems. This is the case for the Netherlands (until June 1998), Germany and France. Before June 1998, spin-offs in the Netherlands were seen as a distribution of income or capital and they were taxed accordingly. Under the pressure of some large Dutch companies spin-offs were no longer taxed from June 1998. Instead the fiscal claims were passed on to the future.[21] This opened the way for one of the largest European spin-offs in which the Dutch company KPN spun-off its postal division TNT Post Groep.[22] Besides that, two other relatively large spin-offs could be realized. In Germany spin-offs can be arranged in a tax-neutral way. However, if more than 20% of the shareholders transfer their shares within 5 years after the spin-off, the spin-off will still be taxed (Zaman, 1998). In France, a problem occurs in the sense that it is not possible for the company to ask for approval from the tax authorities before the transaction is carried out. This uncertainty is probably the cause of the low number of spin-offs that were announced in France. In the period from January 1987 to September 2000 a mere total of seven spin-offs were announced in France.

Chapter 5

The Competitive Challenge in Banking

Arnoud Boot and Anjolein Schmeits

5.1. Introduction

Over the last few decades, the liberalization and deregulation of the financial sector have dramatically changed the financial landscape. Interbank competition has heated up and banks face increasing competition from non-banking financial institutions and the financial markets. Mutual funds, like Fidelity and Merrill Lynch, compete fiercely for the banks' core deposit base. Commercial paper, medium-term notes and other financial market innovations challenge the banks' traditional lending products. The past 25 years have shown a spectacular proliferation of new financial instruments. Examples of such financial innovations are plentiful: zero-coupon bonds, collateralized mortgage obligations, eurodollars, warrants, callable bonds and all kinds of derivatives (from plain-vanilla interest-rate swaps to collars and caps). Many of these product innovations may have been infeasible if it were not for contemporaneous advances in financial market microstructure and trading practices. The ongoing revolution in information technology (IT) has improved information dissemination and enhanced overall market liquidity. Consequently, the business of banking is changing rapidly. "Traditional" relationship banking is under siege. The proliferation of financial innovations, advances in securitization and underwriting push funding to the financial markets. Does this tilt the comparative competitive advantage to the transaction-oriented financial markets?

The challenge for bankers is to draw the right conclusions. Fads need to be distinguished from long-term trends. While banks — on average — have been quite profitable in the last few years, their real competitive strength has been questioned. In particular, many suggest that the banks' traditional comparative advantage in relationship banking has been diluted by transaction-oriented finance available in the financial markets. This begs the question: What is the future of relationship-based bank lending? And, more generally, what should be the competitive positioning of banks? Our core message is that the fundamentals of banking have *not* changed. For many of the modern "funding vehicles", bankers' traditional skills are indispensable. In many other cases, bank loans may continue

Advances in Corporate Finance and Asset Pricing
Edited by L. Renneboog
© **2006 Elsevier B.V. All rights reserved.**
ISBN: 0-444-52723-0

to be the optimal instruments. The threat to banks may therefore come from bankers themselves. They may falsely interpret modern banking (and their own future) as transaction- rather than relationship-oriented. As *The Economist* put it over 10 years ago in the context of the experience of securities firms:

> Perhaps the worst feature of the 1980s — which has subsequently returned to haunt the securities firms — was the abandonment by most of them of the old relationships with their customers. [...] 'The aim was to do a deal, any deal', remembers one manager who prefers not to be named (*The Economist*, April 15, 1995, *Special section: A survey of Wall Street*, p. 13).

Indeed, as we will argue, banks' strategic choices may have undermined rather than strengthened their competitiveness. In particular, banks may have neglected relationship finance and relationship-oriented activities in general. Consequently, relationship banking may have suffered as a self-fulfilling prophecy. Not surprisingly (with hindsight), Citigroup's retail banking head Steven S. Freiberg seeks to reinvigorate Citigroup's banking retail operations by emphasizing Citi to think "locally".[1]

Our evaluation, however, would be incomplete without considering the positioning of banks in a broader context. Important questions here are: How will banks evolve? What is the optimal size of banks (scale)? And which activities are optimally combined (scope)? A related question is about the role of alliances and joint ventures, and the value of outsourcing or, more generally, specialization *within* the value chain. This relates to the potential optimality of the disaggregation of the value chain. These questions have no easy answers. The financial services industry is going through a major transition, and only at the end of the process, we may have some hope of finding somewhat more definitive answers.

One source of (potential) tentative answers is the evidence on mergers and acquisitions in banking. The motivations for mergers seem obvious to many bank executives, and many consultants. The popular press points to the increasingly competitive environment of banking as the trigger for the observed developments. With competition in commercial banking heating up, banks feel forced to quickly and significantly increase efficiency. A shortcut to achieving efficiency gains could be a cost-saving motivated merger with another bank. A horizontal merger may allow banks to exploit efficiencies of scale through elimination of redundant branches and back-office consolidation. Moreover, increased competitive pressure and diminishing margins in commercial banking could invite banks to look outside their traditional domain. Some non-banking activities may offer higher margins, so expanding scope may become attractive.

However, these popular explanations have their limitations. The empirical evidence on scale and scope economies in banking is far from conclusive. It is questionable whether these economies are large enough to justify consolidation and scope expansion on the scale that we have observed. Moreover, ample research in corporate finance points at the existence of a "diversification discount". On average, diversification seems to destroy value. There is substantial empirical evidence that improvements in operating performance and stock returns have been experienced by firms that have refocused.

We will examine the existing empirical evidence on scale and scope economies in banking. One conclusion that we will draw is that this evidence is of little help in assessing the optimal positioning of banks, and their configuration of activities. An issue in this context is that the literature needs to differentiate more between the various activities (services and products) of financial intermediaries. Scale and scope economies have been looked at too generically. From a deeper level of understanding, we can then move on to discussing the (potential) optimality of the disaggregation of the value chain, and the desirability of alliances and outsourcing in particular.

The organization of this chapter is as follows. In Section 5.2, we analyze the economics of banking, and seek to identify the comparative economic advantages of banks, particularly in the context of funding corporations. Our analysis identifies relationship-oriented banking as the key characteristic of value-enhancing financial intermediation. Section 5.3 discusses the future of relationship banking and particularly the desired responses of banks to increased competition. In Section 5.4, we discuss scale and scope economies in banking, and also include a brief summary of the extant empirical evidence. Section 5.5 addresses the potential disaggregation of the value chain, including the role of alliances, joint ventures and outsourcing. Section 5.6 concludes this chapter.

5.2. The Economics of Banking[2]

5.2.1. *Traditional versus Modern Banking*

Traditional commercial banks hold non-marketable or illiquid assets that are funded largely with deposits. There is typically little uncertainty about the value of these deposits, which are often withdrawable on demand. The liquidity of bank liabilities stands in sharp contrast to that of their assets, reflecting the banks' *raison d'être*. By liquifying claims, banks facilitate the funding of projects that might otherwise be infeasible.

The banks' assets are illiquid largely because of their information sensitivity. In originating and pricing loans, banks develop proprietary information. Subsequent monitoring of borrowers yields additional private information. The proprietary information inhibits the marketability of these loans. The access to information is the key to understanding the comparative advantage of banks. In many of their activities banks exploit their information and the related network of contacts. This relationship-oriented banking is a characteristic of value-enhancing financial intermediation. The relationship and network orientation does not only apply to traditional commercial lending but also to many areas of "modern banking".

One might be tempted to interpret modern banking as transaction-oriented. So does an investment bank — generally considered a prime example of modern banking — facilitate a firm's access to public capital markets. The investment bank's role could be interpreted as that of a broker; that is, matching buyers and sellers for the firms' securities. In this interpretation investment banks just facilitate transactions, which would confirm the transaction orientation of modern banking. The investment banks' added value would then be confined to their networks, that is, their ability to economize on search or matching costs.

As a characterization of modern banking, however, this would describe their economic role too narrowly. Investment banks do more. They — almost without exception — *underwrite* those public issues, that is, absorb credit and/or placement risk. This brings an investment bank's role much closer to that of a commercial bank engaged in lending; the processing and absorption of risk is a typical intermediation function similar to that encountered in traditional bank lending.[3]

In lending, a bank manages and absorbs risk (e.g., credit and liquidity risks) by issuing claims on its total assets with different characteristics from those encountered in its loan portfolio. In financial intermediation theory, this is referred to as *qualitative asset transformation*.[4] Underwriting by an investment bank can be interpreted analogously; risk is (temporarily) absorbed and is channeled through to the claim holders of the investment bank. The role of investment banks is therefore more than purely brokerage. Underwriting requires information acquisition about the borrower, which is supported by a relationship orientation. A relationship orientation will therefore still be present in investment banking, both in the direction of investors ("placement capacity") and towards borrowing firms.

What will also be true, however, is that in investment banking relationships depend much less on local presence. Nevertheless, public debt issues are relatively hands off with few interactions between financiers and borrowers over time (Berlin & Mester, 1992; Rajan & Winton, 1995). The full menu of financing options for borrowers includes many other products with varying degrees of relationships. In the continuum between bank loans and public debt issues, we can find, for example, syndicated loans. These are offered by investment banks and commercial banks alike, and involve several financiers per loan. Generally, only the lead banks have a relationship with the borrower, and the relationship intensity is somewhere in-between a bank loan and a public debt issue (see Dennis & Mullineaux, 2000; Sufi, 2005).

It is important to note that the relationship aspect does not only involve funding, but also includes various other financial services, for example, letters of credit, deposits, check clearing and cash management services. We will not focus on these services *per se*, but one should keep in mind that these services can expand the information available to the intermediary. As some have argued, the information that banks obtain by offering multiple services to the same borrower may be valuable in lending (Degryse & Van Cayseele, 2000). For example, the use of checking and deposit accounts may help the bank in assessing the firm's loan repayment capability. Thus, the scope of the relationship may affect a bank's comparative advantage.

5.2.2. Are Bank Loans Special?

Some see public capital market financing as a superior substitute for bank lending. This, however, stated as such, is unwarranted. Bank lending has distinct comparative advantages. In particular, it may support enduring close relationships between debtor and financier that may mitigate information asymmetries. This has several components. A borrower might be prepared to reveal proprietary information to its bank, while it would have never disseminated this information to the financial markets (Bhattacharya & Chiesa, 1995). A bank might also be more receptive to information because of its role as enduring and dominant lender. This amounts to observing that a bank might have better incentives to invest in information acquisition. While costly, the substantial stake that it has in the funding of the borrower, and its, hopefully, enduring relationship — with the possibility of information reusability over time — increase the value of information.[5]

Another feature is that relationship banking could accommodate an intertemporal smoothing of contract terms (see Allen & Gale, 1997), including accepting losses for the bank in the short term that are recouped later in the relationship. Petersen and Rajan (1995) show that credit subsidies to young or *de novo* companies may reduce the moral hazard problem and informational frictions that banks face in lending to such borrowers. However, subsidies impose losses on the bank. Banks may nevertheless provide funding if they can expect to offset these losses through the long-term rents generated by these borrowers. The point is that without access to subsidized credit early in their lives, *de novo* borrowers would pose such serious adverse selection and moral hazard problems that no bank would lend to them. Relationship lending could make such subsidies and accompanying loans feasible because the proprietary information generated during the relationship produces rents for the bank later in the relationship and permits the early losses to be offset. The importance of intertemporal transfers in loan pricing is also present in Berlin and Mester (1999). They show that rate-insensitive core deposits allow for intertemporal smoothing in lending rates. This suggests a complementarity between deposit taking and lending. Moreover, the loan commitment literature has emphasized the importance of intertemporal tax-subsidy schemes in pricing to resolve moral hazard (Boot, Thakor, & Udell, 1991) and also the complementarity between deposit taking and *commitment* lending (see Kashyap, Rajan, & Stein, 1999).

The bank–borrower relationship is also less rigid than those normally encountered in the financial market. The general observation is that a better information flow facilitates more informative decisions. In particular, relationship finance could allow for more flexibility and possibly value-enhancing discretion. This is in line with the important ongoing discussion in economic theory on rules versus discretion, where discretion allows for decision-making based on more subtle — potentially non-contractible — information.[6] Two dimensions can be identified. One dimension is related to the nature of the bank–borrower relationship. In many ways, it is a mutual commitment based on trust and respect. This allows for *implicit* — non-enforceable — long-term contracting. An optimal information flow is crucial for sustaining these "contracts". Information asymmetries in the financial market, and the non-contractibility of various pieces of information, would rule out long-term alternative capital market funding sources as well as *explicit* long-term commitments by banks. Therefore, both bank and borrower may realize the added value of their relationship, and have an incentive to foster the relationship.[7]

The other dimension is related to the structure of the explicit contracts that banks can write. Bank loans are generally easier to renegotiate than bond issues or other public capital market funding vehicles. The renegotiation allows for a qualitative use of flexibility. Sometimes this is a mixed blessing because banks may suffer from a soft-budget constraint: borrowers may realize that they can renegotiate *ex post*, which could give them perverse *ex ante* incentives. In reality, bank loans often have priority to resolve this problem. With priority, a bank may strengthen its bargaining position and thus become tougher.[8] The bank could then credibly intervene in the decision process of the borrower when it believes that its long-term interests are in danger. For example, the bank might believe that the firm's strategy is flawed, or a restructuring is long overdue. Could the bank push for the restructuring? If the bank has no priority, the borrower may choose to ignore the bank's wishes. The bank could threaten to call the loan, but the borrower — anticipating the adverse consequences not only for himself but also for the bank — realizes that the bank would never carry out such a threat. When the bank has priority, the prioritized claim may insulate the bank from these adverse consequences. It could now *credibly* threaten to call the loan, and enforce its wishes upon the borrower. This identifies an important advantage of bank financing: *timely intervention.*[9]

These observations highlight the complementarity of bank lending and capital market funding. Prioritized bank debt facilitates timely intervention. This feature of bank lending is valuable to the firm's bondholders as well. They might find it optimal to grant bank debt priority over their own claims, and in doing so delegate the timely intervention activity to the bank.[10] Consequently, the borrower may reduce its total funding cost by accessing both the bank-credit market and the financial market.

Diamond (1991) and Hoshi, Kashyap, and Scharfstein (1993) further develop arguments highlighting the complementarity of bank lending and capital market funding. Hoshi, Kashyap, and Scharfstein (1993) show that bank lending exposes borrowers to monitoring, which may serve as a certification device that facilitates simultaneous capital market funding.[11] Diamond (1991) shows that borrowers may want to borrow first from banks in order to establish sufficient credibility *before* accessing the capital markets. Again, banks provide certification and monitoring. Once the borrower is "established", it switches to capital market funding. In this explanation, there is a *sequential* complementarity between bank and capital market funding. In related theoretical work, Chemmanur and Fulghieri (1994) show that the quality of the bank is of critical importance for its certification role. This suggests a positive correlation between the value of relationship banking and the quality of the lender.

The overall conclusion is that bank lending potentially facilitates more informative decisions based on a better exchange of information. While not universally valuable, this suggests a benefit of relationship-oriented banking.[12]

5.2.3. Securitization: A Threat to Bank Lending?

Securitization is an example of a financial innovation — or an innovation in funding technology — that suggests a potential gain of (transaction-oriented) markets at the expense of bank lending. Is this true? We first evaluate the economics of securitization.

Securitization is an example of unbundling of financial services. It is a process whereby assets are removed from a bank's balance sheet. More specifically, banks would no longer permanently fund assets; instead, the investors buying asset-backed securities would provide funding. Asset-backed securities rather than deposits would then fund dedicated pools of bank-originated assets. As we will emphasize, securitization does not signal the demise of banks, even if it becomes an economically more important innovation (and thus substantially reduces the banks' on-balance sheet assets). To see this point, one needs to analyze the traditional lending function in some detail.

The lending function can be decomposed into four more primal activities: origination, funding, servicing and risk processing. Origination subsumes screening prospective borrowers, and designing and pricing financial contracts. Funding relates to the provision of financial resources. Servicing involves the collection and remission of payments as well as the monitoring of credits. Risk processing alludes to hedging, diversification and absorption of credit, interest rate, liquidity and exchange-rate risk. Securitization decomposes the lending function such that banks would no longer fund the assets, but continue to be involved in the primal activities.

The economics of securitization dictates that the originating bank *credit enhances* the issue. Credit enhancement is typically achieved through the provision of excess collateral or with a letter of credit. Effectively this means that the originating bank continues to bear the consequences (losses) if the securitized assets do not perform. The credit enhancement reduces the riskiness of the asset-backed claims from the investors' perspective, but — more importantly — it addresses conflicts of interest rooted in the originating bank's proprietary information. With private information in possession of the originating bank, the market requires assurances that the bank will not exaggerate the quality of the assets it seeks to sell. As with a warranty in product markets, credit enhancement discourages misrepresentation by requiring the originator to absorb a portion of the losses owing to default. Similarly, credit enhancement signals the market that the originator will perform a thorough credit evaluation and an undiminished monitoring effort. Credit enhancement, therefore, reduces the information sensitivity of securitized claims by enhancing their marketability.[13]

What this implies is that securitization could lead to a *reconfiguration* of banking. Banks would continue to originate and service assets, while also processing the attendant risks in order to sustain these activities. Banks would still screen and monitor borrowers, design and price financial claims, and provide risk management services. As such, securitization would preserve the incremental value of banks.[14]

How important will securitization become? We can only give a very tentative answer. Until recently, the securitization market in Europe was small, but it is now growing rapidly. In the US, securitization has been important for a long time, but mainly for car loans, mortgages and credit card receivables. The standardization and modest size of these credits allow diversification of idiosyncratic risks upon pooling. Private-information distortions — as discussed above in the context of credit enhancement — are thought to be less severe for these standardized credits.

What can be said for the larger, more customized and heterogeneous commercial loans? These tend to be more information sensitive. Their quality is therefore more dependent on the rigor of initial screening and subsequent monitoring. Hence, the pooling of commercial loans does less to dissipate their information sensitivity, attenuating the benefits of securitization. These considerations, however, do not preclude the securitization of business credits, but they merely elevate the cost. For example, with more information-sensitive assets, the originating bank may need to retain a larger portion of the credit risk; credit enhancement becomes more important. If the information sensitivity is too severe, credit enhancement, short of total recourse, may not overcome the private-information problem. Thus, the potential advantages of securitization would largely be lost, and traditional bank lending would continue to dominate. However, for an increasing array of moderately information-sensitive assets, securitization might become the preferred intermediation technology.

In fact, over the last few years several successful examples of transactions involving the securitization of business credits have emerged. Including synthetic transactions (default swaps), the European volume of collateralized debt obligations (CDOs, securitization of business credits) has grown from €40 billion in 1999 to €128 billion in 2001. Moreover, a new market for the securitization of working capital (via asset-backed commercial paper, ABCP conduits) is rapidly coming to maturity.[15]

As our discussion of the economics of securitization suggests, even if securitization would become more prevalent, banks could continue to play an important role for most of the primal activities that were previously combined in bank lending. More importantly, the comparative advantage of banks rooted in proprietary information about their clientele could be preserved. However, the message is not totally comforting for banks. In particular, the securitization of loans may greatly benefit from standardization in the origination (lending). This may weaken the bank–borrower relationship somewhat. The securitization trend does also force banks to think about their market positioning. A key question is whether securitization skills (structuring, but also placement capacity with (end) investors) need to be developed. In other words, can the commercial bank continue just to originate assets (and let others bring in the securitization skills), or do securitization skills need to be developed in-house? For most commercial banks, it will be very difficult to develop placement capacity. Also, the sheer size needed will make this a difficult proposition. Some structuring skills, however, and a better feeling for the financial markets might become indispensable.

5.3. Relationship Banking: The Strategic Challenge

We have argued that relationships may facilitate a continuous flow of information between debtor and creditor, which could guarantee an uninterrupted access to funding. Some, however, believe that a more competitive environment may threaten relationships; others have argued the exact opposite. The question then is: How does increased interbank competition and/or more intense competition from the financial market affect relationship banking?[16]

We first consider the viewpoint that more competition implies less relationship banking. The argument here is that with more competition, borrowers might be tempted to switch to other banks or to the financial market. When banks anticipate a shorter expected "life span" of their relationships they may respond by reducing their relationship-specific investments. More specifically, anticipated shorter relationships inhibit the reusability of information, and thus diminish the value of information (Chan, Greenbaum, & Thakor, 1986). Banks may then find it less worthwhile to acquire (costly) proprietary information, and relationships suffer. Interestingly, shorter or weaker relationships may then become a self-fulfilling prophecy. This argument highlights the negative spiral that may undermine relationship banking. An important observation is that this negative spiral might be self-inflicted. While competitive banking challenges relationships, the bankers' response — cutting back on information acquisition — may actually damage relationship banking the most.

A complementary negative effect of competition on relationship banking may come from the impact that competition has on the intertemporal pricing of loans. Increased credit market competition could impose constraints on the ability of borrowers and lenders to intertemporally share surpluses (see Petersen & Rajan, 1995). In particular, it becomes more difficult for banks to "subsidize" borrowers in earlier periods in return for a share of the rents in the future. Thus, the funding role for banks that Petersen and Rajan (1995) see in the case of young corporations (see our discussion in Section 5.2.2) may no longer be sustainable in the face of sufficiently high competition.[17] This implies that excessive interbank competition *ex post* may discourage bank lending *ex ante*.[18]

An alternative view is that competition may actually *elevate* the importance of a relationship orientation as a distinct competitive edge. This may somewhat mitigate the negative effect that pure price competition would otherwise have on bank profit margins. Boot and Thakor (2000) show that a relationship orientation can alleviate these competitive pressures, because it can make a bank more *unique* relative to its competitors.[19] A more competitive environment may then encourage banks to become more client-driven and customize services, thus focusing more (rather than less) on relationship banking.[20]

Relationships may foster the exchange of information, but may simultaneously give lenders an information monopoly and undermine competitive pricing.[21] Transaction-oriented finance, however, may give little incentive to acquire information but is potentially subject to more competition. There might be no winners in this process; for example, transaction-oriented finance may not be feasible where relationship-oriented finance retreats. More specifically, markets for transaction-oriented finance may fail when problems of asymmetric information are insurmountable. This argument is used by some to highlight the virtues of (relationship-oriented) bank-dominated systems (e.g., Germany and Japan) vis-à-vis market-oriented systems.[22]

What this discussion indicates is that the impact of competition on relationship banking is complex; several effects need to be disentangled. What seems to have emerged, though, is that greater lender competition may very well elevate the value of relationship banking. Pure price competition is an unattractive alternative. A relationship orientation can alleviate competitive pressures. Thus, a more competitive environment should encourage banks to become client-driven, and customize services. Since a relationship orientation may earn banks a substantial added value, banks would then isolate themselves from pure price competition. However, truly creating an added value in relationship banking may require skills that banks do not (yet) have. Without those skills a retreat from relationship banking (including, for example, downsizing of the branch network) might be unavoidable.

As discussed in Section 5.2, bank lending, securitization of loans and underwriting of public capital market issues may all benefit from a relationship orientation. The distinction between relationship-oriented finance and transaction-oriented finance, or between bank-dominated systems and market-oriented systems, may therefore be less well defined than it appears. What might be true is that a bank-dominated system invites oligopolistic behavior such that competition is contained (and relationships preserved) while a market-dominated system suppresses competition less.

The overall message is that the comparative advantage of banks is rooted in relationships (note that this is directly related to "information", see Section 5.2.2), and that this is of particular importance in a more competitive environment.

5.4. The Consolidation Trend in Banking: Rationales and Empirical Evidence

5.4.1. Recent Developments

We have witnessed an unprecedented restructuring and consolidation trend in the financial services industry across the globe. In the last decade, mergers in the US have led to a consolidation of money center banks (e.g., the Chase Manhattan and Chemical Bank merger, prior to the subsequent merger with J.P. Morgan) and the emergence of regional powerhouses (e.g., the expansion strategies of BankOne and Nationsbank and their mergers with, respectively, First Chicago/NBD and BankAmerica). Recently, a merger brought together BankOne and J.P. Morgan Chase, and Bank of America further enlarged its footprint by acquiring Fleet Boston. In Europe, mergers have been prominent as well. While cross-border mergers are relatively infrequent — with exceptions in Scandinavia and across the Dutch–Belgian border (e.g., the acquisition of the Belgian Bank BBL by the Dutch financial conglomerate ING)[23] — on a domestic scale, mergers typically involve large universal banks and are often spectacular (e.g., the marriage of the Union Bank of Switzerland and Swiss Bank Corporation, and the acquisition of Paribas by Banque National de Paris). More recently, a somewhat higher level of activity has been observed; for example, ABN AMRO has been successful in acquiring control over the Italian bank Banca Antonveneta.

The coincidence of the consolidation trend in the financial sector with increased competition have led many to believe that the massive restructurings in banking are a response to a more competitive environment. That is, as commercial banking becomes more competitive, banks need to examine all possible ways to eliminate inefficiencies from their cost structures, for example, by merging with other banks and realizing *scale efficiencies* through elimination of redundant branches and back-office consolidation. Moreover, the diminishing margins in commercial banking have invited banks to look outside their traditional domain. Some non-banking activities may offer higher margins and make *scope expansion* look attractive. The key question addressed in this section is whether these responses indeed create value.

The recent trend on banks' inclination to expand scope is somewhat mixed. For example, while we have seen a spectacular cross-industry merger of Citicorp and Travelers, bringing together insurance activities with bank-oriented financial services, more recently, Citigroup has been divesting its insurance assets. Similarly, Credit Suisse expanded into insurance by acquiring the insurance company Winterthur, but lately has been divesting these assets. Some European banks (e.g., ING in the Netherlands), however, continue to center their strategies around *bancassurance*; that is, combining banking and insurance activities. While there does not seem to be a consensus on the added value of bancassurance, banks do define their scope quite broadly, and by some measures scope expansion might have become more prevalent over time.[24]

Scale and scope economies are often cited as one of the main reasons behind the current merger and acquisition wave in banking. But are scale and scope economies truly present? And could they rationalize the current restructuring in the industry? In the next subsection, we summarize the empirical evidence on scale and scope economies.

5.4.2. Empirical Evidence on Scale and Scope

Existing empirical evidence is quite generic. One conclusion that can be drawn is that the existing studies do not really differentiate between which activities in combination could offer scope benefits, nor do they focus on which activities generate economies of scale.

Scale and scope economies in banking have been studied extensively. A survey article by Berger, Demsetz, and Strahan (1999) concludes that, in general, the empirical evidence cannot readily identify substantial economies of scale or scope. Illustrative is Saunders (2000). He cites 27 studies, 13 of which found diseconomies of scope, 6 found economies of scope and 8 were neutral.[25] In particular, scale economies could not be found beyond a relatively small size of banks as measured by total assets (i.e., beyond $100 million up to $10 billion in total assets). The story on scope economies is even more negative. Diseconomies of scope are quite prevalent.

An important caveat is that this research mainly involves US studies using data from the 1970s and 1980s. The results therefore do not capture the dramatic structural and technological changes in banking that since then have taken place. Furthermore, they reflect the historic fragmentation of the US banking industry due to severe regulatory constraints on the type of banking (banks could engage in commercial banking or investment banking, but not both) and the geographic reach of activities (limits on interstate banking) till the deregulation in the 1990s (see Calomiris & Karceski, 1998).

5.4.2.1. Diversification discount   A large empirical literature in corporate finance documents that the diversification associated with conglomeration destroys value. Berger and Ofek (1995) find that diversified firms trade, on average, at a 13–15% discount relative to a portfolio of specialized single-segment firms. Many articles suggest that this "diversification discount" arises from investment inefficiencies caused by inefficient cross-subsidies between the divisions in a conglomerate firm (see Lamont, 1997; Shin & Stulz, 1998).[26]

While this literature addresses the impact of conglomeration in general, some recent studies examine the existence of a diversification discount for financial institutions. Laeven and Levine (2005) confirm the existence of a diversification discount in banks that combine lending and non-lending financial services, and suggest that the potential economies of scope in financial conglomerates are not large enough to compensate for potential agency problems and cross-subsidies.

Rajan, Servaes, and Zingales (2000) emphasize that, even though conglomerates trade at a discount on average, 39.3% of the conglomerates trade at a premium. They show that the interrelation between activities within the conglomerate is of crucial importance. Diversified firms can trade at a premium if the dispersion between activities is low.[27] High dispersion induces inefficiencies. This points at the importance of focus within the conglomerate.

The sources of inefficiencies in combining banking activities are often subtle. In the box we have included an illustration that focuses on the potential value destruction in combining relationship banking and proprietary trading. These activities are very heterogeneous and highlight Rajan, Servaes, and Zingales' (2000) conclusion that dispersion between activities in a diversified firm has a negative impact.

An Illustration of the Downside of Conglomeration: Combining Relationship Banking and Proprietary Trading

An important issue is what the costs and benefits are of combining different activities. We focus on the question how relationship banking is affected by the banks' increased involvement in trading-related activities. The extreme manifestation of this is proprietary trading.

First, note that banks like to *combine* many different activities. This distinguishes banks from many of their competitors, for example, non-banking financial institutions like mutual funds and finance companies (see Merton, 1993). The latter often choose to specialize and therefore are much more transparent. Banks generally choose to diversify their activities. Although few would readily deny that some degree of diversification is necessary, banks seem to engage in a very broad variety of activities. The question that arises is what is the optimal conglomeration of bank activities?

This question is of particular importance because self-inflicted opaqueness may come to haunt banks in a more competitive environment. Outsiders — including the banks' financiers — may not be able to assess the performance of banks sufficiently. More importantly, opaqueness gives outsiders very little control over the bank. Bank managers, therefore, may have excessive discretion. This may elevate a bank's cost of funds.[28]

Till recently, the opaqueness even meant that bankers themselves did not really know the profitability of many of their activities. Cross-subsidies were the rule, and internal cost accounting was rudimentary. Recently some improvements have been made. Banks by now have a better understanding of the costs and benefits of different lines of their businesses. Some of the implicit or explicit cross-subsidies are now recognized. While cross-subsidies may sometimes be an optimal competitive response, often they will not be sustainable in a competitive environment.

Banks face a challenge in that they may need to become more transparent. This is in apparent conflict with the current practices in banking. Banks increasingly combine transaction- and relationship-based activities. Trading activities within banks have grown enormously (see Berger, Kashyap, & Scalise, 1995) and seem sometimes in conflict with the "traditional" relationship-oriented activities. These developments have broadened the activities of banks and may have reduced transparency. An interesting example is proprietary trading, an activity that has gained importance, and — on paper — seems to have contributed significantly to the profitability of banks in recent years.

A noteworthy example of a banking institution where proprietary trading gained importance rapidly was the Barings Bank, a British bank with a long tradition in corporate banking. Some interpret the Barings debacle as a meltdown caused by a clash of cultures: aggressive and ambitious traders versus traditional and conservative bankers. For them, better internal controls and external supervision aimed at aligning incentives seem obvious remedies. We believe that the economics of banking dictate a more fundamental analysis, one that transcends the specifics of Barings and sheds light on the banks' strategic choices in general.

Our analysis will highlight that in the absence of market discipline banks may only arbitrarily allocate capital to their different activities and charge a cost per unit of capital that is even more arbitrary. This line of argument implies that the proprietary trading activity is free-riding on the bank at large. This — as we will show — may have three consequences: (i) proprietary trading appears more profitable than it really is, (ii) a proprietary trading unit does not sufficiently internalize risks, and (iii) other — mainly relationship-oriented — activities of banks face an unfairly high cost of funds. The implications are twofold. First, proprietary traders may operate with little market discipline. Consequently, the only corrective mechanisms are internal controls and external supervision. Second, banks may become less competitive in their relationship-oriented activities. Thus, proprietary trading could undermine the banks' real competitive edge. We now turn to a more detailed analysis of the trading activity.[29]

Banks' trading activities have been a considerable source of earnings in the last few years. But has it been as profitable as some believe? The trading activity involves substantial risks, thus establishing the fair risk-adjusted cost of funds is important. Banks try to resolve this by allocating (costly) capital to the trading unit. Thus, the trading unit's funding cost is artificially grossed up by adding the cost of its "capital at risk". This internal capital allocation process is far from perfect, and actually might also be flawed.[30]

The presumption in these internal capital allocations is generally that capital has one price. A bank's cost of capital might be set, for example, at 15%. Some believe that capital is twice as expensive as (risk-free) financial market debt financing. Whatever the presumption, capital does *not* have one price. Standard capital structure theory tells us that the per unit cost of capital depends on the risks that this capital is exposed to. More risk generally implies a higher cost of capital. Two important implications now follow. First, the per unit cost of capital will *not* be the same for all of the bank's activities. The level of risk *and* the risk characteristics will determine the unit cost of capital for each of the activities. Applying a bank's cost of capital to its proprietary trading unit is therefore wrong. Given the generally well-diversified, and thus low risks, found in the bank at large, the (non-diversifiable) risks taken in the trading unit dictate a much higher cost of capital.

The second implication is more general: banks should not choose to engage in certain activities solely because they have the capital. The critical observation is that "putting capital to use" increases the per unit cost of capital. Therefore, engaging in proprietary trading to exploit the bank's capital will elevate the cost of this capital, and as a consequence increase the cost of funds for the bank at large. Banks that consider themselves "overcapitalized" and decide to put this capital to use may thus not create value at all. This argument may also explain why banks consider capital (prohibitively?) expensive. If potential investors anticipate that banks will put their capital to use at all cost, they will gross up their required return accordingly. Banks then can issue equity only at discount prices. These beliefs and anticipations create a perverse equilibrium. Given the bankers' state of mind — fixed priced, expensive capital that needs to be put to use as quickly as possible — the market responds rationally by charging a high price for capital. And given these anticipations by the market, the bankers' beliefs are justified and confirmed in equilibrium.[31]

The arguments above explain why proprietary trading has been granted an artificially low cost of capital, at the expense of a (potentially) prohibitively high cost of capital for the bank as a whole. Other — mainly relationship-oriented activities — are then implicitly taxed and falsely appear not profitable. The general lesson from the discussion in this box is that the rather opaque nature of the banking business easily distorts decision-making. This suggests that focus may have distinct benefits. In the next section, we further analyze this issue.

5.4.2.2. Recent evidence   Recently, and using more recent data, DeLong (2001) looked at the shareholder gains — that is, the immediate announcement effects — from focused versus diversifying bank mergers in the US between 1988 and 1995. She found that focused mergers, both on the level of activity and geography, have positive announcement effects. Moreover, focus in activities was shown to be more important than geographic focus, albeit the latter was important as well.[32] Activity-diversifying mergers had no positive announcement effects. These results point at the presence of scale rather than scope economies. While this study focuses on relatively small US banking institutions (market cap of the acquirer approximately $2 billion, and market cap of target less than $100 million), recent European evidence on much larger institutions confirms the desirability of geographic focus.[33]

An alternative approach for analyzing scale and scope economies is to focus on structural differences between financial conglomerates and specialized institutions. Several studies have looked at the relative cost and profit efficiency (e.g., Berger & Humphrey, 1997; Berger & Mester, 1997). Van der Vennet (2002) has looked at this in the European context. He finds somewhat higher cost and profit efficiency for conglomerates and universal banks. This may look surprising in light of earlier comments. However, these efficiency differences cannot readily be translated in scale and scope economies. The banking industry is changing rapidly and the (traditional) inefficiencies in banking are coming under attack from competitive pressure and technological advances. Differences in efficiency may just reflect differences in the state of adjustment of these institutions, translating into temporarily diverging levels of X-efficiency, rather than point at scale and scope economies.

5.4.2.3. Further interpretation   With respect to the interpretation of the empirical evidence on scale and scope, some general observations can be made. First, scale and scope economies are empirically often dominated by changes in managerial efficiency. For example, inefficiencies in managing larger organizations may mitigate possible scale and scope benefits.[34] Second, scale and scope economy effects are difficult to disentangle from changes in market power. Increasing scale and scope may facilitate market power, and thus elevate profitability in the *absence* of scale and scope economies. Moreover, alternative distribution networks (e.g., direct banking) and the proliferation of financial markets may have reduced the effective market power of locally concentrated financial institutions, and elevated the contestability of markets. Third, to the extent that mergers may change the structure and dynamics of the industry, the abnormal stock returns associated with merger announcements reflect such changes. This makes event studies on bank mergers harder to interpret.

Finally, the level of aggregation in most studies is high and may obscure benefits of scale and scope. In particular, one should look at what *type* of mergers and acquisitions involve scale and scope benefits. For example, Flannery (1999) points at recent research that suggests that mergers with both a geographic and activity focus are most value enhancing.[35] Similarly, in analyzing scope and scale issues one should focus on the type of activities. What are the scale economies in each activity? And what product-mix offers true scope economies?[36]

5.4.3. Problems with Realizing Economies of Scale and Scope

It is important to observe that technological and regulatory frictions affect the potential realization of scope and scale economies. For example, a merger between two financial institutions may not readily lead to scale and scope economies because the integration of computer systems may take time.

A similar argument can be made with respect to regulatory constraints. If regulators force banking and insurance activities to be operated separately, potential scope economies may suffer. This problem was most acute in the US where up to recently insurance and banking activities could not be combined under one corporate roof. In many other countries, regulations were less stringent but could still have a major impact on the feasibility of realizing scope economies.

In the end, implementation issues are crucial as well. As the evidence shows, there are enormous differences between the best practice and "average practice" of financial institutions. This points at the importance of managerial ability. Cultural differences between merged entities play an important role as well. Also conflicts of interest between activities might be important, and dictate functional separation of activities.

A final barrier may come from political considerations. Many countries seek to protect their domestic financial institutions, and, if needed, help create "national champions" to preserve domestic ownership and control. Table 5.1 summarizes the main barriers to realizing scope and scale economies.

5.4.4. Sources of Scale and Scope Economies

We will now seek to uncover the main sources of scale and scope economies. We see the following two primary sources:[37]

1. IT-related economies.
2. Reputation and marketing/brand name-related benefits.

5.4.4.1. IT-related benefits   The first source, IT, is most likely of great importance. IT has two primary effects. First, it allows for a disaggregation of activities, breaking up the traditionally integrated value chain. One important manifestation of this is that it facilitates a centralization of supporting activities (particularly, infrastructure and trading-related activities, e.g., clearing, settlement and custody). This offers potential scale economies in those disintegrated activities, which (see Section 5.5) could also have implications for specialization within the value chain, and outsourcing in particular. Related to this is that it could widen the scope of control, that is, facilitate a flatter, and potentially larger organization. Second, it has profound implications for the interface with clients. More specifically, it facilitates a more efficient and effective utilization of databases over ranges of services and customers. That is, client-specific information may allow for scope economies and facilitate a competitive advantage to financial institutions that can offer a range of services to their clientele. Similarly, possibilities for reusability of information across customers may have increased.

IT helps in identifying client-related needs. Scope economies, therefore, apply to all products that could be sold to the same client group. Examples for bank-insurance conglomerates include: life insurance features in mortgages, asset management/private banking services combined with life insurance, commercial credits in combination with industrial risk insurance and export financing together with export credit insurance.

This also points at distribution network related benefits. These benefits may be rooted in IT developments. In particular, IT developments may facilitate scale economies in running a sizeable distribution network. Simultaneously, scope economies might become much more visible. For example, IT facilitates an increasing array of financial products and services to be offered through the same distribution network. Customers may attach value to "one-stop shopping", which encourages some financial institutions to offer a broader package of financial services tailored to particular customer categories.

5.4.4.2. Reputation and brand name/marketing   The second source for scale and scope economies is linked to brand name/marketing and reputation. Scope benefits may be present in the joint marketing of products to customers. Brand image is partially marketing related, but is also related to the notions of "trust", "reputation" and "confidence". These notions play an important role in the financial services industry. Increasingly, financial service providers offer services that crucially depend on their reputation. For example, the growing importance of off-balance sheet claims puts great emphasis on the ability of financial institutions to honor these *contingent* liabilities. But also the success of modern "virtual" distribution channels (Internet) may depend crucially on reputation. Under certain conditions, increasing scale and scope allows financial institutions to capitalize more on their reputation. That is, a wider scope (and/or scale) may help a financial institution to put its reputational capital to work (see Boot, Greenbaum, & Thakor, 1993).

A concrete example here is the Dutch bank-insurance conglomerate ING that offers direct banking services in, for example, Spain. The name of ING is linked in advertisements explicitly to the Nationale Nederlanden brand name, its insurance subsidiary, a well-known and respected institution in Spain. This type of branding "externality" is also used by players entering the financial services arena from other industries (e.g., supermarkets leveraging their brand name for financial services offerings). Again, some link can be made to IT, which clearly helps in the extent to which the brand name and reputation can be leveraged.

5.4.5. Evaluation

We may conclude that the primary sources of economies of scale and scope are related to back-office support functions and distribution. Much of this is induced by IT. The importance of the distribution network is quite clear and should be considered a primary source of scale and scope economies. For example, on the demand side, the proliferation of savings products and their link to pensions, mutual funds and life insurance clearly pushes for joint distribution, and thereby facilitates economies of scope. However, a word of caution is warranted. IT developments might have made it possible to better exploit potential scope economies with multiple product offerings to a particular customer group, using new direct distribution channels with relatively easy access to (formerly) distant customers. The very same IT developments offer also very good possibilities for focused single-product players. Interfaces (may) come up that help bundle the product offerings of specialized providers, thereby becoming a substitute for the integrated provider. The lesson is that only very well-managed integrated financial services firms may realize positive scope economies. The execution (X-efficiency) is probably more crucial than ever before, since inefficiencies will be exploited by single-product players. What this means is that it is very unlikely that (ultimately) a single strategy will dominate in the financial services sector.

The same arguments apply for the vertical disintegration of the value chain. Ultimately, it does not seem unrealistic to expect the emergence of, for example, product specialists without distribution network. The scale economies and the benefits coming from focus could be substantial (see also McKinsey & Company, 2002). However, specializing in one segment of the value chain might for now be too risky a strategy. Banking is too much in turmoil and specialization within the value chain may lead to an overly vulnerable dependence on other players.[38]

In the particular context of bank-insurer mergers several other comments can be made. An important issue is the potential benefits coming from asset management. Some argue that the income stream from asset management is relatively stable, and hence a welcome addition to the otherwise erratic revenue stream of financial institutions. There might be some truth in this, but this benefit, at least from a corporate finance perspective, cannot be really large. That is, diversification for purely financial reasons could also be accomplished by individual investors in the financial market. Thus, unless the synergies with other business lines are substantial, an independent asset management operation is a credible alternative.

Similarly, people argue that bank-insurance combinations have distinct benefits on the funding side. Diversification may allow for a more effective use of equity capital. Also direct funding synergies may apply. The mismatch between assets and liabilities on the bank's balance sheet (short-term funding, long-term lending) might be the reverse of that of an insurer (long-term obligations). Again, corporate finance theory is skeptical about the validity of these arguments.

Another argument for combining life insurance and banking is that it could augment the total asset management pool, and thus offer scale economies. While this might be true, more recently banks and insurers have learned that the asset management operation requires distinct skills and is not "automatically" profitable as a passive spin-off from other (feeding) activities. Thus, synergies are present, but not necessarily dominant. This is not to say that combining banking and insurance with an appropriate customer focus could not be value enhancing. As stated earlier, combining banking and insurance could offer synergies in distribution. This builds on the distribution network related benefits discussed earlier.

However, as discussed earlier, other factors may undermine the possibility for realizing scope benefits. For example, due to national tax regulations life insurance needs to be tailored to each specific country. Also other differences exist between countries in terms of (corporate) culture, law, etc. These complications make it important to have well-focused operations outside the home market and abstain from scope-expanding strategies that would complicate the operation even more. In some cases this also means that one should abstain from broad cross-border acquisitions, and only choose to go cross-border where the specific activity at hand requires this.[39]

These observations help understand the reconfiguration of many European financial institutions. In particular, it becomes increasingly questionable to rationalize a universal banking strategy based on some company-wide synergy argument. Scope economies need to be carefully examined, and linked directly to specific market segments across clients, products and geographic areas of operations (see also Smith & Walter, 1997).

5.5. Alliances, Joint Ventures and the Disaggregation of the Value Chain

More recently, alliances and joint ventures appear to have become more important in banking. An interesting example is the joint venture that ABN AMRO set up with the insurer Delta Lloyd. In fact, ABN AMRO sold its insurance activities to the joint venture in the hope that in the alliance with Delta Lloyd the bank would be better at selling insurance products via its own distribution network. ABN AMRO's motive is clear. The stand-alone nature of the joint venture together with the expertise from the insurer Delta Lloyd creates focus, urgency, and better accountability and incentives in the insurance operations. It helps resolve the inefficiencies associated with trying to mix insurance and banking cultures.[40] As we highlighted in Section 5.4.4, the IT revolution has clearly been helpful in making it possible to have a smooth interface between the more separated insurance activity and ABN AMRO's banking operations. In this sense, it is an example of disintegration of the value chain.

We expect that vertical disintegration of the value chain will gain in importance over the coming years (see also Berlin, 2002). Vertical disintegration allows for greater specialization, and hence focus with potential gains in scale economies as well. Alliances and joint ventures could play an important role in this process. They may introduce durable, yet flexible cooperative structures facilitating interactions between the different parties in the value chain. An example is the opening up of a bank's distribution network to products from others. In that way, institutions could exploit their local presence by capitalizing on their distribution network; simultaneously, product specialists may emerge that feed products into these distribution networks.

The applicability of this idea is broader. Financial institutions rooted in strong local relationships may gain access to more "distant" asset management services that are scale intensive and globally, rather than locally oriented. It may well be possible to offer some of these services in an alliance (i.e., to "join forces") and still capitalize on customer-related synergies. While some will argue that a merger with these institutions would allow for a smoother operation of these services, we would like to take issue with this point of view.

First, for several reasons, cross-border mergers may not (yet) be feasible. A focused alliance would create valuable linkages between institutions with immediate synergy benefits (see above), but could also allow the possibly nationally rooted partners to "get to know" each other. In that sense, it would be an intermediate phase. As a second argument, the alliance model based on asset management and/or specific investment banking activities may, if properly designed, combine the benefits of an integrated universal banking structure and a stand-alone type of organization of those activities. For example, the alliance partners all have a limited exposure to these activities, putting them together helps maintain focus. In particular, cultural conflicts and distractions associated with trying to build up (or buy) an investment bank next to running the relationship-rooted regional bank are prevented.[41] Obviously, the alliance model does not come without cost. The important task is to identify a clearly defined portfolio of activities that would become part of the alliance. This will not be investment banking in the broadest sense of the word. Similarly, in the case of asset management, the alliance partners would each maintain their own proprietary access to the customers, but join forces in the asset management operations including research and back-office activities. Maintaining proprietary access by the individual alliance partners preserves customer-related scope economies.

The same arguments could be made for bank-insurance combinations. That is, banks could choose to engage in an alliance with an insurer, rather than merge. The joint venture of ABN AMRO and Delta Lloyd discussed at the beginning of this section is an example of this. It is also possible to distribute insurance products via a bank's distribution network based on a license agreement. An outright merger may not be needed. The IT revolution (see Section 5.4.4) now makes a smooth interface between (semi) independent entities possible.

We believe that joint ventures and alliances will gain importance in the future. Economies of scale and benefits of focus could be obtained in this way. The trend towards outsourcing of back-office functions fits neatly as well. Also this points towards a disintegration of the value chain. However, it will help if the level of uncertainty in the industry comes down a little. Vertical disintegration (and specialization) now may create an unpredictable dependence on other parties in the value chain.

5.6. Conclusion

This chapter highlights *the* major challenges facing "modern" banks: How to identify and protect their true comparative competitive advantages. We believe that relationship banking offers distinct benefits, and see it as the banks' *raison d'être*. However, relationship banking has suffered from the proliferation of transaction-oriented banking. We have argued that the optimal response might be to invest *more* in relationships. Banks then may isolate themselves from pure price competition.

We have also looked at the positioning of banks in general. The insights from existing empirical research on scale and scope advantages in banking proved rather limited. We argued, however, that the developments in IT over the last decade may have fundamentally changed the benefits of scale and scope. In particular, we see substantial scale and scope economies in distribution, and scale economies in back-office functions. We also envision a further disintegration of the value chain, and expect a proliferation of joint ventures, alliances and outsourcing.

What we have emphasized only little is that the current uncertain state of the banking industry, where the choices made by the various players are very unpredictable, makes it

difficult for each individual bank to make clear choices. For example, specialization somewhere within the value chain could make a bank very dependent on the behavior of banks
upstream or downstream in that same value chain. In a sense, banks hold each other
hostage. Such strategic considerations make it also difficult to extrapolate from choices
that we currently observe in the banking sector.[42]

Future research should be directed at further developing the basic themes of this chapter. While we may have provided some important insights in the functioning of banking
institutions and their optimal competitive responses, the financial sector largely remains a
black box.

Endnotes

1. See "Thinking Locally at Citigroup", *Business Week*, October 24, 2005, pp. 50–51.
2. The analysis in this section follows Boot (2003).
3. From this perspective, it is not surprising that several European banks are currently integrating their debt capital market activities with their corporate lending operations. Previously, the debt capital market activities
   were typically linked to equity capital market operations (within their investment banking divisions). The
   commitment to equity-linked investment banking activities is being reduced or even dismantled by many
   players in the industry.
4. In this chapter, we do not focus on the costs and benefits of the mismatch on the banks' balance sheets. See
   Calomiris and Kahn (1991) and Diamond and Rajan (2001) for theories that rationalize the asset and liability structure of banks.
5. Diamond (1984) introduces intermediaries as delegated monitors. See Chan, Greenbaum, and Thakor (1986)
   for a discussion on information reusability, and James (1987), Lummer and McConnell (1989) and Gande
   and Saunders (2005) for empirical evidence on the informational value of bank financing. See also the recent
   "stories" provided by Berlin (1996) supporting the special role of banks.
6. See, for example, Simon (1936) and Boot, Greenbaum, and Thakor (1993).
7. Mayer (1988) and Hellwig (1991) discuss the commitment nature of bank funding. Boot, Thakor, and Udell
   (1991) address the *credibility* of commitments. Schmeits (2005) formally considers the impact of discretion
   (flexibility) in bank loan contracts on investment efficiency.
8. See Dewatripont and Maskin (1995) on the issue of soft-budget constraints. Diamond (1993), Berglöf and
   Von Thadden (1994), and Gorton and Kahn (1993) address the priority structure. Boot (2000) provides a survey of relationship banking.
9. One could ask whether bondholders could be given priority and allocated the task of timely intervention.
   Note that bondholders are subject to more severe information asymmetries and are generally more dispersed
   (i.e., have smaller stakes). Both characteristics make them ill-suited for an "early intervention task".
10. The bondholders will obviously ask to be compensated for their subordinated status. This — ignoring the
    timely intervention effect — is a "wash". In other words, the priority (seniority) and subordination features
    can be priced. That is, as much as senior debt may *appear* to be "cheaper" (it is less risky), junior or subor-
    dinated debt will appear to be more expensive.
11. Empirical evidence provided by James (1987) and Slovin, Sushka, and Hudson (1988) supports the certifi-
    cation role of banks. Other evidence can be found in Houston and James (1995).
12. See Petersen and Rajan (1994) and Houston and James (1995) for empirical evidence. The relationship
    feature also has drawbacks. There are two primary costs to relationship banking (see Boot, 2000): the soft-
    budget constraint problem and the hold-up problem. The soft-budget constraint problem has to do with the
    potential lack of toughness on the bank's part in enforcing credit contracts that may come with relationship-
    banking proximity. The problem is that borrowers who realize that they can renegotiate their contracts *ex post*
    may have perverse incentives *ex ante* (see Dewatripont & Maskin, 1995; Bolton & Scharfstein, 1996). As
    discussed above, the seniority structure of bank loans could mitigate this problem. The hold-up problem has
    to do with the information monopoly the bank generates in the course of lending, which may allow banks to

extend loans to borrowers at non-competitive terms in the future. More specifically, the proprietary information on borrowers that banks obtain as part of their relationships may give them an informational monopoly. In this way, banks could charge *ex post* high loan interest rates (see Sharpe, 1990; Rajan, 1992). The threat of being "locked in", or informationally captured by the bank, may make the borrower reluctant to borrow from the bank. Potentially valuable investment opportunities may then be lost. Alternatively, firms may opt for multiple bank relationships. This may reduce the informational monopoly of any one bank, but possibly at a cost. Ongena and Smith (2000) show that multiple bank relationships indeed reduce the hold-up problem, but worsen the availability of credit.

13. The reputation of the originating bank will be equally important. Moreover, accreditation by credit rating agencies could also add to the marketability of the securitized claims (see also Boot, Milbourn, & Schmeits, 2006). Gorton and Pennachi (1995) provide an economic rationale for bank loan sales and securitization.

14. See also Boyd and Gertler (1994). They argue that banks have not lost importance. Their argument is that a substitution from on-balance sheet to off-balance sheet banking may have (falsely) suggested a shrinking role for banks. As in the description of securitization in the text, much of the banks' value added in the primal activities would be preserved.

15. As a caveat, some of this activity in securitization is undoubtedly induced by capital arbitrage; the new Basle II capital requirements may mitigate this somewhat.

16. Another threat is the better dissemination of information. This, in itself, could reduce the value of (previously) proprietary information in the hands of banks, and possibly reduce the value of relationship banking.

17. An extensive empirical literature focuses on the effect of consolidation in the banking sector on small business lending. This consolidation may in part be a response to competitive pressures (see also Section 5.4). The effects on small business lending, however, are not clear-cut. Sapienza (2002) finds that bank mergers involving at least one large bank result in a lower supply of loans to small borrowers by the merged entity. However, Berger, Saunders, Scalise, and Udell (1998) show that the actual supply of loans to small businesses may not go down after bank mergers, since they invite entry of *de novo* banks that specialize in small business lending.

18. Berlin and Mester (1999) provide a related, albeit different argument. Their analysis suggests that competition forces banks to pay market rates on deposits, which may complicate the potentially value-enhancing smoothing of lending rates.

19. In Boot and Thakor (2000) banks choose between "passive" transaction lending and more intensive relationship lending. Transaction lending competes head-on with funding in the financial market. Competition from the financial market (as well as interbank competition) will lead to more resource-intensive relationship lending, and reduce transaction lending. The rationale for this is — as hinted at above — to mitigate the margin-reducing effects of price competition. The *absolute* level of relationship lending is, however, non-monotonic in the level of competition: initially competition increases relationship lending, but when competition heats up "too much", investments in bank lending capacity will suffer and that may start to constrain relationship lending.

20. In related work, Hauswald and Marquez (2005) focus on a bank's incentives to acquire borrower-specific information in order to gain market share, and Dinç (2000) examines a bank's reputational incentives to honor commitments to finance higher-quality firms.

21. The informational monopoly on the "inside" lender's side may be smaller if a borrower engages in multiple banking relationships. This would mitigate the possibilities for rent extraction by informed lenders and induce more competitive pricing (see Sharpe, 1990, and also Petersen and Rajan, 1995). Similarly, Schmeits (2005) shows that competition reduces the hold-up problem associated with the bank's informational monopoly. This allows for the use of price discretion in bank loan contracts; that is, banks that produce information on borrowers can optimally adapt a borrower's lending terms to "soft" (or non-verifiable) information in the course of lending (see Section 5.2.2). In the absence of lender competition, such discretion may not be feasible, since the rent extraction by the bank may be prohibitively high. Importantly, the use of contractual discretion in relationship lending also requires that the bank's quality (skill) as an information producer is sufficiently high. Other recent articles also address the importance of a relationship focus in the face of increased interbank and/or financial market competition.

22. A fascinating academic literature focuses on the design of financial systems; see Allen (1993), Allen and Gale (1995), and Boot and Thakor (1997). One objective of this literature is to evaluate the pros and cons of bank-dominated versus financial market-dominated systems.

23. Some noteworthy cross-border mergers that go beyond these culturally aligned regions are HSBC's purchase of Crédit Commercial de France in 2000, Bank Austria's acquisition of Germany's HypoVereinsbank in 2000

and the purchase of Abbey National, Britain's sixth largest bank, by Banco Santander Central Hispano of Spain. The Spanish bank BBVA, may succeed in its bid to acquire Banca Nationale del Lavoro. Italy's largest bank UniCredit is in talks with the HypoVereinsbank.

24. For example, Bankers Trust, with its activities aimed at the corporate market, put itself in the arms of a scope-expanding universal bank (Deutsche Bank). Furthermore, major investment banks are redefining their domain by offering traditional commercial banking products like commercial and industrial loans, and by moving into retail brokerage (see the union of Salomon Brothers (investment bank) and Smith Barney (brokerage) within Travelers. Similarly, Credit Suisse bought the US stockbroker DLJ, and UBS bought Paine-Webber).

25. See also Shaffer and David (1991), Cornett and Tehranian (1992), Mester (1992), Mitchell and Onvural (1996), and Clark (1996).

26. For example, Berger and Ofek (1995) find that conglomerate firms overinvest in industries with limited investment opportunities, as measured by a low Tobin's q ratio. In the context of the oil industry, Lamont (1997) has shown that diversified companies tend to subsidize and overinvest in poorly performing segments. Furthermore, Shin and Stulz (1998) have shown that investment by segments of a highly diversified firm is larger and less sensitive to their own cash flow than that in unrelated firms, and is also relatively insensitive to the quality of their investment opportunities.

27. These conclusions are roughly consistent with Boot and Schmeits (2000), who argue that heterogeneity of activities is generally bad for conglomeration.

28. Securitization could be interpreted as a mechanism that seeks to enhance accountability and transparency by giving the market a direct claim on a specific group of assets. Dewatripont and Tirole (1995) discuss the benefits of securitization in the context of these transparency arguments.

29. It is important to realize that much of modern (investment) banking is relationship oriented. Proprietary trading is one of the few activities that is not. The trading involves arbitrage between different markets and/or different financial products. Arbitrage does, strictly speaking, not involve risk. However, on an intra-day basis, traders do not cover (all) their positions, and thus accept considerable risk. This is a type of speculation. Banks also speculate on an inter-day basis; this is "real" speculation. They may use their "vision" and try to benefit from anticipated developments in interest rates, exchange rates, etc.

30. The capital allocations are typically based on Economic Capital, VaR and RAROC-type methodologies.

31. Another compelling argument is that banks' credit ratings have become increasingly important due to the proliferation of off-balance sheet banking. The viability of banks in their off-balance sheet activities (e.g., writing guarantees as in underwriting and securitization) necessitates sufficient capitalization and high credit ratings (see Boot, Milbourn, & Schmeits, 2006, for a general analysis of the *raison d'être* of credit ratings).

32. Geographic expansion in the US often involves buying up neighboring (focused) retail banks, which allow for economies on IT systems, management processes and product offerings. Relative to the European scene, where geographic expansion often implies buying up big universal banks across the border, fewer barriers to an effective integration exist. This may explain the more favorable US evidence.

33. Beitel and Schiereck (2001), analyzing mergers between European financial institutions between 1988 and 2000, show that domestic (intra-state) mergers on average have significantly positive combined (bidder plus target) announcement effects, but weaker so in the last few years (1988–2000). They also found that diversifying domestic mergers (particularly between banks and insurers) had on average a positive value impact. In line with this evidence, the Citigroup-Travelers merger resulted in an increase in the stock prices of both merger partners (Siconolfi, 1998). The latter insight is also confirmed in other European studies on bank-insurer mergers; for example, Cybo-Ottone and Murgia (2000) find a positive effect on combined value. A key question is what role market power plays in explaining the value gains in these mergers.

34. Berger (2000) offers an illustration by observing that managerial ability to control costs creates a differentiation in bank performance that may well dominate the potential scale economies. The difference between an "average" bank and the "best practice bank" is about 20% of the costs of the average bank, while cost scale economies in the 1980s did not exceed 5%. Berger (2000) argues that managerial ability may have a similar effect on revenue efficiency. The arguments for this might be subtle. For example, a potential impediment for relationship lending follows from the literature on "soft" information and organizational structure. Consolidation may undermine the incentives of banks to produce and utilize soft information. In particular, recent research has shown that large banks are less capable in using soft information (see Berger & Udell, 2002; Stein, 2002; and for empirical evidence, Berger, Miller, Petersen, Rajan, & Stein, 2005). Larger (more centralized) banks base their credit approval decisions more on hard (verifiable) information, whereas smaller (more decentralized) banks can more easily use soft information. This may be particularly important

for the financing of smaller and informationally opaque firms, and also has implications for optimal decision-making structure of larger financial institutions (see Stein, 2002, and Liberti, 2003). These arguments also point at the importance of proximity in relationship banking (see Degryse & Ongena, 2005).

35. An important issue is whether this only points at market power benefits or whether also true efficiency gains could be at work.

36. Surprisingly, this type of research is yet hard to find. A lot of research has been done on potential conflicts of interest in universal banking. To some extent, this is activity specific (investment banking versus commercial banking). However, this research is of very limited interest for this study because it ignores the question of complementarity between activities. This is not really surprising, because the literature is solely motivated by the Glass-Steagall regulation in the US (see Kroszner & Rajan, 1994; Puri, 1996). See Ramirez (2002) for some evidence on scope economies in pre-Glass-Steagall Act US banking. In a similar spirit, Drucker (2005) shows that junk-rated firms and companies in local lending relationships are more likely to select an integrated (universal) commercial-investment bank when they expect to issue public debt in the future. This revealed preference by firms that issue informationally sensitive securities for commercial-investment bank relationships suggests that there are benefits from the bank's ability to use private information from lending in investment banking.

37. Two other sources can be identified (see Boot, 2003): financial innovation related economies and diversification benefits. Ceteris paribus, large institutions could better recoup the fixed costs of financial innovations. Innovations could be marketed to a larger customer base and/or introduced in a wider set of activities. For financial innovations, scale and scope might be particularly important given the rapid imitation by competitors. Only for a short period of time does a true competitive advantage exist. A wider scope and larger scale may help recoup the fixed costs in this short period of time. Diversification benefits are more controversial. In many cases, conglomeration may lead to a valuation discount. This points at (anticipated) inefficiencies (see Section 5.4.2). Also corporate finance theory tells us that investors can choose to diversify and that this does not need to be done at the firm level. However, some bank activities (see our discussion about securitization in Section 5.2.3) benefit from a better rating, which suggests that diversification could be valuable.

38. On the benefits of vertical (dis)integration in the financial services industry there is little empirical work. An interesting exception is a recent article by Berger, Cummins, Weiss, and Zi (2002), who look at profit scope economies in combining life and non-life in the insurance industry. They find that conglomeration (and hence scope) *might* be optimal for larger institutions that are primarily retail/customer focused and have vertically integrated distribution systems.

39. In contrast to domestic mergers, the expected cost savings and economies of scale in cross-border mergers are rather modest. Domestic mergers benefit from the closures of branches and the cuts in the number of employees and other fixed costs. Cross-border mergers are likely to bring only a few savings from the eventual integration of IT systems, back offices, and perhaps the design and marketing of some financial products. But in general, even banks that have bought subsidiaries abroad tend to run them as separate banks. For example, Citigroup has not integrated its banking operations in various European countries, and nor have Nordea (the result of a merger of four Scandinavian banks), Deutsche Bank, HSBC or any of the smaller banks with subsidiaries in Central and Eastern Europe (see *The Economist*, May 19, 2005, *Special survey on international banking*).

40. The particular construction at hand gives ABN AMRO also the benefit of maintaining a direct link to insurance (and the knowledge involved). The fact that the insurance products are sold under the ABN AMRO brand name may give it a stronger bargaining position in the future vis-à-vis Delta Lloyd.

41. The experience of some Western banks is that top management gets fully distracted by the investment banking activities and as a result spends disproportionately little time on the often more profitable non-investment banking activities.

42. Boot (2003) explains the rather broad strategies of banking institutions by emphasizing that in the current uncertain environment banks may want to keep their options open. The domestic consolidation wave helps underwrite this strategy in that it creates "deep pockets".

References

Allen, F. (1993). Stock markets and resource allocation. In: C. Mayer, & X. Vives (Eds), *Capital markets and financial intermediation*. Cambridge: Cambridge University Press.

Allen, F., & Gale, D. (1995). A welfare comparison of the German and U.S. financial systems. *European Economic Review, 39*, 179–209.

Allen, F., & Gale, D. (1997). Financial markets, intermediaries and intertemporal smoothing. *Journal of Political Economy, 105*, 523–546.

Beitel, P., & Schiereck, D. (2001). *Value creation and the ongoing consolidation of the European banking market.* Working paper, University of Witten/Herdecke.

Berger, A. (2000). Efficiency in banking: Professional perspectives. In: A. Saunders (Ed.), *Financial Institutions Management* (pp. 300–301). New York: McGraw-Hill.

Berger, A., Cummins, J., Weiss, M., & Zi, H. (2002). Conglomeration versus strategic focus: Evidence from the insurance industry. *Journal of Financial Intermediation, 9*, 322–362.

Berger, A., Demsetz, R., & Strahan, P. (1999). The consolidation of the financial services industry: Causes, consequences and implications for the future. *Journal of Banking and Finance, 23*, 135–194.

Berger, A., & Humphrey, D. (1997). Efficiency of financial institutions: International survey and directions for future research. *European Journal of Operational Research, 98*, 175–212.

Berger, A., Kashyap, A., & Scalise, J. (1995). The transformation of the US banking industry: What a long, strange trip it's been. *Brookings Papers on Economic Activity, 2*, 55–218.

Berger, A., & Mester, L. (1997). Inside the black box: What explains differences in the efficiencies in financial institutions? *Journal of Banking and Finance, 21*, 895–947.

Berger, A., Miller, N., Petersen, M., Rajan, R., & Stein, J. (2005). Does function follow organizational form? Evidence from the lending practices of large and small banks. *Journal of Financial Economics, 76*, 237–269.

Berger, A., Saunders, A., Scalise, J., & Udell, G. (1998). The effects of bank mergers and acquisitions on small business lending. *Journal of Financial Economics, 50*, 187–230.

Berger, A., & Udell, G. (2002). Small business credit availability and relationship lending: The importance of bank organizational structure. *Economic Journal, 112*, 32–53.

Berger, P., & Ofek, E. (1995). Diversification's effect on firm value. *Journal of Financial Economics, 37*, 39–65.

Berglöf, E., & Von Thadden, E. (1994). Short-term versus long-term interests: Capital structure with multiple investors. *Quarterly Journal of Economics, 109*, 1055–1084.

Berlin, M. (1996). For better and for worse: Three lending relationships. *Business Review Federal Reserve Bank of Philadelphia*, December, 3–12.

Berlin, M. (2002). We control the vertical: Three theories of the firm. *Business Review Federal Reserve Bank of Philadelphia*, September, 13–22.

Berlin, M., & Mester, L. (1992). Debt covenants and renegotiation. *Journal of Financial Intermediation, 2*, 95–133.

Berlin, M., & Mester, L. (1999). Deposits and relationship lending. *Review of Financial Studies, 12*, 579–607.

Bhattacharya, S., & Chiesa, G. (1995). Proprietary information, financial intermediation, and research incentives. *Journal of Financial Intermediation, 4*, 328–357.

Bolton, P., & Scharfstein, D. (1996). Optimal debt structure and the number of creditors. *Journal of Political Economy, 104*, 1–25.

Boot, A. W. A. (2000). Relationship banking: What do we know? *Journal of Financial Intermediation, 9*, 7–25.

Boot, A.W.A. (2003). Consolidation and strategic positioning in banking with implications for Europe. *Brookings-Wharton Papers on Financial Services*, Washington.

Boot, A.W.A., Greenbaum S., & Thakor, A. (1993). Reputation and discretion in financial contracting. *American Economic Review, 83*, 1165–1183.

Boot, A.W.A., Milbourn T., & Schmeits, A. (2006). Credit ratings as coordination mechanisms. *Review of Financial Studies, 19*, 81–118.

Boot, A.W.A., & Schmeits, A. (2000). Market discipline and incentive problems in conglomerate firms with applications to banking. *Journal of Financial Intermediation, 9*, 240–273.

Boot, A.W.A., & Thakor, A. (1997). Financial system architecture. *Review of Financial Studies, 10*, 693–733.

Boot, A.W.A., & Thakor, A. (2000). Can relationship banking survive competition? *Journal of Finance, 55*, 679–713.

Boot, A.W.A., Thakor, A., & Udell, G. (1991). Credible commitments, contract enforcement problems and banks: Intermediation as credibility assurance. *Journal of Banking and Finance, 15*, 605–632.

Boyd, J., & Gertler, M. (1994). Are banks dead, or are the reports greatly exaggerated? *Federal Reserve Bank of Minneapolis Quarterly Review*, Summer.

Calomiris, C., & Kahn, C. (1991). The role of demandable debt in structuring optimal banking arrangements. *American Economic Review, 81*, 497–513.

Calomiris, C., & Karceski, J. (1998). Is the bank merger wave of the 90s efficient? Lessons from nine case studies. Working paper, Columbia University.

Chan, Y., Greenbaum, S., & Thakor, A. (1986). Information reusability, competition and bank asset quality. *Journal of Banking and Finance, 10*, 255–276.

Chemmanur, T., & Fulghieri, P. (1994). Reputation, renegotiation, and the choice between bank loans and publicly traded debt. *Review of Financial Studies, 7*, 475–506.

Clark, J. (1996). Economic cost, scale efficiency, and competitive viability in banking. *Journal of Money, Credit and Banking, 28*, 342–364.

Cornett, M., & Tehranian, H. (1992). Changes in corporate performance associated with bank acquisitions. *Journal of Financial Economics, 31*, 211–234.

Cybo-Ottone, A., & Murgia, M. (2000). Mergers and shareholder wealth in European banking. *Journal of Banking and Finance, 24*, 831–859.

Degryse, H., & Van Cayseele, P. (2000). Relationship-lending within a bank-based system: Evidence from European small-business data. *Journal of Financial Intermediation, 9*, 90–109.

Degryse, H., & Ongena, S. (2005). Distance, lending relationships and competition. *Journal of Finance, 60*, 231–266.

DeLong, G. (2001). Stockholder gains from focusing versus diversifying bank mergers. *Journal of Financial Economics, 59*, 221–242.

Dennis, S., & Mullineaux, D. (2000). Syndicated loans. *Journal of Financial Intermediation, 9*, 404–426.

Dewatripont, M., & Maskin, E. (1995). Credit and efficiency in centralized and decentralized economies. *Review of Economic Studies, 62*, 541–555.

Dewatripont, M., & Tirole, J. (1995). *The prudential regulation of banks*. Cambridge MA: MIT Press.

Diamond, D. (1984). Financial intermediation and delegated monitoring. *Review of Economic Studies, 51*, 393–414.

Diamond, D. (1991). Monitoring and reputation: The choice between bank loans and directly placed debt. *Journal of Political Economy, 99*, 689–721.

Diamond, D. (1993). Seniority and maturity of debt contracts. *Journal of Financial Economics, 33*, 341–368.

Diamond, D., & Rajan, R. (2001). Banks and liquidity. *American Economic Review, 91*, 422–425.

Dinç, S. (2000). Bank reputation, bank commitment, and the effects of competition in credit markets. *Review of Financial Studies, 13*, 781–812.

Drucker, S. (2005). *Information asymmetries and the effects of banking mergers in firm-bank relationships*. Working paper, FDIC Center for Financial Research.

Flannery, M. (1999). Comment on Milbourn, Boot and Thakor. *Journal of Banking and Finance, 23*, 215–220.

Gande, A., & Saunders, A. (2005). *Are banks still special when there is a secondary market for loans?* Working paper, New York University.

Gorton, G., & Kahn, J. (1993). *The design of bank loan contracts, collateral, and renegotiation.* NBER working paper no. 4273.

Gorton, G., & Pennachi, G. (1995). Banks and loan sales: Marketing nonmarketable assets. *Journal of Monetary Economics, 35*, 389–411.

Hauswald, R., & Marquez, R. (2005). Competition and strategic information acquisition in credit markets. *Review of Financial Studies*, forthcoming.

Hellwig, M. (1991). Banking, financial intermediation and corporate finance. In: A. Giovanni, & C. Mayer (Eds), *European financial integration.* Cambridge: Cambridge University Press.

Hoshi, T., Kashyap A., & Scharfstein, D. (1993). *The choice between public and private debt: An analysis of post-deregulation corporate financing in Japan.* NBER working paper no. 4421.

Houston, J., & James, C. (1995). Bank information monopolies and the mix of private and public debt claims. *Journal of Finance, 51*, 1863–1889.

James, C. (1987). Some evidence on the uniqueness of bank loans. *Journal of Financial Economics 19*, 217–235.

Kashyap, A., Rajan, R., & Stein, J. (1999). *Banks as liquidity providers: An explanation for the co-existence of lending and deposit-taking.* Working paper, University of Chicago.

Kroszner, R., & Rajan, R. (1994). Is the Glass-Steagall Act justified? A study of the US experience with universal banking before 1933. *American Economic Review, 84*, 810–832.

Laeven, L., & Levine, R. (2005). *Is there a diversification discount in financial conglomerates?* NBER working paper no. W11499.

Lamont, O. (1997). Cash flow and investment: Evidence from internal capital markets. *Journal of Finance, 52*, 83–109.

Liberti, J. (2003). *Initiative, incentives and soft information. How does delegation impact the role of bank relationship managers?* Working paper, London Business School.

Lummer, S., & McConnell, J. (1989). Further evidence on the bank lending process and the reaction of the capital market to bank loan agreements. *Journal of Financial Economics, 25*, 99–122.

Mayer, C. (1988). New issues in corporate finance. *European Economic Review, 32*, 1167–1183.

McKinsey & Company (2002). Europe's banks: Verging on merging. *McKinsey Quarterly, 3*.

Merton, R. (1993). Operation and regulation in financial intermediation: A functional perspective. In: P. Englund (Ed.), *Operation and regulation of financial markets.* Washington: Economic Council.

Mester, L. (1992). Traditional and non-traditional banking: An information-theoretic approach. *Journal of Banking and Finance, 16*, 545–566.

Mitchell, K., & Onvural, N. (1996). Economies of scale and scope at large commercial banks: Evidence from the Fourier flexible functional form. *Journal of Money, Credit and Banking, 28*, 178–199.

Ongena, S., & Smith, D. (2000) What determines the number of bank relationships? Cross-country evidence. *Journal of Financial Intermediation, 9*, 26–56.

Petersen, M., & Rajan, R. (1994). The benefits of lending relationships: Evidence from small business data. *Journal of Finance, 49*, 1367–1400.

Petersen, M., & Rajan, R. (1995). The effect of credit market competition on lending relationships. *Quarterly Journal of Economics, 110*, 407–443.

Puri, M. (1996). Commercial banks in investment banking: Conflict of interest or certification role? *Journal of Financial Economics, 40*, 373–401.

Rajan, R. (1992). Insiders and outsiders: The choice between informed and arm's length debt. *Journal of Finance, 47*, 1367–1400.

Rajan, R., Servaes, H., & Zingales, L. (2000). The cost of diversity: The diversification discount and inefficient investment. *Journal of Finance, 55*, 35–80.

Rajan, R., & Winton, A. (1995). Covenants and collateral as incentives to monitor. *Journal of Finance, 50*, 1113–1146.

Ramirez, C. (2002). Did banks' security affiliates add value? Evidence from the commercial banking industry during the 1920s. *Journal of Money, Credit and Banking, 34*, 391–411.

Sapienza, P. (2002) The effects of banking mergers on loan contracts. *Journal of Finance, 57*, 329–367.

Saunders, A. (2000). *Financial institutions management*. New York: McGraw-Hill.

Schmeits, A. (2005). *Discretionary contracts, competition and bank–firm relationships*. Working paper, Washington University in St. Louis.

Shaffer, S., & David, E. (1991). Economics of superscale in commercial banking. *Applied Economics, 23*, 283–293.

Sharpe, S. (1990). Asymmetric information, bank lending, and implicit contracts: A stylized model of customer relationship. *Journal of Finance, 45*, 1069–1087.

Shin, H., & Stulz, R. (1998). Are internal capital markets efficient? *Quarterly Journal of Economics, 113*, 531–552.

Siconolfi, M. (1998). Big umbrella: Travellers and Citicorp agree to join forces in $83 billion merger. *Wall Street Journal*, April 7.

Simon, H. (1936). Rules versus authorities in monetary policy. *Journal of Political Economy, 44*, 1–30.

Slovin, M., Sushka, B., & Hudson, C. (1988). Corporate commercial paper, note issuance facilities and shareholder wealth. *Journal of International Money and Finance, 7*, 289–302.

Smith, R., & Walter, I. (1997). *Global banking*. Oxford: Oxford University Press.

Stein, J. (2002). Information production and capital allocation: Decentralized versus hierarchical firms. *Journal of Finance, 57*, 1891–1921.

Sufi, A. (2005). *Information asymmetry and financing arrangements: Evidence from syndicated loans*. Working paper, University of Chicago.

Van der Vennet, R. (2002). Cost and profit efficiency of financial conglomerates and universal banks in Europe. *Journal of Money, Credit and Banking, 24*, 254–282.

Appendix

Table 5.1: Possible barriers to realizing scale and scope economies.

Barrier	Examples
Technological barrier	• Incompatible computer systems • Conflicting distribution channels
Regulatory barrier	• Explicit limitations on activities • Regulatory-induced Chinese walls
Managerial barrier	• Lack of leadership • Cultural differences • Conflicts of interest
Political considerations	• National "flagship" attitude

Chapter 6

Consolidation of the European Banking Sector: Impact on Innovation[1]

Hans Degryse, Steven Ongena and Maria Fabiana Penas

6.1. Introduction

We investigate whether innovation and growth in Europe (as envisioned in the "*Lisbon Agenda*") are hurt by the deepening integration of its financial sector. At first the question may strike one as odd. Is not the integration of the financial sector supposed to increase the efficiency of financial intermediation and almost by definition deliver more growth?

We will argue that the impact of integration on growth is not always straightforward and positive, and that there may be instances where integration actually hampers growth. In particular we highlight the problems financial integration may create for breakthrough innovation. Financial integration, by escalating competition and consolidation in the European banking sector, may jeopardize the funding of those perennial radical innovators such as start-ups and other small and young firms. However weighing the current evidence, we conclude these problems may at most be transitory.

We unfold our argumentation in a number of intermediate steps (Figure 6.1 provides a basic road map). We briefly review the literature on growth, distilling that innovation and financial development are the key ingredients of growth. Europe lags the USA in innovation. To trigger more breakthrough innovations, small firms need access to resources to prosper in Europe. However, small firm financing may be jeopardized by the integration of the European banking sector. Fiercer interbank competition may undermine vital intertemporal risk sharing between bank and innovator, while banking consolidation may create behemoth banks unwilling or unable to handle small firm loan applications. However weighing the current evidence, we argue that competition and relationship finance are not necessarily inimical and that other existing or *de novo* banks may accommodate the denied loan applicants. We also stress the key role the rapidly deepening venture capital markets in Europe will play.

The rest of this chapter proceeds as follows. Section 6.2 reviews the theories of economic growth that emphasize innovation and financial development, the challenges for

Advances in Corporate Finance and Asset Pricing
Edited by L. Renneboog
© 2006 Elsevier B.V. All rights reserved.
ISBN: 0-444-52723-0

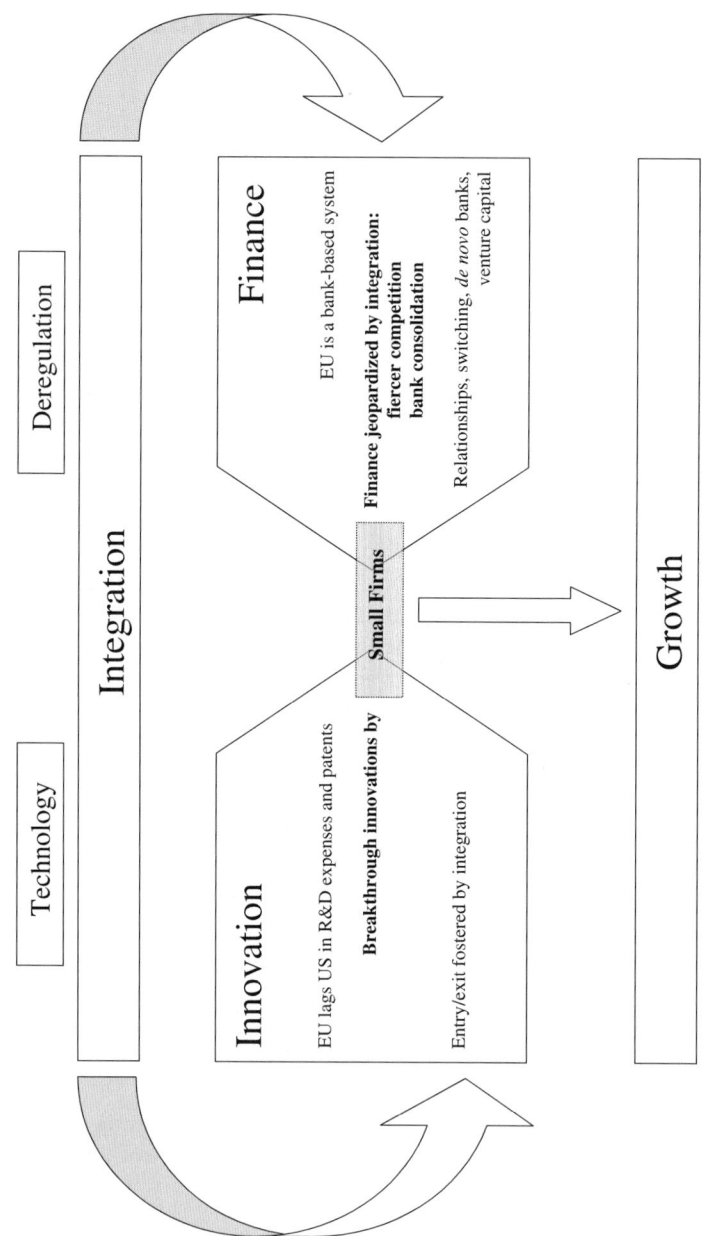

Figure 6.1: Innovation, finance, small firms and growth (A road map for the chapter).

Europe, and the key ingredients of the Lisbon Agenda. Section 6.3 analyses the impact of deregulation and technology on the integration of the European banking sector, in order to explain in Section 6.4 the impact of integration on the financing of innovation. Section 6.5 takes a step back and discusses alternatives to bank finance. Section 6.6 concludes this chapter.

6.2. Lisbon: Agenda of Growth and Innovation

6.2.1. Theories of Economic Growth and Innovation: Role for Finance?

6.2.1.1. Exogenous and endogenous technological change   Technological progress is a key driver of economic growth in most macro-economic theories. In neoclassical models (e.g., Solow, 1956), the long-run steady-state growth rate is driven by exogenous technological change as capital is assumed to be subject to diminishing returns. This exogenous technological change is left unexplained and is labelled the "Solow residual" or the "total factor productivity" growth; that is, the growth net of the capital- and labour-related components.

The *endogenous* growth models, in contrast, do not rely on exogenous technological progress to explain long-run growth. The "AK" models, for example, assume that output is a linear function of inputs. Hence the AK models depart from the diminishing returns to capital assumption of the neoclassical models. This departure permits continued growth as long as capital and labour are abundantly available.

Other endogenous growth models (the so-called "R&D-based models") allow the "shift term" or the technological progress to depend on the general stock of knowledge available to the firms. This stock depends on the ideas produced by the firms or reflects "learning by doing". Profit-maximizing R&D firms produce ideas that introduce new processes and products that are used as inputs in the production of the final goods. Special attention in this part of the literature is given to the modelling of the R&D sector because: (1) the degree of competition in the final goods market and R&D sector influences the production of ideas and (2) there is a public good aspect to the production of ideas due to knowledge spillovers. Grossman and Helpman (1991), for example, model international knowledge spillovers due to international trade in intermediate goods. Aghion, Bloom, Blundell, Griffith, and Howitt zoom in on the micro-organization of the final goods sector and the R&D sector, and highlight the role of contracts, institutions and the industrial organization of these sectors in explaining economic growth.

Investment in the knowledge infrastructure by both public and private agents is crucial for technological progress. The literature on "National Innovation Systems" highlights the interaction between the different elements of an "innovation system". That is, technological progress depends on the ability to combine new knowledge produced with the knowledge already available and the actions of the various actors in the innovation system (see e.g., Freeman, 1987). Hence the literature on "National Innovation Systems" stresses that economic growth not only hinges on the growth of inputs but also on the efficiency of the innovation system.

6.2.1.2. Finance and growth   The discussed macro-models only allow for a limited role of finance in explaining long-run economic growth. Policymakers and economists nowadays generally agree that financial development — delivering a well-functioning financial system — contributes to economic growth. King and Levine (1993), for example, focus on the link between financial system development and growth for 80 countries for the period 1960–1989, and report that the relative size of the financial sector in 1960 is positively associated with economic growth over the period 1960–1989. As the initial size of the financial sector may reflect the expectation of future economic potential, subsequent work controls for the endogenous effects of economic growth on financial development. But the effect of financial development on growth remains robust (see e.g., Levine, Loayza, & Beck, 2000).

But what is the transmission mechanism driving this robust finding? The theories discussed so far allow for an impact through: (1) the channel of capital accumulation (as in the neoclassical growth models) and/or (2) the channel of productivity gains through knowledge creation (as in the endogenous growth theory).

Rajan and Zingales (1998), for example, look at the relationship between financial development and industry- or firm-level growth. They find that industries that depend more on external finance grow relatively faster in countries with more developed financial systems. They also document that younger firms in higher-productivity sectors tend to depend more on external finance. Precisely these firms enjoy the benefits of the lower cost of financing from a well-developed financial system. Hence financial development may improve productivity growth by reducing the cost of external finance for those young firms that generate the new ideas. Other evidence suggests that financial liberalization improves the efficiency of investment fund allocation and consequently that financial development also spurs improved capital accumulation (Galindo, Schiantarelli, & Weiss, 2005).

Do different financial market structures produce varying results? That is, does the composition of the financial system — bank- or market-based — for a given level of financial development influence growth? Bank-based systems may be better in providing monitoring. Market-based systems may be superior in allocating capital, in avoiding soft-budget constraint problems and in curtailing hold-up by individual financiers.

It is well documented that the continental European countries are more bank-based financial systems, whereas the UK and the USA tend towards a market-oriented financial system (for a review see Allen & Gale, 2000). The empirical evidence on the performance of bank- versus market-based financial systems on the other hand is mixed. Levine (2002), for example, finds that the structure of the financial system is irrelevant for growth. Ergungor (2003), on the other hand, finds that countries with a more flexible judicial system and that are more market-oriented grow faster. He finds that the channel linking judicial flexibility and output growth stems from the growth of the capital stock. That is a more flexible judicial system and a more market-oriented financial system lead to more capital-intensive investment.

6.2.2. Empirical Work on Economic Growth and Innovation and the Role of Small Firms

The recent emergence of the knowledge economy has called for a concerted effort to improve innovation performance. We start by highlighting the differences between Europe

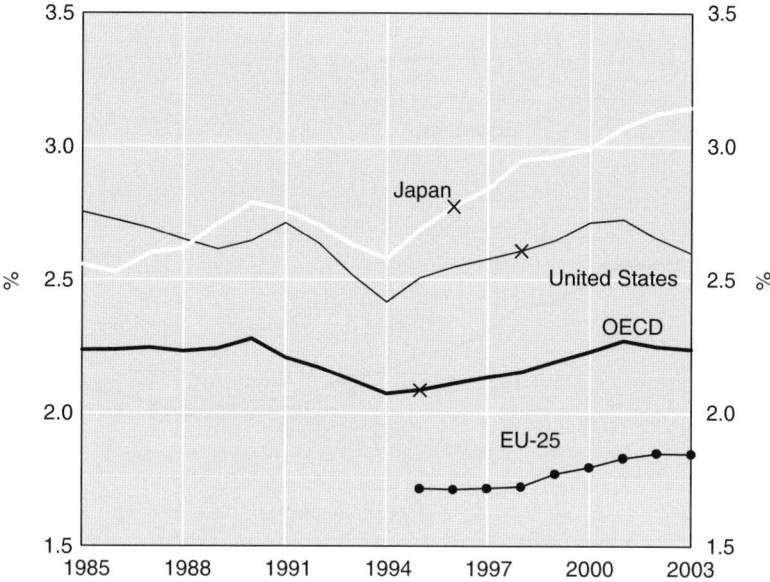

Figure 6.2: Gross domestic expenditures on R&D (as % of GDP). *Source*: OECD (2005) *Main Science and Technology Indicators*.

and the USA in terms of innovation performance. For that purpose, we look at two indicators, an input and output indicator of innovation.

Inputs are typically proxied by R&D expenditures relative to gross domestic product (GDP). Figures 6.2–6.4 provide data on different measures of gross expenditures of R&D. Figure 6.2 shows that the EU-25 spends less than 2% of its GDP on R&D expenditures, while Japan and the USA spend more than 3% and 2.5%, respectively. This expenditure gap is persistent over time although the difference in spending between the EU and the USA has declined somewhat during the last few years. Figures 6.3 and 6.4 indicate that the gap exists both in government- and in industry-financed R&D expenditures.[2]

Patent-based indicators are one measure of technological *output*. Although using patents as indicator may have severe limitations, analysis of patents learns that: (1) the patent share of the EU-25 in the sum of EU-25, Japanese and US patents, has slightly declined from 27% to 23% over the period 1990–2000, and is considerably lower than the patent share of the USA (which decreases marginally from 39% in 1990 to 38% in 2000); (2) the EU-25 has a strength in "Mechanical Engineering" and "Materials", and a major weakness in "Biotechnology"; (3) the EU-25 is persistently lagging behind in "Information, Communication and Technology" and (4) the EU-25 is catching up in "Consumer Electronics". In sum, the comparison of both input and output indicators of innovation reveals that the EU-25 trails the USA.

But what are the determinants of R&D expenditures and the propensity to patent? A large theoretical and empirical literature has emerged that looks at the link between innovation, firm size and market structure. Theoretical work initiated by Schumpeter and

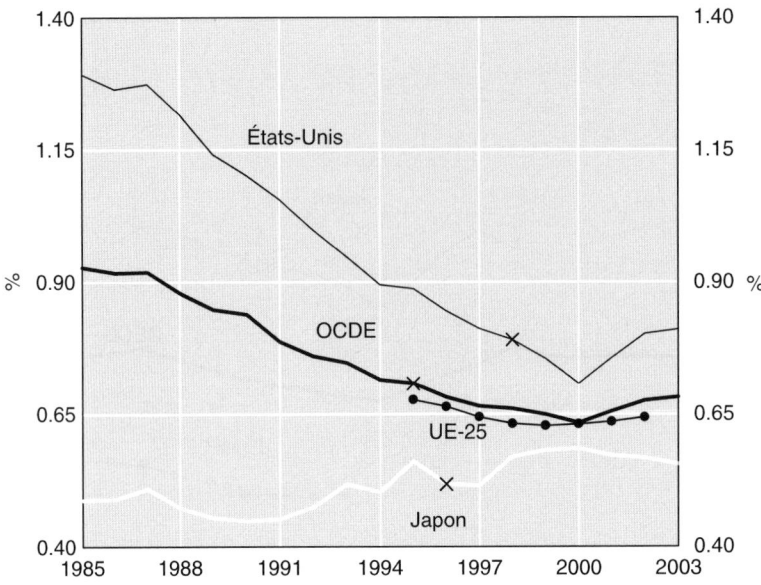

Figure 6.3: Government-financed gross domestic expenditures on R&D (as % of GDP).
Source: OECD (2005) *Main Science and Technology Indicators*

Arrow points to different results. Schumpeter (1942), on the one hand, argues that it is the large firm in a concentrated sector, that is the engine of technological progress. Cosy competition preserves rents and spurs innovation. Arrow (1962), on the other hand, argues that innovation will only take place in a competitive sector. He considers drastic innovations and finds that competition pushes firms to innovate more.

Empirical research also has intensively looked at the relation between innovation, firm size and market structure. Symeonidis (1996) provides an early review of the developing literature and concludes that:

> On the whole, there is little empirical support for the view that large firm size or high concentration are factors generally associated with a higher level of innovative activity.

However, more recent theoretical and empirical work suggests an inverted-U relationship between competition and innovation (see e.g., Boone & van Damme, 2004; Aghion et al., 2005). Hence an intermediate degree of competition will stimulate innovation the most. The theoretical models (e.g., Gilbert & Newbery, 1982) now incorporate dynamic aspects of innovation taking into account the technological distance between leader and laggards (and including the possibility of "leapfrogging innovations") as well as knowledge spillovers. These new models deliver interesting predictions related to the heterogeneity between "incremental innovations" and "breakthrough innovations". Incumbent firms enjoy a comparative advantage in incremental innovations, whereas new entrants

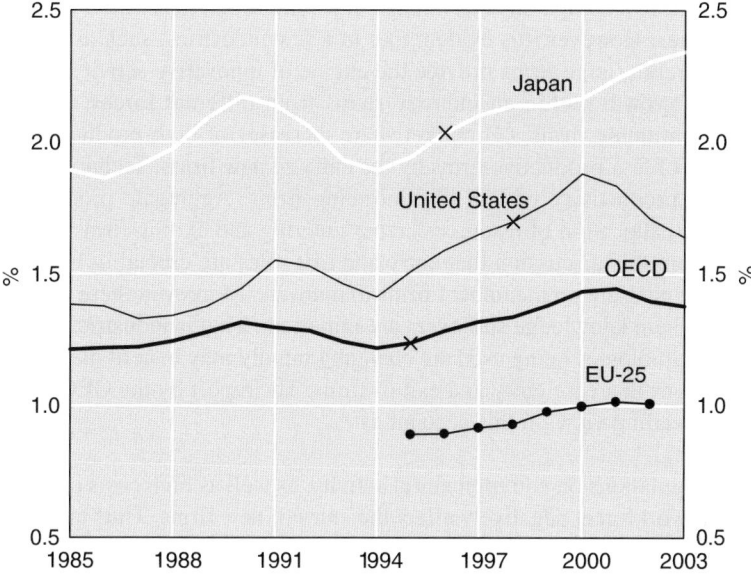

Figure 6.4: Industry-financed gross domestic expenditures on R&D (as % of GDP). *Source*: OECD (2005) *Main Science and Technology Indicators*.

(typically small firms) have a comparative advantage in fundamental breakthrough innovations. Baumol (2004) argues that:

> Breakthrough inventions are contributed disproportionately by independent inventors and entrepreneurs, while large firms focus on cumulative, incremental (and often invaluable) improvements.

Based on an analysis of data from the US Small Business Administration, he concludes that:

> It is a plausible observation, then, that perhaps *most* of the revolutionary ideas of the past two centuries have been, and are likely to continue to be, provided more often by these independent innovators who, essentially, operate small business enterprises.

As "breakthrough inventions" are most important in explaining productivity growth, small firms play a special role. For example, a recent report by the OECD (2003) argues that small firms foster innovation more than large firms do. The OECD does not stand alone in this view of the world (e.g., WorldBank, 2004). Growth is usually associated with new entrants who drive out old and obsolescent firms. The new entrants typically introduce new technologies and indirectly foster technological progress by prodding incumbent firms to also adopt the new technologies. Firm dynamics are thus important in explaining industry growth.

It might appear that only small firms can be innovative in a radical sense. This is not the case. The relative innovative advantage of small and large firms is industry specific.

Small firms do have a comparative advantage in breakthrough innovation over larger firms in most industries. However it is evident that in a few industries, such as pharmaceutical products and aircraft, large firms provide the engine of innovative activity.

Productivity growth within an industry stems from different forces: (1) productivity gains within continuing firms, (2) market share increases of high-productivity firms and (3) the removal of less-productive firms by the entry of new firms. Technological progress determines the productivity growth of continuing firms. Aggregate productivity is also affected by the reallocation of resources across entering and exiting firms.

It is clear from this discussion that entry and exit rules are crucial in boosting productivity by putting pressure on incumbent firms to innovate. Moreover, these rules may affect the industries where knowledge spillovers are important. That is industries where the general-purpose technologies being used are changing rapidly may benefit more from product market regulations that ease entry and exit of firms. The report by the OECD (2003) summarizes the prevailing view on this account as:

> Strict regulations on entrepreneurial activity, as well as high costs of adjusting the workforce, negatively affect the entry of new firms. Thus in the US, low administrative costs of start-ups and not unduly strict regulations on labour adjustments are likely to stimulate potential entrepreneurs to start on small scale, test the market and, if successful with their business plan, expand rapidly to reach the minimum efficient scale. In contrast, higher entry and adjustment costs in Europe may stimulate a pre-market selection of business plans with less market experimentation.

We think that it is on this margin that European integration may play a key role in facilitating firm entry and exit. The financial system also plays a role in this part of the innovation process. The report by the OECD (2003) stresses:

> The more market-based financial system may lead to lower risk aversion to project financing in the US, with greater financing possibilities for entrepreneurs with small or innovative projects, often characterized by limited cash flows and lack of collateral.

We will develop this argument further in Section 6.5 where we discuss finance and innovation in Europe.

6.2.3. Lisbon Agenda

At the European Council in March 2000 in Lisbon, the ambition was stated to make Europe by 2010 "the most competitive and dynamic knowledge-based economy in the world, capable of sustainable economic growth with more and better jobs and greater social cohesion".

The Lisbon Strategy initially consisted of an economic pillar and a social pillar. The economic pillar consists of reforms to promote productivity, innovation and competitiveness. The Lisbon Agenda and its different action plans lead to 10 different central policy areas or priorities.[3] This resulted in specific quantitative targets most notably to raise the overall EU employment rate to 70%, the EU female employment rate to 60% and the employment rate for older workers (with an age between 55 and 64 years) to 50% by 2010.

Special attention was given to improving productivity. Innovation is a cornerstone of the "Lisbon Strategy" to stimulate productivity. The discussion above reveals that the innovation performance of the EU remained low compared to the USA and Japan. It is argued that the Union's relatively low expenditures on R&D explains part of Europe's innovation weakness. The Barcelona European Council of March 2002 sets the target R&D to GDP ratio of 3% by 2010 where two-thirds are to be financed by the private sector.

6.3. The Impact of Deregulation and Technology on the Integration in the European Banking Sector

In this section we review how the two fundamental drivers of integration, *deregulation* and *technological advances*, may escalate competition and spur consolidation in the European banking sector. In Section 6.4, we discuss how changes in competition and consolidation in the banking sector may affect the financing of innovation in Europe. Figure 6.5 provides a road map to both Sections 6.3 and 6.4.

6.3.1. Impact of Deregulation

6.3.1.1. Impact of deregulation on competition
(a) The beneficial effects of deregulation on competition

The impact of deregulation in Europe has been substantial and profound. Most regulatory borders are by now removed and in principle the European banking market should be open for business for all banks chartered in the EU and provided with the single passport of the European Second Banking Directive.

The evidence on the beneficial effects of deregulation on competition in general is substantial (Degryse & Ongena, 2005a; Strahan, 2005). A recent article by Demirguc-Kunt, Laeven, and Levine (2004), for example, uses data from banks covering 72 countries examines the impact of banking regulation on bank net interest margins. The information on commercial banking regulation is taken from Barth, Caprio, and Levine (2001). Regulatory variables include the fraction of entry that is denied, a proxy for the degree to which banks face regulatory restrictions on their activities in, for example, securities markets and investment banking, and a measure of reserve requirements. They also employ an indicator of "banking freedom", taken from the Heritage Foundation, which provides an overall index of the openness of the banking industry and the extent to which banks are free to operate their business.

The results in Demirguc-Kunt, Laeven, and Levine (2004) indicate that restrictive banking regulation substantially hikes net interest margins. For example, a one standard deviation increase in entry or activity restrictions, reserve requirements, or banking freedom, result, respectively, in 50***, 100***, 51*, and 70*** basis points (bp) extra for the incumbent banks.[4]

However, when including, in addition to the bank-specific and macro-economic controls, also an index of property rights, the regulatory restrictions turn insignificant and do

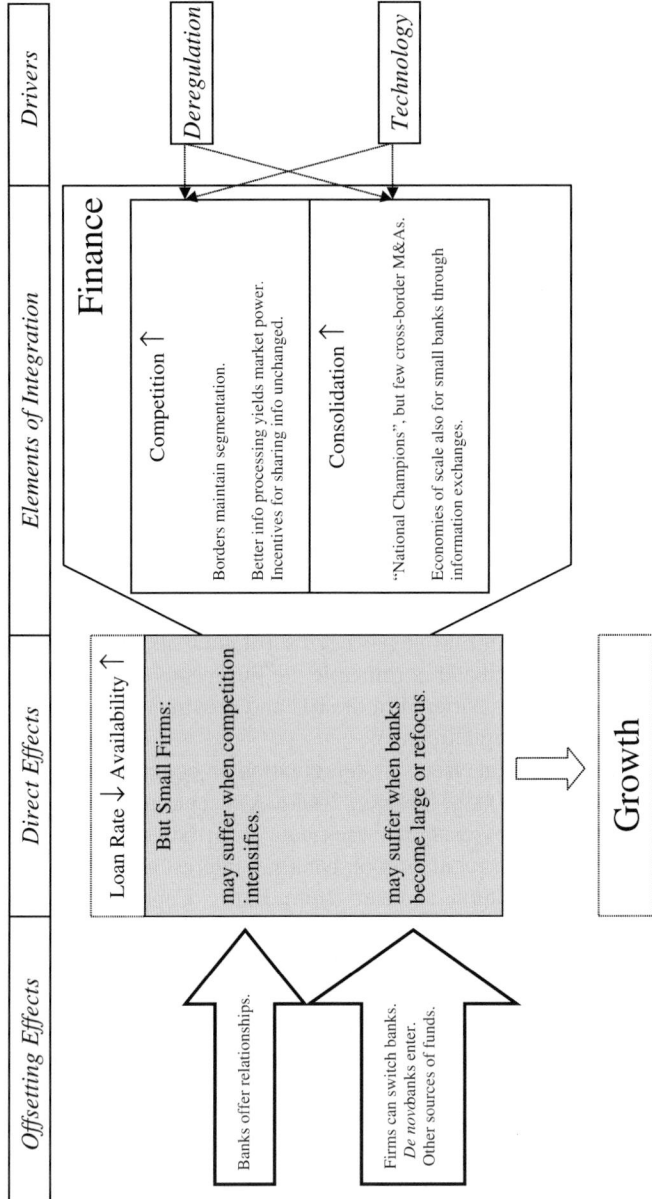

Figure 6.5: Integration and small-firm finance (A road map For Sections 6.3 and 6.4).

not provide any additional explanatory power. Demirguc-Kunt, Laeven, and Levine interpret this result as indicating that banking regulation reflects something broader about the competitive environment. Their interpretation fits with findings in Kroszner and Strahan (1999), and more recently Garrett, Wagner, and Wheelock (2004), who investigate the political and economic drivers of bank branching deregulation across US states, and with results in Jayaratne and Strahan (1996) showing that loan rates decrease with 30** bp on average following deregulation.

There is also evidence directly pertaining to the case of European deregulation. Cetorelli (2004), for example, shows that the enhanced competition following the relaxation on cross-border restrictions in Europe in the early 1990s led to better credit availability as average firm size declined after reform, and that this decline was concentrated in bank-dependent industries. Bertrand, Schoar, and Thesmar (2004) analyse the effect of banking system deregulation on French firms and industrial structure. They find that credit availability to bank-dependent industries increased following deregulation. And Giannetti and Ongena (2005) employ a large panel containing almost 60,000 firm-year observations on listed and unlisted companies in Eastern European economies to assess the differential impact of foreign bank presence on firm growth and financing. They find that lending by foreign (locally based) banks makes bank credit in the country cheaper (firm interest payments decrease) and more widely available (the use of trade credit decreases), consequently foreign bank lending stimulates the growth in domestic firm leverage.

(b) Limits to the effects of deregulation on competition

While under the European Second Banking Directive in principle the European banking market should be open for business for all banks chartered in the EU, in practice things are not that simple, as both exogenous and endogenous economic borders remain formidable barriers (Degryse & Ongena, 2004). Exogenous economic borders arise because of differences in, for example, legal origin and system, supervisory and corporate governance practices, political framework, language or culture. Take differences in legal systems and practices. Europe contains within its national boundaries all the (former) standard bearers from all major legal regimes, creating work for corporate lawyers but headaches and costs for bank management. Another example: the variation in banking supervisory practices within the EU is as large as the variation in the world (Barth, Caprio, & Levine, 2001). Needless to say it is close to zero within the US. Differences in corporate governance and the mutual structure of a few key banks in Europe create further barriers to integration. And then we have not touched yet on the undeniably profound differences in politics, language and culture within the EU.

Endogenous economic borders, on the other hand, are mainly informational and may well be affected by deregulation and technological developments, but the extent to which remains unclear. Informational borders arise because of the formation of bank–firm relationships, adverse selection or information sharing between (a group of) banks. Endogenous (informational) economic borders also remain quite high in Europe and hence Europe may face specific problems when it comes to reducing informational asymmetries. Making more accounting and other "hard" information available, for example, could in principle alleviate some of the informational asymmetries. But "hardening" of information may also be more problematic in Europe than in the USA, as it is not clear that all information that is already hardened is equally reliable across Europe. For example, La Porta,

Lopez-de-Silanes, Shleifer, and Vishny (1998) report a *Rating on Accounting Standards* that ranges between 36 and 83 for countries in Europe and between 24 and 76 for the rest of the world (the US score equals 71 while the average for all the countries is 61). In addition, a lot of local knowledge is often still needed to correctly interpret the "hard facts" often transforming "hard information" into "soft information".

As a result of both exogenous and endogenous economic borders retail loan markets in Europe remain surprisingly segmented, in contrast to wholesale capital markets in both Europe and the USA (Danthine, Giavazzi, & von Thadden, 2001; Adam, Jappelli, Menichini, Padula, & Pagano, 2002). For example, the distance at which banks lend internationally in Europe, and hence cross border, has not at all increased over time in Europe in contrast to the USA where the distance at which banks lend internationally has steadily increased (Buch, 2004).

6.3.1.2. Impact of deregulation on consolidation   Deregulation may not only spur competition but also the consolidation of the banking sector. Jayaratne and Strahan (1998) and Stiroh and Strahan (2003), for example, find that following deregulation of restrictions on in-state branching in the USA, the market share of large banks (following consolidation) increased, while the price of credit declined (see also Berger, Demsetz, & Strahan, 1999).

However, deregulation under the European Second Banking Directive has so far only resulted in domestic merger activity, creating the so-called "National Champions". This creation of National Champions may partly be the result of the existence of informational borders (Degryse & Ongena, 2004). Outside banks seeking to acquire a local bank find it more difficult than incumbent banks to assess the value of the loan portfolio of the possible target banks. As a result of the winner's curse problem, outside banks refrain from stepping in and most mergers and acquisitions (M&As) activity, driven by for example (revenue and cost) scale and scope considerations, occurs between domestic banks.

However as the domestic banks increase in size, diversify, and possibly partly refocus their lending towards larger firms (a key issue we return to later) they become easier-to-value targets. If this is indeed the case we contend that the informational asymmetries facing the outside acquiring banks may actually endogenously decrease over time as possible target banks that are shielded within the bordered area prosper, grow and merge among themselves resulting in a further diversification of their loan portfolios.

At some point national competition policy concerns may ultimately hinder further domestic consolidation. As further local mergers come under scrutiny of competition policy authorities, winner's curse problems may further decrease, facilitating cross-border M&As. Hence one could argue that informational borders and the accompanying winner's curse problem have a tendency to partly and endogenously self-destruct, that M&As may become the optimal route of entering a market long before cross-border servicing or direct entry are economically feasible, and that "National Champions" will almost inevitably metamorphose into "European Champions".

Again to the extent that the rush towards building "National Champions" was the result of a winner's curse problem, the trend may have run its course (Danthine, Giavazzi, & von Thadden, 2001). It is, therefore, the time that the National Champions start naturally spilling across borders as well. But we should note that: (1) cost savings are often impossible in cross-border mergers and (2) current cross-border mergers have produced negative combined cumulative abnormal returns.[5]

Nevertheless to facilitate cross-border M&As, further national supervisors need to treat domestic and cross-border merger candidacies more equally (Barros, Berglöf, Fulghieri, Gual, Mayer, & Vives, 2005; Walkner & Raes, 2005). Indeed, in a few high-profile cross-border M&A attempts that took place in Europe, national supervisors wielded their informal and/or formal mandate in the bank merger review process to derail or maim the planned cross-border bank merger. The role of banking supervisors in the merger review process is a natural and undisputable proper corollary to: (1) its licensing mandate (capital requirements, "fit and proper management", etc.); (2) its role in the bank default or restructuring process and (3) its general engagement and responsibility for the maintenance of banking sector stability (Carletti & Hartmann, 2003). However, it appears as if in a number of these recent instances national banking supervisors were mobilized or swayed by domestic political interests to block European cross-border bank mergers, fielding arguments of improper management or financial instability as only the flimsiest of excuses.[6] Further pressure from the European executive branch and judicial system, and enhanced national supervisory independence should put a stop to such rather dubious practices.

6.3.2. Impact of Technology

6.3.2.1. Impact of technology on competition   The impact of technological advances on banking competition is not as straightforward as may seem at first sight. Of course, developments in *communication* technology may undermine the "tyranny of distance", intensify competition in banking markets, and improve overall conditions and credit availability. For example, on-line banking spurs competition and diminishes the impact of distance on rates in Bouckaert and Degryse (1995). And Vesala (2000) indeed find that loan mark-ups were decreasing substantially in recent years in Finland, in lock step with the rapid development of Internet and mobile banking in that country. On the other hand, Corvoisier and Gropp (2001) find only a small increase in contestability in European loan markets in recent years despite technological advances in many countries and despite an increase in contestability in deposit markets.

An article by Hauswald and Marquez (2003) offers a potential explanation for these differential findings. In their model better access to information by banks leads to more competition and lower loan rates, but the improved ability by banks to *process* information actually leads to higher loan rates and higher bank profits as banks are better able to "carve out a niche" and generate informational rents.

There are quite a few other takes on how advances in communication technology and increased capacity for information need not imply more exchange of information and hence competition. First, take information exchange *inside the banks*. Wilhelm (2001), for example, argues that loan officers have limited incentives to transfer information, as they are the content originators but also the monopolists in the human capital needed to create proper credit assessments. Hence loan officers may try to tie the now commodity-like distribution (sending reports by e-mail) to its origination. They can do so by arguing some information that cannot be hardened or is too sensitive to move through the bank (or branch) organization.

The advances in communication technology and increased capacity for information also need not imply more exchange of information *between firms and banks*. For example, Yosha (1995) and Bhattacharya and Chiesa (1995) have argued that firms choose the type and the number of financiers on the basis of concerns for confidentiality vis-à-vis product market competitors regarding proprietary information (R&D results, etc.). Similar concerns refrain firms from giving the chosen financier(s) more specific information or limit the format in which the information is transferred (e.g., firms prefer to provide oral presentations rather than supply full-fledged project manuals; improved communication technology has not altered this desire).

Finally, technological developments not necessarily enhance sharing of information *between banks*. While technological progress shapes the structure of the information sharing industry itself (e.g., as it allows exploiting economies of scale), the degree of information sharing or incentives to share information may remain unaffected. Concerns about free riding between banks and adverse selection, and moral hazard at the firm level have long been recognized as a driver of the determination of the optimal degree of information sharing. Even dramatically lower costs of information sharing may not alter such fundamental strategic calculations (Padilla & Pagano, 1997; Bouckaert & Degryse, 2004). Similarly, Vercammen (1995), for example, argues that it is optimal for information sharing bureaus to limit the number of years of credit history that is maintained in the database. Not for technological reasons (e.g., the cost of data storage) but because the incentive of the borrowers for compliance is reduced as credit histories lengthen and the value of a negative piece of information is reduced. And indeed in all European countries surveyed by Jappelli and Pagano (2003) the public credit register eventually "forgets" though the precise memory system varies from country to country. Again, it seems unlikely that technological developments will alter these specific trade-offs.

Now of course technological developments could directly affect competition from capital markets as individual investors can more cheaply obtain and process information. In this way increased capital market competition may push the natural habitat of bank financing towards more opaque firms (Berger & Udell, 1993; Greenbaum & Emmons, 1998; Mannonen 2001).

However, increased capital market competition also leads, for example, to changes in bank orientation away from relationship banking towards more transactional banking and more bank industry specialization (Boot & Thakor, 2000). In contrast, they argue that more interbank competition leads to more relationship lending.[7] Hence any reorientation in Boot and Thakor (2000) alters both financing habitats and informational needs of the banks and possibly affects the impact of technology on the availability of credit.

6.3.2.2. Impact of technology on consolidation   Berger (2003) investigates how advances in technology, in particular in communication and information processing, substantially alter current practices in the banking sector. He argues that recent technological developments affect banking in four areas: (1) the monitoring and risk management of loans; (2) the offering of traditional banking services, through for example improvements in credit scoring; (3) the management of staff and (4) the provision of new services over the Internet.

Economies of scale in each of these areas seem to have spurred bank consolidation (Strahan, 2005). Indeed, there is evidence that large banks implement new technologies, such as credit scoring, securitization and Internet banking faster than small banks (Furst, Lang, & Nolle, 2002; Akhavein, Frame, & White, 2005). In addition, large banks also use older technologies such as telephone and mail more than small banks (Berger, Miller, Petersen, Rajan, & Stein, 2005b).

On the other hand, it is not entirely impossible that small banks can tap into these new information technologies quickly by turning to information exchanges, thereby circumventing scale issues. Kallberg and Udell (2003), for example, show that information exchanges, in particular Dun & Bradstreet in the USA, collect information on potential borrowers' credit history that is actually valuable in predicting future firm failure.

In any case, the recent advances in technology arguably enhance the availability of credit. For example, credit scoring seems to enhance lending to small businesses and to improve the pricing of risks limiting credit rationing (Frame, Srinivasan, & Woosley, 2001; Berger, Frame, & Miller, 2005a), while securitization may reduce the funding costs of, for example, credit card loans and mortgages (Allen, McAndrews, & Strahan, 2002). However consolidation of banks could of course in principle overturn these positive effects, an issue we investigate in the next section.

6.4. The Impact of Integration in the European Banking Sector on the Financing of Innovation

6.4.1. Impact of Competition on the Financing of Innovation

There is ample empirical work investigating the impact of bank market concentration on bank loan rates (Gilbert & Zaretsky, 2003). Though this impact is mostly positive, the magnitude of the impact of the concentration index on loan rates varies widely (Degryse & Ongena, 2005a). Nevertheless, the bottom-line seems to be that lower bank market concentration lowers the cost of credit.

But there are other dimensions one should consider when assessing the impact of competition in the banking sector on the financing of innovative firms. Petersen and Rajan (1995), for example, in their seminal paper investigate the effects of competition between banks not only on the loan rate but also on the availability of bank credit to different types of firms. Petersen and Rajan model shows how especially firms with uncertain future cash flows are negatively affected by competition between banks. Banks may be unwilling to invest in relationships by incurring initial loan losses that may never be recouped in the future (as firms can later on obtain a low loan rate in a competitive banking or financial market).

Petersen and Rajan provide empirical evidence on the impact of concentration both on loan rates and availability of credit. They document that young firms — having uncertain future cash flows — in more concentrated banking markets in the USA obtain substantially lower loan rates than firms in more competitive banking markets. The loan rates decreases by more than 150** bp for *de novo* firms, if the Herfindahl–Hirschman Index (HHI) increases by 0.10. They also document somewhat easier access to bank credit in more concentrated markets, but even for young firms the effects seem modest economically speaking and statistically not always significant. An increase of 0.1 in the HHI roughly augments the percentage trade credit paid before the due date by between 1.5*** and 3*** per cent across all firms and by around 2* to 8 per cent for young firms.

However, it is not clear how the evidence provided by Petersen and Rajan (1995) translates to a European setting. On the one hand, Herrera and Minetti (2005), for a sample of 4000 Italian manufacturing firms, find that the probability that firms innovate is positively affected by the length of the credit relationship with the bank, highlighting the importance that bank–firm relationships could have in channelling resources to the most innovative projects. On the other hand, Angelini, Di Salvo, and Ferri (1998), for a sample of small Italian firms, record no economically significant effect on perceived access to credit.

A complicating factor in interpreting results is that substantial differences exist in the characteristics and the degree of development of the European national banking markets. Take for example the number of bank–firm relationships. Ongena and Smith (2000) document a large cross-country variation in the number of relationships. They find that roughly speaking the number of relationships increases "going south", from 1 in Northern to 15 in Southern Europe. There is further substantial variation in duration of relationships across countries. For example, small US and Belgian firms report relationships to last between 5 and 10 years on average, while small Italian and French firms report 15 years or more.

While theoretical work is continuing to explore this surprising cross-country variation in the basic characteristics of bank–firm relationships (e.g., Detragiache, Garella, & Guiso, 2000; Carletti, 2004; von Rheinbaben & Ruckes, 2004), it is clear that this key feature of a national banking market may determine how changes in the degree of market-wide competition affect the pricing and availability of credit for small and innovative firms. If small firms have many relationships to start with, then changes in the degree of market-wide competition *per se* may not affect their financing conditions much. On the other hand, if the lack of competition sustains small and innovative firms to have few and intense relationships, then fiercer competition may undermine not only these relationships but also the financing of these firms. These firms could be further negatively affected if their main banks succumb to competitive pressures. However, we leave the issue of relationship severance due to bank distress to the next section.

6.4.2. Impact of Consolidation on the Financing of Innovation

6.4.2.1. Short-run effects of consolidation   According to standard thinking, mergers that result in increased market power should raise prices or diminish service quality, resulting in a decline in customer welfare, while gains to efficiency should reduce prices or raise the quality of services, enhancing customer welfare. The welfare implications are straightforward. Mergers harm customers if increased market power offsets the efficiency gains that are passed on to borrowing firms.

But there are exceptions to this standard trade-off. For instance, bank market power may actually benefit certain types of borrowers. As already indicated Petersen and Rajan (1995) argue that concentrated credit markets are required for financing firms with highly uncertain future cash flows. In contrast to Petersen and Rajan (1995), and also discussed earlier, Boot and Thakor (2000) model shows how competition can increase investments in relationship lending. Boot and Thakor view relationship lending as a way to offer a differentiated product that is less subject to price competition.

Even within a competitive market, merger-related efficiency gains need not lead to welfare enhancement for all types of customers (Karceski, Ongena, & Smith, 2005). For example, in an acquisition where the target bank is considered undervalued because it is poorly run, target bank borrowers may be receiving loans at below-cost rates. Part of the reason for the target bank's poor performance is that it makes negative net present value loans. Efforts by new management to improve efficiency could result in higher loan rates to borrowers that received below-cost loans, or denial of credit altogether.

Even when borrowers are profitable to their banks, consolidating banks may exploit efficiencies that negatively impact certain types of borrowers. Berger and Udell (1996), Peek and Rosengren (1996), and Sapienza (2002) find that as banks grow in size, they tend to focus more on financing larger firms. Stein (2002) provides a theoretical explanation for this "size effect in lending," where large banks lend to large firms and small banks lend to small firms.

Large hierarchical banks in Stein (2002) only succeed when information is "hard" enough to flow freely inside the bank. On the other hand, only loan officers at small banks may have the proper incentives to collect and take advantage of "soft" information (that cannot "travel" so easily up the chain of command), precisely the type of information that could be needed to advance relationship banking.[8] Hence the organizational structure of small, decentralized banks is well suited to loan decisions based on "soft" information, such as trust and reputation, which is critical in lending to small firms. If bank consolidation leads to greater organizational complexity, Stein's argument implies that merging banks will seek efficiency gains by shifting their emphasis to large-firm lending. Consequently, without alternative sources of financing, small borrowers of merging banks could be harmed as banks become larger and more complex. And indeed Bonaccorsi di Patti and Gobbi (2003) find evidence credit availability to small firms decreases following a merger.

In addition, borrowers of target banks may be negatively impacted when the merged bank adopts the strategic focus or takes on the characteristics of the acquiring bank. Acquisitions commonly result staff turnover that favour acquirer employees or management, or the adoption of organizational structures and policies familiar to the acquirer. The dismissal of key employees could upset existing lending relationships. In addition, when a bank merger results in changes in the lending policies of the target bank, borrowers comfortable with the previously prevailing system may become confused or dissatisfied with the new post-merger lending practices. Degryse, Masschelein, and Mitchell (2005) analyse Belgian bank mergers and indeed report that: (1) target bank borrowers are more likely to discontinue their relationship and (2) credit availability of single-relationship borrowers who continue at the target bank is negatively affected.

6.4.2.2. Long-run effects of consolidation   It is not clear whether or not we need to expect consolidation to have long-run detrimental effects on the financing of innovative firms. Firstly, Berger, Saunders, Scalise, and Udell (1998), for example, show that the initial decrease in small lending following an M&A is offset by credit supplied by other banks in the same local market. Similarly Garmaise and Moskowitz (2005) establish that the negative effects of reductions in competition following large bank mergers (large mergers are thought to be exogenous to the local market that is being studied) dissipate after 3 years. Similar diffusion of effects is found on the deposit side in the years following Italian bank mergers (Focarelli & Panetta, 2003). Secondly, entry of *de novo* banks may be encouraged by high intermediation margins providing prospective borrowers with additional and actually quite sympathetic sources of funding. There is evidence for the USA on this account. Berger, Bonime, Goldberg, and White (2004), for example, show that the formation of *de novo* banks is higher in markets following consolidation, while DeYoung, Goldberg, and White (1999) find that *de novo* banks focus their lending on small firms. Finally, innovative firms may increasingly tap into alternative sources of finance, that is, venture capital for example.

6.5. Finance and Innovation in Europe

6.5.1. Different Types of Innovation and Sources of Finance

As pointed out in Section 6.2.2, innovations can be classified as being either *incremental* or *breakthrough*. Incremental innovation exploits already existing technology, focuses on cost or feature improvements of existing processes or products, improves competitiveness within markets or industries, and most importantly, the level of uncertainty involved is low. This type of innovations can be evaluated from the perspective of the mainstream business, using traditional evaluation methods and criteria. Banks play a useful role in the financing of these activities.

However, while incremental projects follow a formal and predictable route, a high level of uncertainty is typical of breakthrough innovation projects, which requires flexibility and creativity. When a new technology is introduced there are not only uncertainties about the effectiveness of the technology (which focuses on products and processes with unprecedented performance features), but also about the best management strategies to follow. Diversity of opinion among investors is a characteristic of such projects. Allen and Gale (1999) argue that markets have considerable advantages over intermediated finance when there is no uniformity of initial beliefs among investors:

> A large number of people participate directly in the investment decision. This is costly because each investor has to acquire information to make the decision, but it has the great advantage that each investor makes his own decision based on his own information and his own prior. This ability to agree to disagree allows innovative projects to be financed.

Examples of market finance include initial public offerings (IPOs), private equity market and venture capital firms (though the latter have some features of intermediaries, Allen and Gale considered them under market finance because the small number of investors in each firm and the large number of firms makes it likely that homogeneous beliefs prevail among the investors in a single venture capital firm as opposed to heterogeneity of beliefs among the investors in a bank).

On the other hand with intermediated finance, the decision to invest is delegated to a manager. If there is diversity of opinion some investors will disagree with the manager and may be unwilling to provide funds leading to underfunding of good projects. Moreover a loan officer would tend to apply traditional evaluation methods and criteria, which is inappropriate for radical projects and may lead to premature rejection of good ideas. Hellman (1997) argues that credit committees in banks tend to make decisions to lend based on their assessment of the degree of certainty that the principal will be repaid. And as argued in Section 6.4.2.1, the delegated credit decision process typical of large banks where credit officers make decisions based on hard data, Stein (2002) effectively discourages lending against untested future performance.

In contrast, venture capital has played a key role in the financing of technology-based small firms. It is a special form of financial intermediation with private or institutional investors providing funds to the venture capitalist that allocates them across ventures and provides corporate governance and other services to the entrepreneur. Venture capitalists are willing to accept high levels of risk for high potential profits, do not require collateral or charge interest payments, provide medium- or long-term capital, and most importantly, contribute to the management of the firm by closely overseeing investee firms, by being active board members who step in and control when times get difficult (Lerner, 1995), and by helping in the professionalization of the start-up firm (Hellman & Puri, 2002).

Consistent with the framework developed above and based on a sample of Silicon Valley high-technology start-ups, Hellman and Puri (2000) find that venture-backed firms pursue more radical product and process innovations than non-venture-backed firms. They also find that venture-backed firms are faster in developing their products and bringing them to the market. Finally Kortum and Lerner (2000), also for a sample of US firms, find that venture-backed firms not only produce more patents than non-venture-backed firms, but that these patents are more valuable (more frequently cited by other patents).

However many large banks provide venture capital. Do they play the same role in financing breakthrough innovations as independent venture capitalists? Hellman, Lindsay, and Puri (2005) analyse venture capital data for the USA for the period 1980–2000 and find that banks behave differently from independent venture capitalists. Banks invest less frequently in earlier rounds, syndicate more and invest in larger deals. They also find strong support for the hypothesis that banks strategically invest in venture capital seeking complementarities with their traditional loan business and that this behaviour is mutually advantageous for companies and banks. Specifically, they find that banks invest in deals where the observable characteristics suggest a higher probability of future loan activity, that having a prior venture capital relationship significantly increases a bank's chance of becoming a company's lender, and that firms also benefit by means of lower interest rates from relationship loans than non-relationship loans.

6.5.2. Venture Capital in Europe

6.5.2.1. Europe versus the USA   Bottazzi and Da Rin (2002) summarized the main differences in venture capital between the USA and Europe. They report that Europe invests significantly less in venture capital as a percentage of GDP, a difference that widened further in 2000, when Europe invested 17% compared with 78% for the USA. There is also high cross-country variability in venture capital intensity in Europe (with the Netherlands and the UK being the largest investors, 80% and 38%, respectively). Moreover, while Europe invests less, it supports almost twice the number of companies, leading to significantly smaller amounts invested per company.

They also report that although the amount invested in the early stages in Europe has been increasing since 1997, the total amount invested in the early stage is considerably less than in the USA (in 2000 Europe invested one-fifth of US investment in the early stage).

In a comparative micro-level study of the performance of venture financing in the USA and Europe, Hege, Schwienbacher, and Palomino (2003) also find that the fraction of the total investment devoted to the initial round is higher in the USA than in Europe and that this fact has a significant impact on firm performance. They conclude that US venture capitalists have a better capacity to screen projects and to add value to innovative firms, and that European venture capitalists are more deal-makers and less active monitors. Also compared to Asia, Europe invests a smaller percentage in the early stage, as reported by Allen and Song (2003).

Interestingly there are also profound differences in the funding of venture capitalists, which is certainly related to the fact that Europe is a bank-based system and the USA is a market-based economy. Bottazzi and Da Rin (2002) report that institutional investors, mainly pension funds, contribute about two-thirds of all funds in the USA, compared to one-third in Europe. The largest contributors in Europe are financial institutions, mainly banks that provide another third of the funds.

6.5.2.2. Empirical evidence on European venture capital   In a recent paper Bottazzi, Da Rin, and Hellman (2004) undertake a survey of European venture capital firms for the period 1998–2001 and they report several interesting findings. Firstly, the European venture capital market is surprisingly integrated. Approximately a quarter of all venture capital firms have partners from foreign countries, and a quarter of investments are made in foreign countries, being the USA the most popular destination for foreign investments. Also a third of all European venture capitalists had some work experience in the USA.

Secondly, new entrants in the industry invest more in the seed stage, monitor their investments more closely, have more prior professional experience and are more likely to have a business education and a masters degree.

Finally, and consistent also with Mayer, Schoors, and Yafeh (2004), they find that corporate-owned venture capital firms invest more in early-stage companies, while bank-owned venture capital firms invest more in later-stage activities, and are less likely to frequently monitor their firms or sit on the board of directors.

6.5.3. Impact of European Financial Integration on the Venture Capital Market

Many of the characteristics of venture capital in Europe are related to the fact that Europe is a bank-based economy. In this sense the consolidation of the banking industry that is leading to larger and more diversified financial institutions, could allow banks to increase the funds devoted to high-risk activities such as investments in the venture capital market. However, it is clear from the above discussion that banks are strategic followers rather than leaders in this market. The positive impact of consolidation will be most probably felt in the late stages, when the firm may need additional funding to reach industrial scale production, upgrade facilities and later on when preparing for sale or IPO. Probably bank consolidation will not induce a larger supply of funds for the earlier stages when the firm explores the viability of the project and when it begins to design its organization and corporate strategy.

In this latter respect, the evidence provided by Bottazzi, Da Rin, and Hellman (2004) about the characteristics of new entrants in the industry being more willing to invest in the early stages and to get involved in the management are also encouraging. European integration leading to simplification of tax rules and removal of barriers to cross-country investments will surely help to increase the level of integration already achieved by the industry and could provide private venture capitalists with a boost.

6.6. Conclusion

In this chapter, we address the question whether the *"Lisbon* Agenda" is hurt by the deepening integration of the European financial sector. The Lisbon Agenda sets the stage for growth and innovation, to make Europe by 2010 "the most competitive and dynamic knowledge-based economy in the world, capable of sustainable economic growth with more and better jobs and greater social cohesion". Recent theoretical and empirical work highlights that, precisely, start-ups and other small and young firms are crucial in generating breakthrough innovations in most sectors.

Are small firms hurt by the integration of the European financial sector? The integration of the European banking sector through deregulation and technological progress has mainly led to increased banking competition but also to domestic banking consolidation. Fiercer interbank competition could undermine vital intertemporal risk sharing between bank and innovative firms. Banking consolidation leads to larger banks that may be unwilling or unable to handle loan applications by small innovative firms, as existing information in bank–firm relationships may evaporate.

However, weighing the current evidence we conclude that: (1) competition and relationship finance are not necessarily inimical and (2) based on USA evidence, other existing or *de novo* banks may accommodate the reduced credit availability over time and (3) the deepening venture capital markets in Europe may play a key role in "filling up the potential financing gap".

Endnotes

1. We received valuable comments from Ivan Mortimer-Schutts. We gratefully acknowledge financial support from the Groupe d'Economie Mondiale at Sciences Po and AEI-Brookings (Paris).
2. These numbers do not take into account other government support such as financial incentives, government payments as part of contracts and procurement, and public support to research infrastructures (see Dosi, Llerena, & Labini, 2005).
3. They are (1) extend and deepen the Internal Market, (2) ensure open and competitive markets inside and outside, (3) improve European and national regulation, (4) expand and improve European infrastructure, (5) increase and improve investment in Research and Development, (6) facilitate innovation, the uptake of ICT and the sustainable use of resources, (7) contribution to a strong European industrial base, (8) attract more

people into employment and modernize social protection systems, (9) improve the adaptability of workers and enterprises and the flexibility of labour markets, and (10) providing incentives for the acquisition of skills, knowledge and human capital.

4. We star the coefficients to indicate their significance levels: *** significant at 1%, ** significant at 5%, and * significant at 10%.

5. A nice recent study by Beitel, Schiereck, and Wahrenburg (2004), for example, documents that the combined cumulative abnormal returns for stocks of bidder and target bank in cross-border bank M&As in Europe over the last few decades is actually zero or negative! This finding stands in stark contrast with other industries where the combined CARs of cross-border M&As are typically found to be positive. Hence investors seemingly evaluate cross-border bank M&As as destroying value. A recent paper by Campa and Hernando (2004) suggests the (lingering) effects of regulation may play a role. Their study shows that the combined CARs of M&As are typically lower in industries, such as banking, that until recently were under government control or are still or were most heavily regulated. CARs of cross-border M&As in these industries are actually negative, evidence in line with Beitel et al. (2004).

6. Domestic mergers also heighten the too-big-to-fail concern, especially when national governments have a policy of protecting National Champions. This policy can lead to large banks taking excessive risk, in particular when facing difficulties. See Vives (2001) for a review of the European cases and Kane (2000) and Penas and Unal (2004) for US evidence.

7. Degryse and Ongena (2005b) and Elsas and Krahnen (1998) provide empirical evidence broadly supporting both hypotheses.

8. Berger et al. (2005b) provide suggestive evidence corroborating elements of Stein's model. They find, for example, that large banks have less exclusive and shorter relationships and interact more impersonally with their borrowers. Liberti (2002) documents how delegation increases monitoring efforts by relationship managers.

References

Adam, K., Jappelli, T., Menichini, A., Padula, M., & Pagano, M. (2002). *Analyse, compare, and apply alternative indicators and monitoring methodologies to measure the evolution of capital market integration in the European Union*. Centre for Studies in Economics and Finance, Salerno IT.

Aghion, P., Bloom, N., Blundell, R., Griffith, R., & Howitt, P. (2005). Competition and innovation: An inverted-U relationship. *Quarterly Journal of Economics, 120*, 701–728.

Akhavein, J., Frame, W.S., & White, L.J. (2005). The diffusion of financial innovations: An examination of the adoption of small business credit scoring by large banking organizations. *Journal of Business, 78*, 577–596.

Allen, F., & Gale, D. (1999). Diversity of opinion and financing of new technologies. *Journal of Financial Intermediation, 8*, 68–89.

Allen, F., & Gale, D. (2000). *Comparing financial systems*. Cambridge: MIT Press.

Allen, F., McAndrews, J., & Strahan, P. (2002). E-Finance: An introduction. *Journal of Financial Services Research, 22*, 5–27.

Allen, F., & Song, W. (2003). *Venture capital and corporate governance*. Wharton Financial Institutions Center, Philadelphia.

Angelini, P., Di Salvo, R., & Ferri, G. (1998). Availability and cost of credit for small businesses: Customer relationships and credit cooperatives. *Journal of Banking and Finance, 22*, 925–954.

Arrow, K.J. (1962). *Economic welfare and the allocation of resources for innovation*. Princeton: Princeton University Press.

Barros, P.P., Berglöf, E., Fulghieri, P., Gual, J., Mayer, C., & Vives, X. (2005). *Integration of European banks: The way forward*. Centre for Economic Policy Research, London.

Barth, J.R., Caprio, G., & Levine, R. (2001). The regulations and supervision of banks around the world: A new database. World Bank, Washington, DC.

Baumol, W.J. (2004). *Education for innovation: entrepreneurial breakthroughs vs. corporate incremental improvements*. National Bureau for Economic Research, Boston, MA.

Beitel, P., Schiereck, D., & Wahrenburg, M. (2004). Explaining M&A success in European banks. *European Financial Management, 10*, 109–140.

Berger, A.N. (2003). The economic effects of technological progress: evidence from the banking industry. *Journal of Money, Credit, and Banking, 35*, 141–176.

Berger, A.N., Bonime, S.D., Goldberg, L.G., & White, L.J. (2004). The dynamics of market entry: The effects of mergers and acquisitions on entry in the banking industry. *Journal of Business, 77*, 797–834.

Berger, A.N., Demsetz, R., & Strahan, P. (1999). The consolidation of the financial services industry: causes, consequences, and implications for the Future. *Journal of Banking and Finance, 23*, 135–194.

Berger, A.N., Frame, W.S., & Miller, N.M. (2005a). Credit scoring and the availability, price and risk of small business credit. *Journal of Money, Credit, and Banking, 37*, 191–222.

Berger, A.N., Miller, N.M., Petersen, M.A., Rajan, R.G., & Stein, J.C. (2005b). Does function follow organizational form? Evidence from the lending practices of large and small banks. *Journal of Financial Economics, 76*, 237–269.

Berger, A.N., Saunders, A., Scalise, J.M., & Udell, G.F. (1998). The effects of bank mergers and acquisistions on small business lending. *Journal of Financial Economics, 50*, 187–230.

Berger, A.N., & Udell, G.F. (1993). Securitization, risk and the liquidity problem in banking. In: M. Klausner, & L.J. White (Eds), *Structural change in banking*. New York: University Salomon Center.

Berger, A.N., & Udell, G.F. (1996). Universal banking and the future of small business lending. In: A. Saunders, & W. Ingo (Eds), *Financial system design: The case for universal banking*. Homewood: Irwin Publishing.

Bertrand, M., Schoar, A., & Thesmar, D. (2004). *Banking deregulation and industry structure: Evidence from the French banking reforms of 1985*. University of Chicago, Chicago.

Bhattacharya, S., & Chiesa, G. (1995). Proprietary information, financial intermediation, and research Incentives. *Journal of Financial Intermediation, 4*, 328–357.

Bonaccorsi di Patti, E., & Gobbi, G. (2003). *The effects of bank mergers on credit availability: Evidence from corporate data*. Bank of Italy, Rome IT.

Boone, J., & van Damme, E. (2004). *Marktstructuur en innovatie*. TILEC Tilburg University, Tilburg.

Boot, A.W.A., & Thakor, A.V. (2000). Can relationship banking survive competition? *Journal of Finance, 55*, 679–713.

Bottazzi, L., & Da Rin, M. (2002). Venture capital in Europe and the financing of innovative companies. *Economic Policy, 17*, 229–269.

Bottazzi, L., Da Rin, M., & Hellman, T. (2004). The changing face of the European venture capital industry: Facts and analysis. *Journal of Private Equity, 7*, 26–53.

Bouckaert, J., & Degryse, H. (1995). Phonebanking. *European Economic Review, 39*, 229–244.

Bouckaert, J., & Degryse, H. (2004). Softening competition by inducing switching in credit markets. *Journal of Industrial Economics, 52*, 27–52.

Buch, C.M. (2004). Distance and international banking. Forthcoming in *Review of International Economics*.

Campa, J.M., & Hernando, I. (2004). Shareholder value creation in European M&As. *European Financial Management, 10*, 47–81.

Carletti, E. (2004). The structure of bank relationships, endogenous monitoring, and loan rates. *Journal of Financial Intermediation, 13*, 58–86.

Carletti, E., & Hartmann, P. (2003). Competition and stability: What's special about banking? In: P. Mizen (Ed.), *Monetary history, exchange rates and financial markets: Essays in honour of charles goodhart*. Cheltenham: Edward Elgar.

Cetorelli, N. (2004). Real effects of bank competition. *Journal of Money, Credit, and Banking, 36,* 543–558.

Corvoisier, S., & Gropp, R. (2001). *Contestability, technology, and banking.* European Central Bank, Frankfurt.

Danthine, J.-P., Giavazzi, F., & von Thadden, E.-L. (2001). European financial markets after EMU: A first assessement. In: C. Wyplosz (Ed.), *EMU: Its impact on Europe and the world.* Oxford: Oxford University Press.

Degryse, H., Masschelein, N., & Mitchell, J. (2005). *SMEs and Bank lending relationships: The impact of mergers.* CentER Tilburg University, Tilburg.

Degryse, H., & Ongena, S. (2004). The impact of technology and regulation on the geographical scope of banking. *Oxford Review of Economic Policy, 20,* 571–590.

Degryse, H., & Ongena, S. (2005a). Competition and regulation in the banking sector: A review of the empirical evidence on the sources of bank rents. In: A.W.A. Boot, & A.V. Thakor (Eds), *Handbook of corporate finance: Financial intermediation and banking.* London: North Holland.

Degryse, H., & Ongena, S. (2005b). *The impact of competition on bank orientation and specialization.* Tilburg University, Tilburg.

Demirguc-Kunt, A., Laeven, L., & Levine, R. (2004). Regulations, market structure, Institutions, and the cost of financial intermediation. *Journal of Money, Credit, and Banking, 36,* 563–583.

Detragiache, E., Garella, P.G., & Guiso, L. (2000). Multiple versus single banking relationships: Theory and evidence. *Journal of Finance, 55,* 1133–1161.

DeYoung, R., Goldberg, L.G., & White, L.J. (1999). Youth, adolescence, and maturity of banks: Credit availability to small business in an era of banking consolidation. *Journal of Banking and Finance, 23,* 463–492.

Dosi, G., Llerena, P., & Labini, M.S. (2005). *Evaluating and comparing innovation performance of the United States and the European Union.* TrendChart Policy, Brussels.

Elsas, R., & Krahnen, J.P. (1998). Is relationship lending special? Evidence from credit-file data in Germany. *Journal of Banking and Finance, 22,* 1283–1316.

Ergungor, O.E. (2003). *Financial system structure and economic development: Structure matters.* Federal Reserve Bank of Cleveland, Cleveland.

Focarelli, D., & Panetta, F. (2003). Are mergers beneficial to consumers? Evidence from the market for bank deposits. *American Economic Review, 93,* 1152–1171.

Frame, W.S., Srinivasan, A., & Woosley, L. (2001). The effect of credit scoring on small-business lending. *Journal of Money, Credit, and Banking, 33,* 813–825.

Freeman, C. (1987). *Technology and economic performance, lessons from Japan.* London: Pinter.

Furst, K., Lang, W.W., & Nolle, D.E. (2002). Internet banking. *Journal of Financial Services Research, 22,* 95–117.

Galindo, A., Schiantarelli, F., & Weiss, A. (2005). *Does financial liberalization improve the allocation of investment? Micro evidence from developing countries.* Boston College, Boston.

Garmaise, M.J., & Moskowitz, T.J. (2005). Bank mergers and crime: The real and social effects of credit market competition. Forthcoming in *Journal of Finance.*

Garrett, T.A., Wagner, G.A., & Wheelock, D.C. (2004). *A spatial analysis of state banking regulation.* Federal Reserve Bank of St. Louis, St. Louis, MO.

Giannetti, M., & Ongena, S. (2005). *Financial integration and entrepreneurial activity: Evidence from foreign bank entry in emerging markets.* European Central Bank, Frankfurt.

Gilbert, R.A., & Zaretsky, A.M. (2003). Banking antitrust: Are the assumptions still valid? *Review of the Federal Reserve Bank of St. Louis,* 29–52.

Gilbert, R.J., & Newbery, D.M.G. (1982). Preemptive patenting and the persistence of monopoly. *American Economic Review, 72,* 514–526.

Greenbaum, S.I., & Emmons, W.R. (1998). Twin information revolutions and the future of financial intermediation. In: Y. Amihud, & G. Miller (Eds), *Bank mergers and acquisitions*. New York: Kluwer.

Grossman, G.M., & Helpman, E. (1991). Trade, knowledge spillovers, and growth. *European Economic Review, 35,* 517–526.

Hauswald, R., & Marquez, R. (2003). Information technology and financial services competition. *Review of Financial Studies, 16,* 921–948.

Hege, U., Schwienbacher, A., & Palomino, F. (2003). Determinants of venture capital performance: Europe and the United States. RICAFE, Amsterdam.

Hellman, T. (1997). Venture capital: A challenge for commercial banks. *Journal of Private Equity, 1,* 49–55.

Hellman, T., Lindsay, L., & Puri, M. (2005). *Building relationships early: Banks in venture capital.* UBC, Vancouver BC.

Hellman, T., & Puri, M. (2000). The interaction between product market and financing strategy: The role of venture capital. *Review of Financial Studies, 13,* 959–984.

Hellman, T., & Puri, M. (2002). Venture capital and the professionalization of start-up firms: Empirical evidence. *Journal of Finance, 57,* 169–198.

Herrera, A.M., & Minetti, R. (2005). *Informed finance and technological change: Evidence from credit relationships.* Michigan State University, Lansing, MI.

Jappelli, T., & Pagano, M. (2003). Public credit information: A European perspective. In: M.J. Miller (Ed.), *Credit reporting systems and the international economy.* Cambridge: MIT Press.

Jayaratne, J., & Strahan, P.E. (1996). The finance-growth nexus: Evidence from bank branch deregulation. *Quarterly Journal of Economics, 111,* 639–670.

Jayaratne, J., & Strahan, P.E. (1998). Entry restrictions, industry evolution, and dynamic efficiency: Evidence from commercial banking. *Journal of Law and Economics, 41,* 239–274.

Kallberg, J.G., & Udell, G.F. (2003). The value of private sector business credit information sharing: The US case. *Journal of Banking and Finance, 27,* 449–469.

Kane, E. (2000). Incentives for banking megamergers: What motives might regulators infer from event study evidence? *Journal of Money, Credit, and Banking, 32,* 671–701.

Karceski, J., Ongena, S., & Smith, D.C. (2005). The impact of bank consolidation on commercial borrower welfare. *Journal of Finance, 60,* 2043–2082.

King, R.G., & Levine, R. (1993). Finance and growth: Schumpeter may be right. *Quarterly Journal of Economics, 108,* 713–737.

Kortum, S., & Lerner, J. (2000). Assessing the contribution of venture capital to innovation. *RAND Journal of Economics, 31,* 674–692.

Kroszner, R.S., & Strahan, P.E. (1999). What drives deregulation? Economics and politics of the relaxation of bank branching restrictions. *Quarterly Journal of Economics, 124,* 1437–1467.

La Porta, R., Lopez-de-Silanes, F., Shleifer, A., & Vishny, R.W. (1998). Law and finance. *Journal of Political Economy, 106,* 1113–1155.

Lerner, J. (1995). Venture capitalists and the oversight of private firms. *Journal of Finance, 50,* 301–318.

Levine, R. (2002). Bank-based or market-based financial systems: Which is better? *Journal of Financial Intermediation, 11,* 1–30.

Levine, R., Loayza, N., & Beck, T. (2000). Financial intermediation and growth: Causality and causes. *Journal of Monetary Economics, 46,* 31–77.

Liberti, J.M. (2002). *Initiative, incentives and soft information: How does delegation impact the role of bank relationship managers?* University of Chicago, Chicago, IL.

Mannonen, P. (2001). *Advancing information technology and financial intermediation.* Research Institute of the Finnish Economy, Helsinki.

Mayer, C., Schoors, K., & Yafeh, Y. (2004). Sources of funds and investment activities of venture capital funds: Evidence from Germany, Israel, Japan and the United Kingdom. Forthcoming in *Journal of Corporate Finance*, 10.

OECD (2003). *The sources of economic growth in the OECD countries*. Organization for Economic Cooperation and Development, Paris.

Ongena, S., & Smith, D.C. (2000). What determines the number of bank relationships? Cross-country evidence. *Journal of Financial Intermediation, 9*, 26–56.

Padilla, A.J., & Pagano, M. (1997). Endogenous communication among lenders and entrepreneurial incentives. *Review of Financial Studies, 10*, 205–236.

Peek, J., & Rosengren, E.S. (1996). Small business credit availability: How important is the size of lender? In: A. Saunders, & W. Ingo (Eds), *Financial system design: The case for universal banking*. Homewood: Irwin Publishing.

Penas, M.F., & Unal, H. (2004). Gains in bank mergers: Evidence from the bond markets. *Journal of Financial Economics, 74*, 149–179.

Petersen, M.A., & Rajan, R.G. (1995). The effect of credit market competition on lending relationships. *Quarterly Journal of Economics, 110*, 406–443.

Rajan, R.G., & Zingales, L. (1998). Financial dependence and growth. *American Economic Review*, 559–586.

Sapienza, P. (2002). The effects of banking mergers on loan contracts. *Journal of Finance*, 329–368.

Schumpeter, J.A. (1942). *Capitalism, socialism, and democracy*. New York: Harper and Brothers.

Solow, R. (1956). A contribution to the theory of economic growth. *Quarterly Journal of Economics*, 65–94.

Stein, J. (2002). Information production and capital allocation: Decentralized versus hierarchical firms. *Journal of Finance, 57*, 1891–1922.

Stiroh, K., & Strahan, P. (2003). Competitive dynamics of deregulation: Evidence from US banking. *Journal of Money, Credit, and Banking, 35*, 801–828.

Strahan, P. (2005). Bank structure and lending: What we do and do not know. In: A.W.A. Boot, & A.V. Thakor (Eds), *Handbook of corporate finance: Financial intermediation and banking*. London: North Holland.

Symeonidis, G. (1996). *Innovation, firm size and market structure: Schumpeterian hypotheses and some new themes*. Organization for Economic Cooperation and Development, Paris.

Vercammen, J.A. (1995). Credit bureau policy and sustainable reputation effects in credit markets. *Economica, 62*, 461–478.

Vesala, J. (2000). Technological transformation and retail banking competition: Implications and measurement. Bank of Finland, Helsinki.

Vives, X. (2001). Restructuring financial regulation in the European Monetary Union. *Journal of Financial Services Research, 19*, 57–82.

von Rheinbaben, J., & Ruckes, M. (2004). The number and the closeness of bank relationships. *Journal of Banking and Finance, 28*, 1597–1615.

Walkner, C., & Raes, J.-P. (2005). *Integration and consolidation in EU banking: An unfinished business*. European Commission Directorate-General for Economic and Financial Affairs, Brussels.

Wilhelm, W.J. (2001). The Internet and financial market structure. *Oxford Review of Economic Policy, 17*, 235–247.

WorldBank (2004). *World Bank Group support for small business*. World Bank, Washington, DC.

Yosha, O. (1995). Information disclosure costs and the choice of financing source. *Journal of Financial Intermediation, 4*, 3–20.

PART 2

CORPORATE GOVERNANCE

Chapter 7

Transatlantic Corporate Governance Reform

Joseph McCahery and Arman Khachaturyan

7.1. Introduction

The reduction in barriers to trade and the liberalization of financial markets, transportation and telecommunications have created the basis for the increase in flows of factors of production between jurisdictions. With the prospect of more capital mobility, it becomes conventional wisdom that national governments are prompted to perform their economic policy functions more efficiently. Indeed, the EU and US have developed successful policy strategies over time to encourage more competitive capital, product and labor markets while erecting few barriers that could deter substantial benefits. Nevertheless, many scholars view current efforts with a mixture of skepticism and optimism, arguing that the system of rules and institutions has insufficient incentives and capacity to foster equilibrium levels of efficient investments. At the same time, most serious proponents of liberalization accept that the separate interests within each country may lead to divergences in the optimal outcome with respect to standards. Consequently, much of the debate over finding agreement on the level of optimal standards is thought to turn on whether, all things considered, regulators can press for agreement on the level of standards to set. Underlying this fundamental policy question is the concern that the capacity to come to agreement on higher standards will lead to substantial benefits.

The EU and US are enjoying increased and unprecedented integration of their economies. Together they account for the largest share of international capital and banking flows, levels of trade, investments and securities transactions. If anything, this transatlantic economic partnership reflects the common will and commitment to strengthen transatlantic relations by upgrading the institutional framework of dialog, identifying specific challenges, reducing transatlantic trade barriers and promoting bilateral trade. The US–EU summit of 2004 further confirmed the common commitment toward the establishment of a multilateral trading system governed by rules, as well as policies to produce strong and sustained economic growth, and to create the cooperative means and best practices to reinforce the underlying basis of the transatlantic economic partnership.

While there are a number of financial and regulatory difficulties that are sufficient to pose a threat to increased transatlantic trade and efficient transatlantic capital markets, the EU and

Advances in Corporate Finance and Asset Pricing
Edited by L. Renneboog
ISBN: 0-444-52723-0

US launched the Regulatory Cooperation and the Financial Markets Regulatory Dialogue in 2002. The initiative is designed to promote transatlantic trade through establishing a better quality regulation and minimize the divergences in the laws and policies of the two jurisdictions. A similar function is also served by the establishment of the Regulatory Dialogue as a forum for discussion of issues of bilateral corporate governance and financial market regulation, which have recently been given increased preference in national regulatory policies.

The high-profile corporate fallouts of recent years have underscored the interconnection and interdependency of transatlantic economies and the need for regulators to work cooperatively to create timely and effective solutions to improve transatlantic auditing and governance policies. Whereas corporate governance failures usually occur at the national level, there is no denying that the recent financial scandals at Enron and Parmalat involved questionable dealings (Special Purpose Entities (SPEs), improper swap arrangements and flaws in financial disclosure) that took on a global dimension. These scandals provoked a variety of responses and brought the issue of transatlantic governance and accountability to the attention of law-makers and the public. Responding rapidly to the corporate scandals, the US Congress enacted the Sarbanes-Oxley Act (hereafter referred to as SOXA) in 2002, the most comprehensive legislative package in the history of US corporate regulation since the Securities Acts of 1933 and 1934.

The SOXA introduced sweeping reforms in corporate governance systems of publicly traded companies aimed at increasing the disciplinary systems of managers and gatekeepers. In an attempt to restore public trust and confidence in corporate accounting and reporting, the SOXA was designed to improve the governance and accountability of boards, managers and gatekeepers by inducing increased oversight and monitoring of US-listed companies and reputational intermediaries. In addition to the audit reforms, the SOXA put in place a number of measures specifically designed to counter the governance failures. These include requiring Chief Executing Officers (CEOs) and Chief Financial Officers (CFOs) to certify, on pain of criminal penalties, their firms' periodic reports and the effectiveness of internal controls; the imposition of obligations on corporate lawyers to report any evidence of suspected violations of securities law; the prohibition of corporate loans to managers or directors; restrictions on stock sales by executives during 'blackout periods'; and requiring firms to establish an independent audit committee, of which at least one member must be a financial expert. At the same time, the NYSE and NASDAQ quickly proposed new corporate governance guidelines.

The wave of US regulatory reform that followed the collapse of Enron has spilled over into Europe. Most directly, the SOXA applies to non-US firms that are listed on a US exchange and obliges EU audit firms to register with the US Public Accounting Oversight Board (PCAOB). This extraterritorial application has triggered widespread criticism in Europe. An indirect effect of the events in the US has been to provoke a host of parallel reforms in the EU. Interestingly, EU policy-makers quickly responded to the US scandals by accelerating their own company law modernization and corporate governance reform program that was earlier instituted by the Commission through the High Level Working Group, chaired by Professor Jaap Winter. EU regulators were motivated by a concern to ensure that US collapses are not replicated in Europe, a desire to ensure that domestic and EU legislation reflect best practice and the need to give credibility to claims of regulatory parity for the purposes of negotiations over the extraterritorial impact of US law.

In their second report, the Group recommended strengthening mandatory disclosure obligations for listed companies, granting special investigation rights to minority investors and considering the introduction of a disqualification sanction for directors associated with misleading disclosures. Besides these reforms, the Group suggested the development by EU member states of UK-style codes of best practice, primarily enforced by markets through 'comply or explain' mechanisms, improved investor access to corporate information through the use of electronic dissemination facilities and the strengthening of shareholders' rights to vote via electronic means.

Taking up the recommendations of the High Level Group to establish a new framework for corporate governance, the EU launched its Action Plan in May 2003.[1] The Action Plan is intended to give a fresh and ambitious impetus to EU company law harmonization and is meant to meet three challenges in the area of corporate governance:

1. improving the integrity and accountability of board members;
2. restoring the auditors' credibility;
3. promoting fair presentation of the company through sound and reliable accounting and hence, restoring investor confidence and fostering efficiency and competitiveness of businesses in the EU.

This chapter examines the major transatlantic regulatory challenges posed by the latest spate of regulation promulgated on both sides of the Atlantic. While some question whether the reforms are optimally designed to limit future financial frauds or whether they pose excessive burdens for small businesses, EU and US policy-makers, in contrast, contend that it is important to work out cooperative solutions for improving governance performance overall. The development of a 'transatlantic practice' is underway and regulators, lawyers and other parties in the fields of accounting, corporate law and securities regulation are influencing its development, leading to the adoption of common standards and convergence in legal techniques to solve similar problems.

Despite these substantive reforms, corporate law remains a domestic matter. Interestingly, securities regulators, who have been developing the recent regulatory innovations, have been a significant influence on the developments that have taken place in EU company law. Similar incursions into the terrain of US corporate law were not significant until legal changes were introduced by the SOXA in 2002. To be sure, impediments remain on both sides of the Atlantic, and questions remain as to whether and how adoption of common standards and convergent measures will influence transatlantic market developments. This policy briefly concludes by arguing that regulatory diversity rather than harmonization will be more conducive toward the establishment of a truly transatlantic marketplace. See Table 7.1 for an overview of the main characteristics of the principal actors on the corporate governance stage of the USA and selected EU member states.

7.2. Transatlantic Regulatory Challenges

In the post-scandal era, the EU and US have continued to face increased transatlantic regulatory challenges. These challenges stem in part from the corporate fallouts and the subsequent regulatory responses, and more comprehensively from the ambition to design an international regulatory and supervisory system of cooperation in accounting and auditing.

Whereas the EU's reform moves remain nascent and have been treated with indifference in the US, the cross-border implications of the SOXA and its 'moral DNA' for US-listed

Table 7.1: Main characteristics of transatlantic corporate governance players.

Country	US	UK	Germany	France	Italy
Employees	Flexible labor Low unionization Employment at will	Flexible labor market	Work councils Co-determination High skills Non-flexible labor market	Work councils Low unionization Short-term contracts	Long-term contracts Rigid labor market Medium skills
Shareholders	Institutional investors and individuals Dispersed	Institutional investors Dispersed	Other non-financial companies Banks	Foreign investors State	State Families
Government	Liberal policies Arms length Weak takeover barriers	Liberal policies Arms length Weak takeover barriers	Protectionist policies Medium takeover barriers	Protectionist policies Interventionist Medium takeover barriers	Protectionist policies Interventionist Strong takeover barriers
Boards of Directors	High activism High percentage of outsiders due to investor pressure	High activism High percentage of outsiders determined by law	Moderate activism Stakeholders as a significant minority Medium size	Moderate activism Minority outsiders Medium size	Low activism Large % of insiders Medium size
Top Management Team	Professional (finance/MBA) background Some foreign-born management Open labor markets	Semi-professional background Some foreign-born management Open labor markets	Technical background Few foreign-born managers Closed labor markets (long term)	Common educational backgrounds State links Few foreign-born managers Closed labor markets (long term)	Non-professional No foreign-born management Closed labor markets (long term)

Source: Mastering Corporate Governance. *Financial Times*, May 27, 2005.

European companies have raised apprehensions and objections in the EU for creating 'unnecessary extraterritorial consequences' and 'unnecessary difficulties'. EU policy-makers and businesses alike have expressed growing discontent that the extension of SOXA requirements to US-listed European companies is costly and might possibly oblige these European companies to de-list from major US markets such as NYSE and NASDAQ. Moreover, the SOXA has been perceived as an attempt to export US corporate governance rules with disregard to the distinct legal and institutional framework in the EU and the very virtue of the EU's approach to regulatory reform. Against this background, a number of pending transatlantic regulatory challenges remain high on the agenda of policy-makers on both sides of the Atlantic. We turn next to the most significant reform measure that has emerged from the governance crises.

7.2.1. Internal Controls

The first transatlantic regulatory challenge relates to compliance with SOXA's internal controls standards. According to the SOXA, management of a US-listed company is required to file a report that should state:

1. management's responsibilities for establishing and maintaining adequate internal controls and procedures over financial reporting;
2. management's assessment about the effectiveness of the company's internal controls as of the end of the company's most recent fiscal year, including a statement as to whether the controls are effective;
3. any 'material weaknesses' in internal controls that management has identified;
4. the framework used by management to evaluate the effectiveness of the company's internal controls;
5. an outside auditor's attestation to and report on management's evaluation of the company's internal controls and procedures for financial reporting.[2]

Moreover, managers are responsible for creating, maintaining and regularly evaluating the effectiveness of a system of 'disclosure controls and procedures'. As noted above, the CEO and CFO are accountable for reliability and accuracy of both the financial and non-financial information contained in their periodic reports and internal accounting controls. They must personally certify for compliance and take personal responsibility (criminal penalties) for non-compliance.[3]

Whereas the Securities and Exchange Commission (SEC) states that such internal controls standards and compliance measures are necessary to enhance US investor confidence and promote deep and liquid capital markets, critics note that the new reporting demands of SOXA Section 404 are perceived in the EU as imposing unjustified costs and time-consuming transitions on all US-listed EU companies. For many types of firms, these regulations impose costs but bring few benefits to investors.

Following intense lobbying efforts from the EU and European businesses and faced with possible de-listing of European companies from the US capital markets, the SEC has recently granted a year-long reprieve to non-US-listed companies from SOXA's internal controls standards. As a result, European companies have to implement US internal controls standards by July 15, 2006.

7.2.2. Auditing Standards

The second transatlantic regulatory challenge concerns the recent shift in auditing standards. In an effort to create a more independent and accountable audit environment, the SOXA puts significant emphasis on the regulation of not only accounting and auditing practices of a registered public accounting firm but also that of any Certified Public Accountant (CPA) associated therewith, and any CPA working as an auditor of a publicly traded company. The SOXA establishes a direct reporting responsibility between the auditor and the audit committee of the issuer, subjects audit and non-audit services to pre-approval by the audit committee, limits non-audit services to be provided by an auditor to the issuer, clearly defines rules for audit and non-audit service fees, regulates the conflict of interest between the auditor and the issuer, and requires more frequent rotation of lead and review audit partners.

Moreover, following the SOXA's enactment, the SEC ended a long era of self-regulation and established PCAOB as a regulator. Subject to SEC oversight and aimed at protecting public interest in 'informative, accurate and independent audit reports' for publicly traded companies, the function of PCAOB is to:

1. register public accounting firms;
2. establish, or adopt, by rule, 'auditing, quality control, ethics, independence and other standards relating to the preparation of audit reports for issuers';
3. conduct inspections of accounting firms;
4. conduct investigations and disciplinary proceedings, and impose appropriate sanctions;
5. perform such other duties or functions as necessary or appropriate;
6. enforce compliance with the Act, the rules of the Board, professional standards and the securities laws relating to the preparation and issuance of audit reports, and the obligations and liabilities of accountants with respect thereto.[4]

As we have already seen, the fact that PCAOB authority extends to any non-US accounting firm that 'prepares and furnishes' audit and accounting services to any US-listed company has further sharpened the focus of transatlantic regulatory dialog and became one of the major points of contention between the USA and EU.[5] EU policy-makers and industry groups have expressed their discontent that any European accounting firm that provides material services to publicly traded companies in the US should supply its work papers upon the request of the PCAOB or the SEC and be subject to their controls. Moreover, the fact that European accounting companies that do not issue audit reports but are still substantially involved in the process of their preparation are treated as a public accounting firms, for SOXA purposes, is likely to cause continued irritation in the EU until convergence or equivalence has been achieved.

Even though EU policy-makers and European businesses have insisted on mutual recognition of equivalent systems of auditing, the SEC remains skeptical of European audit practices, which may impede progress in this area. The SEC takes the view that EU standards, which are largely national and rely on enforcement by national-level regulators, are not adequate in most respects and contrast poorly to the level of regulation in place in the US. While the SEC acknowledges that there may be some variation in standards, the US investor is nevertheless entitled to the same level of protection no matter whether the party invests in a domestic or foreign company publicly traded in the US.

7.2.3. Accounting Standards

The third challenge in the transatlantic regulatory dialogue relates to the introduction of a single set of global accounting standards. As of January 1, 2005, all listed European companies have to comply with reporting requirements of the International Financial Reporting Standards (IFRS). EU-listed US companies publish their financial statements according to the US Generally Accepted Accounting Principles (GAAP). Whereas EU policy-makers have expressed their willingness to extend the mutual recognition principle to EU-listed US companies reporting in US GAAP, and hence, granting equivalence to US GAAP with the IFRS, the SEC has been so far reluctant to judge the equivalence of IFRS with US GAAP.

The SEC requires that all US-listed companies, including European ones, have to reconcile accounting differences arising from IFRS with US GAAP. This virtually means that US-listed European companies should report according to US GAAP. The position of the SEC reflects the fact that despite the markedly improved quality of transparency and disclosure in the EU since the introduction of more stringent listing rules on national stock exchanges and the enforcement of the IFRS, enforcement of accounting rules in the EU is still national and there is no EU enforcement body. In some new member states there is very weak enforcement of accounting rules. Moreover, even though the Committee of European Securities Regulators (CESR) plays an important role, it does not have 'EU enforcement leverages' or the necessary authority to allow for accounting standards across both sides of the Atlantic offering equivalence.

Nevertheless, the transatlantic regulatory dialog has already produced positive results with regard to accounting standards. Taking into consideration the transition to IFRS, the SEC has already eased disclosure of historical results by US-listed European companies. Finally, the SEC and EU policy-makers have recently announced a road map that would eliminate the reconciliation requirement for US-listed European companies by 2009.

7.2.4. De-Listing and Deregistration

As a consequence of sweeping changes in corporate governance, accounting and auditing practices in the US and their across-the-board application to all US-listed companies, the cost of regulatory compliance, possible de-listing and deregistration from the US markets by European companies became yet another challenge on the EU and US regulatory agenda. EU policy-makers and business groups alike have warned that they might decide to de-list and deregister because of high regulatory costs and costly transitions that US-listed EU companies will face. Nevertheless, de-listing is not a simple task for European companies with more than 300 shareholders. Indeed, such companies are unable to deregister pursuant to Rule 12(e) and consequently must remain listed on the exchange.

Even though most EU-listed companies would not rush to de-list if the barriers were dropped, EU policy-makers have long argued that the SEC should take actions to ease the process of deregistration from the SEC for European companies with more than 300 shareholders. Currently, the SEC is examining ways whether such European companies can be exempted from some corporate governance requirements. It may be an argument to recommend that EU-listed companies may opt out of the US measures if the SEC, having assessed all details, is satisfied that the parallel EU measures are sufficient.

7.2.5. International Regulatory and Supervisory Cooperation

The next challenge in the transatlantic regulatory dialog refers to the long-running dispute as to greater EU representation and participation in international standards-setting bodies. The EU is keen to have more involvement in the International Accounting Standards Board (IASB) and in the International Auditing and Assurance Standards Board (IAASB) to be able to influence governance thereof as well as the reform process in accounting and auditing initiated by these bodies.

The fact that the PCAOB might 'overrule' the IAASB by extending its system of inspections and investigations to US-listed foreign companies and issue standards independently from those developed by the IAASB as evidenced by the PCAOB Release 2003-023 on 'Proposed Auditing Standard on Audit Documentation and Proposed Amendment to Interim Standards on Auditing',[6] elevated concerns in the EU as to the future of global standards setting in accounting and auditing.

The debate in this area is heating up, but 'the fight' moves into another round with no concrete results so far.

7.3. A Transatlantic Road Map

The new US audit and accounting regulatory environment (particularly by limiting the role of the profession) will probably have a major influence on future efforts to establish a convergence model for a global auditing and accounting profession. While the EU's approach offers different regulatory menus, we should expect substantial convergence in the area of governance and disclosure.

Turning our attention to the introduction of new regulatory frameworks, it is important to keep in mind that measures should be left sufficiently flexible in order to accommodate the wide range of firms and corporate law regimes. The more innovative and adaptable a legal system is, the more likely it will be able to supply firms with measures that they require while ensuring an adequate level of investor protection.

In this context, the US legislative reforms introduced in wake of the 2002 governance scandals impose a number of new statutory measures that seek to improve the level of transparency of accounts, ensure auditor independence, and limit the abusive actions taken by boards and officers. While such measures have surely taken away some of the shortcomings of the original corporate law regime governing listed firms in the US, they may suffer from several shortcomings as we have seen. In this context, EU-listed firms do not have the possibility of opting out of the EU regime. Those who support the introduction of a lower regulatory regime can cite the benefit of allowing investors and firms to enjoy different levels of protection, which is likely to correspond to the diverse needs of investors for information and legal protection. In this respect, the issue of flexibility and reliability of different measures should be examined and assessed.

For the EU, the emphasis on increased use of recommendations by regulators can provide a coherent foundation for reform. Another beneficial aspect might be the use of less intrusive self-regulatory measures that could speed up the process of reform while taking into account the dynamic changes in the market. From this perspective, the role of the EU would be to ensure a certain level of coordination between the member states, and make it possible to provide for certain minimum standards. Either way, focusing solely on directives and other hard law measures, as opposed to flexibility and national-level decision-making, is to ignore arguably the key policy issues for firms for years to come.

Finally, the transatlantic dimension of corporate governance reform represents a unique experiment in corporate law reform. While it is unclear whether EU–US cooperation has make it easier for firms to comply with regulation, made it more attractive for new investment or protected the interests of minority shareholders sufficiently, there may be good reasons to support more extensive cooperation between the EU and US since it may eventually affect capital mobility, and hence, drive product and labor market reforms, leading in turn to lower costs of capital. In this respect, some level of regulatory competition may be necessary to ensure the high rate of flexibility and innovation necessary to create an effective system of corporate law. On the other hand, the increasing trend toward adoption of similar techniques and institutions, accompanied by extensive interest group pressures, may create additional incentives for directors and managers to adopt internal organizational forms that are more efficient. Whether the EU and US will create an effective transatlantic regulatory environment in the various areas of corporate law will depend on how successful the parties are in striking a balance between fostering regulatory competition in some areas to favor heterogeneity of issuers, investors, creditors and to allow them to choose between possible governance structures, while introducing limited harmonization in other areas.

Endnotes

1. European Commission Communication (2003). Modernizing Company Law and Enhancing Corporate Governance in the European Union — A Plan to Move Forward, COM(2003)284 final, May 21.
2. For more details, see SOXA Section 404: Management Assessment of Internal Controls.
3. For more details, see SOXA Sections 302 and 906: Corporate Responsibility for Financial Reports.
4. For more details see Section 103 of the SOXA: Auditing, Quality Control, and Independence Standards and Rules.
5. For more details see Section 106 of the SOXA: Foreign Public Accounting Firms.
6. For more details, see http://www.pcaobus.org/Rules_of_the_Board/Documents/BriefingPaper2003-023.pdf

Chapter 8

The Role of Self-Regulation in Corporate Governance: Evidence and Implications from the Netherlands

Abe de Jong, Douglas DeJong, Gerard Mertens and Charles Wasley

8.1. Introduction

It is well known that agency problems are associated with the separation of ownership from control in corporations (Berle & Means, 1932; Jensen & Meckling, 1976; Fama & Jensen, 1983a,b). To mitigate these problems, corporate governance mechanisms have evolved that enable companies to raise funds in debt and equity markets. Corporate governance plays a crucial role in determining where, in what form and at what cost capital is provided by outside investors (e.g., Price Waterhouse, 1997; Shleifer & Vishny, 1997; La Porta, Lopez-de-Silanes, Shleifer, & Vishny, 1998; Financial Times, 2000a).

It is generally recognized, particularly by the European Union (EU) countries, that investors, both foreign and domestic, consider the quality of corporate governance when making investment decisions (e.g., Weil, Gothshal, & Manges, 2002). In response, EU countries have initiated self-regulation efforts to improve corporate governance practices and thereby promote investor interests. The nature of the initiatives has differed from country to country and their overall success or failure is an open question. As such, it is of interest to determine when self-regulation (via market forces) is sufficient to promote change, as well as when legal action is required to enforce contracts between owners and managers of capital (Alchian, 1950; Stigler, 1958; Shleifer & Vishny, 1997).

This chapter assesses the effectiveness of the Netherlands' self-regulation initiative as outlined in the Peters Committee report (see, Committee on Corporate Governance, 1997).

The rationale for studying the Netherlands is two-fold. The first is the intense international interest shown by investors and policy-makers in this private sector initiative. With its *perceived* ability to balance alternative interests within the firm, the Dutch structure has been proposed as an alternative for the EU (e.g., Financial Times, 2000b). Further, outside Europe, the International Monetary Fund funded a project for Indonesia that has the Dutch

Advances in Corporate Finance and Asset Pricing
Edited by L. Renneboog
© 2006 Elsevier B.V. All rights reserved.
ISBN: 0-444-52723-0

corporate governance model as part of its focus, and the Korean government used the Peters Committee report during deliberations on corporate governance. Finally, the United States' Securities and Exchange Commission (SEC) closely followed the Dutch "experiment" in self-regulation. All of this interest suggests the success or failure of self-regulation to promote effective corporate governance that enhances firm value is an important issue to investors and policy-makers.

The Netherlands' initiative (hereafter, the Peters Committee) focuses on self-regulation through transparency and monitoring. Based on an agreement between the Association of Securities Issuing Companies and Euronext Amsterdam in 1996, a Committee on Corporate Governance was formed. The committee was chaired by J. Peters (retired Chief Executive Officer, CEO of Aegon) and its members included representatives from the business community, Euronext Amsterdam, security issuing companies, academics and a platform of investors (stockholder and pension representatives). The charge of the Peters Committee was to initiate debate and suggest change in the balance of power between a firm's management and investors in the Netherlands.

In June 1997, the Peters Committee issued recommendations designed to increase the effectiveness of management, supervision and accountability to investors in Dutch corporations (see, Committee on Corporate Governance, 1997). A key element of the report was its reliance on self-enforcement, through market forces, to implement and enforce its recommendations. Not unexpectedly, the Dutch government was interested in seeing the changes taking place. The Dutch Minister of Finance stated "… in the case too little is done with the recommendations, the question arises whether legislation is needed" (NRC Handelsbad, July 24, 1997). One year after the effective date of the report, the Peters Committee completed a project to assess the impact of its initial report (Monitoring Corporate Governance in Nederland, 1998).

In this chapter we evaluate the impact of the Peters Committee's recommendations by analyzing the Tobin's Q (TQ) of Dutch companies listed on Euronext Amsterdam over the 5-year period prior to, and 3-year period after the release of the report. The data we study include variables on organizational form, voting rights, board characteristics, outside block-holders and debt/financing characteristics. We use an event study to assess investors' reactions to various events (e.g., the release of the Peters Committee monitoring report). We also document constraints on investor rights in the Netherlands and actions by major investors that not only impact firm value, but also temper the potential success of the self-regulation initiative.

When domestic firms in the Netherlands reach a certain size, they are legally required to organize as a *structured regime*. The *structured regime* requires a supervisory board comprised of outsiders. A key aspect of this board is that it takes numerous powers from shareholders. For example, the supervisory board elects the members of the management board (i.e., management) as well as electing its *own* members. Due to the greater separation of ownership from control, we hypothesize the structured regime has a negative relation with firm value. The results support this hypothesis as firms under the legally required structured regime exhibit, on average, a significantly lower TQ. A *voluntarily retained structured regime* is a management choice for multi-national firms with more than 50% of their employees outside the Netherlands. Firms electing this organizational form also exhibit, on average, a significantly lower TQ. Contrary to the role of outside monitoring, we find outside and industrial shareholders have a negative influence on firm value in the Netherlands. Thus, outside institutions do not play a significant monitoring role (although there is no evidence of collusion). We also document the presence of takeover defenses in the Netherlands and their negative effects on firm value.

The monitoring problems we document suggest a pessimistic outcome for the Netherlands' self-regulation initiative, even with the government's "threat" of potential legislation. Consistent with this pessimism, we fail to document any positive share price effects to actions taken by the Peters Committee. To the contrary, our event study results suggest that the market was pessimistic about any substantive evolution of corporate governance practices in the Netherlands, and reacted negatively to the release of the Peters Committee monitoring report. A notable feature of our findings is the disciplining role of the new listings market in the post-Peters period. In the post-Peters report period, new listings have favorable and significant corporate governance characteristics when compared to new listings in the pre-Peters period.

A further rationale to study the Netherlands self-regulation initiative is 13 of the 15 EU countries have initiated codes of corporate governance (these initiatives are outlined in more detail in the following section). The codes differ by whether compliance is "required" or voluntary, whether there is monitoring or not (i.e., whether information reported by companies is independently verified or not), and if there was monitoring, whether it was with or without enforcement. Our findings of no significant improvements in corporate governance resulting from the Netherlands self-regulation initiative (which is characterized by voluntary compliance, monitoring and no enforcement) cast doubt on the success of 10 out of the 13 initiatives by other EU countries because they are based on voluntary compliance, monitoring and *no* enforcement. Further, if monitoring with enforcement is a necessary condition for success, the outcomes of two additional initiatives merely requiring compliance are also questionable. A notable exception to these 12 EU initiatives is the United Kingdom's (UK) successful Cadbury Committee and report. However, this initiative was characterized by mandatory compliance, monitoring and enforcement.[1]

The outcomes of the EU self-regulation initiatives noted above, and the recently passed German corporate governance legislation that excludes monitoring and enforcement confirm La Porta, Lopez-de-Silanes, Shleifer, and Vishny's (2000) skepticism about substantive legal/political action because of the intense opposition from the self-interested parties involved (and to a lesser extent the lack of appreciation for the importance of investor rights).

The remainder of the chapter is organized as follows. The next section presents a framework for integrating the self-regulation initiative in the Netherlands with similar self-regulation initiatives in other markets. Section 8.3 provides a description of Dutch corporate governance practices and outlines hypotheses on the relation between corporate governance characteristics and firm value. Section 8.4 describes the data and Section 8.5 reports our results. Section 8.6 concludes and discusses the implications of our findings.

8.2. Self-Regulation Corporate Governance Initiatives

To place our study of the Netherlands' self-regulation corporate governance initiative in a broader context with other countries, we present a framework for analyzing and comparing

Table 8.1: A classification and comparison of corporate governance initiatives and codes for 15 EU countries.[1]

Country[2]	Anti-director index Minimum = 0 Maximum = 6	Code of corporate governance	Compliance		Monitoring (i.e., independent verification)		No monitoring[3] (i.e., no independent verification)		
			Required: explain non-compliance	Voluntary	With enforcement	Without enforcement	Self-reporting	Official survey	No official follow-up
Netherlands	2.0	Yes		Yes		Yes			
UK	5.0	Yes	Yes		Yes				
Italy	1.0	Yes	Yes				Yes		
Ireland	4.0	Yes	Yes				Yes		
Spain	4.0	Yes		Yes				Yes	
Belgium	0.0	Yes		Yes				Yes	
Portugal	3.0	Yes		Yes				Yes	
France	3.0	Yes		Yes				Yes	
Denmark	2.0	Yes		Yes					Yes
Finland	3.0	Yes		Yes					Yes
Sweden	3.0	Yes		Yes					Yes

Greece	2.0	Yes		Yes
Germany	10	Yes		Yes
Austria	2.0	No		
Luxemburg	N/A	No		

1. *Source:* Weil, Gothshal, and Manges (2002). "A comparative study of corporate governance codes relevant for the EU and its members, final report (on behalf of the European Commission, Internal Market Directorate General)."

2. Since there are numerous initiatives in some countries, we chose the initiative with the explicit or implicit backing of the government. Variable definitions are as follows: anti-director index (which ranges from 0 to 6) is a index formed by adding 1 when:
   –the country allows shareholders to mail their proxy vote to the firm,
   –shareholders are not required to deposit their shares prior to the general shareholders' meeting,
   –cumulative voting or proportional representation of minorities in the board of directors is allowed,
   –an oppressed minorities mechanism is in place,
   –the minimum percentage of share capital entitling a shareholder to call for an extraordinary shareholders' meeting is less than or equal to 10% (the sample median in the study cited),
   –shareholders have pre-emptive rights that can be waived only by a shareholders' vote.
   See Table 8.2 in La Porta, Rafael, Lopez-de-Silanes, Shleifer, and Vishny (1998), which details a country's compliance with each of the six criteria that make up the anti-director index. A "Yes" entry in the remaining columns of the table indicates the presence of the item in the particular country's code of corporate governance.

3. Self-reporting means firms in non-compliance with the requirements must "voluntarily" report their non-compliance. Official survey means the group responsible for the corporate governance initiative conducted an official follow-up survey that firms were asked to complete. However, there was no independent verification of the information firms provided. No official follow-up means there was no official follow-up or officially sanctioned follow-up to the publication of the respective code of corporate governance.

it with similar initiatives in other (EU) countries. The Internal Market Directorate General of the European Commission underwrote a study of corporate governance codes of the EU and its members (see, Weil, Gotshal, & Manges, 2002). For EU members, the study provides a detailed description of each initiative, the issuing or sponsoring body, the legal basis for compliance, and the objectives, scope and companies covered. From this information we can classify the corporate governance initiatives by whether compliance was required or voluntary, whether there was monitoring or not (whether companies' information was independently verified or not), and if there was monitoring, whether it was with or without legal enforcement. Table 8.1 summarizes the results of our classification.

At one extreme is the highly successful Cadbury Committee in the UK (row 2 of the table). While the Cadbury Report started as a voluntary code, it recommended a mandatory compliance report. The London Stock Exchange adopted the recommendations and firms were required to provide reasons if they did not comply with the Cadbury Committee's recommendations. Reviews of the compliance report by outside auditors were also required and there was the threat of litigation if companies did not comply with the guidelines. Dedman (2000) and Dahya, McConnell, and Travlos (2002) find significant changes in board structure and management characteristics following the Cadbury Committee's recommendations, as well as an increase in firms' average performance. Stiles and Taylor (1993) document that significant changes took place within a year of the Cadbury Committee's recommendations.

With the exception of Italy and Ireland (rows 3 and 4 of Table 8.1), which require compliance like the UK, all of the remaining countries with a corporate governance code rely on voluntary compliance. Included in this set is the corporate governance code put forth in the Netherlands by the Peters' Committee (row 1 of Table 8.1). As stated above, the Peters' Committee advocated self-regulation of Dutch corporate governance practices via voluntary compliance, and monitoring without enforcement. Differences in the structure and implementation of the initiatives summarized in Table 8.1 make it impossible to perform a detailed comparative analysis of their (likely) outcomes with any degree of accuracy. As noted above, we use this framework simply to place the Peters Committee's corporate governance initiative in a broader context with other European countries. Nonetheless, using this classification framework, and based on the results we report below for the Netherlands, we can conjecture about the likely outcomes. If monitoring with enforcement is a necessary condition for success (e.g., UK), then the Italian and Irish initiatives requiring compliance can be evaluated. Specifically, the UK condition of monitoring with enforcement casts some doubt on the likelihood of success for Italy and Ireland. The remaining corporate governance initiatives summarized in rows 5–13 of Table 8.1 (for Spain, Belgium, Portugal, France, Denmark, Finland, Sweden, Greece and Germany), are weaker than the Netherlands in that compliance is voluntary, with no monitoring. The results we report below for the Netherlands lead us to be skeptical about the success of the initiatives in these nine countries.

Table 8.1 also presents information about investor rights based on La Porta, Lopez-de-Silanes, Shleifer, and Vishny's (1998) anti-director index. The value of the index ranges from 0 to 6 with a low (high) value indicating a low (high) level of shareholder rights.[2] Since it is somewhat arbitrary deciding at what point on the scale a country shifts from anti-shareholder to pro-shareholder, we refrain from making precise statements and comparisons along such lines. Instead, we make the following general observations. Consistent with the discussion in the previous paragraph, the UK (index of 5.0) ranks quite high on the scale. Conversely, the Netherlands (index of 2.0) and the remaining countries (except Ireland and Spain) have values of 3.0 or lower. The *lower* index values for these countries (including the Netherlands), in conjunction with the point we made in the prior paragraph about the voluntary nature of compliance, with no monitoring, of the corporate governance codes in these countries, lead us to further doubt the likely success of these countries' corporate governance initiatives. We should mention that Ireland has since mandated independent monitoring with enforcement. These general observations are consistent with Dyck and Zingales (2004) who document the value of control, as measured by the premium paid for controlling blocks of shares, in the countries just considered.

Further evidence of the lack of success with self-regulation-based corporate governance initiatives is illustrated by Germany's recently enacted corporate governance legislation (the final form of the legislation excludes monitoring and consequently effective enforcement). A lack of success with self-regulation initiatives confirms La Porta, Lopez-de-Silanes, Shleifer, and Vishny's (2000) skepticism about substantive legal/political action due to intense opposition from the self-interested parties involved. On the other hand, the lack of success is somewhat contrary to evidence suggesting governance mechanisms maintaining day-to-day accountability of management and boards are more efficient than relying on alternatives such as the market for corporate control (Franks & Mayer, 1996; Barca & Becht, 2001; Gugler, 2001).

8.3. Dutch Corporate Governance

8.3.1. Legal Structure

Current Dutch company law was enacted in 1971 after a government committee (Verdam Committee, 1965) issued a proposal for company law reform in 1965 and a draft law based on the report in 1968.[3] Its starting point is a shareholder-controlled firm with both a supervisory and management board. Shareholders elect members of the supervisory board and management boards and approve the annual accounts. Dividend policy is set by management with the consent of the supervisory board and is formally approved by shareholders. Shareholders vote on such issues as mergers and acquisitions. All votes are taken at the Annual Meeting of Shareholders and physical presence is required (voting by proxy is not part of the Dutch structure).

A full "structured regime" is legally required for Dutch companies with more than 100 employees, a legally installed work council and book value of shareholders' equity in excess of 11.4 million euros. The full structured regime requires the supervisory board to take over the following powers from shareholders: establishing and approval of the annual accounts, the election of the management board and the election of the supervisory board itself (called co-optation). The supervisory board also has the authority over major decisions made by the management board. The most prevalent exception to the full structured regime is Dutch multinationals with more than 50% of their employees outside the Netherlands. Such companies file and obtain an exemption from the full structured regime.

However, such a company may voluntarily retain the full structured regime, and Dutch multinationals typically do, even though there is no legal requirement.[4]

Turning to the two boards and the works council, a Dutch company operates under a two-tier management structure consisting of a Supervisory Board and a Management Board.[5] The supervisory board is "independent" of the company and comprised entirely of "outsiders." These outsiders primarily consist of "professional managers" and can (and often do) include past members of management. With the rare exception of a retired politician, politicians and regulators are not members of a supervisory board. Board members receive a fixed payment (dependent on the firm's size) for their services and very few hold shares in the company. Thus, reputation is important for getting and keeping such positions, which suggests supervisory board members are likely to be risk averse. The law requires the board to serve the firm's interest. However, under the structured regime, the supervisory board has very few restrictions on its ability to determine its own composition, re-appointments and other organizational matters, including the management board. The law requires that the management board serve at the pleasure of the supervisory board.[6]

The management board makes up the company's management team and is responsible for attaining the company's objectives, its strategy and policy and the ensuing results. Labor is not required to have an "outside" representative on the supervisory board nor is labor a member of the management board (Company Law of 1971). The legally installed works council, which is required when a company has more than 100 employees, has a right to relevant information and to advise on such major issues as transfers of ownership, plant closings and major investments. While this is more than a formality, the management board decides and can overrule the advice of the works council. The works council's permission is only required for changes in social arrangements (e.g., pensions, working hours, wages and safety rules). If the council disagrees with a firm's proposals on social arrangements, the firm must obtain a local judge's decision to proceed.

8.3.2. Voting Rights

At the time of organization, a company has an authorized capital structure consisting of ordinary shares. Such shares have voting, dividend and trading rights. When the company's organization and size require the full structured regime, the supervisory board is granted the rights (detailed above) previously held by shareholders. Shareholders still vote on mergers and acquisitions and dividend policy under the structured regime.

A company can have a second type of security called "Certificates." In fact, under the structured regime, the supervisory board can request the exchange of ordinary shares for certificates. A trust office administers the certificates when issued or initiates a certification process where certificates are exchanged for ordinary shares. The trust office is comprised of members from the company (supervisory board and management board) and the "outside" (not from the company). While the chairman and majority of the trust office members must be outsiders, in practice, the trust office is always friendly to a existing management. The trust office is given responsibility for the ordinary shares associated with the certificates. Through the process of certification, legal, but not "economic" ownership of the ordinary shares is transferred to the trust office (Slagter, 1996). Certificate holders have dividend rights, can freely trade their certificates and can attend the General Meeting of Shareholders, but they cannot vote. The trust office holds all voting rights including approval of the dividend policy. The prevailing type of certificate is the limited exchangeable certificate. Once issued, these certificates can be exchanged for ordinary shares up to a maximum percentage of 1% of outstanding equity capital. However, once exchanged for ordinary shares, holders lose trading privileges for the exchanged shares. Ordinary shares can be reconverted to certificates, but then voting rights are lost.

As takeover defenses, companies may have additional types of securities in their capital structure. The most common takeover defense is "protective preference shares." Management can issue such shares to a friendly trust office or outside investor during a hostile takeover. Preference shares are sold at nominal value to the trust office or friendly investor with an obligation to pay only 25% of the amount upfront. Preference shares have voting rights and are restricted to a maximum of 50% or 100% of the current outstanding nominal capital depending on the anti-takeover amendments in place. Special voting privileges are also granted through "priority shares" which give their holders special rights in situations such as merger approval, new public offerings, charter amendments and company liquidation. The provisions of Euronext Amsterdam 1997 only allow a company to have two of the three takeover defenses noted above (certificates, priority shares and protective preference shares).

Prior research finds that firm value is adversely affected by constraints placed on shareholders' voting rights and by management's attempt to prevent changes in corporate control (e.g., Malatesta & Walking, 1988; Stulz, 1988). In the Netherlands, the legally required structured regime is used to directly limit shareholder's influence. Similarly, the voluntarily retained structured regime also directly limits shareholder rights. However, the voluntarily retained structured regime is essentially a supervisory and management board choice. Other explicit constraints on shareholder influence occur through the use of certificates, and preference and priority shares, which as takeover defenses mitigate the market for corporate control.

To help to put the sour discussion of voting rights and the takeover market in the Netherlands in a broader context and link our discussion to related research Maeijer and Geens (1990) enumerate anti-takeover measures in 11 European countries. Non-voting shares (certificates in the Netherlands) are used in France and Belgium, while priority shares are present in the UK and Germany. In Germany specific shares may even have rights to appoint managerial and supervisory board members. Unlike the Netherlands, none of the 11 countries has preference shares as a takeover defense. Voogd (1989) presents a detailed review of takeover defenses in the Netherlands and identifies over 50 measures that are or have been used in the Netherlands. However, most of the measures are used by very few firms, or are not used anymore. Voogd (1989) identifies six measures which are widely used. The four measures we use include, the structured regime, priority shares, preferred shares and certificates, along with binding appointments and voting limits. Binding appointments imply the right to appoint board members is granted to a specific party (not the shareholders).[7] Voting limits occur only in 6% of Voogd's 1989 sample, thus aren't widely used. Finally, stock markets of similar size and liquidity (to the Netherlands) in Europe face similar problems affecting disciplining takeovers. For example, Maeijer and Geens (1990) show legal measures are present in most countries and other countries have structural defenses like cross-holdings and pyramids (also see Becht, 1999).

8.3.3. Monitoring

The literature suggests major outside shareholders may constrain management's deviation from value-maximizing behavior (e.g., Agrawal & Knoeber, 1996; Cho, 1998; Holderness & Sheehan, 1988; Morck, Shleifer, & Vishny, 1988; La Porta, Lopez-de-Silanes, & Shleifer, 1999). However, the ability to generalize these findings to the Netherlands is questionable, particularly for structured regime firms. We consider the influence of a major outside shareholder, and also the influence of major shareholdings by financial institutions (i.e., banks, insurance companies and pension funds, etc.) and industrial firms. Shareholdings by financial institutions can have a positive or negative impact on firm value (Pound, 1988). The effect will be positive if they are more efficient monitors than atomistic shareholders. It will be negative if they collude with management. While McConnell and Servaes (1990) find a positive relationship in the US, in the Netherlands financial institutions are known for their passive attitude. With regard to industrial firm shareholdings, the effect may be positive due to improved monitoring, or negative due to collusion and/or attempts to influence decisions for their own benefit.[8]

Two final factors related to monitoring are debt markets and cross-listing. Debt markets can discipline management's deviation from value-maximizing behavior (Jensen & Meckling, 1976). To help to put the strength of bondholder/creditor rights in the Netherlands in a broader context we draw on work by La Porta, Lopez-de-Silanez, Shleifer, and Vishny (1998). La Porta, Lopez-de-Silanez, Shleifer, and Vishny (1998) develop a measure of creditor protection in 49 countries. The measure is composed of four items:

1. No automatic stay on assets (i.e., a restriction exists in the law that prevents secured creditors from gaining possession of their security).
2. Secured creditors are paid first (i.e., secured creditors are ranked first in the distribution of the liquidation, which mean the absolute priority rule applies).
3. Restrictions exist for going into reorganization (i.e., reorganization is only allowed after consent of creditors).
4. Management does not stay on in reorganization (i.e., an official is appointed who is responsible for the business during reorganization).

Each of these four items is derived from countries' bankruptcy and reorganization laws. The Netherlands scores 2 out of 4 on this measure of creditor protection because secured creditors are paid first, and restrictions exist for going into reorganization. Other (French-origin) firms' score an average of 1.58, the US scores 1 and the sample average for all 49 countries is 2.3. A score of 2 implies debt-holders in the Netherlands have a stronger position than US peers, but overall (i.e., internationally), they do not have many rights. While La Porta, Lopez-de-Silanes, and Shleifer (1998) describe the *legal* rights of creditors, *actual* practices may differ in the Netherlands. Couwenberg (1997) explores four cases of bankruptcy and finds co-operative debt-holders in the sense that debt contracts are renegotiated. Couwenberg (1997) concludes creditors have influential positions in the Netherlands, suggesting debt has a disciplining effect in cases of bankruptcy.

Finally, it is important to recognize the disciplining aspects of listing on an exchange outside the Netherlands. For example, UK and US listings require more company and compensation disclosure than Euronext Amsterdam (Lins, Strickland, & Zenner, 1999). Our empirical tests include a variable capturing cross-listings in the USA and UK.

8.3.4. The Peters Committee

The Peters Committee issued its preliminary conclusions in October 1996. Its final recommendations were published in June 1997, which as expected, were similar to the preliminary report (the report is available at www.ecgi.org). The report made a major appeal to re-evaluate the numerous constraints placed on the rights of shareholders in the Netherlands. The committee spoke specifically to the accountability of the supervisory and management boards under the structured regime. However, the report did not address the inherent problems of the structured regime. Instead, the committee focused on how to make the structured regime relatively more accountable to shareholders without changing shareholders' fundamental rights. Clearly, this is likely to be a difficult task, because shareholders have very few rights to begin with under the full structured regime. The committee's monitoring report of December 1998 contained all of the corporate governance information collected on the companies for 1997 (1 year after the release of the committee's formal report). The "monitoring report" was an attempt by the committee to assess the extent to which Dutch firms were complying with the recommendations contained in the original Peters Committee report.

8.4. Research Design

Data from 1992–1999 (covering both the pre- and post-Peters Committee periods) are used to examine organizational form, voting rights and monitoring relationships. By collecting data from the post-Peters period (i.e., 1997–1999), we are able to conduct tests to assess the impact of the committee's recommendations on the corporate governance variables outlined above. To do so, we use the results from the pre-Peters period as a benchmark. As a means to further assess the impact of the Peters Committee's recommendations, we compare governance characteristics of new listings during the pre-Peters period with those during the post-Peters period to see if any improvements in shareholder rights are observed. Lastly, using event study techniques, we evaluate the impact of various corporate governance-related events and announcements related to the Peters Committee and Dutch government during the 1996–1999 period and afterwards.

8.4.1. Sample

Our sample contains all non-financial firms listed on Euronext Amsterdam from 1992–1999. We exclude financial firms because of their regulatory structure. We start our sample selection with the yearly overviews of all securities listed at Euronext Amsterdam (Gids bij de Officiële Prijscourant van de Amsterdamse Effectenbeurs). There are 208 firms listed for at least one calendar year from 1992–1999. Three firms are dropped because their annual reports are not available. For the remaining 205 firms, we collect data from 1992 (or the year following the firm's listing) through 1999. Since we focus on the Peters Committee and its implications, we exclude 26 firms that were only listed during the pre-Peters period (1992–1996) and 39 firms that were only listed during the post-Peters period (1997–1999). The final sample contains 140 firms with 1035 firm-year observations.

Financial data, including bank debt and board compensation, are obtained from Statistics Netherlands (Centraal Bureau voor de Statistiek) and the Review and Analysis of Companies in Holland (REACH) dataset. We use annual reports to identify board members and to obtain information missing from Statistics Netherlands and REACH. Data on ownership structure are obtained from the leading Dutch financial daily newspaper (Het Financieele Dagblad) that annually publishes a list of exchange-listed firms and their stakeholders (in accordance with the notifications for The Law on Disclosure of Shareholdings, Wet Melding Zeggenschap). Information about takeover defenses and cross-listings are from the yearly overviews of all securities listed at Euronext Amsterdam (Gids bij de Officiële Prijscourant van de Amsterdamse Effectenbeurs). Data on structured regimes are obtained from the Monitoring Corporate Governance in Nederland (1998) and Honée, Timmerman, and Nethe (2000), which provide structured regime classifications for 1997 and 1999. For years prior to 1997, we use the firm's annual report for 1992 to make the classification. The annual reports allowed us to investigate whether the supervisory board established the annual accounts and whether the firms met the criteria for the structured regime. If we found a difference between 1992, 1997 or 1999, we investigated all annual reports from 1992–1999. In cases of inconsistency, we contacted the firm.

8.4.2. Variable Definitions and Summary Statistics

Along with some descriptive statistics, Table 8.2 lists the variables used in our empirical tests along with the abbreviations used to refer to them in the text and later tables. Table 8.3 presents descriptive statistics for three sub-samples, no structured regime, legally required structured regime and voluntarily retained structured regime.

TQ measures firm value and performance (Lindenberg & Ross, 1981). TQ is the dependent variable in our regression tests and is measured as the book value of liabilities plus the market value of equity, divided by the replacement cost of the firm's assets (see, Perfect & Wiles, 1994).[9] Also appearing in Table 8.2 are several control variables. These variables are firm size measured as the book value of total assets (BVTA), growth measured as the log of one plus (growth) the 3-year historical growth rate of the firm's book value of assets and leverage (LEV) measured as long-term debt divided by book value of assets. Based on the prior research, in a regression with TQ as the dependent variable, the coefficient on BVTA will be negative and those on GROWTH and LEV will be positive.[10]

Turning to our independent variables, the first deals with cross-listing. XLIST takes on the value 1 (0) if the firm is (is not) listed on an exchange in the UK or USA. The organizational form of the sample firms is addressed by the next two variables. SR takes on a value of 1 (0) if the firm is (is not) a legally required structured regime while SR_V takes on a value of 1 (0) if the firm has (has not) voluntarily retained the structured regime. We capture limitations on shareholder rights by using PRIO which takes on a value of 1 (0) in

Table 8.2: Variable definitions and descriptive statistics for the variables used in the empirical tests. The sample consists of 140 Dutch firms over the 1992–1999 period (sample size is 1035 observations, 806 observations for bank debt).

Variable	Description	Variable name	Mean	Median	Minimum	Maximum	Standard deviation
TQ	Market value of total assets/replacement value of total assets	TQ	1.576	1.228	0.524	23.323	1.472
Total assets	BVTA in 1,000,000 NLG	BVTA	3133.0	452.0	3.79	109863.0	9961.0
Growth	The 3-year historical growth of total assets	GROWTH	0.428	0.224	-0.760	9.810	0.930
LEV	Long-term debt/BVTA	LEV	0.136	0.115	0.0	0.660	0.123
Listing abroad	Dummy variable with value of 1 for listing on a stock exchange in the UK and/or USA, 0 otherwise	XLIST	0.160	0.0	0.0	1.0	0.360
Structured regime	Dummy variable with value of 1 for presence of legally required structured regime, 0 otherwise	SR	0.473	0.0	0.0	1.0	0.500
Voluntary structured regime	Dummy variable with value of 1 for presence of voluntarily retained structured regime, 0 otherwise	SR_V	0.132	0.0	0.0	1.0	0.339

Table 8.2: Continued.

Variable	Description	Variable name	Mean	Median	Minimum	Maximum	Standard deviation
Priority shares	Dummy variable with value of 1 for presence of priority shares, 0 otherwise	PRIO	0.390	0.0	0.0	1.0	0.490
Preference shares	Dummy variable with value of 1 for presence of preference share option, 0 otherwise	PREF	0.604	1.0	0.0	1.0	0.489
Certificates	Dummy variable with value of 1 for presence of certificates, 0 otherwise	CERT	0.370	0.0	0.0	1.0	0.480
Interlocks with banks Inter-locks with financials	The number of inter lock-ing directorates with banks The number of interlocks with financial institutions	BANK_ILOCK FIN_ILOCK	0.780 1.080	0.0 0.0	0.0 1.0	8.0 9.0	1.160 1.560

Largest block-holder	The stake of the largest block-holder	OSIDE_EQ	22.10	13.33	0.0	94.00	19.35
Financial institution block-holdings	The stake of block-holdings by banks, insurance companies, pension funds and institutionalized venture capitalists	INSTI_EQ	12.68	8.20	0.0	90.73	14.95
Bank block-holdings	The stake of block-holdings by banks	BANK_EQ	7.66	5.14	0.0	67.35	10.41
Industrial block-holdings	The stake of industrial block-holders	INDUS_EQ	10.22	0.0	0.0	93.17	20.32
Insider block-holdings	The stake of supervisory and management board block-holdings	INSIDE_EQ	6.16	0.0	0.0	97.05	17.15
Bank debt	Long-term bank debt/BVTA	BANK_D	0.072	0.003	0.0	0.44	0.089

Table 8.3: Select descriptive statistics for sub-samples with no structured regime, a legally required structured regime and a voluntarily retained structured regime. The sample consists of 140 Dutch firms over the 1992–1999 period (sample size is 1035 observations, 806 observations for bank debt). See Table 8.2 for variable definitions.

Variable	No. of structured regime n = 408				Legally required structured regime n = 490				Voluntarily retained structured regime n = 137			
	Mean	Median	Minimum	Maximum	Mean	Median	Minimum	Maximum	Mean	Median	Minimum	Maximum
TQ	1.890	1.378	0.50	23.323	1.290	1.107	0.524	9.516	1.660	1.381	0.848	6.347
Total assets	5200.0	169.0	3.790	109863.0	1275.0	469.0	33.0	19205.0	3627.0	1052.0	9.0	31481.0
Growth	0.490	0.238	−0.760	9.810	0.329	0.199	−0.630	8.510	0.596	0.352	−0.410	9.090
LEV	0.111	0.085	0.0	0.460	0.144	0.122	0.0	0.660	0.180	0.185	0.0	0.530
Listing abroad	0.190	0.0	0.0	1.0	0.100	0.0	0.0	1.0	0.250	0.0	0.0	1.0
Priority shares	0.48	0.0	0.0	1.0	0.35	0.0	0.0	1.0	0.25	0.0	0.0	1.0
Preference shares	0.42	0.0	0.0	1.0	0.75	1.0	0.0	1.0	0.61	1.0	0.0	1.0
Certificates	0.28	0.0	0.0	1.0	0.48	0.0	0.0	1.0	0.26	0.0	0.0	1.0

Interlocks with blanks	0.52	0.0	0.0	5.0	0.87	0.0	0.0	8.0	1.24	1.0	0.0	5.0
Interlocks with financials	0.80	0.0	0.0	8.0	1.14	1.0	0.0	9.0	1.69	1.0	0.0	7.0
Largest block-holder	25.33	15.00	0.0	94.00	20.36	13.53	0.0	82.62	18.71	9.42	0.0	67.35
Financial institution block-holdings	7.99	0.0	0.0	90.73	16.81	12.68	0.0	90.73	11.84	8.94	0.0	73.17
Bank block-holdings	5.43	0.0	0.0	58.28	9.26	6.57	0.0	49.99	8.61	5.34	0.0	67.35
Industrial block-holdings	11.56	0.0	0.0	93.17	9.89	0.0	0.0	93.17	7.41	0.0	0.0	62.00
Insider block-holdings	11.08	0.0	0.0	97.05	3.11	0.0	0.0	68.30	2.41	0.0	0.0	46.93
Bank debt	0.054	0.010	0.0	0.380	0.079	0.048	0.0	0.440	0.102	0.098	0.0	0.340

the presence (absence) of priority shares, PREF which is set to 1 (0) if the firm can (cannot) issue and place protective preference shares and CERT which is set to 1 (0) when the firm has (has not) issued certificates.

The role of the debt market as a disciplining mechanism is first captured by focusing on financial institutions (e.g., banks, insurance companies and pension funds, etc.). In particular, we consider LEV, and FIN_ILOCK, which is the number of interlocking directorates with financial institutions. We next focus on banks by using BANK_D, which is measured as the firm's bank debt (long-term bank debt divided by total assets) and BANK_ILOCK, which is the number of bank interlocking directorates on the supervisory board. Both measures of interlocking directorates reflect the number of relationships (interlocks) with banks or financial institutions, with bank interlocks being a subset of financial institutional interlocks. Due to data availability we do not have a complete set of BANK_D observations for all firms.

The remaining (five) independent variables capture the concentration and identity of outside shareholders as well as insider holdings. OSIDE_EQ is the stake of the largest outside block-holder owning 5% or more of the shares, INSTI_EQ is the sum of all institutional block-holdings (banks, insurance companies and pension funds, etc.), BANK_EQ is the sum of all bank block-holdings and INDUS_EQ is the sum of the block-holdings by the industrial firms. To isolate the influence of outside shareholders, we must control for the sum of the block-holdings by insiders, supervisory and management board members (INSIDE_EQ).[11]

The definitions of block-holder control rights follow Barca and Becht (2001) where nine European countries are studied (see, De Jong, Kabir, Marra, & Röell, 2001 for a detailed description of the Dutch data). La Porta, Lopez-de-Silanes, and Shleifer (1999) study voting rights using dummy variables for specific features such as pyramids and cross-holdings. In the Netherlands, deviations from one-share-one-vote are certificates, priority shares and preferred shares. Certificates take away all control rights, priority shares take away voting rights on specific issues, while preferred shares dilute voting rights in specific circumstances. We use the cash flow rights and control for the deviations from one-share-one-vote using three dummy variables.

Several aspects of the descriptive statistics in Table 8.2 are worth noting. Forty-seven percent of the observations in the sample have structured regimes and 13.2% have voluntary structured regimes. With regard to cross-listings, 16.0% of the sample observations are drawn from years where a firm is listed in the USA and/or UK. Turning to the variables reflecting limitations on shareholders' rights, 39.0%, 60.4% and 37.0% of the sample observations are associated with priority shares, preference shares and certificates, respectively.

Comparison of select variables across regime status in Table 8.3 reveals the following. Firms with *no structured regime* tend to have higher mean and median values of TQ when compared to firms with a *legally required structured regime,* or firms with a *voluntary structured regime.* Mean and median values for the former are 1.89 and 1.38, compared to 1.29 and 1.11, and 1.66 and 1.38 for the other two groups, respectively. Based on median values of total assets, firms with *no structured regime* tend to be smaller (169.0) than firms with a *legally required structured regime* (469.0) and firms with a *voluntary structured regime* (1052.0).[12]

8.4.3. Regression Model

We use the following regression model to test relationships between the governance and control variables described above and the firm value (TQ):

TQ = f (Organizational form, limits on voting rights, debt market, outside block-holders and control variables.)

All regression *t*-statistics are based on White's heteroskedastic corrected standard errors and the estimation of the model incorporates fixed firm and year effects.[13]

8.5. Results

We first estimate regressions to test the relationships hypothesized in Section 8.3. Next we isolate the impact the Peters Committee recommendations had on the corporate governance variables and the relation between these variables and TQ. Lastly, we report the results of our event study analysis.

8.5.1. Regression Results for the 1992–1999 Period (Pre- and Post-Peters Committee)

Our initial regressions are based on the 1992–1999 period and the results are reported in Tables 8.4 and 8.5. Referring to model 1 in Table 8.4, consistent with prior research the coefficient on firm size is negative and that on growth is positive. The coefficient on LEV, the remaining control variable, is insignificant.[14] The disciplining role of cross-listing is confirmed by the positive and significant coefficient on the cross-listing variable. As discussed in a more detail below, this result appears to be driven by firms listed in the USA.

Models (2) and (3) in Table 8.4 address the impact of organizational form on TQ. Consistent with our most important hypothesis, the legally required structured regime has a significant negative impact on TQ. After controlling for the other shareholder rights variables (see model 3), the structured regime reduces TQ by 0.555. Similar results are found for firms voluntarily retaining the structured regime (TQ is reduced by 0.639). It is important to view the effect of the required structured regime as distinct from the voluntarily retained structured regime because the former is not a managerial choice while the latter is.

The impact of takeover defenses is addressed by model (3). Consistent with our predictions, the coefficients for priority shares, preference shares and certificates are negative and significant. As described in Section 8.3, certificates have a direct affect on shareholder rights, while preference shares represent potential protection against a takeover. Priority shares deal with specific circumstances that constrain shareholder rights.

We turn next to the regressions reported in Table 8.5, which analyze ownership structure and relations with financial institutions. Model (1) focuses on the monitoring role of major block-holders. The coefficients for the major outside shareholder, industrial block-holders and financial institutions are negative and significant. A large outside or industrial block-holder can force management to undertake activities that benefit the block-holder at the expense of other shareholders. For example, an industrial firm may act to reduce the competition between the companies or influence the prices at which

Table 8.4: The relation between TQ and shareholder rights.

	Predicted sign	Model (1)		Model (2)		Model (3)	
Constant		0.937	(5.28)***	1.145	(5.61)***	1.861	(4.45)***
Y93		0.281	(2.95)***	0.300	(3.12)***	0.306	(3.12)***
Y94		0.339	(3.64)***	0.391	(3.99)***	0.399	(4.02)***
Y95		0.295	(3.17)***	0.348	(3.63)***	0.332	(3.43)***
Y96		0.406	(3.42)***	0.477	(4.14)***	0.424	(3.66)***
Y97		0.504	(3.74)***	0.600	(4.43)***	0.539	(3.95)***
Y98		0.389	(2.94)***	0.487	(3.94)***	0.415	(3.14)***
Y99		0.431	(2.38)***	0.535	(2.76)***	0.456	(2.48)***
BVTA	−	−0.001	(−3.42)***	−0.001	(−3.45)***	−0.001	(−3.45)***
log (1+GROWTH)	+	2.257	(3.88)***	2.116	(3.96)***	2.019	(4.11)***
LEV	+	0.130	(0.15)	0.474	(0.59)	0.667	(0.40)
XLIST	+	2.362	(4.12)***	2.391	(4.19)***	2.261	(4.41)***
SR	−			−0.546	(−2.37)***	−0.555	(−2.52)***
SR_V	−			−0.682	(−2.43)***	−0.639	(−2.41)***
PRIO	−					−0.667	(−2.61)***
PREF	−					−0.357	(−1.97)**
CERT	−					−0.365	(−1.61)**
N		1035		1035		1035	
Adjusted R^2		0.408		0.418		0.433	

Notes: The table reports the results of fixed-effects regressions focusing on shareholder right variables. The dependent variable is TQ and all other variables are defined in Table 8.2. The regressions contain year dummies (Y93–Y99) that are shown and firm dummies that are not. The sample consists of 1035 observations for 140 firms over the 1992–1999 period (t-values are in parentheses).
Significance levels: * (10% level), ** (5% level) and *** (1% level) based on a one-tailed test.

Table 8.5: The relation between TQ and ownership structure and financial institution characteristics.

	Predicted sign	Model (1)		Model (2)	
Constant		1.401	(5.77)***	1.447	(5.72)***
Y93		0.310	(3.21)***	0.312	(3.22)***
Y94		0.384	(4.02)***	0.388	(4.02)***
Y95		0.350	(3.69)***	0.355	(3.70)***
Y96		0.501	(4.65)***	0.493	(4.61)***
Y97		0.632	(4.83)***	0.618	(4.78)***
Y98		0.505	(4.07)***	0.498	(3.99)***
Y99		0.566	(2.84)***	0.557	(2.83)***
BVTA	−	−0.001	(−3.80)***	−0.001	(−3.89)***
log (1+GROWTH)	+	1.849	(4.22)***	1.850	(4.25)***
LEV	+	0.261	(0.35)	0.343	(0.46)
XLIST	+	2.418	(4.75)***	2.469	(4.70)***
SR	−	−0.568	(−2.67)***	−0.514	(−2.65)***
SR_V	−	−0.825	(−2.67)***	−0.754	(−2.66)***
OSIDE_EQ	+	−0.005	(−1.35)*	−0.006	(1.47)*
INDUS_EQ	+\−	−0.009	(−1.71)**	−0.008	(−1.73)**
INSIDE_EQ	+	0.028	(1.92)**	0.028	(1.90)**
INSTI_EQ	+\−	−0.019	(−3.87)***	−0.019	(−3.87)***
FIN_ILOCK	+			−0.081	(−1.53)*
N		1035		1035	
Adjusted R^2		0.463		0.465	

Notes: The table reports the results of fixed-effects regressions focusing on ownership structure and financial institution variables. The dependent variable is TQ and all other variables are defined in Table 8.2. The regressions contain year dummies (Y93–Y99) that are shown and firm dummies that are not. The sample consists of 1035 observations for 140 firms over the 1992–1999 period (*t*-values are in parentheses).

Significance levels: * (10% level), ** (5% level) and *** (1% level) based on a one-tailed test.

transactions occur between the companies. The negative coefficient for financial institutions is consistent with the collusion story in Pound (1988) and the passive attitude of Dutch financial institutions (later in this section we provide additional evidence on the collusion interpretation). Finally, as expected, the coefficient on insider holdings is positive and significant.

Model (2) in Table 8.5 focuses on financial institutions. Relative to model (1), we include the same ownership variables and also add interlocking directorates with financial institutions. The financial institutions driving institutional holdings and interlocking directorates are essentially banks, insurance companies, pension funds and large venture capitalists. The coefficient for interlocking directorates is negative and significant, reinforcing the effect previously documented for financial institutions.

8.5.2. Some Sensitivity Tests

To investigate the influence of banks we include block-holdings by banks, interlocks with banks and long-term bank debt divided by the total debt.[15] For this analysis we have 709 observations (due to missing observations for bank debt and firms with 0 debt). The fixed-effect regression results (not tabled) show a negative coefficient for bank debt of -0.191 (significant at the 5% level). Due to the reduced number of observations (low power), other variables become insignificant. Without the firm fixed effects (results not tabled), the coefficient for bank debt remains significantly negative (at the 1% level), bank block-holdings is also significantly negative (at the 5% level) as they are interlocks (at the 1% level). Thus, the disciplinary role of bank debt is absent, consistent with the previously cited management entrenchment argument of de Jong and Veld (2001) and Zwiebel (1996).[16]

We next address the relationship between ownership structure and takeover defenses. We know ownership concentration may be a takeover defense as well as provide monitoring. In our sample, the block-holdings of the largest outside equity-holder and the number of takeover defenses used (i.e., the number of takeover defenses used from certificates, priority and preference shares) are negatively correlated (-0.254). When we interact these two measures (regressions not tabled), the coefficient is insignificant. The coefficient on the number of takeover defenses itself is negative and significant (as expected), since individually all three defenses were already negative. However, no new insight is obtained by viewing ownership concentration as a takeover defense.

We also investigated whether institutional investors "collude" with entrenched management and supervisory board members by focusing on a setting where this could occur, namely, takeovers. In the Netherlands preference shares are often placed with friendly institutional investors during takeover attempts. Therefore, we expect institutional investors' ownership is more likely to induce entrenchment in firms that can issue preference shares. Specifically, we consider the interaction between preference shares and institutional holdings. While the coefficient for this interaction term is positive and significant, it is very small, too small to compensate for the significant and negative effects of preference shares and institutional holdings. Thus, there is no evidence of collusion between boards and institutions in potential takeover situations.

Finally, we analyze in more detail firms with a secondary listing on US/UK exchanges (Karolyi, 1998; Petotti & Cordfunke, 1998; Doidge, Karolyi, & Stulz, 2001). When we split the cross-listings in our sample into two groups, UK and USA, the effect is still significant for US listings, but not for UK listings. In the UK, all Dutch firms are listed at Stock Exchange Automated Quotation System (SEAQ) International of the London Stock Exchange. UK rules for a secondary listing are less strict than for domestic UK firms and this includes exemption from the Combined Code containing the principles of good governance. The USA has different disclosure requirements for the different types of ADRs (American Depository Receipt). Level 1 ADRs are traded over the counter with minimum SEC disclosure, are exempt for SEC filings, and allowed to use home country accounting. Level 2 ADRs are exchange-listed securities without capital raising capabilities. Level 2 ADRs require full SEC registration and reporting under the Exchange Act of 1934 and must include an annual Form 20-F reconciling financial statements to US requirements. Level 3 ADRs also require full SEC disclosure, but add compliance with the applicable exchange's-listing rules. Splitting the US listings into Level 3 and those below, both groups remain significant, but the coefficient for Level 3 firms is larger by a factor of more than four. This is consistent with the SEC's full required disclosure and adherence to exchange's-listing requirements.

8.5.3. Summary

With regard to organizational form and voting rights, the legally required structured regime, the voluntarily retained structured regime and takeover defenses all have a negative effect on firm value (TQ). Contrary to effective monitoring, major outside and industrial shareholders negatively influence firm value. Financial institutions also fail in their monitoring role, although there is no indirect evidence of collusion. Given the importance of the supervisory board and its influence over the management board under the structured regime (and operations of the firm in general), a logical question to ask is whether our results are affected by the omission of supervisory and management board characteristics. To address this, we collected data on the absolute size of the supervisory board, its size relative to the management board, its shareholdings (previously included in selected regressions as part of insider block-holdings), compensation of its members and the interlocking directorates the firm's board members have with other firms. We also collected analogous data for the management board. Including these variables in the regressions (not tabled) does not alter the basic tenor of our results.[17] As an alternative to a fixed-effects model, we also estimated regressions where firm-specific averages (based on 8 years of data) were used to measure the dependent and independent variables. While the significance of the coefficients was reduced due to the reduction in sample size, the signs of the coefficients are unchanged. We also ran regressions on a year-by-year basis and none of the significant coefficients changes signs when compared to the reported results. Finally, we also ran regressions with industrial fixed effects using the industrial classifications of Statistics Netherlands (similar to Standard Industrial Classification, SIC codes). The inferences are unchanged.

8.5.4. Univariate and Regression Results for 1997–1999 Period (Post-Peters Committee)

8.5.4.1. Univariate tests To gain an overall perspective on the impact of the Peters Committee, we compare corporate governance characteristics, pre- and post-Peters Committee. It could be entrenched that the management has the capability to forestall changes in a firm's corporate governance. One way to investigate this is to perform the same comparison as before using the same firms as before (i.e., those firms listed over both the pre- and post-Peters period, 1992–1999). It could also be the case that change manifests itself not through existing firms, but through the market for new listings. Accordingly, for new listings, we compare governance characteristics pre- and post-Peters. Finally, to ensure our results are not sensitive to the characteristics of the firms that were de-listed, we compare governance characteristics of the de-listed firms pre- and post-Peters.

For the firm characteristics and sample detailed in Tables 8.2 and 8.3 (and supervisory and management board characteristics), we compared their values in 1992–1996 to those in 1997–1999 using a *t*-test. The results are reported in Table 8.6. The comparisons show

Table 8.6: Properties of corporate governance characteristics in the pre- and post-Peters Committee periods.

Variable	1992–1996		1997–1999		Differences	
	Mean	Standard Deviation	Mean	Standard Deviation	Difference	*t*-value
TQ	1.395	0.962	1.868	2.032	0.473	(5.09)***
Total assets	2705.0	9214.0	3824.0	11039.0	1119.0	(1.76)*
Growth	0.262	0.572	0.695	1.272	0.433	(7.47)***
LEV	0.140	0.127	0.129	0.116	−0.010	(−1.30)
Listing abroad	0.13	0.34	0.19	0.39	0.05	(2.40)**
Structured regime required	0.48	0.50	0.47	0.50	−0.01	(−0.19)
Structured regime voluntarily retained	0.11	0.32	0.16	0.37	0.05	(2.19)**
Priority shares	0.41	0.49	0.34	0.48	−0.01	(−2.29)**
Preference shares	0.62	0.49	0.58	0.50	−0.04	(−1.32)
Certificates	0.39	0.49	0.35	0.48	−0.04	(−1.46)
Interlocks with banks	0.82	1.23	0.72	1.03	−0.11	(−1.43)
Interlocks with financials	1.08	1.59	1.07	1.51	−0.01	(−0.08)
Largest block-holder	23.17	19.82	20.38	18.45	−2.78	(−2.26)**
Financial institution block-holdings	12.56	14.89	12.86	15.08	0.29	(0.31)
Bank block-holdings	7.38	10.13	8.13	10.83	0.75	(1.13)
Industrial block-holdings	10.91	21.03	9.11	19.08	−1.80	(−1.40)
Insider block-holdings	6.59	17.46	5.47	16.64	−1.12	(−1.03)
Bank debt	0.071	0.089	0.073	0.088	0.003	(0.43)

Notes: A comparison of the means (two-tailed *t*-test) of the corporate governance variables in the pre-Peters (1992–1996) and post-Peters Committee (1997–1999) periods. The sample consists of 1035 observations, 639 for the pre-Peters and 396 for the post-Peters period. See Table 8.2 for variable definitions.
Significance levels: * (10% level), ** (5% level) and *** (1% level) based on a one-tailed test.

significant increases for TQ, book value of assets, growth, cross-listings on US/UK exchanges and voluntarily retained structured regimes. Significant decreases are noted in the holdings of the largest outside block-holder and the use of priority shares.[18] We also compared firm characteristics in 1996 to those in 1997 (results not tabled). The only significant change was growth, which increased.

We also compared new listings in the pre-Peters period (21 firms) to those in the post-Peters period (39 firms). Though the sample size is small, there are substantive differences in these firms. Post-Peters new listings have a significantly lower number of takeover defenses and interlocking directorates with financial institutions and banks, lower equity holdings by financial institutions and banks, a lower proportion of voluntarily retained structured regimes (though no difference in the legally required structured regime), more insider equity holdings and lower holdings by the largest outside block-holder. On balance, these findings suggest the new listings market appears to be a disciplinary force in the post-Peters period. Finally, we compared the 26 firms de-listed in the pre-Peters period to the 20 firms de-listed in the post-Peters period. We found no significant differences in the corporate governance characteristics of these firms.

8.5.4.2. Regression tests   In Table 8.7, we perform two regressions, one for the 1992–1999 period (both the pre- and post-Peters periods) and one comparing the pre- and post-Peters periods. The first regression includes all significant variables from Tables 8.4 and 8.5 because these are the variables that change significantly from the pre- to the post-Peters period.

To test for changes over time between 1992–1996 and 1997–1999, the second regression interacts the governance variables with a dummy variable having a value of 1 in 1997–1999 and 0 otherwise. The left-hand column of Table 8.7 contains the coefficients for the 1992–1996 period, while the right-hand column contains the coefficients for the variables interacted with the 1997–1999 dummy variable. The results in the right-hand column show the coefficient on the required structured regime is significantly negative, indicating the already negative effect of this variable on firm value became more pronounced in 1997–1999. The coefficients for certificates, the major outside block-holder and interlocking directorates with financial institutions become negative and significant in the post-Peters period. The coefficient for industrial holdings is significantly positive, which implies that while the overall influence of industrial holdings is still negative, its influence is smaller in the post-Peters period.

Overall, the findings suggest the use of priority shares (univariate tests) dropped, and the adverse effects of industrial holdings (regression tests) were reduced for firms spanning the pre- and post-Peters periods. In addition, the disciplining role of the new listings market changes for the better in the post-Peters period.

8.5.5. Stock Price Reactions to Corporate Governance Events in the Netherlands

8.5.5.1. Background   The above univariate analysis of governance characteristics and regressions using TQ illustrate little evidence can be found for a positive impact from the recommendations contained in the Peters Committee report. However, the Peters Committee did not operate in isolation, as there were additional Dutch government and EU events with the potential to affect corporate governance practices and firm value. In this

Table 8.7: The relation between TQ and corporate governance characteristics in the pre- and post-Peters Committee periods.

	Predicted sign	Results for 1992–1999		Results for 1992–1996 versus 1997–1999			
				1992–1996		1997–1999	
Constant		2.117	(4.99)***	1.853	(4.56)***		
Y93		0.319	(3.30)***	0.308	(3.37)***		
Y94		0.396	(4.11)***	0.363	(4.00)***		
Y95		0.341	(3.55)***	0.317	(3.59)***		
Y96		0.444	(4.20)***	0.456	(5.07)***		
Y97		0.556	(4.32)***			1.199	(3.74)***
Y98		0.427	(3.32)***			1.080	(3.25)***
Y99		0.483	(2.56)***			1.138	(2.68)***
BVTA		−0.001	(−3.85)***	−0.001	(−4.26)***	0.001	(0.73)
log (1+GROWTH)	+	1.788	(4.29)***	1.578	(2.88)***	0.357	(0.39)
LEV	+	0.496	(0.67)	−0.552	(−0.82)	−0.771	(−0.85)
XLIST	+	2.348	(4.92)***	2.161	(5.25)***	0.272	(0.56)
SR	–	−0.542	(−2.86)***	−0.356	(−2.03)**	−0.613	(−3.11)***
SR_V	–	−0.692	(−2.66)***	−0.523	(−2.18)**	−0.196	(−0.78)
CERT	–	−0.236	(−1.30)*	−0.030	(−0.16)	−0.283	(−2.06)**
PRIO	–	−0.669	(−2.91)***	−0.722	(−3.18)***	0.031	(0.19)
PREF	–	−0.316	(−1.94)**	−0.232	(−1.51)*	−0.115	(−0.67)
OSIDE_EQ	+	−0.007	(−1.66)**	−0.004	(−0.81)	−0.007	(−1.40)*
INDUS_EQ	–/+	−0.008	(−1.51)*	−0.013	(−2.45)***	0.007	(1.38)*
INSTI_EQ	–/+	−0.020	(−3.92)***	−0.019	(−3.78)***	0.002	(−0.48)
INSIDE_EQ	+	0.026	(1.88)**	0.024	(2.05)**	0.004	(0.61)
FIN_ILOCK	+	−0.081	(−1.55)*	−0.020	(−0.40)	−0.137	(−2.21)**
N		1035		1035			
Adjusted R²		0.478		0.497			

Notes: The table reports the results of fixed-effects regressions for the governance variables for the 1992–1999, 1992–1996 and 1997–1999 periods. The dependent variable is TQ and all other variables are defined in Table 8.2. The regressions contain year dummies (Y93–Y99) that are shown and firm dummies that are not shown. The sample consists of 1035 observations for 140 firms over the 1992–1999 period (*t*-values are in parentheses).
Significance levels: * (10% level), ** (5% level) and *** (1% level) based on a one-tailed test.

section, we use event study techniques to assess investors' reactions to the various events associated with corporate governance practices in the Netherlands. In a sense, the event study analysis provides a direct market test of the premise underlying the Peters Committee, namely, self-regulation of corporate governance practices relying on market forces are sufficient to promote changes that enhance shareholder value.

Table 8.8 lists 18 events associated with corporate governance in the Netherlands starting with the formation of the Peters Committee in 1996 and ending in 2003 with the

Table 8.8: Event study results.

Event	Description	Average return F-statistic (P-value)
1	On February 13, 1996 Van Ittersum, chairman of the Amsterdam Stock Exchange, announces a committee for code of best practice on corporate governance.	-0.04% 0.03 (0.855)
2	On February 28, 1996 the Ministries of Finance, Law and Economic Affairs and VvdE (shareholders) and VEUO (exchange-listed firms) agree to an arrangement on takeover defenses	-0.08% 0.08 (0.773)
3	On March 15, 1996 there is an announcement of the members of Committee Corporate Governance. Given the Dutch consensus approach, all the parties are represented on committee.	0.04% 0.03 (0.859)
4	On October 28, 1996, the publication of the preliminary conclusions of the Peters Committee took place.	-0.04% 0.04 (0.838)
5	On June 25, 1997, the publication of the final conclusions of the Peters Committee took place. Conclusions are similar to the preliminary report.	-0.01% 0.00 (0.960)
6	On March 17, 1998 the Foundation for Corporate Governance Research by Pension Funds is founded. Its goal was to improve the influence of shareholders and to increase accountability by management.	-0.005% 0.00 (0.99)
7	On April 18, 1998, an announcement of a "Communication Channel" for shareholders. A small group of (11) firms form a private sector initiate or experiment in "voting by proxy" using a system designed and owned by the participating firms.	0.01% 0.00 (0.976)
8	On May 19, 1998, an announcement of the firms participating in the "Communication Channel" for shareholders.	-0.4% 1.01 (0.315)
9	On December 3, 1998 the Peters Committee's monitoring report is presented. This is the major event because it contains all the corporate governance information collected by the committee on Dutch companies.	-0.8% 7.38 (0.007)

Table 8.8: Continued.

Event	Description	Average return F-statistic (P-value)
	During this meeting the Minister of Finance announces legislation on proxy voting will be proposed to the cabined of ministers. The proposed legislation is independent of the private sector initiative.	
10	On April 29, 1999, a proposal to introduce proxy voting is approved by 'Ministerraad', which means it is approved by the "cabinet" of ministers and will be sent to parliament for consideration.	−0.1% 0.20 (0.654)
11	On May 10, 1999 the Minister of Finance replies to the Peters Committee report in a "nota" to the "Tweede Kamer" (parliament) — firms should provide more information on compensation and stock transaction by managers; proxy voting should be possible and limitations on voting power should be banned. No specific proposals are mentioned and the article described the reply as a "wensenlijstje" (list of wishes).	−0.05% 0.04 (0.840)
12	On June 23, 1999, a new EU Directive is released which states that majority shareholders have to make a bid on the remaining shares of the company. certificates and preference share are allowed in a firm's capital structure.	−0.1% 0.27 (0.601)
13	On September 1, 2002 a new law became effective requiring firms to disclose information regarding their remuneration of individual management board and supervisory board members.	0.04% 0.03 (0.86)
14	On December 15, 2002 a new law became effective facilitating proxy voting by allowing shareholders to register 7 days before the shareholders meeting instead of immediately before the meeting (see also event 7 where 11 firms began to allow proxy voting).	−0.07% 0.07 (0.753)
15	On December 18, 2002, a second monitoring report related to the Peters Committee's recommendations on corporate governance in the Netherlands was published.	0.005% 0.00 (0.99)
16	During 2002, the ministers of Dutch finance and economic affairs invited the Dutch employers association, Amsterdam Stock Exchange, Association of Stock.	−0.01% 0.04 (0.982)
17	Issuing Companies, Foundation for Corporate Governance Research by Pension Funds and the Association of Stockholders to establish a new corporate	−0.03% 0.05 (0.87)

Table 8.8: Continued.

Event	Description	Average return F-statistic (P-value)
18	governance committee. The task of the committee was to develop a new corporate governance code. The process began in March 10, 2003 (event 16), a concept code was presented on July 1, 2003 (event 17) and the final code was released on December 9, 2003 event (18).	−0.04 0.03 (0.91)

Notes: For each event, we test the null hypothesis and the mean abnormal return is 0. The right-hand column reports the mean risk-adjusted return for each particular event and below it are the associated *F*-statistic and *P*-value. Results are based on a sample of Dutch firms with security return data available over the January 1, 1996–December 31, 2003 period. Events during the 1996–1999 (2002–2003) periods are based on a sample of 123 (97) firms. The sample is smaller in 2002–2003 due to mergers, acquisitions, etc. Estimation is based on the SUR method described in Schipper and Thompson (1983, 1985). The data sources for the key events related to Dutch corporate governance practices are Het Financieele Dagblad (the leading Dutch financial daily newspaper, equivalent to the *Financial Times* in the UK and *The Wall Street Journal* in the USA), the preliminary and final reports of the Peters Committee, and the monitoring report that assessed the impact of the final report of the Peters Committee.

release of a report of a second committee on Dutch corporate governance practices (i.e., a follow-up committee to the original Peters committee). The data sources are the Dutch equivalent of the Financial Times (Het Financieele Dagblad), the preliminary and final version of the Peters Committee's first report, the Peters Committee's monitoring reports and the subsequent committee on Dutch corporate governance practices that followed-up the Peters Committee.

8.5.5.2. Event study analysis   The event study method used is an application of Zellner's (1962) Seemingly-Unrelated-Regression (SUR) methodology (see, Schipper & Thompson, 1983; 1985 for a detailed discussion). The returns-generating process of each firm is:

$$R_{it} = \alpha_i + \beta_i R_{mt} + \sum_{k=1}^{18} \gamma_{ik} D_{ikt} + \varepsilon_{it,}$$

where R_{it} is the return to security i on day t, R_{mt} is the return to the market index on day t, D_{ikt} is a dummy variable that takes on a value of 1 on the day before and day of the announcement of event k ($k = 1, 2, \ldots, 18$) and 0 on all other days, α_i is the model intercept of firm i, β_i is the slope coefficient or systematic risk of firm i, γ_{ik} is the abnormal return of firm i associated with event k, and ε_{it} is a random disturbance. For each firm the disturbances are assumed independent and identically distributed over time, but may be heteroscedastic and correlated in cross-section. The firm-specific parameters of the model are estimated using daily stock return data from January 1, 1996 to December 31, 2003. The market index used is a value-weighted index of all firms traded on Euronext Amsterdam (results using alternative market indices yield similar results). Events during the 1996–1999 (post-1999) period are based on a sample of 123 (97) firms. The sample is smaller in the later years due to mergers and acquisitions, etc.

The test of interest is the significance of the mean abnormal return of the sample firms at the time of each event. In particular,

$$H_0 : \sum_{i=1}^{N} \gamma_{ik} = 0, \quad (k = 1, 2, \ldots, 18),$$

where k denotes events and N denotes the number of firms. Since the sum is a scalar multiple of the cross-sectional average, this test is equivalent to a test on the cross-sectional average abnormal return. The significance of the sample mean abnormal return to each event is assessed using the F-test outlined in Schipper and Thompson 1985. To save space, the key findings are discussed in the text, while details of the results (i.e., a detailed description of each event, F-statistics and P-values for all 18 events) are reported in Table 8.8.

Of the 18 events, only event 9 (the release of the Peters Committee's monitoring report and the related corporate governance information it contained about Dutch firms) is associated with a significant stock price reaction. The sample-wide mean abnormal return is -0.8% (F-statistic = 7.38 and P-value = 0.007). There is a pervasive negative reaction to this event as 78% of the firms have a negative stock return. One interpretation of these results is that, based on the (negative) corporate governance information released in the Peters Committee's monitoring report, the market was disappointed with firms' lack of progress in their governance practices.[19]

On balance, the market's reaction to the release of the monitoring report (event 9) is one of disappointment about the substantive change in Dutch corporate governance practices. The other 11 events through 1999, which generated no significant investor reaction, dealt mainly with the other activities of the Peters' Committee including the release of its recommendations, private and government proposals on proxy voting and the Minister of Finance's reply to the monitoring report (see, Ministry of Finance, 1999), the latter of which was described as a "wish list" by the financial press. The six post-1999 events consist of follow-up activities associated with the "wish list" (e.g., proxy voting and compensation disclosure), the results of the second monitoring report of the Peters Committee in 2002, and the release of the new corporate governance code by the committee that followed the Peters Committee. A key aspect of the new corporate governance code is that it failed to address shareholder rights. Overall, the event study evidence suggests that the market was skeptical about the substantive evolution of corporate governance practices in the Netherlands.

8.6. Conclusions and Implications

The Netherlands and the structure of the Peters Committee's initiative on corporate governance provide an ideal setting to investigate the role of self-regulation. For self-regulation to succeed, shareholders must have voting rights. Under the "pure" form of the structured regime, shareholders in the Netherlands lose their ability to *directly* monitor the supervisory and management boards. However, the market for corporate control still functions since shareholders vote on mergers and acquisitions. With shareholder voting rights restricted permanently or via takeover defenses in Dutch firms, shareholders lose their ability to initiate change via the market for corporate control. These points highlight the basis for our findings on the Peters Committee's lack of success, and the market's skepticism about the evolution of Dutch corporate governance practices. They also cast considerable doubt on the Dutch corporate governance model as a framework for other countries.

It is often argued the market provides management with incentives to change because of the penalty assessed to firms with poor governance and performance. This argument is predicated on the assumption that there are mechanisms in place to facilitate change. In Dutch firms where the supervisory and management boards already controlling the voting rights, it is doubtful whether change will take place without exchange or government action to restore voting rights to shareholders. It is equally doubtful whether the prospects for change are any different for existing firms in the long run without voting rights for shareholders (one of the major recommendations of the Peters Committee). A possible exception is the disciplining role of the market for new listings where there are relatively fewer entrenched parties who control voting rights. Our results suggest self-regulation, which relies on monitoring without enforcement by either exchanges or governments, or where there is limited or no outside monitoring, is unlikely to be successful. The results also cast considerable doubt on the success of other (similar) self-regulation initiatives undertaken by EU countries.

Acknowledgement

Reprinted from *Journal of Corporate Finance*, *11*(3), 2005, 473–503: The role of self-regulation in corporate governance: Evidence and implications from the Netherlands, by Abe de Jong, D. DeJong, G. Mertens, and C. Wasley, with permission from Elsevier.

Endnotes

1. In a study motivated in part by the recommendations of the Cadbury Committee, Dahya and McConnell (2003) find "announcement period stock returns indicate that investors appear to view appointments of outside directors and outside CEOS as good news." The authors conclude "Apparently, boards with more outside directors make different (and perhaps better) decisions.

2. The anti-director index ranges from 0 to 6 and is formed by adding 1 when each of the following applies, when:
   1. the country allows the shareholders to mail their proxy vote to the firm,
   2. shareholders are not required to deposit their shares prior to the general shareholders' meeting,
   3. cumulative voting or proportional representation of minorities in the board of directors is allowed,
   4. an oppressed minorities mechanism is in place,
   5. the minimum percentage of share capital entitling a shareholder to call for an extraordinary shareholders' meeting is less than or equal to 10% (the sample median in the study cited)
   6. shareholders have pre-emptive rights that can be waived only by a shareholders' vote. See Table 8.2 in La Porta, Rafael, Lopez-de-Silanes, Shleifer, and Vishny (1998), which details a country's compliance with each of the six criteria that make up the anti-director index.

3. The Verdam Committee referred to the then situation as "no longer acceptable" due to inadequate control of management's activities, and their propensity to misstate the firms' financial position and to violate the position of shareholder, debtholders and employees (Verdam Committee, 1965). This was the major driving force to restructure company's law (Mertens, 1997). Slagter (1996) documents the desire for more co-determination (*medezeggenschap*); meaning all stakeholders' interests should be represented in a fair way. The law also dealt with financial reporting requirements, the right of enquiry, a works council and the establishment of the enterprise chamber at the Amsterdam court (Zeff, van der Wel, & Camfferman, 1992).

4. Companies required to apply the structured regime have statutes detailing the exact rights and duties of the supervisory board. If a company no longer meets these criteria (e.g., due to its international scope) and wants to change to another organizational form, its statutes must be changed. The management board, supervisory board or the annual shareholders meeting may suggest a change in the statutes. However, the supervisory board still has most of the legal powers and shareholders usually have a limited say. This could be one of the reasons why a relatively large number of the largest publicly Dutch-listed companies apply the structured regime on a voluntary basis.

5. Presently, the two-tier structure is used in Denmark, Germany, Netherlands and France (which gives firms the option of choosing either the one- or two-tier structure, eight of the CAC40 in France use the two-tier structure). However, implementation differs across countries. In Germany, the supervisory board exerts substantial independent influence on management. In the Netherlands, there is a close relationship between the management and the supervisory boards so as to include the management board's influence on appointments to the supervisory board.

6. Under the *no structured regime*, at the annual meeting shareholders can nominate and elect supervisory board members. Under the *structured regime*, nominations for supervisory board members may be proposed and rejected by shareholders, but election is by the supervisory board. Large investors can influence the outcomes by refusing to approve the financial statements and supervisory board nominations (Chirinko, van Ees, Garretsen, & Sterken, 2003).

7. Unfortunately, this information is only available from the articles of association and we do not have access to such data. This is unlikely to bias our results because holders of priority shares normally receive binding appointment rights and we already include priority shares in our tests.

8. Cantrijn and Vente (1997) sent questionnaires to Dutch institutional investors. The responses showed such investors perceive liquidity to be more important than exercising control. Moreover, institutions exercising supervision over a firm's investment and remuneration policies were cited by only 20% and 33% of the respondents, respectively.

9. In the Netherlands, firms either present replacement values or historical costs in their annual reports. If replacement values are presented no adjustment is required. If historical costs are presented, we adjust the value to estimate replacement value. To do this, we assume, in the base year, the replacement value equals the historical cost. For each subsequent year, we adjust this replacement value by adding new investments and corrections for the growth in capital good prices, and by subtracting depreciation. Growth in capital good prices is based on the price index of investment goods provided by the Statistics Netherlands.

10. A positive coefficient for leverage confirms the disciplinary role of leverage (see, McConnell & Servaes, 1990). De Jong and Veld (2001) document the absence of this role in the Netherlands due to managerial entrenchment. The absence of this result is also consistent with the "debt avoidance" hypothesis articulated by Zwiebel (1996).

11. Since Dutch Law on Disclosure of Shareholdings requires the notification of shareholdings when thresholds of 5%, 10%, 25%, 50%, or 66.7% are passed, we do not have information for shareholdings below 5%. The percentage of firm-year observations with insider block-holdings in our data set is 16.7%. This is not a high percentage, but some block-holdings are over 80% and thus significantly influence the average.

12. A curious feature of the descriptive statistics in Table 8.3 is the average total assets for the "No Structured Regime" sample exceeds that of the "Legally Required Structured Regime" sample. The difference is due to an outlier and the firm is Royal Dutch, which is the Dutch part of the dual-listed firm Royal Dutch/Shell. Since more than 50% of the firm's employees are employed outside the Netherlands, it is exempt from the structured regime, and has not chosen to voluntarily adopt the structured regime.

13. A feature of panel data like that used in this study is over time there are likely to be unobserved factors affecting the behaviour of the dependent variable that cannot be identified or measured and included in the model. A common approach to control for such factors is to incorporate firm-specific intercepts into the regression model. The resulting fixed-effects regression assumes the impact of the unobserved factors is constant through time for a given firm, but different across firms. An analogous argument motivates using year-specific intercepts.

14. This result differs from the McConnell and Servaes (1990) that documents a positive influence. Our result is explained by results in de Jong and Veld (2001), which document, in a sample of debt and equity issues, that Dutch firms avoid LEV when its disciplinary role is most valuable. Thus, an insignificant effect is consistent with the absence of LEV as a disciplinary factor for Dutch firms.

15. We remove INSTI_EQ and FIN_ILK, because these variables are by definition highly correlated with bank equity and bank interlocks, respectively.
16. The negative impact of bank-holdings contrasts with the positive and significant findings for Germany (Gorton & Schmid, 2000). One explanation for the difference is bank-holdings are higher in Germany than the Netherlands. Further, the typical German supervisory board is more powerful than in the Netherlands and a banker is often chairman of the supervisory board (not so in Netherlands). The proxy voting system where by banks vote individual investors shares (that are deposited with the bank) and the constraints placed on other shares amplify a German bank's influence, particularly relative to a Netherlands bank where there is no proxy voting and bank-holdings are equally affected by voting constraints. Finally, at that time covered by our sample period, the Netherlands provided tax incentives for banks holding equity securities so long as holdings exceeded 5%. Thus, there is a tax incentive to hold (at least) 5%, but not a lot more. All this makes for a more benign block-holder.
17. The results are also robust to alternative specifications of the dependent variable (e.g., market-to-book value of assets or equity). The correlation between TQ and the market-to-book value of total assets is 0.998 and that between TQ and the market to book value of equity is 0.545.
18. For supervisory and management board comparisons, the only significant change is board compensation, which increased.
19. Based on personal discussions with Peters Committee staff members, this interpretation is consistent with their view that Peters himself, built up market expectations about substantive change that was not realized given the data that were released.

References

Agrawal, A., & Knoeber, C.R. (1996). Firm performance and mechanisms to control agency problems between managers and shareholders. *Journal of Financial and Quantitative Analysis, 31*, 377–398.

Alchian, A. (1950). Uncertainty, evolution and economic theory. *Journal of Political Economy, 58*, 211–221.

Barca, F., & Becht, M. (2001). *The control of corporate Europe.* Oxford: Oxford University Press.

Becht, M. (1999). European corporate governance: Trading off liquidity and control. *European Economic Review, 43*, 1071–1083.

Berle, A., & Means, G. (1932). *The modern corporation and private property.* New York: Macmillan.

Cantrijn, D., & Vente, J. (1997). Institutionele beleggers en corporate governance in Nederland. *Bedrijfskunde, 69*, 51–60.

Chirinko, R., van Ees, H., Garretsen, H., & Sterken, E. (2003). *Investor protection and concentrated ownership: Assessing control mechanisms in the Netherlands.* Working paper.

Cho, M.-H. (1998). Ownership structure, investment, and corporate value: An empirical analysis. *Journal of Financial Economics, 47*, 103–121.

Committee on Corporate Governance (1997). *Corporate governance in the Netherlands.* Amsterdam: Secretariat Committee on Corporate Governance.

Couwenberg, O. (1997). *Resolving financial distress in the Netherlands.* Unpublished Ph.D. dissertation, Groningen University.

Dahya, J., McConnell, J., & Travlos, N.G. (2002). The Cadbury committee, corporate performance and management turnover. *Journal of Finance, 57*, 461–483.

Dedman, E. (2000). An investigation into the determinants of UK board structure before and after Cadbury. *Corporate Governance: An International Review, 8*, 133–153.

De Jong, A., Kabir, R., Marra, T., & Roell, A. (2001). Ownership and control in the Netherlands. In: F. Barca, & M. Brecht (Eds), *The Control of Corporate Europe.* Oxford: Oxford University Press.

De Jong, A., & Veld, C. (2001). An empirical analysis of incremental capital structure decisions under managerial entrenchment. *Journal of Banking and Finance, 25*, 1857–1895.

Doidge, C., Karolyi, A., & Stulz, R. (2001). *Why are foreign firms listed in the U.S. worth more?* Working paper.

Dyck, A., & Zingales, L. (2004). Private benefits of control: An international comparison. *Journal of Finance, 59*, 533–596.

Fama, E., & Jensen, M. (1983a). Separation of ownership and control. *Journal of Law and Economics, 26*, 301–325.

Fama, E., & Jensen, M. (1983b). Agency problems and residual claimants. *Journal of Law and Economics, 26*, 327–349.

Financial Times (2000a). *McKinsey report — investors pay premiums for well-governed companies.*

Financial Times (2000b). *Breaking the bank's consensus.*

Franks, J., & Mayer, C. (1996). Hostile takeovers and the correction of managerial failure. *Journal of Financial Economics, 40*, 163–181.

Gorton, G., & Schmid, F. (2000). Universal banking and performance of German firms. *Journal of Financial Economics, 58*, 29–80.

Gugler, K. (2001). *Corporate governance and economic performance.* Oxford: Oxford University Press.

Holderness, C.G., & Sheehan, D.P. (1988). The role of majority shareholders in publicly held corporations. *Journal of Financial Economics, 20*, 317–346.

Honée, H.J.M.N., Timmerman, L., & Nethe, M.Y. (2000). *Rapport inzake de toepassing van de structuurregeling; zeggenschapsverhoudingen en Nederlandse beursvennootschappen.* Report for Ministry of Finance.

Jensen, M.C., & Meckling, W.H. (1976). Theory of the firm: Managerial behaviour, agency costs and ownership structure. *Journal of Financial Economics, 3*, 305–360.

Karolyi, A. (1998). Why do companies list shares abroad: A survey of the evidence and its managerial implications. *Financial Markets, Institutions and Instruments, 7*, 1–60.

La Porta, R., Lopez-de-Silanes, F., & Shleifer, A. (1999). Corporate ownership around the world. *Journal of Finance, 54*, 471–517.

La Porta, R., Lopez-de-Silanes, F., Shleifer, A., & Vishny, R.W. (1998) Law and finance. *Journal of Political Economy, 106*, 1113–1155.

La Porta, R., Lopez-de-Silanes, F., Shleifer, A., & Vishny, R.W. (2000). Investor protection and corporate governance. *Journal of Financial Economics, 58*, 3–27.

Lindenberg, E.B., & Ross, S.A. (1981). Tobin's q ratio and industrial organization. *Journal of Business, 54*, 1–32.

Lins, K., Strickland, D., & Zenner, M. (1999). *Do non-US firms issue stock on U.S. equity markets to relax capital constraints?* Working paper.

Maeijer, J.J.M., & Geens, K. (1990). *Defensive measures against hostile takeovers in the common market.* Dordrecht: Nijhoff Publishers.

Malatesta, P.H., & Walking, R.A. (1988). Poison pill securities: Stockholder wealth, profitability and ownership structure. *Journal of Financial Economics, 20*, 347–376.

McConnell, J.J., & Servaes, H. (1990). Additional evidence on equity ownership and corporate value. *Journal of Financial Economics, 27*, 595–612.

Mertens, G.M.H. (1997). *The impact of financial reporting regulation on financial accounting method choice.* Unpublished dissertation, University of Maastricht.

Ministry of Finance (1999). Kabinetsreactie op het rapport van de Monitoring Commissie Corporate Governance.

Monitoring corporate governance in Nederland (1998). *Bericht van de Monitoring Commissie Corporate Governance en de uitkomsten van het onderzoek verricht door het Economisch Instituut Tilburg.* Deventer: Kluwer.

Morck, R., Shleifer, A., & Vishny, R.W. (1988). Management ownership and market valuation: An empirical analysis. *Journal of Financial Economics, 20*, 293–315.

NRC Handelsbad (1997). *Minister keeps new legislation up his sleeve after advice 'Peters.'* Zalm: shareholder remains rightless.

Perfect, S.B., & Wiles, K.W. (1994). Alternative constructions of Tobin's Q: An empirical comparison. *Journal of Empirical Finance, 1*, 313–341.

Pound, J. (1988). Proxy contests and the efficiency of shareholder oversight. *Journal of Financial Economics, 20*, 237–265.

Price Waterhouse (1997). *Converging cultures: trends in corporate governance.*

Schipper, K., & Thompson, R. (1983). The impact of merger-related regulations on the shareholders of acquiring firms. *Journal of Accounting Research, 21*, 184–221.

Schipper, K., & Thompson, R. (1985). The impact of merger-related regulations using exact distributions of test statistics. *Journal of Accounting Research, 23*, 408–415.

Stulz, R.M. (1988). Managerial control of voting rights: Financing policies and the market for corporate control. *Journal of Financial Economics, 20*, 25–54.

Shleifer, A., & Vishny, R.W. (1997). A survey of corporate governance. *Journal of Finance, 52*, 737–783.

Slagter, W.J. (1996). *Compendium van het Ondernemingsrecht.* Deventer: Kluwer, p. 210.

Stigler, G. (1958). The economies of scale. *Journal of Law and Economics, 1*, 54–71.

Stiles, P., & Taylor, B. (1993). Benchmarking corporate governance: The impact of the Cadbury code. *Long Range Planning, 26*, 61–71.

Verdam Committee (1965). *Herziening van het ondernemingsrecht. Rapport van de commissie ingesteld bij beschikking van de Minister van Justitie van 8 April 1960.* Den Haag: Staatsuitgeverij (pp. 119–125).

Voogd, R.P. (1989). *Statutaire beschermingsmiddelen bij vennootschappen.* Deventer: Kluwer.

Weil, Gothshal & Manges (2002). *Comparative study of corporate governance codes relevant to the European Union and its members.* Final Report on behalf of the European Commission, Internal Market Directorate General.

Zeff, S.A., van der Wel, F., Camfferman, C. (1992). *Company financial reporting: A historical and comparative study of the Dutch regulatory process.* Amsterdam: Elsevier Science Publishers (171–181).

Zellner, A. (1962). An efficient method of estimating seemingly-unrelated-regressions and tests for aggregation bias. *Journal of American Statistical Association, 57*, 348–368.

Zwiebel, J. (1996). Dynamic capital structure under managerial entrenchment. *American Economic Review, 86*, 1197–1215.

Chapter 9

Shareholder Lock-in Contracts: Share Price and Trading Volume Effects at the Lock-in Expiry

Peter-Paul Angenendt, Marc Goergen and Luc Renneboog

9.1. Introduction

During the late 1990s, many Western European countries saw the emergence of stock market segments attracting high-growth and high-technology firms. Their initial success was followed by a painful downfall in 2000 from which they are still to recover. Several markets were even closed down or restructured (see Goergen, Khurshed, McCahery, & Renneboog, 2002). In this chapter, we focus on initial public offerings (IPOs) on the French *Nouveau Marché*. A firm that wishes to go public seeks one or more investment banks to act as its underwriter(s). The responsibilities of the underwriter are to sell the shares to the public, to take up any unwanted shares and to take care of the legalities of the deal. There is usually asymmetric information between the existing shareholders, the underwriter and the public. To reduce such asymmetric information, lock-in contracts can be used.[1] Such agreements are arrangements between the existing shareholders of the issuing firm and the lead underwriter or stock exchange, whereby the shareholders agree not to sell a certain percentage of their shares for a specified period after the IPO (Espenlaub, Goergen, & Khurshed, 2001: 1235). The duration of the lock-in agreement and the percentage of shares locked in may signal the commitment of the pre-IPO shareholders who hold on to (part of) their shares at the IPO. In practice, the company and the underwriter may exempt certain shareholders (usually only the shareholders holding small stakes) from the lock-ins while enforcing more stringent lock-ins on the other insiders and new shareholders. Further, some stock markets, such as the French *Nouveau Marché*, impose minimum lock-in contracts. Conversely, the main stock market segments in the UK and USA do not have any such requirements, such that all existing lock-in agreements on these markets are voluntary arrangements.

The *Nouveau Marché* was a segment of the French stock market, specializing in high-growth and high-technology companies. Since these firms are characterized by high

Advances in Corporate Finance and Asset Pricing
Edited by L. Renneboog
© 2006 Elsevier B.V. All rights reserved.
ISBN: 0-444-52723-0

uncertainty, *La Bourse de Paris* decided to impose lock-in agreements on the firms' insiders. Until 1 December 1998, the *Nouveau Marché* required all IPO firms to lock in their insiders with 80% of their shareholdings for 3 years. The precise definition of insiders was determined on a company-by-company basis when the firm filed its IPO prospectus. Usually, the insiders were defined as the founders and the executives. With effect of 1 December 1998, *La Bourse de Paris* introduced new lock-in rules for the *Nouveau Marché (Instruction NM3-02)*. From this date, firms planning to go public on the *Nouveau Marché* had two options. They could either lock in their insiders with 80% of their holdings for 1 year or lock in their entire holdings for 6 months. Figure 9.1 reproduces the lock-in agreement for *Qualiflow Société Anonyme (SA)*, which went public on 10 October 2000. The first paragraph of the agreement states that the company's executives — the founder is one of them — have chosen a stricter lock-in agreement than the minimum requirement. The second paragraph of the agreement shows that the other shareholders are locked in voluntarily.

New minimum lock-in requirements came into force on 15 September 2003. Since then, only the managing directors, and not all the insiders, have had to lock in their entire holding for 1 year. Additionally, shares bought by any shareholder during the year preceding the admission to a flotation also had to be locked in for 1 year. Unfortunately, the impact of this change cannot be investigated, as there were no IPOs from the day the new regulation came into force until the market's closure in February 2005.

The literature on lock-in agreements used to be restricted to studies on US IPOs, most of which document significant abnormal negative returns around the expiry of lock-ins. Recently, however, studies on the expiries of lock-in agreements have been conducted for UK, German and Italian IPOs. So far, the number of French studies is limited to two. Ducros (2001) explains how French firms choose between two alternative lock-in requirements for a small sample of IPOs on the *Second Marché* and the *Nouveau Marché*. Similarly, Goergen, Renneboog, and Khurshed (2005) focus on the reasons explaining the differences in the lock-in characteristics across IPOs on the *Neuer Markt* and the *Nouveau Marché*. This chapter is the first to conduct an event study on the lock-in expiry in the population of *Nouveau Marché* IPOs. The high degree of variability in the lock-in characteristics and the fact that the *Nouveau Marché* had mandatory lock-in agreements for insiders, which changed after a few years, has created a particularly rich dataset. Further, US studies have found higher negative abnormal returns and larger increases in trading volume for venture-capital (VC)-backed

Commitment to retain securities

Pursuant to the operating rules of the Nouveau Marché, shareholding executives have made a commitment to retain 100% of the stake they hold in the capital of the Company on the date of the initial listing for a period of one year after the Company's shares are listed for trading on the Nouveau Marché.

In addition, the other shareholders have undertaken to retain 80% of the shares of the Company in their possession after the offering for a period of 8 months from the date on which the shares of the Company are listed for trading on the Nouveau Marché.

Figure 9.1: Example of a lock-in agreement. *Source:* Offer prospectus of *Qualiflow SA.*

firms. Unlike US studies, the nature of our data makes it possible to identify specific shareholder types, including VCs, and their lock-in characteristics.

Section 9.2 gives an overview of the market environment and institutional setting on the *Nouveau Marché* and compares it to those of other European growth markets. Section 9.3 reviews the existing literature on lock-in agreements and states the hypotheses. Section 9.4 describes the sample and the variables. The methodology is explained in Section 9.5, while Section 9.6 discusses the results and Section 9.7 concludes this chapter.

9.2. Market Environment and Institutional Setting

This section starts by describing the emergence of the *Nouveau Marché* and similar markets during the previous decade. It then reviews the institutional setting of the *Nouveau Marché* with a focus on lock-in requirements. Finally, VC financing and corporate governance in France are discussed.

9.2.1. European Growth Markets

The access to capital for young European firms with high growth opportunities has been limited compared to their US counterparts. On 1 March 1996, the stock exchanges of Brussels and Paris formed *Euro.NM*, which stands for the *European New Market*. Its ambition was to become the pan-European stock market for growth companies, similar to what National Association of Securities Dealers Automated Quotations (NASDAQ) is in the USA. Over the years, three additional stock markets (located in Amsterdam, Frankfurt and Milan) joined the *Euro.NM*.

France was the first continental European country to introduce a growth segment, the *Nouveau Marché*, which opened on 14 February 1996. The first company that obtained a listing was *Infonie SA*, which had its IPO on 20 March 1996. In total, 177 companies (166 domestic and 11 foreign companies) were listed. Even though new regulation was introduced in September 2003 (see the appendix), there have been no new listings since March 2002.[2] The *Nouveau Marché* became part of *Euronext Paris* in September 2000 and was dissolved in February 2005. The 128 remaining companies were transferred to the newly created *Eurolist Small Caps*, *Eurolist Mid Caps* or *Eurolist Large Caps*, according to their size. The *Nouveau Marché* index was calculated until 30 June 2005.

The *Euro.NM* markets in the Netherlands, Belgium and Italy were less successful in attracting new listings. Conversely, on Germany's *Neuer Markt* a total of 345 listings (275 domestic and 70 foreign companies) were introduced. On 1 January 2003, *Deutsche Börse* restructured its segments; the *Neuer Markt* ceased to exist and its companies were transferred to other segments.

All five *Euro.NM* markets had their own performance and price indices. On 16 January 1998, they were combined into the *Euro.NM* index, which was computed until 1 January 2001 when the *Euro.NM* group fell apart. The markets themselves prefer to state that the collapse was caused by the emergence of *Euronext* in September 2000. Goergen, McCahery, and Renneboog (2002), however, claim that the inability to harmonize five sets of listing rules, the involvement of five different national regulators and inefficient cross-border trading led to the dissolution of the *Euro.NM* markets (see also Bottazzi & Da Rin, 2002).

Most other European countries also set up growth markets, but with mixed success. The *Alternative Investment Market* (AIM), which was introduced in the UK in June 1995, attracted the most listings. Another growth market is the electronic stock market *European Association of Securities Dealers Automated Quotation* (*EASDAQ*), which was set up in October 1996 by more than 60 European and American financial institutions, as well as NASDAQ (Manigart & De Maeseneire, 2000). Based in Brussels, it was the first pan-European stock market offering international growth companies and investors seamless cross-border trading, clearing and settlement within a unified market infrastructure. In 2001, NASDAQ became its majority shareholder and EASDAQ was hence renamed *NAS-DAQ Europe*. However, the slump in demand for technology stocks took its toll and led to the market's closure in November 2003. The London Stock Exchange tried to convince 30 of the remaining companies to transfer to London. Nevertheless, most of the firms decided to be listed on one of the national segments of *Euronext* in order to offer their investors a more liquid trading platform. The downfall of NASDAQ Europe is said to be caused by a lack of liquidity; the bid-ask spread was often more than 10%.

Table 9.1 reports the numbers of new listings on the new and the main stock markets between 1996 and 2003. It is remarkable that the number of new listings on the five *Euro.NM* markets exceeded that on the main markets. However, even combined, the number of European listings is still substantially lagging that of NASDAQ.

9.2.2. Lock-in Requirements

Table 9.2 shows the different lock-in requirements on several European and US stock markets, including the *Euro.NM* markets. The main market segments in the USA, the UK and continental Europe do no require any lock-ins. However, all the growth markets impose lock-in contracts. The main reason for this is that young and high-growth firms face much larger information asymmetries (Goergen, McCahery, & Renneboog, 2002).

Empirical studies show that the vast majority of firms have lock-in agreements even in countries where they are not compulsory, such as the USA (Mohan & Chen, 2001) and the UK (Espenlaub, Goergen, & Khurshed, 2001). Further, firms which go public on stock markets with minimum lock-in requirements often choose longer periods than those required. Goergen, Renneboog, and Khurshed (2005) find that 57% of the lock-in contracts of 268 German firms that went public on the *Neuer Markt* between 1997 and 2000 chose lock-in periods longer than the required minimum of 6 months. Companies about to be listed on the *Nouveau Marché* have to publish their lock-in agreements in the IPO prospectus. Therefore, the dates at which the different pre-IPO shareholders are released from their lock-in agreements are known by the public prior to the IPO.

9.2.3. VC Financing

Gompers and Lerner (1999) argue that in order to have a well-functioning stock market one needs a well-developed VC sector. Contrary to Europe, the USA and the UK have a relatively long history of VC financing. However, Megginson (2004) states that VC funding has rapidly

Table 9.1: New listings on European and US stock markets (1996–2004).

Country	Market	1996	1997	1998	1999	2000	2001	2002	2003	2004
Belgium	*Nieuwe Markt*	—	2	6	6	3	0	0	4	0
	Eerste Markt	12	17	21	23	9	12	3	12	1
France	*Nouveau Marché*	18	20	43	32	52	10	2	0	0
	Premier Marché[1]	2	4	8	8	13	7	2	4	12
	Second Marché[1]	32	44	76	33	18	12	5	4	13
Germany	Neuer Markt	—	14	45	135	139	11	1	—	—
	Amtlicher Handel[2]	6	10	15	30	13	5	1	—	—
	Geregelte Markt[2]	6	4	14	10	11	7	3	—	—
Italy	*Nuovo Mercato*	—	—	—	6	34	5	0	0	0
	Mercato di Borsa[3,4]	14	13	25	31	16	13	8	4	2
The Netherlands	Nieuwe Markt	—	5	8	2	2	0	0	0	2
	Officiële Markt[1,5]	7	16	13	16	6	3	2	2	0
UK	AIM[6]	145	107	75	102	277	177	160	162	355
	LSE[6]	282	178	157	134	210	127	68	39	58
USA	NASDAQ[7,8]	680	494	273	485	397	66	66	63	170
	NYSE[7,8]	88	87	68	49	48	40	44	42	69

Notes: New listings comprise IPOs as well as spin-offs, admissions with no public offering, dual listings and transfers from other domestic stock markets. The Euro.NM markets are put in italic.

Sources: [1]www.euronext.com.
[2]Leven (2003).
[3]Giudici (2001) for 1996–2001.
[4]www.borsaitalia.it for 2002–2004.
[5]Beursplein 5 for 1996 and 1997.
[6]www.londonstockexchange.com.
[7]Aussenegg, Pichler, and Stomper (2002) for 1996–2000.
[8]www.nasdaq,com for 2001–2004; others from lists sent by stock exchanges.

Table 9.2: Lock-in requirements on several European and US stock markets.

Market	Lock-in requirements
Nieuwe Markt/ Nouveau Marché (Brussels, Belgium)	All managing shareholders have to be locked in for at least 80% of their shares for at least 1 year.
Nouveau Marché (Paris, France)	Until 1 December 1998, all insiders (executives and founders) had to lock in at least 80% of their shares for at least 3 years. Between 1 December 1998 and 15 September 2003, all insiders (executives and founders) had to choose between locking in all their shares for at least 6 months and locking in at least 80% of their shares for at least 1 year. If the firm was less than 2 years old insiders had to be locked in with all their shares for at least 2 years. From 15 September 2003 until closure, all executives had to lock in all their shares for at least 1 year. Shares bought by any shareholder during the year preceding admission also had to be locked in for 1 year.[1]
Neuer Markt (Frankfurt, Germany)	All initial shareholders have to lock in all of their shares for at least 6 months. The company is not allowed to issue new shares during this period.
Nuovo Mercato (Milan, Italy)	All managing shareholders and founders have to lock in at least 80% of their shares for at least 1 year. At least 80% of the shares bought by other shareholders, holding at least 2% of the equity, during the 12 months preceding the IPO also have to be locked in for at least 1 year. Firms which have been exempted by the stock exchange from providing financial accounts for at least 1 entire year must lock in all the shares held by their initial shareholders for 1 year and 80% of those shares for another year.
Nieuwe Markt (Amsterdam, the Netherlands)	Until 24 November 2000, all shareholders holding at least 5% of the shares outstanding were locked in depending on the firm's published results. They were locked in for 100% until the company had reported positive operating and net income for 1 year. Then 50% of their shares remained locked in until the company had at least 3 years of positive operating and net income in a 5-year period. From 24 November 2000 until closure, all founders, managers and supervisory board members had to lock in at least 80% of their shares for at least 360 days.
Euronext (pan-European)	Until 4 April 2005, there was no harmonization of listing rules. Firms applying for a listing had to comply with the requirements on the Dutch, Belgian, French or Portuguese market. Lock-in

Table 9.2: Continued.

	requirements did not exist on these markets, with the exception of the growth segments.
	Since 4 April 2005, the lock-in requirements have been decided on a company-by-company basis only in case the applicant does not comply with certain other listing requirements. This applies to all participating markets.[2]
EASDAQ/NASDAQ Europe (Brussels, Belgium)	Insiders had to lock in at least 80% of their shares for at least 6 months.
AIM (London, UK)	Insiders have to lock in all their shares for at least 1 year.[3]
LSE (London, UK)	Until January 2000, mineral companies and scientific research-based companies, which were less than 3-year old, had to lock in all incumbent shareholders for up to 2 years.
	Since January 2000, there have been no minimum lock-in requirements. However, mineral companies, scientific research-based companies and innovative high-growth companies, with less than 3 years of trading history, must display in a prominent way in their prospectus whether they have a lock-in agreement in place, and if they do not have such an agreement, the reasons for its absence.[4]
US markets	SEC Rule 144 imposes certain restrictions on the sale of restricted securities, that is, securities that have been directly purchased in a private placement from the issuing firm before the IPO. Sales of these shares are not allowed during the first year of ownership. After 1 year, during any 3-month period, the sale cannot exceed 1% of the shares outstanding and the average weekly trading volume of the past 4 weeks. NASD rules also prevent VCs who have a private investment in the issuing firm from selling their shares during a 90-day period and underwriters who have received shares as compensation for 1 year.

Source: Goergen, Renneboog, and Khurshed (2005) unless specified otherwise:
[1]Euronext Paris Notice No. 2003-2869.
[2]www.euronext.com.
[3]Goergen, Khurshed, McCahery, and Renneboog (2002).
[4]Espenlaub, Goergen, and Khurshed (2001).

increased in most continental European and some Asian countries since 1997. Figure 9.2 shows that, during the stock market peak of the late 1990s the US outpaced Europe, whereas since 2002 investments by the European VC industry have exceeded those by its US counter-part. However, there are still marked differences in terms of the development of the VC sector across Europe. In 2004, the VC investments in the UK alone accounted for 26% of the total

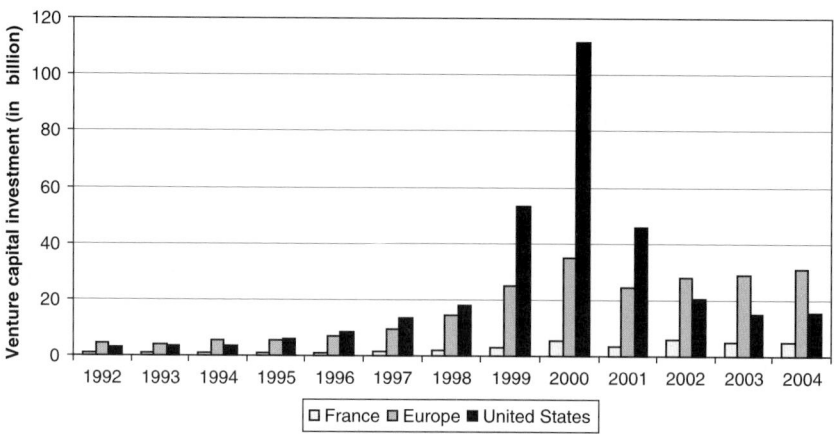

Figure 9.2: Development of a VC culture. The figures for the USA were converted into Euros using end of year exchange rates. The amounts for the years prior to 1999 are in ECU. All amounts are nominal as published annually by AFIC, European Venture Capital Association (EVCA) and National Venture Capital Association (NVCA). *Sources*: www.afic.asso.fr; www.evca.com; www.nvca.org and Datastream.

European VC investments, while France, Germany and the Netherlands accounted for 17%, 14% and 9%, respectively.[3] Goergen, Renneboog, and Khurshed (2005) find that a higher proportion of *Nouveau Marché* IPOs than *Neuer Markt* IPOs are VC backed. VCs in France are also more frequently represented on the boards of the firms they invest in.

National VC associations exist in North America, Europe and certain Asian and South-American countries. There are currently 35 such associations. The French Private Equity Association (*Association Française des Investisseurs en Capital* (*AFIC*)) has been active since 1984 and had 212 members at the time of writing this chapter.

9.2.4. Corporate Governance in France

Companies aspiring to a listing on the *Nouveau Marché* have to be public-limited firms (*SA*) as defined by the 1966 French Business Law. Kremp and Sevestre (2001) state that the law gives companies a choice between a one-tier board and a two-tier board structure. The one-tier board consists of the board of directors (*conseil d'administration*), which is appointed by the annual general meeting of shareholders. The board of directors appoints a chairman/CEO (*président directeur général* (*PDG*)), who is responsible for the daily operations of the company. The two-tier board consists of a supervisory board (*conseil de surveillance*) and a management board (*directoire*). The annual general meeting appoints the members of the supervisory board, which in turn appoints the members of the management board including its chairman. The management board is responsible for the daily operations of the company. Its members have stricter reporting obligations than the chairman/CEO of the one-tier board. Kremp and Sevestre (2001) find that 75% of the French blue-chip companies forming the CAC40 index have a one-tier board. The Vienot II Report states that less than 3% of all corporate firms in France chose the two-board system.

Corporate governance in France has gone through several major changes in recent years. The Vienot I Report (1995), the Vienot II Report (1999) and the Bouton Report (2002) all give recommendations for changes in corporate governance regulation in France. After the European Commission's recommendation that all EU Member States should design a code of reference concerning corporate governance, the French Association of Private Companies (*Association Française des Entreprises Privées* (AFEP)) and the French Employers' Association (*Mouvement des Entreprises de France* (MEDEF)) published 'The Corporate Governance of Listed Corporations'[4] in October 2003. This report combines the recommendations from the Vienot and Bouton reports and has become the benchmark for corporate governance in France. The report allows the separation of the offices of chairman and CEO for firms that have chosen a one-tier board. In case the board of directors opts for this separation, the company's rules of operation need to define clearly the tasks of both posts. The CEO is then referred to as the *directeur général exécutif*. Other propositions from the report refer to the maximum reporting delays of company results. Semi-annual results are to be reported no later than 2½ months after the end of the first half of the financial year. Provisional annual results have to be published within a month after the close of the financial year, while the final results should be disclosed within 3 months after the close. Furthermore, the annual report of all listed companies has to disclose the company's compensation policies (including any stock option and stock purchase schemes), the aggregate amount of compensation for all the corporate officers and the individual attendance fees paid to the non-executive directors. Disclosure obligations for companies listed on the *Nouveau Marché* were increased along with the introduction of stricter disclosure requirements in September 2003 (see the appendix).

Another interesting aspect of French corporate governance is that ownership and control are not always identical (see Goergen, Renneboog, & Khurshed, 2005). French law allows the use of a clause in a firm's articles of association such that the long-term shareholders are attributed double voting rights. The company is given discretion to decide how long the holding period ought to be before shareholders qualify to obtain double voting rights. Subsequently, the period can only be changed at the annual general meeting. Wymeersch (1994) states that these structures are set up for reasons of control leverage. The control structure and a change therein can have a substantial impact on company performance as shown by Dherment and Renneboog (2002).

9.3. Reasons for the Price Effect at the Expiry of Lock-in Agreements

Lock-in agreements and the effect of their expiries on stock prices have only recently been examined. Table 9.3 summarizes the results from such event studies. Most studies on the USA, Germany and Italy report significantly negative abnormal returns and increased trading volume. In contrast, Espenlaub, Goergen, and Khurshed (2001) report insignificant abnormal returns for the UK.

9.3.1. Fundamental Reasons

Leland and Pyle (1977) argue that if managers are risk averse, they will want to diversify their portfolios. Hence, it is expected that insiders sell part of their stakes as soon as they

Table 9.3: Overview of literature on lock-in expiry anomalies.

Author (year)	Market	Period	Sample Size	Abnormal return on expiry day	Event window for CAAR	CAAR	Increased trading volume at expiry
Ofek and Richardson (2000)	USA	1996–1998	1053	−1.15%***	[−4, 0]	−2.03%***	Yes
Field and Hanka (2001)	USA	1988–1997	1948	−0.90%***	[−1, 1]	−1.50%***	Yes
Bradley, Jordan, Yi, and Roten. (2001)	USA	1988–1997	2529	−0.74%***	[−2, 2]	−1.61%***	Yes
Brav and Gompers (2003)	USA	1988–1996	2749	−0.12%	[−1, 1]	−0.79%[a]	Yes
Ofek and Richardson (2003)	USA	1998–2000	305	−1.99%***	[−4, 0]	−4.11%***	Yes
Brau, Carter, Christophe, and Key (2004)	USA	1988–1998	3049	−0.38%[a]	[−4, 0]	−1.53%[a]	Yes
Espenlaub, Goergen, and Khurshed (2001)	UK	1992–1998	52	−0.71%	[0, 1]	−0.96%	—
Nowak and Gropp (2000)	Germany	1997–1999	142	−0.19%	[−1, 30]	−7.95%***	Yes
Bertoni, Giudici, Randone, Rochira, and Zanoni (2002)	Italy	1999–2001	45	−1.40%	[−5, −1]	−1.42%*	Yes

Notes: Statistical significance level at ***1%, *10% and [a]an undisclosed significance level.

are released from the lock-in. According to Ofek and Richardson (2000), this so-called *diversification hypothesis* is the main reason for insiders to sell part of their stakes at the lock-in expiry. Gompers and Lerner (1999) add that VCs have similar incentives. Although they often use IPOs as an exit route, they frequently retain part of their holdings at the IPO and, therefore, have to wait until the lock-in period has expired to sell the remainder of their shares.

The diversification hypothesis in isolation does not explain all the abnormal returns around the lock-in expiry. As long as the demand curves for shares are horizontal, different levels of supply do not influence the share price. Field and Hanka (2001) suggest that, just like markets for most products, stocks have downward sloping demand curves. They call this concept the *demand curve hypothesis*. Especially those firms facing high uncertainty and asymmetric information are likely to have downward sloping demand curves for their shares. A supply shock shifts the equilibrium to a point where a higher quantity of shares are sold at a lower price. Field and Hanka (2001) also study the signalling effect of insider sales. If insiders sell more shares at the lock-in expiry than the market has anticipated, the market interprets this as a lack of insider confidence in the firm.

The combination of the above reasons explains the negative abnormal returns and increased trading volume after the lock-in expiry. In addition, there are two reasons why negative share price reactions may already occur prior to the lock-in expiry. First, the *anticipation theory* states that, if abnormal returns are likely to occur after the lock-in expiry, outside investors have an incentive to sell their shares already before the expiry in order to pre-empt the price pressure created by insiders' sales. In the presence of downward sloping demand curves, share prices will be lower and trading volume will be higher. However, Ofek, and Richardson (2000) discard this argument as being weak, as this effect should then already be incorporated on the first trading day. Their argument is based on the semi-strong form of the *efficient market hypothesis* (EMH) which states that all public information about the firm is already reflected in its share price.

Hypothesis 1: At the lock-in expiry, there are negative abnormal returns and trading volume is higher.

9.3.2. The Impact of Shareholder Types and of the Control Structure

Given that shareholders' expectations about the firm's prospects vary, we expect the trading around the lock-in expiry to depend on the type of large shareholders.

9.3.2.1. Insiders Lock-in agreements protect outside investors from being exploited by insiders trading on private information. By the time the lock-in agreement has expired, the information asymmetry may already be less pronounced such that it will be more difficult for insiders to expropriate outside investors.

Until 15 September 2003, the *Nouveau Marché* imposed lock-ins on the shares held by all the insiders of a firm. Even though the regulator did not define the term insiders and left the definition to each individual firm, executives (top managers) and founders were virtually always considered insiders and subject to lock-in contracts. Hence, this is also the definition of insiders we adopt. The executives are most likely to have superior knowledge about the quality of the firm, as they are in charge of the firm's daily operations. If the founders are still involved in running the firm, they too are likely to have superior knowledge. Insider sales may increase agency problems, which may have a negative impact on firm value.

Hypothesis 2: At the expiry of insider lock-ins, the abnormal returns are more negative and trading volume is higher.

9.3.2.2. Venture capitalists   Field and Hanka (2001) find that VCs sell a significantly larger percentage of their shareholdings during the first year after the IPO than other pre-IPO shareholders. Therefore, it is likely that companies with VC backing show larger negative abnormal returns and larger increases in trading volume around the expiry.

Hypothesis 3: At the expiry of VC lock-ins, the abnormal returns are more negative and trading volume is higher.

9.3.3. The Choice of Lock-in Contracts and the Signalling of Shareholders' Commitment

The signals of shareholders' commitment (and hence firm quality) that may have an impact on the price effect at the lock-in expiry are the length of the lock-in period, the percentage of shares locked in, the degree of underpricing, the underwriter's reputation and VC certification.

9.3.3.1. The length of the lock-in period and the percentage of shares locked in   Courteau (1995) argues that insiders can signal their firm's superior quality via the duration of the lock-in period and the percentage of shares locked in. The signal is credible as it is costly for the insiders of low-quality firms to be locked in for longer periods, as the share price may decrease to its true value when more information about the firm becomes available.[5]

Hypothesis 4a: Abnormal returns at the lock-in expiry are less negative and trading volume is lower if the lock-in period is longer.

Hypothesis 4b: Abnormal returns at the lock-in expiry are less negative and trading volume is lower if a higher percentage of shares are locked in.

9.3.3.2. Underpricing   Firms can also underprice to signal their quality. In a separating equilibrium, a high-quality firm will underprice more, lock in for a longer period, or lock in a larger percentage of the shares outstanding. As such, these devices may be substitute signals. Underpricing is costly as it consists in selling the firm's shares below their real value such that underpricing constitutes a credible signal. If a firm does not want to lock in its shareholders for a longer period, it needs to underprice more to signal quality.

Hypothesis 5: Firms with large underpricing at the flotation experience less negative abnormal returns and lower trading volume at the lock-in expiry.

9.3.3.3. Underwriter reputation   The most reputable underwriters may not risk bringing a low-quality firm to the market. Underwriters may provide price support at the expiry of the lock-in agreements of other types of shareholders and may avoid price pressure at their own expiry to avoid price declines. Therefore, firms with reputable underwriters are less likely to show negative abnormal returns and increased trading volume during the days around the expiry of the lock-in agreement.

Hypothesis 6: Firms with reputable underwrites have less negative abnormal returns and less trading volume at the lock-in expiry.

9.3.3.4. VC reputation   As is the case with underwriters, VCs may also certify firm quality. They do not only provide the necessary capital but their presence also signals the firm's quality as VCs usually also monitor the firm closely and are involved in the firm's major (investment) decisions (Barry, 1994; Jain & Kini, 2000).

Hypothesis 7: Firms with VC-backing experience less negative abnormal returns and less trading volume at the lock-in expiry.

9.4. Data Description

9.4.1. Number of IPOs and Distribution Across Sectors

On the *Nouveau Marché*, 177 firms went public between the stock exchange's launch on 20 March 1996 and its closure in February 2005. Thirty firms are excluded for at least one of the following reasons. Companies of foreign origin are excluded as they may be subject to different corporate regulations and different accounting standards. We also exclude seasoned equity offerings, rights issues and firms operating in the financial sector. This reduces our sample to 147 firms.

Figure 9.3 shows the number of IPOs in each quarter. There was a slow but steady rise in the number of new listings during the first 5 years. However, after the burst of the so-called Internet bubble during Spring 2000, the number of new listings per quarter dropped steeply, with only two new listings since September 2001.

Table 9.4 shows the distribution of the IPOs across standard industrial classification (SIC) industrial sectors. The vast majority of the IPOs are from the service sector, followed by slightly less than a quarter from the manufacturing sector. The majority of the service-oriented firms offer software packages or other computer-related services. Nearly half of the manufacturing firms produce either electrical equipment or measurement instruments.

9.4.2. Ownership, Control and Issue Size

Based on the information collected from the IPO prospectuses, the shareholders of each firm are classified as insiders and outsiders. As mentioned above, we define insiders (as does the *Nouveau Marché*) as executives and founders. For the firms with a two-tier board, the distinction between executives and non-executives is straightforward. The members of the management board are executive directors, whereas those of the supervisory board are non-executive directors. For companies with a one-tier board, executive directors are members of the *conseil d'administration* who exert a management function in the firm. The remaining members of the board of directors are the non-executive directors. Shareholders are classified as VCs if they are a member of at least one national VC association. Banks that hold shares in

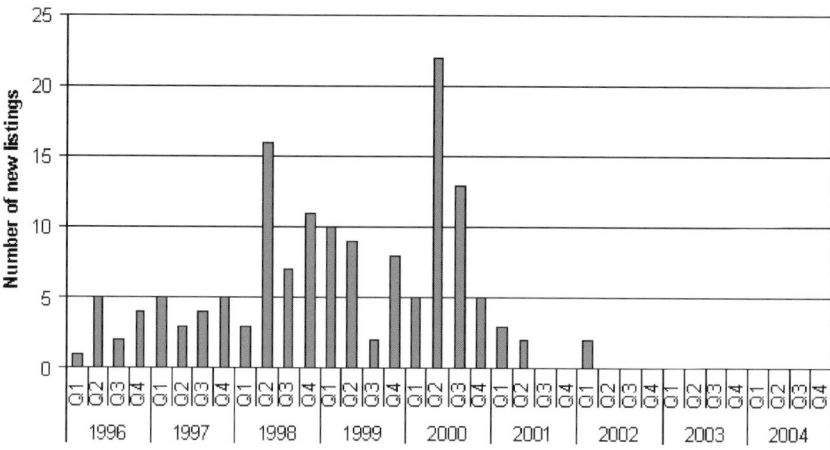

Figure 9.3: Number of IPOs by quarter. We exclude firms of foreign origin, seasoned equity offerings, rights issues and firms operating in the financial sector. *Source*: www.euronext.com

Table 9.4: Distribution of the French *Nouveau Marché* IPOs across industries.

Primary SIC Code	Industry	Number	%
0100-0999	Agriculture, forestry, fishing, hunting and trapping	0	0.00
1000-1499	Mining	0	0.00
1500-1799	Construction	0	0.00
2000-3999	Manufacturing	35	23.81
4000-4999	Transportation, communications, electric, gas and sanitary services	7	4.76
5000-5199	Wholesale trade	10	6.80
5200-5999	Retail trade	7	4.76
6000-6799	Finance, insurance and real estate	0	0.00
7000-8999	Services	88	59.86
9100-9999	Public administration	0	0.00
Total	—	147	100.00

Source: Thomson One Banker.

the firm and are part of the underwriter syndicate of that particular firm are identified as underwriters. Others include all shareholders who do not fit in any of the above categories. This category includes primarily minority stakeholders such as business partners and employees.

Table 9.5 shows the percentage of ownership and control by category of shareholder before and after the IPO. Insiders hold on average 65% of the control rights and 64% of

Table 9.5: Ownership and control.

| | | Insiders | Non-executives | Outsiders | | |
				VCs	Underwriters	Others
Before the IPO	Ownership (%)	64.35	19.02	15.84	2.42	12.72
	Control (%)	65.36	18.77	15.58	2.46	12.14
	Number of firms with ownership held by …	147	98	84	23	143
After the IPO	Ownership (%)	46.86	13.86	10.86	1.90	9.22
	Control (%)	50.93	14.11	10.95	1.96	9.11
	Number of firms with ownership held by …	147	99	86	24	143

Notes: Shareholders are classified into insiders and four non-excluding categories for outsiders. Insiders include executives and founders. Others include all shareholders who do not fit in any of the other categories and includes primarily minority stakeholders such as business partners and employees.

the cash flow rights immediately prior to the IPO. Immediately after the IPO, their control rights and cash flow rights are reduced to 51% and 47%, respectively. As mentioned above, ownership and control are different from each other as many firms (in fact 75%) have a clause in their articles of association granting double votes to shareholders who hold on to their shares for a long time (which is at the discretion of the firm but is frequently 2 years and can extend to 4 years) and have registered their ownership with the firm.

More than 80% (118) of the firms in the sample have at least one shareholder who is both an executive and founder.[6] The second most important class of shareholders consists of the non-executive directors who hold shares in 67% (99) of the companies after the IPO. VCs hold on average about 16% of the equity. In total, 59% (86) of the firms in the sample were backed by 72 different VCs.

Table 9.6 shows that the firms differ in terms of the percentages of primary and secondary shares offered at the IPO. Some companies offer merely 10% of their shares for sale, whereas others double the shares outstanding by large primary issues. This suggests that some companies are mainly interested in being listed, whereas the main interest of other firms is attracting additional capital to finance investment opportunities. The mean percentage of primary shares is substantially larger than that of secondary shares.[7] This is congruent with the fact that most of the sample firms belong to a growth segment.

9.4.3. Over-Allotment Options

Nearly 48% of the IPOs provide their underwriter with an over-allotment option, the so-called *Greenshoe option*. The option gives the underwriter the right to offer additional shares to the market in case of high demand. These additional shares can be primary or secondary shares, or a mix of both types. For only 46% of the firms with an over-allotment option, this option was actually exercised. These figures are rather low compared to those for the *Neuer Markt* where 89% of the IPOs had an over-allotment option, and more than 81% of these were at least partially exercised (see also Goergen, Renneboog, & Khurshed, 2005).

Table 9.6: Percentage of secondary and primary shares offered in the IPO.

Variable	Mean (%)	Median (%)	Range (%)	Standard deviation (%)
Secondary shares offered/ total shares after IPO	5.10	2.80	[0.00, 38.09]	6.57
Primary shares offered/ total shares after IPO	23.16	21.39	[0.00, 48.46]	8.28
Total shares offered/ total shares after IPO	28.26	27.67	[9.87, 53.13]	9.01
Primary shares offered/ total shares offered	83.19	87.00	[0.00, 100.00]	19.22

Notes: Secondary shares are shares sold by the pre-IPO shareholders. Primary shares are newly issued shares.

9.4.4. Lock-in Contracts

As nearly half of the 147 firms in the sample had two or more lock-in agreements in place, the total number of lock-in contracts (252) exceeds the number of companies. Twenty-one per cent of our sample firms locked in all the old shareholders who retained shares at the IPO. Six companies even locked in some of the new shareholders. Table 9.7 shows the different types and frequencies of lock-in agreements for the sample. Panel A shows the contracts that lock in 100% of the shares of a specific type of shareholder (e.g. 6 months for 100%). Panel B reports the statistics for the agreements locking in only part of the shares held by a shareholder (e.g. 12 months for 80%), while Panel C concentrates on staggered agreements. These are contracts that lock in part or all of the shares of a specific shareholder type for an initial period, followed by one or more periods during which a lower percentage of his shares remains locked in. Panel D shows some special cases.

The influence of lock-in regulation is reflected in the frequency of the type of contracts used (the legally determined minimum contracts are put in bold). Panel A shows that the most frequently chosen lock-in agreement for IPOs before 1 December 1998 is 36 months with 80% of the shares locked in, which was the minimum requirement at that time. From 1 December 1998 onwards, companies were given the choice between two legal minimums: 12 months with 80% of the shares locked in and 6 months with 100%. The two requirements together cover 61% of the lock-in contracts for insiders. Importantly, a substantial number of contracts deviates from the minimum requirements.

Table 9.8 shows the average percentage of shares locked in for each shareholder category.[8] More than 80% of the insiders' shares are locked in which reflects the stock exchange's regulation. Only two companies exempt their insiders from a lock-in as they only retain a tiny share stake. Further, non-executive directors, VCs and underwriters have voluntary locked in large percentages of their equity. Out of all the shares held by the old shareholders after the IPO, more than 77% are locked in. While this seems a high proportion, it is lower than the 95% found by Field and Hanka (2001) and the 93% found by Brau, Carter, Christophe, and Key (2004) for US IPO firms. Table 9.8 also reports that 56% of all the shares outstanding are locked in after the IPO.

9.4.5. Timing of Lock-in Expiries

For the USA, Ofek and Richardson (2003) find that an unprecedented number of shares were unlocked during the months leading up to the crash on NASDAQ in March 2000. They argue that there is a causal relationship between the number of lock-in expiries around the time of the crash and the market crash itself. As the *Nouveau Marché* index has experienced an even more extreme rise and fall, it is interesting to examine whether there is a similar correlation. Figure 9.4 depicts the quarterly number of lock-in expiries and the evolution of the *Nouveau Marché* index.

The number of lock-in expiries was highest during the last quarter of 2000 and in 2001. The peaks in the number of expiries are accompanied by a substantial drop in the *Nouveau Marché* index. Unlike Ofek and Richardson (2003) for the USA, most of the lock-in

Table 9.7: Types and frequencies of lock-in contracts.

Type of lock-in agreement	Insiders				Outsiders			
	IPO before 1 December 1998		IPO after 1 December 1998		IPO before 1 December 1998		IPO after 1 December 1998	
	Number	%	Number	%	Number	%	Number	%
Panel A: All the shares are locked in								
6 months for 100%	3	4.23	**20**	**20.00**	11	22.92	21	20.19
Between 6 and 12 months for 100%	1	1.41	1	1.00	4	8.33	3	2.88
12 months for 100%	1	1.41	10	10.00	8	16.67	22	21.15
More than 12 months for 100%	2	2.82	2	2.00	0	0.00	4	3.85
Panel B: Only part of the shares are locked in								
Less strict than 12 months for 80%	0	0.00	1	1.00	1	2.08	4	3.85
12 months for 80%	1	1.41	**41**	**41.00**	1	2.08	21	20.19
12 months for more than 80% but less than 100%	0	0.00	5	5.00	0	0.00	4	3.85
36 months for 80%	**53**	**74.65**	2	2.00	13	27.08	1	0.96
36 months for more than 80% but less than 100%	1	1.41	0	0.00	0	0.00	0	0.00
Panel C: Staggered agreements								
Less strict than 6 months for 100%; then staggered	1	1.41	3	3.00	1	2.08	7	6.73
6 months for 100%; then staggered	3	4.23	11	11.00	3	6.25	13	12.50
Stricter than 6 months for 100%; then staggered	3	4.23	1	1.00	1	2.08	2	1.92
Panel D: Other types of agreements								
Not to sell below 120% of offer price for 6 months	0	0.00	0	0.00	2	4.17	0	0.00
Others	2	2.82	3	3.00	3	6.25	2	1.92
Sum of the different types of contracts	71	100.00	100	100.00	48	100.00	104	100.00

Notes: The figures in bold relate to the minimum lock-in requirements during each period. These requirements are only applicable to insiders. For staggered agreements only the first period is taken into account.

Table 9.8: Average percentage of shares locked in by category of shareholder.

Shareholder type	Number of firms	Mean (%)	Median (%)	Standard deviation (%)
Insiders (executives and founders)	147	82.31	80.00	16.18
Outsiders				
Non-executive directors	82	68.37	90.62	41.99
VCs	83	67.34	100.00	43.90
Underwriters	23	74.25	100.00	41.71
Others	143	45.59	49.54	43.20
All old shareholders	147	77.21	79.99	18.41
All the shares outstanding that are locked in	147	55.63	56.23	14.84

Notes: The percentages refer to the ratios of the shares locked in for a particular category of shareholders over the total number of shares owned by that category immediately after the IPO. The means and medians for a specific shareholder category are based on all the firms in which that category of shareholder holds share stakes. If a particular shareholder fits in both the insider and outsider categories (e.g. a founder who is also a non-executive), we categorize him as an insider only. Insiders include executives and founders. Others include all shareholders who do not fit in any of the other categories. This category includes primarily minority stakeholders such as business partners and employees. It should be noted that the different outsider categories may overlap. For example, a VC who is also a non-executive will be counted in the VC category as well as the non-executive category.

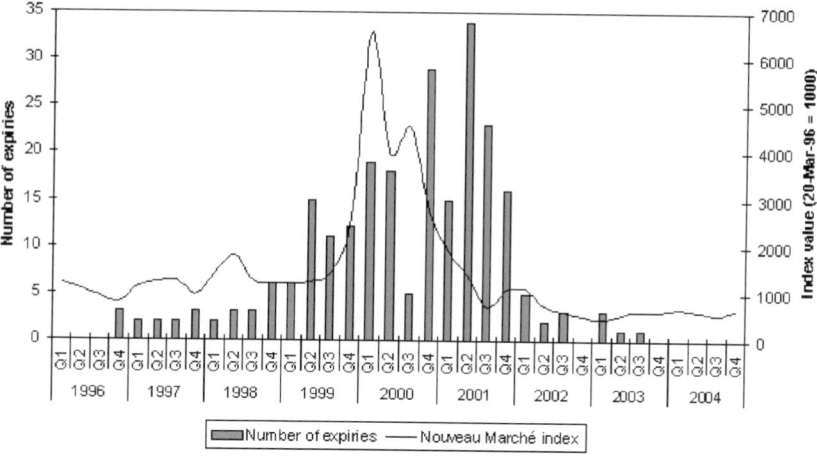

Figure 9.4: Number of expiries per quarter plotted against the *Nouveau Marché* index. The bars represent the quarterly number of lock-in expiries. In total, there were 251 different expiry dates planned. Still, as seven expiries did not occur due to delistings before the expiry, only 244 are shown.

expiries in France take place at least half a year after the market crash. Therefore, the increasing number of lock-in expiries has worsened the strong downward movement of the *Nouveau Marché* in 2000 and 2001 but has not caused it. Figure 9.5 depicts that the sudden increase in the number of lock-in expiries in 2001 is largely the result of the reduction

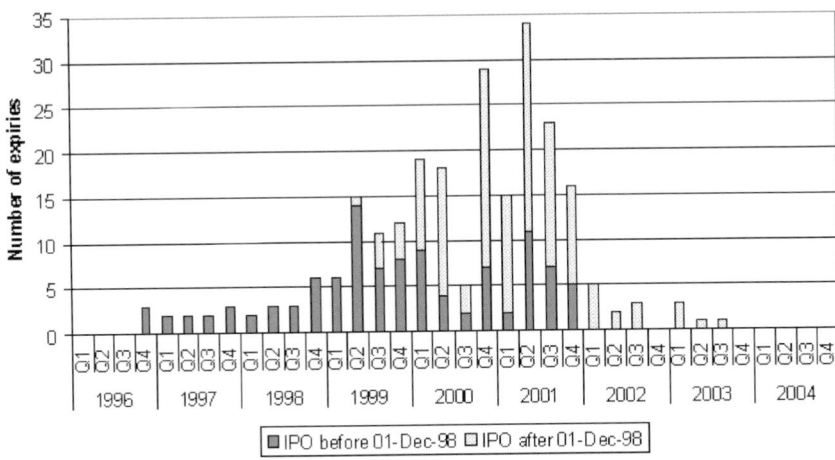

Figure 9.5: Time of lock-in expiry and the change in lock-in regulation.

in the duration of the minimum lock-in requirement following the regulatory change of 1 December 1998.

9.4.6. Pricing of IPOs

Except for *Datatronic SA*, all French IPOs went public via the book-building method. This procedure consists of three stages. During the first stage, the underwriter approaches institutional investors in order to determine a price range. In the second stage, the actual book-building stage, investors are asked to apply for shares by stating a price within the price range and a quantity of shares. Finally, the underwriter determines a strike price using the book. Any investor who bid for shares at a price equal to or exceeding the strike price will be allocated shares.[9] Underpricing is the percentage difference between the closing price on the first day of trading and the offer price. Table 9.9 shows that first-day underpricing is around 21% and ranges from 27% to 241%. Underpricing is slightly higher (by about 25%) if the closing price at the end of the first week rather than the first day of trading is used.

9.4.7. Underwriter Reputation

Underwriter reputation is based on the percentage of total market capitalization brought to the *Nouveau Marché* by each lead underwriter during the entire period 1996–2002. Underwriter reputation is given in Table 9.10: in terms of turnover, the most important underwriter was Crédit Lyonnais, followed by BNP Paribas, FleetBoston and Société Générale. More than two-thirds of the firms (99) had more than one underwriter. On average, the 147 firms in our sample chose two underwriters with a maximum of eight underwriters per firm.

Table 9.9: Book-building ratio and underpricing.

Variable	Sample size	Mean	Median	Minimum	Maximum	Standard deviation
Book-building ratio	146	0.54	0.95	−3.44	1.48	0.78
First-day underpricing	147	21.28%	9.43%	−26.99%	240.91%	41.73%
First-week underpricing	147	24.75%	9.15%	−20.95%	264.55%	47.74%

Notes: The book-building ratio is the position of the final offer price within the range of the book. Underpricing is percentage difference between the closing price after the first day or week of trading and the offer price. *Sources*: IPO prospectuses and Datastream.

9.4.8. VC Reputation and Influence

Our first measure of VC reputation hinges on the number of national VC associations a VC is registered with as a member. We also distinguish between domestic VCs, that is, those recognized by AFIC only, and international VCs who are recognized by at least one foreign VC association. In addition, we distinguish between VCs who are recognized by the USA or UK VC associations and those who are not. As the VC industry has been established for a longer time in the UK and USA, VCs from these two countries may be more experienced than VCs from other countries. Further, monitoring by a VC may be more efficient if the VC holds a seat on the firm's board of directors. We use several measures to capture VC influence: we record (i) whether or not VCs have a representative on the board of directors (dummy variable) and (ii) whether VCs have large board influence (they hold more than a quarter of the board seats) or little influence (they hold less than 25% of the seats).

9.4.9. Board Structure

Twelve per cent of the IPOs have a two-tier board at the time of IPO. Compared to Kremp and Sevestre (2001) who find that 25% of the French blue-chip companies in the CAC40 index have a two-tier board, this percentage is low. However, the percentage is much more substantial than that reported by the Vienot II Report which states that less than 3% of all firms in France have a two-tier board.

9.4.10. Other Variables

Uncertainty is proxied by the firm's age, its size, the ratio of intangibles over total fixed assets and the share price volatility. Age is calculated as the number of days between the date when the company was formed as a private limited company, a *Société à Responsabilité Limitée* (SARL), and the date of the IPO. Age ranges from less than 1 to more than 80 years with an average of 11 years. Goergen, Renneboog, and Khurshed (2005) report that the average age of IPOs on the *Neuer Markt* is about 13 years.[10]

Table 9.10: Reputation measure of lead-underwriters active on the *Nouveau Marché*.

Rank	Lead underwriter	%
1	Crédit Lyonnais	15.35
2	BNP Paribas	9.79
3	FleetBoston Robertson Stephens International	9.51
4	Société Générale	9.28
5	Credit Suisse First Boston (Europe)	8.79
6	Oddo-Pinatton Corporate	8.40
7	BNP Banque Nationale de Paris	5.21
8	Crédit Agricole Indosuez/Lazard	4.69
9	Oddo et Cie	4.66
10	Banque Paribas	4.59
11	CIC — Crédit Industriel et Commercial	4.18
12	Ferri — Groupe ING-BBL	3.89
13	Pinatton Finance	3.74
14	ABN AMRO Rothschild	3.30
15	Europe Finance et Industrie	2.95
16	Crédit du Nord	2.78
17	Merrill Lynch Capital Markets France	2.35
18	Natexis Capital	2.14
19	Lehman Brothers International (Europe)	2.05
20	Meeschaert-Rousselle (Fortis Bank)	1.98
21	Caisse Centrale des Banques Populaires	1.63
22	Aurel-Leven	1.56
23	CCF Charterhouse	1.47
24	JP Morgan Securities	1.15
25	Banque de Vizille	0.93
26	Ernst and Young Corporate Finance	0.55
27	Cyril Finance Gestion	0.37
28	Hambrecht and Quist Saint Dominique	0.32
29	KBC Securities France	0.27
30	KBL France	0.20
31	CDC Bourse	0.13

Note: Banque Nationale de Paris merged with Banque Paribas in 1999 and Oddo et Cie merged with Pinatton Finance in 2000.

Size is measured as the market capitalization at the offer price. The mean size is €80 million, while the median firm is worth €46 million. We also use the first-day market capitalization as an alternative measure for size. Information on the value of intangibles and fixed assets is taken from Thomson One Banker. Due to limited data availability, the ratio of intangibles over fixed assets can only be calculated for 86 companies and averages around 49%. The mean daily share price volatility is calculated using the share prices during the 180-day period between the IPO and expiry, ending 30 days before the expiry date. The volatility on a daily basis is high (1.4%). As the NASDAQ index reached its peak at 5049 points on 10 March 2000, this date is frequently taken as the date at which the Internet bubble burst. The *Nouveau Marché* index also reached its all-time high (7481 points) on 10 March 2000. We include a dummy in the regressions which is set to one for IPOs floated after this date.

9.4.11. Data Sources

The data on the characteristics of the lock-in contracts, ownership and control, and age are taken from the IPO prospectuses of the firms. We have set up a unique database covering the prospectuses of all the firms that have gone public on the *Nouveau Marché* since its inception. The prospectuses were obtained from the firms themselves, from Thomson One Banker, and from the French stock exchange. The database contains detailed data on the ownership and control of each shareholder immediately before and after the IPO as well as information on the lock-in contract the shareholder is subject to, if any. Accounting data, share prices and SIC codes were also obtained from Thomson One Banker. The returns and daily trading volume (in value) is obtained from Datastream.

9.5. Methodology

Abnormal returns are calculated for windows of different lengths. All windows lie within the period of 30 days before the day of the expiry (day 0) and 30 days after that day. To avoid contamination, expiries lying within 61 trading days following an earlier expiry are excluded, which results in a sample of 235 expiries. We use the market model to calculate the abnormal returns. We take the period of 210 to 31 trading days before the event day and the Morgan Stanley Capital International (MSCI) France index as the proxy for the market portfolio. The adjusted share prices and index values were obtained from Datastream.[11] In order to adjust for thin trading, we adopt the Dimson (1979) approach and correct for regression to the mean.[12] Cumulative abnormal returns (CARs) and cumulative average abnormal returns (CAARs) are calculated as follows:

$$\text{CAAR}_{t_1,t_2} = \frac{1}{N}\sum_{i=1}^{N}\text{CAR}_{i,t_1,t_2} = \frac{1}{N}\sum_{i=1}^{N}\sum_{t=t_1}^{t_2}\text{AR}_{i,t} = \frac{1}{N}\sum_{i=1}^{N}\sum_{t=t_1}^{t_2}(R_{i,t} - (\alpha_i + \beta_i^{DB}R_{m,t})) \quad (9.1)$$

We use the CARs for the window [−5, 5] as the dependent variable in the regressions.

To test the null hypothesis that the CAARs are equal to zero for a sample of N securities, the following t-statistic is calculated:

$$t_{\text{CAAR}} = \frac{\frac{1}{N}\sum_{i=1}^{N}\text{CAR}_i}{s(\text{CAR}/\sqrt{N})} \quad (9.2)$$

where the numerator is the CAAR and $s(\text{CAR})$ is the standard deviation of the sample's CARs. The t_{CAAR} t-statistic is based on Barber and Lyon (1997). It is Student-t distributed with $N−1$ degrees of freedom, which approaches the normal distribution as N increases.

Daily abnormal trading volume (DAV) is calculated as in Field and Hanka (2001). First, the mean daily trading volume per firm is calculated over the period of day –50 to day –6. Second, for each firm, AV during the event day is computed as the percentage difference between the trading volume on the event day and the mean. The daily average abnormal trading volume (DAAV) is the sample average DAV:

$$
\text{DAAV}_{t_1, t_2} = \frac{1}{N} \sum_{i=1}^{N} \text{DAV}_{i, t_1, t_2} = \frac{1}{N} \sum_{i=1}^{N} \left(\frac{1}{(1 + t_2 - t_1)} \sum_{t=t_1}^{t_2} \text{AV}_{i,t} \right)
$$

(9.3)

$$
= \frac{1}{N} \sum_{i=1}^{N} \left(\frac{1}{(1 + t_2 - t_1)} \sum_{t=t_1}^{t_2} \left(\frac{V_{i,t}}{\frac{1}{45} \sum_{t=-50}^{-6} V_{i,t}} - 1 \right) \right)
$$

The equivalent of Equation (9.2) is also used as a test statistic to determine whether the DAAV is significantly different from zero. For the analysis of the trading volume, the sample only consists of the first expiry for each firm.

9.6. Results

We first discuss the results from the event study based on the abnormal returns, followed by a multivariate analysis of the determinants of the abnormal returns at lock-in expiries. Subsequently, we report the findings related to the analysis of AV. We conclude this section by describing the robustness checks.

9.6.1. Event Study

Table 9.11 reports the CAARs for different windows for both the entire sample as well as the different categories of shareholders. Panel A shows that around the event date (in window [–5, 5]), there are weakly significant abnormal returns. Hence, there is only weak support for Hypothesis 1, which states that there is a negative abnormal return at the expiry.

Panel B distinguishes between different categories of shareholders. The CAARs for the insiders are negative and strongly statistically significant. We find support for Hypothesis 2 as the CAARs for insiders are significantly more negative than the CAARs for outsiders.

However, we reject Hypothesis 3 as CAARs for VCs are not significantly different from zero whatever the window. This result is somewhat surprising in the light of the results from other country studies. Bradley, Jordan, Yi, and Roten (2001) find that VC-backed US IPOs are associated with significantly more negative abnormal returns at the lock-in expiry. Similar results are found by Field and Hanka (2001), Brav and Gompers (2003) and Brau, Carter, Christophe, and Key (2004) for the USA; Espenlaub, Goergen, Khurshed, and Renneboog (2003) for the UK; Bessler and Kurth (2003) for Germany; and Bertoni, Giudici, Randone, Rochira, and Zanoni (2002) for Italy. We proceed by dividing the sample of expiries based on whether the firm was VC backed, regardless of whether VCs were

Table 9.11: CAARs for all expiries and by shareholder type.

Event window	[−30, −1]	[−5, −1]	[−5, 5]	[0, 1]	[0, 5]	[0, 30]	Sample size
Panel A: All expiries for all firms							
All expiries	−1.47%	−0.85%	−2.33%*	−0.72%	−1.48%	−2.91%	235
t-statistics	−0.57	−0.90	−1.72	−1.19	−1.58	−1.33	
Panel B: Expiries by shareholder category							
Insiders	−1.73%	−0.38%	−3.26%**	−1.23%**	−2.87%***	−5.56%**	179
t-statistics	−0.56	−0.33	−2.01	−1.94	−2.66	−2.23	
Outsiders	−0.83%	−2.09%	0.81%	0.73%	2.90%*	5.49%	56
t-statistics	−0.18	−1.47	0.36	0.47	1.67	1.26	
Difference in means	−0.91%	1.71%	−4.07%	−1.96%	−5.77%***	−11.05%**	—
t-statistics	−0.16	0.93	−1.46	−1.18	−2.82	−2.20	
VCs	−4.30%	−1.71%	−3.28%	−1.30%	−1.56%	−3.54%	87
t-statistics	−1.13	−1.44	−1.47	−1.13	−0.93	−0.90	
All others	−0.12%	−0.35%	−1.84%	−0.35%	−1.49%	−2.58%	148
t-statistics	−0.04	−0.26	−1.08	−0.51	−1.36	−1.00	
Difference in means	−4.18%	−1.37%	−1.44%	−0.95%	−0.07%	−0.96%	—
t-statistics	−0.82	−0.77	−0.51	−0.71	−0.04	−0.20	
Non-executives	−1.71%	−1.29%	−5.10%**	−2.54%**	−3.81%**	−5.12%	89
t-statistics	−0.43	−0.94	−2.32	−2.57	−2.44	−1.38	
All others	−1.65%	−0.66%	−0.68%	0.46%	−0.01%	−1.52%	146
t-statistics	−0.49	−0.53	−0.40	0.61	−0.01	−0.56	
Difference in means	−0.05%	−0.63%	−4.42%	−3.00%**	−3.80%*	−3.60%	—
t-statistics	−0.01	−0.34	−1.59	−2.41	−1.96	−0.79	

Notes: CAARs are calculated using the market model with Dimson–Blume betas. The category of insiders includes executives and founders. Statistical significance at ***1%, **5% and *10% level.

Table 9.12: CAARs by signal of firm quality.

Event window	[−30, −1]	[−5, −1]	[−5, 5]	[0, 1]	[0, 5]	[0, 30]	Number of lock-ins
Minimum requirement	−9.52%	−2.95%	−4.51%	−0.97%	−1.56%	−5.63%	59
t-statistics	−1.57	−1.56	−1.54	−0.85	−0.71	−1.12	
Stricter than minimum requirement	−1.71%	0.88%	−4.37%	−2.60%*	−5.25%**	−7.39%	49
t-statistics	−0.29	0.37	−1.22	−1.90	−2.11	−1.49	
Difference in means	−7.82%	−3.83%	−0.14%	1.64%	3.69%	1.77%	—
t-statistics	0.93	1.26	0.03	−0.92	−1,11	−0.25	
Below-median lock-in length	−11.40%	−3.41%*	−7.03%**	−2.29%*	−3.62%	−9.37%	44
t-statistics	−1.66	−1.83	−2.20	−1.95	−1.59	−1.56	
Above-median lock-in length	−3.24%	−0.57%	−2.85%	−1.41%	−2.28%	−1.32%	88
t-statistics	−0.71	−0.33	−1.13	−1.22	−1.23	−0.34	
Difference in means	−8.15%	−2.83%	−4.18%	−0.88%	−1.35%	−8.04%	—
t-statistics	−0.99	−1.11	−1.03	−0.53	−0.46	−1.13	
Below-median % locked in	−0.54%	0.60%	0.33%	0.72%	−0.27%	−2.61%	117
t-statistics	−0.13	0.39	0.16	0.87	−0.21	−0.85	

						N
Above-median % locked in	−2.40%	−2.29%**	−4.96%***	−2.15%**	−2.68%*	−3.20%	118
t-statistics	−0.75	−2.10	−2.90	−2.46	−1.96	−1.02	
Difference in means	1.86%	2.89%	5.30%*	2.87%**	2.41%	0.60%	—
t-statistics	0.36	1.54	1.97	2.39	1.29	0.14	
Below-median underpricing	−0.14%	0.87%	−0.34%	−1.08%	−1.21%	1.67%	120
t-statistics	−0.04	0.65	−0.17	−1.27	−0.84	0.52	
Above-median underpricing	−2.86%	−2.64%**	−4.40%**	−0.34%	−1.76%	−7.68%***	115
t-statistics	−0.74	−2.04	−2.40	−0.40	−1.48	−2.62	
Difference in means	2.72%	3.52%*	4.06%	−0.73%	0.55%	9.34%**	—
t-statistics	0.52	1.88	1.51	−0.60	0.29	2.16	
Top 10 underwriters	−5.07%	−2.60%*	−5.41%**	−0.72%	−2.81%*	−5.52%	111
t-statistics	−1.22	−1.80	−2.50	−0.76	−1.85	−1.58	
Other underwriters	1.75%	0.73%	0.44%	−0.72%	−0.29%	−0.57%	124
t-statistics	0.55	0.60	0.27	−0.93	−0.26	−0.21	
Difference in means	−6.82%	−3.33%*	−5.85%***	−0.01%	−2.52%	−4.95%	—
t-statistics	−1.30	−1.76	−2.16	−0.01	−1.33	−1.12	

Notes: CAARs are calculated using the market model with Dimson–Blume betas: $R_i - (\alpha + \beta^{DB} \times R_m)$. The tests that include the length of the lock-in period are run on the sub-sample of post 1 December 1998 IPOs only.
Statistical significance at ***1%, **5% and *10% level.

released at that particular expiry. We thereby test for the influence of VC backing as the above-mentioned authors do. However, we still do not find any VC influence on abnormal returns at expiry. Panel B also shows that at the expiry of agreements locking in non-executives there is a significantly negative price reaction. The market does not react negatively at the expiries of the lock-in contracts of the underwriters or the other shareholders (business partners and employees). The reason for the former reaction may be that underwriters smooth out their sales over time and do not cluster them at the expiry date as they may want to sustain the price of the IPO they had underwritten.

Table 9.12 investigates whether the various signals of firm quality have an impact on the abnormal returns at the expiry. We find negative abnormal returns for the firms that chose more stringent lock-in agreements for the period after 1 December 1998, but not for those firms that chose contracts that comply exactly with the minimum requirements for the same period.[13] As the differences are not significant, we examine the two core elements of each contract. In France, a lock-in agreement has two dimensions: a firm can signal shareholder commitment by locking in more and by locking in for longer periods of time. When we examine these dimensions individually (although they are intertwined), we find the following: at the expiry of contracts which lock in more shares than the median firm, we find more strongly negative abnormal share price movements than for firms locking in stakes which are lower than the median. This makes intuitively sense (and is also conform to the findings of Brav & Gompers, 2003), as more shares are unlocked. Lock-in contracts with a relatively short length have large abnormal returns at the expiry, while those with a relatively long length do not. This finding is in line with the fact that firms signal shareholder commitment (and hence firm quality) using lock-in length. This provides support for Hypothesis 4a.

Firms with above-median underpricing in the IPO have larger negative abnormal returns at the expiry. This goes against Hypothesis 5, which states that lock-in agreements and underpricing are substitute devices. Still, our finding is in line with the fact that shareholders of heavily underpriced firms do not sell many shares in the IPO, but rather wait until the lock-in expiry (Aggarwal, Krigman, & Womack, 2002). We also find that firms hiring a high-quality underwriter have larger abnormal returns at the lock-in expiry, which does not support Hypothesis 6 (not reported in the tables).

We have also performed several tests on the relation between VC backing/reputation and abnormal returns at the lock-in expiry. We find that VC reputation as such has no influence on abnormal returns at the expiry, which does not support Hypothesis 7. Likewise, the nationality of the VC (French, Anglo-American or other) does not play any role in this context. The abnormal returns around the expiry also do not differ between firms backed by one VC or by a VC syndicate. We do find a difference though when comparing firms in which VCs have substantial influence on the board of directors (the VC holds more than one-quarter of the board seats) and where they have less influence (proxied by only one board seat). If VCs have little board influence, the abnormal returns are significantly more negative than those of firms in which the VCs have a stronger board representation.

9.6.2. Multivariate Analysis

Table 9.13 shows the results from the regressions explaining the determinants of the CARs around the expiry. The dependent variable is the CAR[−5, 5]. The table contains three

Table 9.13: Results multiple linear regressions.

Variable	(1) Minimum contracts	(2) All contracts since change in regulation (1 December 1998)	(3) All contracts more strict than legal minimum since change in regulation (1 December 1998)
Constant	0.055	0.360**	−0.071
Insider contract (dummy)	0.019	−0.053	—
VC contract (dummy)	0.009	−0.007	0.041
Non-executive contract (dummy)	−0.081***	−0.027	−0.044
Length of lock-in period	0.000	0.000	0.000
Percentage of shares locked in	−0.167	−0.411***	0.128
IPO took place after 1 December 1998	−0.169	—	—
Expiry after market crash (10 March 2000)	−0.157*	−0.218*	−0.169
Underpricing	0.000	0.000	0.000
Underwriter reputation	−0.877***	−0.710	−0.836
VC reputation	0.003	0.002	−0.017
VC board influence	0.001	0.003	−0.001
Voting right scheme	0.054	0.064	0.231
Over-allotment option	0.005	−0.059	−0.008
Age	0.006**	0.002	0.000
F-test	2.753*	2.294**	0.480
Adjacent R^2	0.192	0.160	0.210

Notes: The dependent variable is CAR[−5, 5]. The length of the lock-in period is the number of days between the IPO and the expiry. Age is calculated as the firm age in number of days from the date of the creation of the SARL to the date of the IPO. Underpricing is measured in relation to the end of the first trading day. Underwriter reputation is measured as the percentage of total market capitalization brought to the market by the underwriter. VC reputation is measured as the number of recognitions of VC shareholders at national VC associations. Regression (1) includes all expiries before 1 December 1998 and those thereafter that locked in insiders for exactly the minimum requirement. Regression (2) includes all expiries after 1 December 1998. Regression (3) includes all expiries after 1 December 1998 of firms that chose stricter lock-in agreements for insiders than the minimum requirement. Statistical significance at ***1%, **5% and *10% level.

regressions, each of them run on a different sample. Regression (1) is run on the sample including contracts complying with the regulatory minimum contracts. Regression (2) includes all contracts since 1 December 1998. Finally, regression (3) includes only the lock-ins with more stringent terms than the regulatory minimums since 1 December 1998.

As the analysis is performed on the contract level (rather than on the firm level), we include dummy variables capturing the type of contract when it is related to insiders, VCs or non-executive directors. We find that the CARs at the contract expiry (whether an agreement is adhering to the regulatory minimum terms or is more stringent) are not different between insiders and VCs.[14] Hence, we reject Hypotheses 2 and 3.

There is no evidence that the length of the lock-in acts as a signal of firm quality and thereby reduces the negative market reaction at the expiry (Hypothesis 4a). In contrast, the percentage locked in is significantly different from zero, but reflects that the release of a large percentage of locked in shares creates price pressure at the expiry. The regulatory break of December 1998 does not seem to have any influence on the abnormal returns around the expiry. Still, there is evidence of significantly more price pressure when contracts expire after the market crash of the 10 March 2000.

There is no evidence that lock-in contracts and underpricing are substitute signals of firm quality (Hypothesis 5). Further, there is little consistent evidence on the impact of VC or underwriter reputation, voting rights schemes, or the presence of over-allotment options.

9.6.3. AV at Lock-in Expiry

Using Field and Hanka's (2001) method, average abnormal volume (AAV) is calculated for each day during a 101-day event window around the expiry day, resulting in Figure 9.6. There is very high AV during the first 10 days after the lock-in expiry. It is also clear that the increase in trading volume at the lock-in expiry is substantially larger for VC-backed firms, as documented by Bradley, Jordan, Yi, and Roten (2001) and Field and Hanka (2001).

Table 9.14 shows the average AV and the *t*-statistics after eliminating two outliers with very high volume (*European Cargo SA* and *Genset SA*). The table confirms that AV

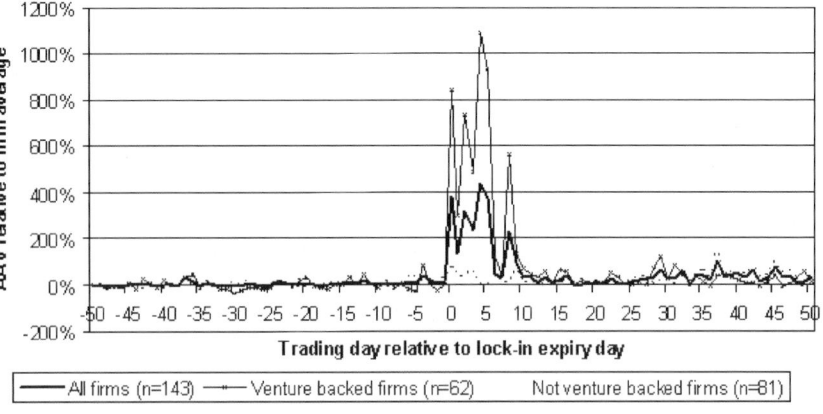

Figure 9.6: AAV at lock-in expiry. The sample is the first lock-in expiry for 143 French IPOs on the *Nouveau Marché* with lock-in expiries from 1996 to 2003. Volume is measured relative to each firm's mean trading volume over days −50 to −6. Firms are only considered to be VC backed if the first expiry relates to the VCs.

Table 9.14: AAV at lock-in expiry.

Day from expiry day	All the firms (%)	*t*-statistic	VC-backed firms only (%)	*t*-statistic	Firms without VC backing only (%)	*t*-statistic
−5	10	0.63	−27	−2.65**	33	1.38
−4	43	0.92	85	0.73	16	1.05
−3	19	1.26	6	0.35	27	1.23
−2	9	0.65	−25	−2.61**	31	1.46
−1	17	1.25	5	0.20	25	1.50
0	96	2.67***	122	2.36**	80	1.63
1	36	1.48	38	1.87*	34	0.91
2	38	2.39**	35	1.38	39	1.94*
3	66	2.11**	60	1.91*	69	1.47
4	16	1.08	40	1.29	1	0.06
5	14	1.10	23	1.08	9	0.53
6	43	1.32	120	1.49	−6	−0.43
7	25	1.63	31	1.42	22	1.02
8	38	1.96*	88	2.23**	6	0.31
9	78	2.96***	91	1.96*	70	2.21**
10	30	1.74*	69	1.86*	5	0.32
11	33	1.57	47	1.74*	24	0.80
12	8	0.66	36	1.33	−9	−0.88
13	29	1.90*	55	2.10**	12	0.66
14	7	0.54	3	0.23	10	0.49
15	22	0.71	63	0.83	−4	−0.26

Notes: The sample is the first lock-in expiry for 141 French IPOs on the *Nouveau Marché* with lock-in expiries from 1996 to 2003. Volume is measured relative to each firm's mean trading volume over days –50 to –6. European cargo SA and Genset SA have been excluded from the initial sample of 143 firms. Both firms are VC backed.
Statistical significance at ***1%, **5% and *10% level.

during the days immediately after the expiry is highly significant and that VC-backed firms show larger and more significant AV. During the first 13 days after the expiry, AV for VC-backed firms ranges from 23% to 122%. Firms without VC backing also have increased trading volume around the expiry, but the increase is statistically significant on only 2 days.

Table 9.15 reports the DAAV around the first lock-in expiry. The table is organized in a similar way as Table 9.11: Panel A reports the DAAVs based on the first expiry for all the firms whereas Panel B reports the DAAVs for the different categories of shareholders. Panel A shows that trading volume increases significantly starting from the day of the expiry. This suggests that substantial amounts of shares that were previously locked in are sold soon after the lock-in expiry, which confirms Hypothesis 1. Our evidence corroborates

Table 9.15: DAAV for first expiries and by shareholder type.

Event window	[−5, −1]	[−5, 5]	[0, 1]	[0, 5]	[0, 30]	[20, 50]	Number of lock-ins
Panel A: First expiries for all firms							
All expiries	19%	33%***	66%**	44%***	28%***	30%***	141
t-statistics	1.48	2.77	2.35	2.73	3.26	3.14	
Panel B: First expiry							
per shareholder category							
Insiders	17%*	36%***	69%**	52%**	30%***	37%***	108
t-statistics	1.73	2.66	1.99	2.56	3.02	3.14	
Outsiders	28%	22%	56%	18%	22%	9%	33
t-statistics	0.60	0.91	1.41	0.99	1.25	0.62	
Difference in means	−12%	14%	13%	35%	9%	28%	—
t-statistics	−0.24	0.49	0.25	1.28	0.44	1.48	
VCs	11%	35%**	81%***	55%***	49%***	25%*	54
t-statistics	0.37	2.00	2.71	2.90	2.89	1.75	
All others	25%**	32%**	57%	38%	16%*	33%**	87
t-statistics	2.09	1.98	1.36	1.60	1.69	2.60	
Difference in means	−14%	3%	24%	17%	33%*	−8%	—
t-statistics	−0.46	0.13	0.47	0.57	1.74	−0.42	
Non-executives	17%	30%	67%	41%	36%**	31%**	58
t-statistics	0.63	1.44	1.15	1.49	2.27	2.16	
All others	21%*	35%**	65%***	46%**	23%**	30%**	83
t-statistics	1.77	2.48	2.64	2.34	2.35	2.29	
Difference in means	−4%	−5%	3%	−5%	13%	0%	—
t-statistics	−0.13	−0.19	0.04	−0.16	0.72	0.02	

Notes: The sample consists of the first lock-in expiry of 141 French IPOs on the *Nouveau Marché* with lock-in expiries from 1996 to 2003. Volume is measured relative to each firm's mean trading volume over days −50 to −6. Desk SA was delisted 14 days after its first and only lock-in expiry; therefore, the samples for the window [20, 50] does not include this observation.
Statistical significance at ***1%, **5% and *10% level.

the findings for the USA by Field and Hanka (2001), and Ofek and Richardson (2003) (see also our Table 9.3 above). Panel B reports the DAAVs for insiders, VCs and non-executives. The DAAVs are highly significant for insiders and VCs whatever the window (which is in line with Hypotheses 2 and 3), but less though for non-executives.

Table 9.16 reports AV for different sub-samples. We do not find a difference in DAAV at the expiries of lock-in contracts following a regulatory minimum and those with more stringent terms. Contrary to our expectations, we find that contracts locking in for a longer period trigger more abnormal volume. The percentage of shares locked is not found to have an effect on abnormal volume at the lock-in expiry. Hypothesis 5 is supported as firms that are only moderately underpriced show larger increases in trading volume at the expiry. Expiries for firms with a relatively low-quality underwriter have significantly larger increases in trading volume at the expiry than firms with a high-quality underwriter. Thus, we cannot reject Hypothesis 6. We also investigate the impact of VC reputation and board representation on the share trading volume at the lock-in expiry (not shown in the table). We do not find support for Hypothesis 7, as there are no significant differences in trading volume between firms that attracted highly reputable (in the sense of being internationally active and being recognized by VC associations) VCs and those that did not. Partitioning the firms, based on the number of board representatives a VC has, does not yield any different results.

9.6.4. Robustness Checks

As a robustness check we recomputed all abnormal returns using (i) the France-Datastream (DS) Small Companies index, which only includes small cap shares listed on French markets, (ii) and the Eurex-Dow Jones (DJ) Euro Stoxx Small index, which includes approximately 200 small cap shares listed on the main stock markets in the Eurozone and (iii) the DJ Euro Stoxx All Share index. A recalculation of all the results presented above using these different indices does not change any of our conclusions.

We also test for a difference in abnormal return results for the first expiry dates per firm and per shareholder type. We find that VCs tend to use the first opportunity to sell a significant part of their holdings. This is in line with the statement by Gompers and Lerner (1999) that VCs exit the firm at the lock-in expiry. However, we do find that VCs that invested in firms listed on the *Nouveau Marché* keep a minority stake even after the last lock-in expiry. The annual reports of these companies show that most VCs still hold shares 3–4 years after the IPO. Striking is the fact that all 26 expiries for underwriters were simultaneously expiries for VCs. It is likely that underwriters buy the shares that VCs sell at expiry. They thereby show their commitment to support the share price even long after the IPO.

We also tested the influence of the length of the lock-in period on the abnormal returns at expiry by including dummy variables for the different types of minimum requirements for insiders. These results were not significant. First-week underpricing is also used as a robustness check for first-day underpricing, which does not give dissimilar results. In order to prevent an underpricing bias, size is measured in terms of market capitalization at the offer price and subsequent to the first trading day. When extending the share trading benchmark period before the expiry, the AV tends to be larger but similar in terms of significance.

Table 9.16: DAAV by signal of firm quality.

Event window	[-5, -1]	[-5, 5]	[0, 1]	[0, 5]	[0, 30]	[20, 50]	n
Minimum requirement	19%	52%*	116%	79%*	30%**	29%*	48
t-statistics	1.25	1.89	1.54	1.89	2.07	1.87	
Stricter than minimum requirement	3%	26%	24%	46%	41%	47%	22
t-statistics	0.15	1.37	0.88	1.58	1.42	1.58	
Difference in means	17%	26%	91%	33%	-11%	-17%	—
t-statistics	-0.74	-0.77	-1.14	-0.66	0.35	0.52	
Below-median lock-in length	21%	11%	3%	2%	13%	0%	39
t-statistics	0.54	0.51	0.17	0.11	0.96	-0.04	
Above-median lock-in length	34%*	72%**	128%	103%**	48%**	62%***	44
t-statistics	1.97	2.42	1.58	2.27	2.47	2.93	
Difference in means	-13%	-61%*	-125%	-102%**	-35%	-63%***	—
t-statistics	-0.30	-1.68	-1.50	-2.11	-1.46	-2.63	
Below-median percentage locked in	17%	23%***	35%*	29%***	18%***	33%**	70
t-statistics	1.32	2.06	1.86	2.19	1.98	2.29	
Above-median percentage locked in	22%	42%***	96%*	59%***	39%***	28%**	71
t-statistics	0.96	2.03	1.83	2.01	2.62	2.14	

Difference in means	−6%	−19%	−61%	−30%	−21%	4%	—
t-statistics	−0.22	−0.80	−1.09	−0.93	−1.20	0.22	
Below-median underpricing	32%	54%***	104%*	73%**	43%***	47%***	72
t-statistics	1.36	2.53	1.96	2.43	3.36	3.28	
Above-median underpricing	6%	11%	26%*	14%	13%	13%	69
t-statistics	0.58	1.20	1.77	1.42	1.15	1.03	
Difference in means	26%	44%*	77%	58%*	29%*	34%*	—
t-statistics	1.00	1.88	1.41	1.85	1.69	1.80	
Top 10 underwriters	−5%	8%	35%	18%	14%	15%	64
t-statistics	−0.40	0.67	1.65	1.28	1.38	1.33	
Other underwriters	39%*	54%***	92%*	66%**	40%***	43%***	77
t-statistics	1.79	2.79	1.90	2.44	3.00	2.90	
Difference in means	−44%*	−46%**	−57%	−48%	−26%	−28%	—
t-statistics	−1.77	−2.05	−1.08	−1.58	−1.57	−1.50	

Notes: Trading volume is measured relative to each firm's mean trading volume over days −50 to −6. The tests that include the length of the lock-in period are run on the sub-sample of post 1 December 1998 IPOs only. The division criterion of the sample for length, percentage of shares locked-in and level of underpricing is the median.

Statistical significance at ***1%, **5% and *10% level.

Table 9.17: Conclusion.

Hypothesis	Returns		Volume	
	Expected relation	Observed relation	Expected relation	Observed relation
1 All expiries	Negative	Weakly negative	Positive	Strongly positive
2 Expiries for insiders	Negative	Strongly negative	Positive	Not significant
3 Expiries for VCs	Negative	Not significant	Positive	Weakly positive
4 Stricter lock-in contracts	Positive	Not significant	Negative	Not significant
5 Heavily underpriced	Positive	Negative	Negative	Weakly negative
6 Reputable underwriters	Positive	Negative	Negative	Negative
7 VC reputation	Positive	Not significant	Negative	Not significant

9.7. Conclusions

This chapter unveils the variety in lock-in agreements of firms listed on the *Nouveau Marché* stock exchange in France. The lock-in regulation and the changes therein since the inception of the stock exchange are discussed. In addition, the main economic reasons are given why shareholders adopt lock-in agreements that are more stringent than legally required. We relate the abnormal returns and the abnormal volume at the expiry dates of the different types of lock-in contracts to the degree of underpricing, VC reputation and underwriter reputation. We find that the abnormal returns and the trading volume increase at the lock-in expiry (see the summary in Table 9.17); this is especially pronounced at the expiry dates of insider lock-in contracts as insiders are legally required to be locked in. Surprisingly, we do not find significant abnormal returns at the expiries of VC contracts, even though trading volume increases at their lock-in expiry. The fact that VCs may have a large impact on the board of directors (through representation) and/or may be more reputable through international activities does not influence the results. In addition, VC backing has no impact on the abnormal returns or the trading volume. There is no evidence of a positive (negative) relation between abnormal returns (abnormal volume) and more stringent lock-in contracts. If lock-in contracts and the degree of underpricing were substitute signals of firm quality, we would find a positive relation between underpricing and the abnormal returns at expiry. However, it seems that the two signalling devices are complementary.

Acknowledgements

The authors would like to thank Wissam Abdallah and Marie-Thérèse Camilleri-Gilson for excellent research assistance. We are grateful for valuable comments from Anne Högberg Janisch, Marianne Kaefer, Arif Khurshed, Jacob Obrecht and Paul Oranjeboom. Angenendt and Goergen acknowledge financial support from the European Commission Key Action 'Improving the socio-economic knowledge base' through contract number

HPSE-CT-2002-00146 and Renneboog acknowledges support from the European Commission via the 'New Modes of Governance'-project (NEWGOV) led by the European University Institute in Florence; contract number CIT1-CT-2004-506392 and funding from the Netherlands Organization for Scientific Research in the Programme of Shifts in Governance.

Endnotes

1. In American English, they are called lock-up agreements and in French *engagements de conservation*.
2. The IPO of *IDM SA*, which was scheduled for 16 June 2004, was postponed indefinitely.
3. www.evca.com
4. In French, *Le gouvernement d'entreprise des sociétés cotées*.
5. Our data show that there was no signalling via the length of the lock-in period prior to 1 December 1998 as all IPOs prior to that date chose not to exceed the minimum lock-in requirement of 3 years. However, in some companies, the percentages of shares locked in exceeded the minimum requirement over the entire lock-in period.
6. Just over 24% of the firms in the sample have at least one shareholder who is both a non-executive and founder (not reported in the table).
7. Nine firms (6%) do not comply with the listing requirement that at least 50% of total shares offered in the IPO should be primary shares.
8. The means and medians for a specific shareholder category are based on all the firms in which that category of shareholder holds share stakes.
9. For a detailed account of the book-building process, see Cornelli and Goldstein (2001; 2003).
10. We also recorded the date when each firm changed its legal form from a private limited firm to public limited firm (SA). For most firms this date was only a few months before the IPO.
11. Where fewer than 180 daily returns are available, the estimation window can start as early as 110 days before the event day. The exception is *Prosodie SA*, whose α and β parameters were estimated using only 30 daily returns, as the first lock-in expiry took place 3 months after the IPO. We always excluded at least the first 10 trading days after the IPO to avoid a possible bias from any IPO underpricing.
12. Hence, we regress the firm's stock return not only on the contemporaneous market return, but also on that for the 2 previous and the 2 following days. The Dimson β parameters are then calculated as the sum of the five β parameters obtained from these regressions. The problem of thin trading is thereby diminished. Blume (1975a, b) pointed out the problem of reversion to the mean: if the current estimate of β is less (greater) than one, then the subsequent period's estimate of β tends to increase (decline). This tendency to reverse to the mean can be addressed by using a large enough sample, allowing for the actual long-term mean to be determined. We multiply the actual Dimson β parameters by two-thirds and then add a third. These Dimson–Blume β parameters, together with the α parameters from the ordinary least squares (OLS) regressions, are then used to calculate the abnormal returns .
13. We also investigate the difference in CAARs between the two minimum requirements: 100% of the shares locked in for 6 months and 80% of the shares locked in for 1 year. We do not find any statistical difference in the CAARs.
14. The only exception is non-executive directors: the CAARs at the expiry of the minimum contracts are significantly lower when the non-executive directors are restrained from selling (part of) their share stakes.

References

Aggarwal, R.K., Krigman, L., & Womack, K.L. (2002). Strategic IPO underpricing, information momentum, and lockup expiration selling. *Journal of Financial Economics, 66*, 105–137.
Association Française des Entreprises Privées (AFEP) and *Mouvement des Entreprises de France (MEDEF)* (2003). The Corporate Governance of Listed Corporations.

Aussenegg, W., Pichler, P., & Stomper, A. (2002). *Sticky prices: IPO pricing on NASDAQ and the neuer markt*. Working paper, Vienna University of Technology, Massachusetts Institute of Technology and University of Vienna.

Barber, B., & Lyon, J.D. (1997). Detecting long-run abnormal stock returns: The empirical power and specification of test statistics. *Journal of Financial Economics, 43*, 341–372.

Barry, C.B. (1994). New directions in research of venture capital finance. *Financial Management, 23*, 3–15.

Bertoni, F., Giudici, G., Randone, P.A., Rochira, C., & Zanoni, P. (2002). New listings and lock-up agreements. *Borsa Italiana*, BIt Notes 5.

Bessler, W., & Kurth, A. (2003). *The performance of venture-backed IPOs in Germany*. Working paper, Justus-Liebig-University, Giessen.

Blume, M.E. (1975a). Betas and their regression tendencies. *Journal of Finance, 30*, 785–795.

Blume, M.E. (1975b). Betas and their regression tendencies: Some further evidence. *Journal of Finance, 34*, 265–267.

Bottazzi, L., & Da Rin, M. (2002). Venture capital in Europe and the financing of innovative firms. *Economic Policy, 34*, 229–269.

Bouton, D. (2002). Promoting better corporate governance in listed companies. *Mouvement des Entreprises de France (MEDEF)* and *Association Française des Entreprises Privées (AFEP)*.

Bradley, D.J., Jordan, B.D., Yi, H.C., & Roten, I.C. (2001). Venture capital and IPO lockup expiration: An empirical analysis. *Journal of Financial Research, 24*, 465-492.

Brau, J.C., Carter, D.A., Christophe, S.E., & Key, K.G. (2004). Market reaction to the expiration of IPO lockup provisions. *Managerial Finance, 30*, 87–103.

Brav, A., & Gompers, P.A. (2003). The role of lockups in initial public offerings. *Review of Financial Studies, 16*, 1–29.

Cornelli, F., & Goldstein, D. (2001). Bookbuilding and strategic allocation. *Journal of Finance, 56*, 2337–2370.

Cornelli, F., & Goldstein, D. (2003). How informative is the order book. *Journal of Finance, 58*, 1415–1444.

Courteau, L. (1995). Under-diversification and retention commitment in IPOs. *Journal of Financial and Quantitative Analysis, 30*, 487–517.

Dherment-Ferere, I., & Renneboog, L. (2002). Share price reactions to CEO resignations and large shareholder monitoring in listed French companies. In: McCahery et al. (Eds), *Convergence and diversity of corporate governance regimes and capital markets* (pp. 297–324). Oxford: Oxford University Press.

Dimson, E. (1979). Risk measurement when shares are subject to infrequent trading. *Journal of Financial Economics, 7*, 197–226.

Ducros, E. (2001). Asymétrie d'information et engagements de conservation des dirigeants lors des introductions en bourse sur le second et le Nouveau Marché de Paris. Unpublished MSc dissertation, University of Paris Val de Marne (Paris XII) and Ecole Centrale de Paris.

Espenlaub, S., Goergen, M., & Khurshed, A. (2001). IPO lock-in agreements in the UK. *Journal of Business Finance and Accounting, 28*, 1235–1278.

Espenlaub, S., Goergen, M., Khurshed, A., & Renneboog, L. (2003). Lock-in agreements in venture capital backed UK IPOs. In: McCaherty, & L. Renneboog (Eds), *Venture capital contracting and the valuation of high technology firms* (pp. 396–436). Oxford: Oxford University Press.

Field, L.C., & Hanka, G. (2001). The expiration of IPO share lockups. *Journal of Finance, 56*, 471–500.

Giudici, G. (2001). New listings and initial public offerings in Italy. *Banques et Marchés (Association Française de Finance), 55*, 36–42.

Goergen, M., Khurshed, A., McCahery, J.A., & Renneboog, L. (2002). The rise and fall of the European new markets: On the short and long-run performance of high-tech initial public offerings.

In: J. McCaherty, & L. Renneboog (Eds), *Venture capital contracting and the valuation of high technology firms* (pp. 464–492). Oxford: Oxford University Press.

Goergen, M., Renneboog, L., & Khurshed, A. (2005). Explaining the diversity in shareholder lockup agreements. *Journal of Financial Intermediation*. (Forthcoming)

Gompers, P.A., & Lerner, J. (1999). *The venture capital cycle*. Cambridge: MIT Press.

Jain, B.A., & Kini, O. (2000). Does the presence of venture capitalists improve the survival profile of IPO firms? *Journal of Business Finance and Accounting*, 27, 1139–1176.

Kremp, E., & Sevestre, P. (2001). France. In: K. Gugler (Ed.), *Corporate governance and economic performance* (pp. 121–129). Oxford: Oxford University Press.

Leland, H., & Pyle, D. (1977). Information asymmetries, financial structure and financial intermediation. *Journal of Finance*, 32, 371–387.

Leven, F.J. (2003). DAI-Factbook: Statistiken, analysen und graphiken zu aktionären, aktiengesellschaften und Börsen. *Deutsches Aktieninstitut*.

Manigart, S., & De Maeseneire, W. (2000). *Initial returns on EASDAQ and Euro.NM*. Working paper, Vlerick Leuven Ghent management school and Ghent University.

Megginson, W.L. (2004). Towards a global model of venture capital. *Journal of Applied Corporate Finance*, 16, 8–26.

Mohan, N.J., & Chen, C.R. (2001). Information content of lock-up provisions in initial public offerings. *International Review of Economics and Finance*, 10, 41–59.

Nowak, E., & Gropp, A. (2000). *Ist der ablauf der lock-up-frist bei neuemissionen ein kursrelevantes ereignis? Eine empirische analyse von unternehmen der neuen marktes*. Working paper, Johann Wolfgang Goethe University Frankfurt.

Ofek, E., & Richardson, M. (2000). *The IPO lock-up period: Implications for market efficiency and downward sloping demand curves*. Working paper, Stern Business School.

Ofek, E., & Richardson, M. (2003). DotCom Mania: The rise and fall of Internet stock prices. *Journal of Finance*, 58, 1113–1137.

Vienot, M. (1995). The board of directors of listed companies in France. *Conseil national du patronat Français (CNPF)* and *Association Française des Entreprises Privées (AFEP)*, http://www.ecgi.org/codes/documents/vienot1_en.pdf (05-Jun-2005).

Vienot, M. (1999). Recommendations of the committee on corporate governance. *Association Française des entreprises privees (AFEP)* and *mouvement des entreprises de France (MEDEF)*, http://www.ecgi.org/codes/documents/vienot2_en.pdf (05-Jun-2005).

Wymeersch, E. (1994). Aspects of corporate governance. *Journal of Corporate Governance*, 2, 138–149.

Appendix: Listing on the Nouveau Marché

Listing Requirements on the Nouveau Marché during the Sample Period
Except for the minimum lock-in requirements (which were changed on 1 December 1998 — *Instruction NM3-02*), the entry criteria for a listing on the *Nouveau Marché* have remained unchanged during the sample period. The following quantitative criteria are those mentioned in Article P 1.1.31 of the rules applicable to the *Nouveau Marché* and were valid between 21 March 1996 and 15 September 2003:

- The applicant must have individual and consolidated shareholders' equity of at least €1.5 million (or the equivalent in another currency).
- On the initial trading date at the latest, a minimum of 100,000 financial instruments, representing at least €5 million (or the equivalent in another currency) must be held by the public.

- On the initial trading date at the latest, at least half of the publicly held financial instruments must have been distributed through issuance of new financial instruments.
- A minimum number of financial instruments must be made available to the listing advisor/market maker(s) to facilitate market making.
- For equity securities, on the initial trading date at the latest, at least 20% of the company's issued capital must be held by the public.
- The applicant must present an income statement showing a pre-tax profit on ordinary activities for the 12 months prior to the admission decision. The statement must be prepared in accordance with generally accepted accounting principles, without restatements. It must be audited by the company's statutory auditors. Euronext Paris may waive this provision to allow for, *inter alia*, the sector in which the company operates.

Changes in the Listing Requirements on the Nouveau Marché After the Sample Period
The listing requirements were changed on 15 September 2003. Interestingly, the requirement that the capital increase needed to be at least 50% of the issue volume was removed. This criterion had not been strictly enforced, as not all admitted firms complied with it. In addition, the minimum lock-in requirements (Euronext Paris Notice No. 2003-2869) were changed and two articles were added. The first one concerns the possibility of a listed company to be put in the compartiment spécial or special box (Instruction NM3-03, Article 1). This can occur in the following cases:

(a) Where the half-yearly examination of the issuer's situation reveals that during the period under review:
   i. The closing price has been lower than one euro on a regular basis during the previous 6 months. However, registration of the financial instruments in question may be confined to those whose market capitalization, measured during the previous 6 months, is less than €4 million.
   ii. The issuer's market capitalization has been less than Euro 4 million on a regular basis during the previous 6 months.
   iii. The issuer has failed to meet periodic disclosure requirements. In this case, the issuer has 3 months from service of notice by Euronext Paris in which to remedy the failure before being registered in the special box.
(b) Where the issuer has been involved in collective proceedings, within the meaning of Articles L. 620-1 *et seq.* of the Code of Commerce, or in an equivalent procedure in the case of an issuer incorporated outside France, the instruments are registered as soon as the judgement is brought to the attention of Euronext Paris.
(c) Where an event occurs that has a lasting impact on the operations or corporate life of the issuer.

Apparently, this measure was necessary, as 12 companies were singled out within 4 months after the new regulation took effect.
The second new article concerns the extension of the minimum requirements for quarterly reporting of financial information (*Instruction NM3-04*).

Listing Process on the Nouveau Marché

The following schedule that informs potential entrants of events that take place during the listing process is given in the stock market brochure entitled 'Going Public On Le Nouveau Marché'.

Day –120: Choice of a sponsor/market maker
  The issuer shall select a sponsor/market maker who will be in charge of preparing the admission file and selecting the PR agency.
  Preparation of the admission file
  The sponsor/market maker prepares the prospectus and the notice of information   which includes the 3-year business plan.
Day –90: Submission file
  The issuer and the sponsor/market maker submit the file to *Le Nouveau Marché* and the Securities Commission, which will examine the file. This file can be a preliminary file.
Day –45: Submission of the final prospectus to *Le Nouveau Marché* and Securities Commission
Day –30: Decision taken by the Admission Committee of *Le Nouveau Marché* (meetings of the Admission Committee take place twice a month)
Day –21: End of opposition time limit for the Securities Commission
Day –19: Securities Commission Visa on the preliminary operation notice
Day –18: Beginning of the communication drive (RoadShow, investors meetings, 'one-on-ones')
Day –10: Spread price offer decision and beginning of the placement
Day –3: End of placement Securities Commission Visa on the final operation note; Price set up; Beginning of Fixed price offer (OPF) and placement
Day –1: End of the Offer and placement
Day –0: Centralization by *Le Nouveau Marché*; Results of OPF — allocation of shares; issuing — trading
Day +3: Clearing and settlement of day – 0 trades

Chapter 10

The Grant and Exercise of Stock Options in IPO Firms: Evidence from the Netherlands

Tjalling van der Goot, Gerard Mertens and Peter Roosenboom

10.1. Introduction

An Initial Public Offering (IPO) is often the first event in a firm's history at which agency conflicts between management and outside shareholders arise (Beatty & Zajac, 1994; Engel, Gordon, & Hayes, 2002; Baker & Gompers, 2003). The use of stock options can be a possible solution to this agency problem. Managers who own stock (options) continue to bear a substantial part of the wealth consequences of their decisions after the IPO and will therefore be more likely to act in the interest of outside shareholders. However, recent studies have proposed that executives influence the terms of their compensation package to their personal advantage. For example, Bebchuk, Fried, and Walker (2002) and Bebchuk and Fried (2003; 2004) argue that the practice of granting options (at the money or with exercise prices indexed to market movements) could be caused by rent-seeking managers trying to maximize their compensation. The benefits are substantial and the fact that IPO options are treated as being granted at-the-money camouflages their cost. Empirical evidence on grant and exercise behaviour surrounding the IPO can provide more insight into the characteristics of these companies and management motives.

We investigate the grant and exercise of stock options for a sample of 54 Dutch IPO firms in the year of their IPO and 2 years thereafter. To the best of our knowledge, no previous study has investigated both the determinants of the grant and exercise of stock options in the post-IPO period. Engel, Gordon, and Hayes (2002) study post-IPO stock option grants to CEOs in the USA. They report that option grants to CEOs are significantly related to accounting performance (for manufacturing and technology firms) and stock return performance (for internet firms) in non-venture backed IPO firms. However, Engel, Gordon, and Hayes (2002) do not examine option grants and exercises simultaneously as we do in this study. This is important because if employees systematically exercise options before their expiration date, the incentives last for a shorter period of time than is suggested by the maturity of the option (Huddart, 1994; Huddart & Lang, 1996; Hall &

Advances in Corporate Finance and Asset Pricing
Edited by L. Renneboog
© 2006 Elsevier B.V. All rights reserved.
ISBN: 0-444-52723-0

Murphy, 2002). In addition, by examining option grants and exercises of the same firm — in which we include the same explanatory variables — we are able to investigate and compare the effects of these independent variables on either option grants or option exercises.

In the Netherlands, until 2002 companies only had to disclose the aggregate number of option exercises, and the number and exercise price of option grants in their annual report.[1] This limited disclosure requirement is typical for Continental European countries (Ferrarini, Moloney, & Vespro, 2003). As a result, we cannot distinguish between stock options that are granted to management and key employees such as subsidiary managers. This implies that we investigate the stock options held by a wider group of employees (including managers) rather than the CEOs investigated by Engel, Gordon, and Hayes (2002).

Our results show that the ownership stake of managers is decreased by about one-third from 52.1% before IPO to 34.7% in the first year of IPO. From this we conclude that the dilution of the management ownership stake at the IPO is substantial, which gives rise to agency problems. Stock option grants may be used to mitigate the negative effects of this ownership dilution. However, at the end of the second fiscal year after the year of IPO 86% of the stock option grants at the IPO have been exercised. It seems that the incentives from stock options are rather short lived. Our findings show that stock option grants are a positive function of accounting and stock market performance and growth opportunities. We also find a negative but insignificant relation between stock option grants and the level of retained management stock ownership and venture capital (VC) monitoring. Our interpretation of these findings is that it provides only weak evidence that stock options are used to mitigate agency problems. When we investigate the determinants of stock option exercises, we find that the holders of the stock options are more ready to retain stock options when the firm experiences strong stock price performance. Finally, we also document that option holders exercise their options early when there is active trading in the firm's stock and the firm's dividend payout ratio is high.

The remainder of the study is organized as follows. In Section 10.2 we formulate our hypotheses. We describe our data in Section 10.3. The empirical results are given in Section 10.4 and Section 10.5 concludes this chapter.

10.2. Hypotheses and Variable Measurement

In this section we first introduce our hypotheses regarding option grants (Section 10.2.1) and then present subsequent hypotheses on option exercises (Section 10.2.2).

10.2.1. Determinants of Option Grants

First, we use a model to explain the stock options granting behaviour of IPO firms. To capture the stock-based part of a manager's total remuneration, the dependent variable in our option grants model is the value of all stock options that are granted during the fiscal year divided by the sum of the value of the option grants and the fixed compensation during the same year. Hereafter, we will refer to this dependent variable as option grants. The value of the option grants is calculated with the help of the Black and Scholes model (1973) as modified by Merton (1973) for dividends. We investigate a period of up to 3 fiscal years after IPO. In this section we discuss our hypotheses regarding the determinants of stock option grants.

Smith and Watts (1992) argue that firms with valuable growth opportunities require high-quality staff to successfully exploit these opportunities. These high-quality employees can be remunerated with stock-based compensation, such as stock options, which allow them to share in future increases in firm value. At the time of an IPO it is important to competitively reward high-quality employees to prevent them from leaving the firm. For example, Welbourne and Andrews (1996) show that stock option programs and employee profit sharing increase the rate of survival of IPO firms in the USA. We use the market-to-book ratio, which is the market value of the IPO firm's equity plus the book value of its short- and long-term debt divided by the book value of its assets as our proxy for growth opportunities. We predict a positive relation between option grants and the market-to-book ratio.

Hypothesis 1: Stock option grants are positively related to the firm's growth opportunities.

Liang and Weisbenner (2001) analyse stock option grants to employees in the USA. They find that there is a greater demand for options among employees following stock price increases and less willingness to accept stock options when past stock price performance has been poor. Engel, Gordon, and Hayes (2002) report similar findings for option grants to CEOs of US IPO firms. We therefore hypothesize that option grants are a positive function of a firm's accounting performance, measured by its growth rate of net income, and cumulative stock returns.

Hypothesis 2(a): Stock option grants are positively related to the firm's accounting performance.

Hypothesis 2(b): Stock option grants are positively related to the firm's cumulative stock returns.

Management stock ownership can be viewed as a substitute for the use of stock options. If managers own more stock their incentives are already well aligned with those of outside shareholders. This reduces the need for other equity-based rewards such as stock options to mitigate the agency problem. Recent studies document an inverse relation between managerial stock ownership and the use of options (Mehran, 1995; Bryan, Hwang, & Lilien, 2000; Ryan & Wiggins, 2001). Baker and Gompers (1999) examine the determinants of CEO pay and ownership in a sample of US IPO firms from 1978 to 1987. They find that CEOs with large retained ownership sell shares at the time of the offering. However, CEOs who possess little retained ownership and hold options do not tend to sell any shares at the time of the IPO. Baker and Gompers (1999) conclude that option grants increase incentives and help to mitigate agency problems in IPO firms, but only when the CEO does not own much stock. Undiversified managers that already own large shareholdings in the IPO firm may be unwilling to accept stock options, as it would increase the risk exposure of their wealth beyond acceptable levels (Beatty & Zajac, 1994; Toyne, Millar, & Dixon, 2000). We thus hypothesize that option grants are a decreasing function of management ownership.

Hypothesis 3: Stock option grants are negatively related to the percentage of post-IPO management ownership.

Beatty and Zajac (1994) find an inverse relation between the fraction of independent board members and the use of stock options in US IPO firms. They conclude that board monitoring acts as a substitute for stock option grants to top management. Baker and Gompers (2003) find that venture capitalists improve the effectiveness of board supervision in IPO firms. Engel, Gordon, and Hayes (2002) report that venture capitalists reduce the need for pay-to-performance contracting in IPO firms. We, therefore, predict an inverse relation between the grant of options and VC monitoring. We measure VC monitoring as the fraction of non-executive directors affiliated to venture capitalists in a firm's supervisory board.[2]

Hypothesis 4: Stock option grants are negatively related to the percentage non-executive directors affiliated to venture capitalists in a firm's supervisory board.

Subsequently, we add several control variables to our model. We control for risk using the 3-year average standard deviation of daily stock returns volatility from 30 days after IPO until the end of the 3-year period. We omit the first 30 days after IPO because during this period underwriters may have stabilized the stock price of the IPO firm. Our model controls for technology firms by a high-tech dummy that equals one for technology firms and zero otherwise. In order to control for size we include the log of sales and the log of number of employees. The latter is motivated by the evidence provided by Welbourne and Andrews (1996). They show that retaining employees that are key for the success of the company is of great importance for IPO firms. In IPO firms with few employees it may be important to retain these employees with firm-specific knowledge through stock option grants.

We now specify the following model for option grants:

$$
\begin{aligned}
\textit{Option grants}_t = {} & \alpha_0 + \alpha_1 \textit{ market-to-book ratio}_t + \alpha_2 \textit{ growth of net income}_t \\
& + \alpha_3 \textit{ cumulative stock returns}_t + \alpha_4 \textit{ retained ownership after IPO} \\
& + \alpha_5 \textit{ VC monitoring} + \alpha_6 \textit{ volatility}_t + \alpha_7 \textit{ high-tech dummy} \\
& + \alpha_8 \textit{ log (number of employees}_t) + \alpha_9 \textit{ log (sales}_t) + \varepsilon_t
\end{aligned}
\tag{10.1}
$$

where $t = 0$ (year of IPO), $t = 1$ (first fiscal year after IPO) and $t = 2$ (second fiscal year after IPO).

10.2.2. Determinants of Option Exercises

Similar to the option grants model in Section 10.2.1, we specify a model that explains options exercise behaviour of IPO firms. Our measure of option exercises is the number of options exercised as percentage of the number of options outstanding at the beginning of the fiscal year. Hereafter, we will refer to this dependent variable as option exercises. We hypothesize that option exercises are inversely related to the growth opportunities of the IPO firm measured by the market-to-book ratio. As it is costly to exercise stock options early in particular for options of high-growth firms, key employees may be more willing to hold their options in anticipation of future increases in firm value.

Hypothesis 5: Stock option exercises are negatively related to the firm's growth opportunities.

Heath, Huddart, and Lang (1999) report that options are exercised in response to trends. Option exercises are less likely when the firm shows strong accounting and stock price performance because option holders anticipate that the strong accounting and stock price performance will continue in the future.

Hypothesis 6(a): Stock option exercises are negatively related to the firm's accounting performance.

Hypothesis 6(b): Stock option exercises are negatively related to the firm's cumulative stock returns.

Venture capitalists that are represented in the supervisory board are in a position to closely monitor option holders when they exercise their options early. Therefore, venture capitalists play an important role in the context of option exercises. Hence, we hypothesize the following.

Hypothesis 7: Stock option exercises are negatively related to VC monitoring.

Holmström and Tirole (1993) argue that with more market liquidity it becomes easier for an informed party to disguise his private information and personally benefit from it. When market liquidity is high, key employees can easily sell stocks that they have obtained through exercising their options. Although early exercise of options by key employees is a negative signal, this exercise may go largely unnoticed when market liquidity is high and disclosure about stock options is limited. In the sample period that we examine, the option grants and exercises were only published in the firm's annual report. Therefore, it is hypothesized that the exercise of stock options is a positive function of a firm's stock turnover.

Hypothesis 8: Stock option exercises are positively related to the firm's stock turnover.

Maris, Maris, and Yang (2003) argue an employee might exercise his options early if a firm has a high dividend payout. Dividends can only be obtained when the employee possesses the shares. Hence, we hypothesize option exercises are an increasing function of a firm's dividend payout ratio, which is measured by the firm's payout ratio.

Hypothesis 9: Stock option exercises are positively related to the firm's payout ratio.

We have included the same four control variables as in the option grants model. According to Black and Scholes (1973) the value of options is an increasing function of its volatility. Because a high volatility results in a large option value, option exercises and volatility are inversely related. However, a high volatility implies a high firm-specific risk. Assuming risk-averse option holders, option exercises are an increasing function of their volatility. The relation between option exercises and volatility is an empirical question. We control for technology firms by a high-tech dummy that equals one for technology firms and zero otherwise. Again, we have included the log of its sales to control for a firm's size. The number of employees is included to control for retention effects. In IPO firms with few employees we expect that there will be less stock option exercises because these key employees are more likely to be committed to the IPO firm due to firm-specific knowledge. We estimate the following model for option exercises:

$$
\begin{aligned}
Option\ exercises_t = \ & \beta_0 + \beta_1\ market\text{-}to\text{-}book\ ratio_t + \beta_2\ growth\ of\ net\ income_t \\
& + \beta_3\ cumulative\ stock\ returns_t + \beta_4\ VC\ monitoring \\
& + \beta_5\ stock\ turnover_t + \beta_6\ payout\ ratio_t + \beta_7\ volatility_t \\
& + \beta_8\ high\text{-}tech\ dummy + \beta_9\ log\ (number\ of\ employees_t) \\
& + \beta_{10}\ log\ (sales_t) + \varepsilon_t
\end{aligned}
\tag{10.2}
$$

where $t = 0$ (year of IPO), $t = 1$ (first fiscal year after IPO) and $t = 2$ (second fiscal year after IPO).

10.3. Data and Sample Description

The sample consists of firms that have gone public on Euronext Amsterdam during the years 1985–1998. We have hand-collected accounting and stock options data of three subsequent

Table 10.1: Sample construction.

Number of IPOs (1983–1998)		126
IPOs without options	66	
Incomplete or Missing data	6+	
		72−
Number of IPOs examined		54

fiscal years for every firm. The data comes from the IPO prospectuses and the annual reports of the year of IPO and the two following years. Stock prices and stock turnover are from Datastream. We have checked the volume of stocks provided by Datastream with similar data published by ABN-AMRO Bank (1987–2001). In case of discrepancies between both data sources we used the ABN-AMRO data. All monetary amounts are in constant prices of the year 2001 computed with the help of the consumer price index.

Table 10.1 reports that our original sample consists of 126 IPOs on Euronext Amsterdam during 1983–1998 of which 66 IPO firms did not provide stock options. We have only analysed IPO firms that had already issued employee stock options upon listing. Due to incomplete or missing data we have omitted six firms. As a result, our study includes 54 IPOs. Firms that were delisted because of mergers and bankruptcies during the 2 years after IPO remained in the sample until the time of delisting to avoid survivorship bias. Therefore, our final sample consists of slightly less than 162 firm-year observations.

There are 20 IPO firms that report they have provided stock options exclusively to their managers. The remaining firms provided stock options to their managers as well as to other key employees. Due to limited disclosure it was not possible to assess the number of options granted to each of the two categories of employees. However, Duffhues, Kabir, Mertens, and Roosenboom (2002) report that more than 70% of all outstanding options in 1997 are held by managers.

Option grants are measured as the value of the option grants as percentage of the sum of the employees' fixed compensation and the value of the option grants. The latter is the Black and Scholes (1973) value of the stock options that are granted in that year. Figure 10.1 shows that the value of option grants as percentage of the sum of fixed compensation and the value of the outstanding options is increasing from 3% to more than 5%.

We use the market-to-book ratio as our proxy for a firm's growth opportunities. This variable is the market value of the IPO firm's equity plus the book value of its short- and long-term debt divided by the book value of its assets. As can be seen in Table 10.2, the average (median) value of the market-to-book ratio is 5.2 (2.8). The average (median) number of employees is 7403 (521). The average (median) market value of the IPO firms equals €1090 (€ 98.8) million. The volatility of the stock returns is calculated as the average standard deviation of the daily stock returns from 30 days after the IPO until the end of fiscal year 0, 1, or 2, respectively. The average volatility equals 43.2%. The average of the firm's cumulated stock returns, measured from the date of its listing including the IPO firm's first-day return to the end of the fiscal year 0, 1, 2, respectively, is 38.7%.

As can be seen in Table 10.2, the average number of options granted (exercised) is 263,581 (152,427). Due to the exercise of the options the percentage of outstanding shares

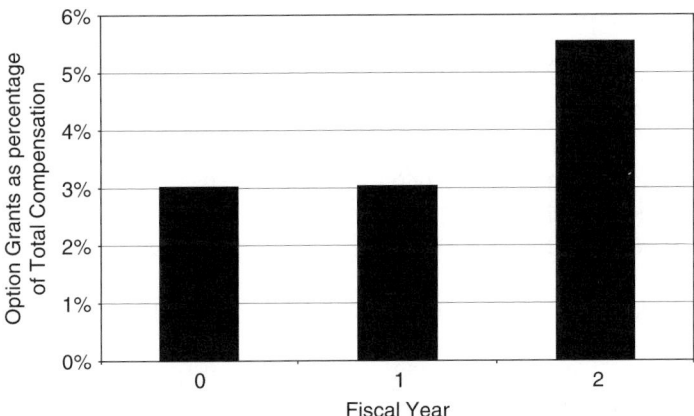

Figure 10.1: Average value of option grants as percentage of the amount of total compensation during the year of IPO and two fiscal years following the IPO.

increases by 0.6 (0.1), on average (median). Figure 10.2(a) and (b) shows that the number and the percentage of option grants and exercises increase during the years. During fiscal years 0–2 the cumulative number of stock options exercised is 461,000 or 86% of the 536,000 options outstanding when the company went public. This shows that any incentives from the stock options at the IPO are short lived and less than the maturity of 5 years suggests.[3] Due to limited disclosure in annual reports, it is not possible to compute the value of the option exercises.

The managers of the IPO firm retain a substantial fraction of the shares outstanding after the IPO. On average, they own 33% of the shares in the years after the IPO. However, before the IPO their stock ownership was much larger. At the time of the IPO management stock ownership goes from an average of 52.1% to 34.7% immediately after the IPO. This underlines the dilution effect that the IPO has on management stock ownership. On average, venture capitalists occupy 8.2% of the supervisory board seats. The number of IPOs with venture capitalists in the supervisory board is 20. Stock turnover is the number of stocks traded per year scaled by the number of stocks outstanding during that year. On average, stock turnover is 6.8%. As reported in Table 10.2, the average (median) dividend payout ratio, defined as dividend paid scaled by a firm's net profit, is 4.4 (13.5) per cent.

10.4. Empirical Results

In the analysis we pool cross-sectional data and estimate the models for options grants and exercises with the help of the Tobit regression method with fixed effects. This method adjusts the regression estimates for observations where the dependent variable has a value of zero, and where the firms of the sample are not homogeneous (fixed effects). There are 58 (63) cases where the number of options granted (exercised) is zero. Our analysis contains three different model specifications: one regression including all explanatory variables, one

Table 10.2: Descriptive statistics.

	Mean	Median	Maximum	Minimum	Standard deviation	Obser-vations
Option grants	0.039	0.009	0.500	0	0.077	159
Option exercises	0.175	0.060	1.379	0	0.251	159
Market-to-book ratio	5.196	2.771	68.639	0.743	7.397	159
Growth rate of net income	0.195	0.238	8.038	−8.199	1.439	159
Cumulative stock returns	0.387	0.243	2.416	−1.210	0.667	162
Volatility	0.432	0.438	0.690	0.150	0.129	162
Retained ownership after IPO	0.330	0.333	0.850	0	0.280	161
VC monitoring	0.082	0.000	0.750	0.000	0.168	162
Stock turnover	0.068	0.050	0.447	0.0005	0.072	160
Dividend payout ratio	0.044	0.135	10.142	−34.268	2.862	159
Number of employees (units)	7403.453	521	139,969	14	23,742.630	159
Sales	815.270	77.128	11,056.100	0.057	2064.873	159
Book value of total assets	576.211	47.746	18,592.190	4.030	2246.792	160
Market value	1090.018	98.807	16,388.490	8.970	3012.791	159
Net income	51.279	5.407	1,276.143	−78.765	175.101	159
Number of exercised options (units)	152,427	5445	4,193,000	0	488,661.800	159
Number of options granted (units)	263,581	19,766	7,712,000	0	819,409.100	159

Notes: Table shows descriptive statistics of firms that went public on Euronext Amsterdam during 1985–1998 and that have stock options outstanding. We follow these firms up to 2 fiscal years after the IPO yielding at least 159 firm-year observations. All money amounts in millions of euros and constant prices of 2001, unless indicated otherwise. *Option grants*: Value of all stock option granted per fiscal year divided by the sum of the value of the option grants and the fixed compensation during the same fiscal year. *Option exercises*: Number of options exercised as percentage of the number of options outstanding at the beginning of the fiscal year examined. *Market-to-book ratio*: The market value of equity plus the long- and short-term debt divided by the book value of a firm's assets of fiscal year t. *Growth rate of net income*: Percentage growth of a firm's net income after tax and interest payments in year t. *Cumulative stock returns*: Stock returns from fiscal year 0 until 1 and 2, respectively. *Volatility*: 3-year average volatility of the daily stock returns in year t. *Retained ownership*: Percentage of retained management ownership after IPO. *VC monitoring*: Percentage of venture capitalists in the board of non-executive directors. *Stock turnover*: Number of annually traded stocks divided by the number of shares outstanding and paid for adjusted for changes in a share's par value in year t. *Dividend payout ratio*: Dividend paid scaled by a firm's net profit (loss) in year t. *Number of employees*: Number of total employees in fiscal year t. *Sales*: Net sales in year t. *Book value of total assets*: Book value of total assets in year t. *Market value*: Number of stocks outstanding and paid for times the stock price at the end of year t. *Net income*: Net income after tax and interest payments in year t. *Number of exercised options*: Number of options exercised during fiscal year t. *Number of options granted*: Number of options granted during fiscal year t.

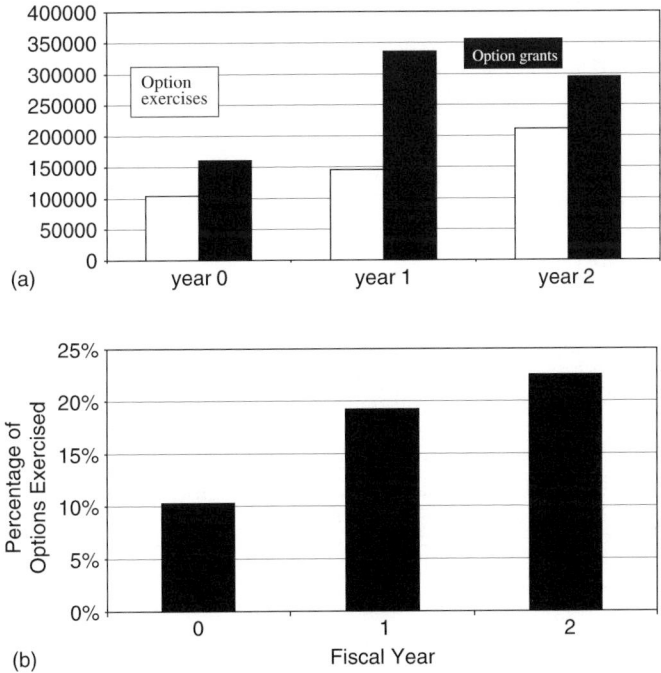

Figure 10.2: (a) Number of stock options granted and exercised during the year of IPO and 2 fiscal years following the IPO. (b) Number of stock options exercised as percentage of the number of employee stock options outstanding at the beginning of the fiscal year.

excluding both corporate governance variables (retained ownership and VC monitoring), and one excluding market and accounting variables (market-to-book ratio, growth of net income and cumulative stock returns). We report heteroskedasticity-consistent *t*-statistics based on White (1980). Variable definitions can be found in the note of Table 10.2.

10.4.1. Option Grants

Table 10.3 shows the empirical results for the option grants model. We find that firms with a higher market-to-book ratio grant more stock options. This is consistent with our first hypothesis. Board members and other key employees are more willing to accept stock option compensation in firms with higher growth opportunities. In addition, we find that option grants are a positive function of the growth rate of a firm's net income and cumulative stock returns. These findings support our second hypothesis. Option grants are used more if the company experiences favourable accounting and stock market performance.

Assuming that stock options are primarily used to address the agency problem we expect fewer option grants when managers own more stock in the company and/or venture capitalists engage in monitoring activities. Management ownership and VC monitoring would already mitigate agency costs reducing the need for costly option grants. We find an

Table 10.3: Tobit fixed effects regression estimates with option grants as dependent variable.

Option grants	Hypotheses	Tobit fixed effects (n = 156)					
		Coefficient	z-statistic	Coefficient	z-statistic	Coefficient	z-statistic
Constant[1]							
Market-to-book ratio	+	0.002	2.265**			0.002	2.472**
Growth rate of net income	+	0.011	2.519**			0.010	2.199***
Cumulative stock returns	+	0.024	2.166**			0.026	2.316**
Retained ownership after IPO	−	−0.056	−1.441	−0.071	−1.611		
VC monitoring	−	−0.072	−1.559	−0.056	−1.060		
Volatility		0.253	2.616***	0.281	3.089***	0.264	2.688****
High-tech dummy		−0.005	−0.280	−0.001	−0.040	−0.002	−0.146
log (number of employees)		−0.011	−0.884	−0.019	−1.560	−0.009	−0.787
log Sales		0.013	1.257	0.019	1.686*	0.014	1.379
Adjusted R-Squared		0.654		0.593		0.630	
Log likelihood		125.331		114.301		123.126	
Average log likelihood		0.793		0.723		0.779	
Left censored observations		58		58		58	

Notes: z-statistics are adjusted for heteroskedasticity (White, 1980).
Statistical significant levels at: *10% level, **5% level and ***1% level, respectively.
[1]The constants of the individual firms of the sample are omitted.

inverse, but statistically insignificant, relation between retained ownership and option grants. Further, we find that monitoring by venture capitalists in the board of non-executive directors is not significantly associated with stock option grants. These findings are directionally consistent with hypotheses 3 and 4. We interpret this as weak evidence that stock options are used to mitigate the agency problem.

Next, we look at our control variables. There is a significantly positive relation between option grants and the volatility of the underlying stock. This is consistent with options having more value when volatility increases, and not with option holders being risk averse. The high-tech dummy is insignificant in all the three regression models. Option grants are a decreasing, though not significant, function of the number of a firm's employees. Option grants are an increasing, but not significant, function of sales.

10.4.2. Option Exercises

We estimate regression model (10.2) using the number of options exercised as percentage of the number of options outstanding at the beginning of the fiscal year as the dependent variable. Table 10.4 shows the regression results. We find that the coefficient of the market-to-book is insignificantly negative. We, therefore, do not find support for hypothesis 5.

The regression results show an inverse but insignificant relation between option exercises and growth of net income. This is inconsistent with hypothesis 6(a), which predicts that option exercises are a decreasing function of a firm's past accounting performance.

In addition we find that cumulative stock returns are positively related to option exercises. This is inconsistent with hypothesis 6(b) that predicted an inverse relationship. The explanation may be that there are two opposing forces. On the one hand, key employees may not want to forfeit the time value of their options by exercising options early when stock price performance has been strong. On the other hand, they may want to cash their gains on the options of which the underlying stock price has increased. In the Netherlands, early exercise may be related to taxes. The Dutch tax authority considers employee stock options as personal income that have to be paid at the moment the options are granted (Veld, 2003). Anecdotal evidence suggests that a majority of the firms provides a loan to the employee who acquires the stock options equal to the taxes due at the time of the option grant. Holders of the options may, therefore, decide to exercise (part of) their options early in order to amortize their debt when the stock price has increased. As reported in Table 10.4, there is an insignificant, inverse relationship between option exercises and VC monitoring.

As predicted by Holmström and Tirole (1993), the empirical results provide strong support for hypothesis 8 that employees exercise more options when trading volume of the underlying shares on the stock market is higher. A higher level of stock turnover makes it easier for employees to disguise private information when they exercise their options and sell the shares on the stock market. Consistent with hypothesis 9 the relation between option exercises and the dividend payout ratio is positive. If the firm has a high dividend payout, option holders exercise early to obtain the dividend.

In all regressions the coefficient of the firm's volatility is significantly negative. A higher volatility implies a higher Black and Scholes option value, which prevents option holders from exercising early because the time value of the options would be forfeited.[4] As

Table 10.4: Tobit fixed effects regression estimates with option exercises as dependent variable.

Option Exercise	Hypotheses	Tobit fixed effects ($n = 156$)					
		Coefficient	z-statistic	Coefficient	z-statistic	Coefficient	z-statistic
Constant[1]							
Market-to-book ratio	−	−0.002	−0.439			−0.003	−0.560
Growth rate of net income	−	−0.039	−1.404			−0.038	−1.411
Cumulative stock returns	−	0.090	1.802*			0.088	1.750*
VC monitoring	−	−0.262	−1.388	−0.267	−1.340		
Stock turnover	+	1.217	3.321***	1.287	3.468***	1.202	3.191***
Payout ratio	+	0.029	3.328***	0.028	3.117***	0.028	3.486***
Volatility		−0.735	−2.415**	−0.758	−2.495**	−0.719	−2.351**
IT-dummy		0.050	0.660	0.064	0.818	0.078	1.059
log (number of employees)		0.066	1.592	0.052	1.319	0.076	1.831*
log sales		−0.061	−1.552	−0.045	−1.221	−0.069	−1.738*
Adjusted R-squared		0.100		0.066		0.099	
Log likelihood		−52.914		−55.950		−53.693	
Average log likelihood		−0.339		−0.344		−0.344	
Left censored observations		63		63		63	

Notes: z-statistics are adjusted for heteroskedasticity (White, 1980).
Statistical significance level at: *10%, **5% and ***1%, respectively.
[1]The constants of the individual firms of the sample are omitted.

can be seen in Table 10.4, the number of employees and the log of sales are significant in one of three regression specifications. The results provide some evidence that option exercises are a decreasing function of a firm's sales and an increasing function of the firm's employees. The coefficient of the IT-dummy is insignificant in all regressions.

As a final point, we check the robustness of our results. After omitting outliers the results for both the option grants and option exercises models are qualitatively similar. Furthermore, regression estimates using the ordinary least squares method for both the option grants and exercises models provide qualitatively similar results.

10.5. Conclusions

This study examines which factors influence the grant and exercise of stock options in the post-IPO period. The IPO is often the first event in a firm's history when agency conflicts arise between management and outside shareholders. Stock options may offer a possible solution to this agency problem. However, the results of our empirical analysis document, among other things, that the incentives of stock option grants at the IPO are short lived. The cumulative number of stock options exercised during the 3 years following the IPO is 86% of the options outstanding when the company went public.

Also, we find that key employees are more willing to be compensated by options when the company shows strong growth opportunities and past accounting and stock price performance. The results of this study also document that option grants are inversely related to retained management ownership and VC monitoring. However, these relations are statistically insignificant. This shows that that management ownership and board monitoring by venture capitalists cannot be viewed as substitutes for stock options. Based on these findings we doubt whether employee stock options are an effective mechanism to mitigate agency problems.

For the same sample of IPO firms we investigate option exercises. We find no support for the hypothesis that option exercises and the firm's growth opportunities and/or net income growth are inversely related. Opposite to our hypothesis, we report that option exercises are an increasing function of cumulative stock returns. One explanation could be that option holders have to pay tax at the moment the options are granted. By exercising the stock options cash is raised to pay the tax due.

Our results indicate a strong positive relation between stock turnover and option exercises, which is consistent with Holmström and Tirole (1993). When stock turnover is high, key employees can sell the shares they receive when exercising their options without it negatively affecting the stock price. Finally, option exercises appear an increasing function of dividend payout. If the firm pays out substantial dividends, key employees have an incentive to exercise their options early so as to receive these dividends.

Acknowledgements

We gratefully acknowledge the helpful comments of Lieke Adema, Piet Duffhues, Noud van Giersbergen, Martin Hoogendoorn, Hans Meijer, Hans van Ophem, participants of the

Financial Accounting Research Seminar of the Amsterdam Graduate Business School, the 2003 Southern Finance Conference at Charleston, the 2004 Eastern Finance Conference at Mystic (CT), and, in particular, Bill Rees on an earlier draft of this chapter. We are much indebted to Pieter Knauff and Fabian Valkenburg for research assistance. All remaining errors are the responsibility of the authors.

Endnotes

1. As of 2002 Dutch companies listed on Euronext Amsterdam are required by law (Title 9, Book 2 of the *Civil code*) to publish information regarding remuneration (including stock options grants and exercises) on an individual basis for board members.
2. Dutch companies have a two-tier board structure. The management board consists of executive directors and is entrusted with the day-to-day management of the company. A Dutch company's supervisory board consists of non-executive directors and is responsible for supervising the policy pursued by the management board.
3. In order to qualify for favourable tax treatment option grants should have a maturity of 5 years or less at the time of the grant. Furthermore, during the years 1987 until 1998 the tax regime required that the stock options were granted unconditionally and had an exercise price equal to the price of the underlying stock. In addition, the owner of the stock options should have the right to exercise the options at any point in time after the grant. Van Sonderen (1996) documents that a majority of listed firms grant employee stock options unconditionally. The taxes due have to be paid when the employees receive their options. Often, firms offer their employees a loan to pay the taxes due.
4. The adjusted R-squared of the option grants regressions are larger than those of the option exercises regressions. An explanation could be that option grants are dependent on firm-specific variables, which are captured by the option grants model. Besides the explanatory variables included in the option exercises model the variance of the option exercises could also be affected by characteristics of the option holders (for instance, their need for liquidity, termination of their job due to resignation or retirement), which are not included in the model.

References

ABN-AMRO Bank (1987–2001). Kengetallen Nederlandse Beursfondsen.

Baker, M., & Gompers, P.A. (1999). *An analysis of executive compensation, ownership and control in closely held firms.* Working paper, Harvard Business School.

Baker, M., & Gompers, P.A. (2003). The determinants of board structure at the Initial Public Offering. *Journal of Law and Economics, 46,* 569–598.

Beatty, R.P., & Zajac, E.J. (1994). Managerial incentives, monitoring, and risk bearing, a study of executive compensation, ownership and board structure in Initial Public Offerings. *Administrative Science Quarterly, 39,* 313–335.

Bebchuk, L.A., & Fried, J.M. (2003). Executive compensation as an agency problem. *Journal of Economic Perspectives, 17,* 71–92.

Bebchuk, L.A., & Fried, J.M. (2004). *Pay without performance: The unfulfilled promise of executive compensation.* Cambridge: Harvard University Press.

Bebchuk, L.A., Fried, J.M., & Walker, D.I. (2002). *Managerial power and rent extraction in the design of executive compensation.* NBER Working paper no. 9068.

Black, F., & Scholes, M. (1973). The pricing of options and corporate liabilities. *Journal of Political Economy, 81,* 637–654.

Bryan, S., Hwang, L., & Lilien, S. (2000). CEO stock-based compensation, an empirical analysis of incentive-intensity, relative mix, and economic determinants. *Journal of Business, 73*, 661–694.

Duffhues, P., Kabir, R., Mertens, G., & Roosenboom, P. (2002). Employee stock option grants and firm performance in the Netherlands. In: J. McCahery et al. (Eds), *Convergence and diversity in corporate governance regimes and capital markets* (pp. 668–678). Oxford: Oxford University Press.

Engel, E., Gordon, E.A., & Hayes, R.M. (2002). The role of performance measures and monitoring in annual governance decisions in entrepreneurial firms. *Journal of Accounting Research, 40*, 485–518.

Ferrarini, G., Moloney, N., & Vespro, C. (2003). *Executive remuneration in the EU, comparative law and practice.* Working paper, European Corporate Governance Institute.

Hall, B.J., & Murphy, K.J. (2002). Stock options for undiversified executives. *Journal of Accounting and Economics, 33*, 3–42.

Heath, C., Huddart, S., & Lang, M. (1999). Psychological factors and stock option exercise. *Quarterly Journal of Economics, 114*, 601–628.

Holmström, B., & Tirole, J. (1993). Market liquidity and performance monitoring. *Journal of Political Economy, 101*, 678–709.

Huddart, S. (1994). Employee stock options. *Journal of Accounting and Economics, 18*, 207–231.

Huddart, S., & Lang, M. (1996). Employee stock option exercises, an empirical analysis. *Journal of Accounting and Economics, 21*, 5–43.

Liang, N., & Weisbenner, S.J. (2001). *Who benefits from a bull market? An analysis of employee stock option grants and stock prices.* Working paper, University of Illinois at Urbana-Champaign.

Maris, B.A., Maris, J.M., & Yang, T.T. (2003). The effects of exercise date uncertainty on employee stock option value. *Journal of Business Finance and Accounting, 5–6*, 669–698.

Mehran, H. (1995). Executive compensation, ownership and firm performance. *Journal of Financial Economics, 38*, 163–184.

Merton, R. (1973). Theory of rational option pricing. *Bell Journal of Economics and Management Science, 4*, 141–183.

Ryan, H.E., & Wiggins, R.A. (2001). The influence of firm- and manager-specific characteristics on the structure of executive compensation. *Journal of Corporate Finance, 7*, 101–123.

Smith, C., & Watts, R. (1992). The investment opportunity set and corporate financing, dividends, and compensation policies. *Journal of Financial Economics, 32*, 263–292.

Van Sonderen, J.C.M. (1996). Werknemersopties. In: C.W.M. van Ballegooijen, C. van Alphen, & H.J.M. Regtering (Eds), *Handboek financiële participatie door werknemers* (pp. 71–88). Deventer: Kluwer Publishers.

Toyne, M.F., Millar, J.A., & Dixon, B.L. (2000). The relation between CEO control and the risk of CEO compensation. *Journal of Corporate Finance, 6*, 291–306.

Veld, C.H. (2003). Analysis of a practical formula for the valuation of employee stock options. *Applied Economics Letters, 10*, 205–208.

Welbourne, T.M., & Andrews, A.O. (1996). Predicting the performance of Initial Public Offerings, should human resource management be in the equation? *Academy of Management Journal, 39*, 891–919.

White, H. (1980). A heteroskedasticity-consistent covariance matrix estimator and a direct test for heteroskedasticity. *Econometrica, 48*, 817–838.

Chapter 11

Institutions, Corporate Governance and Firm Performance

Jos Grazell

11.1. Introduction

In this chapter, the relation between institutions, corporate governance and firm performance is investigated. The emergence of corporate governance questions in the past decade results from accounting scandals in firms, unexpected value redistributions between investors, mismanagement, worker dismissals, excessive remuneration policies and unfair income distribution in general, etc. Hence, it can be expected that several stakeholders try to change the institutions and more specifically the polity. Corporate governance is defined as "a system of procedures and structures that is used to govern and control the firm, within a field of forces of involved stakeholders, with the goal to contribute to the utility of these stakeholders". Evidently, corporate governance regulations, practices and codes are examples of institutions, as institutions are defined as: "A way of thought or action of some prevalence and permanence, which is embedded in the habits of a group or the customs of a people. Institutions fix the confines of and impose upon the activities of human beings (Hamilton, 1932: 84)."

Before we can investigate the relation between institutions, corporate governance and firm performance in more detail, several modes of thinking about institutions will be discussed in the next section. Sections 11.3 and 11.4 deal with the phenomena of corporate governance in general and the corporate governance code in the Netherlands, respectively. In Section 11.5, the relation between institutions, corporate governance and firm performance is discussed and Section 11.6 concludes this chapter.

11.2. Institutions

11.2.1. Institutional Economics

Institutional economics specializes on the examination of institutions and institutional change. It is a complementary field to neoclassical economics that traditionally specializes

Advances in Corporate Finance and Asset Pricing
Edited by L. Renneboog
© 2006 Elsevier B.V. All rights reserved.
ISBN: 0-444-52723-0

in the marginal analyses of choices of economic subjects and that has always ignored the role of institutions. Rutherford (1994) explains that there are two important strands in institutional economics, namely old or original institutionalism (OI) and new institutionalism (NI). Both strands can be subdivided in two sub-streams. The OI has a Veblen-Ayres and a Commons wing, while the NI shows a neoclassical and an Austrian branch (from the Austrian school). The Veblen-Ayres variant of institutionalism concentrates on the distinction between technology and institutions while the Commons branch concentrates around the notion of institutions evolving out of the resolution of conflicting interests. The neoclassical branch of NI explains institutions in terms of the maximizing behaviour of individual economic agents. Maximizing behaviour here means the conscious design of institutions. The Austrian variant focuses more narrowly on the spontaneous, invisible hand development of institutions out of individual action. Insights of the Commons variant of OI, and the neoclassical and Austrian variant of NI will be used here to explain the institutional development around corporate governance practices in the sector of the publicly traded firms. In approach of the Commons, the central idea is that out of scarcity conflicts of interest emerge and that the development of an institutionalized system of rules delivers a degree of order and certainty that is needed for productive efficiency (Rutherford, 1994: 101). The Commons approach does not provide any detailed analysis on how institutions evolve out of individual actions. To find an answer to this question, one could look at prominent modes of thinking in the strand of NI. One of these approaches in new institutional economics (the Austrian approach) explains the emergence of conventions and rules out of the interaction between economic agents. Spontaneously, invisible hand processes produce certain behavioural rules and with game theoretical analysis, it is possible to demonstrate that these rules generated by interaction and adaptation form a Nash equilibrium or even an evolutionary stable strategy (Rutherford, 1994: 110). The other, neoclassical approach consists of a government that rationally designs a system of property rights, and a judicial system that sets and enforces fundamental rules that govern exchange. The state maximizes wealth by assigning property rights to individuals or by redefining the structure of these rights (Rutherford, 1994: 118). With regard to the role of the government in this political process, two opinions are distinguished: namely, the naïve theory and the interest group or rent-seeking theory. This interest group or rent-seeking theory focuses on the redistributive effects of changes in property rights (Rutherford, 1994: 119). A group may invest resources in lobbying and in making political contributions in an attempt to gain a particular change in property rights in its members' favour. Changes in company law and the introduction of or changes in corporate governance codes are examples of these changes in property rights.

11.2.2. Economic and Non-economic Institutions

According to Williamson (1998; 2000: 597), there are four levels of social analysis (see Table 11.1). The first level is the level of embeddedness. Here, one finds informal institutions, customs, traditions, norms, culture and religion. The second level is the institutional environment. The formal rules of the game, for instance property rights, are determined there in the judiciary world of a polity or government bureaucracy. The third level is the sphere of governance. There the play of the game takes place by contracting parties that

Table 11.1: Embedding corporate governance in the economic theories.

	Level (L)	Frequency of change: (in years)	Purpose
L1: Social theory	Embeddedness: informal institutions, customs, traditions, norms, culture and religion	100–1000	Often non-calculative, spontaneous
L2: Economics of property rights/positive political theory	Institutional environment: formal rules of the game, especially property rights (polity, judiciary, government bureaucracy)	10–100	Get the institutional environment right (first order economizing)
L3: Transaction cost economics	Governance: play of the game, especially contract (aligning governance structures with transactions)	1–10	Get the governance structures right (second order economizing)
L4: Neoclassical economics/agency theory	Resource allocation, asset deployment and utility maximization: (prices and quantities, incentive alignment)	Continuous	Get the marginal conditions right (third order economizing)

align governance structures with transactions. Finally, the fourth level of analysis looks at resource allocation, asset deployment and utility maximization. Marginal analysis of costs and benefits determines prices and quantities such that they align the incentives of the economic agents.

Another distinction Williamson (2002: 171) makes is the possibility to look to economic science from two different viewpoints: namely, economics as a science of choice and economics as a science of contract. Neoclassical economics is the science of choice and institutional economics is the science of contract. After that the science of contract is separated in public-ordering and private-ordering. The public-ordering domain looks at the rules of the game, and these are developed by and incorporated in political, legal and thus non-economic institutions. Politics is a structure of complex exchange among individuals, a structure within which persons seek to secure collectively their own privately defined objectives that cannot be efficiently secured through simple market exchanges (Buchanan, 1987: 296). Private-ordering mechanisms are economic institutions that can also be split into two related branches. One branch concentrates on front-end incentive alignment (security design, formal agency theory and formal property rights theory) and the other branch highlights the governance of ongoing, back-end, contractual relations (contract implementation). The private-ordering arrangements or economic institutions are all situated at the third level of social analysis, while the public-ordering mechanisms that contain the non-economic institutions are placed at level two of the social analysis framework. The investigation of these second-level institutions is concentrated in the field of constitutional economics. Traditional neoclassical economics can be characterized as a fourth-level type of analyses of economic problems.

With the help of the social analysis framework, we can explain that the neoclassical branch of NI has the opinion that levels three and two phenomena are deeply influenced by level four forces. OI also states that level one informal institutions determine the resource allocation and need satisfaction process of level four via economic and non-economic institutions. So the difference of opinion between the adherents of OI and NI is about the direction of causality between the distinguished levels in the social analysis framework.

The contractual relation between the firm and its stakeholders can be interpreted as a variation on a theme. In this theme one of the important concepts, namely general- or special-purpose technology, plays an important role via a measure of asset specificity. Also the safeguarding of specific investments measured by the magnitude of safeguards is incorporated as an important concept to develop a simple contracting schema of governance mechanisms.

Williamson (2002: 182) suggests that in a situation where transactions make use of a general-purpose technology, the suitable solution is the unassisted market transaction. If a special purpose technology is the required technology for the parties who transact then without safeguarding the specific investment exists in a situation of unrelieved hazard. In this case, contractual supports take the form of inter-firm contractual safeguards. Credible contracting is then the topical governance mechanism. However, if the contractual supports break down, then it is more efficient to take the transaction out of the market and organize it internally. The general message of the transaction cost theory is: try markets, try hybrids and have recourse to the firm and its hierarchy, and internal organization only when all else fails. This insight can be applied to the relationship of the firm with its sources of finance.

In the situation of general-purpose technology, the capital suppliers and the firm can opt for debt contracts because the bankruptcy procedure gives the bondholders the possibility in the case of default to exercise their pre-emptive claims against the assets in question. Additional safeguards are not necessary here. If special-purpose technology is traded in the transaction then the capital suppliers and the firm should choose equity contracts. Still, if they do not want to be in a situation of unrelieved hazard then contractual support to the equity contracts is required. A safeguarding feature that arises in support of the contract for equity finance is the board of directors. This private-ordering institution can contribute to credible contracting between firm and shareholders.

Suppose that contractual support is given to the equity contract by the introduction of a board of directors which:

- is elected by the pro-rata votes of those who hold tradable shares,
- has the power to replace the management team,
- decides on management compensation,
- has access to internal performance measures on a timely basis,
- can authorize audits in depth for special follow-up purposes,
- is apprised of important investment and operating proposals before they are implemented,
- bears a decision review and monitoring relation to the firm's management.

Consequently, the residual claimant status of the shareholders in both earnings and asset liquidation is brought into line with their residual and ultimate control rights. Hence, this construction reduces the cost of capital given the safeguards for the equity holders. If this board of directors is not strong enough to operate as a safeguard for the equity investors (as the required penalties, information disclosure and verification procedures) are not instituted or enforceable, then this theory suggests integration of the capital suppliers with the firm under one hierarchy. If this solution is not applicable, the firm and its capital suppliers remain in a situation of unrelieved hazard. It is to be expected that the parties concerned, attempt to change the formal institutional rules (like property rights) such that they are able to protect their position and the unrelieved hazardous situation is cancelled. This situation will especially arise for specific-purpose transactions where credible contracting is not possible because of the uncooperative behaviour of one or more involved stakeholders. Examples of changes in formal institutions are changes in company law and the introduction of corporate governance codes. The emergence of these institutional changes via a spontaneous process of stakeholders or via the conscious design of the government under political pressure are captured by the theories of the new institutional economists of the Austrian and the neoclassical wing, respectively.

11.3. Corporate Governance

11.3.1. Introduction

In the previous section, we have defined corporate governance as "a system of procedures and structures that is used to govern and control the firm, within a field of forces of involved stakeholders with the goal to contribute to the utility of these stakeholders". This field of forces contains the mutual monitoring and disciplining of stakeholders to look after the fulfilment of the agreements that were made about achievements and remuneration of each party. Characteristic for these agreements (are shaped in a nexus of contracts) is that employees and bondholders generally have fixed compensation, managers have fixed and variable components in their remuneration, and shareholders are entitled to the residual cash flow rights. Rent-seeking behaviour is the behaviour of economic agents who try to appropriate a larger compensation in comparison to their achievements than is agreed on when the contract was negotiated with the firm. The stakeholder that is best positioned to expropriate the wealth of the firm is the management team, because of its informational advantage. The employees and their unions try to protect themselves by asking for job and income security, bondholders want capital protection and little bankruptcy risk, and share-holders require a rate of return that compensates their exposure to fluctuating cash flows. All these monitoring and disciplining activities ask for institutions that enable these activities and contribute to the utility of the stakeholders. The institutions that facilitate employee and investor protection can emerge either from spontaneous, invisible hand processes via markets and contracts, or they can be designed by a government that changes the property rights under the influence of lobbying activities of interest groups in political processes.

Rent appropriation and rent expropriation are a demonstration of principal-agent problems that can exist between managers and shareholders, between majority, controlling shareholders and minority shareholders, between shareholders and bondholders, and between the employing firm and its employees. If the residual cash flow rights and the residual control rights are not distributed symmetrically between shareholders and management, then there is an important source for an agency problem between these two stakeholders. This rent extraction problem is the basis for the definition of corporate governance by Shleifer and Vishny (1997: 737): "Corporate governance deals with the ways in which suppliers of finance to corporations assure themselves of getting a return on their investment." And they add several questions to this definition like: "How do the suppliers of finance get managers to return some of the profits to them? How do they make sure that managers do not steal the capital they supply or invest it in bad projects? How do suppliers of finance control managers?" Also Shleifer and Vishny state that corporate governance mechanisms are economic and legal institutions that can be altered through the political process. Through private- or public-ordering arrangements, stakeholders intend to get a fair return on invested capital.

11.3.2. The Structure and Evolution of Corporate Governance

Corporate governance is an institutional arrangement that organizes the disciplining and monitoring mechanism within the firm (Table 11.2). This mechanism can be separated in an internal and an external disciplining mechanism and you can divide the system of procedures and structures in three aspects: namely, in a legal, an economic and a social angle.

The corporate governance mechanism is a safeguard mechanism in addition to the equity contract, which makes it for equity holders better possible to earn a return on their investment. We can conclude that the managerial power position has increased substantially during the last decade because this group was able to increase its remuneration level

Table 11.2: Corporate governance disciplining mechanisms.

System of procedures and structures:(→) Disciplining mechanisms:(↓)	Legal	Economic	Social
Internal	Board of directors General meeting of shareholders Work council	Remuneration structure Composition board of directors: Executives and non-executives Internal labour market Ownership structure Control structure	Internal behaviour codes Board of directors: • Remuneration committee • Nomination committee • Audit committee • Strategy committee Corporate culture
External	Structure regime Listing requirements stock exchanges Corporate law Disclosure act financial stakes Corporate governance code	Capital market Take over market Purchasing market Sales market External labour market	Corporate governance committee Associations of investors, firms Monitoring authorities Political process Culture society

substantially in a lot of countries with very different characteristics. Due to the increased power position in management teams, one can expect a counter reaction by equity investors, creditors, employees and other stakeholders by putting more efforts in disciplining and monitoring activities, by renegotiating contracts and by bringing this topic in the political process. This conflict of interest around the remuneration of managers directed us to a situation where the control rights shifted more in the direction of the shareholders. Another development is the increase in the concentration degree of the ownership structure of firms. Large shareholders are better equipped to monitor firms than a large group of small shareholders. The disadvantage of the emergence of large shareholders is that this type of shareholder can expropriate minority shareholders. So, one agency problem is solved by the introduction of another one. That is a frequently returning dilemma in the world of corporate governance. Also, more and more objections against the use of dual-class shares, pyramid/cascade structures in ownership structures and crossholdings which take away the control rights from the shareholder and put it in the hands of management teams which are more entrenched in this way.

Due to this conflict around executive remuneration we register a shift from management-controlled firms to more owner-controlled firms (Grazell, 1992; 1997). The contractual safeguards that support the equity contracts are not sufficient to redress the increased rent extraction effort by the management teams. In many countries, political means are used to try to change the public-ordering mechanism that organizes the relation between the firm and its stakeholders. Proposals from interest groups have arisen to create corporate governance committees, which consist of representatives of the most important stakeholders. In these corporate governance committees negotiations take place between the several stakeholders of the firms and the compromises are moulded in codes of best practice. Even the status of these corporate governance codes is a topic of discussion. Sometimes these corporate governance codes are incorporated in company law, sometimes these codes get a semi-public status and are not enforceable because firms only had to follow the "comply or explain principle". This depended for instance on the legal tradition in these countries. So during a decade of increasing conflict around management remuneration, we witness the development of and the dynamic interaction between private-ordering mechanisms and public-ordering mechanisms to solve the various agency problems.

11.3.3. The Scandals

The increasing conflict around executive compensation was not the only problem that drew the attention of the public. There were also a number of striking scandals in the business world: Maxwell Corporation (1991), Enron (2001), Parmalat (2003) and Ahold (2003). All these scandals were characterized by fraudulent activities of executives who cumulated too many functions within one person. Especially the combination of executive tasks and supervision tasks or even the combination of executive and financial management tasks were unacceptable practices which brought managers at the top into temptation to act without honesty and integrity. Managers who noticed that they could not meet their too ambitious targets searched for escape routes and found these routes in fraudulent activities in their financial reporting systems. All these scandals were similar in this sense that auditors failed to pick up the fraud. Auditing functions and executive tasks were not separated from each other. These scandals were triggers to start an intensive societal debate in a lot of countries on corporate governance practices. This gave an impulse to the design of additional public-ordering devices.

11.3.4. The Development of Codes Around the World

The corporate scandals and fraudulent accounting practices combined with the debates about managerial remuneration led governments and regulators to introduce stronger regulation to reinforce investor confidence in the financial markets. In some countries, legislation and codes addressing corporate governance problems have been in existence for decades, in others governments are just embarking on the development of these codes. In the Anglo-Saxon world the Cadbury report (1992) was one of the first codes of best practice with recommendations on a range of governance practices like the structure and composition of the board of directors and the board committees, and highlighted the importance of non-executive directors (Maier, 2005: 3). Reason for the development of this code was the collapse of the Maxwell Publishing Group. The "comply or explain principle" was established in this code. Other codes were added which resulted in the Combined Code (1998; 2003).

Due to the Enron and WorldCom scandals in the USA, reforms were agreed by the US Congress and the New York Stock Exchange (NYSE). The result was the introduction of the Accounting Industry Reform Act 2002, widely known as the Sarbanes-Oxley Act, and the insertion of corporate governance rules in the listing requirements of the NYSE (Maier, 2005: 4).

Major corporate scandals, and regulatory and legislative responses from governments and regulators are felt worldwide. The principles of good governance that all countries try to develop for their situation converge after a certain time to a kind of standard corporate governance code, which starts to function as a benchmark. The Organization of Economic Cooperation and Development (OECD) took the initiative to summarize all these principles in an OECD Code of Principles of Corporate Governance (1999, 2004). Corporate governance codes address a wide range of structural and behavioural elements, including board accountability, shareholder rights, financial disclosure and internal controls, executive remuneration, and board structure and functioning. The principles of the OECD incorporate all these elements, are non-binding but represent common corporate governance standards of good practice, intended to reflect and inform the corporate governance debate internationally. The principles cover the following issues:

- the basis for an effective corporate governance framework,
- the rights of shareholders and key ownership functions,
- the equitable treatment of shareholders,
- the role of the stakeholders in corporate governance,
- disclosure and transparency,
- the responsibilities of the board.

Rather than advocating particular structures or types of behaviour, the principles identify common elements that underlie good corporate governance everywhere (Maier, 2005: 5).

11.3.5. The Role of Investors

Although the development of a good corporate governance framework as a safeguard to the equity contract is of vital importance the behaviour of the actors itself and the way they fulfil their role cannot be neglected because only the combination of institutions and behaviour makes good governance practices possible. This issue is known in social theory as the agency structure problem (Hodgson, 2004; Scott, 1995). The institutions are the structure within which actors can fill in their actions. These structures constrain but also enable the actions the agent can choose. The principal-agent problem in economic theory is a problem within the agency structure firmament. A good corporate governance structure demands within the possibilities of the agency structure framework from investors as well as managers an active attitude towards their task. From investors is expected that they are active monitors of the firm and that they exhaust every possibility to monitor their company. Especially the large institutional investors have a responsible role to play, because they manage the wealth of millions of stakeholders. From managers a high ethical standard is expected. Only then the residual loss (Jensen & Meckling, 1976) will be limited to a minimum and the trust and confidence in the good working of the institutions of society, that was shaken by the scandals, can be restored.

11.4. Corporate Governance in the Netherlands

In the second half of the 1990s, the Dutch business community felt the need to institute a code of best practice in the field of corporate governance. In 1997, the Committee Corporate Governance produced a report with 40 recommendations. In 2002, a follow-up report was published that reflected the current state of affairs with respect to corporate governance reforms implemented in the Dutch business environment during the earlier 5 years.

In December 2003, a newly installed Corporate Governance Committee published the final Dutch corporate governance code containing principles of good corporate governance and best practice provisions.

11.4.1. Control Issues and Defensive Measures

Dutch listed companies are traditionally well protected against (hostile) takeovers. Since the beginning of the 1990s, however, this protection has been under attack. In 1997, a bill to restrict these measures was sent to parliament, but never became law. At present, a new bill is being prepared, with a view to implementing the 13th European Union (EU) Directive on takeovers. In addition to the pressure coming from the new legislation, Dutch employers are also calling for the dismantling of defensive measures against takeovers. The debate has focused on the extent to which defensive measures should be allowed. In the listing requirements of the Euronext Stock Exchange Amsterdam, a rule is included which limits firms to accumulate defensive measures. Since 1992, firms are not allowed to have more than two of these anti-takeover devices.

11.4.2. The Two-Tier Structure Reform Act of 2004

According to the Dutch Civil Code, a statutory two-tier regime exists in the Netherlands since 1971 that consists of a system in which the supervisory board appoints its own members. At the beginning of the 1990s, this issue was readdressed by several stakeholders such as the Dutch Investors' Association. After advice of the Social Economic Council the Dutch Government decided to change the law by introducing the Two-Tier Structure Reform Act of 2004. The main characteristics of this Act are that the powers of the works council have been altered by an increased right of recommendation and the disappearance of the right to object to certain candidates for the nomination of supervisory board members. In addition, the general meeting of shareholders has been granted the right:

- to appoint the members of the supervisory board,
- to reject any nomination for the appointment of supervisory directors,
- to dismiss the entire supervisory board.

The Two-tier Structure Reform Act came into effect on 1st September, 2004, and will have an important impact on the Dutch corporate governance culture (Groenewald, 2005: 297–300).

11.4.3. The Dutch Corporate Governance Code

The Code contains five chapters with principles and best practices on the role of the managing board, the supervisory board, the shareholders, the general meeting of shareholders, and the internal and the external auditors. One of the provisions on the managing board is that they are appointed for a maximum of 4 years and that they cannot be tenured employees. There are also restrictions on remuneration (such as the conditional grants of stock options to managing directors). The maximum severance pay in the event of dismissal of a managing director is equal to 1 year's salary. With the exception of one supervisory director, all supervisory directors have to be independent. Detailed criteria to ensure such independency are described in the code. The supervisory board will appoint an audit committee, a remuneration committee and a nomination committee. The chairman of the supervisory board will be responsible for the proper functioning of the supervisory board and its committees.

The shareholders can play a role in decisions affecting the identity of the company or concerning large acquisitions and divestments. Depository receipts for shares will no longer able to be used as anti-takeover mechanism. Proxy voting and proxy solicitation will be facilitated. Equal treatment of all shareholders will be secured in the informational contacts of firms with the financial markets. An external auditor is appointed by the general meeting of shareholders on the recommendation of the supervisory board. The audit committee assesses how the external auditor is engaged in the content and publication of financial information. Apart from the external auditor, the internal auditor will work under the responsibility of the managing board. The managing board and supervisory board are together responsible for the company's corporate governance structure and the company's compliance with the code. The annual report should explicitly state whether the company complies with the code and, if it does not, the reasons for its non-compliance (Groenewald, 2005: 301–305).

The "apply or explain" provision has been given a legal basis in the Two-Tier Structure Reform Act of 2004. The enforcement of the "apply or explain" principle will not take place exclusively in the annual report but may also be achieved by an inquiry before the Enterprise Chamber of the Supreme Court into the affairs of the company in the event of an infringement of the code's provisions. In that case, both the managing board and the supervisory board may be held liable for improper management and may be held personally responsible. Even though the code is meant to apply exclusively to listed companies the corporate governance committee has stated that the principles may also be relevant for large non-listed companies (Groenewald, 2005: 307–309).

11.5. Institutions and Corporate Governance Practices as a Determinant of Firm Performance

Firm performance can be measured in diverse ways: accounting returns or market-to-book ratios (q-ratios). We can distinguish three strands of theory by type of firm activity. Information theories state that investments in new technology benefit from the existence of securities markets while traditional investments benefit from the monitoring that banks can provide. In commitment theories, concentrated ownership is associated with activities that involve also investments by stakeholders other than the investors, and dispersed ownership is optimal in investments in new technologies. In control theories, long-term investments are more promoted in concentrated banking systems, while short-term investments are financed in systems with fragmented banking relations. High-risk R&D investments are financed by dispersed ownership systems and lower-risk, and more imitative investments with concentrated ownership systems (Mayer, 2002: 314–315).

The relation between investor protection and corporate valuation is investigated by La Porta, Lopez-de-Silanes, Shleifer, and Vishny (2002). They find that poor shareholder protection is penalized with lower valuations and that higher cash flow ownership by the controlling shareholder improves valuation especially in countries with poor investor protection. Investor protection can be regulated in a code (civil) law system and in a common law system. Code law is according to the concepts of Williamson (2002) a public-ordering device and common law, a private-ordering mechanism. La Porta, Lopez-de-Silanes, Shleifer, and Vishny (2002) find in their study that in countries with common law systems Tobin's q is significantly higher than in countries with civil law systems. Also, the anti-director rights are significantly higher in common law countries. La Porta, Lopez-de-Silanes, Shleifer, and Vishny (2000) distinguish three legal traditions, namely the French, the German and the Scandinavian. Common law countries have the strongest protection of outside investors via the enforcement of private contracts through the court system. Financial markets do not require regulation as long as the contracts are enforced. In many countries such enforcements cannot be taken for granted. In that case, other forms of protecting property rights are considered, such as judicial-enforced laws or even government-enforced regulations because they may be more efficient. At that moment, the country shifts to a code or civil law system. The French civil law countries have the weakest protection for both shareholders and creditors. German civil law and Scandinavian countries fall in between, although they have stronger protection for creditors (La Porta, Lopez-de-Silanes, Shleifer, & Vishny, 2000: 7–8). Remarkable is that the emergence of corporate governance codes takes place in all the countries of the diverse law traditions but that it is to be expected that in the civil law countries the principles of these codes will be integrated in the law itself while in the more common-law-oriented countries the codes play a supportive role in the financial contracts. Whether contracts, court-enforced legal rules or government-enforced regulations are the most efficient form of protecting financial arrangements is largely an empirical question and depends on asset specificity. The consequences of better investor protection are that more dispersed ownership of shares is possible and that the fundamental agency problem between outside investors and controlling shareholders is solved. The existence of controlling shareholders mitigates also the Berle and Means variant of agency problems between outside investors and managers. These equilibrium ownership structures facilitate certain investment policies as we saw earlier in this paragraph when we studied types of activities.

High investor protection encourages also the development of financial markets. When investors are protected from expropriation, the cost of capital decrease, making it more attractive for entrepreneurs to issue securities.

Financial development accelerates economic growth in three ways. First, it increases savings. Second, it fosters through real investment capital accumulation. Third, to the extent that the financiers exercise control over the investment decisions, financial development allows capital to flow towards the more profitable and productive uses, and thus improves the resource allocation (La Porta, Lopez-de-Silanes, Shleifer, & Vishny, 2000: 13–17). Carlin and Mayer (2003) report a strong relation of information disclosure, fragmentation of banking systems and concentration of ownership with the growth of equity-financed and skill-intensive industries. The growth of equity-dependent industries is particularly high in advanced countries with good information disclosure, investor protection and dispersed banking systems. Gugler (2001: 201–205) reports that direct shareholder monitoring has a positive impact on corporate performance. Large shareholders are active monitors in the corporations they control. They have both the incentives and the means to discipline management. Some studies do report beneficial effects of large shareholder monitoring for firm performance, but there are also some that find insignificant or unclear results. This result from the fact that large shareholders are not only effective monitors but also consume private benefits from control at the cost of minority shareholders. Institutional structure does not always mitigate this problem. The conflict between managers and owners, and between controlling shareholders and minority shareholders will only grow in importance. That is why institutional investors like pension funds or mutual funds will play a key role in channelling private savings to productive investment. Efficient allocation processes will be stimulated thanks to these institutional investors by the successful implementation of good governance practices on the European financial markets. An important finding is that all constellations of ownership and control structure (Scott, 1997: 56) involve costs and benefits. Relying on one or a few tools to solve agency conflicts is not optimal. Sole reliance on one mechanism is not optimal but the right mix of direct monitoring by shareholders and board of directors, efficiently designed managerial compensation packages and tight competition in the managerial and product markets yields a better solution (Gugler, 2001: 204–205).

Corporate governance regulation and other legislation are intimately linked to each other. Anti-trust policy, competition policy and regulations about corporate governance influence each other and must be viewed in conjunction. If competition in product markets is weak, managerial discretion over free cash flows is more likely to emerge and corporate governance practices become more important in monopolistic or oligopolistic environments. Since monitoring is a public good in dispersed ownership structures, a carefully composed mix of additional corporate governance means (like monitoring management by board of directors, efficient remuneration contracts, well-functioning takeover markets and clear corporate governance codes) to the individual equity contract is needed. All these services together improve the performance of firms in a lot of countries (Gugler, 2001: 205–212).

11.6. Conclusions

The emergence of corporate governance codes is an important institutional element in a lot of countries and contributes significantly to protection of investors. In civil law countries these codes are public-ordering mechanisms which operate like court-enforced legal rules or government-enforced regulations contract, whereas in common law countries it functions as a private-ordering mechanism that is a contractual safeguard to the equity contract. This encourages the transparency and development of financial markets, increases savings and real investment, and improves the resource allocation and the accumulation of capital. Still, the introduction of these codes imposes transaction costs on firms, which have to comply to all these rules. The frauds and scandals destroyed an important component of immaterial capital namely trust. To rebuild an informal institution like trust between parties on the financial markets will take a lot of time and in the mean time societies have to invest more means in investor protection so that the efficient allocation of savings to the most profitable investment is guaranteed. The disappearance of an informal institution like trust consequently has severe effects on the development of formal institutions and the transaction costs in the financial system. The topicality of this causal direction today makes that it is still possible to gain additional insights from the old institutional economists.

References

Buchanan, J.M. (1987). The constitution of economic policy. *American Economic Review, 77,* 243–250.
Carlin, W., & Mayer, C. (2003). Finance, investment and growth. *Journal of Financial Economics, 69,* 191–226.
Grazell, J. (1992). De scheiding van leiding en eigendom en het prestatievermogen van de onderneming. *Bedrijfskunde, 4,* 361–367.
Grazell, J. (1997). De rol van de grootaandeelhouder. *Bedrijfskunde, 1,* 42–50.
Groenewald, E. (2005). Corporate governance in the Netherlands: From the Verdam report of 1964 to the Tabaksblat Code of 2003. *European Business Organization Law Review, 6,* 291–311.
Gugler, K. (2001). *Corporate governance and economic performance.* Oxford: Oxford University Press.

Hamilton, W.H. (1932). Institutions. In: E.R.A. Seligman, & A. Johnson (Eds), *Encyclopaedia of the social sciences* (pp. 84–89). (Reprinted in G. Hodgson (Ed.). (1993), *Economics of Institutions*, Aldershot: Edward Elgar.

Hodgson, G.M. (2004). *The evolution of institutional economics: Agency, structure and Darwinism in American institutionalism*. New York: Routledge.

Jensen, M.C., & Meckling, W.H. (1976). Theory of the firm: Managerial behaviour, agency costs and ownership structure. *Journal of Financial Economics, 3*, 305–360.

La Porta, R., Lopez-de-Silanes, F., Shleifer, A., & Vishny, R. (2000). Investor protection and corporate governance. *Journal of Financial Economics, 58*, 3–27.

La Porta, R., Lopez-de-Silanes, F., Shleifer, A., & Vishny, R. (2002). Investor protection and corporate valuation. *Journal of Finance, 57*, 1147–1170.

Maier, S. (2005). *How global is good governance?* London: EIRIS Research Report.

Mayer, C. (2002). Financing the new economy: Financial institutions and corporate governance. *Information Economics and Policy, 14*, 311–326.

Rutherford, M. (1994). *Institutions in economics: The old and new institutionalism*. Cambridge: Cambridge University Press (reprinted in 1999).

Scott, J. (1995). *Sociological theory: Contemporary debates*. Cheltenham: Edward Elgar.

Scott, J. (1997). *Corporate business and capitalist classes*. Oxford: Oxford University Press.

Shleifer, A., & Vishny, R.W. (1997). A survey of corporate governance. *Journal of Finance, 52*, 737–783.

Williamson, O.E. (1998). Transaction cost economics: How it works, where it is headed. *The Economist, 146*, 23–58.

Williamson, O.E. (2000). The new institutional economics: Taking stock, looking ahead. *Journal of Economic Literature, 38*, 595–613.

Williamson, O.E. (2002). The theory of the firm as governance structure: From choice to contract. *Journal of Economic Perspectives, 16*, 171–195.

PART 3

CAPITAL STRUCTURE AND VALUATION

Chapter 12

Why Do Companies Issue Convertible Bonds? A Review of the Theory and Empirical Evidence

Igor Loncarski, Jenke ter Horst and Chris Veld

12.1. Introduction

Exchange-listed companies have a wide range of possibilities when they look for new sources of financing. Companies can use equity in the form of internally generated funds or issue new shares of common stock. Alternatively, they can use debt in the form of bank loans or issue bonds. The use of hybrid securities represents yet another possibility. The most well-known hybrid securities are so-called convertible bonds that, at the option of the holder, can be exchanged into shares of common stock of the issuing company. An example of a convertible bond issue is the bond issue by General Motors Corporation in 2003. These bonds pay an annual coupon of 6.25%. Furthermore, on their maturity date, the holder of the bond has the option to choose between receiving the nominal value in cash or converting the bond into 21 shares of the General Motors Corporation stock.[1] Convertible bonds possess characteristics of both equity and debt: they resemble debt, because they pay a fixed coupon interest. On the other hand they resemble equity, because part of the price that is paid for them is for the option to exchange the bonds into shares. The money paid for the option does not have to be paid back by the company, irrespective of future developments of the stock price.

An interesting question is what motivates companies to issue a hybrid security like a convertible bond instead of issuing straight debt or equity. Ross, Westerfield, and Jaffe (2005: 686) state that *"probably there is no other area of corporate finance where real-world practitioners get as confused as they do on the reasons for issuing convertible debt."* The authors observe that practitioners generally argue that convertible bonds offer the possibility to issue equity at a higher price than the currently prevailing stock price and/or that they offer a possibility to attract debt at a low interest rate. The argument that equity can be attracted at a higher price than the stock price at the issuance date of the

Advances in Corporate Finance and Asset Pricing
Edited by L. Renneboog
© 2006 Elsevier B.V. All rights reserved.
ISBN: 0-444-52723-0

convertibles is based on the fact that the conversion price is generally higher than the current stock price. The conversion price is the price for which the holders of the convertible bonds can buy stocks. In the General Motors example the conversion price is $47.62.[2] The conversion price is higher than the stock price at the issuance date of the convertibles, which was $35.94. The second argument that convertibles offer a possibility to attract debt at a low interest rate is based on the fact that the coupon rate on the convertibles is lower than the coupon rate a company would have to pay on ordinary debt. In the General Motors example, the company pays a coupon of 6.25% on the convertible bonds, while the closest comparable straight bond of the same company had a yield to maturity of around 7.5%. However, both these claims are refuted by academics who argue that the conversion price should not be compared to the current stock price, and hence reject the first argument. They also reject the second argument, explaining that the lower coupon interest on convertible bonds is caused by the fact that the holder of a convertible gets the option to buy stock in the future. Since an option is a right and not an obligation, this option has a value, which is paid for by the holder of the convertible by accepting a lower interest rate.

Academic theories in corporate finance concerning the question why companies issue convertible debt are generally based on agency and asymmetric information models. However, surveys among managers responsible for the decision to issue convertibles generally show very little support for these theories. This shows that there is a large divergence between the practitioner's and the academic literature on the question why companies issue convertible bonds. The objective of this chapter is to review the different viewpoints and to see where theory and practice agree, and where the large disagreement lies.

Before going into the question why companies issue convertible bonds, it is useful to give a short overview of the market for these financial instruments. The size of the market for convertible debt varies between the countries considerably, with the US market being the single largest market for convertible bonds in the world, accounting for 30% of all the convertible bond issues in the period 1990–2003, as shown in Table 12.1. The US market is followed by Japan, South Korea and Canada, while the largest Western European markets account only for somewhat more than 9% of the total global issues.

With respect to the popularity of the convertible bonds over time, Table 12.2 shows that globally there are no large variations in the number of issues over time. However, there is an increased popularity of convertible debt between 1993 and 1999 in terms of the number of convertible bond issues, which can again be observed in 2003.

Another interesting difference among different markets is the issue size. As shown in Table 12.3, the largest issue sizes, measured in mean and median values, are in the Western European markets, while the smallest are in South Korea and Australia. The largest variations, measured with the coefficient of variation, are in the German and South Korean market, while the smallest can be observed in Taiwan.[3]

As mentioned before, the objective of this chapter is to overview the theory and empirics on the question why companies issue convertible bonds. This question is very relevant in practice, because convertible bonds are not only frequently used by large exchange-listed companies, but also by young companies that use venture capital. By answering the question why companies issue convertible bonds we can also shed more light on the question

Table 12.1: Number of convertible bond issues in different regions and countries in the period 1990–2003.

Region/country	Number of issues	Percentage of all issues (%)
Europe (all)	*1025*	*14.2*
UK	143	2.0
France	216	3.0
Germany	158	2.2
The Netherlands	152	2.1
US	*2166*	*30.0*
Canada	*280*	*3.9*
Asia (all)	*2967*	*41.2*
Hong Kong	110	1.5
Japan	1632	22.6
Taiwan	185	2.6
South Korea	827	11.5
Australia	*235*	*3.3*
Rest of the World	*535*	*7.4*
World (total)	*7208*	*100.0*

Source: SDC (Securities Data Corporation) New Issues database.

Table 12.2: Yearly breakdown of the number of convertible bond issues in the period 1990–2003.

Year	Number of issues	Percentage of all issues (%)
1990	335	4.65
1991	384	5.33
1992	308	4.27
1993	640	8.88
1994	797	11.06
1995	490	6.80
1996	710	9.85
1997	583	8.09
1998	598	8.30
1999	436	6.05
2000	364	5.05
2001	552	7.66
2002	381	5.29
2003	630	8.74
Total	7208	100.00

Source: SDC New Issues database.

Table 12.3: Descriptive statistics of the issue sizes in different countries and the global market in the period 1990–2003 (the values are in millions of US dollars, except for *N* (number of issues) and *CV* (coefficient of variation).

Country	Mean	Median	Minimum	Maximum	Standard deviation	*N*	*CV*
UK	324.66	159.50	23.40	2026.80	433.10	141.00	1.33
France	404.61	245.70	2.40	3097.20	481.16	215.00	1.19
Germany	149.84	56.40	3.90	5096.30	436.68	154.00	2.91
The Netherlands	368.25	200.90	0.30	2908.30	506.99	151.00	1.38
US	237.55	135.00	0.10	4500.00	331.71	2162.00	1.40
Canada	122.85	87.80	0.00	1500.00	167.92	236.00	1.37
Hong Kong	181.91	115.00	0.40	2500.00	342.48	109.00	1.88
Japan	116.36	65.80	0.10	2851.80	188.49	1632.00	1.62
Taiwan	124.65	100.00	13.20	700.00	100.25	185.00	0.80
South Korea	34.45	12.50	0.20	1317.80	91.38	804.00	2.65
Australia	93.65	8.50	0.10	1500.00	183.41	221.00	1.96
World (Total)	175.46	85.40	0.00	5096.30	307.55	7074.00	1.75

Source: SDC New Issues database.

why companies issue other hybrid financial instruments. These hybrids include convertible preferred stock and warrant-bond loans among others. Convertible preferred stock is preferred stock with an option for the holder to convert it into common stock. A warrant-bond loan is a loan with warrants attached. The most important difference between warrant bonds and convertible bonds is that the warrants in a warrant-bond loan can be detached from the bonds after the issuance. We will not go into the choice that companies can make between different hybrid financial instruments.

A related topic that will shortly be mentioned is that of the call policy of convertible bonds. Convertible bonds are usually callable, which means that the company has a right to call the bonds, and to repay the investor before maturity or conversion. Ingersoll (1977) demonstrates that the optimal moment to call a convertible is when the conversion value equals the call price. The conversion value is the value of the common stock to be received in the conversion exchange. However, in an empirical study he finds that in practice the calls show a delay. On average the conversion value of the bonds is 43.9% above the call price. This finding of Ingersoll has led to a large amount of academic papers on the question why convertible bonds are called late. Given that this is only a side issue in the decision to issue convertible bonds, we will not discuss this topic further.

The chapter is structured as follows. In Section 12.2 we review the theoretical arguments for the issuance of convertible debt. Section 12.3 is dedicated to a review of empirical evidence, based on different types of empirical studies: event studies, cross-sectional analyses and surveys. Section 12.4 concludes the chapter.

12.2. Theoretical Motivations for the Use of Convertible Debt

12.2.1. Capital Structure Irrelevance and Security Choice

In their seminal work on capital structure (ir)relevance Modigliani and Miller (1958) show that the way a firm finances its investments does not matter for the market value of the firm. It is irrelevant whether companies choose to issue equity, straight debt, convertible bond or any other package of securities to finance their investments. Why do investors then in terms of underlying equity valuation of the company react differently to the issue announcements of different types of securities?[4]

Modigliani and Miller build their model based on the assumptions of perfect capital markets[5] and those of perfectly informed agents who trade securities, who share similar information (symmetric knowledge) and are of equal (atomic) size. Their model, although shown not to hold in reality, provides the cornerstone of the capital structure research framework. Perhaps the most crucial assumption is the one about symmetric information and perfect knowledge of the agents. This assumption has inspired numerous later strains of literature. In reality agents possess different information, contracts cannot be written as such to cover for all possible contingencies that might arise and many actions of agents are not observable and/or verifiable. We can describe such a setting with the notion of an asymmetric information framework. In such a setting efficient transmission of funds (contracts) between parties is impaired and can, in the worst case, lead to a complete market collapse (see Akerlof, 1970). The main reasons are adverse selection and agency problems.

The adverse selection problem results in ex-ante unobservable and/or unverifiable type of agents that the other party (principal) in the contract has to choose or determine. The agency problem is a result of ex-post possible opportunistic behaviour of an agent, once the contract has been made, but the actions of the agent are unverifiable and contracts do not cover all possible contingencies. In a financing arrangement (contract) between a firm (agent) and an investor (principal) all these issues play crucial roles and the severity of the adverse selection and the agency problem affects the efficiency of a firm's financing. The worse the adverse selection and agency problems are, the less efficient the financing channel will be, since a first best solution cannot be achieved. A first best solution is the outcome under no adverse selection and agency problems. Put differently, the financing will become more expensive for the firms, because principals cannot differentiate between the agents properly, since bad types can mimic good types. This drives out some positive net present value investment opportunities (Myers & Majluf, 1984) and creates a social dead weight loss, since a first best solution is not implemented. Good type agents thus try to send signals to the principals about their true types in order to differentiate themselves and overcome this issue. In such setting the capital structure, or the way a firm finances itself, is considered to be a signalling device (Heinkel, 1982), but above all the security types that compose the capital structure are considered to be a signalling mechanism (Myers & Majluf, 1984).

Producing a signal has to be costly in order to be perceived as credible. In other words, only the agents that can afford to produce the signal (good types) will do so, while bad types will not mimic them, as the cost of the signal would exceed the benefit (e.g. higher valuation) of representing themselves as good types. Otherwise, the signal can be sent by anyone and types cannot be correctly inferred. For example, a bad type firm will not issue debt, since that increases the probability of the financial distress much more than for a good type firm. In that respect, a capital structure or a degree of leverage can serve as a credible signal of the firm type. Similar is the case of different types of security issues, where there is an equity issue on one end of the spectrum and a straight debt issue on the other. The paradox of both security types is their incompatibility. Namely, equity ownership induces risk taking, due to limited liability. The most an investor can lose are the funds invested, while the upper potential for gains is unlimited.[6] Debt ownership on the other hand induces risk aversion, since the most debt holders can gain is a fixed return. Debt holders are not compensated for additional risk being undertaken by the firm and are therefore faced with a concave payoff function. In the case of the firm's default on debt, when the realized cash flow of the firm is less than the principal, debt holders receive the entire firm's cash flow. In the case where the realized cash flow of the firm is greater than the principal (including a fixed return), debt holders receive only the principal and do not participate on any gains above that value. As mentioned in the introduction, convertible bonds are hybrid instruments, which combine features of straight debt and equity. They are straight debt packaged with a call option on the firm's equity, making it possible for convertible bondholders to participate in potential value gain sharing of the firm.

12.2.2. Theoretical Motivations for Issuing Convertible Debt

There are number of different theoretical explanations as to why companies finance themselves with convertibles. These can be classified into several broader categories:

- Theories based on an asymmetric information framework (Brennan & Kraus, 1987; Brennan & Schwartz, 1988; Kim, 1990; Stein, 1992).
- Theories based on an agency problem framework (Green, 1984; Mayers, 1998; Isagawa, 2000).
- Tax advantage based theories (Jalan & Barone-Adesi, 1995).
- Theories based on managerial entrenchment (Isagawa, 2002).
- Rationing in the equity market (Lewis, Rogalski, & Seward, 2001).

The theoretical explanations show an important distinction between adverse selection models and agency theories on one hand, and the entrenchment theories on the other. The distinction is in the underlying assumptions about the control over financial and investment policies. Adverse selection models and agency theories solve for specific asymmetric information and agency issues between insiders (managers and/or existing shareholders) and outsiders (either new shareholders or bondholders), and assume maximization of the existing shareholder's wealth (in the literature also referred to as the efficient approach). The entrenchment approach on the other hand assumes that financial and investment policies are determined by the entrenched manager (insider), who serves his or her own interests (empire building and different perks among other) and does not necessarily pursue value maximization of the firm.

12.2.2.1. Theories based on the asymmetric information framework   According to Brennan and Kraus (1987) convertible debt can costlessly mitigate investment inefficiencies, which arise due to information asymmetry issues in the framework of Myers and Majluf (1984) and Heinkel (1982). The information asymmetry can either concern the uncertainty regarding returns on investments made by firms (mean of the distribution of returns) or the uncertainty regarding the variance of returns (mean-preserving spread). Brennan and Kraus develop such a single parameter model of information asymmetry. The goal of the firm is to maximize the difference between the value of the funds, obtained from the investors, and a true value of the financing, given the full information about the firm. In the equilibrium each financing strategy[7] is chosen by the worst possible type of firm for that particular financing strategy (this is the so-called "lemons property"). Securities that can lead to such equilibrium include convertible bonds, junior bonds and bonds with warrants. These securities can effectively resolve the issue of adverse selection, as each type of firm reveals itself with the choice of the financing strategy. The strategy depends on the nature of the information asymmetry problem.

Brennan and Schwartz (1988) argue that the only reason investors are willing to pay more for a convertible bond than for a straight bond is because of its hybrid nature. The cost of convertibles is evaluated on a weighted basis of the straight debt component cost of convertibles and the equity option cost of a convertible. Convertible bonds are relatively insensitive to the risk of the issuing company exactly because of their hybrid nature.

Namely, higher risk reduces the value of the straight debt component, but at the same time it increases the value of the equity option component, thus having very limited overall effect on the value of convertibles. Brennan and Schwartz (1988: 59) point out that the relevant risk is " ... *not only the risk of the company's existing operations, but also the risk of any future operations in which the firm may become involved over the life of the bond.*" This relates to the agency cost of straight debt. It arises from the different payoff structures of bondholders and shareholders and limited liability of shareholders (Jensen & Meckling, 1976). With straight debt outstanding, shareholders[8] have strong incentives to increase the risk of the company, which increases the upper potential for gains of shareholders, but reduces the value of straight debt. Convertibles reduce these incentives, as their value is less sensitive to the changes in the riskiness of the underlying equity.[9] Brennan and Schwartz (1988: 59) conclude that " ... *convertibles are most likely to be used by companies which the market perceives as risky, whose risk is hard to assess and whose payment policy is hard to predict.*"

Constantinides and Grundy (1989) present a model in which an issue of a convertible bond, combined with a partial share repurchase, serves as a credible signal of a firm type. This resolves the information asymmetry problem and related underinvestment issue, when the firm is restricted to equity financing. Since the management owns a fraction of the stock in an all-equity firm, they are interested in maximizing the value of the firm's stock. Management may not sell their stock or buy the securities issued by the firm. Constantinides and Grundy show that in the fully revealing equilibrium the payoff of the issued security has to be similar to the payoff of straight debt (concave payoff function) for the low values of the firm's investments. On the other hand, for the high values of the firm's investments, the payoff of the issued security should be similar to the payoff of equity (convex payoff function). Constantinides and Grundy argue that such payoff structure of the security assures the proper signalling incentives for the management (costly signalling). As previously discussed, a convertible bond is a security that conforms to these requirements.

Similarly, in the model of Kim (1990) the convertible bond issue and in particular the conversion ratio serve as a signal of firm's type. The conversion ratio serves as a credible signal of a company's future earnings. In the equilibrium, lower expected future earnings of the worse types induce higher conversion ratios. These imply more shares per bond and thus higher dilution of future earnings, as those have to be shared with a relatively larger share of new shareholders. The model yields a testable hypothesis that abnormal common stock returns at the announcements of the convertible debt issues are negatively related to the conversion ratio, since higher conversion ratios imply worse type firms.

According to Stein (1992) firms issue convertible bonds in order to get equity through the "back door" in situations where informational asymmetries make conventional equity issues unattractive due to high issue costs and dilution (Myers & Majluf, 1984). Stein's rationale resembles that of Constantinides and Grundy (1989), but has a different empirical implication. In the model of Constantinides and Grundy the share repurchase mechanism is a way of signalling type of the firm to the market. This is not the case in Stein's model, where two factors are particularly important: call features of convertibles bonds and increased possibility of financial distress due to excess debt. In a fully separating equilibrium good firms issue debt, medium quality firms issue convertible debt and bad quality firms issue equity. Financing choice therefore serves as the signal to the market. Announcement effects, which are generally found to be negative for all kinds of security-type issues, are according to Stein's model expected to be worst for equity offerings, somewhat better for convertible debt issues and the least negative for straight debt issues. These expectations are in line with the adverse selection models of a capital structure.

12.2.2.2. Theories based on the agency problem framework Maximizing the value of the equity claim and maximizing the value of the firm can, with risky debt outstanding, lead to agency problems (debt holder expropriation). Shareholders have an incentive to substitute projects of lower risk with riskier projects. This is due to their limited liability. Green (1984) develops a model in which option claims issued with debt may mitigate those incentive problems. By addressing the financing and incentive problems simultaneously, the correct incentives can be induced with a convertible bond or debt-warrant combination. This alters the incentives of the equity holders to take risk, as part of the potential gains has to be shared with new shareholders, since option claims on company's equity are issued together with debt. However, Green's analysis abstracts from a number of other incentive (agency) problems, where the most important is the one between management and shareholders. Therefore, the model does not eliminate all the agency costs. The crucial characteristic of convertible and warrant bonds is sharing of the upper potential of the equity gains, while there must be the lower bound of the gains, for which the fixed claim on the debt is paid (the option is not exercised). Only then will such instruments have the desired effect on incentives.

The model of Mayers (1998) is very close to that of Stein (1992), but is different in spirit, since Stein's model is based on asymmetric information about assets in place, whereas Mayers's sequential-financing hypothesis is based on the uncertainty about the value of future investment options. In Stein's model the convertibility feature solves the financing problem at the time of the issue, whereas in Mayers' model convertibility solves a future financing problem. Compared to straight bonds convertible bonds economize on issue costs, because they leave funds in the firm (convertibility feature) and reduce the leverage when the investment option is valuable. On the other hand convertibles control the overinvestment problem (see Jensen, 1986) when the investment option is not valuable. The call provision is an important feature of convertible bonds, when there is uncertainty about the maturity date of the investment option. Mayers notes that existing evidence on convertible bonds supports the sequential-financing hypothesis, but that much of it is also consistent with other theories, since (Mayers, 1998: 88) " ... *investment options provide opportunities for risk-shifting or are a likely source of asymmetric information.*" The sequential-financing hypothesis has no direct implication for stock price reactions at the time of convertible debt announcements. However, as none of the other motivations for the use of convertible debt predicts any additional investment at the time of conversion, evidence of investment-related activity at the time of conversion would support the sequential-financing hypothesis.

In the model of Isagawa (2000) the managerial investment decisions are affected through default risk rather than financing constraints as in Mayers' model. In cases, where managers have empire-building tendencies[10] and fear of default,[11] properly structured convertible debt alleviates managerial opportunism. In essence, the model does not depend on the informational asymmetry problem and thus does not have any testable hypothesis regarding stock price reaction following convertible debt offer announcements.

12.2.2.3. Tax advantage-based theories Jalan and Barone-Adesi (1995) consider convertible bonds as delayed equity financing and motivate their use with a different tax treatment of coupon interest and dividend payments in a setting with market frictions and incompleteness. In such a setting issuing convertible bonds increases the residual equity value of the firm, since the firm benefits from the tax shield as opposed to an up-front equity financing. Cooperation between firms and investors and the fact that firms have repeated need to tap into the financial markets assure that both firms and investors have an incentive to use convertibles and share their benefits. Compared to straight debt, convertible bonds offer much less trade-off between interest tax shields and cost of financial distress. In the case of straight bonds higher interest tax shields are only achievable through higher indebtedness, which increases the probability of financial distress. On the other hand, convertible bonds offer the benefit of the interest tax shields, but do not increase the probability of financial distress as much. Empirical evidence shows that firms tend to delay calls of convertibles, even though this goes against rational explanation (Brennan & Schwartz, 1988). This fact seems to support the tax motivation. By delaying the call, firms leave more benefits to convertible bondholders, thus cooperating in the continuous game, where they repeatedly have to go back to the market for financing. Should they fail to cooperate and share tax benefits with the investors, they would not be able to issue new convertibles and exploit the tax benefits.

12.2.2.4. Theories based on managerial entrenchment Isagawa (2002) analyses the use of convertible bonds in a setting, where an entrenched manager determines the financial policy of the firm. This model is a deviation from the other literature, which mostly assumes that corporate financial policy is chosen such that it maximizes shareholder's wealth. Isagawa builds on the work of Zwiebel (1996) in which the management chooses financial policy based on its own interests. The interests are best served if management remains in control of the firm and undertakes any expansion project (empire building). In the absence of the market for corporate control managers have no incentives to issue debt, since that increases the probability of bankruptcy (and loss of their position). With the existence of the market for corporate control, the manager will issue debt in order to fence the takeover. By doing that and distributing cash dividends, managers can commit not to undertake value-decreasing projects. This, according to Zwiebel, explains why managers would choose to issue debt. When there are no other financing instruments, managers issue straight debt, which increases a probability of bankruptcy and undertake the value-increasing project. By issuing callable convertible debt instead, managers can reduce the probability of bankruptcy. This implicitly assumes that bonds will eventually be converted into equity. A callable convertible bond is thus an effective financial instrument for an entrenched manager, but it is not desirable from the standpoint of the value of a firm. In this model the firm value decreases, since the probability of an inefficient manager being replaced decreases. Isagawa (2002: 266) concludes that " ... *this implies that corporate financial policy itself creates a conflict between the objectives of the management and the owners ...*".

12.2.2.5. Rationing in the equity markets Lewis, Rogalski, and Seward (2001) propose an alternative explanation for the issuance of convertible debt. Their model is in the spirit of the explanation of the rationing in debt markets (see Stiglitz & Weiss, 1981). Lewis et al. argue that there may be cases in which issuers want to issue common stock, but the firm's participation in the equity market is hampered. In case of rationing in debt markets, there is no alternative to raising debt, since straight debt is the most senior security. In case of equity, which is the most junior security, rationing may not necessarily exclude the firm from raising funds with a more senior security such as for example convertible debt.

12.3. Empirical Research

12.3.1. Wealth Effects Associated with Convertible Debt Offering Announcements

It is empirically well documented and consistent with the model of Myers and Majluf (1984) that different security types induce different wealth effects at the time of their announcements. Seasoned equity offerings induce the strongest negative wealth effects[12] of between –2.5% and –4.5% for the US market, while straight debt issues induce only slightly (many times insignificant) negative wealth effects.[13] In Table 12.4 it is shown that convertible debt offerings induce announcement date valuation responses that are between those for equity and straight debt. Using the results of the previous empirical US studies, we have computed the weighted[14] average wealth effect associated with the convertible debt issue announcements in the US market of –1.63%, while the results of individual US studies vary between –0.6% and –3%.

However, the results for the wealth effects associated with the announcements of convertible debt offerings differ across countries and periods. Contrary to studies conducted in the US market, Kang and Stulz (1996) find significant positive abnormal returns in the Japanese market and attribute those to deregulation in Japan during their sample period and different behaviour of Japanese managers, who seem to be less concerned about short-term results than their American counterparts. Similarly to Kang and Stulz, the abnormal returns associated with convertible debt offerings documented by Christensen, Faria, Kwok, and Bremer (1996) in the Japanese market are positive, but insignificant. This is also the only difference they observe between the US and the Japanese market in terms of abnormal stock price reactions to the announcements of different securities, but they offer no clear explanation. De Roon and Veld (1998) also find positive abnormal returns for convertible offering announcements in the Dutch market. They do not find support for the notion that differences in corporate governance structures cause the difference in abnormal returns. In a study of the Taiwanese convertible bond market Chang, Chen, and Liu (2004) find differences in the wealth effects between the first time issuers and seasoned convertible debt offerings, where the wealth effects are significantly positive for the first and negative (but insignificant) for the latter. They suspect that deregulation (similarly as in Japan) could account for the difference, where relaxed criteria for issuance of convertible bonds leads to the issue announcements being interpreted as a signal of the firm becoming more independent from bank financing (Kang & Stulz, 1996).

Table 12.4: Studies of wealth effects associated with convertible debt issue announcements.

Study	Period	Sample size	CAAR (−1, 0) (%)	CAAR (0, 1) (%)
US domestic market				
Dann and Mikkelson (1984)	1970–1979	132	−2.31***	—
Mikkelson and Partch (1986)	1972–1982	33	−1.97***	—
Eckbo (1986)	1964–1981	75	−1.25***	—
Hansen and Crutchley (1990)	1975–1982	67	−1.45***	—
Long and Sefcik (1990)	1965–1984	134	−0.61***	—
Billingsley, Lamy and Smith (1990)	1971–1986	104	−2.04***	—
Kim and Stulz (1992)	1970–1984	259	−1.66***	—
Davidson III, Glascock and Schwarz (1995)	1980–1985	146	−1.40***	—
Jen, Choi and Lee (1997)	1976–1985	158	−2.15***	—
Lewis, Rogalski and Seward (1999)	1977–1984	203	−1.51**	—
Lewis, Rogalski and Seward (2003)	1978–1992	588	−1.09 NA	—
Arshanapalli, Fabozzi, Switzer and Gosselin (2004)	1993–2001	229	−3.07***	−1.92***
Weighted average (sample sizes are weights)			−1.63	
Japanese domestic market				
Kang and Stulz (1996)	1985–1991	561	0.83***	1.05***
Christensen, Faria, Kwok, and Bremer (1996)	1984–1991	35	0.60	—
Taiwanese market				
Chang, Chen, and Liu (2004)	1990–1999	109	0.42	—

Australian market

Magennis, Watts and Wright (1998)	1986–1995	45	−1.08**	—
Dutch market				
De Roon and Veld (1998)	1976–1996	47	0.63**	0.54 NA
UK market				
Abhyankar and Dunning (1999)	1982–1996	129	−1.20***	—
French market				
Burlacu (2000)	1981–1998	141	−0.20***	
Western European markets				
Dutordoir and Van de Gucht (2004)	1990–2002	188	−1.35***	−1.54***
German and Swiss markets				
Ammann, Fehr and Seiz (2005)	1996–2003	55	−0.18	−1.36**

Notes: CAAR denotes cumulative average abnormal return.
***: denotes significance at 1% level; **: denotes significance at 5% level; NA: not reported.

Apart from country and period specific differences in studies, most of the variation in the size of the wealth effects is attributable to issuer- and issue-specific factors due to the hybrid nature of convertible debt. More specifically, convertible debt can be structured such that it is either more equity- or more debt-like, by adjusting the characteristics of the issue. These include conversion price, maturity and call protection period among others. Typically, convertibles with shorter maturities or call protection periods and lower conversion prices are more likely to be in the money sooner and be converted into equity, which makes them more equity-like. Longer maturities or call protection periods and high conversion prices are the characteristics, which make a convertible issue more debt-like. This effectively provides an important measure. Firstly, by estimating whether the issue is more equity- or more debt-like, it is possible to capture an important explanation for the different size of the wealth effect associated with the announcement of a convertible debt issue. Secondly, it gives a useful test for the theoretical motives behind issues of convertibles. Almost all researchers agree to the following reasoning. Cases, where most of the convertibles are indeed more debt-like, suggest that convertibles are structured such as to resolve issues mostly associated with substitutions for straight debt (risk-shifting hypothesis of Green, 1984; risk estimation of Brennan & Kraus, 1987; Brennan & Schwartz, 1988). On the other hand, if the convertibles are more equity-like, this could be interpreted as support for delayed equity and signalling motives (relating to theories of Kim, 1990 and Stein, 1992). Although the reasoning that convertible bonds are a substitute for either debt or equity seems straightforward, it could be the case that they are neither or perhaps something else, which so far has not been theoretically proposed. This is also the most important point that future empirical research should address. The structure of the convertible debt issue on the other hand does not have any direct implication for the sequential-financing model of Mayers (1998) and Isagawa's idea behind the control of managerial opportunism (2000) and managerial entrenchment (2002).

For the measurement of the size of the equity component in a particular convertible debt issue, different authors propose several measures, which are summarized in Burlacu (2000). The measure mainly used in the most recent literature is the so-called delta[15] (see Burlacu, 2000; Dutordoir & Van de Gucht, 2004). The delta measure relates to the price sensitivity of a convertible bond to the underlying equity and takes values between 0 and 1. A value closer to 1 indicates that the sensitivity of convertible bond price with respect to changes in the price of underlying equity is high, which makes the convertible bond more equity-like. Therefore, we expect that more debt-like offerings of convertible bonds are associated with less negative abnormal returns and more equity-like offerings with more negative abnormal returns. Indeed, all the studies using the delta measure to determine the characteristic of the convertible bond issue find that issues with higher delta value induce more negative wealth effects. This is consistent with the more equity-like nature of such issues.

12.3.2. Convertible Debt Structure and Empirical Tests of Theoretical Motives

Stein (1992) finds support for his model in managerial motives, since in the earlier survey research most managers stated that convertible debt is issued in the function of "delayed equity". The surveys do not support the implications of the signalling model of

Constantinides and Grundy (1989), since no firm in the surveys uses the proceeds to repurchase stock. They rather use the proceeds for capital expenditures, general corporate spending and debt refinancing. Empirical evidence (Essig, 1991) suggests that high debt-to-equity ratio firms, firms with high informational asymmetries and high-growth potential are significantly more likely to use issue convertible debt. Call provisions seem to be crucial, since most of the firms force conversion in a short time after the issue date or call protection expiration. Mikkelson and Partch (1986) document that convertible bond issues with high bond ratings (A and above) have very negative wealth effects associated with the announcements of convertible debt issues, whereas issues with lower ratings essentially exhibit no wealth effects. At first, this finding seems difficult to reconcile with theory. However, Stein argues that the greater the potential for financial distress (lower bond rating), the more credible is convertible debt as a signal of optimism, since without the conversion into equity companies would be left with a debt overhang.

Davidson, Glascock, and Schwartz (1995) investigate Kim's signalling hypothesis and Stein's delayed equity motivation on a sample of 146 convertible bond issues in the US market between 1980 and 1985. Davidson, Glascock, and Schwartz propose the use of the expected time until the convertible becomes at-the-money as a proxy that captures both Kim's and Stein's equity-related motives for issuing convertible debt. On one hand it depends upon the conversion ratio, which is perceived as the signal sent to the market in Kim's model. On the other hand it depends on the market's expectations about the firm's growth rate, which relates this measure to Stein's delayed equity argument. Davidson, Glascock, and Schwartz (1995) argue that a relatively low-conversion ratio compared to the market's expectations about the growth will result in a relatively short expected time for the option becoming at-the-money, effectively making the convertible issue more equity-like and vice versa. Firstly, their results show that the average expected time for the convertible options to become at-the-money is less than 1.5 years. Secondly, the shorter the expected time until the convertible bond becomes at-the-money (more equity-like as conversion is more likely), the more negative the wealth effect associated with the announcement is. The authors interpret the first result as support for Stein's delayed equity motive and the second result as being consistent with Kim's conversion prices signalling mechanism.

Based on Stein's argument for the use of convertible debt Jen, Choi, and Lee (1997) test two hypotheses using a sample of 158 convertible issues in the US market between 1976 and 1985. The first "growth funding" hypothesis states that companies with large and growing capital needs and limited debt capacity are more likely to issue convertibles and thus create a future equity base with lower flotation and information costs (less dilution due to information asymmetries). The second "expected cost of financial distress" hypothesis states that issuers with high expected costs of financial distress and limited additional debt capacity will have a greater incentive to reduce the interest coupon (due to the conversion option) and lower the probability of financial distress by issuing convertibles. Both hypotheses together yield the idea that high-growth companies with limited debt capacity and high expected costs of financial distress are more likely to issue convertibles. The market is expected to react more favourably to convertible issues announced by such companies than to the issue announcements made by low-growth companies. Jen, Choi, and Lee find two-day abnormal returns to be significantly negative (i.e. –2.15%) for the whole sample. They also note a stock price run-up prior to announcement date. Using a standard cross-sectional regression analysis, where they regress the cumulative average abnormal returns on a set of independent variables, they find support for the two hypotheses and thus Stein's "backdoor-equity" argument. Firms issue convertible debt because of the high-growth potential and limited debt capacity (costly or unavailable debt financing), while at the same time managers believe that equity prices do not properly reflect the firm's value and new equity issues would not be favourable to the existing shareholders (costly equity financing).

Similarly to Davidson, Glascock, and Schwartz (1995), Magennis, Watts, and Wright (1998) explore Kim's signalling hypothesis on a sample of 45 convertible issues in the Australian market between 1986 and 1995. To measure, whether the convertible issue is more equity- or debt-like, they use the expected time for the convertible options to become at-the-money as the proxy measure. The longer the expected time to at-the-money of the conversion option is, the more debt-like the convertible issue is. The size of the abnormal returns should be positively related to the expected time of the convertible option to become at-the-money. Magennis, Watts, and Wright indeed find this relationship to be positive and significant. This yields support for Kim's signalling hypothesis. However, they claim that convertibles are not simply substitutes for equity or debt, but rather "... *a 'ready-made' capital structure*" (Magennis, Watts, & Wright, 1998: 313), as a single convertible issue can be a " ... *simple and cheaper alternative (to separate debt and equity issues)*" (Magennis, Watts, & Wright, 1998: 314).

Lewis, Rogalski, and Seward (1999) investigate Stein's backdoor-equity hypothesis and Green's risk-shifting hypothesis on a sample of 203 convertible issues on the US market between 1977 and 1984. If the hypothesis of risk-shifting holds, convertible debt issuers must have higher agency costs than straight debt issuers. Should the Stein's hypothesis be correct, convertible debt issuers must have higher adverse selection and financial distress costs than common equity issuers. Lewis et al. classify convertible debt offers as either debt- or equity-like by estimating the probability of conversion of convertible bond into equity at the maturity.[16] They confirm the findings of previous studies of announcement dates wealth effects, where the most negative effects are for equity issues, a bit less negative for con-vertibles issues and somewhat neutral for straight debt issues. Firms that issue convertibles are smaller in terms of capitalization (size is often seen as proxy for information asymme-try), riskier in terms of total risk, with better pre-issue stock performance and more finan-cial slack (consistent with the model of Myers & Majluf, 1984) and with highly profitable growth opportunities. Firms that issue debt-like convertibles are smaller than those that issue straight debt, have higher market-to-book ratios, lower cash flows, lower dividend payouts, higher stock volatility and higher leverage before the issue. These findings about debt-related costs are consistent with the hypothesis that firms use debt-like convertibles to control for the asset-substitution (risk-shifting) problem. The equity-related financing costs indicate that debt-like convertibles are issued when future economic conditions are expected to be good (good growth opportunities). Investment opportunities are significantly more profitable for equity-like convertible debt issuers than for common equity issuers. Equity-like convertible issuers have more financial slack than common equity issuers, which according to Myers and Majluf (1984) implies greater adverse selection costs. Lewis et al. see this as evidence that issuing equity-like convertibles instead of common equity mitigates information asymmetry problems. Common stock issuers are riskier, both in terms of systematic and total firm risk, than firms that issue equity-like convertibles. Overall, the effects of equity-related costs are consistent with the backdoor-equity hypothesis, since the adverse selection costs are higher for equity-like convertible issuers than for common equity issuers.

In the follow-up paper Lewis et al. investigate long-run performance of companies issuing convertible debt. Lewis et al. argue that issuers might be using the convertible debt market because they were "rationed out" of the equity market. As mentioned in Section 12.2.2.5 this provides another motive for issuing convertible debt. On a sample of 566 convertible debt issues in the US market from 1979 to 1990 they find deteriorating operating performance of the issuers of convertible bonds following the convertible debt issue compared to the matched sample of non-issuing firms. However, the difference in operating performance is not significant as in the case for equity issuing firms compared to the matched sample of non-issuing firms. Lewis et al. interpret these findings as evidence somewhat contradicting the arguments of Green (1984) and Mayers (1998). Lewis et al. argue that in Green's and Mayers' models it is implicitly assumed that one of the consequences of a convertible debt issue would be that firms invest only in positive net present value projects. Given a relatively deteriorating performance of convertible bond issuers, they conclude that convertible debt does not completely resolve risk shifting and/or managerial discretion (overinvestment problem). On the other hand, they see the findings as support for Stein's delayed equity motive, as firms may choose a convertible debt issue over an equity issue when they expect improved operating performance in the future. Lewis et al. consider the findings on relative operating performance of convertible versus equity issuers as support for their alternative explanation for the use of convertible debt due to the rationing in the equity market. This rationing means that some firms are allowed to access the equity market, but only if their post-issue performance proves to be sufficient.

Mayers (1998) empirically tests the proposed "sequential-financing" rationale for convertible debt issues. If the sequential-financing hypothesis holds, firms will exhibit intensive investment-related activity at the time of calls of convertible bonds. Mayers documents that issuers of convertible debt have higher than industry median leverage, higher market-to-book ratios, higher R&D costs relative to sales and a lower than industry median ratio of tangible to total assets. For these companies convertible debt represents 30% of total debt on average. Somewhat contrary to the sequential-financing hypothesis is the large size of the firms in the sample, since the sequential-financing hypothesis is based on the issue cost economization, which is more important for smaller firms. Compared to a matching sample of non-issuing firms, Mayers finds statistically significant larger capital expenditure changes for companies that issued and called convertible debt in the call year and in the year following the call. Calls of convertibles that precede significant changes in financing activity seem to be an important breakpoint. This breakpoint signals an increased rate of new financing, with straight debt being the most popular instrument. Mayers argues that this evidence does not support Stein's model, since calls are not being executed to avoid possible financial distress, as new debt is issued shortly after the calls. This, combined with increased investment activities, gives support to the sequential-financing hypothesis.

In their analysis of 129 convertible debt issues on the UK market in the period 1982–1996 Abhyankar and Dunning (1999) find limited support for Stein's model and for the risk-estimation arguments of Brennan and Kraus (1987), and Brennan and Schwartz (1988). Similarly as in some other studies (e.g. McConnell & Muscarella, 1985) they observe a positive effect on abnormal returns in firms, which use the proceeds to finance capital expenditure, while a negative effect is observed in firms, which dedicate the proceeds to refinancing, mergers and acquisitions and general expenditure.

Chang, Chen, and Liu (2004) test Mayers' sequential-financing hypothesis based on a sample of 109 issues of Taiwanese firms. They develop and test two implications directly related to Mayers' model. The first implication is related to the overinvestment problem. If convertibles are an effective way to mitigate this issue, they are more valuable in cases, where current investments and future investment options are highly positively correlated. According to Chang, Chen, and Liu this is a feature generally found in firms with focused activities and more volatile cash flows (since they are not diversified). Therefore, such companies will benefit more from the use of convertibles. Essig (1991) documents volatility of corporate cash flows to be positively related to the use of convertible debt. The second testable prediction refers to the net new financing (gross proceeds less refinancing) that companies will rise during the life of convertible bond. If indeed Mayers' hypothesis holds, companies want to avoid costly external financing when capital needs are high and should therefore mostly rely on internal funds during the life of the convertible bond. Chang, Chen, and Liu find support for both implications related to the sequential-financing motivation for the issue of convertible securities. The difference in size of the wealth effects associated with the announcement of the convertible debt issue between companies with more- and less-focused activities is significant. The wealth effects for the subsample of companies with focused activities are significantly positive, while negative and not significant for those with less-focused activities.

In another paper Lewis, Rogalski, and Seward (2003) use a sample of 588 convertible debt issues in the US market in the period 1972–1992. They attempt to reconcile the diverging evidence on the motives for convertible debt issues and determinants of stock price reactions to convertible debt announcements. They analyze the impact of issuer characteristics on the size of the wealth effect associated with the announcement of convertible debt offers. They again split the issues according to the previously mentioned delta measure into more equity- and more debt-like issues. Lewis et al. find support for the risk-shifting motive proposed by Green (1984), as investment-related issuer characteristics do not affect the investor reactions for the debt-like offers. They do not document strong support for the risk-estimation argument proposed by Brennan and Schwartz (1988), as leverage negatively affects abnormal returns for issuers that are neither equity- nor debt-like. They find strong support for Stein's (1992) backdoor-equity hypothesis, as good industry-adjusted-growth opportunities of the issuers positively affect abnormal returns, especially if they invest the proceeds in new projects. Following a strain of the literature on market timing (e.g. Bayless & Chaplinsky, 1996) they analyze the impact of the market, issue and issuer characteristics on abnormal returns for subsamples of cold, normal and hot market periods of security offerings. They show that the size of the wealth effect associated with the announcement of convertible debt issue also depends on the aggregate volume of the issues in the seasoned equity markets. Moreover, firm-specific factors seem to be more important in periods of cold equity markets, when investors more closely analyze these factors than in periods of more attractive equity issues.

Similar to the analysis of Lewis, Rogalski, and Seward (2003) is the study of Dutordoir and Van de Gucht (2004), conducted on 222 convertible debt issues on 8 Western European markets in the period 1990–2002. They explicitly test Brennan and Kraus' (1987) and Stein's (1992) motivations for the use of convertible debt. Dutordoir and Van de Gucht document strong support for the Brennan and Kraus' model and only limited support for Stein's backdoor-equity motivation. In the analysis they point to certain differences between the US and Western European markets, as the convertible issues on Western European markets seem to be more debt-like and firms are much larger than those on the US market.

In Table 12.5 empirical research related to theoretical motivations for the issue of convertible debt is summarized. The summarized studies use issue, accounting and stock prices information to capture issuer- and issue-specific characteristics. In the studies a cross-sectional analysis is mostly used as the research method; while Lewis, Rogalski, and Seward (1999) for example also used a multinomial logit model in their study to investigate security choice decision. As the table shows, the most frequently tested motivation was Stein's "backdoor-equity" explanation for the use of convertible debt. The support for it (and Kim's hypothesis as well) has consistently been documented. Green's (1984) and Mayers' (1998) agency cost resolution-based arguments have also been explored and generally supported, but with some studies finding contradictory or mixed evidence. Tax motivation and managerial entrenchment explanations have not been tested directly to our knowledge, while little and mixed evidence has been found to support Brennan and Kraus (1987), and Brennan and Schwartz (1988) motivations for the use of convertible debt. One of the reasons for this disparity in popularity of individual motives might be in the ease of deriving and applying meaningful empirical tests. To find support for Stein's motivation, most of the researchers rely on establishing whether the largest share of convertible bonds in the sample is equity-like. All the other theoretical motivations are more difficult to address, as the nature of convertible debt is very complex.

12.3.3. Survey Evidence

There have not been many surveys on convertible debt issues. The first survey was done by Pilcher (1955), followed by Brigham (1966) and Hoffmeister (1977), while the latest surveys include Billingsley and Smith (1996), Graham and Harvey (2001) and Bancel and Mittoo (2004). The survey by Bancel and Mittoo (2004) has been conducted on an international scale (European countries), while other surveys have been done for the US market. The sample sizes vary substantially across the surveys.

Pilcher's (1955) sample includes 22[17] responding presidents of corporations, Brigham (1966) bases his conclusions on a sample of 22 responding firms, Hoffmeister's (1977) survey is composed of 55 respondents, Billingsley and Smith (1996) have a sample of 88 responding firms, Graham and Harvey (2001) base their survey on 392 responses from chief financial officers (CFOs) and Bancel and Mittoo (2004) have a sample of 29 firms from 8 countries.

Table 12.5: Theoretical motivations for issuing convertible debt and related empirical research.

	Asymmetric information based				Agency cost based		Managerial entrenchment	Tax	Equity rationing
	BK (1987)	BS (1988)	K (1990)	S (1992)	G (1984)	M (1998)	I (2002)	JBA (1995)	LRS (2001)
Davidson, Glascock, and Schwartz (1995)			+	+					
Jen, Choi, and Lee (1997)				+					
Magennis, Watts, and Wright (1998)			+						
Mayers (1998)						+			
Lewis, Rogalski, and Seward (1999)				+	+				
Abhyankar and Dunning (1999)			0	0					
Lewis, Rogalski, and Seward (2001)			0	+	−	−			+
Lewis, Rogalski, and Seward (2003)				+	+				
Chang, Chen, and Liu (2004)						+			
Dutordoir and Van de Gucht (2004)	+			0					

Notes: BK (1987) refers to Brennan and Kraus (1987); BS (1988) refers to Brennan and Schwartz (1988); K (1990) refers to Kim (1990); S (1992) refers to Stein (1992); G (1984) refers to Green (1984); M (1998) refers to Mayers (1998); I (2002) refers to Isagawa (2002); JBA (1995) refers to Jalan and Barone-Adesi (1995); LRS (2001) refers to Lewis, Rogalski, and Seward (2001).
+: strong support; 0: limited support; −: contradicting evidence.

In most of the surveys questions were grouped into the following broader categories:

- Rationales (reasons) for issuing convertible securities
- Financing alternatives
- Use of funds
- Conversion policy
- Other factors

It is important to note the difference between the questions about the motives for the use of convertible debt, put forward by practitioners and the theoretical motives, put forward by academics. In general, two distinctive motivations are put forward by practitioners. Namely, practitioners seem to consider convertible debt as the cheaper source of financing than straight debt, as it bears a lower coupon rate. Closely related to this view is also the role of the conversion option as the so-called "deal sweetener", which helps to achieve a lower coupon rate and sell otherwise hard to sell debt issue. Secondly, practitioners traditionally consider convertible debt to be a way of selling the equity at a premium, as the conversion price is higher than the current stock price. As previously mentioned, both views are refuted by academics, who offer other motives for the use of convertible debt.

As theoretical motivations for the use of convertible debt only started to emerge in the late-1980s, early surveys do not rely on any theoretical motivation for the issuance of convertible debt, but rather rely on the mentioned general perceptions among investors and managerial communities. Pilcher (1955) asked managers about the primary motivation for issuing convertible securities, where raising a common equity and "sweetening" (with conversion option) the senior security (debt) were offered with possible answers. Eighty-two per cent of respondents said that the prime motivation for the issue of convertibles was to raise equity. Brigham (1966) based the questions on the primary interest in either equity or debt, where a company was not able to issue one of those and opted for convertibles instead. Seventy-three per cent of the respondents claimed that their primary interest was in equity. He also asked questions about equity undervaluation, concerns about equity dilution, high cost of straight debt and targeting a particular investor's group. Sixty-eight per cent of respondents claimed that convertibles were the way to sell the equity at a premium, while only 27% stated that convertibles were issued in order to "sweeten" otherwise difficult to sell straight debt issue. Hoffmeister (1977) related the questions to interest rate reduction (cost of debt in Brigham, 1966), perceived undervaluation of equity, enhancement of an otherwise difficult to sell issue (marketability in Pilcher, 1955 and debt sweetening) and popularity of convertible debt at the time, equity dilution and a favourable accounting treatment. Seventy per cent of those surveyed found the issuance of delayed equity as an important feature of convertible debt, while 58% claimed that reducing the interest cost was an important consideration. Somewhat more than a quarter of the respondents said that marketability of the issue also played an important role. Interestingly, Hoffmeister also found some differences between large- and medium-sized firms, where the managers of large firms more often stated cheaper debt as the motivation for the use of convertibles, while the managers of medium-sized firms perceived delayed equity as a more important reason.

By the time of the Billingsley and Smith (1996) survey several theoretical motivations for the issuance of convertible bonds emerged. They used the questionnaire to test whether the theories about delayed equity (Stein, 1992) and risk shifting[18] (Green, 1984) in fact drive a firm's decision to issue convertible securities. Aside from the questions related to practical motivations for the use of convertible debt, which were asked in previous surveys,[19] they also asked questions about delayed equity and bondholder protection. On top of those, they also pose a question about the advice of an investment banker and the popularity of convertible debt at the time. The lower coupon rate compared to straight debt was cited as the primary motivation for the issuance of convertibles by most of the mangers, while managers in general offered mixed responses regarding the sale of equity at a premium. The survey is also the first that explicitly asks about the ranking of other financing alternatives that were considered. Managers most often claimed that straight debt was the primary alternative to convertibles, while equity issuance came second. Billingsley and Smith document a strong support for Stein's delayed equity argument, while almost no support for Green's risk-shifting argument.[20] Surveyed managers also gave high importance to the window of opportunity for the issuance of the securities.

Among the questions regarding capital structure, payout policy and capital budgeting Graham and Harvey (2001) asked the surveyed CFOs specific questions about convertible bonds. The questions were aimed at testing the risk-estimation models of Brennan and Schwartz (1977) and Brennan and Schwartz (1988), the risk-shifting model of Green (1984) and the sequential-financing model of Mayers (1998),[21] as well as the delayed equity model of Stein (1992). Similarly to previous surveys they also ask questions about equity dilution, lower coupons on convertibles and popularity of convertible securities at the time. Fifty-eight per cent of the respondents viewed convertible debt as an inexpensive way to issue delayed equity, while more than 40% of the surveyed chief executive officers (CEOs) found a lower coupon rate to be an important motive for the issue of convertible debt. Graham and Harvey find support for the risk-estimation argument, since more than 40% of those surveyed stated that issuing convertibles was a way to attract investors unsure about the riskiness of the company. Similarly as in the study of Billingsley and Smith (1996), Graham and Harvey did not document any support for Green's risk-shifting argument.

The survey by Bancel and Mittoo (2004) encompasses the widest spectrum of theoretical motivations. Aside from delayed equity, risk-shifting motives and the risk-estimation models, they also formulate questions with respect to the signalling model of Constantinides and Grundy (1989), which is closely related to that of Stein (1992). Bancel and Mittoo (2004) also ask questions about the relationship between a convertible debt issue and rating requirements, call provisions, dilution concerns, importance of covenants, tax advantage of convertibles,[22] reducing the risk of hostile takeover,[23] popularity of convertible debt at the time and tapping a group of international investors. They find strong support for Stein's delayed equity argument, since around 86% of respondents were stated "delayed equity" as the most important or very important reason for the issue of convertibles. Around 55% of respondents claim that the signalling role of convertibles is an important feature, which gives further support both to Stein and Kim (1990) models. Somewhat less support is documented for the sequential-financing hypothesis (Mayers, 1998), as only about 28% of the managers find the call feature of convertibles important and the same percentage claim that they would force the conversion as and when future investment opportunities occur. Limited support is shown for the risk-estimation (Brennan & Kraus, 1987, Brennan & Schwartz, 1988) motivations for the use of convertible debt, as only about 21% of the respondents claim that the most important reason for the issue of convertibles is to attract investors, unsure about the risk of the firm. The same weak support is documented for the tax-based explanation[24] (Jalan & Barone-Adesi, 1995), while no support is found for Isagawa's (2002) managerial entrenchment motivation and Green's (1984) risk-shifting argument.

In the surveys managers were also asked to state and rank the financing alternatives to convertible debt at the time of the issue. These financing alternatives range from simple equity and straight debt to preferred stock (convertible and non-convertible), private placements and synthetic convertible debt (debt with warrants). Bancel and Mittoo (2004) find that for the most of the companies convertible debt is the alternative to straight debt. The result is somewhat in conflict with the responses relating to the question of delayed equity, where over 80% of the managers found that motive to be the most or very important. On the other hand, this result is in line with the findings of Dutordoir and Van de Gucht (2004) for the Western European markets, where most of the convertible bonds are structured to be more debt-like.

Bayless and Chaplinsky (1996) present a model of window of opportunity for seasoned equity offerings. They show that negative price reactions in hot equity markets are lower than in cold equity markets and attribute this difference in part to reduced levels of informational asymmetries. The same reasoning could then also be applied to convertible bond issues. Bancel and Mittoo (2004) surveyed managers on how the market conditions affected their decision to issue convertibles, by asking them about the importance of the different factors (overvaluation and undervaluation of equity, levels of interest rates, volatility of the stock market, among others). Most of the respondents claim that high stock market volatility, which translates into a higher value of the conversion option and low interest rates were the key factors that affected the timing of the convertible debt issue.

In Table 12.6 a summary of survey evidence relating to the theoretical motivations for the use of convertible debt is presented. With respect to practical motivations for the issue of convertible debt, surveys in general find strong to moderate support for both "cheap" debt argument and the motivation based on selling the equity at the premium. The importance of these two arguments, which are most often put forward by practitioners, varies over time. For example, Hoffmeister (1977) notes that the shift he observes from delayed equity financing toward a desire to reduce debt interest cost is consistent with the highest interest rates experienced in 30 years at the time. Nevertheless, both practical motivations have remained very important arguments for managers. With respect to theoretical motivations for the use of convertible debt, all the surveys find strong evidence for the delayed equity motivation. In the latest two surveys some support for the risk-estimation argument and the sequential-financing hypothesis is documented, while no support is found for the managerial entrenchment and risk-shifting argument for the use of convertible debt in particular.[25] The survey questions do not differ much between (in particular the recent) surveys and aim at the most direct tests of different theoretical motivations for the use of convertible debt. Although this direct approach is useful for the interpretation of the results, some questions, which are too direct (e.g. the question on risk shifting or bondholder expropriation), might invoke answers that do not reflect the true state of affairs. The

Table 12.6: Theoretical motivations for issuing convertible debt and related survey research.

Survey		P (1955)	B (1966)	H (1977)	BS (1996)	GH (2001)	BM (2004)
Sample size		22	22	55	88	392	29
Practical motives	Lower coupon rate than on straight debt/deal "sweetener"	0	0	+	+	0	+
	sell equity at the premium	+	+	+	0	+	0
Theoretical motives	Asymmetric information based BK (1987)					+	0
	BS (1988)					+	0
	K (1990)				+		+
	S (1992)					+	+
	Agency cost based G (1984)				−	−	−
	M (1998)					+	+
	Managerial entrenchment I (2002)						−
	Tax motivation JBA (1995)						0
	Equity rationing LRS (2001)						

Notes: BK (1987) refers to Brennan and Kraus (1987); JBA (1995) refers to Jalan and Barone-Adesi (1995); BM (2004) refers to Bancel and Mittoo (2004); LRS (2001) refers to Lewis, Rogalski, and Seward (2001); BS (1988) refers to Brennan and Schwartz (1988); GH (2001) refers to Graham and Harvey (2001); P (1955) refers to Pilcher (1955); K (1990) refers to Kim (1990); I (2002) refers to Isagawa (2002); B (1966) refers to Brigham (1966); S (1992) refers to Stein (1992); H (1977) refers to Hoffmeister (1977); G (1984) refers to Green (1984); BS (1996) refers to Billingsley and Smith (1996); M (1998) refers to Mayers (1998).
+: strong support; 0: limited support; −: no support.

weakness of more indirect questions of course is that the results might be subject to different interpretations.

12.4. Conclusion

In this chapter we have summarized and reviewed the most relevant up-to-date literature on the motives for the issuance of convertible debt. The evidence is far from being conclusive and unanimous as to why companies choose to issue convertible debt and how these motives affect investor reactions to convertible debt issue announcements. However, there exist some findings, which are common to all the empirical research.

First of all, the wealth effects associated with the convertible debt issue announcements are generally negative and in between those for straight debt and equity. Secondly, convertible debt can be structured to be either more debt- or equity-like. Convertible issues that are more equity-like induce stock market responses at the issue announcements closer to those, documented for equity issues. This is consistent with the adverse selection model of Myers and Majluf (1984). Thirdly, Stein's (1992) delayed equity motive, Kim's (1990) signalling theory, Mayers' (1998) sequential-financing argument and Green's (1984) risk-shifting hypothesis are the most investigated theoretical argumentations for the use of convertible debt versus straight debt and/or equity. The support for the delayed equity and signalling models found in cross-sectional analyses is corroborated in the surveys. Some support is documented for the risk-shifting hypothesis in the cross-sectional empirical analysis, but is completely refuted in the surveys. Limited evidence is provided for Brennan and Kraus (1987) and Brennan and Schwartz (1988) risk-estimation explanations, both in cross-sectional analyses and surveys. Tax-based motivation for the use of convertible debt (Jalan & Barone-Adesi, 1995) and Isagawa's (2002) managerial entrenchment argument have not been investigated in cross-sectional analyses and surveys yield no support either. Finally, to a large extent surveys reveal that managers still find a lower coupon rate of convertible debt to be an important argument for its issuance, although the importance of this motive varies over time. Given that convertibles include a conversion feature (that comes at a price), a view that convertibles are a cheaper source of financing than straight debt is deceptive. The same is true for the practitioners' view that convertibles provide means of selling the equity at a premium.

Based on a review on the theoretical and empirical literature on why companies issue convertible bonds we can conclude that there are large discrepancies between theory and practice. The practical point of view shows up in surveys among managers that were responsible for issuing convertible bonds. These surveys show that they base themselves on irrational motives. The theoretical literature presents a number of rational motives. These rational motives are confirmed in some of the cross-sectional studies, but they are not confirmed in the survey studies. There are two possible explanations for the different outcomes of the survey and cross-sectional studies. The first explanation is that the surveys are sensitive to the question contents. Therefore they may not yield reliable results. It is often argued that "*managers act smarter than they speak*". Therefore they may follow rational motives, without being aware of this. The second explanation is that the proxies in the cross-sectional studies may be weak. For example, it is very hard to measure a concept of informational asymmetry using only stock market and/or accounting data. In our view, future research in this field should aim for an approach that captures the best of both worlds. Such an approach would ideally combine the different techniques in one study. More specifically, besides using surveys to ask direct questions, it is also possible to use them to find proxies for variables that are used in cross-sectional studies. This approach was used before by De Jong and Van Dijk (2003) in a study on the capital structure of Dutch companies and by De Jong, Van Dijk, and Veld (2003) in a study on the dividend and share buy-back policies of Canadian firms. We believe that such an approach may bridge the gap between theory and practice.

Endnotes

1. The data on these convertible bonds is taken from the SDC New Issues database.
2. This is the nominal value of the bonds divided by the conversion ratio. The conversion ratio is the number of shares that is acquired when the bonds are converted. In this example it is 21. This leads to a conversion price of $1,000/21 = $47.62.
3. Note that the number of issues in Table 12.3 can be different than the reported number of issues in Table 12.2. This is due to missing information on issue sizes for some of the issuers in the SDC database.
4. For the empirical evidence on wealth effects associated with announcements of different securities see Section 12.3.
5. No frictions and discriminating taxes among others.
6. This creates a convex payoff function.
7. Note that Brennan and Kraus make a distinction between securities and financing. They consider securities "*to be basic claims traded in the capital markets*", while financing in their terminology refers "*to the complete set of financial decisions by a firm at a point in time*".
8. Here, we can also think of the management that acts in the interests of shareholders, if we set aside the agency costs of equity.
9. Note that this second argument of Brennan and Schwartz should essentially be classified in the moral hazard framework.
10. This relates to the so-called overinvestment problem related to free cash flow. See Jensen (1986).
11. This relates to the so-called underinvestment problem related to debt. See Myers (1977).
12. See for example Masulis and Korwar (1986), Mikkelson and Partch (1986) and Asquith and Mullins (1986).
13. See for example Dann and Mikkelson (1984) and Eckbo (1986).
14. The weights are sample sizes of the US studies.
15. Under standard Black–Scholes assumptions for the probability of conversion (option being in-the-money), the delta measure is computed as:

$$\Delta = e^{-\delta T} \cdot N \left[\frac{\ln\left(\frac{S}{X}\right) + \left(r - \delta + \frac{\sigma^2}{2}\right) \cdot T}{\sigma \cdot \sqrt{T}} \right]$$

where S is the current price of the underlying stock, X is the conversion price, δ is the continuously compounded dividend yield, r is the continuously compounded yield on a selected "risk-free" bond, σ is the annualized stock return volatility, T is the initial maturity of the bond and $N(.)$ is cumulative standard normal probability distribution.
16. This is estimated using the standard Black–Scholes assumptions, where the underlying stock follows a geometric Brownian motion.
17. There were actually 75 respondents, but only 22 are for companies that issued convertible debt. Others were from companies that issued convertible preferred stock.

18. Billingsley and Smith (1996) actually do not mention Green (1984) explicitly, but the question they ask is a direct test of Green's risk-shifting proposition.
19. Lower coupon rates versus straight debt, over and undervaluation of stock at the time.
20. Note that results of the survey also depend on the way questions are asked. In most cases where questions denote negative meaning, we do not believe that answers are equally truthful as with the other questions. This might also provide an alternative explanation to finding no support for certain issues.
21. The test of Mayers' model was not related to a direct question in the survey.
22. Note that this is implicitly related to Jalan and Barone-Adesi (1995) argument, although Bancel and Mittoo do not mention them.
23. Note that this is implicitly related to the managerial entrenchment motivation by Isagawa (2002), although Bancel and Mittoo do not explicitly relate the survey question to Isagawa's argument.
24. They find that this motivation is more important for the low-growth companies.
25. Veld (1994) has done a survey for warrant-bond loans in the Netherlands. His findings are similar to those of the studies for convertibles. He finds support for the practical motives, but not for theoretical motives, such as for Brennan and Schwartz (1988) and Green (1994). His study does not include questions on the Stein (1992) model.

References

Abhyankar A., & Dunning, A. (1999). Wealth effects of convertible bond and convertible preference share issues: An empirical analysis of the UK market. *Journal of Banking and Finance, 23,* 1043–1065.

Akerlof, G.A. (1970). The market for "lemons": Quality uncertainty and the market mechanism. *Quarterly Journal of Economics, 84,* 488–500.

Ammann, A., Fehr, M., & Seiz, R. (2005). New evidence on the announcement effect of convertible and exchangeable bonds. *Journal of Multinational Financial Management* (in press).

Arshanapalli, B., Fabozzi, F.J., Switzer, L.N., & Gosselin, G. (2004). *New evidence on the market impact of convertible bond issues in the U.S.* Working paper, Indiana University Northwest, Yale University, and Concordia University.

Asquith, P., & Mullins, Jr., D.W. (1986). Equity issues and offering dilution. *Journal of Financial Economics, 15,* 61–89.

Bancel, F., & Mittoo, U.R. (2004). Why do European firms issue convertible debt? *European Financial Management, 10,* 339–373.

Bayless, M., & Chaplinsky, S. (1996). Is there a window of opportunity for seasoned equity issuance? *The Journal of Finance, 51,* 253–278.

Billingsley, R.S., Lamy, R.E., & Smith, D.M. (1990). Units of debt with warrants: Evidence of the 'penalty-free' issuance of an equity-like security. *The Journal of Financial research, 13,* 187–199.

Billingsley, R.S., & Smith, D.M. (1996). Why do firms issue convertible debt? *Financial Management, 25,* 93–99.

Brennan, M.J., & Kraus, A. (1987). Efficient financing under asymmetric information. *The Journal of Finance, 42,* 1225–1243.

Brennan, M.J., & Schwartz, E.S. (1988). The case for convertibles. *Journal of Applied Corporate Finance, 1,* 55–64.

Brigham, E.F. (1966). An analysis of convertible debentures: Theory and some empirical evidence. *The Journal of Finance, 21,* 35–54.

Burlacu, R. (2000). New evidence on the pecking order hypothesis: The case of French convertible bonds. *Journal of Multinational Financial Management, 10,* 439–459.

Chang, S.C., Chen, S.S., & Liu, Y. (2004). Why firms use convertibles: A further test of the sequential-financing hypothesis. *Journal of Banking and Finance, 28,* 1163–1183.

Christensen, D.G., Faria, H.J., Kwok, C.C.Y., & Bremer, M. (1996). Does the Japanese stock market react differently to public security offering announcements than the US stock market? *Japan and the World Economy*, *8*, 99–119.

Constantinides, G.M., & Grundy, B.D. (1989). Optimal investment with stock repurchase and financing as signals. *Review of Financial Studies*, *2*, 445–465.

Dann, L.Y., & Mikkelson, W.H. (1984). Convertible debt issuance, capital structure change and financing-related information: Some new evidence. *Journal of Financial Economics*, *13*, 157–186.

Davidson III, W.N., Glascock, J.L., & Schwartz, T.V. (1995). Signalling with convertible debt. *Journal of Financial and Quantitative Analysis*, *30*, 425–440.

De Jong, A., & Van Dijk, R. (2003). *Determinants of leverage and agency problems.* Working paper, Erasmus University Rotterdam.

De Jong, A., Van Dijk, R., & Veld, C. (2003). The dividend and share repurchases of Canadian firms: Empirical evidence based on an alternative research design. *International Review of Financial Analysis*, *12*, 349–377.

De Roon, F., & Veld, C. (1998). Announcement effects of convertible bond loans and warrant bond loans: An empirical analysis for the Dutch market. *Journal of Banking and Finance*, *22*, 1481–1506.

Dutordoir, M., & Van de Gucht, L. (2004). *Is there a window of opportunity for convertible debt issuance? Evidence for Western Europe.* Working paper, Katholieke Universiteit Leuven.

Eckbo, E. (1986). Valuation effects of corporate debt offerings. *Journal of Financial Economics*, *15*, 119–151.

Essig, S.M. (1991). *Convertible securities and capital structure determinants.* Unpublished Ph.D. thesis, Graduate School of Business, University of Chicago.

Graham, J.R., & Harvey, C.R. (2001). The theory and practice of corporate finance: Evidence from the field. *Journal of Financial Economics*, *60*, 187–243.

Green, R.C. (1984). Investment incentives, debt, and warrants. *Journal of Financial Economics*, *13*, 115–136.

Hansen, R.S., & Crutchley, C. (1990). Corporate earnings and financings: An empirical analysis. *Journal of Business*, *63*, 347–371.

Heinkel, R. (1982). A theory of capital structure relevance under imperfect information. *The Journal of Finance*, *37*, 1141–1150.

Hoffmeister, J.R. (1977). Use of convertible debt in the early 1970s: A reevaluation of corporate motives. *Quarterly Review of Economics and Business*, *17*, 23–32.

Ingersoll, J. (1977). An examination of corporate call policies on convertible securities. *The Journal of Finance*, *32*, 463–478.

Isagawa, N. (2000). Convertible debt: An effective financial instrument to control managerial opportunism. *Review of Financial Economics*, *9*, 15–26.

Isagawa, N. (2002). Callable convertible debt under managerial entrenchment. *Journal of Corporate Finance*, *8*, 255–270.

Jalan, P., & Barone-Adesi, G. (1995). Equity financing and corporate convertible bond policy. *Journal of Banking and Finance*, *19*, 187–206.

Jen, F.C., Choi, D., & Lee, S.H. (1997). Some new evidence on why companies use convertible bonds. *Journal of Applied Corporate Finance*, *10*, 44–53.

Jensen, M.C. (1986). Agency costs of free cash flow, corporate finance, and takeovers. *The American Economic Review*, *76*, 323–329.

Jensen, M.C., & Meckling, W.H. (1976). Theory of the firm: Managerial behaviour, agency costs and ownership structure. *Journal of Financial Economics*, *3*, 305–360.

Kang, J., & Stulz, R. (1996). How different is Japanese corporate finance? An investigation of the information content of new security issues. *Review of Economics Studies*, *9*, 109–139.

Kim, Y.C., & Stulz, R.M. (1992). Is there a global market for convertible bonds? *Journal of Business*, *65*, 75–91.

Kim, Y.O. (1990). Informative conversion ratios: A signalling approach. *Journal of Financial and Quantitative Analysis*, *25*, 229–243.

Lewis, M., Rogalski, R.J., & Seward, J.K. (1999). Is convertible debt a substitute for straight debt or for common equity? *Financial Management*, *28*, 5–27.

Lewis, M., Rogalski, R.J., & Seward, J.K. (2001). The long-run performance of firms that issue convertible debt: An empirical analysis of operating characteristics and analyst forecasts. *Journal of Corporate Finance*, *7*, 447–474.

Lewis, M., Rogalski, R.J., & Seward, J.K. (2003). Industry conditions, growth opportunities and market reactions to convertible debt financing decisions. *Journal of Banking and Finance*, *27*, 153–181.

Long, M.S., & Sefcik, S.E. (1990). Participation financing: A comparison of the characteristics of convertible debt and straight bonds issued in conjunction with warrants. *Financial Management*, *19*, 23–34.

Magennis, D., Watts, E., & Wright, S. (1998). Convertible notes: The debt versus equity classification problem. *Journal of Multinational Financial Management*, *8*, 303–315.

Masulis, R.W., & Korwar, A.N. (1986). Seasoned equity offerings: An empirical investigation. *Journal of Financial Economics*, *15*, 91–118.

Mayers, D. (1998). Why firms issue convertible bonds: The matching of financial and real investment options. *Journal of Financial Economics*, *47*, 83–102.

McConnell, J.J., & Muscarella, C.J. (1985). Corporate capital expenditure decisions and the market value of the firm. *Journal of Financial Economics*, *14*, 399–422.

Mikkelson, W.H., & Partch, M.M. (1986). Valuation effects of security offerings and the issuance process. *Journal of Financial Economics*, *15*, 31–60.

Modigliani, F., & Miller, M.H. (1958). The cost of capital, corporation finance and the theory of investment. *The American Economic Review*, *48*, 261–297.

Myers, S.C. (1977). Determinants of corporate borrowing. *Journal of Financial Economics*, *5*, 147–175.

Myers, S.C., & Majluf, N.S. (1984). Corporate financing and investment decisions when firms have information that investors do not have. *Journal of Financial Economics*, *13*, 187–221.

Pilcher, J.C. (1955). Raising capital with convertible securities. *Michigan Business Studies*, *12*, University of Michigan.

Ross, S.A., Westerfield, R.W., & Jaffe, J. (2005). *Corporate finance*. New York: McGraw-Hill Irwin.

Stein, J.C. (1992). Convertible bonds as backdoor equity financing. *Journal of Financial Economics*, *32*, 3–21.

Stiglitz, J.E., & Weiss, A. (1981). Credit rationing in markets with imperfect information. *The American Economic Review*, *71*, 393–410.

Veld, C. (1994). Motives for the issuance of warrant-bond loans by Dutch companies. *Journal of Multinational Financial Management*, *4*, 1–24.

Zwiebel, J. (1996). Dynamic capital structure under managerial entrenchment. *The American Economic Review*, *86*, 1197–1215.

Chapter 13

The Financing of Dutch Firms: A Historical Perspective[1]

Abe de Jong and Ailsa Röell

13.1. Introduction

Dutch financial markets and institutions were shaped by a unique mix of divergent influences. Elements of the mix include a stock exchange culture dating back to the Dutch Golden Age of sea borne trading dominance, a legal system handed down from a brief period of French occupation, and strong influences from neighbouring Germany as well as England and the USA.

In this chapter we provide an explorative study of the financing of Dutch exchange-listed firms in the twentieth century. We review the most relevant literature and provide a comparative analysis of Dutch listed firms over the course of the twentieth century by focusing on 3 years spaced at 35-year intervals: 1923, 1958 and 1993.

Received wisdom about financial structure has changed significantly over the twentieth century. The general opinion in our first year, 1923, is well represented in the doctoral thesis of a prominent financial economist of the time, Polak (1921). Polak argues that in setting their financial structure firms consider liquidity as a key driver. Firms aim to optimize liquid assets, relative to equity and interest and repayments on loans, while taking into account the collection period of accounts receivable and the turnover of accounts payable. The danger of a shortage of liquidity — and of an inability to meet short-term obligations — is considered more relevant than the cost of excessive liquidity.

Our second sample year is 1958, the year in which Nobel laureates Modigliani and Miller published the irrelevance theorems that were to revolutionize thinking about financial structure. However, at the time these theoretical constructs had not yet made their way into Dutch academe or practice. Speight and Duffhues (1966, Chapter 6) give a good overview of the consensus view of on financial structure at the time. A key idea is that maturities of debt are matched with those of the assets, that is, short debt is used for current assets, while long-debt finances fixed assets. Another viewpoint is the determination of the external financing needs (investments minus internal financing) in comparison with

Advances in Corporate Finance and Asset Pricing
Edited by L. Renneboog
© 2006 Elsevier B.V. All rights reserved.
ISBN: 0-444-52723-0

availability, where much attention is paid to specific financial instruments. Duffhues (1997, Chapter 4) provides an elaborate overview of these so-called golden balance sheet rules.

Finally, the viewpoint taken in 1993 as well as current thinking are also well described in Duffhues (1997) textbook. Building on Modigliani and Miller's (1958) irrelevance theorems, costs and benefits of debt and equity financing, such as tax costs and bankruptcy inefficiencies, are described. In this framework, each firm has an optimal debt ratio that minimizes the cost of capital. An interesting and unique intuition in the work of Duffhues is that a relatively large range of debt ratios near the single optimal value exists in which the cost of capital is nearly constant. Duffhues (1997: 283) refers to this as the "flat bottom of the bath tub" in which it is rational to let the debt ratio fluctuate.

This chapter first describes in brief the historical development of Dutch industrial finance in Section 13.2. The remaining of the chapter provides a comparative analysis of the financial characteristics of Dutch firms in the twentieth century, focusing on the years 1923, 1958 and 1993. A general description of the data and its sources is given in Section 13.3, presenting a wide array of financial characteristics of the firms. This is followed in Section 13.4 by an analysis of networks of influence. Section 13.5 discusses determinants of the capital structure in the 3 years of our sample. Section 13.6 concludes.

13.2. Historical Overview

13.2.1. General Introduction

The Dutch have some claim to a pioneering role in stock exchange capitalism. The first shareholdings in a Dutch corporation came into being in 1602, when the *Vereenigde Oostindische Compagnie* (*VOC*), the first great limited-liability joint stock company in the world, was founded. The initial investors were, in 1602, unaware of their destiny: ostensibly, they were contributing money to a limited-term partnership which would send out a series of merchant ships to the East Indies, with a liquidating dividend promised at the end of 20 years. To the investors' dismay (and despite their vociferous protests), in 1622 the company's directors (who reported to the government rather than to the shareholders) decided to prolong the company's charter, thus shelving the liquidation and keeping this astonishingly lucrative[2] enterprise going for many years.

By the middle of the seventeenth century the Netherlands had developed an active shareholding culture, with speculation in *VOC* shares and even derivatives trading a widespread popular pursuit. In the eighteenth century, the fortunes of the Dutch East India trade declined, and the *VOC* finally went under in 1799. Even so, the wealth amassed by the Dutch during the Golden Age was still largely undissipated, and primarily invested in a wide range of international government securities. A spate of defaults, notably by the French government, reduced this wealth and seriously undermined confidence in securities investment, but even in the nineteenth century there were still many wealthy rentier families whose riches were primarily held in the form of securities.[3]

In the early nineteenth century the Dutch nation emerged from the French occupation of 1795–1813; it assumed its present geographical contours with the separation of Belgium from the Netherlands in 1830. The first half of the nineteenth century was a period of continued economic stagnation: Dutch investment in infrastructure and the new steam-driven manufacturing technologies was minimal, and the country's industrial development lagged far, far behind that of Belgium, Germany, France and, of course, England. This period of retarded growth has been studied intensively by economic historians, and the consensus now seems to be that it cannot be attributed to a shortage of capital or to Dutch investors' supposed preference for foreign investments above domestic industry. Other factors seem more likely culprits. One was the disarray of government finances: the new Kingdom of the Netherlands inherited from the French a crushing debt burden of 420% of net national income, with concomitantly high interest rates on government paper; the situation was not brought under control until around 1850 (see Jonker, 1996). Another was the need to redefine the traditional division of labour within the low countries: the Southern provinces, now Belgium, had traditionally specialized in manufacturing while the North focused on commerce. Thus there was no strong manufacturing base to build on. Then there were the steep transport costs related to the extra cost of providing a proper infrastructure, with adequate drainage and flood defences, in such low-lying and water-logged territory; and various other factors such as the high cost of raw materials, and the high wage levels and the poor education of the citizenry.

Industrial development started coming to life in the second half of the nineteenth century, with new shareholder capital raised for a number of enterprises such as railway construction, *albeit* rather laboriously, buffeted by the vicissitudes of international political developments and the business cycle. The main source of capital for industry during that period seems to have been retained earnings, supplemented with contributions by members of the founding families and closely connected wealthy individuals. Interestingly, rather the meagre contribution of publicly raised equity was not offset by long-term bank loan finance: such financing was also very scarce throughout the country's industrialization.

The long period of stagnation of the eighteenth and early nineteenth centuries, and the short period of French hegemony, create a natural break in capital market traditions and institutions. Only very late in the nineteenth century did substantive modern industrial development get-off the ground, and therefore much of our enquiry into the origins of current corporate ownership and financing patterns and can start there, without going back all the way to the Dutch Golden Age. We turn now to the historical role of the stock exchange, banks and private financing in providing capital for industry.

13.2.2. Equity Financing and the Role of the Stock Market in Industrial Finance

The Amsterdam stock exchange was a sophisticated and active market throughout the nineteenth century. The *prolongatie* system funnelled large amounts of savings to the market. The market was overcrowded, open and competitive: the principle of unrestricted public access was carefully upheld by the city authorities, and premises were shared with commodities trading. However, the stock exchange did not initially play much of a direct role in the financing of industry. The bulk of the official list seems to have been made up of foreign state loans, American railway stocks, American industrial shares and colonial securities. The first date at which domestic industrial stock was officially listed on the Amsterdam stock exchange is generally reported to be a brewery listing in 1889, though

Jonker (1996) suggests this date is misleading; four industrial issues (from a sugar refinery, a shipyard and an engineering firm) were already quoted in the early 1880s. In any case a listing meant little before 1903, when listing requirements and a vetting process by the *Vereeniging voor Effectenhandel* (set up in 1876 to oversee the market and instil investor confidence) were formalized.

Meanwhile there was a large and active unlisted securities market on which domestic securities were both auctioned and directly placed; an example of a prime unlisted stock traded there during the last decades of the nineteenth century is Heineken. Shares were often initially privately placed, and Jonker (1996) cautions that a lack of domestic industrial stock exchange listings should not be interpreted as a definitive indicator of investor disinterest. A number of *naamloze vennootschappen (NVs)* set up in the 1840s and 1850s found ready backers; they did not seek a listing until the end of the century. By 1937/1939, private placements still encompassed 16.6% of bond issues and 4.8% of equity issues; and private "underhand" loans remained important right up until the eve of World War II: in 1938, institutional investors' portfolios still contained equal amounts of underhand loans and listed securities (Renooij, 1951: 186 and 190). Clearly, then, the Amsterdam stock exchange was not the sole venue for primary issues or for secondary trading. The dearth of domestic industrial listings cannot be interpreted as a sign of structural impediments to equity financing.

Van Zanden (1987; 1998) points out that external finance, *albeit* not obtained from the general public, played a major part in the industrialization of Amsterdam. Initially, money for capital-intensive new ventures would be supplied by the city's traditional trading elite. For example, merchants set up two companies for steamship transport and shipbuilding in hopes of stimulating trade. Similarly, rich and successful entrepreneurial dynasties would move into related industries: for example, the profits from sugar refining were ploughed back into beer brewing and flour milling concerns. Meanwhile, the government and King William I at times provided crucial credit lines. And in 1883 Amsterdam's financial elite contributed a capital of ƒ0.5 million for a banking venture, the *Finantieele Maatschappij voor Nijverheidsondernemingen*, whose explicit purpose was to provide finance for industry in the form of credit, in anticipation of repayment when a public share issue was completed.

Still, it is fair to say that infusions from a network of family, friends and business associates, complemented by retained earnings, were, in the Netherlands as in most other countries, the dominant source of risk capital for much of industry in the late nineteenth century. For example, the textile industry developing in the East and South of the country was almost exclusively financed in this way. The exception, rather than the rule, were large, capital-intensive infrastructure projects like railways, which typically relied on an initial primary issue of shares to the general public, sometimes combined with some form of limited government support, to get-off the ground.

13.2.3. The Role of Banks

A surprising feature of Dutch financial history (particularly when contrasted with the emergence of powerful universal banks in Germany in the late nineteenth century) is the negligible role played by banks in the financing of industrial growth, not just in the early period of industrialization of the late nineteenth century but well into the twentieth century. Dutch economic historians attribute the patchy record of late nineteenth century banking initiatives — banks were set up, but many failed, and the industry remained exceedingly fragmented well into the twentieth century — to a number of causes.

One major cause was the dominance of the *prolongatie* system of financing, which flourished throughout the late nineteenth and early twentieth century. *Prolongatie* refers to short-term callable margin loans, on the face of it a rather unlikely source of industrial finance. As a legacy from the successes of the Golden Age, the nineteenth-century Netherlands still had a strong stock market culture and a well-developed network of local agents (notaries, lawyers and brokers) who would collect savings from wealthy individuals and channel them to the stock exchange. Much of the money was not invested in securities directly, but made available to firms or other investors in the form of short-term margin loans. These, though of course callable at short notice, were typically rolled over or "prolonged", whence their name. They were backed by securities, commodities or other exchange-traded collateral. Thus industry and trade in effect obtained direct short-term capital in a very fragmented way, via margin loans provided by investors without the intermediation of a banking system. The *prolongatie* loans were considered safe, the interest rate was attractive and roughly tracked the London discount rate (hovering between 3% and 5% between 1820 and 1860, see Jonker (1996) Figure 12.4, p. 96). The system worked so smoothly that intermediation and liquidity transformation by a nascent banking system was effectively crowded out. This remained the case well into the twentieth century, as argued by Jonker (1995). On the eve of World War I, the amount outstanding on *prolongatie* at any point in time was around 400 million guilders; more than double the known deposits of all the banks taken together. Jonker (1996, see Figure 9.2, p. 191) points out that the short-term interest rate on the Amsterdam exchange remained at or above the yield on government bonds until nearly 1920, effectively precluding substantive profitable deposit taking by banks. The *prolongatie* market did not disappear until short rates fell dramatically towards the end of the 1920s.

Another brake on banking development was Dutch savers' distrust of financial institutions. The sovereign bond defaults of the late eighteenth century and the parlous state of government finances in the early nineteenth century (with government debt hovering around a staggering 400% of national income) meant that even the paper money circulated by the *Nederlandsche Bank* (*NB*) (set up in 1814 at the behest of King Willem I, an energetic supporter of initiatives to revive the Dutch economy) was long considered an unsafe substitute for specie. Private banking institutions were considered even more dubious; a view confirmed when the first wave of new banking ventures of the 1860s was followed by a spate of banking failures in the long recessionary period starting in 1870.

The industrial boom that started in 1895 precipitated a period of intense interest in industrial finance in the early twentieth century, right up until 1920. During this period many new companies were listed and public share offerings were readily absorbed. Banks, for this short period only, were prepared to offer long-term financing to industry. Meanwhile, a wave of banking consolidation from 1911 onwards, together with a major shakeout of minor and regional banks in the crisis that started in 1920 (in 1920–1922 a total of bad debts amounting to nearly 10% of the assets of the biggest five banks was written-off), left the general banking industry dominated by the "Big Five" banks.

Financing for industry completely dried up in the deflationary 1920s and did not revive until after World War II. Banks' reluctance to provide long-term financing for industry was the subject of intense debate; whilst large companies could fill the gap by issuing stocks and bonds, small and medium-sized enterprises were seriously constrained. The government went so far as to attempt to set up a bank for industrial finance in 1935 (it succumbed to the bad economic climate). The banks limited their role to collecting deposits (though, as Jonker (1995) shows, in the interbellum years Dutch banking deposits, and in particular time deposits, were still extraordinarily low relative to the total money supply compared with neighbouring countries), making short-term loans (maturities of over 3 months were avoided as much as possible), and underwriting new issues. While they dominated the new issue market from the 1930s onwards, they acted only as a conduit, never retaining equity stakes in industry or making long-term loan commitments.

In short the Dutch banks most resembled the British banks, not the universal banks of neighbouring Belgium and Germany, as stressed in Van Goor and Koelewijn's (1995) overview of Dutch banking in the twentieth century. Dutch bankers focused on mercantile finance and consistently veered away from long-term commitments. As "general" banks they did do a lot of underwriting and investment banking business (also carried out by some private specialized firms); there was no counterpart of the Glass-Steagall Act formally mandating the separation of commercial and investment banking.

In 1945, the *Herstelbank* (bank for reconstruction), a joint venture between the government and the financial sector, was set up to fill the perceived gap in finance for long-term investment by providing long-term loans (a subsidiary, the *Nationale Participatie Maatschappij*, was created to take equity stakes). It played an important role in the recovery of Dutch industry over the decade following World War II. Perhaps its example (and that of its various successors), together with other government policies, stimulated the commercial banks' slow evolution towards medium- and long-term lending in the 1950–1960 period. Meanwhile, banks did adhere to the fundamental principle of non-engagement in industry; and indeed, industry spokesmen at the time explicitly expressed reservations about bank influence on commercial and strategic decision-making.

The boom years of 1955–1970 saw a period of increased diversification, as specialized institutions such as the mortgage banks lost ground. A spate of large-scale bank mergers led to a fear that banks had too much market power and were exposing themselves to an unacceptably wide range of risks. Thus starting in 1971 the *NB*, as industry regulator, put out a number of unofficial directives (some of which were later codified in the *Wet Toezicht Kredietwezen 1978*) that prohibited mergers of general banks with insurance companies or mortgage banks, restricted bank participation in the equity of other companies (financial or non-financial) to 5% without explicit permission from the *NB*, and limited the value of share stakes held by banks to 60% of their capital.

The 1980s were a difficult period of retrenchment for the banks, and again the accusations that banks were excessively cautious led to the adoption of various government measures (such as loan guarantees) to encourage the provision of risk-taking capital. Meanwhile the international expansion of Dutch industry brought with it a continuing trend towards the formation of large banking conglomerates offering a wider range of financial services.

In 1990 banking and insurance regulation was radically loosened. Participation in the European Union (EU) has meant that Dutch banks' market power is no longer considered a threat. As an immediate consequence, more mergers in 1991 created the three current giant banks (ABN-Amro, ING Bank and Rabobank). And restrictions on banking-insurance alliances were lifted in accordance with EU practice. This has led to the formation of conglomerate groups holding substantial share stakes in large numbers of companies. Thus a gradual trend away from the Anglo-Saxon model and towards a more Continental style of banking is in evidence.

13.2.4. Non-bank Institutional Investors: Insurance Companies and Pension Funds

Insurance companies and pension funds have played a role in taking equity stakes, absorbing bond issues and providing long-term loans at least since the beginning of the twentieth century. Our data for 1993 show that both the *ING Bank* and the *AEGON* insurance group had substantial long-term stakes in other companies (note that *ING* was formed in 1991 by a merger involving amongst others the large insurance company *Nationale Nederlanden*).

Institutional investors rose to a prominent place in the Dutch capital markets during the early decades of the twentieth century.[4] Traditionally, nineteenth century life insurers had invested primarily in securities that were judged to be particularly safe and liquid; many of them invested exclusively in Dutch government bonds, and indeed, many were restricted to do so by their statutes. The twentieth century saw a gradual lifting of these restrictions, but investment in private issuers' securities remained only a small fraction of their investments. In the pre-World War I burst of enthusiasm for industrialization, a typical life insurer, *Eerste Nederlandsche*, invested as much as 4% of its assets in banking and 7% in manufacturing securities; these were predominantly bonds rather than equity. Interest in privately issued securities then dwindled down to almost zero, until it revived in the late 1930s; by 1939, the precursor companies of *AEGON* held about 5% of their assets in manufacturing company securities, whilst over time the balance had shifted from bonds to equity (Gales, 1986). Still, round 1950 life insurers' investment in industrial securities remained modest, indeed, the proportion was lower than at the turn of the century. Insurers did also make some contributions to industrial finance in the form of direct long-term loans (*onderhandse leningen*)[5] and mortgages. But the trend towards equity and non-government bonds did not gather force until the second half of the twentieth century.

Regarding pension funds, to illustrate their contribution to equity financing, consider the combined Philips pension funds, founded in 1913, described in Appendix 2d of Van Nederveen Meerkerk and Peet (2002). Equity comprised a mere 2% of the fund's total investment in 1925; most of the fund was invested in (government) bonds. By 1950, equity took a 7% share, rising to 28% in 1975 and 46% in 2000. By then, the Philips pension fund was holding ƒ16,771 million in equity, together with ƒ106 million in venture participations. Here again we see very modest interest in risk-bearing capital in the first half of the century, with a marked shift towards investment in corporate equity in the second half of the century.

In any case, it does not seem to be the case that institutional equity ownership has been matched by an active role in corporate decision-making. The discussion surrounding the recent management crises at *Ahold* and other major Dutch companies gives some insight into why the independent, public sector employee pension fund *Algemeen Burgerlijk Pensioenfonds* (*ABP*) is one of the few Dutch institutional investors to attempt an activist stance. As pointed out by an insurance company spokesman, banks and insurance companies are not only shareholders: for them, the firm in which they invest is at the same time a (potential) client: "You are in a difficult position if you want to present a new contract to the management board whilst you have voted against one of their proposals the day before."[6] Meanwhile, activism by private companies' pension funds is likely to be reined in by the parent company's management, in return for reciprocal restraint by their counterparts' pension funds. Institutional shareholder activism thus remains somewhat limited in scope and potential.

13.2.5. Governance and Control

Dutch attitudes to the role of corporations have evolved considerably over the course of the twentieth century. In the beginning of the century, corporations were seen as vehicles for shareholder's wealth creation. Over the course of the century, firms became to be seen as more independent entities oriented towards continuity, stability and the interests of multiple stakeholders, as expressed in a salient *Hoge Raad* (Supreme Court) decision of 1949. It is perhaps the relative homogeneity of the Dutch population that has fostered a sense of solidarity, expressed in a preference for consensus decision-making and a generous welfare system. The corporatist model of centralized, consensual economic decision-making, known as the *Poldermodel*, was very successful in the reconstruction of the Dutch economy after World War II. In particular, centralized collective bargaining made possible a lengthy period of wage restraint that contributed substantially to economic growth. In return, employee representation in decisions regarding job security and employment is considered appropriate. And indeed, any corporate restructuring that involves the loss of jobs imposes a significant cost on the public purse in the form of unemployment and/or disability pay. This means that corporate decision-making has a direct public interest dimension. Not surprisingly, the stakeholder view of corporate governance, which sees shareholders as just one of many interested parties entitled to a say in decision-making, dominates Dutch public opinion.

The *structuurregeling* or "structured regime", introduced in 1971, was designed to increase worker participation by imposing a carefully defined control structure on all larger firms (roughly speaking, those with at least 100 employees). Such firms must set up an *ondernemingsraad* or company council (to be referred to as *OR*), a body created to represent and consult the views of employees.[7] These and other large firms (those with capital and reserves of at least ƒ25 million) are also obliged to set up a Supervisory Board (*raad van commissarissen*) with some powers that might otherwise be held by the shareholders' meeting. Such a board appoints new members itself by co-optation (unless the Shareholders' Meeting or Council object), and the statutes may determine that one or more are to be government appointees. The board supervises important managerial decisions, appoints and dismisses the management board (*raad van bestuur*), establishes and approves the yearly accounts (De Jong, DeJong, Mertens, & Wasley 2005).

A perhaps unintended side effect of the *structuurregime* is that, because it gives shareholders almost no say in the appointment or removal of supervisory board members and management, it protects entrenched management to an excessive degree. The co-optation system is currently the topic of intense public debate and unlikely to survive in its current form.

The most recent developments in the Netherlands are two best practices codes for publicly listed firms. The first code was put forth by the Peters Committee, named after former

Aegon-CEO Jaap Peters, in 1997. This code contains 40 recommendations, about the role of management, supervisory boards and, most importantly, a reconsideration of the role of capital in governance. As 39 (out of the 40) recommendations did not involve legal changes, the code's implementation relies on self-regulation. De Jong, DeJong, Mertens, and Wasley (2005) shows that this effort failed, as no observable changes were present and stock market reactions, if present, were negative. After the irregularities with *Ahold*, an initiative was taken to restore investors' confidence in the Dutch market. In March 2003 a committee chaired by Morris Tabaksblat, former CEO of *Unilever*, started work on a new code, releasing a final draft in December 2003. Following the example of the successful UK codes, the comply-or-explain principle is introduced, which forces firms to explain to shareholders the rationale for any deviations from best practices. Although the contents of the code largely overlap with the Peters Committee's ideas, the outlook for enforcement is more promising.

13.3. Empirical Analysis: The Data

13.3.1. The Sample of Firms

Our study focuses on all domestic firms that have equity officially listed on the Amsterdam stock exchange in the years examined. It should be pointed out that this concept is somewhat different from the usual definition of "listed firms" for the Netherlands, which also includes firms whose bonds only are listed. Traditionally, many of the security issues listed and traded on the Amsterdam exchange have been bonds; though the proportion of listed firms that list only their bonds and not their stock as well is relatively small (e.g. 17% in 1910). One reason to exclude these firms from our sample is that they are somewhat less likely to comply with the obligation to publish annual accounts.

The universe of firms for which we present data also excludes the financial sector. In 1923 this sector comprises mainly banks and mortgage banks. In the second half of the century insurance firms and collective investment vehicles such as mutual funds are important additional constituents of this group. Our main data sources for information about the non-financial firms are *Van Oss' Effectenboek* for 1923 and 1958, and the electronic database REACH (Review and Analysis of Companies in Holland) for 1993.

It should be noted that many of the largest Dutch firms are not listed, so that our sample cannot be said to represent all the most important Dutch companies. Sluyterman and Winkelman (1993) identify the 100 largest Dutch firms in terms of their assets. Even though they point out that their methodology probably under-represents privately held firms because their balance sheet data are harder to obtain and their accounting practices are generally more conservative, they still find that only about three-fourth of these firms are listed. Agricultural firms (and their food-processing outgrowths) in particular are often organized as cooperatives, as are the banks that specialize in agricultural loans (the *Rabobank* and its precursors).

13.3.2. The Three Sample Years

Our data were gathered for 3 years spaced at 35-year intervals: 1923, 1958 and 1993. In choosing these particular years we were influenced by at least two considerations.

Firstly, we would like to have years that were in some sense typical of an epoch:

- 1923 comes towards the end of the first great boom in industrial development; it is still a year of relative prosperity, predating the subsequent collapse in share prices, the depression and the Second World War.
- 1958 is a year in which the economic dislocation wrought by the war has receded: post-war reconstruction is virtually complete, and a new era of prosperity and growth has set in.
- 1993 is a year in which the impact of EU membership has already shaped many developments.

Secondly, our aim was to try and pick years which as much as possible enabled us to complement rather than duplicate the available body of work on Dutch economic history.

13.3.3. Data Availability

For most limited-liability companies, the publication of annual accounts was not legally required in the Netherlands until 1928. However, from 1909 the stock exchange's *Fondensreglement* required all companies that wished to list their stocks or bonds to make available to shareholders' annual published accounts comprising the balance sheet and profit- and loss-statements. By 1910, about 80% of listed firms complied in whole or in part, though the level of compliance was considerably lower (around 50%) among manufacturing firms. By 1923, our first sample year, compliance (as measured by the availability of accounts in *Van Oss' Effectenboek*) had risen considerably.

For 1923 and 1958 the way we investigate family influence and control is by tracking the identities of the management and the board of directors, both available for much of the late nineteenth and the twentieth century from published sources.[8]

13.3.4. Summary Statistics

As shown in Table 13.1, the number of firms on the Amsterdam Stock Exchange's official list has actually declined over the last few decades studied. The decline in numbers is off-set by a substantial increase in size; the average book value of assets increased more than hundredfold over the 70 years from 1923 to 1993, a period during which prices (as measured by the gross domestic product (GDP) deflator) rose by a factor of 12. To some extent these trends are attributable to mergers and consolidation; but a tendency to limit the Exchange's Official List to very large and liquid companies may also play a role.

The data regarding the 3-year growth in assets show that 1923 followed on a difficult period; indeed, there had been a serious economic downturn, and overall stock market equity prices had fallen by about one-half during the immediately preceding decade.

The median return on assets (ROA) fluctuated between a low of 4.7% in 1923 and a high of 11.3% in 1958, down to 7.4% in 1993. ROA in 1923 is net profits/equity; in other years operating income/book value total assets.

The median payout ratio of 0.31 that we obtain for 1923 is somewhat on the low side both in historical and international perspective. In the nineteenth century, the norm was to

Table 13.1: Summary statistics.
Medians are reported in parentheses below the means.

	1923		1958		1993	
Book value total assets (× f1000)	13,673 (3158)		79,700 (9314)		2,286,000 (360,000)	
Past 3-year growth book value total assets	−0.077 (−0.074)	n = 303	0.161 (0.102)	n = 318	0.170 (0.080)	n = 141
Return on assets	0.073 (0.047)	n = 317	0.159 (0.113)	n = 321	0.073 (0.074)	n = 143
Payout ratio	0.375 (0.311)	n = 300	0.716 (0.440)	n = 323	0.369 (0.363)	n = 143
Debt/total assets	0.300 (0.280)		0.339 (0.325)		0.535 (0.536)	
Fixed assets/total assets	0.552 (0.578)		0.404 (0.352)		0.381 (0.355)	
Cash and liquid assets/ total assets	0.114 (0.050)		0.124 (0.084)		0.107 (0.041)	
Age	21.80 (18)	n = 317	47.12 (46)	n = 333	48.75 (36)	n = 84
Managerial board size	2.158 (2)		2.318 (2)		2.776 (2)	
Supervisory board size	4.874 (5)		4.540 (4)		5.167 (5)	
Family firm: (former) firm name equals board member's surname	28.1%		27.6%		6.3%	
Family firm: at least two board members with same surname	31.5%		29.1%		5.6%	
Family firm based on both criteria	16.4%		16.2%		1.3%	
Family firm based on at least one criterion	43.2%		40.5%		10.4%	
Number of firms	317		333		143	

pay out most or all of its earnings, perhaps with some retentions from extraordinary profits to create a reserve for use in smoothing dividends in bad years. In the first two decades of the twentieth century, it gradually became accepted practice to retain earnings for the purpose of expansion. However, payout ratios were generally still very high; and Post (1972, Table 5) cites a payout ratio of 0.78 in 1923 for all Dutch *NV*s (not just listed ones). One point to note is that 1923 was not a good year for the economy, coming at the end of the depression of 1921–1923. Many of the firms in our data set made losses, and nearly half of the firms passed their dividend; the median payout ratio for the firms that did pay out a non-zero dividend was 0.75, which is very close to Post's figure.

Our data source, *Van Oss' Effectenboek*, sometimes gives fairly detailed information about the disposition of profits, both as stipulated in the company charters and as carried out *ex post*. A striking feature of the 1923 data is the substantial proportion that is statutorily destined for the executives and directors in the form of *tantièmes* or profit-sharing agreements. The norm for statutory payouts of this nature is in the region of 15% of profits, which suggests that such payments should perhaps be interpreted in part as a reflection of the ownership rights of the individuals concerned rather than just as remuneration for executive effort. But in practice, the actual payments made often fall far short of the profit sharing payouts stipulated *ex ante* in the company statutes.

By 1958 the mean (median) payout ratio was 0.72 (0.44), declining to 0.37 (0.36) in 1993. Payout ratios declined secularly until the 1980s, as firms chose to retain earnings to finance expansion. A probable contributing factor was the introduction of a corporation tax, phased in around 1941. A classical system is in force: corporate earnings are taxed at 35%, whether distributed or not, and dividends are subsequently taxed as personal income at a heavy 60% marginal rate, while there is no capital gains tax. Indeed, of the 33 countries studied by La Porta, Lopez-de-Silanes, Shleifer, and Vishny. (1998), the Netherlands tax regime has the rock bottom ratio of net-of-tax payout from dividends relative to capital gains. Accordingly, one would expect Dutch personal investors to have little enthusiasm for dividend payouts, and a preference for retained earnings. Such a preference would be less likely on the part of those institutional investors that are exempted from income tax. While the Dutch tax system does not attempt to mitigate the double taxation of dividends at the corporate and personal income tax levels, it has traditionally been exceptionally careful in ensuring that inter-corporate dividends are not double-taxed at the corporate level. This feature of the tax regime is one reason why the Netherlands (and in particular the Netherlands Antilles) is popular as a base for international holding companies.

Leverage as measured by the ratio of debt to total assets exhibits a marked increase from a median of 0.32 in 1958 to 0.54 in 1993. Again, the corporate tax shield from debt may explain this increase in leverage in the post-war half century.

The sizes of the managerial and supervisory boards remained fairly constant over the 70-year period studied. Meanwhile, founding family influence seems to have declined dramatically. Our proxies for family influence are two: one is the presence of board members with the founding family surname; the other is multiple board members with a common surname. These indicators of family presence declined only slightly from 1923 to 1958; but there was a large reduction from 1958 to 1993. Both criteria for family influence dropped by a factor of about 5, from roughly 30% to 6%, leaving only a total of 10.4% of firms in 1993 still exhibiting one or both indicators of family influence.

13.4. Networks of Influence: Interlocking Board Memberships

13.4.1. Boards and Networks

In this section we will focus on the phenomenon of interlocking directorates, that is, of having the same individual occupy board seats in multiple firms. Two aspects of this practice will be looked at:

Firstly, the number of appointments per board member is studied. Members with multiple appointments may have reputational capital, that is, they may be excellent managers or monitors. On the other hand, multiple appointments may reduce the time available for individual firms, reducing the effectiveness. Pritchard, Ferris and Jagannathan (2003) provide recent evidence in US firms and find no negative effects of multiple appointments. For the Netherlands, there is no evidence relating network relationships to firm performance but a wealth of descriptive evidence regarding interlocking directorates. To name but two prominent studies, Schijf (1993) describes networks in 1886 and 1902 and Stokman, Wasseur and Elsas (1985) focus on networks in 1976 in the context of an international comparative project.

A second aspect of interlocking directorates that is of particular interest is the relation between banks and non-financial firms. Bank relations may bring expertise to the board of non-financial firms. Besides, bank relations may offer monitoring, which reduces contracting costs. On the other hand, banks may abuse their power and information to expropriate wealth from other lenders and shareholders; recent studies on US firms are Booth and Deli (1999), and Kroszner and Strahan (2001). The relations between banks and non-financials have been studied in the Netherlands by, among others, Van den Broeke (1988) and Jonker (1989). Van den Broeke selects four industrial firms and one bank, and describes the interlocking directorships. The bank, *Rotterdamsche Bankvereeniging*, has joint board member with three out of four firms through eight interlocks in the period 1918–1939; even though throughout this period it did not make a single long-term loan to any of the firms concerned, in line with Dutch banking practice at the time. Jonker (1989) selects eight banks and measures interlocks with non-financial exchange-listed firms in 1910, 1923, 1931 and 1940. For example, in 1923, the eight banks had 43 board members and these persons held 431 board positions outside the banks.

Interlocking directorships can involve both executive and supervisory board members. Dutch firms have dual board systems on the German model. The first tier comprises the executive board (*Directeuren* or *Raad van Bestuur*): the management team that is responsible for the firm's strategy and daily operations. These executives are supervised by the second tier, the supervisory board (*Raad van Commissarissen* or *Raad van Toezicht*).

In 1923, supervisory boards were not a legal requirement (Bos 1923: 34). Nonetheless, all exchange-listed firms in 1923 do have a supervisory board. The members are normally appointed by the shareholders' meeting. In special cases, the owners of preferred shares, priority shares or bonds have the right to appoint all or a limited number of supervisors. Intermediate arrangements existed where other parties than the shareholders propose members, while the shareholders can reject the proposal.

In 1993, a supervisory board is a legal obligation for firms that adopt the so-called *structuurregeling* or structured regime, introduced in 1971. This regime is compulsory for firms that meet size criteria (in particular, those that have more than a cut-off number of domestic employees). In 1993, again, all the listed firms have supervisory boards.

13.4.2. Data Sources

Our aim is to describe the relevance of interlocks for non-financial firms. First, we describe the interlocks with other non-financial firms. Second, we focus on interlocks between banks and non-financials.

The focus for non-financial firms is simply on all exchange-listed firms. For 1923 and 1958 we use *Van Oss' Effectenboek*. For 1993 we mainly use *REACH* and *Jaarboek Nederlandse Ondernemingen*.

For the identification of board members of banks we do not want to restrict ourselves to listed banks, because especially in 1923, several important banks were unlisted partnerships. Therefore we select the largest banks. For 1923 we use the *Financieel Adresboek voor Nederland* issued by *J.H. de Bussy*. This book contains the section *Financiëele instellingen in Nederland* with for each financial institution its name, its placed equity and reserves, and the names of its board members. The book includes listed and non-listed institutions. For 1958 we use the same book and collect bank information from the section *Bank- en credietwezen*. For 1993 we use *Omzetcijfers 1993*, issued in 1994 by *Het Financieele Dagblad*. This guide contains the banks and other financial institutions in the Netherlands, including total assets. The board members of most banks are in the *Jaarboek Nederlandse Ondernemingen* and, if not, obtained from annual reports.

For 1923 we identify 504 banks, of which 423 banks have available a book value of equity (placed equity plus reserves). Total equity value is 1319 million guilders. The first 60 firms have 1213 million guilders of equity value, or 92% of the total. The smallest firm in the selection of 60 has equity worth 200,000 guilders. Of these 60, 32 are listed on the Amsterdam stock exchange. The five largest banks have 49% of the total equity value and the 10 largest 67%.

In 1958, we traced 148 banks, with total equity value of 1099 million guilders. The largest 50 banks have 96% (1061 million guilders). The five largest banks have 48% of the total equity value and the 10 largest 69%.

In 1993, we have 71 banks (general and savings banks) and for 56 we have a book value of total assets. Total value is 1,309,788 million guilders. We select the 11 largest banks, but exclude two banks for governmental financing. We also include three smaller banks that are known for longstanding relations with non-financials. The 11 banks have a total asset value of 1,084,151 guilders, or 91% (excluding governmental banks). The difference with 1923 is striking and in particular caused by the dominance of three large banks: *ABN-AMRO, Rabobank* and *ING*.

13.4.3. Results and Analysis

Table 13.2 describes the interlocks of board members of non-financial listed firms for 1923, 1958 and 1993.

The first six rows in Table 13.2 describe our sample of (non-financial) firms and banks. The average board size has fluctuated somewhat: the average total number of board

Table 13.2: Boards and interlocks.

	1923	1958	1993
Number of firms	317	333	143
Number of managerial board members	684	772	397
Number of supervisory board members	1545	1512	739
Number of banks	57	50	12
Number of managerial board members	238	159	60
Number of supervisory board members	432	361	122
Firms: umber of managerial board members			
With one interlock	137	127	38
With two interlocks	56	38	13
With three interlocks	32	21	6
With four interlocks	39	6	3
With five interlocks	11	19	0
With more than five interlocks	61	25	0
Total interlocks	1248	599	94
Average number of interlocks	1.82	0.78	0.24
Firms: number of supervisory board members			
With one interlock	371	328	170
With two interlock	205	175	89
With three interlocks	136	131	90
With four interlocks	141	69	32
With five interlocks	49	77	6
With more than five interlocks	170	220	0
Total interlocks	3440	3606	776
Average number of interlocks	2.23	2.39	1.05

members per firm decreased slightly from 7.03 in 1923 to 6.86 in 1958, increasing by 1 to 7.94 by 1993. It is important to notice that the number of banks in our sample declines from 57 to 12 over the 70-year period studied; as mentioned in our discussion of the data selection procedure, ongoing concentration in the banking system means that the proportion of total banking equity value represented by our sample remains roughly constant at over 90%. Not surprisingly, as the banks in the 1993 sample are so much larger, they have more board members: 15.2 on average, as opposed to 11.7 (10.4) in 1923 (1958). Meanwhile for both banks and industrial firms, the ratio of supervisory board members to management board members remained fairly steady, ranging between 1.82 and 2.27.

Table 13.2 shows us whether board members have more or less additional board seats. For managerial board members (including the chairman), our findings indicate that members in 1923 held many more positions than in 1958 or 1993: the average number of interlocks dropped from 1.82 in 1923 down to 0.24 in 1993. For supervisory board members the average number of interlocks decreased less dramatically, in the post-war period the average number fell by roughly one half. In 1923 we also find quite a few board members with more than five interlocks; by 1993, no board member had more than five additional seats.

In the remaining of this section we focus on industrial-firm board members who have affiliations with banks.

Table 13.3 contains the frequency distributions of bank interlocks in firms. Banking interlocks were more widespread in the earlier periods of our investigation: the proportion of firms with no bank interlocks was 40% (39%) in 1923 (1958), rising to 55% in 1993. Thus in 1923 and 1958, presence of bankers was more widespread than in 1993. In 1923, 12 firms even had 10 or more bankers on the board. The average number of board member with a bank affiliation decreases from 0.60 (0.61) in 1923 (1958) to 0.45 in 1993. However, it should be noted that the significant concentration in the banking industry over the 1958–1993 period would have led to a decline in the number of bank board members available for positions on industrial firm boards.

The use of interlocks by banks is illustrated in Table 13.4, which lists all banks with at least 10 (15) interlocks in 1958/1993 (1923). It is clear that there has been a substantial decline in the latter period of the century in the number of major-bank board members that sit directly on industrial-firm boards.[9]

Table 13.5 further documents the decline in interlocks, contrasting banks' and other industrial firms' board members' role on industrial-firm boards. Industrial-firm interlocks have declined steeply over the 70 years of our investigation; the overall decline in the average number of interlocks is by roughly a half. While multiple supervisory board memberships are still very common, interlocks involving management board members in particular have fallen steeply. Indeed, by 1993 there was no industrial firm in our sample sharing a common management board member with a bank or o[ther industrial firm.

Meanwhile, the role of banks in industrial firm board interlocks was falling even more rapidly than that of industrial peers. Again, bank-industry interlocks involving a management

Table 13.3: Frequency distribution bank interlocks.

	1923	1958	1993
Fraction of firms with			
No bank interlocks	40.38%	39.34%	55.24%
One bank interlock	22.08%	26.43%	25.87%
Two bank interlocks	12.30%	13.81%	9.09%
Three bank interlocks	7.89%	6.61%	5.59%
Four bank interlocks	5.05%	5.11%	3.50%
Five bank interlocks	4.42%	3.00%	0.70%
Six bank interlocks	1.26%	0.90%	0%
Seven bank interlocks	0%	1.20%	0%
Eight bank interlocks	0.63%	0.60%	0%
Nine bank interlocks	2.21%	0.90%	0%
Ten or more bank interlocks	3.79%	2.10%	0%
Average number of bank interlocks	0.596	0.607	0.447

Table 13.4: Banks and their interlocks.

Banks	Interlocks
1923 (over 15)	
Rotterdamsche Bankvereeniging	119
Nationale Bankvereeniging	56
Bank voor Indië	55
De Twentsche Bank	50
Nederlandsche Handel-Maatschappij	43
Hollandsche Bank voor Zuid-Amerika	31
Koloniale Bank	31
De Nederlandsche Bank	26
Kas-Vereeniging	26
Amsterdamsche Bank	19
Bank-Associatie Wertheim & Gompertz 1834 en Credietvereeniging 1853	18
Nederlandsch Indische Handelsbank	16
1958 (over 10)	
Rotterdamsche Bank N.V.	149
De Nederlandsche Bank N.V.	73
De Twentsche Bank N.V.	63
Nederlandsche Handel-Maatschappij N.V.	51
Amsterdamsche Bank N.V.	46
Nationale Handelsbank N.V.	20
Bank voor Handel en Scheepvaart N.V.	20
N.V. Export-Financiering-Maatschappij	19
N.V. Nederlandsche Bankinstelling voor Waarden belast met Vruchtgebruik en Periodieke Uitkeringen	19
Van Mierlo en Zoon N.V.	19
Nederlandse Overzee Bank N.V.	14
N.V. Hollandsche Disconteeringsmaatschappij van 1939	12
N.V. Hollandsche Koopmansbank	12
Kas-Associatie N.V.	11
Maatschappij voor Middellang Crediet N.V	11
Hollandsche Bank Unie N.V.	11
1993 (over 10)	
ABN-AMRO	34
Internationale Nederlanden Bank (ING)	18
Nationale Investeringsbank	18
MeesPierson	14

board member fell very steeply, far more so than those involving two supervisory boards. A further decline in bank interlocks over the period 1976–1996 is documented by Heemskerk, Mokken and Fennema (2003), who find that finance-industry interlocks declined by almost 40% over that period, outpacing the 25% decline in overall interlocks.

Table 13.5: Interlocks at firm level.
Average number of interlock and in parentheses fraction of firms with at least one interlock.

Own firm — other firm — type of other firm	1923	1958	1993
Supervisory board — supervisory board — industrial	5.997 (83.9%)	6.327 (79.9%)	3.441 (74.1%)
Supervisory board — management board — industrial	1.079 (46.7%)	0.901 (42.3%)	0.454 (37.8%)
Management board — supervisory board — industrial	1.530 (31.5%)	0.921 (24.6%)	0.454 (20.3%)
Management board — management board — industrial	1.000 (25.6%)	0.366 (12.3%)	0 (0%)
Supervisory board — supervisory board — bank	1.202 (46.7%)	1.285 (53.7%)	0.622 (40.6%)
Supervisory board — management board — bank	0.461 (29.0%)	0.198 (17.4%)	0.077 (7.7%)
Management board — supervisory board — bank	0.293 (11.4%)	0.201 (8.4%)	0.084 (7.7%)
Management board — management board — bank	0.287 (3.8%)	0.012 (0.9%)	0 (0%)

13.5. Financing

In this section we conduct a cross-sectional regression analysis of the determination of the capital structure of the firms in our three sample years. The dependent variable is the debt ratio, that is, debt over total (book value) assets. The explanatory variables are intended to represent several theories. The logarithm of the book value of total assets is a measure of firm size, which proxies for bankruptcy costs. We expect that larger firms have more debt, both because their business is more diversified and because of economies of scale in bankruptcy procedures. The historical growth rate is a measure for the firm's growth opportunities. According to existing empirical work for U.S. firms (e.g. Smith and Watts 1992) leverage is lower in firms with larger growth potential.

Fixed assets have two potential relations with debt. First, fixed assets can be collateralized in debt contracts, reducing expected bankruptcy costs. Thus fixed assets as a fraction of total assets would positively affect the debt ratio. Second, the maturity matching principle relates fixed assets to equity and long-term debt and current assets to current debt. Thus, we now expect a negative relation between fixed assets and debt. The ROA has a mechanical relation with capital structure because the fraction of profits that is retained increases equity; ROA is thus expected to reduce debt.

Liquidity, measured as cash and liquid assets, is an important element in the traditional literature. We expect that firms with higher liquidity can match these funds with larger future obligations from debt. In the contemporary literature liquidity reserves reduce the bankruptcy probability and allow the use of more debt financing.

We also include a dummy variable for family firms. Although we have no strong prior about this variable, we are interested in the result for the early periods in which family control was widespread in listed firms.

The interlocking directorates are distinguished along two criteria. First, the interlocks are separated out by board type, that is, whether the management board member is, in the other company, on the management board (*RvB–RvB*) or on the supervisory board (*RvB–RvC*); Similarly for supervisory board members (the two resultant categories are *RvC–RvB* and *RvC–RvC*). Second, we treat interlocks with industrial and financial firms separately.

The results of our regressions confirm the expected positive effect of firm size on debt; and the coefficients are significant in 1923 and 1993. The historical growth rate is significant in 1958, but does not have the predicted sign. Apparently, growing firms had less equity in 1958; a result that is more consistent with the pecking order theory of capital structure than with static trade-off theory. For fixed assets we reject the bankruptcy cost hypothesis. Instead a negative effect is found, which is significant in 1958. This evidence is in line with the matching principle of fixed assets with equity financing. The coefficients for ROA are significantly negative in 1923, corroborating the expected mechanical relation (Table 13.6).

A striking result emerges for liquidity, which is significantly negatively related with leverage in all three sample years. We hypothesized a positive relation. Both the traditional reasoning and contemporary trade-off theory cannot provide an explanation for this consistent pattern; again, the pecking order theory of financing seems more consistent with the evidence.

Table 13.6: Regression analysis for debt ratio.

	1923		1958		1993	
	(1)	(2)	(1)	(2)	(1)	(2)
Intercept	−0.135* (−1.92)	−0.155* (−2.02)	0.386*** (5.45)	0.361*** (4.33)	0.512*** (10.01)	0.475*** (8.61)
Log (book value)	0.062*** (7.58)	0.072*** (7.60)	0.006 (0.81)	0.002 (0.18)	0.016* (1.97)	0.019* (1.76)
Past 3-year growth book value total assets	0.011 (0.62)	0.005 (0.30)	0.055* (1.90)	0.051* (1.70)	0.037 (1.20)	0.032 (1.02)
Fixed assets/total assets	−0.060 (−1.44)	−0.064 (−1.45)	−0.152*** (−3.70)	−0.149*** (−3.38)	−0.076 (−1.18)	−0.085 (−1.29)
Return on assets	−0.141*** (−3.23)	−0.156*** (−3.55)	−0.005 (−0.07)	0.019 (0.282)	−0.276 (−1.45)	−0.251 (−1.31)
Cash and liquid assets/total assets	−0.343*** (−4.34)	−0.340*** (−4.20)	−0.366*** (−4.48)	−0.343*** (−4.07)	−0.255** (−2.28)	−0.244** (−2.28)
Dummy family firm		−0.070** (−2.39)		0.061* (2.02)		—

Dummy interlock RvC–RvC/industrial	−0.028 (−0.92)		0.040 (1.28)		0.029 (0.74)
Dummy interlock RvC–RvB/industrial	0.001 (0.03)		0.003 (0.12)		0.046 (1.48)
Dummy interlock RvB–RvC/industrial	−0.051* (−1.90)		−0.046 (−1.60)		−0.027 (−0.72)
Dummy interlock RvB–RvB/industrial	−0.038 (−1.48)		0.065 (1.77)*		—
Dummy interlock RvC–RvC/bank	0.017 (0.73)		0.022 (0.86)		−0.027 (−0.81)
Dummy interlock RvC–RvB/bank	−0.034 (−1.41)		0.025 (0.82)		−0.023 (−0.44)
Dummy interlock RvB–RvC/bank	0.034 (0.87)		0.020 (0.41)		−0.022 (−0.37)
Dummy interlock RvB–RvB/bank	0.014 (0.24)		0.109 (0.77)		—
Adj R^2	0.22	0.09	0.10	0.05	0.05
Observations	302	308	308	141	141

Notes: White heteroscedasticity-consistent *t*-values. Observations with payout < 0 removed.
Statistically significant levels at: ***1%, **5% and *10% indicated.

The dummy for family firms only has sufficient variation in 1923 and 1958. In both years the coefficients are significant, but the sign changes from negative in 1923 to positive in 1958. A possible explanation is that in 1923, family firms had still only very recently emerged onto the publicly listed market, and their traditional reliance on internally generated (equity) funding is still in evidence. In contrast, by 1958 their relatively high debt ratio could result from a reluctance to dilute family control by seeking outside equity finance for the substantial growth and reconstruction, taking place in the immediate aftermath of World War II (see Sluyterman 2003: 198). We also investigate interlocking directorates to measure the impact of firm–bank relationships. Interestingly, we find no significant impact of bankers on the board on leverage.

Finally the adjusted R^2s are between 0.05 in 1993 and 0.24 in 1923. We see two reasons for this relatively low explanatory power of our regressions. The first reason is our model setup: we may have omitted relevant variables in our regressions, and measurement error will influence our analysis. The second reason stems from the intuition in the work of Duffhues (1997) that a relatively large range of debt ratios near the single optimal value exists ("flat bottom of the bath tub") in which the cost of capital is nearly constant. As within this range it is rational to let the debt ratio fluctuate, we cannot expect our regressions to predict leverage perfectly.

13.6. Conclusions

Our chapter gives a bird's-eye overview of financing of Dutch listed firms over the past century. We provide a historical sketch from the literature and an exploratory empirical analysis for 1923, 1958 and 1993. The role of banks in the control and financing of Dutch industry seems to have been rather secondary, and more British than German in nature. We document the presence of widespread firm–bank relations through interlocking directorates in Dutch firms. However, we find no effect from these interlocks on capital structure choice. Furthermore, our empirical analysis on the determinants of leverage shows strong fluctuation over the century. Firm size, growth, fixed assets and profitability all exhibit in one or two years the expected relations with leverage. We find a consistently negative effect of liquidity on leverage in all three years, which is puzzling from the viewpoint of static trade-off theory.

Endnotes

1. Paper prepared for the Liber Amicorum of Piet Duffhues entitled "Advances in Corporate Finance and Asset Pricing". The paper is adapted from "Financing and control in The Netherlands: a historical perspective", 2005, in: The History of Corporate Governance around the World: Family Business Groups to Professional Managers, R. Morck (Ed.), NBER. We thank Henry van Beusichem and Esther Koomen for excellent research assistance.
2. By the time of its last dividend in 1782, an initial investment of ƒ100 in the *VOC* would have yielded ƒ360 033.33 in payouts (Steensgaard, 1982). Steensgaard gives an insightful discussion of how the novel corporate form of the *VOC* made this enduring profitability possible, for example by facilitating long-term investments in the military protection of trading routes and monopolies.

3. The rentier class were popularly referred to as coupon-cutters: "... ces rentiers hollandais que le peuple appelle ironiquement *coupon-knippers*, parce qu'ils n'ont rien à faire, sauf à detacher les coupons semestriels de leurs fonds publics", Emile de Laveleye, L'économie rurale en Néerlande, *Revue des deux mondes, 49,* 1864, p. 329.

4. Renooij (1951: 63) reports figures illustrating the rising importance of such investors: between 1900 and 1939, deposits with private savings banks rose from ƒ80 to ƒ515 million, those with the state *Rijkspostspaarbank* from ƒ85 to ƒ670 million, while the capital of the life insurance companies rose from ƒ130 to ƒ1359 million. Meanwhile various social insurance funds were founded in the first quarter of the century in response to social legislation; and by 1939, the *Algemeen Burgerlijk Pensioenfonds* (the government employees' pension fund) held ƒ794 million in assets, the railway workers' and miners' pension funds held a combined ƒ203 million, private industry's *Ongevallenfonds* and *Invaliditeits- en Ouderdomsfonds* together some ƒ491 million, while the self-employed's voluntary *Ouderdomsfonds B* held ƒ68 million.

5. These were exempt from stamp duty until 1939, and hence a popular substitute for bonds in the interwar period. The major place taken by direct long-term private loans in institutional investors' portfolios is distinctive to the Netherlands and Germany.

6. D. Brilleslijper, Delta Lloyd spokesman, in *FEM Business,* 20 September 2003.

7. It has a right to relevant information, a right to advise on major decisions (e.g. transfers of ownership, relocation and important investments); it can delay decisions it disagrees with for 1 month and appeal to the *ondernemingskamer* (company chamber) of the Amsterdam Court. Its permission is required for changes to social arrangements (pensions, working hours, wages, safety rules) and if it disagrees the employer must obtain a local judge's decision to go ahead.

8. This information is in principle available for all public limited companies (*naamloze vennootschappen*) from both the yearbooks of *NV*s compiled by Van Nierop and Baak over the period 1880–1948 and from the yearbooks relating to listed securities, *Van Oss' Effectenboek* 1903–1978 (later continued as *Effectenboek*).

9. Our data do not allow us to determine whether all or part of this decline may be offset by the placement of bank officials from below the board level on industrial firm boards.

References

Booth, J.R., & Deli, D.N. (1999). On executives of financial institutions as outside directors. *Journal of Corporate Finance, 5,* 227–250.

Bos, J.W. (1923). *Over commissarissen van naamlooze vennootschappen.* Doctoral dissertation, Rijksuniversiteit Groningen.

Duffhues, P.J.W. (1997). *Ondernemingsfinanciering en vermogensmarkten.* Amsterdam: Wolters-Noordhoff.

Gales, B.P.A. (1986). *Werken aan zekerheid: een terugblik over de schouder van AEGON op twee eeuwen verzekeringsgeschiedenis.* AEGON Verzekeringen, 's-Gravenhage.

Heemskerk, E., Mokken, R., & Fennema, M. (2003). From stakeholders to shareholders? Corporate governance networks in the Netherlands 1976–1996. University of Amsterdam. http://users.fmg.uva.nl/heemskerk/publications/stakeholderPreprint_2003.pdf.

De Jong, A., DeJong, D., Mertens, G., & Wasley, C. (2005). The role of self-regulation in corporate governance: Evidence and implications from the Netherlands. *Journal of Corporate Finance, 11,* 473–503.

Jonker, J. (1989). Waterdragers van het kapitalisme; nevenfuncties van Nederlandse bankiers en de verhouding tussen bankwezen en bedrijfsleven, 1910–1940. *Jaarboek voor de geschiedenis van bedrijf en techniek, 6,* 158–190.

Jonker, J. (1996). Merchants, bankers, middlemen: The Amsterdam money market during the first half of the nineteenth century. *NEHA Series III-24,* Amsterdam.

Jonker, J.P.B. (1995). Spoilt for choice? Statistical speculations on banking concentration and the structure of the Dutch money market, 1900–1940. In: Y. Cassis, G.D. Feldman, & U. Olsson (Eds),

The evolution of financial institutions and markets in twentieth century Europe (pp. 187–208). Aldershot: Scolar Press.

Kroszner, R.S., & Strahan, P.E. (2001). Bankers on the boards: Monitoring, conflicts of interest, and lender liability. *Journal of Financial Economics, 62,* 415–452.

La Porta, R., Lopez-de-Silanes, F., Shleifer, A., & Vishny, R.W. (2000). *Agency problems and dividend policy around the world. Journal of Finance, 55,* 1–33.

Modigliani, F., & Miller, M.H. (1958). The cost of capital, corporation finance, and the theory of investment. *American Economic Review, 48,* 261–297.

Polak, N.J. (1921). *Eenige grondslagen voor de financiering van de onderneming.* Doctoral dissertation, Handels-Hoogeschool, Rotterdam.

Post, J.G. (1972). *Besparingen in Nederland 1923–1970: Omvang en verdeling.* Doctoral dissertation, University of Amsterdam, Amsterdam.

Pritchard, A.C., Ferris, S.P., & Jagannathan, M. (2003). Too busy to mind the business? Monitoring by directors with multiple board appointments. *Journal of Finance, 58,* 1087–1112.

Renooij, D.C. (1951). *De Nederlandse emissiemarkt van 1904–1939.* Amsterdam: De Bussy.

Schijf, H. (1993). *Netwerken van een financieel-economische elite: Personele verbindingen in het Nederlandse bedrijfsleven aan het eind van de 19e eeuw.* Amsterdam: Het Spinhuis.

Sluyterman, K.E. (2003). *Kerende kansen: Het Nederlandse bedrijfsleven in de twintigste eeuw.* Amsterdam: Boom.

Sluyterman, K.E., & Winkelman, H.J.M. (1993). The Dutch family firm confronted with Chandler's dynamics of industrial capitalism, 1890–1940. *Business History, 35,* 152–183.

Smith, C.W., & Watts, R.L. (1992). The investment opportunity set and corporate financing, dividend, and compensation policies. *Journal of Financial Economics, 32,* 263–292.

Speight, H., & Duffhues, P.J.W. (1966). *Industriële efficiency; een economische benadering ten behoeve van het management.* Amsterdam: Agon Elsevier.

Steensgaard, N. (1982). The Dutch East India Company as an institutional innovation. In: M. Aymard (Ed.), *Dutch capitalism and world capitalism* (pp. 235–257). Cambridge: Cambridge University Press.

Stokman, F.N., Wasseur, F.W., & Elsas, D. (1985). The Dutch network: Types of interlocks and network structure. In: F.N. Stokman, R. Ziegler, & J. Scott (Eds), *Networks of corporate power: A comparative analysis of ten countries.* Cambridge: Polity Press.

Van den Broeke, W. (1988). Vermogensstructuren en netwerkrelaties in het Nederlandse bedrijfsleven 1890–1940. *Jaarboek voor de geschiedenis van bedrijf en techniek, 5,* 154–171.

Van Goor, L., & Koelewijn, J. (1995). Le système bancaire néerlandais: Étude rétrospective. In: M. Lévy-Leboyer (Ed.), *Les banques en Europe de l'Ouest de 1920 à nos jours* (pp. 153–175). Comité pour l'histoire économique et financière, Ministère de l'Économie et des Finances, Paris.

Van Nederveen Meerkerk, E., & Peet, J. (2002). *Een peertje voor de dorst: geschiedenis van het Philips pensioenfonds.* Amsterdam: Aksant.

Van Zanden, J.L. (1987). *De industrialisatie in Amsterdam 1825–1914.* Bergen: Octavo.

Van Zanden, J.L. (1998). *The economic history of the Netherlands 1914–1995: A small open economy in the "long" twentieth century.* London and New York: Routledge.

Chapter 14

Corporate Financing in the Netherlands

Rezaul Kabir

14.1. Introduction

Raising capital through security offerings is an important event in the financing pattern of
listed corporations. The use of different types of securities and their effect on firm value
varies from country to country due to differences in financial systems and institutional factors. According to Brealey, Myers, and Allen (2006), companies face two basic financing
decisions: How much profit should be ploughed back into the business rather than paid out
as dividends? What proportion of the deficit should be financed by borrowing rather than
by an issue of equity? These are the central corporate financing decisions for each and every
firm. Companies can raise capital internally by retaining earnings or attract funds externally
from the capital market. The two principal external sources of raising capital are equity and
debt. These come from either private sources like bank loans and private placements, or
public sources like issuing new securities in domestic and foreign capital markets.

   Along with an analysis of bank loans and, to a limited extent, private placements, the
investigation of security offerings to the public has been a fascinating area of academic
research in corporate finance. By deciding to issue one or another type of security, firms
are constantly changing its capital structure. It is widely known that under strict assumptions of perfect capital market, capital structure of firms does not affect value of the firms.
As long as the total cash flow generated by the assets of the firm remains unchanged,
financing decisions do not change the overall firm value. Studies have relaxed these
assumptions one by one and shown their relevance in real (and imperfect) world affecting
firm value. The real world shows interplay of different factors that determines the ultimate
value consequence of capital structure decisions. Capital structure decisions of firms are
believed to be used as an attempt to reduce taxes and bankruptcy costs, and/or as signalling, bonding or control devices. Indirect test on the support of these theoretical postulates is made on the basis of survey research (Graham & Harvey, 2001; Brounen, De Jong,
& Koedijk, 2004). On the other hand, direct empirical test of validity of these factors is
performed by looking at the change in market value of common stocks and examining the
determinants of the value change. This chapter discusses some of these empirical tests.

Advances in Corporate Finance and Asset Pricing
Edited by L. Renneboog
© 2006 Elsevier B.V. All rights reserved.
ISBN: 0-444-52723-0

Several studies examine the effect on shareholder wealth when changes in capital structure take place due to issuance of equities and debts. Ross, Westerfield, and Jaffe (2005: 550) note the following: "It seems reasonable to believe that new long-term financing is arranged by firms after positive net present value projects are put together. As a consequence, when the announcement of external financing is made, the firm's market value should go up." The empirical evidence, on the other hand, demonstrates a decline in share price at the announcement of common stock and convertible bond offerings, and an insignificant stock price movement at the announcement of straight debts. The analysis of the reasons of this seemingly anomalous empirical result has been a constant source of scientific research.

The purpose of this chapter is to analyze the valuation effect of financing decisions of Dutch firms by specifically examining different types of security offerings. I proceed as follows. First, I review the main features of the Dutch financial system and show how it differs from some other major financial systems. I also present some stylized facts of corporate financing in the Netherlands. I provide information on internal and external financing as well as the capital structure of Dutch firms. Many scholars point out that the observed differences in financial systems can explain the differences in firms' corporate financing behaviour. Second, I analyze the stock market valuation effect of different types of security offerings made by Dutch firms. I relate these effects with several theoretical explanations put forward to explain firm's capital structure choice. An evaluation of the determinants of the valuation effect is also made. Third, I explore the long-term impact of stock offerings by focusing on fundamental performance measures. Such an analysis allows us to evaluate, if real firm performance is consistent with the stock market-based performance.

14.2. Dutch Financial System

In this section, I focus on the salient features of the Dutch financial system and illustrate how it is different from some other major financial systems. In general, the Dutch system is a mixture of the Anglo-American (capital market-based and dispersed ownership-oriented) and the German (bank-based and concentrated ownership-oriented) systems. Capital market control, competition and shareholder wealth maximization characterize the Anglo-American system. On the other hand, the German system is characterized by bank control and stakeholder wealth maximization.

14.2.1. Private and Public Capital Market

Public corporations in the Netherlands are quite small in number, but very large in size. There are about 2000 public limited companies, of which about 200 are listed on the stock exchange. On the other hand, there are more than 150,000 private limited companies. The role of public capital market is also limited as far as the issue of new securities is concerned. Relatively few Dutch firms issue shares and bonds publicly. The total value of share issues by non-financial corporations on the Amsterdam stock exchange amounted to be almost 2 billions of euros in 1993. This was only 1.5% of total stock exchange value of all quoted shares on the Exchange. A total of 146 Dutch industrial firms have listed their shares on the Amsterdam stock exchange during 1984–1999. After reaching a peak of 15 billions euros in 2000 (which was mainly due to the widespread listing of dot-com firms), the value of share issues fell to nearly 1 billion euros in 2004. A sharp decline has taken place in the number of companies going public.

Table 14.1 provides information on the listed companies in the Netherlands and compares with those of some other countries. We observe that there are 392 domestic and foreign companies listed in Amsterdam with a total market capitalization of $640 millions. This is much smaller than Germany and Paris, not to speak of London, New York and Tokyo. The total stock market capitalization of Dutch firms is equal to almost half of the country's gross domestic product (GDP). This is also less compared to the German stock market capitalization of about 60% and nearly 200% for the US. A unique feature of the Dutch capital market is the dominance by a handful of very large companies. Fifteen companies including Royal Dutch, Unilever, Philips, Elsevier, Ahold, Akzo-Nobel, ING and ABN-AMRO represent about 70% of total market capitalization. The major multinational company Royal Dutch alone accounts for almost 20%.

Roosenboom (2002) observes that companies of a wide range of sizes and numerous industry groups go public in the Netherlands. The median initial public offering comprises 22 million euro worth of shares with a minimum of 3 millions euro and maximum of 1477 millions of euro. The average Dutch company does not use its IPO to raise large amount of new equity capital. Instead, the larger part of the proceeds goes to pre-IPO owners that cash out by selling (part) of their existing shares. This phenomenon contrasts sharply with that of the US. For Dutch firms, the average IPO underpricing, measured as the offer-to-close return on the first day of trading, is 9.5%. This compares to an average underpricing of 11% reported for Germany, 12% for the UK and 14% reported for France and the US.

Table 14.1: The relative position of the Dutch capital market.

Countries	Number of companies with shares listed	Stock market capitalization	Top 10 market capitalization
Euronext Amsterdam	392 (356)	640 (375)	
Euronext Brussels	265 (269)	182 (119)	35.3%
Euronext Paris	966 (891)	1447 (587)	
Deutsche Börse	989 (−)	1270 (665)	44.3%
London	2364 (2623)	2612 (1642)	44.0%
NYSE	2862 (2476)	11535 (6842)	20.0%
Tokyo	2096 (1833)	3157 (3011)	22.2%

Notes: The table compares some important features of the Dutch capital market with those of some other countries. It presents the number of companies with domestic and foreign shares listed, the market capitalization (in millions of dollars) of shares of domestic companies, and the market capitalization (in millions of dollars) of top 10 domestic companies. The figures are for the year 2000 and those within brackets are for the year 1996.
Source: World Federation of Exchanges.

The major proportion of Dutch firms is privately financed. Bank loans are thought to play the most significant role in the external finance of Dutch corporations. Firms rely more on bank loans because of difficulties in accessing the public securities market at attractive terms. De Haan and Hinloopen (2003) perform a long time-series analysis of the amount of funds obtained externally (private loans and issuing securities) by Dutch non-financial companies. They find that private loans always dominate external sources of funds. The respective proportions have changed somewhat during the 1990s due to the booming security market of these years.

14.2.2. Role of Banks

The banking system is extremely concentrated in the Netherlands. The share of three main commercial banks (ABN-AMRO, ING and Rabobank) in total bank assets is more than two-third. This concentration is very high, compared to, say Germany, where the share of the main three banks is less than one-quarter. Banks have been the major source of funds for Dutch firms. The banking literature suggests that bank loans have both benefits and costs for firms. Empirical studies on Dutch bank loans are not available as it is difficult to find information on long-term loans provided to firms. Chirinko, Van Ees, Garretsen, and Sterken (1998) analyze short-term bank loans and report that the median short-term bank loans as a percentage of total assets is 6%.

Dutch banks also engage in both commercial and investment banking businesses. Although there is no restriction of banks owning shares of companies, their average shareholdings are not significant. Bank's representatives usually take seat on the supervisory boards of many firms. As pointed out by Chirinko, Van Ees, Garretsen, and Sterken (1998), this is not the result of the banks being a shareholder, but it merely reflects informal linkages through networks. Such a networking provides Dutch financial institutions with the opportunity to gather information about a firm and is also a potential means to exercise indirect control on the firm. There is also much similarity with Germany where bank equity holdings are relatively low, but the power is enormous especially through proxy voting and representation on supervisory boards (Gorton & Schmid, 2000).

14.2.3. Corporate Governance

Two main aspects of corporate governance that receive most attention are the ownership structure and the board structure of firms. Like many other industrialized countries, ownership and control among the listed companies in the Netherlands are not always separated. Only a few owners with significant blocks of shares may effectively control the affairs of several companies. Therefore, studies of ownership concentration have gained prominence.

Among the Continental European countries, Dutch companies have a relatively low concentration of ownership. The median size of the largest ownership block is 18%; for the top three block holders together, the figure is 34%; for all large block holders, it is 48%. A relatively large number of firms have ownership stakes in the 25–50% and 50–75% ranges. The average ownership stakes of banks, insurance companies and other financial institutions are 7%, 10% and 15%, respectively. More than 50% of Dutch firms have a bank as a block holder. In one-third of firms, an insurance company is another block holder. Individuals and corporations have average stakes of 10% and 2.5%, respectively. This scenario is different from Belgium and Germany where cross-holdings by corporations play an important role. Renneboog (2000) finds that the largest direct shareholder controls 43% in the average Belgian listed company. Holding companies, industrial corporations own 33% and 15% of the voting rights, respectively. In Germany, individual and families, industrial companies and financial institutions are the dominant shareholders.

An important feature of the Netherlands is that voting rights are different from ownership rights. This means that ordinary shareholders do not have the rights which are considered as normal in many other countries. When voting rights are taken into consideration, the Netherlands can be considered as one with a relatively high concentration. The average size of the largest voting stake is much higher due to the fact that blocks of shares are controlled by administrative office that holds the original common shares and issues depository certificates instead. The use of administrative office is one of the several anti-takeover measures adopted by Dutch listed companies. Certificate holders, in addition to dividends, retain the right to attend and speak at shareholders' meetings, to challenge the legitimacy of company decisions, and to call for extra meetings just like any shareholder. But they have no vote; the voting rights attached to their shares can only be exercised by the administrative office. These two classes of shares are not traded simultaneously on the exchange. It is also important to note that other categories of owners, such as banks, insurance companies and pension funds have, on average, very few voting rights. A detailed analysis of these and other anti-takeover measures in the Netherlands is given in Kabir, Cantrijn, and Jeunink (1997).

The board structure of many European companies reflects the idea that the firm should act in the interest of all stakeholders, not just the owners. In this spirit, Dutch firms have two-tire boards of directors. Many firms are legally obliged to appoint a supervisory board whose members are appointed by co-optation (i.e. the incumbents elect new members) with no direct shareholder input. The supervisory board in turn names a management board. The management board controls day-to-day functions. It also influences the composition of the supervisory board. Therefore, one can raise question on the degree of independence of the Dutch supervisory board. Many individuals are usually members of several supervisory boards.

The median size of the management board is two, while that of the supervisory board is five. The largest management board has 14 members and the largest supervisory board has 11 members. There are 20% of Dutch firms in which block holders or their relatives are members of the supervisory or the management board. The average ownership stakes of the management board members, the supervisory board members and their relatives are 5%, 2% and 1%, respectively. In a few firms members of the supervisory board hold ownership stakes but those of the management board do not. German companies have also a supervisory board. The main difference with Germany is that one-half of the supervisory board's members are elected by employees, including management and staff as well as trade unions. The other half of the supervisory board represents shareholders, often including bank executives.

14.3. Financing by Dutch Firms

Dutch firms, like firms in many other industrialized countries, prefer internal funds to external funds. De Haan and Hinloopen (2003) analyze financing techniques used by Dutch companies. They collect time-series data of Dutch non-financial companies for the years 1984–1997. From a sample consisting of 1915 annual observations, they find that 43% of firms do not require any form of financing. In 1085 (57%) cases, companies do use one or another type of financing method. The distribution of financing techniques is shown in Figure 14.1. We can see that pure internal financing is used in 45% cases whereas external financing is used in 40% cases. The rest belong to a combination of internal and external financing. If external financing is obtained, we observe that the most common source is financing by means of private debt (51%). The remaining proportion is divided among issuing equity (20%), bonds (15%) and hybrid financing (18%). The overwhelming dominance of internal finance is also observed in the UK and the US.

The empirical analysis of De Haan and Hinloopen (2003) indicates that the choice between internal and external financing depends on the availability of internal cash flow and liquid assets. Firms with sufficient internal funds are less likely to acquire external finance. When firm require external funds, it is found that profitable firms and smaller firms are more likely to use private debt than public security offerings. Smaller firms are more dependent on banks for external funds, while larger firms have easier access to capital market.

Like most continental European markets, the corporate bond market is relatively under-developed in the Netherlands. De Haan and Hinloopen (2003) mention several institutional factors to explain this phenomenon. The supply side of the Dutch capital market is dominated by institutional investors (pension funds, life insurance companies), which until recently invest mostly in relatively risk-free long-term government bonds and loan. They were legally restricted to invest in risky assets. Since the lifting of legal barriers, pension funds have increased their investment in risk-bearing assets like shares. The corporate bond market, however, does not have the necessary infrastructure to take advantage of this new development. There is an increasing need for market analysts and rating agencies to assess the quality of companies.

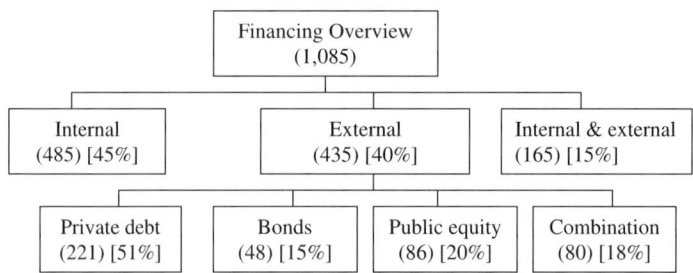

Figure 14.1: Types of financing used by Dutch listed companies. The table presents information on the different types of financing used by a sample of 153 non-financial Dutch listed companies during the period 1984–1997. *Source*: De Haan and Hinloopen (2003).

It is also important to get an idea on the extent of debt and equity financing used by Dutch corporations. Past research has used a number of different definitions of leverage. These vary depending on long-term, short-term or hybrid nature of debt. Empirical literature uses these different measures because different theories of capital structure have different implications for different types of debt. The capital structure of Dutch firms is analyzed by De Jong (1999). He uses several measures of leverage. Long-term debt ratio is calculated as the book value of long-term debt divided by the book value of total assets. Alternative definitions of leverage are long-term debt over market value of total assets, total debt over book value of total assets and total debt over the market value of total assets. Short-term debt is defined as short-term debt over the book value of total assets.

The empirical findings are presented in Table 14.2. We find that the median long-term debt ratio in the Netherlands is 14%. Measuring long-term debt in terms of market value indicates a slightly lower figure. It is difficult to compare this and other measures of leverage internationally. As pointed out by Rajan and Zingales (1995), international comparisons of this sort are extremely difficult due to accounting differences among countries. For example, the treatment of reserves and pensions liabilities has different consequence on the actual amount of debt and equity used by firms. Rajan and Zingales (1995) adjust for these items. The long-term debt ratio in the Netherlands is comparable to that of Germany (0.10), France (0.16), Italy (0.12) and the UK (0.12), but low in comparison with the US (0.23) and Canada (0.28). As for the Dutch IPO firms, Roosenboom (2002) reports that the median long-term debt in the financial year before the IPO is only 6%.

We also see that Dutch firms tend to rely more on short-term finance. The average short-term debt ratio is 35%. Short-term debt accounts for the bulk of total debt financing. It allows banks to frequently monitor firms and to exercise potential monopoly power in case of loan renegotiations. UK firms appear to have a similar degree of reliance on short-term firms. But, Dutch firms rely more on short-term finance than German firms. It is believed that trade credits play an important part of short-term debt.

While Germany and the Netherlands are examples of bank-oriented financial systems and listed firms in these two countries appear to have similar aggregate leverage structures,

Table 14.2: Capital structure of Dutch firms.

Variable	Mean	Median	Standard deviation
Long-term debt ratio (book value)	0.161	0.142	0.126
Long-term debt ratio (market value)	0.133	0.112	0.114
Total debt ratio (book value)	0.513	0.526	0.157
Total debt ratio (market value)	0.411	0.400	0.177
Short-term debt ratio	0.352	0.363	0.165

Notes: The table reports summary statistics for leverage of a sample of Dutch listed firms over the period 1992–1997. Long-term debt ratio is long-term debt over total assets. Total assets is the book value of total assets. Market value is the book value of total assets minus the book value of common equity plus the market value of common equity. Total debt ratio is total debt over total assets. Short-term debt ratio is short-term debt over book value of total assets.
Source: De Jong (1999).

there are some important differences. First, the largest firms in Germany tend to have lower leverage ratios compared to the Netherlands, and second, the financing of firms in Germany appears to be more long-term than the Netherlands.

14.4. Wealth Effect of Security Issues

Published empirical studies on capital structure choice in general indicate that the effect of taxes and bankruptcy costs appear to play a minor role in explaining the financing behaviour of corporations. Most studies rather conclude that information and agency considerations are more dominant factors. According to Grinblatt and Titman (2002), a firm's choice of debt or equity conveys information for two reasons. First, managers will avoid increasing a firm's leverage if they have information indicating that the firm could have future financial difficulties. Hence, a debt issue can be viewed as a signal that managers are confident about the firm's ability to repay the debt. Second, managers are reluctant to issue what they believe underpriced share. Hence, an equity issue might be viewed as a signal that the firm's shares are not underpriced, and therefore may be overpriced.

A number of studies from several countries examine stock price reaction to the announcement of new security issues. In this section, I review the results obtained from the Netherlands and compare them with prior studies.

14.4.1. Equity Offerings

Listed corporations typically raise additional external equity capital either from existing shareholders or from new investors. The first method, known as rights issue, is widely used in diverse European and international capital markets. The second flotation method, commonly known as general cash or public offers, is the usual practice in the US. In line with other European countries, rights issue is the usual practice in the Netherlands. Corporate charters provide existing shareholders the pre-emptive right to purchase new issues of common equity. Another special feature is that Dutch firms always adopt standby rights offer method. Thus, investment banks or other financial institutions guarantee the execution of any unexercised rights.

During the period 1983–1998, there were about 90 seasoned equity offerings made by Dutch listed firms. Of these issues, almost 20% were general cash offers while the rest were rights issues. The non-rights equity issues were made jointly on international stock markets and/or related to organizational restructuring. Firms issuing rights offerings are on average much smaller than firms issuing general equity. The proceeds obtained from equity issues are used in repaying debt, restructuring operations, new investments, financing takeovers or simply to improve solvency.

Kabir and Roosenboom (2003) perform a detailed analysis of a sample of 58 rights issues in the Netherlands. Descriptive information on the issue-size and the issue-price is presented in Table 14.3. The monetary amount of an equity issue is standardized using the firm's market value of common equity on the day before announcement. It is found that the average equity issue represents 21% (median = 16%) of firm's outstanding common equity. This is roughly similar to issues in the US and UK. The offer price of equity issues

Table 14.3: Issue-size and issue-price of seasoned equity issues.

Variable	Mean	Median	Standard deviation
Issue-size	0.212	0.159	0.184
Issue-price (−1)	0.868	0.877	0.098
Issue-price (−1, −10)	0.872	0.883	0.099

Notes: The table reports summary statistics for issue-size and issue-price of a sample of seasoned equity offerings in the Netherlands. Issue-size is expressed as relative to the market value of equity on the day before the announcement. Issue-price is expressed as relative to the closing stock price of 1 day before the issue announcement as well as the average of closing stock prices for 10 days before the announcement.
Source: Kabir and Roosenboom (2003).

is, on average, set below the market price prevailing during the days before the announcement. The average issue-price (subscription price discount) is 88% (13%). This is slightly less than the average offer-price discount observed in case of insured rights offerings in the US (20%) and in the UK (17%). The average subscription price discount is remarkably higher in Norway (about 50%) and Greece (38%).

Empirical result on shareholder wealth effect of announcements of equity offerings is presented in Table 14.4. Excess stock returns are estimated after adjusting for each stock's systematic risk estimated from the market model. The results show that the stock price announcement effect is significantly negative. On the day of the announcement of rights issue (day 0), the average excess decline is about 2%. An additional half a percent decline takes place on the day after the announcement. In two days time, shareholders of rights issuing firms suffer an average abnormal wealth reduction of about 2.8%. The result is also consistent with that found earlier by Levis (1995) and Slovin, Sushka, and Lai (2000) for the UK; Bohren, Espen Eckbo, and Michalsen (1997) for Norway; and Gajewski and Ginglinger (2002) for France. In contrast to these findings, Kang and Stulz (1996) and Tsangarakis (1996) observe a positive valuation effect in Japan and Greece, respectively. It is possible that the positive stock price effect is caused by distinct institutional features of these stock markets like the absence of an active market for rights and highly concentrated / affiliated ownership structure of firms.

The results presented in Table 14.4 also show that Dutch companies issue equity after an increase in stock price. Similar result is found by De Jong and Veld (2001). Equity issue announcements usually take place together with other kinds of news announcements. A robustness check of confounding events does not change the direction of average price reaction. It is also observed that equity issuing firms with new investment plans experience a statistically significant decline in their stock price. However, the magnitude of the stock price decline is smaller than that obtained for the total sample.

Which firm-specific factors can explain this decline in stock return of equity issuing firms? Cross-sectional regression analyzes help us to investigate this question. The results are shown in Table 14.5. The announcement period cumulative excess stock return is used as the dependent variable. The explanatory variables are used to proxy three different hypotheses: the information asymmetry (Myers & Majluf, 1984), the free cash flows (Jensen, 1986) and the window of opportunity hypotheses (Choe, Masulis, & Nanda, 1993;

Table 14.4: Shareholder wealth effect of seasoned equity issues.

Period	Excess return	t-statistic
−60, −1	3.27	1.98*
0, +1	−2.79	−7.89**
+2, +30	−2.55	−1.76*
0, +30	−5.34	−3.71**

Notes: The table shows cumulative average excess stock returns for various periods surrounding the announcement (day 0) of seasoned equity issues. Excess returns are calculated after adjusting for each stock's systematic risk estimated from the Market Model, and are expressed in percentages. Statistically significant levels at: *10% and **5% indicated.
Source: Kabir and Roosenboom (2003).

Table 14.5: Determinants of excess stock return.

Model	Intercept	Issue-size	Issue-price	M/B	GDP	Adj. R^2
1	−0.01	−0.11**				0.06
2	−0.29**		0.31**			0.17
3	−0.25*	−0.05	0.27*			0.17
4	−0.40**		0.42**	0.01		0.26
5	−0.34**	−0.02	0.31**	0.01	0.01	0.24

Notes: The table reports results where the two-day announcement period excess stock return is regressed on various explanatory variables. The explanatory variables are: issue-size = the monetary amount of rights issue/market value of equity on the day before announcement; issue-price = the offer price/stock price on the day before the issue announcement; M/B = the ratio of market to book value of total assets; GDP = a dummy variable set to 1 if the issue occurs in years of relatively high growth rate of GDP.
Statistically significant levels at: *10% and **5% indicated.
Source: Kabir and Roosenboom (2003).

Bayless & Chaplinsky, 1996). It is observed that (in model 1) that the announcement period excess stock return is inversely related to the relative size of the rights issue. In this univariate analysis, the magnitude of the issue-size coefficient is −0.11 and it is statistically significant. The finding indicates that as the relative size of the rights issue increases, a larger decline in the stock price takes place. The result supports the prediction of the information asymmetry hypothesis that larger equity issues signal more negative information thereby depressing stock prices more.

A significant positive relationship is observed between the announcement period excess stock return and the relative offer price. The univariate regression coefficient of the variable is 0.31 (model 2) and is statistically significant. The result is again consistent with the information asymmetry hypothesis which posits that higher quality firms use higher subscription price, or smaller discounts, as a signal of quality, and therefore, experience a less negative price decline. Prior studies (e.g. Slovin, Sushka, & Lai, 2000) also find significant relationship between offer price discount and announcement period stock returns. When both the issue-size and the issue-price variables are used in a bivariate regression framework (model 3), the coefficient of issue-size variable is found to be statistically insignificant. This is caused by a statistically significant correlation between the two explanatory variables.

The overinvestment of free cash flows hypothesis predicts that stock return will be positively related with issuing firms' market to book ratio of total assets. The results of models 4 and 5 in Table 14.5 show that although the coefficient of the market to book ratio is positive, it is statistically insignificant. To determine whether corporate managers utilize the opportunity of favourable economic conditions to issue new equity, the relationship between announcement period stock return and the annual growth rate of GDP is investigated. As can be seen in model 5, the GDP growth rate is insignificantly related to stock returns. The above findings, therefore, fail to support the overinvestment hypothesis as well as the window of opportunity hypothesis.

14.4.2. Other Security Offerings

Besides equity, companies can choose to issue pure debt or hybrid securities that have both equity and debt components, like convertibles and warrants. By issuing bonds, a firm receives additional external funds but increases its leverage and external disciplining by bondholders. The capital market, therefore, interprets bond issues as a mixed signal. The fact that a firm needs new financing indicates a shortage of internal funds which investors consider as bad news. On the other hand, the higher leverage is a signal that the company is confident about its ability to meet higher interest obligations and thereby to generate higher cash flows.

De Jong and Veld (2001) analyze 98 issues of straight debt during the period 1977–1996. They also make a comparative analysis with equity issuing firms. The results indicate that debt-issuing firms are more profitable than equity issuing firms, and companies issue debt after a decline in stock price. The wealth effect of debt announcements, as shown in Table 14.6, is positive (0.51%) but statistically insignificant. The finding generally supports that of prior studies from the US. De Jong and Veld (2001) also examine the determinants of abnormal stock returns associated with debt issues. They find that, consistent with theoretical prediction, announcement period abnormal return is positively related with firms' growth opportunities. But, in contrast to the expectation, they also find that firms with a relatively large amount of short-term funds like cash and other liquid assets, and using the proceeds to repay short-term debt, experience higher abnormal returns. Their study also reveals that the size of debt issue has no relationship with abnormal stock returns.

An analysis of financing by convertibles and warrants is made by De Roon and Veld (1998). A convertible bond gives its owner the right to *exchange* the bond for other securities, mostly stocks. The owner of a convertible bond owns a bond and a call option on the firm's stock. On the other hand, a company issues warrants that give its owner the right to *buy* other securities, mostly new shares. The main difference is that warrants are separately traded securities, while in case of convertibles, the bond and the conversion right are always traded together. During 1976–1996, there were 62 convertible bonds issues and

Table 14.6: Shareholder wealth effect of debt, convertible and warrant issues.

	Debt	Convertible	Warrant
Day (−1, +1)	0.51 (0.95)	0.23 (1.01)	1.35 (2.17)[**]
Sample size	98	47	19
Pre-issue excess return	−0.047 (12 months)	7.63 (8 months)	8.03 (8 months)
Source	De Jong and Veld (2001)	De Roon and Veld (1998)	De Roon and Veld (1998)

Notes: The table shows excess stock returns for various periods associated with the announcement of issues of debt, convertible and warrant. Excess returns are calculated after adjusting for each stock's systematic risk (for debt issues) and adjusting for the stock market index return. The excess returns are expressed in percentages. Statistically significant levels at: **5% indicated.

22 warrant bonds issues in the Netherlands. De Roon and Veld (1998) collect detailed information on 47 convertibles and 19 warrants. They find that the mean market value of new equity as a fraction of the market value of the outstanding equity is 22% for convertible bonds and 15% for warrants. The issues are, on average, large in relation to the outstanding equity.

The effect of financing by issuing convertible bonds and warrants is empirically examined by performing an event study. The results presented in Table 14.6 show that the average abnormal stock return from day −1 to day +1 is 0.23% for convertible bonds and 1.35% for warrants. The former is statistically insignificant while the latter is significant. These results are in line with the results for Japan, but inconsistent with the results obtained from the US. An issue of convertible in the US is usually associated with significant negative impact on shareholder wealth. Looking at the abnormal stock returns prior to issues, De Roon and Veld (1998) observe that Dutch firms issue both securities after a period of positive stock price gains. They also find that Dutch companies generally announce the issue of convertibles or warrants at the presentation of annual results or at the announcement of strategic news on mergers or takeovers. After correction for this confounding news, it is found that the announcements of neither convertibles nor warrants have any significant effect on shareholder wealth.

14.5. Long-term Performance

It is also interesting to examine the long-term performance of firms following security issues. Spiess and Affleck-Graves (1995) find significant stock price under-performance during the post-equity issue years. Loughran and Ritter (1997) report that the operating performance of equity issuing firms decline afterwards. Similar decline in performance is reported by Lee and Loughran (1998) for a sample of convertible debt offerings in the US.

For the Netherlands, the long-term operating performance is analyzed by Kabir and Roosenboom (2003). They investigate if the post-issue operating performance of firms is consistent with the stock price effect observed during equity issue announcement. If raising additional capital by means of equity offerings leads to an improvement in firm's real performance, then the previously documented negative stock price announcement effect should be considered as an anomalous finding. On the other hand, if stock price changes are forward looking and correct, then post-rights issue operating performance would show deterioration.

The excess operating performance of firms subsequent to a sample of rights issues in the Netherlands is reported in Table 14.7. Abnormal or excess operating performance is calculated as the difference in return on assets between issuing firm and median non-issuing firm (during the preceding 5 years). Median abnormal *levels* of operating performance for the period beginning with the year of rights issue up to 5 years after right issue is presented in the table. The results reveal that each performance measure is negative in post-issue years. Many of these excess declines are statistically significant. Equity issuing firms systematically experience an abnormal decline in subsequent operating performance. The magnitude of cumulative average return on assets varies from –6.2% to –9.1%. The results indicate that the earlier observed value decline in the stock market at the time of announcement of equity issue comes from the expected deterioration in future operating performance of firms. These results are robust to alternative methodologies, and consistent with prior studies mainly from the US.

In order to examine the determinants of the decline in operating performance of equity issuing firms, Kabir and Roosenboom (2003) perform a cross-sectional regression analysis. They use the post-issue cumulative excess operating performance of firms as the dependent variable. The explanatory variables are used to proxy the information asymmetry, the free cash flows and the window of opportunity hypotheses (the same hypotheses used to explain stock price performance). The results are presented in Table 14.8. The size of equity issue is not observed to have a statistically significant relationship with long-run firm performance. But, the issue-price variable is significantly positively related to post-issue operating

Table 14.7: Long-run operating performance of companies after seasoned equity issues.

	Year 0	Year 1	Year 2	Year 3	Year 4	Year 5
Net income/Total assets	−0.5	−0.5	−1.3*	−1.1*	−1.2	−1.4*
Cash flow/Total assets	−1.5	−0.3	−3.2*	−2.0	−1.2	−0.9
EBIT/Total assets	−0.4	0.3	−0.3	−0.1	−2.1**	−2.1*
EBITDA/Total assets	0.3	−0.2	−1.3*	−2.1	−2.2**	−3.3

Notes: The table reports median abnormal levels of operating performance of firms for 5 years after equity issue. The figures are expressed in percentages. Abnormal measures are calculated as the difference in performance between issuing firm and median non-issuing firm. Four different performance measures are calculated: the ratios of net income to average total assets, cash flow (net income plus depreciation plus the change in current assets excluding the change in cash minus the change in current liabilities plus the change in current maturities of long-term debt) to the average of total assets, earnings before interest and taxes (EBIT) to the average of total assets, and earnings before interest, taxes and depreciation and amortization (EBITDA) to average total assets. Statistically significant levels at: *10% and **5% indicated.
Source: Kabir and Roosenboom (2003).

Table 14.8: Determinants of long-run excess operating performance.

Dependent variable	Intercept	Issue-size	Issue-price	M/B	GDP	Adj. R²
Net income/Total assets	−1.01**	−0.03	0.82**	0.18**	0.03	0.14
Cash flow/Total assets	−0.81	−0.08	0.54	0.19	0.13*	0.09
EBIT/Total assets	−0.76**	−0.17	0.54**	0.21**	0.06	0.14
EBITDA/Total assets	−0.86**	−0.15	0.65*	0.19*	0.08	0.11

Notes: The table reports results where the cumulative abnormal level of operating performance for 5 years after equity issue is regressed on various explanatory variables. The explanatory variables are: issue-size = the monetary amount of equity issue/market value of equity on the day before announcement; issue-price = the offer price/stock price prevailing one day before the issue announcement; M/B = the ratio of market to book value of total assets; GDP = a dummy variable set to 1 if the issue occurs in years of relatively high growth rate of GDP. Statistically significant levels at: *10% and **5% indicated.
Source: Kabir and Roosenboom (2003).

performance of firms. The findings provide support for the asymmetric information hypothesis. The market to book ratio is significantly positively related to various measures of return on assets. The regression coefficient is around 0.2 and remains stable among different specifications. The observed performance decline experienced by rights issuing firms receives support from the overinvestment of free cash flows hypothesis. The relationship between the GDP growth rate and the operating performance of equity issuing firms is also examined. All but one regression coefficients are found to be statistically insignificant. Conducting tests using other proxy variables in both univariate and multivariate framework do not produce any significant result. The findings, therefore, fail to support the window of opportunity hypothesis.

14.6. Conclusion

This chapter makes an analysis of corporate financing decisions of Dutch listed companies. It reviews some of the institutional features of the Dutch capital market, and discusses the empirical studies that measure the effect on shareholder wealth and long-term operating performance of firms.

Most Dutch companies have a preference for internal funds. This is nothing exceptional. Countries with market-oriented financial system like the UK and the US also show similar pattern. Overall, there appears to be some managerial aversion to external financing either to avoid disciplining from the banks or the capital market. If external financing has to be used, there is preference for debt financing rather than equity financing. The pecking order theory of financing, therefore, receives empirical support.

Dutch listed companies mostly make rights offerings in order to attract new equity capital. The empirical evidence indicates that a significant decline in shareholder wealth takes place when companies announce rights issues. The most widely accepted explanation of this finding is that new equity issues convey information about the value of the issuing firm. Although theoretically there appears to be no incentive for managers to issue rights when the firm is overvalued, in practice it does happen. Managers possess valuable information that outside investors lack. The prevailing differences in the Dutch financial system with respect to Anglo-Saxon system do not result in a dissimilar stock market reaction.

The post-issue operating performance of equity issuing firms conveys information on the real value of the firm. The empirical analysis of long-run performance suggests that companies issue shares when these are over-valued. Firms display poor operating performance for several years after they issue new equity. There are indications that firms with greater information asymmetry, higher possibilities of overinvestment of free cash flows exhibit deteriorating operating performance.

An examination of shareholder wealth effect of debt financing by Dutch corporations does not reveal a statistically significant change. Similarly, announcements of financing by means of convertibles and warrants show no significant effect on firm value. Overall, the empirical evidence on the valuation effect of public security offerings in the Netherlands suggests that the prevailing differences in financial system do not lead to a pronounced different result.

References

Bayless, M., & Chaplinsky, S. (1996). Is there a window of opportunity for seasoned issuance? *Journal of Finance, 60*, 253–278.

Bohren, O., Espen Eckbo, B., & Michalsen, D. (1997). Why underwrite rights offerings? Some new evidence. *Journal of Financial Economics, 46*, 223–261.

Brealey, R., Myers, S., & Allen, F. (2006). *Principles of corporate finance*. New York: McGraw-Hill Irwin.

Brounen, D., De Jong, A., & Koedijk, K. (2004). Corporate Finance in Europe: Confronting theory with practice. *Financial Management, 33*, 71–1001.

Chirinko, B., Van Ees, H., Garretsen, H., & Sterken, E. (1998). *Networks and financial institutions in the Netherlands: Corporate governance and the delta model*. Working paper, University of Groningen.

Choe, H., Masulis, R., & Nanda, V. (1993). Common stock offerings across the business cycle: Theory and evidence. *Journal of Empirical Finance, 1*, 3–33.

De Haan, L., & Hinloopen, J. (2003). Preference hierarchies for internal finance, bank loans, bond, and share issues: Evidence for Dutch firms. *Journal of Empirical Finance, 10*, 661–681.

De Jong, A. (1999). *An empirical analysis of capital structure decisions in Dutch firms*. Unpublished Ph.D. dissertation, Tilburg University.

De Jong, A., & Veld, C. (2001). An empirical analysis of incremental capital structure decisions under managerial entrenchment. *Journal of Banking and Finance, 25*, 1857–1895.

De Roon, F., & Veld, C. (1998). Announcement effects of convertible bond loans and warrant-bond loans: An empirical analysis for the Dutch market. *Journal of Banking and Finance, 22*, 1481–1506.

Gajewski, J.F., & Ginglinger, E. (2002). Seasoned equity issues in a closely held market: Evidence from France. *European Finance Review, 6*, 291–319.

Gorton, G., & Schmid, F. (2000). Universal banking and the performance of German firms. *Journal of Financial Economics, 58*, 29–80.

Graham, J., & Harvey, C.R. (2001). The theory and practice of corporate finance: Evidence from the field. *Journal of Financial Economics, 60,* 187–243.

Grinblatt, M., & Titman, S. (2002). *Financial markets and corporate strategy.* New York: McGraw-Hill Irwin.

Jensen, M. (1986). Agency costs of free cash flow, corporate finance, and takeovers. *American Economic Review, 76,* 323–329.

Kabir, R., Cantrijn, D., & Jeunink, A. (1997). Takeover defenses, ownership structure and stock returns in the Netherlands. *Strategic Management Journal, 18,* 97–109.

Kabir, R., & Roosenboom, P. (2003). Can the stock market anticipate future operating performance? Evidence from equity rights issues. *Journal of Corporate Finance, 9,* 93–113.

Kang, J., & Stulz, R. (1996). How different is Japanese corporate finance? An investigation of the information content of new security issues. *Review of Financial Studies, 9,* 109–139.

Lee, I., & Loughran, T. (1998). Performance following convertible bond issuance. *Journal of Corporate Finance, 4,* 185–207.

Levis, M. (1995). Seasoned equity offerings and the short- and long-run performance of initial public offerings in the UK. *European Financial Management, 1,* 125–146.

Loughran, T., & Ritter, J. (1997). The operating performance of firms conducting seasoned equity offerings. *Journal of Finance, 52,* 1823–1850.

Myers, S., & Majluf, N. (1984). Corporate financing and investment decisions when firms have information investors don't have. *Journal of Financial Economics, 13,* 187–221.

Rajan, R., & Zingales, L. (1995). What do we know about capital structure? Some evidence from international data. *Journal of Finance, 50,* 1421–1460.

Renneboog, L. (2000). Ownership, managerial control and the governance of companies listed on the Brussels stock exchange. *Journal of Banking and Finance, 24,* 1959–1995.

Roosenboom, P. (2002). *Corporate governance mechanism in IPO firms.* Unpublished Ph.D. dissertation, Tilburg University.

Ross, S., Westerfield, R., & Jaffe, J. (2005). *Corporate finance.* New York: McGraw-Hill Irwin.

Slovin, M., Sushka, M., & Lai, K. (2000). Alternative flotation methods, adverse selection and ownership structure: Evidence from seasoned equity issuance in the U.K. *Journal of Financial Economics, 57,* 157–190.

Spiess, D., & Affleck-Graves, J. (1995). Underperformance in long-run stock returns following seasoned equity offerings. *Journal of Financial Economics, 38,* 243–267.

Tsangarakis, N. (1996). Shareholder wealth effects of equity issues in emerging markets: Evidence from rights offerings in Greece. *Financial Management, 25,* 21–32.

Chapter 15

Syndicated Loans: Developments, Characteristics and Benefits

Ger van Roij

15.1. Introduction

Syndicated loans are granted by a syndicate of banks and are based on a joint loan agreement. This credit instrument originated in the 1970s of the last century and quickly developed as the most attractive and important international financing instrument until the early 1980s. However during the debt problems of the 1980s this loan type disappeared almost completely. However since the late 1980s/early 1990s the syndicated loan re-emerged as one of the most important global funding instruments today. In this chapter, the main characteristics of syndicated loans and loan syndications are explained; a syndicated loan combines important aspects of bilateral loans and bonds in a flexible way. The existence of a secondary market has stimulated the interest of non-bank financial institutions in syndicated loans as an investment outlet. Furthermore this market has contributed to the integration of syndicated loan markets and of bond markets. We also explain the benefits of syndicated loans for borrowers, banks and non-bank investors, and for the financial system as a whole.

15.2. Developments since the early 1970s

The development of the modern syndicated loan market since the early 1970s is often divided into three broad periods. In the 1970s of the 20th century the syndicated loan developed to the most important international credit instrument. This period ended with the outbreak of the international debt crisis (Mexico 1982) after which the significance of the syndicated loan reduced rapidly and capital market instruments emerged strongly and took over the role of the syndicated loans to a large extent. But since the late 1980s/early 1990s until today there is a clear revival and an increasing use of the syndicated loan as a funding instrument in many sectors in many countries.

Advances in Corporate Finance and Asset Pricing
Edited by L. Renneboog
© 2006 Elsevier B.V. All rights reserved.
ISBN: 0-444-52723-0

The development of the international syndicated loan market until the early 1980s of the last century is closely connected with the existence and structure of the Eurocurrency market in the 1970s on the one hand and balance of payments disequilibria on the other hand. Eurocurrency markets, especially Eurodollar markets emerged in the late 1950s/early 1960s. In essence these markets consisted of banks which accept deposits denominated in non-resident currencies (especially in US dollars by non-US banks including branches of US banks abroad). This created the possibility for these banks to supply dollar denominated loans. Generally these markets were allowed to operate outside domestic regulations. The banking systems of many industrial countries participated in these markets, which showed high growth rates since the markets emergence.[1] Within the Eurodollar system the international interbank market was of a crucial importance. Only a small number of big banks in industrial countries (including the overseas branches of US banks) had access to non-bank deposits in a systematic way. Many banks could only participate in this market via the interbank market. This market was used as an investment outlet for the surplus funds of big banks and — on balance — as a funding market for an overwhelming majority of other banks (Mentré, 1984; van Roij, 1989).

International financial disequilibria emerged in the 1970s because of the oil crisis of 1973 and high growth rates of many emerging market economies, especially in Latin America. These events resulted in high current account disequilibria in the world economy. Capital flows, needed to finance these disequilibria, could only be channeled by the international banking system. International capital markets did not really exist in the 1970s and many regulations in many countries made it for non-residents impossible in practice to borrow in domestic capital markets. However commercial banks of industrialized countries were well able to intermediate between surplus and deficit countries, especially via the Eurodollar system, which was well developed in the late 1960s and which could deal well with a growing demand of credit from deficit countries. McDonald (1982: 30) concludes: "By 1968 the Euro market had come of age. The deposit market was stable, growing and free of U.S.-inspired regulations..." and "banks had become confident in providing their clients 5–7 year medium term loans, based upon 3–6 months deposits. When coupled with the increasing borrower appetite for larger credit facilities, the birth of the Euro syndications business was inevitable". The amounts involved were rather small in the early 1970s (less than $10 billion in 1971), but tops $100 billion in 1979 and $178 billion in 1981 (McDonald, 1982: 27).

The "Euro syndications business" consisted of syndicated loans (with generally a medium- or long-term maturity), supplied by a group of banks after managing banks agreed with the borrowers on principal, interest rate conditions and other terms. As many participating banks in the loan only could borrow in the short-term interbank deposit market, the interest rate related to the loan was very often a London interbank offering rate (LIBOR), augmented with a risk premium. In this way the interest rate risk was shifted from the banks to the borrowers.

After the outbreak of the debt crisis in 1982 and the resulting problems for many countries and banks the significance of the syndicated loan market almost disappeared immediately after the early 1980s. During the following years the possibility for emerging markets to borrow new money on a large scale was very limited because of their problematic domestic economic situation and their debt. Moreover international operating banks had to take care of healthier balance sheets. Furthermore international fixed- and floating-rated bonds, commercial paper market programs and medium-term notes showed high growth rates and became very attractive, especially for high-qualified borrowers. They became much less dependent on bank loans and could easily switch to international capital markets (Euro bonds, foreign bonds). So the syndicated loan could not maintain its imposing position, built up in the 1970s, in the decade after the outbreak of the debt crisis. However since the late 1980s/early 1990s, the syndicated loan market has been revitalized very strongly. The following driving forces can be mentioned (Armstrong, 2003: 12; Gadanecz, 2004: 77):

- Leveraged buy-outs, acquisitions and corporate restructurings in the late 1980s were financed by large and risky syndicated loan arrangements, underwritten and distributed by US banks. These activities stimulated the emergence of large syndication banks, operating like investment banks, with a strong focus on fee income. These banks act in practice as intermediaries between borrowers and participating banks.
- In the 1990–1991 recession the syndicated loan market became attractive for high-qualified borrowers, as banks reduced their lending to risky borrowers. They could borrow large amounts of money within a short time period at favorable terms to finance acquisitions and other strategic transactions. Top-tier corporate borrowers became interested and were stimulated to switch to the syndicated loan market.
- The introduction of credit ratings on loans and the development of standardized price and rate-of-return indexes. These have improved transparency and facilitate comparisons with many other financial assets. These developments have stimulated strongly the interest of non-financial institutions in the syndicated loan market as investors.
- The development of secondary markets and the emergence of new risk-transferring techniques like asset securitization and credit derivatives have also stimulated insurance companies, pension funds and mutual funds to enter into the market. They make it much easier to adjust investment portfolios continuously according to a change in preferences or market developments.

So since the late 1980s/early 1990s, syndicated loans have re-emerged, not only for risky borrowers and projects, but also for high-qualified borrowers. Some information about the development of the syndicated loan market is given in Figure 15.1 (total) and Table 15.1 (international credit facilities). Comparing figures roughly one may probably conclude that the international component in the global syndicated loan market is substantial (60–80% in recent years).[2]

Syndicated loans are used on a large scale for general corporate purposes of high- and less-qualified companies, as back-up facility for commercial paper programs, for refinancing, merger, acquisition and buy-out financing, and to finance projects in utilities, transportation, mining, energy, construction, telecommunications, automobile and retail sectors in industrial countries and emerging markets (Armstrong, 2003: 12; Gadanecz, 2004: 78; 2005: 29). Nowadays about a third of all international financing (including bond, commercial paper and equity issues) is accounted by the international syndicated loan market (Gadanecz, 2004: 78). So the market has a real global nature, and is very popular and important for many companies and projects in many countries all over the world.

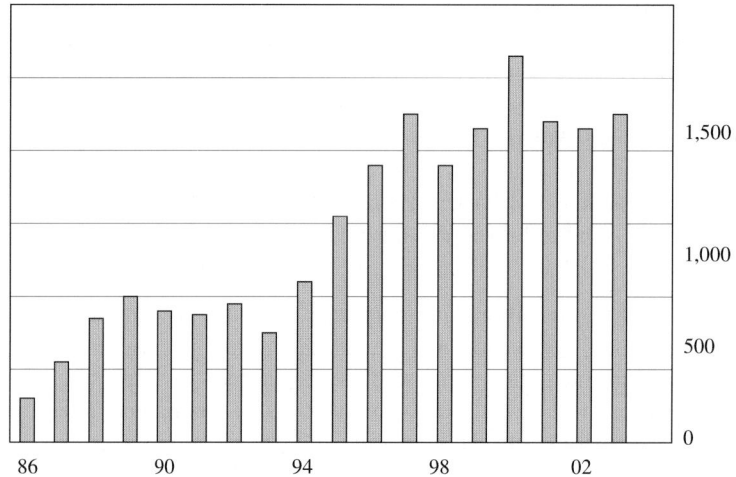

Figure 15.1: Syndicated lending since the 1980s. Gross signings (in billions of US dollars). Total of international and domestic syndicated credit facilities. *Source*: Dealogic Loanware, Euromoney, BIS (in Gadanecz, 2004: 76).

Table 15.1: Announced/signed international credit facilities (in billions of US dollars*).

	1993	1994	1995	1996	1997	1998	1999	2000	2001	2002	2003	2004
Residents of all countries	221	252	311	901	1136	905	1026	1465	1389	1294	1241	1812
Developed countries	171	200	250	800	976	820	958	1328	1280	1198	1130	1630
Off-shore centers	10	14	17	20	33	8	9	40	36	28	24	44
Eastern Europe	3	2	5	8	18	14	11	20	13	13	22	35
Developing countries	35	35	40	73	108	77	59	95	71	71	87	128

Notes: *Figures are derived from tables announced (or signed) syndicated credit facilities by Nationality of Borrower, *BIS Quarterly Review*, August 1996, February 1997, November 1999, March 2001, 2003 and 2005. Country groups and figures are not always comparable. For details see *BIS Quarterly Reviews*.

15.3. Characteristics

15.3.1. *Loans and Loan Syndicates*

A syndicated loan refers to a term loan, a credit facility or revolving facilities extended to a borrower by two or more banks. As stated in many publications the loan agreement is incorporated in one document, implying equal terms and conditions for all lenders. The agreement is the result of negotiations between the arranging bank or leading bank and the borrower. Co-managers are often involved especially when large transactions have to be dealt with. The leading bank produces a memorandum which contains relevant information with respect to the borrower, amount of the loan, maturity, interest rates, transferability and so on. Next this memorandum is distributed over to other banks that are invited to participate in the loan. If they accept they become participating banks (junior banks) and will receive a direct claim on the borrower. Generally the arranging bank will act as an agent (or correspondent) bank for the participating banks. This implies this bank will service and administrate the loan.

A loan can be underwritten (for the full amount or partly) by the lead manager(s) or can be arranged on a "best efforts" basis. This last possibility is usual, while it offers an opportunity for the arranger(s) to change the terms of the loan (if desired) to attract higher commitments or additional participating banks (Nini, 2004: 5). The maturity amounts from short term (e.g. 1–5 years), but longer maturities are also possible. Generally a benchmark interest rate (e.g. LIBOR, Euro interbank offered rate or Euribor) added up with a spread is applied, as far as the loan is drawn. Apart from the interest payments the borrower has to pay fees to the banks. Well-known fees are arrangement fees, commitment fees, participations fees, utilization fees and agency fees; sometimes other kinds of fees apply too (Gadanecz, 2004: 80). The benchmark interest rate can be considered as a compensation for the funding cost of the banks; spreads and fees compensate for other cost and for risks the lenders can be confronted with. Generally guarantees, collateral and restrictive covenants are used to limit risks for the lending banks. Very often the lead bank is a commercial bank that has a close and long relationship with the borrower. About 200 institutions have a market share of about 90%, although the role of investment banks is increasing (Gadanecz, 2004: 83). The possibilities for investment banks to originate, underwrite and distribute a loan have increased in recent years, especially in the USA, since distinctions between commercial and investment banking activities have been blurred because of deregulation. However there are some specific problems for investment banks. Generally they do not want to retain a part of the loan they underwrite like many commercial banks do as an arranger. Furthermore investment banks have an aversion to back-up lines and revolving facilities because of the risk of a large and unexpected use by borrowers, which can result in funding problems for the lending investment bank. Responsible for this attitude of investment banks are their relative small balance sheets, higher funding cost and different traditional business models (Basset & Zakrajšek, 2003: 488). Besides one can state that commercial banks are better positioned to provide liquidity insurance (back-up lines, loan commitments) to borrowers than other financial institutions including investment banks. In case of turmoil in the commercial paper markets and in bond markets, the need for liquidity by borrowers increases, but deposit inflows occur at banks. So banks can provide funds, as securities markets are closed or too expensive (Saidenberg & Strahan, 1999: 4–5).

The syndicate to which a loan will be sold is organized by the arranging bank. According to Dennis and Mullineaux (2000: 424–425) the possibility to sell a loan in a syndication context and the proportion of the loan that will be sold depend among others on the quality and reputation of the arranging bank, and especially on the character and the quality of the information about the borrower in the market. Much public information (e.g. ratings) and high transparency contribute to the possibility to sell loan participations to many and different kind of investors. However with limited transparency "… debt contracts tend to be marketed to investors with specialized monitoring skills who rely on contractual characteristics and seller reputation to resolve information asymmetry and agency problems" (Dennis & Mullineaux, 2000: 425). This indicates a much smaller investment basis for information-problematic loans compared with more transparent loans.

Information problems connected with international syndicated loans to fund projects in emerging market economies are reduced by the participation of local banks. Almost always these loans are arranged by banks from industrial countries, so by foreign banks from an emerging market viewpoint. The role of local banks in the syndicated loan market is a very limited one. According to Nini (2004: 5) local banks in Latin America and Eastern Europe, for example, do not participate in loans to borrowers outside their local region and they provide only 6% of the funding to local borrowers. Since local banks can be considered as natural suppliers of funds to local borrowers, Nini suggests that heavy capital constraints may be responsible for this. However even the small representation of local banks in a syndicate is very important. Generally they have better capabilities to screen and monitor local borrowers than foreign banks. So their preparedness to participate in a syndicate is a positive signal for other (foreign) banks. As a consequence, this reduces borrowing cost significantly, roughly 10% of the average spread, compared with the costs that would have been charged by a syndicate without local banks. It implies a syndicate can supply more funds at a given risk premium or reduce the required spread connected with a given loan amount. It also indicates a relatively advantage in supplying riskier loans to local borrowers, who are more opaque to foreign banks (Nini, 2004: 16).

Syndication programs for borrowers in emerging markets and developing countries have been set up also by multilateral international organizations as the International Finance Corporation and the Inter-American Development Bank. Participating banks often enjoy some advantages with respect to extended loans in such a program because of the official status of these organizations, which reduces country risk.

Syndicated loans can be considered as hybrid financial instruments, which combine important aspects of bilateral loans and bonds (Dennis & Mullineaux, 2000; Armstrong, 2003: 24; Gadanecz, 2004: 78). Bilateral loans are "relationship loans", bonds are "transaction loans".[3] Dennis and Mullineaux (2000: 405) state "… relationship loans embody information specific to the borrower and bank, while transactions loans are analogous to debt sold in the capital market. Syndicated loans typically involve elements of both kinds of financing in the sense that the lead bank screens and monitors the borrower in a relationship — like context, but then sells or underwrites some or all of the loan in a capital-market-like setting". So the lead bank behaves partly as a relationship bank (monitoring, screening) and partly as an investment bank (selling loans to participating banks similar to bond selling). Some important aspects of different loan instruments are summarized in Table 15.2.

Due to the hybrid character, in practice, many syndicated loans can be situated somewhere between bilateral loans on the one hand and bond market finance on the other hand. But in extreme situations such a loan can almost be identical to one of these. "A loan fully syndicated to a large number of participants is functional similar to capital market finance"

Table 15.2: Loan instrument characteristics, from a borrower's perspective.

	Bilateral loans	Syndicated loans	Bond markets
Loan size	Lowest	Larger	Similar to syndicated loans
Public information disclosure	Lowest	Medium	Highest
Driving factor	Relationship	Relationship or transaction	Transaction
Covenants	Extensive and frequently renegotiated	Extensive but less frequently renegotiated	Fewer and looser covenants/rarely renegotiated
Borrowing rate	Floating rate	Floating rate	Fixed rate
Funding	Revolving credit fully funded term loan	Revolving credit or fully funded term loan	Fully funded term obligation

Source: Armstrong (2003: 24).

(Dennis & Mullineaux, 2000: 406). Analogously one can state that a loan extended by a syndicate of two banks is almost similar to a traditional relationship loan extended by one bank.

15.3.2. Secondary Markets

A secondary market for syndicated loans emerged in the mid-1980s, especially in less-developed country debt, which became distressed after the outbreak of the debt crisis in 1982. Sellers and buyers mainly consisted of commercial banks with international loan portfolios. This market has been used by banks to restructure their loan portfolios to reduce risk concentration and to increase diversification. Thomas and Wang (2004: 231) conclude: "The market merely increased the scale of existing practices of the internal syndications market". In this way much experience in bank loan trading developed in the 1980s of the last century.

In many recent and contemporary loan agreements the transferability of loan participations is incorporated explicitly, increasing the possibility of secondary market trading. In practice large commercial and investment banks operate as market makers by publishing bid and offer prices and in this way create liquidity. Market liquidity has increased in the course of time among others by standardization of loan trading documentation, bank loan ratings, code of conduct and price publications under influence of professional associations (Thomas & Wang, 2004: 233). Trading volumes are increasing but remain modest compared to new loan arrangements: about 10–20% in Europe and in the USA in 2003 (Gadanecz, 2004: 84). Problems are relatively high cost connected with the transfer of ownership and required documentation (Basset & Zakrajšek, 2003: 489–490). Market segments consist of distressed loans (price below 90% of the issuance price) and (near) par loans (price higher than 90%), which consist of leveraged- and investment-grade loans. Trade activity concentrates especially in below investment-grade and distressed loans (Basset & Zakrajšek, 2003: 490; Thomas & Wang, 2004: 234). Due to the existence of secondary markets and connected market activity, there exists much price transparency for many loans. This stimulates an active management of loan portfolios at banks. It stimulates also the interest of non-banks in investments in corporate loans. Although credit risks can be bought and sold in secondary markets by loan trading, other risk-transferring instruments are available too, especially credit derivatives, which are used on a large scale in recent years.

Activities in secondary markets have contributed to more convergence in spreads on bank loans and on bonds, especially in the higher-risk segments and banks use bond prices, among others, as a help to determine the credit quality of their borrowers. Interest rates on used credit lines have become more dependent on credit ratings. As a consequence nowadays there exists a close relationship between risk prices and premiums in both markets (Basset & Zakrajšek, 2003: 490). This can be considered as an integration stimulating development between loan and bond markets, particularly between the high-leveraged loan markets on the one hand and the junk bond market on the other hand.[4] In their empirical study about the integration of both markets Thomas and Wang (2004: 319) conclude: "Our findings broadly support the hypothesis that syndicated loan pricing has substantially changed in recent years. Increasingly it is integrated with bond markets. Prior to 1993 bank liquidity affected loan spreads: the more money banks had, the less they charged their HLT (high-leveraged-transaction) borrowers. Following 1993, that relationship ended ... HLTs are now priced relative to disintermediated securities markets where institutional investors are major players".

Banks use secondary markets to sell risk full and distressed loans. This allows an acceleration of charge-offs and an improvement of the quality of their loan portfolios and balance sheets. Institutional investors like insurance companies, pension funds, high-yield mutual funds, hedge funds and special purpose investment vehicles are purchasers of loans in the secondary markets if their price reflects the riskiness of the borrower in a correct way. Generally these organizations are not or less interested in low-risk–low-yield loans but prefer higher-yield investments. So a relative large part of the more risky syndicated loans are appearing as assets on the balance sheets of many non-bank financial institutions (Basset & Zakrajšek, 2003: 488–489).

15.4. Benefits

Benefits of syndicated loans (including credit facilities) for borrowers, banks and investors are closely connected with their main characteristics of course. These benefits have also consequences for the financial system.

Companies that need a large amount of funds are able to borrow on the basis of one loan agreement with the arranging bank(s) instead of a number of different agreements. The latter implies building up and maintaining a loan relationship with more banks, which will imply higher cost generally. Furthermore the alternative of a loan like a bond issue may not be possible or too expensive. So the syndicated loan may offer the borrower the best available low-cost opportunity if much money is needed.

A syndicated loan can be structured with much flexibility. Depending on the needs and wishes of the borrower it can be tailor made similar or almost similar to a bilateral loan. So it can show many relationship characteristics. On the other hand the loan agreement may contain more standardized features and resemble bond funding. So a syndicated loan can combine advantages of different extreme funding possibilities and credit facilities for borrowers. Besides it can be arranged within a short-time period and in a discrete way, which may be important in some cases. A company that borrows from a syndicate of banks might build up new relations with other banks, without disturbing the relationship with the arrangement bank, supposing this bank has a long relationship with the borrower. This may increase borrowing conditions in the future or it can give access to the use of other financial instruments from banks on favourable conditions.

The benefits for banks depend on the role of a bank in a syndicate. Leading banks that are confronted with liquidity and/or capital constraints, or with too high concentration risks can maintain and intensify relations with borrowers by originating loans, distributing parts of the loan and by fulfilling the agency function. Next to interest income they receive different kinds of fee income connected with the organization of a bank syndicate, by which bank loans can compete better with the bond market. Lending banks (especially the smaller ones) can use loan participations to diversify extensively their loan portfolio. They can build up a more optimal and more tailor-made portfolio with participations in loans to corporates in sectors and regions they do not have access to with bilateral loans. Due to the existence of secondary markets it is relatively easy to change the structure of a portfolio and to adapt it to changed circumstances. Generally participating banks not only receive interest income but also some fee income. At last participations may help to start relations with new clients.

Earlier it has been stated that the syndicated loan market has taken the interest of many and different kinds of institutional and other investors. Price and risk transparency have been of great importance in this respect. According to Armstrong (2003: 24) many non-bank financial institutions in the USA consider syndicated loans, especially the longer-term higher-yielding ones as attractive assets. Referring to a study of Madan (Armstrong, 2003: 25), this popularity is based on three characteristics of these loans.

First, a low volatility of the returns on investment compared with other assets. This allows investors to more leverage (with e.g. derivatives) to amplify returns without great risks. A second reason consists of the floating interest rate on syndicated loans. It implies a very limited or even negligible influence of interest rate changes on the market value of the loans, even not if they have a long maturity. For some investors this is an important issue, for example, if they mark their portfolios to market regularly because of market conventions or regulations (Basset & Zakrajšek, 2003: 490). Therefore assets like syndicated loans can be used to reduce the volatility of the market value of an asset portfolio. Finally, in case of default the recovery rates of bank loans are substantially higher than high-yield bonds. This implies a lower credit risk on bank loans than on comparable high-yielding bonds.

The development and growth of an impressive syndicated loan market since the late 1980s/early 1990s is an important structural and innovative change in credit market together with the emergence of a market in credit derivatives in more recent years.

This implies the benefits of credit market innovations for the financial system can be attributed partly to the syndicated loan market too. The Bank for International Settlements (BIS, 2005: 117–118) stresses three benefits particularly. Innovations have created more complete markets giving investors greater diversification opportunities. Furthermore the BIS states that credit market innovations have resulted in greater market integration, both in terms of the investor base and with regard to other assets. Finally it is stated that new financial instruments have increased liquidity in credit markets. The three benefits can fully be attributed to the syndicated loans too as explained in this chapter.

The beneficial effects of the developments mentioned should be according to the BIS (2005: 118) "… lead … to a general reduction in financial risk in the long run and in particular to lower average credit spreads. Better diversifications of portfolios should reduce single-name risk premiums, and the increased depth and breadth of the market should lower liquidity premiums". Perhaps one can state there are no benefits without risks and uncertainty, of which product complexity and market functioning under stress stand out (BIS, 2005: 118). In this context the BIS gives special attention to the often very complex Collateral Debt Obligations (CDO) contracts, often issued by special purposes vehicles of banks and often combined with Credit Default Swaps. In general syndicated loans can be considered as less complex (at least in principle) and exist much longer than CDOs. Therefore it may be concluded that the structural positive contribution of the syndicated loan market to the credit market is less doubtful than those of more recent and more complicated credit instruments.

15.5. Conclusion

The syndicated loan market has evolved as one of the most important global funding instruments, combining characteristics of single bank loans and bonds funding in a flexible way. Syndicated loans are useful and attractive for many and different kinds of borrowers in many sectors and countries. The emergence of secondary markets has contributed to an increasing role of non-bank financial institutions as investors in syndicated loan participations. It has also stimulated market liquidity, and the integration of bank loan markets and bond markets. As a consequence, more opportunities have arisen for risk diversification, market integration and increased market liquidity.

Endnotes

1. Statistical evidence about these markets is given in the Annual Reports of the BIS from the mid-1960s onwards.
2. If the nationality of at least one bank differs from the nationality of the borrower, a loan is considered to be an "international" one.
3. Expressions by Boot and Thakor (2000).
4. Junk bonds have high yields because the borrower has a low credit rating and has to pay a high-risk premium. The comparison with high-leveraged-syndicated loans therefore is obvious.

References

Armstrong, J. (2003). *The syndicated loan market: Developments in the North American context.* Working paper, Bank of Canada.

Bank for International Settlements (2005). 75th Annual Report.

Basset, W.F., & Zakrajšek, E. (2003). Recent developments in business lending by commercial banks. *Federal Reserve Bulletin*, December, 477–492.

Boot, A.W.A., & Thakor, A.V. (2000). Can relationship banking survive competition? *The Journal of Finance*, 55, 679–713.

Dennis, S.A., & Mullineaux, D.J. (2000). Syndicated loans. *Journal of Financial Intermediation*, 9, 404–426.

Gadanecz, B. (2004). The syndicated loan market: Structure, development and implications. *BIS Quarterly Review*, December, 75–89.

Gadenecz, B. (2005). Refinancing boosts syndicated lending to record levels. *BIS Quarterly Review*, March, 29.

McDonald, R.P. (1982). *International syndicated loans*. London: Euromoney Publications.

Mentré, P. (1984). *The fund, commercial banks and member countries*. Occasional paper, 26th International Monetary Fund.

Nini, G.P. (2004). *The value of financial intermediaries: Empirical evidence from syndicates loans to emerging market economies*. International Finance Discussion Paper Federal Reserve Board, version 9/29/2004.

van Roij, G.P.L. (1989). The international interbank market and the stability of the banking system. In: J.J. Sijben (Ed.), *Financing the world economy in the nineties* (pp. 107–153). Deventer: Kluwer Academic Publishers.

Saidenberg, M.R., & Strahan, P.E. (1999). Are banks still important for financing large business? *Current Issues in Economics and Finance*, 5, 106, Federal Reserve Bank of New York.

Thomas, H., & Wang, Z. (2004). The integration of bank syndicated loan and junk bond markets. *Journal of Banking and Finance*, 28, 299–329.

Chapter 16

The Bank's Choice of Financing and the Correlation Structure of Loan Returns: Loans Sales versus Equity

Vasso Ioannidou and Yiannos Pierides

16.1. Introduction

Financial institutions have been selling loans among themselves for over a century. Although this market existed for many years, it grew slowly until the early 1980s, when it entered a period of spectacular growth. For example, the volume of loans sold by US banks grew from less than $20 billion in 1980 to $280 billion in 1989 (see Saunders, 1999). Between 1990 and 1994, the volume of loan sales fell almost equally dramatically, as a result of the credit crunch associated with the 1990–1991 recession. In recent years, however, the volume of loan sales has expanded again.

This dramatic increase in loan sales during the 1980s gave raise to a literature that tries to explain why banks sell loans and what types of loans they sell under different conditions. In general, this literature motivates loans sales either as a cheaper source of finance or as a way to diversify a bank's portfolio.[1] Selling loans could be cheaper than issuing equity or raising deposits for many reasons.

In particular, the cost of equity is generally perceived to be much greater than the cost of deposits due to various capital market imperfections. For example, tax benefits on the interest paid to deposits, high transaction costs of issuing equity, and the "bank safety net" (e.g., access to deposit insurance and the discount window) are among the many regulatory induced imperfections. The presence of asymmetric information and agency costs, however, are probably the most popular explanations. The seminal contribution by Myers and Majluf (1984) shows that internally generated funds (which have no issue costs and information problems) are generally preferred to externally generated funds. If external funds are needed, deposits are usually preferred to equity. This is because in the presence of asymmetric information, the bank's existing shareholders may be reluctant to issue equity since it may sell at a discount. The more recent literature on loan sales, however, suggests that in

Advances in Corporate Finance and Asset Pricing
Edited by L. Renneboog
ISBN: 0-444-52723-0

some cases loan sales are cheaper than deposits and thus equity. For example, a bank can reduce its regulatory tax burden by selling assets without recourse.[2] Loan sales without recourse provide a funding source that is not subject to deposit insurance premiums or reserve requirements. Also, by shrinking the balance sheet, loan sales allow a bank to reduce its capital requirement (e.g., Pavel & Phillis, 1987; Pennacchi, 1988). James (1988) shows that loan sales with recourse or backed by standby letters of credit could still be cheaper than risky debt, since they have payoff characteristics similar to secured debt.

This chapter contributes to the literature that motivates loans sales as a cheaper source of finance by examining how the correlation structure of loan returns affects the bank's choice of financing. In the papers mentioned above, only the expected value (and not the correlation structure) of loan returns enters the analysis. Here, the opposite is true. In particular, we consider two cases with different correlation structures, but the same expected returns. We show that even in a set-up where all agents are risk neutral, the correlation structure of loan returns could affect the bank's choice of financing.

In particular, we consider a Myers and Majluf's set-up where a bank that must raise its capital ratio and can choose between issuing equity and selling loans in the secondary market. In the first period of the model, when the bank must increase its capital ratio, there is asymmetric information about the quality of its loans and a positive probability of default in the next period. Like in the Myers and Majluf's set-up, the bank's portfolio consists of two loans, whose value can increase or decrease in the second period. Changes in the market value of a loan could be thought as changes in the probability of repayment. The bank knows what will happen to its loans in the second period, but the perspective investors (who consider buying loans or equity from this bank) do not. Hence, they have to base their decisions on expected values. We assume that the two loans have the same expected value, but one is riskier than the other. In this set-up, the risky loan determines whether the bank will be able to repay its debt in full or not (i.e., if the value of the risky loan decreases, the bank will default). The less risky loan does not determine default, but it determines the bank's portfolio in the second period and thus the price investors are willing to pay for equity. Since equity holders are residual claimants, the value of the bank's portfolio in the second period determines the amount of equity that will be used to repay the bank's debt. The higher this amount, the lower the price investors are willing to pay for equity, which implies that the correlation structure of loan returns affects the cost of issuing equity.

Hence, to examine how the correlation structure of loan returns affects the bank's choice of financing, we consider two cases: one in which the two loans are positively correlated and one in which the two loans are negatively correlated. Given the set-up as described earlier, the only difference between the two cases is the correlation structure of loan returns. In both cases, the expected value of the bank's portfolio is the same and in both cases there is a positive probability of default.

The results suggest that if the bank's loans are not all positively correlated, the bank will always prefer to sell loans in the secondary market instead of issuing equity. The intuition for this result is simple. If a bank's portfolio is not made up with loans that all appreciate or depreciate at the same time, there will always be a loan that the bank could sell at a price above its true value (i.e., its "lemon"). In the absence of any reputation costs from the secondary market, selling a lemon results in a gain for the bank's existing shareholders. Issuing equity, instead, involves a loss for the bank's existing shareholders. The size of the loss could depend on the correlation structure of loan returns, but it is always a loss. Even if we were to introduce reputation costs from selling lemons, the bank will still prefer to sell loans instead of equity, since it could sell a riskless combination of loans at zero cost for the bank's existing shareholders instead of issuing equity at a loss. The only case where the bank would consider issuing equity is one in which all loans are positively correlated with each other and after the new equity issue there is still a positive probability of default. When all loans are positively correlated, there is no strategy that results in a gain for the bank's existing shareholders. There is also no riskless combination of loans that could lead to zero loss. Hence, all strategies involve a loss for the bank's existing shareholders and the bank will simply choose the strategy with the minimum loss. We show that if after issuing equity there is still a positive probability of default, issuing equity could be the optimal strategy.

Theories of financial intermediation predict that loan sales should not be possible, since such a market would be a "lemons" market (e.g., Diamond, 1984; Boyd & Prescott, 1986). However, there are a number of possible explanations why this market exists and why it has not shut down. For example, Gorton and Pennacchi (1995) show that loan sales could be incentive compatible if the selling bank retained a fraction of the loan or it gave loan buyers an implicit guarantee to repurchase the loan at a previously agreed price if the quality of the loan deteriorates. In addition, the loan sales market would not shut down if not all loans supplied in this market are lemons. Loan sales would still occur if some "constrained" banks were forced to supply profitable projects. This reasoning is similar to Akerlof's (1970) argument that, as long as some individuals must sell their cars every year, the used car market will not shut down because not all cars will be lemons. Here, the loan sales market is not a lemons market because "constrained" banks (i.e., the weakest banks in the model) find it optimal to supply loans at a price below their true value in order to postpone bankruptcy.

This chapter is organized as follows. Section 16.2 presents the assumptions underlying the model. Section 16.3 describes the expected payoffs from each strategy assuming that the bank is willing to issue equity or sell any of its loans regardless of which state occurs. Section 16.4 describes the equilibrium and Section 16.5 concludes this chapter.

16.2. A Model of Bank Financing Choice

Consider a model with two periods, period 1 and period 2, and a bank with two loans, loan 1 and loan 2. We define L_i^B the book value of loan i in period 1 and L_i^M the market value of loan i in period 1, where $i = 1, 2$. Similarly, we define D^B and E^B the book values of debt and equity in period 1, and D^M and E^M their corresponding market values in period 1. Clearly,

$$D^B + E^B = L_1^B + L_2^B, \qquad (16.1)$$

$$D^M + E^M = L_1^M + L_2^M, \qquad (16.2)$$

where the market value of each loan in period 1 is equal to its expected value in period 2 conditional on whatever information the market has in period 1. For simplicity, we assume that in period 1 the two loans have the same market value,

$$L_1^M = L_2^M, \qquad (16.3)$$

and that the bank's portfolio is balanced with respect to each loan,

$$L_1^B = L_2^B. \tag{16.4}$$

Suppose that due to market or regulatory constraints, the bank must increase its capital ratio from its current level $d = E^B/(L_1^B + L_2^B)$ to a new level $c > d$ and that this increase must be accomplished in period 1. In general, a bank can increase its capital ratio by increasing the numerator of its capital ratio (i.e., by issuing equity) and/or by decreasing the denominator (i.e., by selling loans, not initiating new loans and not renewing old loans). Here, we assume that the bank can decrease the denominator of its capital ratio only by selling loans and that it has enough of each loan as to be able to sell only one of the two loans to satisfy its new capital requirement.[3] Hence, the bank can satisfy its new capital requirement by pursuing one of the following strategies:

  (i) issue E of new equity,
 (ii) sell proportion b of loan 1,
(iii) sell proportion b of loan 2,
 (iv) sell proportion $\omega_1 b$ of loan 1, $\omega_2 b$ of loan 2, and $(1-\omega_1 b-\omega_2 b)$ of E, where $(0 \le \omega_1, \omega_2 < 1)$.

  If strategy (i) is pursued, E must be such that:

$$c = \frac{E + E^B}{L_1^B + L_2^B}. \tag{16.5}$$

Instead, if strategy (ii) is pursued, b must be such that:

$$c = \frac{E^B + b(L_1^M - L_1^B)}{L_2^B + (1 - b)L_1^B}, \tag{16.6}$$

where $b(L_1^M - L_1^B)$ is the gain or loss from the sale of loan 1. Note that the cash from the sale is kept on the balance sheet until period 2, when it is used to repay debt. In other words, the bank does not use this money to buy or issue new loans since this would defy the reason for which the loans were sold in the first place (i.e., to increase its capital ratio). Similarly, if strategy (iii) is pursued, b must be such that:

$$c = \frac{E^B + b(L_2^M - L_2^B)}{L_1^B + (1 - b)L_2^B}. \tag{16.7}$$

Combining Equations (16.1) and (16.3)–(16.6) we get the following relationship between E and b:

$$E = \frac{b(2L_1^M - D^B)}{(2 - b)}. \tag{16.8}$$

Following Myers and Majluf (1984), we assume that both, the bank's managers and the investors, are risk neutral and that the bank's management acts for the best interest of the existing shareholders.[4] Like in Myers and Majluf's set-up, the existing shareholders are passive (i.e., they "sit tight" if new stock is issued, which implies that any new issue goes to a different group of investors). In period 1, the bank managers must decide which strategy to pursue in order to maximize the existing shareholder's (i.e., those who hold shares of the bank at the beginning of period 1) wealth.

To formalize this maximization problem, we define V_2 the market value of the existing shareholder's wealth in period 2 and V_{2j} the market value of V_2 given the choice of strategy j in period 1. The optimal strategy is chosen from the set $I = \{I_1, I_2, I_E, I_\omega\}$ of possible strategies in period 1, where I_E is the strategy of selling equity, I_1 is the strategy of selling proportion b of loan 1, I_2 is the strategy of selling proportion b of loan 2, and I_ω is the mixed strategy.

Hence, the bank manager's maximization problem can be written as,

$$\max_{j \in I} V_2. \tag{16.9}$$

If two or more strategies result in the same V_2 we assume that the bank management chooses the strategy that maximizes the wealth of existing shareholders in period 1. To formalize this, we define V_1 the market value of existing shareholders wealth in period 1 and V_{1j} the value of V_1 given the choice of strategy j in period 1. Hence, when more than one strategy solves Equation (16.9), the chosen strategy should also solve:

$$\max_{j \in I^*} V_1, \tag{16.10}$$

where I^* is the set of strategies that solves Equation (16.9).

We will now describe the investors' maximization problem. In period 1, the investors purchase loans or equity in order to maximize their wealth in period 2. However, they are at an informational disadvantage. In period 1, the bank's managers know the values of the two loans in period 2, while the investors do not observe these values until period 2. In period 1, the investors know what are the possible values in period 2 and thus they form expectations upon which they base their decisions in period 1. Note that this chapter takes this information asymmetry as given and sidesteps the question of how much information managers should release. Hence, the underlying assumption is that transmitting information is prohibitively costly. Obviously, the distortions introduced because of the asymmetric information would disappear if the managers could convey their special information to the market.

Suppose that in period 2 there are two equally possible states of nature for each loan: the market value of loan 1 can increase or decrease by $\delta\alpha$ and the market value of loan 2 can increase or decrease by α, where $0 < \delta < 1$ and $\alpha > 0$. Hence, in period 1 the expected value of loan 1 and loan 2 are equal to L_1^M and L_2^M, respectively. Given Equation (16.3) the two loans have the same expected value in period 1, but loan 2 is riskier. If we assume that the correlation structure of loan returns is *negative* (i.e., in period 2, one of the two loans appreciates whereas the other loan depreciates), then Table 16.1 describes the possibilities with which investors are faced in period 2.

According to Table 16.1, there are two equally possible states of nature in period 2: the "high-quality scenario" and the "low-quality scenario". The high (low) quality scenario is

Table 16.1: The correlation structure of loan returns is negative.

Market value in period 1	Market value in period 2	
	High-quality scenario	Low-quality scenario
Loan 1 L_1^M	$L_1^M(1 - \delta\alpha)$	$L_1^M(1 + \delta\alpha)$
Loan 2 L_2^M	$L_2^M(1 + \alpha)$	$L_2^M(1 - \alpha)$

one in which the average market value of the bank's loan portfolio increases (decreases) from period 1 to period 2. Given our set-up, the value loan 2 in period 2 determines which scenario will prevail in period 2.

If, instead, we assume that the correlation structure of loan returns is *positive* (i.e., in period 2, both loans appreciate or depreciate), then Table 16.2 describes the possibilities with which investors are faced in period 2.

In Table 16.1, the correlation coefficient (ρ) between the two loans is equal to -1, while in Table 16.2 it is equal to 1. Since the bank has only two loans, the correlation coefficient between loan 1 and loan 2 fully characterizes the correlation structure of the bank's loan portfolio. It is important to point out that the expected value of the bank's portfolio is the same across the two correlation structures.

The risk neutral investors are willing to purchase a security offered by the bank if the security's expected return is at least equal to the expected return from their best alternative. Here, if the investors do not purchase the security offered by the bank, they can invest their funds in a riskless asset that pays a real interest rate R, where R is normalized to 0. In addition, it is assumed that capital markets are perfect and efficient with respect to publicly available information and that there are no transaction costs in issuing equity or selling loans. Hence, in equilibrium the investors will buy the security offered by the bank at a price that will imply an expected return of zero (i.e., equal to the return from their best alternative).

Finally, we assume that bank debt is risky: regardless of whether $\rho = -1$ or 1, there is a positive probability of bankruptcy.[5] In particular, we assumed that all bank debt matures in period 2 and that even if $\rho = -1$ the bank would default on its debt if the low-quality scenario would prevail. This implies that the following conditions hold:

$$L_1^M(1 - \delta\alpha) + L_2^M(1 + \alpha) > D^B, \qquad (16.11)$$

$$L_1^M(1 + \delta\alpha) + L_2^M(1 - \alpha) < D^B. \qquad (16.12)$$

The first inequality states that if $\rho = -1$ and the high-quality scenario is realized, the market value of the two loans in period 2 exceeds the face value of the bank's debt and thus the bank will be able to pay its debt in full. Since $R = 0$, the amount of debt that has to be repaid in period 2 is equal to the face value of debt in period 1, D^B. The second inequality, instead, states that if $\rho = -1$ and the low-quality scenario is realized, the market value of the bank's portfolio in period 2 is lower than the face value of its debt. Hence, the bank, in this case, will go bankrupt.

Table 16.2: The correlation structure of loan returns is positive.

Market value in period 1	Market value in period 2	
	High-quality scenario	Low-quality scenario
Loan 1 L_1^M	$L_1^M(1 + \delta\alpha)$	$L_1^M(1 - \delta\alpha)$
Loan 2 L_2^M	$L_2^M(1 + \alpha)$	$L_2^M(1 - \alpha)$

Given Equations (16.11) and (16.12) we know that the following conditions also hold:

$$L_1^M(1 + \delta\alpha) + L_2^M(1 + \alpha) > D^B, \tag{16.13}$$

$$L_1^M(1 - \delta\alpha) + L_2^M(1 - \alpha) < D^B. \tag{16.14}$$

This implies that if the $\rho = 1$, the bank will be able to repay its debt if the high-quality scenario prevails while it will default on its debt if the low-quality scenario is realized.

The choice of security to sell in period 1, however, could improve or worsen the bank's ability to repay its debt. For example, suppose that $\rho = 1$ and that the bank's managers know that the low-quality scenario will prevail in period 2 and they choose to sell proportion b of loan 2. If the investors do not know which scenario will prevail, they are willing to buy loan 2 at its expected value, L_2^M.[6] Hence, V_{2l_2} is given by:

$$V_{2l_2} = \max\{0, bL_2^M + L_1^M(1 - \delta\alpha) + (1 - b)L_2^M(1 - \alpha) - D^B\},$$

which might be positive or zero depending on the parameter values. If $V_{2l_2} > 0$, selling loan 2 prevents the bank from a sure bankruptcy. The intuition is simple: because of asymmetric information the bank is able to sell loan 2 at a favourable price before a major loss in its market value. However, if the investors knew that the low-quality scenario would prevail they would be willing to pay only $bL_2^M(1 - \alpha)$. Hence, V_{1l_2} and thus V_{2l_2} would immediately drop to zero since it is common knowledge that under these conditions the bank will be bankrupt in period 2. In particular, V_{2l_2} is given by:

$$V_{2l_2} = \max\{0, bL_2^M (1 - \alpha) + L_1^M(1 - \delta\alpha) + (1 - b)L_2^M(1 - \alpha) - D^B\}$$

$$\Rightarrow V_{2l_2} = \max\{0, L_1^M(1 - \delta\alpha) + L_2^M (1 - \alpha)\}.$$

Given Equation (16.14), we know that:

$$V_{2l_2} = 0.$$

In some cases, selling a certain security might worsen the bank's ability to repay its debt. For example, suppose that $\rho = -1$ and the bank's managers know that the high-quality scenario will prevail and they choose to sell loan 2. Since the investors do not know which scenario will prevail, they are willing to buy loan 2 at its expected value, L_2^M. Hence, V_{2I_2} is given by:

$$V_{2I_2} = \max\{0, bL_2^M + L_1^M(1 - \delta\alpha) + (1 - b)L_2^M(1 + \alpha) - D^B\},$$

which might be positive or zero depending on the parameter values. If $V_{2I_2} = 0$, selling loan 2 worsens the bank's ability to repay its debt (i.e., before the sale the bank was able to repay its debt for sure, while after the sale it is not always able). The intuition is simple: because of the asymmetric information the bank can only sell loan 2 at its expected value which is below the value that will have in period 2.

16.3. Expected Payoffs

We will now calculate the existing shareholder's gain/loss from each strategy assuming that the investors are willing to buy any of the three securities at their expected values (i.e., the choice of security to sell does not signal to investors which scenario will be realized in period 2). We show later that this condition holds at the equilibrium.

The existing shareholder's gain/loss from each strategy will be calculated under two *alternative* assumptions, depending on whether issuing new equity helps the bank to avoid bankruptcy under the low-quality scenario.

Assumption 1: In period 2 the bank can repay its debt in full under the low-quality scenario if it issues an amount E of new equity in period 1. This implies that:

$$L_1^M(1 + \delta\alpha) + L_2^M(1 - \alpha) + E > D^B,$$

when $\rho = -1$.

$$L_1^M(1 - \delta\alpha) + L_2^M(1 - \alpha) + E > D^B,$$

when $\rho = 1$.

Assumption 2: In period 2 the bank cannot repay its debt in full under the low-quality scenario if it issues an amount E of new equity in period 1. This implies that:

$$L_1^M(1 + \delta\alpha) + L_2^M(1 - \alpha) + E < D^B,$$

when $\rho = -1$.

$$L_1^M(1 - \delta\alpha) + L_2^M(1 - \alpha) + E < D^B,$$

when $\rho = 1$.

Given that equity holders are residual claimants (i.e., in the event of bankruptcy they receive whatever is left after the repays its debt in full), the price they are willing to pay for equity depends on whether in period 2 there is positive probability of bankruptcy or not. Next we derive the price that investors are willing to pay for E.

16.3.1. Negative Correlation

Table 16.3 describes the existing shareholder's gains/losses under each possible scenario when the correlation structure of loan returns is negative.

The calculations for strategies I_1 and I_2 are straightforward. For example, suppose that under the *high-quality scenario* the bank sells proportion b of loan 1 for its expected value in period 2, bL_1^M. In this case, the bank's existing shareholders will gain $bL_1^M \delta\alpha$, since the market value of loan 1 will decrease by $\delta\alpha$ in period 2. Instead, if the bank sells proportion b of loan 2 for its expected value, bL_2^M, the bank's existing shareholders will forgo the increase in the value of loan 2 in the next period. Hence, their loss from strategy I_2 will equal $-bL_2^M\alpha$. Since $L_1^M = L_2^M$, the loss from strategy I_2 can be written as $-bL_1^M\alpha$ in order to facilitate comparison with loss/gain from I_1. The gains/losses under the *low-quality scenario* can be derived in a similar way.

The expected gains/losses from strategies I_1 and I_2 are *feasible*, since in the absence of signalling, the investors are willing to buy loan 1 or loan 2 at their expected prices. For example, buying loan 1 at its expected price, L_1^M, is a fair deal for investors since the expected payoff from this transaction is equal to the opportunity cost of their money. In particular, since the existing shareholder's gain is equal to the investor's loss and vice versa, the investor's expected gain is:

$$\text{Investor's expected gain} = 0.5(bL_1^M\alpha\delta) + 0.5(-bL_1^M\alpha\delta) = 0.$$

Given that $R = 0$ and that investors are risk neutral, an expected gain of zero is one that satisfies investors. It is straightforward to show that the same is true for loan 2.

The calculations of the shareholder's gains/losses from I_E are more complicated and deserve some discussion. Recall from the definitions that V_{1I_E} is the market value of the existing shareholders wealth in period 1 if the bank sells new equity in period 1. Clearly, V_{1I_E} will be determined by the price at which the new investors are willing to buy new equity. In particular, new shareholders realize that the market value of debt increases when new equity is issued and adjust the price they are willing to pay for E.[7] However, since in period 1 investors do not know which scenario will be realized in period 2, they calculate the expected value of debt after the equity issue, D_{new}^M, by assigning a probability of 0.5 to each of the two possible scenarios.

Table 16.3: Existing shareholder's gains/losses when $\rho = -1$.

Strategy	High-quality scenario		Low-quality scenario	
	Assumption 1	Assumption 2	Assumption 1	Assumption 2
I_1	$bL_1^M\delta\alpha$	$bL_1^M\delta\alpha$	$-bL_1^M\delta\alpha$	$-bL_1^M\delta\alpha$
I_2	$-bL_1^M\alpha$	$-bL_1^M\alpha$	$bL_1^M\alpha$	$bL_1^M\alpha$
I_E	$-bL_1^M\alpha(1-\delta)/2$	$-E$	$bL_1^M\alpha(1-\delta)/2$	E
I_ω	0	0	0	0

Under *Assumption 1*, the market value of debt in period 1 increases from its initial level D^M to its risk free level D^B, since the equity issue enables the bank to repay its debt in full under the low-quality scenario. Hence, D^M_{new} is given by:

$$D^M_{new} = 0.5D^B + 0.5D^B = D^B.$$

The new shareholders want this increase in debt value to be paid by the existing shareholders. In other words, they want V_{1I_E} to be worth its pre-issue market value, E^M, minus the increase in the market value of debt, D^B–D^M:

$$V_{1I_E} = E^M - (D^B - D^M). \tag{16.15}$$

Given that $D^M = 0.5D^B + 0.5[L^M_1(1 + \delta\alpha) + L^M_2(1 - \alpha)]$, we can express V_{1I_E} as,

$$V_{1I_E} = E^M - 0.5\{D^B - [L^M_1(1 + \delta\alpha) + L^M_2(1 - \alpha)]\}, \tag{16.16}$$

where $D^B - [L^M_1(1 + \delta\alpha) + L^M_2(1 - \alpha)]$ measures the shortfall of existing funds that will be covered with funds from the new equity issue if the low-quality scenario is realized. Since in period 1 the investors do not know which scenario will prevail in period 2, they are willing to buy the new equity if the existing shareholders pay the expected shortfall, $0.5\{D^B - [L^M_1(1 + \delta\alpha) + L^M_2(1 - \alpha)]\}$. This means that in the event of bankruptcy the new shareholders will only loose $0.5\{D^B - [L^M_1(1 + \delta\alpha) + L^M_2(1 - \alpha)]\}$.

Under these conditions, the new shareholders will pay E for new shares if they receive a proportion k of the total shares outstanding after the new equity issue:

$$k = \frac{E}{V_{1I_E} + E}. \tag{16.17}$$

Since the total market value of all shares after the new equity issue is $V_{1I_E} + E$, the market value of the existing shareholders shares is $(1 - k)(V_{1I_E} + E)$, which is equal to V_{1I_E}, where V_{1I_E}, is determined by Equation (16.16).

For a given amount E, these equations determine the price of each share. In particular, the higher the increase in the market value of debt, $D^B - D^M$, the higher the proportion k of the total shares that the new shareholders get for a given amount E, and thus the lower the price of each share. Moreover, it is clear from Equation (16.16) that the price of each share depends on the market value of the bank's portfolio in the low-quality scenario. In particular, the lower the value of the bank's loan portfolio in the worst-case scenario the larger the shortfall and thus the lower the price the new shareholders are willing to pay for each share. *This implies that under Assumption 1 the correlation structure of loan returns affects the price of new equity*. Everything else equal, the value of the bank's portfolio in the low-quality scenario is lower when $\rho = 1$, than when $\rho = -1$. When $\rho = 1$ both loans depreciate in value, while when $\rho = -1$ one loan depreciates and the other appreciates mitigating the total drop.

If new equity is issued under these conditions, the gain to the bank's existing shareholders will be given by the difference between the value of new equity in period 1 and the value of new equity in period 2. This implies that under the *high-quality scenario* the existing shareholder's loss is given by:

$$\text{Existing shareholder's loss} = E - k[L_1^M(1 - \delta\alpha) + L_2^M(1 + \alpha) - D^B + E]. \quad (16.18)$$

Substituting Equations (16.2), (16.3), (16.8), (16.15) and (16.17) into (16.18) we get:

$$\text{Existing shareholder's loss} = -\frac{b}{2}L_1^M\alpha(1 - \delta).$$

Similarly, under the *low-quality scenario* the existing shareholder's gain is:

$$\text{Existing shareholder's gain} = \frac{b}{2}L_1^M\alpha(1 - \delta).$$

We will now calculate the existing shareholder's gain/loss from selling equity under Assumption 2. Under *Assumption 2*, new shareholders know that in period 1 the market value of debt after an equity issue will increase from D^M (the original level) to some new level D_{new}^M. In this case, $D_{new}^M < D^B$ since the bank will not be able to repay its debt for full if the low-quality scenario prevails. Hence, V_{1I_E} is given by:

$$V_{1I_E} = E^M - (D_{new}^M - D^M), \quad (16.19)$$

where,

$$D_{new}^M = 0.5D^B + 0.5[L_1^M(1 + \delta\alpha) + L_2^M(1 - \alpha) + E], \quad (16.20)$$

$$D^M = 0.5D^B + 0.5[L_1^M(1 + \delta\alpha) + L_2^M(1 - \alpha)]. \quad (16.21)$$

Using Equations (16.20) and (16.21) we can express V_{1I_E} as,

$$V_{1I_E} = E^M - 0.5E, \quad (16.22)$$

where E is the amount of new equity that will be lost in period 2 if the low-quality scenario prevails. Like before the investors are willing to buy the new shares if this amount is shared with the existing shareholders. Note that in this case, the amount that both existing and new shareholders will loose is fixed and does not depend on the value of the bank's portfolio in period 2. This also implies that the price of each share is fixed.

Under these conditions, the existing shareholder's loss under the *high-quality scenario* is:

$$\text{Existing shareholder's loss} = E - k[L_1^M(1 - \delta\alpha) + L_2^M(1 + \alpha) - D^B + E]. \quad (16.23)$$

Substituting Equations (16.2), (16.3), (16.8), (16.17), (16.19), and (16.20) into (16.23) we get:

$$\text{Existing shareholder's loss} = -E.$$

Similarly, under the *low-quality scenario* the existing shareholder's gain is given by:

$$\text{Existing shareholder's gain} = E.$$

Buying equity is a fair deal for investors since their expected payoff is equal to the opportunity cost of their money. In particular, under *Assumption 1*, the investor's expected gain is:

$$\text{Investor's expected gain} = 0.5\left[\frac{b}{2}L_1^M(1+\delta)\right] + 0.5\left[-\frac{b}{2}L_1^M(1+\delta)\right] = 0,$$

while under *Assumption 2* is:

$$\text{Investor's expected gain} = 0.5E + 0.5(-E) = 0.$$

Finally, we consider the mixed strategy, I_w, which involves selling a riskless combination of the three securities (i.e., a combination that has the same value in period 1 and period 2 regardless of which scenario prevails). Such combination must be considered because it eliminates the asymmetric information problems and thus it could potentially dominate the other strategies. In particular, a combination $\omega_1 b$ of loan 1, $\omega_2 b$ of loan 2, and $(1-\omega_1-\omega_2)$ of equity is riskless, if it involves no loss or gain at each possible scenario (i.e., it has the same value in period 1 and period 2 regardless of which scenario prevails). Under *Assumption 1*, this implies that ω_1 and ω_2 must satisfy the following equations:

$$\omega_1 b L_1^M \delta\alpha - \omega_2 b L_2^M\alpha - (1-\omega_1-\omega_2)\frac{b}{2}L_1^M\alpha(1-\delta) = 0, \tag{16.24}$$

and

$$-\omega_1 b L_1^M \delta\alpha + \omega_2 b L_1^M\alpha - (1-\omega_1-\omega_2)\frac{b}{2}L_1^M\alpha(1-\delta) = 0. \tag{16.25}$$

Equations (16.24) and (16.25) imply that I_ω is riskless if:

$$\omega_1 - \omega_2 = \frac{1-\delta}{1+\delta}.$$

Similarly, under *Assumption 2* it can be shown that I_ω involves no risk if:

$$\omega_1 b L_1^M \delta\alpha + \omega_2 b L_1^M\alpha = (1-\omega_1-\omega_2)E.$$

16.3.2. *Positive Correlation*

Table 16.4 describes the existing shareholder's gains/losses when $\rho = 1$. The calculations are not presented since they are similar to those described in the previous section for $\rho = -1$. All expected gains reported in Table 16.4 are feasible for the same reasons explained in the previous section. Note, however, that Table 16.4 does not report the results for a mixed strategy. This is because no such riskless combination exists when $\rho = 1$.

16.4. Equilibrium

We now derive the bank's optimal choice of security to sell at the equilibrium assuming that the bank's managers and the investors are rational economic agents maximizing their objective functions conditional on whatever information they have in period 1.

16.4.1. *Negative Correlation*

Comparing the gains/losses reported in Table 16.3 we can rank the bank's preferences. Table 16.5 shows the bank's preferences in descending order.

Given the above ranking of preferences, if the bank's managers know that the high-quality scenario will prevail they would like to sell loan 1, irrespective of whether Assumption 1 or 2 holds. This is because I_1 is the only strategy that results in a gain for the bank's existing shareholders. On the contrary, if the bank's managers know that the low-quality scenario will prevail and Assumption 1 holds, they would like to sell loan 2, since it is the strategy with the largest gain. If, instead, they know that the low-quality

Table 16.4: Existing shareholder's gains/losses when $\rho = 1$.

Strategy	High-quality scenario		Low-quality scenario	
	Assumption 1	Assumption 2	Assumption 1	Assumption 2
I_1	$-bL_1^M \delta\alpha$	$-bL_1^M \delta\alpha$	$bL_1^M \delta\alpha$	$bL_1^M \delta\alpha$
I_2	$-bL_1^M \alpha$	$-bL_1^M \alpha$	$bL_1^M \alpha$	$bL_1^M \alpha$
I_E	$-bL_1^M \alpha(\delta + 1)/2$	$-E$	$bL_1^M \alpha(\delta + 1)/2$	E

Table 16.5: Descending order of preferences when $\rho = -1$.

	High-quality scenario	Low-quality scenario
Assumption 1	I_1, I_ω, I_E, I_2	I_2, I_E, I_ω, I_1
Assumption 2	I_1, I_ω, I_E, I_2	I_2, I_E, I_ω, I_1 if $bL_1^M \delta\alpha > E$
		I_E, I_2, I_ω, I_1 if $bL_1^M \delta\alpha < E$

scenario will prevail and Assumption 2 holds, they would like to sell loan 2 or equity depending on whether $bL_1^M \delta \alpha$ is greater or smaller than E.

However, the bank's first best strategy under each scenario cannot be the equilibrium solution. In particular, the bank's first best choice under the high-quality scenario is *always different* from its first best strategy under the low-quality scenario. Hence, if the bank chooses anything else other than I_1 it will give the signal to investors that it is the low-quality scenario that will prevail. In that case, they are willing to buy the security offered by the bank, only at the price they think it will have in period 2. Under these circumstances, it is straightforward to show that the bank will always choose its first best strategy under the high-quality scenario in order to postpone bankruptcy for one period. This leads to Proposition 1.

Proposition 1: When $\rho = -1$, the unique equilibrium is one in which proportion b of loan 1 is sold.

Proof: It will be shown that under each possible scenario the bank will not deviate from the postulated equilibrium. The proof is divided in two steps:

Step 1: *It will be shown that if the bank's managers know that the high-quality scenario will prevail, they have no incentive to deviate from the postulated equilibrium.* Suppose that the bank's managers sell proportion b of loan 1, V_{2I_1} is given by:

$$V_{2I_1} = \max\{0, bL_1^M + (1 - b)L_1^M(1 - \delta\alpha) + L_2^M(1 + \alpha) - D^B\}, \qquad (16.26)$$

which is positive since Equation (16.11) holds.

Given the out of equilibrium belief, if the bank chooses to sell anything other than I_1 it will give the signal to investors that it is the low-quality scenario that will prevail in period 2. For example, if the bank decides to sell proportion b of loan 2, it will be able to sell it only at $bL_2^M(1 - \alpha)$ because the investors will not be willing to pay more that the value of loan 2 under the low-quality scenario. This also means that the investors will think that the bank's condition is described by:

$$bL_2^M(1 - \alpha) + L_1^M(1 + \delta\alpha) + (1 - b)L_2^M(1 - \alpha) - D^B$$

$$\Rightarrow L_1^M(1 + \delta\alpha) + L_2^M(1 - \alpha) - D^B,$$

which according to Equation (16.12) is negative. In other words, if the bank chooses I_2, it will make investors believe that it will be bankrupt in period 2. Hence, the market value of its equity will immediately drop to zero (i.e., $V_{1I_2} = 0$ and thus $V_{2I_2} = 0$). Given that $V_{2I_1} > V_{2I_2}$, the bank will not deviate by selling loan 2.

The bank's managers will also not deviate by issuing equity. Given the out of equilibrium belief, an equity issue signals to investors that the low-quality scenario will prevail. Under such circumstances, investors are unwilling to buy equity because they think that their payoff in period 2 will be less than the amount they contributed in period 1. To prove this, note that if the bank issues new equity, the market value of both old and new stake in period 2 under the low-quality scenario is:

$$L_1^M(1 + \delta\alpha) + L_2^M(1 - \alpha) + E - D^B.$$

Investors believe that this value is less than E because under the low-quality scenario:

$$L_2^M(1 + \delta\alpha) + L_2^M(1 - \alpha) < D^B.$$

Thus, investors will not buy new equity worth E in period 1 even if they are offered 100% ownership. In other words, if investors think that equity in period 2 will have zero market value, they are not willing to buy equity for any positive price. Hence, selling new equity is not feasible. This also implies that the only feasible mixed strategy, I_ω, is one for which $\omega_1 + \omega_2 = 1$. However, the bank will not deviate from the postulated equilibrium by choosing I_ω for the same reasons it will not choose I_2.

Step 2: *It will be shown that if the bank's managers know that low-quality scenario will prevail, they do not have an incentive to deviate from the postulated equilibrium* because selling anything other than loan 1 will give the signal to investors that the low-quality scenario will prevail. For the same reasons as in step 1, selling loan 2, when investors think that the low-quality scenario will prevail results in: $V_{1I_1} = V_{2I_2} = 0$.

If, instead, the bank chooses to sell proportion b of loan 1, V_{2I_2} is given by:

$$V_{2I_2} = \max\{0, bL_1^M + (1 - b)L_1^M(1 + \delta\alpha) + L_2^M(1 - \alpha) - D^B\} = 0.$$

However, since I_1 does not signal to investors that the low-quality scenario will prevail, $V_{2I_1} > 0$. Given that $V_{2I_2} = V_{2I_1} = 0$ and $V_{2I_1} > V_{2I_2}$, the bank will not deviate from the postulated equilibrium by selling loan 2. For the same reasons as in step 1, selling equity at any positive price is not feasible and strategy I_ω is not preferred over I_1 since it will lead to $V_{1I_\omega} = V_{2\omega} = 0$.

It should be emphasized that I_1 is the optimal strategy since this is a one-shot model where there are no reputation effects from selling lemons. However, it is easy to see how our results would change if there were to introduce reputation costs. In that case, the bank's optimal strategy will be I_ω, instead of I_1, if the present discounted value of future reputation costs is equal or greater to the gain from I_1.

16.4.2. Positive Correlation

Comparing the gains/losses reported in Table 16.4 we can rank the bank's preferences. Table 16.6 shows the preferences of each bank in descending order of preference.

Given the ranking of preferences shown in Table 16.6, if Assumption 1 holds and the bank's managers know that the high-quality scenario will prevail, they would like to sell

Table 16.6: Descending order of preferences when $\rho = 1$.

	High-quality scenario	Low-quality scenario
Assumption 1	I_1, I_E, I_2	I_2, I_E, I_1
Assumption 2	I_E, I_1, I_2 if $bL_1^M\delta\alpha > E$	I_2, I_1, I_E if $bL_1^M\delta\alpha > E$
	I_1, I_E, I_2 if $bL_1^M\delta\alpha < E$	I_2 or I_E, I_1 if $bL_1^M\delta\alpha < E$

loan 1 in order to minimize the loss for their existing shareholders. On the contrary, if they know that the low-quality scenario will prevail, they would like to sell loan 2 in order to maximize the gain for their existing shareholders. Similarly, if Assumption 2 holds and the bank's managers know that the high-quality scenario will prevail, they would like to issue equity if $bL_1^M \delta \alpha > E$ and they would like to sell loan 1 if $bL_1^M \delta \alpha < E$. Instead, if they know that the low-quality scenario will prevail they would like to sell loan 2 if $bL_1^M \delta \alpha > E$ and they would like to sell loan 2 or to issue equity if $bL_1^M \delta \alpha < E$.

Also in this case, the bank's first best choice under the high-quality scenario is always different from its first best choice under the low-quality scenario. Hence, if the bank deviates from its first best choice under the high-quality scenario it will give the signal that it is the low-quality scenario that will prevail and the investors will adjust their price. It is straight-forward to show that under these conditions the bank will not find it profitable to deviate from its first best strategy under the high-quality scenario, even if they know that it is the low-quality scenario that will prevail in period 2. This leads to Propositions 2 and 3.

Proposition 2: When $\rho = 1$ and Assumption 1 holds, the unique equilibrium is one in which proportion b of loan 1 is sold.

Proposition 3: When $\rho = 1$ and Assumption 2 holds, then the unique equilibrium depends on the relationship between $bL_1^M \delta \alpha$ and E. If $bL_1^M \delta \alpha < E$, the proportion b of loan 1 is sold at the equilibrium. Instead, if $bL_1^M \delta \alpha > E$, then equity will be issued at the equilibrium.

Formal proofs of Propositions 2 and 3 are not presented because they are very similar to the proof of Proposition 1. The rational of all three propositions is straightforward. At the equilibrium the bank's managers will always choose to follow the first best strategy under the high-quality scenario because they will otherwise give the signal to investors that it is the low-quality scenario that will prevail in period 2. This out of equilibrium belief is possible because the first best strategy under the high-quality scenario is always different from the first best strategy under the low-quality scenario.

16.5. Conclusions

This chapter examines how the correlation structure of loan returns affects a bank's choice of financing in a Myers and Majluf's set-up with asymmetric information. In particular, we consider a bank that must raise its capital ratio and can choose between issuing equity and selling loans in the secondary market. In the first period of the model, when the bank must increase its capital ratio, there is asymmetric information about the quality of its loans and a positive probability of default in the next period. Contrary to previous studies in the literature, only the correlation structure of loan returns (and not the expected values) enters the analysis. The results suggest that even in a set-up where all agents are risk neutral, the correlation structure of loan returns could have important implications on the bank's choice of financing and the cost of issuing equity.

In particular, we show that the bank will always find it optimal to sell loans in the secondary market instead of issuing equity, if its loans are not all positively correlated with each other. The intuition for this result is simple. If a bank's portfolio is not made up with loans that all appreciate or depreciate at the same time, there will always be a loan that the bank can sell at a price above its true value (i.e., its "lemon"). In particular, in the absence of any reputation costs from the secondary market, selling a lemon results in a gain for the bank's existing shareholders. Instead, issuing equity involves a loss for the bank's existing shareholders. The size of the loss could depend on the correlation structure of loan returns, but it is always a loss. Note that even if we were to introduce reputation costs from selling lemons, the bank will still prefer to sell loans instead of issuing equity, since it could sell a riskless combination of loans at zero cost for the bank's existing shareholders instead of issuing equity at a loss.

When all loans are positively correlated with each other, there is no strategy that results in a gain for the bank's existing shareholders. There is also no riskless combination of loans that could lead to zero loss. All feasible strategies involve a loss for the bank's existing shareholders. Hence, the bank will choose the strategy with the minimum loss. If issuing equity eliminates the probability of default in the second period, the loss from issuing equity will always be larger than the loss from selling a loan. The loss from an equity issue depends positively on the variance of the bank's total loan portfolio, while the loss from selling a loan depends only on its own variance. Given that all loans are positively correlated with each other, the variance of the bank's portfolio is always larger than the variance of any one of its loans. Hence, selling a loan is always cheaper. In fact, the bank will sell its less risky loan (i.e., the one that will have to sell at a lower discount). If instead, the probability of default in the second period is positive, the loss from selling equity does not depend on the variance of a bank's loan portfolio, but is fixed and equal to the amount raised from the equity issue. The bank will issue equity if this amount is lower than the loss from selling its less risky asset.

The model highlights that a bank will find it optimal to issue equity — instead of selling loans in the secondary market — only if all bank loans are positively correlated with each other and there is a positive probability of default in the future. In practice, however, it is unlikely that a bank loans would either all increase or decrease in value at the same time. This might happen occasionally but is unlikely to happen on a consistent basis. If it did, it would imply that some banks are consistently undervalued or overvalued. It is more likely that a bank will have favourable inside information for some of its loans and unfavourable inside information for some of its other loans. As far as this is true, the results suggest that the bank will always prefer to sell loans instead of equity. Whether it will choose to sell a lemon or a riskless combination of loans it depends on whether there are reputation costs.

Endnotes

1. Berger and Udell (1993) provide a comprehensive review of this literature up to 1993. For more recent papers, see Carlstrom and Samolyk (1995), Gorton and Pennacchi (1995), Demsetz (2000), Jones (2000), Dahiya, Puri, and Saunders (2003), and Cebenoyan and Strahan (2004).

2. If the loan is sold without recourse, not only it is removed from the bank's balance sheet, but the bank has no explicit liability if the loan eventually goes bad (i.e., the buyer bears all the credit risk). Instead, if the loan is sold with explicit recourse, under certain conditions the buyer can put the loan back to the selling bank. Thus, the bank retains a contingent credit risk liability.

3. Since the purpose of this chapter is to study the bank's choice of financing under different assumptions about the correlation structure of loan returns, this assumption guarantees that the bank's choice is constrained by factors other than those analyzed in this chapter.

4. The shareholders and the investors would behave as if they are risk neutral if they hold sufficiently large and diversified portfolios to achieve perfect risk pooling.
5. Having a positive probability of default for both cases (i.e., $\rho = -1$ or 1) it is necessary in order to make the two cases comparable.
6. This is true only if the bank's choice of security to sell does not signal to investors which scenario will prevail in period 2. In Section 16.4, we show that this is true in equilibrium since the bank's optimal strategy is the same regardless of which scenario (high or the low) will be realized in period 2.
7. Since debt holders are senior claimants while equity holders are residual claimants, an equity issues makes more funds available to repay the bank's debt.

References

Akerlof, G. (1970). The market for lemons: Quantitative uncertainty and the market mechanism. *The Quarterly Journal of Economics, 84,* 488–500.

Berger, A.N., & Udell, G. (1993). Securitization, risk, and the liquidity problem in banking. In: M. Klausner, & L. White (Eds), *Structural changes in banking* (pp. 227–291). Homewood: Irwin.

Boyd, J.H., & Prescott, E.C. (1986). Financial intermediary-coalitions. *Journal of Economic Theory, 38,* 211–232.

Carlstrom, C.T., & Samolyk, K.A. (1995). Loan sales in response to market-based capital constraints. *Journal of Banking and Finance, 19,* 627–647.

Cebenoyan, S.A., & Strahan, P.E. (2004). Risk management, capital structure and lending at banks. *Journal of Banking and Finance, 28,* 19–43.

Dahiya, S., Puri, M., & Saunders, A. (2003). Bank borrowers and loan sales: New evidence on the uniqueness of bank loans. *Journal of Business, 76,* 563–582.

Demsetz, R.S. (2000). Bank loan sales: A new look at the motivations for secondary market activity. *Journal of Financial Research, 23,* 192–222.

Diamond, D. (1984). Financial intermediation and delegated monitoring. *Review of Economic Studies, 51,* 393–414.

Gorton, G.B., & Pennacchi, G.G. (1995). Banks and loan sales, marketing nonmarketable assets. *Journal of Monetary Economics, 35,* 389–411.

James, C. (1988). The use of loan sales and standby letters of credit by commercial banks. *Journal of Monetary Economics, 22,* 1183–1200.

Jones, D. (2000). Emerging problems with the Basel Capital Accord: Regulatory capital arbitrage and related issues. *Journal of Banking and Finance, 24,* 35–58.

Myers, S.C., & Majluf, N.S. (1984). Corporate financing and investment decisions when firms have information that investors do not have. *Journal of Financial Economics, 12,* 187–221.

Pavel, C., & Phillis, D. (1987). Why commercial banks sell loans: An empirical analysis. *Federal Reserve Bank of Chicago Economic Perspectives, 14,* 3–14.

Pennacchi, G.G. (1988). Loan sales and the cost of bank capital. *The Journal of Finance, 43,* 375–396.

Saunders, A. (1999). Loan sales and other credit risk management techniques. In: A. Saunders (Ed.), *Financial institutions and management a modern perspective* (pp. 648–663). Chicago: Irwin.

Chapter 17

Shareholder Value and Growth in Sales and Earnings

Luc Soenen

17.1. Introduction

The relentless search for growth and the $3.5 billion acquisition in 2000 of US Foodservice appear to be among the factors that led to massive accounting problems at the Dutch retailer Ahold NV. Ahold was determined to maintain earnings growth of at least 15% annually. The company drove its executives to continue meeting tough-growth targets even as the global supermarket operator ran out of good acquisition opportunities in recent years (Wall Street Journal, February 26, 2003). The company ended up with 12 billion euro in debt, it certainly got bigger but not better for its many stakeholders.

A similar experience was recently reported by Ghemawat (2004) regarding Coca-Cola's growth targets causing enormous troubles. Coke's top executives clung stubbornly to the company's long-term volume growth rates of 7–8%. After it ran through two CEOs and various strategies, advertising campaigns, and pursued several takeover attempts, it saw its market value plummet. In December 2003, Coca-Cola announced that it would stop giving analysts guidance based on volume growth rates. It finally figured out that a company could not simultaneously maximize its growth rate and the present value of its total profit stream.

The quest for growth is not new but symptomatic for so many companies. Unfortunately, the pursuit of growth, to become the number one in the business has very often resulted in disappointing consequences for its shareholders. The fastest way to grow is through merger and acquisition. Although a big acquisition can inflate a company's top line it is hardly fair to call this growth. Real growth depends on innovations, for example, when a company runs out of innovation, it runs out of growth (Hamel & Getz, 2004). Deal making through Mergers and Aquisition (M&A) was used to increase revenues at companies such as Enron, Tyco, Worldcom, Vivendi, and DaimlerChrysler but is unlikely to produce above-average growth for more than a few years at a time. Publicly available data (Wall Street Journal, March 9, 2005) shows that of the 172 companies that spent time on Fortune's list of the 50 largest

Advances in Corporate Finance and Asset Pricing
Edited by L. Renneboog
© 2006 Elsevier B.V. All rights reserved.
ISBN: 0-444-52723-0

companies between 1955 and 1995, only 5% were able to sustain a real, inflation-adjusted annual growth rate of more than 6% across their entire tenure in this group.

As companies find it increasingly harder to achieve and sustain growth, they have placed their faith in acquisitions and alliances to boost sales, profits, and importantly, stock prices (Dyer, Kale, & Singh, 2004). These authors and others, for instance Fuller, Netter, and Stegemoller (2002), conclude that acquisitions of public firms on average either destroy or do not add shareholder value while alliances typically create very little wealth for shareholders.

Too many companies have focused on the top line of the income statement ignoring the bottom line. Growth without profitability cannot be sustained. The challenge remains to turn growth into profits, preferable simultaneously. Bigger by itself may not make economic sense, but then do you know of a firm that wants to stop growing?

17.2. Growth and the Creation of Shareholder Value

The fact that managers pursue corporate growth and diversification as a primary objective, even at the expense of shareholder value, is well established (see Aggarwal & Samwick, 2003). Early on Seymour Tilles, Vice President at BCG (1963) noted: many managers have a view of their companies' future that is strikingly analogous to the child's view of himself. When asked what they want their companies to become over the next few years, the reply "bigger". So why do managers almost blindly pursue corporate growth?

Several reasons for pursuing corporate growth have been identified in the literature. By pursuing corporate growth, managers might be pursuing their own personal wealth at the expense of shareholders. This is the classic agency problem of financial contracting (Jensen & Meckling, 1976). Since managers essentially hold a call option on the underlying assets of the firm, this asymmetric incentive structure might induce them to take actions that are not in the best interests of shareholders. Given this agency cost scenario, therefore, managers grow their companies because by doing so they expect to grow their own remuneration, regardless of the effects of such growth on shareholder value. Another reason for corporate growth relates to the fact that managers are not fully diversified as they typically hold large wealth positions in the firms they manage, for example, their salary, executive stock options, and direct stock holdings are all dependent upon the performance of their company. In other words, they are exposed to significant idiosyncratic risk (Jin, 2002). Since they cannot fully diversify exogenously to their own firm, managers may attempt to diversify endogenously through corporate growth. Managers may use the corporate assets under their control to buy other companies, to form alliances, and thereby diversify their own wealth position. For example, May (1995) finds that CEOs with more wealth tied up in their own firm's equity engage in acquisitions that are more diversifying.

There is significant evidence that managers pursue corporate growth at the expense of shareholder value for reasons other than personal wealth or risk reduction. Along with big remuneration come power, job security, and celebrity status. With millions of dollars of incentive pay as well as oversized reputations at stake most successful CEOs are at risk of losing it all because they have committed themselves to unrealistic targets. This is because managers succumb to a tendency of overconfidence about the likely outcome of their decisions. Evidence of overconfidence bias has a pedigree in financial economics dating back to Roll's "Hubris Hypothesis" (1986), in which he explains shareholder-value-destroying corporate acquisitions in terms of managerial overconfidence in corporate acquisition decisions. Managers simply overestimate the probability of success and underestimate the probability of failure.

In "just say no to wall street", for example, Jensen and Fuller (2002) argue that the power of market analysts lead managers to frame their decisions too narrowly. Managers focus entirely on meeting analysts' expectations. Senior management's presumed obsession with anticipated quarterly earnings growth limits its innovation productivity, which is according to Hamel and Getz (2004) the only source of long-term sustainable real growth. Thus the power of market analysts is inducing managers to frame their decisions in terms of sales and earnings growth to meet analysts' expectations, rather than in terms of shareholder value creation.

Associating creation of shareholder value with growth in earnings, sales, or other metrics is commonplace in the investment industry, and the use of such metrics has greatly influenced managerial compensation schemes and thus provided impetus to M&As as well as internal growth.

Traditional incentives schemes compensation is often tied to the manager's ability to beat budgeted increases in earnings or sales, but a formal mechanism for determining whether growth activities enhance returns to shareholders is lacking. Jensen (1989) and Murphy (1985) discussed the undesirable consequences of tying executive pay and managerial compensation to measures of corporate growth. The modern "value-based approaches" remove this ambiguity; in these approaches, managers' compensation depends on metrics that are consistent with shareholder value wealth maximization. Such value-based metrics as economic value added (EVA), market value added (MVA), return on invested capital, and cash flow return on investment (ROI) — all claim to align management and shareholder interests. Although EVA has gained wide acceptance in both the investment community and corporate boardrooms, it remains an open question whether this value-based performance measure is truly in line with shareholder interests.

In this chapter, we are concerned with two broad questions that are of considerable theoretical and practical interest. First, what is the relationship between earnings (or sales) growth and measures of corporate profitability? Understanding the nature of this relationship will shed light on whether there is an optimal growth that maximizes profitability. Moreover, if companies with high earnings (sales) growth also generate high EVA, then either growth rates or EVA can be used in managerial compensation schemes. The second question is: does maximizing such a performance metric as EVA maximize shareholder wealth or stated differently, is there a risk-adjusted premium to investing in the equity of companies that experience high earnings (sales) growth and generate positive EVA?

17.3. Corporate Growth and Performance[1]

To examine the relationship between growth and company performance we use data from the annual Compustat files on US companies for the period 1990 through 2000. Following standard practice, we exclude data for American Depository Receipts, utilities, and financial, governmental or unclassifiable institutions. We also exclude companies with annual net sales, total assets, and common equity less than $1 million. The final sample consists of approximately 2156 companies a year.

We consider two broad measures of growth, each of which represents a different view of a company's ability to expand the sales and earnings growth rate. Sales growth is measured as the average of quarterly sales growth rates over the past 20 quarters. Similarly, earnings growth is measured as the average of earnings growth rates over the past 20 quarters. Earnings are defined as net of interest, dividends, and taxes but before depreciation. For each calendar year, we sort the data and assign companies to quartiles of sales and earnings growth rates, with the first quartile containing the companies with the slowest growth rates.

To investigate the link between measures of growth and corporate profitability, we examine return on equity (ROE) and ROI as the two classic measures of corporate profitability. ROE is defined as income before extraordinary items divided by common equity. ROI is calculated as income before extraordinary items divided by total invested capital, which is the sum of total long-term debt, preferred stock, minority interests, and common equity. For the newer value-based measures we use EVA and its variant MVA. We follow the methodology described by Yook (1999) to calculate EVA. Since EVA does not account for growth opportunities inherent in the companies' investment decisions, we introduce MVA to capture this effect. In effect, MVA measures the difference between what investors have put in and what they expect to take out. One disadvantage of MVA is that it may be biased by over- or under-valuation of a company's growth opportunities as reflected in its stock price. To facilitate comparisons of companies and comparisons over time, we normalize EVA, MVA, and other dollar-denominated variables by the net asset value (NAV) of the company. NAV is defined as total assets – cash and marketable securities.

These metrics measure performance from a corporate finance perspective rather than the point of view of shareholder wealth creation. Therefore, following Bacidore, Boquist, Milbourn, and Thakor (1997), we use Jensen's alpha, which measures "abnormal returns" given the company's systematic risk, to assess the impact of performance on shareholders' wealth.

As can be seen from Table 17.1, high sales growth rates are accompanied by high volatility. For the sample as a whole, the correlation between sales and earnings growth is negative. The negative correlation can be seen for the first three quartiles of earnings but reverses in the fourth quartile. This inverted U-shaped relationship shows that for a majority of companies, faster earnings growth is not synonymous with faster sales growth.

Somewhat surprisingly, we find that, on average, companies destroy value, as measured by EVA. Companies in the inner-quartile range, however, have better results. MVA increases across the quartiles of both measures. This result is not surprising as MVA represents the difference between the market value and book value of the company's capital, and as such, it reflects the market expectations about the company's future growth prospects. The 1990–2000 period covered one of the longest bull markets in US history. The "irrational exuberance" expressed by many market participants is reflected in the positive relationship between MVA and growth rate, whereas the inner-quartile EVA is always negative. The classic measures, ROE and ROI, show a highly non-linear relationship between growth and performance, on average, companies in the inner quartiles performed

Table 17.1: Company characteristics by sales and earnings.

Measure	All firms	Quartiles of annual sales growth rate				Quartiles of annual earnings growth rate			
		Q1	Q2	Q3	Q4	Q1	Q2	Q3	Q4
Sorting variable									
Mean sales growth rate (%)	49.50	−3.36	11.77	26.13	166.51	57.58	40.61	32.02	67.93
Standard deviation sales growth rate (%)	79.05	29.71	29.20	40.21	220.65	92.95	68.98	48.18	106.31
Performance measures									
EVA/net assets	−0.11	−0.11	−0.05	−0.06	−0.23	−0.15	−0.09	−0.06	−0.15
MVA/net assets	1.04	0.42	0.70	1.12	1.93	0.85	0.92	1.26	1.11
ROE (%)	−1.40	−4.01	5.30	2.54	−9.63	−10.06	1.82	7.21	−4.64
ROI (%)	3.42	−1.79	3.27	−1.65	14.11	1.55	0.04	5.85	6.26
Financial attributes									
Size (total assets, $ millions)	825.75	1068.70	1053.30	751.62	416.94	537.70	1061.90	1100.50	600.16
Market/book	1.85	1.49	1.71	1.93	2.30	1.75	1.77	2.00	1.90
Total debt/total equity (%)	71.42	77.92	72.07	67.53	68.03	78.36	73.45	61.35	72.57
P/E	11.54	9.91	12.70	14.83	8.69	6.85	12.30	16.72	10.28

Table 17.1: Continued.

Measure	All firms	Quartiles of annual sales growth rate				Quartiles of annual earnings growth rate			
		Q1	Q2	Q3	Q4	Q1	Q2	Q3	Q4
Asset-pricing parameters									
Annualized CAPM alpha (%)	-8.66	-18.81	-8.46	-0.98	-6.23	-6.37	-15.19	-1.32	-11.75
CAPM beta	1.00	1.00	1.00	1.00	1.00	1.00	1.00	1.00	1.00
Idiosyncratic risk	56.39	51.93	47.99	55.87	70.15	67.52	50.29	43.86	63.98
Standard deviation of monthly returns	58.16	53.84	50.05	57.59	71.54	69.01	52.23	45.97	65.53
Sample size	23720	5986	5992	5923	5819	5920	5944	5947	5909

better. If we consider ROI in isolation, however, we find the first indication that maximizing growth may lead to maximum performance.

The next group of variables in Table 17.1 provides a broad picture of the companies' financial attributes by quartile. Small companies, measured by the value of total assets, generate the highest sales growth but not necessarily the highest earnings growth. Interestingly, the largest companies (on average) generate relatively high earnings growth (third quartile) with the lowest mean and standard deviation of sales growth rate. This finding is consistent with the evidence presented in Perez-Quiros and Timmerman (2000), who found that large and diversified companies are less vulnerable to cyclical market variations than small companies; small companies display a high degree of asymmetry in their riskiness between recession and expansion states.

As we move from the first to the third quartile of sales growth, both company size and the debt-to-equity ratio fall monotonically, but moving from the first to the third quartile of earnings growth is accompanied by an increase in company size and a fall in the debt-to-equity ratio. The ratio reaches its minimum in the third quartile of both partitioning measures, which suggests that these companies more likely rely on equity financing. These results are consistent with Myers' (1993) findings that the debt ratio tends to be lower in high-growth industries, even when the need for external capital may be great.

A common measure whether a company is likely to have projects providing positive net present value in the future is the ratio of the market value of the company's assets to the book value of its assets (MV/BV). Table 17.1 shows that MV/BV increases monotonically across sales growth quartiles, which suggests that companies with high sales growth rate also posses significant growth options. The ratio is relatively stable across the earnings quartiles, however, with companies in the third quartile having moderately better growth prospects. The "trailing" price/earnings (P/E) ratio reported in Table 17.1 is also indicative of a company's future growth opportunities and should rise with earnings. This ratio shows an inverted U-shaped relationship, however, for both partitioning measures, it reaches a maximum in the third quartile and falls in the fourth quartile. In other words, investors are prepared to pay the highest price per dollar of earnings for companies in the inner quartiles.

The final panel of Table 17.1 shows our results for the parameters of the capital asset-pricing model (CAPM) for the sample and partitioned portions. To estimate the CAPM alpha and beta parameters, we use the previous 60-months' excess returns for each company and the market (S&P 500 Index) returns over the yield on 3-month US T-bills. Since each sub-sample represents a well-diversified portfolio, Table 17.1 shows that the average beta for all data partitions is close to unity. The annualized alpha, which once again tends to follow an inverted path across the quartiles, reaches its maximum at the third quartile for both the sales growth and earnings growth groups. Interestingly, the companies in the third quartile of earnings growth have the lowest level of total and idiosyncratic risk.

These results point to a complex and often inverted U-shaped relationship between performance and growth. Company's performance improves with sales and earnings growth up to the third quartile and then declines in the fourth quartile. In fact, the companies in the third quartile of both growth measures appear to be the most likely to enhance corporate performance and maximize shareholder value.

Ramezani, Soenen, and Jung (2002) further investigate the relationship between growth and performance as measured by EVA, using a multivariate regression model. I report here the major findings of this analysis, the reader is referred to the original publication for detailed statistical results. The general conclusion is that there is a distinct pattern of "decreasing returns" to rapid growth, in that EVA significantly increases as we move to the third quartile of growth and declines in the fourth quartile. As Opler, Pinkowitz, Stulz, and Williamson (1999) showed, corporate cash holdings have significant implications for a company's performance and ability to capitalize on growth opportunities. The companies in the fourth quartiles of both growth measures had relatively higher cash holdings than companies in the other quartiles. Volatility, measured as the standard deviation of sales growth, is indicative of operational risks and evidently contributes negatively to managers' ability to enhance EVA. A large corporate cash holding also decreases EVA because most companies realize a lower rate of return on their cash holdings than on other internal or external investment opportunities. This finding is consistent with Jensen's (1986) conjecture that managers with substantial free cash holdings are more likely to engage in "empire building", which destroys shareholder value and hinders performance. Company size, measured by the logarithm of a company's total assets, contributes positively to EVA. All else being equal, EVA increases with MV/BV and P/E as well as the company's current cash flow and acquisition expenditures. The ratio of R&D expense to sales, which is a measure of potential financial distress (see Opler, Pinkowitz, Stulz, & Williamson, 1999), negatively influences EVA. These control variables are all proxies commonly used to measure corporate flexibility and the existence of growth options. The ratio of fixed assets to net assets, a proxy for a company's operational flexibility, is associated with lower EVA values. As predicted by Myers's financing hierarchy model, small companies (the fourth quartile based on sales growth) need to retain a larger portion of net income than large companies to fund future growth and are thus less likely to pay dividends. Companies that paid dividends or had high net profit margins had higher EVA. Access to credit market, determined by whether the company's bonds were rated lowers the cost of debt, which raises long- and short-term debt, has a negative impact on EVA.

To summarize, there is an inverted U-shaped relationship between EVA and measures of sales and earnings growth. The estimated regression coefficients are statistically and economically significant and support the results from the univariate analysis. Therefore, maximizing growth is not necessarily consistent with maximizing shareholder wealth. That is, shareholder value is a concave function of growth. Hence, the prevalent fascination with unbounded sales and earnings growth can be questioned.

17.4. Conclusion

The investment industry demands that managers maximize sales and earnings growth over time. This prescription is based on the presumption that growth is synonymous with shareholder value creation. The empirical results indicate that although the corporate profitability measures generally rise with earnings and sales growth, an optimal point exists beyond which further growth destroys shareholder value. As an investor you would receive the highest risk-adjusted returns by buying the stock of firms that persistently produced moderate sales and earnings growth rates. Had you focused on the high fliers (the fourth-quartile firms), your risk-adjusted returns would have been negative. The message of this chapter is quite simple: investing in the fastest growing firms is a very risky proposition. Pursuing such a strategy will most likely lead to shareholder value destruction. The most effective strategy is to invest in firms that demonstrate moderate and persistent sales and earnings growth rates. Managers must therefore move away from the obsessive focus on meeting quarterly earnings per share targets and instead adopt sustainable strategies and set realistic targets; if necessary, just say no to wall street.

The financial press is replete with examples of once rapidly growing companies that have "gone south". Recent crises have shown that growth without profitability cannot be sustained. The empirical results show that corporate managers need to abandon the habit of blindly increasing company size and investors need to carefully consider the drawbacks of diseconomies of scale (see Ghemawat & Ghadar, 2000), managers need to make a fundamental shift in their strategic orientation from "growth now, profitability later" to "profitable growth now". That is, growth should not be the input to strategic planning but the outcome of a sound investment strategy that is geared to accepting value-creating projects.

Endnotes

1. The empirical results reported are those published in Ramezani, Soenen, and Jung (2002). Similar empirical evidence was reported in an earlier study by Soenen and Duffhues (2001).

References

Aggarwal, R.K., & Samwick, A.A. (2003). Why do managers diversify their firms? *Journal of Finance, 58*, 71–118.

Bacidore, J.J., Boquist, J.A., Milbourn, T.T., & Thakor, A. (1997). The search for the best financial performance measure. *Financial Analysts Journal, 53*, 11–21.

Dyer, J.H., Kale, P., & Singh, H. (2004). When to ally & when to acquire. *Harvard Business Review, 82*, 109–115.

Fuller, K., Netter, J., & Stegemoller, M. (2002). What do returns to acquiring firms tell us? Evidence from firms that make many acquisitions. *Journal of Finance, 57*, 1763–1793.

Ghemawat, P. (2004). The growth boosters. *Harvard Business Review, 82*, 35–40.

Ghemawat, P., & Ghadar, F. (2000). The dubious logic of global megamergers. *Harvard Business Review, 78*, 65–72.

Hamel, G., & Getz, G. (2004). Funding growth in an age of austerity. *Harvard Business Review, 82*, 76–84.

Jensen, M. (1986). Agency costs of free cash flow: Corporate finance, and takeovers. *American Economic Review, 76*, 323–329.

Jensen, M. (1989). Eclipse of the public corporation. *Harvard Business Review, 67*, 61–74.

Jensen, M., & Fuller, J. (2002). Just say no to wall street. *Journal of Applied Corporate Finance, 14*, 41–46.

Jensen, M., & Meckling, W.H. (1976). Theory of the firm: Managerial behaviour, agency costs and ownership structure. *Journal of Financial Economics, 3*, 305–360.

Jin, L. (2002). CEO compensation, diversification and incentives. *Journal of Financial Economics, 66*, 29–63.

May, D.O. (1995). Do managerial motives influence firm risk-reduction strategies? *Journal of Finance*, *50*, 1291–1308.

Murphy, K. (1985). Corporate performance and managerial remuneration. *Journal of Accounting and Economics*, *7*, 16–39.

Myers, S.C. (1993). Still searching for optimal capital structure. *Journal of Applied Corporate Finance*, *6*, 4–14.

Opler, T., Pinkowitz, L., Stulz, R., & Williamson, R. (1999). The determinants and implications of corporate cash holdings. *Journal of Financial Economics*, *52*, 3–46.

Perez-Quiros, G., & Timmerman, A. (2000). Firm size and cyclical variations in stock returns. *Journal of Finance*, *55*, 1229–1262.

Ramezani, C., Soenen, L., & Jung, A. (2002). Growth, corporate profitability, and value creation. *Financial Analysts Journal*, *58*, 56–67.

Roll, R. (1986). The hubris hypothesis of corporate takeovers. *Journal of Business*, *59*, 198–216.

Soenen, L.A., & Duffhues, P.J.W. (2001). On the relationship between growth, profitability and shareholder value creation. *Tijdschrift voor Corporate Finance*, *6*, 6–17.

Tilles, S. (1963). The manager's job — a systems approach. *Harvard Business Review*, *41*, 73–81.

Yook, K. (1999). Estimating EVA using Compustat PC Plus. *Financial Practice and Education*, *9*, 33–37.

PART 4

ASSET PRICING AND MONETARY ECONOMICS

Chapter 18

The Term Structure of Interest Rates: An Overview

Peter de Goeij

18.1. Introduction

A large part of the investment portfolios of financial institutions as well as many individuals consists of fixed-income securities such as bonds and mortgages. Pension funds, for example, usually invest a large portion of their portfolio in government bonds, while insurance companies typically hold large amounts of fixed-income securities and mortgage banks have both fixed-income assets (the mortgages) and fixed-income liabilities.

There are several reasons to devote attention to fixed-income securities. First, fixed-income securities markets have developed separately from equity markets. They have their own institutional structure and terminology. Second, the markets for treasury securities are extremely large, regardless of whether size is measured by quantities outstanding or quantities traded. Therefore, good empirical research will provide us with better understanding of the types of risks that are involved in this kind of markets. Finally, many assets can be seen as combinations of fixed-income securities and derivative securities. Examples of these assets are bond options, interest rate swaps, interest swaptions, caps and floors. To be able to correctly determine the prices of these assets, a better understanding of the term structure of interest rates is of great importance. The market prices of fixed-income securities are by definition linked to the term structure. Term-structure models are also relevant in other areas in economics. In the field of monetary economics for example, the analysis of how long-term interest rates would change as a result of short interest rate targeting behaviour by the Central Bank is the topic of many studies.

The primary focus of this overview is on discrete-time models and on empirical implementation (using US data). Although most of the current research on interest-rate modelling is formulated in a continuous-time framework, for sake of convenience a discrete-time approach is used throughout this chapter.

The remainder of this chapter is organized as follows. In Section 18.2, some notation and terminology is introduced that will be used throughout this chapter. Section 18.3

Advances in Corporate Finance and Asset Pricing
Edited by L. Renneboog
© 2006 Elsevier B.V. All rights reserved.
ISBN: 0-444-52723-0

briefly explains how, in theory, bond prices can be calculated. Next, Section 18.4 provides an extensive overview of the (empirical) literature on term-structure modelling. Insights are provided to the expectation hypothesis of the term-structure, short interest-rate modelling, affine-yield models and the linking of the "financial" and "macroeconomic" term-structure literature. Finally, Section 18.5 concludes this chapter.

18.2. Definitions, Notation and Statistics

Interest is a payment (received) for borrowing (lending) funds over a period of time. Thus an interest rate is the amount of interest per unit of time as a fraction of the total amount of the funds. Zero-coupon bonds, also referred to as *discount bonds*, promise to pay a fixed amount of money, the *face value*, at a certain date in the future, the *maturity date*, assuming that the bond issuer will not default on his loan.[1] The length of time to the maturity date is referred to as the *maturity* of the bond. For example, US Treasury bills with maturity up to and including 12 months are discount bonds.

The yield to maturity of a bond is the fictional, constant, known, annual, interest rate that justifies the quoted price of a bond, assuming that the bond does not default (see Cochrane, 2001: 348). If P_{nt} is the price at time t of a discount bond that makes a single payment of $1 at time $t + n$ (the maturity date) and if Y_{nt} is the yield to maturity, we have:

$$P_{nt} = \frac{1}{(1 + Y_{nt})^n}. \tag{18.1}$$

Hence, the yield to maturity can then be calculated as:

$$1 + Y_{nt} = P_{nt}^{-\frac{1}{n}}. \tag{18.2}$$

It is common in the empirical literature to work with log-arithmetic or continuously compounded variables. This has the advantage that it transforms the non-linear relationship (18.2) into a linear one. Taking logs, we can write Equation (18.2) as:

$$y_{nt} = -\frac{1}{n} p_{nt}, \tag{18.3}$$

where $y_{nt} = \log(1 + Y_{nt})$ and $p_{nt} = \log(P_{nt})$. Note that for small values of Y_{nt}, $y_{nt} \approx Y_{nt}$.

The *term structure of interest rates*, also known as the *yield curve*, describes the relation between yields at different maturities at a certain point in time. It is the function that relates yields to the maturity. Yield curves can be upwards sloping, downward sloping or humped-shaped functions of the time to maturity. Examples of such types of yield curves, using fictional data, are shown in Figure 18.1. First, and this is the most common case, the yield curve is *upwards* sloping: the yield of the shorter maturities is lower that of higher maturities as is shown in the upper-left graph of the figure. Second, occasionally the yield curve is *hump shaped:* it rises first and then falls at longer maturities. An example of such a yield curve is shown in the upper-right graph of the figure. Finally, the lower-left graph of the figure shows an *inverted* yield curve, and is characterized by a downward sloping curve over the whole range of maturities. The shape of the yield curve can change day by day and this

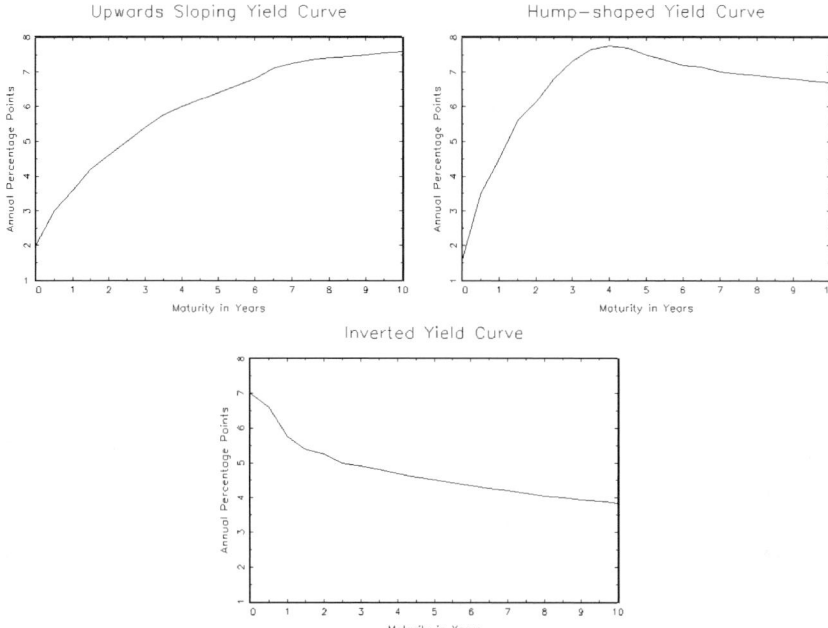

Figure 18.1: Different yield curve shapes. Notes: The upper-left graph shows a upward sloping yield curve, the upper-right graph shows a hump shaped yield curve, while in the lower-left graph a downwards sloping yield curve is shown. Fictional data is used to make the graphs.

is obviously an important risk that has to be taken into account when determining an investment strategy.

To illustrate some stylized facts of the term structure for the US, we consider continuously compounded zero-coupon interest rate data, taken from McCulloch and Kwon (1993). This data set covers the period 1947:12 to 1991:2. Due to the Treasury accord of March 4, 1951, the data before that date are less reliable and therefore, like in Campbell and Shiller (1991), the observations prior to 1952:1 are not taken into account. We update the data by including data from Duffee (2002), which results in a data set that covers the period 1952:1 to 2000:12, for a total of 588 observations. Table 18.1 presents some descriptive statistics of the US yield data.

Table 18.1 shows that the average yield curve is upward sloping: the 1-month yield is about 5.16% and this gradually increases to about 6.63% for the 10-year discount bond. The sample standard deviations in Table 18.1 form the basis for the average *volatility curve*. This curve indicates how the variance of the yield curve behaves over the different maturities. From Table 18.1, we can see that this volatility curve is hump shaped. Furthermore, for each maturity there is a large difference between the minimum and maximum interest. This indicates that the general level of the yield curve has changed significantly during the sample

Table 18.1: Descriptive statistics of US yields.

Maturity	Mean	Standard deviation	Minimum	Maximum
1	5.160	2.789	0.249	16.210
2	5.339	2.840	0.485	16.010
3	5.462	2.863	0.615	15.999
6	5.686	2.899	0.685	16.511
12	5.894	2.887	0.847	16.345
36	6.256	2.795	1.412	15.825
60	6.430	2.762	1.770	15.696
84	6.553	2.748	2.072	15.283
120	6.626	2.724	2.341	15.065

Notes: The maturity is measured in months. The table reports the sample mean, standard deviation, minimum and maximum using data from McCulloch and Kwon (1993) and Duffee (2002), which cover the period 1952:1 to 2000:12. All yields are given as percentages per annum, are on a continuous compounding basis and represent the last business day of the month.

period. This can be seen more clearly if we focus on the *time-series* dimension of the term structure. Figure 18.2 shows the time series of the 1-month and the 10-year US yields. In general, the level of the short maturity yield is lower than the level of the longer maturity yield. However, at some periods we can see that the 1-month yield is higher than the 10-year yield. During these periods there was an inverted yield curve.

Yields should not be confused with returns. Returns are calculated over a fixed holding period, for example a month. Define $(1 + R_{n,t+1})$ as the gross one-period holding return on an n-period bond purchased at time t and sold at time $t + 1$ (see, for example, Shiller, 1990). At $t + 1$, the bond will then be a $(n - 1)$-period bond with price $P_{n-1,t+1}$. Therefore, the *holding return* is defined as:

$$1 + R_{n,t+1} = \frac{P_{n-1,t+1}}{P_{nt}}. \tag{18.4}$$

which will be referred to the *return* in the remainder of this chapter. Due to the inverse relationship between bond prices and yields (see definition (18.1)), we can rewrite Equation (18.4) as:

$$1 + R_{n,t+1} = \frac{(1 + Y_{nt})^n}{(1 + Y_{n-1,t+1})^{n-1}}. \tag{18.5}$$

From Equations (18.4) and (18.5), it can be confirmed that the return is high when the price on the bond bought at time t is low (when its yield is high), and the price on the bond sold at time $t + 1$ is high (when its yield is low). In logs, we calculate the log return $r_{n,t+1} = \log (1 + R_{n,t+1})$ as:

$$r_{n,t+1} = P_{n-1,t+1} - P_{nt} \tag{18.6}$$

$$= ny_{nt} - (n - 1)y_{n-1,t+1}.$$

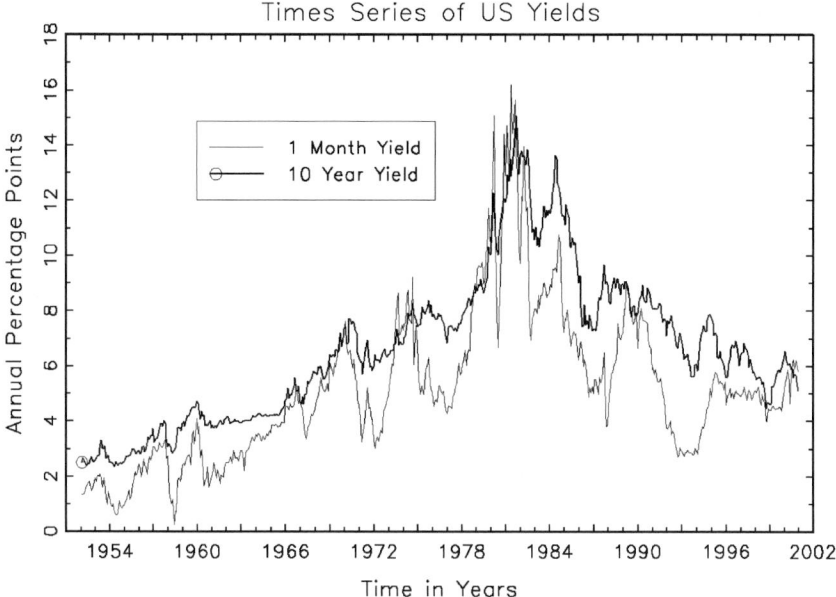

Figure 18.2: Time-Series Graphs of 1-Month and 10-Year Yields. *Notes*: Time-series graphs of the 1-month and the 10-year yield. The data are taken from McCulloch and Kwon (1993) and Duffee (2002) and cover the period 1952:1 to 2000:12.

Note that for small values of $R_{n,t+1}$, $r_{n,t+1} \approx R_{n,t+1}$. Unlike the log yield, the log return is not known in advance because it depends on the uncertain price at which the discount bond can be sold in the next period. Only when the investor holds the bond to maturity, the log return will be equal to the log yield. Table 18.2 shows some summary statistics of the returns on the zero-coupon bonds.

From Table 18.2, we can see that for maturities up to 12 months, the average returns are increasing with maturity. For a maturity of 3–7 years, the average return increases from about 0.49% per month to almost 0.50% per month. For a maturity of 10 years, the return is slightly more than 0.49% per month. The differences in return between maturities are quite small. In the table we can see that the unconditional variance of the log returns is increasing with maturity. The standard deviations of the bond returns are in general lower than for the bond yields. Both the skewness and excess kurtosis are larger than zero. This indicates that the distribution of log returns for each maturity separately, is skewed to the right and has "fat" tails.

In contrast to discount bonds, *coupon bonds* have *coupon payments*, normally a certain fraction of the face value, at equally spaced times up to and including the maturity date, while on the maturity date, the principal is paid (back) as well. The majority of the bonds that are issued by governments and (large) corporations are coupon bonds. Examples of such bonds are the US Treasury notes and bonds that have a maturity above 12 months at issue date. Bonds that are issued by companies like, for example, IBM, GE and AT&T are

Table 18.2: Descriptive statistics of US discount bond returns.

Maturity	Mean	Standard deviation	Minimum	Maximum	Skewness	Excess Kurtosis
2	0.4452	0.2349	−0.0169	1.5810	1.1826	5.365
3	0.4596	0.2494	−0.1337	1.8927	1.4387	6.964
6	0.4809	0.3184	−0.4993	3.0852	2.3612	14.655
12	0.5021	0.5006	−1.6677	4.6909	1.8539	14.918
36	0.4895	1.1586	−6.3394	8.5803	0.5305	10.284
60	0.4952	1.6861	−8.8364	9.6300	0.2487	7.397
84	0.4959	2.1161	−10.0860	10.4020	0.2050	5.950
120	0.4912	2.7700	−11.5100	12.7120	0.3419	5.758

Notes: The maturity is measured in months. The table reports the sample mean, standard deviation, minimum, maximum, skewness and excess kurtosis of monthly log returns on US discount bonds. The returns are calculated according to Equation (18.6) using data from McCulloch and Kwon (1993) and Duffee (2002), which cover the period 1952:1 to 2000:12. All returns are given in percentages per month.

referred to as *corporate bonds*. Prices of these bonds are in general different than those of treasury bonds with the same maturity. These differences in price are due to the difference in the risk of default between a company and government.

In the US, coupon payments on Treasury bonds are made every 6 months. However, the coupon rates for these instruments are normally quoted at an annual rate; thus a 5% Treasury bond actually pays 2.5% of the face value every 6 months up to and including the maturity date. Coupon bonds can be seen as packages of discount bonds: several discount bonds with the face value equal to the value of one coupon payment and a final coupon bond with its face value equal to the principal plus one coupon payment. This way of splitting up a coupon bond is not only theoretically convenient. The principal and interest components of US Treasury bonds have been traded separately under the Treasury's STRIPS (Separate Trading of Registered Interest and Principal Securities) programme since 1985.

In contrast with discount bonds, the price of a coupon-paying bond not only depends on its maturity n and time t, but also on its coupon payments. If we define one period as the time interval between coupon payments and c as the coupon payment per period,[2] the price of a coupon bond, P_{nt}^{c}, that pays a coupon c in each period plus the principal (which is normalized at 1 for convenience) at the maturity date, is given by:

$$P_{nt}^{c} = \frac{c}{(1 + Y_{1t})} + \frac{c}{(1 + Y_{2t})^2} + \cdots + \frac{1 + c}{(1 + Y_{nt})^n}$$

$$= \frac{1}{(1 + Y_{nt})^n} + \sum_{i=1}^{n} \frac{c}{(1 + Y_{it})^i}.$$

(18.7)

The *yield to maturity* of this coupon bond is defined as the (interest) rate $\widetilde{Y}_{nt}$ that solves:

$$P_{nt}^c = \frac{c}{1 + \widetilde{Y}_{nt}} + \frac{c}{(1 + \widetilde{Y}_{nt})^2} + \cdots + \frac{1 + c}{(1 + \widetilde{Y}_{nt})^n}$$

$$= \frac{1}{(1 + \widetilde{Y}_{nt})^n} + \sum_{i=1}^{n} \frac{c}{(1 + \widetilde{Y}_{nt})^i}.$$

(18.8)

In general, $\widetilde{Y}_{nt}$ will be different from Y_{nt}, unless $c = 0$. For US Treasury bonds coupon payments are made every 6 months. Therefore, Y_{nt} is the 6-month yield and the annual yield quoted to the public is $2 \times \widetilde{Y}_{nt}$. Note that Equation (18.8) cannot be solved analytically. Instead it must be solved numerically, but since all future payments are positive there is a unique positive real solution for $\widetilde{Y}_{nt}$ (see also Campbell, Lo, & MacKinlay, 1997). If the price of a coupon bond equals 1 (the principal) at a certain period t, the yield to maturity of the coupon bond equals the nominal coupon interest rate (as mentioned "on the bond"). In general, however, as prices vary over time, yields to maturity also change over time.

18.3. Pricing Zero-Coupon Bonds

Every asset-pricing model should be able to correctly price stocks *and* bonds.[3] From the asset-pricing literature it is known that in an economy that does not admit arbitrage opportunities, there exits a (positive) *stochastic discount factor M* also known as the *pricing kernel*, such that the expectation of the product of this stochastic discount factor and the gross return on the asset i is equal to 1:

$$E_t\{M_{t+1}(1 + R_{n,t+1})\} = 1,$$

(18.9)

where $E_t\{.\}$ denotes the expectation operator, conditional on the information available at time t, I_t (see Harrison & Kreps, 1979).

Fixed-income securities, such as discount bonds, have deterministic cash flows. Therefore, only time-variation in the discount rates makes them covary with the stochastic discount factor. The only source that can determine this time-variation stems from the time-series behaviour of the stochastic discount factor. Therefore, term-structure models are equivalent to time-series models for the stochastic discount factor (see Cochrane, 2001, Chapter 19).[4]

To obtain an expression in terms of prices, we combine Equations (18.9) and (18.4) to obtain:

$$P_{nt} = E_t\{M_{t+1}P_{n-1,t+1}\}.$$

(18.10)

A discount bond pays its face value at the maturity date, and if the face value is normalized to 1, $P_{0t} = 1$. Using this property, we can recursively solve Equation (18.10) to express the n-period bond price as the expected product of n successive one-period stochastic discount factors:

$$P_{nt} = E_t\{M_{t+1}M_{t+2}\cdots M_{t+n}\} = E_t\{M_{t+n}^n\}.$$

(18.11)

This expression shows that the price of a discount bond is solely depending on the time-series properties of the stochastic discount factor as stated above. Expressions (18.9)–(18.11) are equivalent, but it depends on the type of model which is the most convenient to work with (see Campbell, Lo, & MacKinlay, 1997). Note that Equation (18.11) states that the price of the n-period bond is the conditional expectation of the n-period stochastic discount factor: M_{t+1}^n, such that for an investor with a horizon of n periods, a n-period discount bond is riskless (Campbell, 2000). Or to put it in other words: a bond that is bought at the issue date, and that is kept until its maturity date does not contain any risk for the (n-period horizon) investor.

Equation (18.11) shows that in *theory* it should be relatively easy to calculate the prices of discount bonds. If the time-series process of the stochastic discount factor M_{t+1}, is known, you can in principle find the price of any bond by chaining together the (one-period) discount factors. However, this chaining together can be hard to do and much of the analytical machinery in term-structure models centres on this technical question (see Cochrane, 2001: 347).

18.4. Interpreting the Term Structure of Interest Rates

There is a large empirical literature that tests statements about expected-return relationships among bonds without deriving these statements from a fully specified equilibrium model. On the other hand, there is also a large literature on fully specified general-equilibrium models of the term structure on interest rates. This section tries to provide an overview of the most important topics in the term-structure literature.

18.4.1. The Expectation Hypothesis of the Term Structure

The expectation hypothesis of interest rates has been studied for more than a century. In its log form, the expectation hypothesis can be formulated in a number of ways.[5] Here, the most common definition is used, which states that the log yield on an n-period discount bond equals the expected sum of n successive log yields of one-period bonds that are rolled over for n periods:

$$y_{nt} = \frac{1}{n} \sum_{i=0}^{n-1} E_t\{y_{1,t+i}\}. \tag{18.12}$$

This definition is closely related to the explanation given by Irving Fisher (1896): "*The investor who holds a bond a long time realizes an interest which is an "average" of the oscillating rates of those who speculate during the interim.*"

The expectation hypothesis assumes that an investor does not bear a risk premium. Therefore the literature refers to Equation (18.12) as the *pure expectation hypothesis*. Definition (18.12) can also be extended to cover cases that incorporate risk premiums that vary over maturity, but not over time (see, for example, Campbell and Shiller, 1991). This *expectation hypothesis* is similar to Equation (18.12), augmented with a time-invariant term premium (Φ_n):

$$y_{nt} = \frac{1}{n} \sum_{i=0}^{n-1} E_t\{y_{1,t+i}\} + \Phi_n. \tag{18.13}$$

Equation (18.13) can be obtained by assuming the existence of a constant risk premium that is defined as the difference between the expected log return on an *n*-period bond and the one-period log yield:

$$\phi_n = E_t\{r_{n, t+1}\} - y_{1t}.$$ (18.14)

Combining this definition with Equation (18.6) we obtain:

$$\phi_n = ny_{nt} - (n-1)E_t\{y_{n-1, t+1}\} - y_{1t},$$

which can be solved for y_{nt}:

$$y_{nt} = \frac{1}{n}y_{1t} + \frac{n-1}{n}E_t\{y_{n-1, t+1}\} + \frac{1}{n}\phi_n.$$ (18.15)

Using backwards substitution of Equation (18.15) in itself we obtain Equation (18.13), where Φ_n is defined as:

$$\Phi_n = \frac{1}{n}\sum_{i=0}^{n-1}\phi_{n-i}.$$ (18.16)

As mentioned in the previous section, a model for the term structure is obtained by formulating a time-series model for the stochastic discount factor. Consider Equation (18.9):

$$E_t\{M_{t+1}(1 + R_{n,t+1})\} = 1.$$

This equation can be written as:

$$\text{Cov}_t\{M_{t+1}, (1 + R_{n,t+1})\} + E_t\{M_{t+1}\} E_t\{(1 + R_{n,t+1})\} = 1.$$

When the returns and the stochastic discount factor are log-normally distributed, taking logs this equation implies (see, for example, Bekaert, & Hodrick, 2001):

$$E_t\{m_{t+1}\} + \frac{1}{2}\text{Var}_t\{m_{t+1}\} + E_t\{r_{n,t+1}\} + \frac{1}{2}\text{Var}_t\{r_{n,t+1}\} + \text{Cov}_t\{m_{t+1}, r_{n,t+1}\} = 0,$$ (18.17)

where $m_{t+1} = \log(M_{t+1})$; and $\text{Var}_t\{.\}$ and $\text{Cov}_t\{.\}$ denote the variances and covariances conditional on time *t* information. Using Equation (18.6) for $n = 1$, and substituting it into Equation (18.17) we obtain:

$$y_{1t} = -\left[E_t\{m_{t+1}\} + \frac{1}{2}\text{Var}_t\{m_{t+1}\}\right].$$ (18.18)

Then, combining Equations (18.17) and (18.18) we have:

$$E_t\{r_{n,t+1}\} - y_{1t} = -\left[\frac{1}{2}\text{Var}_t\{r_{n,t+1}\} + \text{Cov}_t\{m_{t+1}, r_{n,t+1}\}\right].$$ (18.19)

Note that the left-hand side of this equation corresponds to the right-hand side of Equation (18.14). However, the right-hand side of Equation (18.19) is not necessarily constant over time. Therefore, defining a time-varying risk premium as:

$$\phi_{nt} = -\left[\frac{1}{2}\,\mathrm{Var}_t\,\{r_{n,t+1}\} + \mathrm{Cov}_t\,\{m_{t+1},r_{n,t+1}\}\right] \tag{18.20}$$

and go through steps (18.14) and (18.15) again, we obtain:

$$y_{nt} = \frac{1}{n}\sum_{i=0}^{n-1} E_t\{y_{1,t+i}\} + \Phi_{nt} \tag{18.21}$$

where,

$$\Phi_{nt} = \frac{1}{n}\sum_{i=0}^{n-1} E_t\{\phi_{n-i,t+i}\}. \tag{18.22}$$

For $\Phi_{nt} = \Phi_n$, Equations (18.13) and (18.21) are equal. Bekaert, Hodrick, and Marshall (2001) and Bekaert and Hodrick (2001) derive the assumptions that are needed for the stochastic discount factor such that the expectation hypothesis is valid. Their derivations show that for the expectation hypothesis to hold we need to assume that all second and higher-order conditional moments of the log-pricing kernel are constant.

Various studies have investigated the expectation hypothesis of the term structure of interest rates. Campbell and Shiller (1991) and Bekaert, Hodrick, and Marshall (2001) for example, use Equations (18.13) and (18.15) to derive simple linear relationships that can easily be tested empirically. First, the regression equation:

$$y_{n-1,t+1} - y_{nt} = \alpha_0 + \alpha_1 \frac{1}{n-1}\,(y_{nt} - y_{1t}) + \varepsilon_{t+1}, \tag{18.23}$$

should hold with $\alpha_0 = -\frac{1}{n-1}\,\phi_n$, $\alpha_1 = 1$ and $\varepsilon_{t+1} = y_{n-1,t+1} - E_t\{y_{n-1,t+1}\}$. Equation (18.23) describes a simple regression model where ε_{t+1} can be interpreted as an error term. Therefore, the first way to test Equation (18.13) is to run a regression of $(y_{n-1,t+1} - y_{nt})$ on a constant and the adjusted spread $\frac{1}{n-1}\,(y_{nt} - y_{1t})$ and testing whether the slope coefficient α_1 is equal to 1. A second regression-based test of the expectation hypothesis, is to rewrite Equation (18.13). This results in the regression equation:

$$\frac{1}{n}\sum_{i=0}^{n-1} y_{1,t+i} - y_{1t} = \beta_0 + \beta_1\,(y_{nt} - y_{1t}) + \varepsilon_{t+n-1} \tag{18.24}$$

which must hold with $\beta_0 = -\Phi_n$, $\beta_1 = 1$ and $\varepsilon_{t+n-1} = \frac{1}{n}\sum_{i=0}^{n-1}(y_{1,t+i} - E_t\{y_{1,t+i}\})$. Therefore, the second simple way of testing the expectation hypothesis is to run the ordinary least square (OLS) regression in Equation (18.24) and test whether the slope coefficient β_1 is equal to 1.

Using our data set for the US, we estimate Equations (18.23) and (18.24), the results of which are presented in Table 18.3. The estimates for α_1 in the regression (18.23) are all significantly different from 1 and negative. These estimates are in clear violation with those we expected from the derivations above. The estimates for the constant term α_0 for $n=2$ and 3 are negative and significantly different from zero, which is in line with the theory. However, for the other maturities, the estimates for α_0 are positive and even significantly positive for the maturity of 10 years.

The estimates for the constant term β_0 for Equation (18.24) all have their expected negative sign. However, only for the shorter maturities, up to 1 year, they are significantly different from zero. The estimates for the β_1 coefficients are all positive. Except for a maturity of 10 years all estimates are significantly different from 1. Although these results are not in line with what we would expect from theory, they are in line with what is found in other studies for the US (see Fama & Bliss, 1987; Campbell & Shiller, 1991; Bekaert, Hodrick, & Marshall, 2001; Bekaert & Hodrick, 2001).

There are a number of econometric difficulties with the regressions (18.23) and (18.24). Bekaert, Hodrick, and Marshall (2001) show that "peso problems" — inconsistencies between the frequency distributions of what agents thought at a certain point in time and what actually materialized — result in increased dispersion of the estimates, leading the model to be rejected too strongly. In addition, Bekaert and Hodrick (2001) argue that the standard tests tend to reject the null of the expectation hypothesis even when it is true. However, they find that even after correcting for the small-sample properties, the data remain inconsistent with the expectation hypothesis. Campbell and Shiller (1991) mention that the existence of time-varying risk premiums can explain the poor empirical results. However, it appears that the rejection of the expectation hypothesis seems to be a typical US phenomenon. Bekaert and Hodrick (2001) for example, cannot reject the expectation hypothesis for the UK and Germany.

Table 18.3: Regression results for expectation hypothesis equations.

n (months)	$\hat{\alpha}_0$	se $(\hat{\alpha}_0)$	$\hat{\alpha}_1$	se $(\hat{\alpha}_1)$	$\hat{\beta}_0$	se $(\hat{\beta}_0)$	$\hat{\beta}_1$	se $(\hat{\beta}_1)$
2	-0.171	(0.031)	-0.006	(0.178)	-0.085	(0.016)	0.497	(0.095)
3	-0.097	(0.039)	-0.123	(0.258)	-0.136	(0.036)	0.477	(0.130)
6	0.018	(0.039)	-0.698	(0.396)	-0.166	(0.062)	0.352	(0.142)
12	0.046	(0.042)	-1.146	(0.544)	-0.203	(0.108)	0.328	(0.169)
36	0.056	(0.043)	-1.600	(1.128)	-0.418	(0.368)	0.460	(0.255)
60	0.052	(0.034)	-2.166	(1.333)	-0.539	(0.385)	0.553	(0.256)
84	0.051	(0.029)	-2.733	(1.440)	-0.470	(0.472)	0.558	(0.271)
120	0.047	(0.024)	-3.452	(1.672)	-0.352	(0.637)	0.569	(0.342)

Notes: The data are taken from McCulloch and Kwon (1993) and Duffee (2002), which cover the period 1952:1 to 2000:12. The standard errors are between parentheses. The standard errors for the $\hat{\alpha}$-coefficients are corrected for heteroscedasticity according to White (1980). The standard errors for the $\hat{\beta}$-coefficients are corrected for the overlapping samples according to Newey and West (1987), with lag $n-1$. For maturities above 1 year, the approximation $y_{n-1,t+1} \approx y_{n,t+1}$ is used.

The general conclusion that can be drawn from Table 18.3 is that the expectation theory fails to explain the dynamic behaviour of the term structure. These results are typically taken as evidence of time-varying risk premiums. As explained above, the expectation hypothesis allows for risk premiums that vary over maturity. This implies that the parameters α_0 and β_0 in Equations (18.23) and (18.24), respectively, do not vary with time t. This can be easily tested using a Chow-test. Table 18.4 presents the results of these Chow-tests using an equal two- and three-way split of the data.

The results of Table 18.4 show that there is some statistical evidence for time-varying risk premiums. For Equation (18.23), it can be seen that for a maturity of 12 months the test rejects at the 5% significance level in case of three subsamples. In addition, for Equation (18.24) there is more evidence against constant risk premiums, as the test rejects at the 5% significance level for longer maturities.

Attempts with simple general-equilibrium models that include time-varying risk premiums have been shown to be unable to explain the sign, the magnitude, or the variability of observed risk premiums. However, Dai and Singleton (2002) argue that the stochastic risk premiums and not stochastic interest rate volatility is the key to the failure of the expectation hypothesis. They present evidence for the US that a particular model within the class of affine-yield models (see below for more details) is able to match the findings of Campbell and Shiller (1991), but they cannot explain the question of what economic mechanism is at work. Wachter (2005) proposes a general-equilibrium model that captures the empirical results of Campbell and Shiller (1991) and links them to investor preferences and aggregate consumption. Her model includes external habit persistence in line with Campbell and Cochrane (1999) and allows for time-varying risk premiums in the bond market. Wachter's model is also able to reproduce the empirical findings on the expectation hypothesis of Campbell and Shiller (1991).

Table 18.4: Chow test results for expectation hypothesis equations.

n (months)	Equation (18.23)		Equation (18.24)	
	Two subsamples	Three subsamples	Two subsamples	Three subsamples
2	0.238	0.111	0.264	0.143
3	0.378	0.080	0.285	0.125
6	0.872	0.203	0.614	0.388
12	0.341	0.003	0.572	0.314
36	0.870	0.384	0.390	0.053
60	0.794	0.344	0.113	0.002
84	0.787	0.349	0.003	0.000
120	0.708	0.315	0.000	0.000

Notes: The table represents the *p*-values of the chow test for the constant terms in the Equations (18.23) and (18.24) using either two or three subsamples that are each equal in size.

18.4.2. Modelling the Short-Term Interest Rate

In Section 18.3, it has been shown that interest-rate models can be represented by a time-series model for the stochastic discount factor. For the short-term interest rate, this relationship is particularly simple, as Equation (18.10) for $n = 1$, simplifies to:

$$y_{1t} = E_t\{M_{t+1}\}. \tag{18.25}$$

A term-structure model only guarantees the absence of arbitrage opportunities when a time-series process for the stochastic discount factor is formulated and the pricing relation (18.10) is used to derive the price implications for discount bonds (see Cochrane, 2001: 356). Several studies, like Vasicek (1977) and Cox, Ingersoll, and Ross (henceforth CIR) (1985) derive one-factor equilibrium term-structure models, in which the short-term interest rate is the only factor. A much simpler approach would be to formulate a time-series model for the short-term interest rate and then to derive the implications for the entire term structure. However, in this case absence of arbitrage is not guaranteed.

18.4.2.1. A time-series approach A partial list of models for the short interest rate is: Merton (1973), Brennan and Schwartz (1977), Vasicek (1977), Dothan (1978), CIR (1985), Constantinides and Ingersoll (1984), Schaefer and Schwartz (1984), Sundaresan (1984), Longstaff (1989), Hull and White (1990), and Longstaff and Schwartz (1992). Econometric models for the short-term interest rate imply certain time-series dynamics for the instantaneous interest rate r. Such dynamics are typically formulated by the continuous-time stochastic differential equation:

$$dr = (\alpha + \beta r)dt + \sigma r^\gamma dB, \tag{18.26}$$

where B is a standard Brownian motion. The first term on the right-hand side is referred to as the *drift*, while the second term is referred to as the *diffusion*. These dynamics imply that the conditional mean (drift) and variance (diffusion) of changes in the short-term rate depend on the level of r. Chan, Karolyi, Longstaff, and Sanders (1992) estimate several specifications for the short-term interest-rate model (18.26). As the *instantaneous* interest rate is not observed, they approximate the differential equation by a discrete-time econometric specification:

$$y_{1,t+1} - y_{1t} = \alpha + \beta y_{1t} + \varepsilon_{t+1} \tag{18.27}$$

$$E_t\{\varepsilon_{t+1}\} = 0, E_t\{\varepsilon_{t+1}^2\} = \sigma^2 y_{1t}^{2\gamma}. \tag{18.28}$$

This discrete-time model has the advantage of allowing the variance of interest changes to depend directly on the level of the interest rate in a way consistent with the continuous-time model.

Table 18.5 presents the parameter restrictions for the models that were estimated by Chan, Karolyi, Longstaff, and Sanders (1992). In Merton (1973) the interest-rate model was

Table 18.5: Parameter restrictions of alternative models for the short-term interest rate.

Model	α	β	σ	γ
Merton	–	0	–	0
Vasicek	–	–	–	0
CIR SR	–	–	–	0.5
Dothan	0	0	–	1
GBM	0	–	–	1
Brennan–Schwartz	–	–	–	1
CIR VR	0	0	–	1.5
CEV	0	–	–	–

Notes: The unrestricted model is $dr = (\alpha + \beta r)dt + \sigma r^{\gamma}B$.
"–" indicates that there are no restrictions for that parameter, while a number indicates the fixed value of the variable in question.

used to model discount bond prices. The stochastic process for the riskless rate is simply a Brownian motion with drift. The Vasicek model is the simple mean reverting process used by Vasicek (1977) to derive an equilibrium model for discount bond prices. CIR SR is the square-root process, which appears in the CIR (1985) single-factor general-equilibrium term-structure model. This model has been used extensively in developing valuation models for interest-rate sensitive contingent claims. The Dothan model is developed by Dothan (1978) and GBM stands for Geometric Brownian Motion used by Black and Scholes (1973) to derive expressions for the prices of options. Brennan and Schwartz (1977) used their model to derive a numerical model for convertible bond prices. The CIR VR model was introduced by CIR (1980) in their study of variable-rate (VR) securities. Finally, Cox and Ross (1976) introduced the constant elasticity of variance (CEV) process.

Table 18.6 presents descriptive statistics for the 1-month yield and the monthly changes in the 1-month yields, similar to Chan, Karolyi, Longstaff, and Sanders (1992). The unconditional average level of the 1-month yield is 5.16% annually with a standard deviation of 2.79%. Although the autocorrelations in the interest rate levels decay slowly, those of the month-to-month changes are almost zero and are in general negative. This offers some evidence that the short interest rate is stationary. All these findings are more or less consistent with Chan, Karolyi, Longstaff, and Sanders (1992).

Table 18.7 presents the estimation results for the models described in Table 18.6 when using our US dataset. The estimates are similar to those found by Chan, Karolyi, Longstaff, and Sanders (1992) and were obtained using Generalized Method of Moments (GMM) on the set of Equations (18.27) and (18.28), using a constant and y_{1t} as instruments. The models that are estimated vary in their explanatory power for interest rate changes. The tests for overidentifying restrictions suggest that the Merton, Vasicek and CIR SR models are misspecified, while the remaining models are not statistically rejected at the 5% significance level. Similar to Chan, Karolyi, Longstaff, and Sanders (1992), only the models where the γ parameter is larger or equal to 1 are not rejected. Furthermore, differences in the minimized GMM criterion values between models with the same value of γ are generally much

Table 18.6: Descriptive statistics for the 1-month discount bond yield.

Variables	Mean	Standard Deviation	ρ_1	ρ_2	ρ_3	ρ_4	ρ_5	ρ_6
y_{1t}	5.160	2.788	0.976	0.951	0.927	0.909	0.893	0.878
$y_{1,t+1} - y_{1t}$	0.008	0.590	0.018	−0.019	−0.115	−0.064	−0.015	−0.063

Notes: The table reports the sample mean, standard deviations, and autocorrelations of the monthly discount bond yield. The results are obtained from data taken from McCulloch and Kwon (1993) and Duffee (2002), which cover the period 1952:1 to 2000:12. The variable y_{1t} denotes the 1-month yield per annum and $y_{1,t+1} - y_{1t}$ denotes the monthly change. ρ_j denotes the autocorrelation coefficient of order j.

Table 18.7: Estimates of alternative models for the short-term interest rate.

Model	α	β	σ^2	γ	χ^2_{df}	df
Unrestricted	0.1308	−0.0239	0.0017	1.4210	—	—
	(0.0767)	(0.0180)	(0.0012)	(0.1741)		
Merton	0.0229	0	0.1715	0	13.2750	2
	(0.0163)		(0.0211)		[0.0013]	
Vasicek	0.0219	0.0003	0.1701	0	14.0406	1
	(0.0720)	(0.0170)	(0.0210)		[0.0002]	
CIR SR	0.0447	−0.0005	0.0414	0.5	10.6135	1
	(0.0724)	(0.0171)	(0.0049)		[0.0011]	
Dothan	0	0	0.0082	1	6.6163	3
			(0.0008)		[0.0852]	
GBM	0	0.0056	0.0080	1	4.7656	2
		(0.0038)	(0.0008)		[0.0923]	
Brennan–Schwartz	0.0846	−0.0139	0.0080	1	3.9630	1
	(0.0732)	(0.0173)	(0.008)		[0.0465]	
CIR VR	0	0	0.0012	1.5	6.45060	3
			(0.0001)		[0.0916]	
CEV	0	0.0060	0.0025	1.3213	2.7864	1
		(0.0038)	(0.0018)	(0.1918)	[0.0951]	

Notes: The parameters are estimated by GMM with the following moment conditions

$$\frac{1}{T} \sum_{t=1}^{T} ((y_{1,t+1} - y_{1t}) - \alpha + \beta y_{1t})z_t = 0$$

$$\frac{1}{T} \sum_{t=1}^{T} ([(y_{1,t+1} - y_{1t}) - \alpha + \beta y_{1t}]^2 - \sigma^2 y_{1t}^{2\gamma})z_t = 0$$

with a constant and y_{1t} as instruments z_t. The estimates were obtained using data from McCulloch and Kwon (1993) and Duffee (2002), which cover the period 1952:1 to 2000:12. χ^2_{df} represents the test statistic for the test of overidentifying restrictions, with df degrees of freedom. Standard errors are between parentheses, while p-values are between square brackets.

smaller than differences in models with different values of γ. The statistical importance of the estimates of the volatility parameters σ^2 and γ, as shown in Table 18.7, suggests that the relation between interest rate volatility and the level of y_{1t} is an important feature for any dynamic model of the short-term interest rate. The prices of interest rate derivatives, like call and put options, are a function of the volatility of the short interest rate. Therefore a careful specification of this volatility seems to be important to calculate correct prices for such derivatives.

18.4.2.2. Short-term interest rate volatility   The models that were estimated in the previous subsection are nested within the stochastic differential Equation (18.26). This equation puts some parametric restrictions upon the form of the drift (mean) and diffusion (volatility) process of the short-term interest rate. As shown by the empirical results presented in Table 18.7 above, the functional form of these processes is important for the statistical success of the model. Several studies, like Aït-Sahalia (1996a,b) and Koedijk, Nissen, Schotman, and Wolff (1997) investigate to what extent the effects of these parametric restrictions on the functional form determine the empirical results.

Aït-Sahalia (1996a) uses a semi-parametric estimation technique to estimate a model for the instantaneous interest rate. In the first step he estimates the linear drift function with OLS. In the second step he uses a non-parametric estimation technique to estimate the diffusion process. He shows that using this estimation technique, it results in more realistic estimates for call option prices.

Koedijk, Nissen, Schotman, and Wolff (1997) take a different approach. They extend the most general model of Chan, Karolyi, Longstaff, and Sanders (1992) by augmenting the discrete-time model with a quadratic term:

$$y_{1,t+1} - y_{1t} = \alpha_0 + \alpha_1 y_{1t} + \alpha_2 y_{1t}^2 + e_{t+1}, \tag{18.29}$$

where $e_{t+1} = \varepsilon_{t+1}\sqrt{h_{t+1}}$ is the prediction error of the short-term interest rate and h_{t+1} is its conditional variance. The error term ε_{t+1} is normalized to have unit variance, while the conditional variance is assumed to be of the form:

$$h_{t+1} = \sigma_{t+1}^2 y_{1t}^\gamma,$$

which differs from the specification used by Chan, Karolyi, Longstaff, and Sanders (1992) by the time-varying nature of σ_{t+1}. This is assumed to be generated by the GARCH(1,1) process:

$$\sigma_{t+1}^2 = \beta_1 + \beta_2 \varepsilon_t^2 + \beta_3 \sigma_t^2. \tag{18.30}$$

Their empirical results suggests that the inclusion of a GARCH effect in addition to the inclusion of a quadratic effect in the specification of the mean, is relevant for the pricing of short-term discount bond options. This would imply that the parametric specification of the short-term interest rate, see Equation (18.26) above, is too restrictive.

The findings of Koedijk, Nissen, Schotman, and Wolff (1997) are similar to the results of Aït-Sahalia (1996b), where different non-linear models for the short-term interest rate are estimated and compared with each other. Similar to Koedijk, Nissen, Schotman, and Wolff (1997), Aït-Sahalia (1996b) uses a general non-linear expression for the drift to allow for higher-variance elasticities. The change of the drift function completely changes the non-parametric estimates for the diffusion process as well. This is a strong indication that both the diffusion process and the (parametric) form of the drift are very important to find the appropriate process for the short interest rate. Lubrano (2000) continues this line of research and estimates both the drift and diffusion processes non-parametrically.

18.4.2.3. Regime switches in short-term interest rates

Based on the results from the studies presented in the previous subsection, it appears that the main source of rejecting existing models is the strong non-linearity in the drift. It seems that a non-linear specification for the drift function has a large impact on the behaviour of the non-parametric estimates of the diffusion process. However, the non-parametric models of Aït-Sahalia (1996a,b) and Lubrano (2000) are in general over-parameterized and may have poor small sample properties (see Pritsker, 1998; Ang & Bekaert, 2002a). Chapman and Pearson (2000) for example, show that the findings of Aït-Sahalia (1996a) might be entirely spurious, primarily because of the lack of data at the extremes of the interest rate range where the non-linearities are found. However, we cannot deny the empirical evidence indicating non-linearities in the short-term interest rate. These findings have lead several researchers to use regime-switching models. The most important feature of regime-switching models is the existence of an unobserved state (a regime variable) that follows a Markov chain and governs the switching between two (or more) potential linear processes. Hamilton (1994, Chapter 22) provides a concise but excellent overview of regime-switching models.

Several studies, mainly focusing on US data,[6] have found that regime-switching models with state dependent transition probabilities between regimes can replicate patterns of non-linear drift and volatility functions. Gray (1996), for example, develops a generalized regime-switching (GRS) model of the short-term interest rate. His model allows the short rate to exhibit both mean reversion and heteroscedasticity. Gray finds two different regimes in US short-term interest rates. In the first regime, the short rate essentially follows a random walk during periods of low volatility. In the second regime, there is some evidence of mean reversion at high levels of the interest rate during periods of high volatility. Furthermore, the high-volatility regime is characterized by a higher sensitivity to recent interest rate shocks than the low-volatility regime. The GRS model performs well both in-sample and out-of-sample. Bekaert, Hodrick, and Marshall (2001) and Ang and Bekaert (2002a,b) use multivariate regime-switching models for interest rates. In addition, they extend the model by using information from short rates and term spreads (the difference between the short interest rate and an interest rate with a longer maturity) for up to three different countries. The empirical results of these studies show that the term spread is an important factor in the probability of changing from one regime to another.

Regime-switching models are important tools in modelling the non-linearities of short-term interest rates. However, although it is interesting to find and model these non-linear patterns, we should attempt to understand what economic forces drive them (see Ang & Bekaert,

2002a). It could be possible that the non-linearities are induced by shifts in expected inflation, or changes in unemployment levels. A recent paper by Bansal and Zhou (2002) for example, finds that regimes are intimately related to business cycles, thereby indicating that there is indeed a close link between modelling interest rates and the macroeconomy (see also Section 18.4.4).

18.4.3. Affine-Yield Models

During the past 10–15 years, a wide range of empirical studies have appeared that focus on the time-series and cross-sectional dimensions of the term structure simultaneously. Examples include Longstaff and Schwartz (1992), Chen and Scott (1993), Pearson and Sun (1994), Jegadeesh and Pennacchi (1996), De Jong and Santa-Clara (1999), Dai and Singleton (2000) and De Jong (2000). These studies use a panel data approach to estimate the models' parameters. All these studies investigate the implications of *affine-yield models*[7] of the term structure. Affine models are particularly attractive because they can be analytically solved. In general, such an affine-yield model can be written as:

$$y_t = a_n(\theta) + b'_n(\theta)x_t, \tag{18.31}$$

where y_t is an n-dimensional vector of (log) yields, $a_n(\theta)$ is an n-dimensional vector, $b_n(\theta)$ is a $K \times n$ matrix, x_t is a K-dimensional vector of factors and θ is a vector of unknown parameters (see Duffie & Kan, 1996; Dai & Singleton, 2000, for more details). The relationship between $a_n(\theta)$, $b_n(\theta)$ and the parameters θ depends on the assumptions that are made about the stochastic discount factor M_{t+1}.

When we assume joint log-normality of the stochastic discount factor and returns, and take logarithms of the general bond pricing relationship (18.10), we obtain (see also Campbell, Lo, & MacKinlay, 1997):

$$p_{nt} = E_t\{m_{t+1} + p_{n-1,t+1}\} + \frac{1}{2} \text{Var}_t\{m_{t+1} + p_{n-1,t+1}\}$$

$$= E_t\{m_{t+1}\} + \frac{1}{2} \text{Var}_t\{m_{t+1}\} + E_t\{p_{n-1,t+1}\} + \frac{1}{2} \text{Var}_t\{p_{n-1,t+1}\}$$

$$+ \text{Cov}_t\{m_{t+1}, p_{n-1,t+1}\}. \tag{18.32}$$

Now, let m_{t+1} be represented by the sum of its conditional expectation and an innovation term ε^*_{t+1}:

$$m_{t+1} = E_t\{m_{t+1}\} + \varepsilon^*_{t+1}, \tag{18.33}$$

where $E_t = \{\varepsilon^*_{t+1}\} = 0$ by construction. To construct an interest-rate model that belongs to the class of affine term-structure models, particular assumptions about the conditional expectation and innovation term in Equation (18.33) have to be made. In most studies, it is assumed that the conditional expectation is the sum of the unobserved factors x_{it}, $i=1,...,K$:

$$E_t\{m_{t+1}\} = -\sum_{i=1}^{K} x_{it}, \tag{18.34}$$

where the minus sign is for convenience only, so that Equation (18.33) can thus be rewritten as:

$$m_{t+1} = -\sum_{i=1}^{K} x_{it} + \varepsilon^*_{t+1}. \tag{18.35}$$

In addition, some assumptions about the unobserved factors have to be made. Typically it is assumed that the time-series process of the factors can be represented by:

$$x_{i,\,t+1} = \mu_i + \phi_i x_{it} + \sigma_i(.)\,\xi_{i,\,t+1}, \quad i=1,\,...,\,K \tag{18.36}$$

where $\xi_{i,\tau+1}$ are error terms with zero mean and unit variance. The factor x_i follows an AR(1) process when $\sigma_i(.) = \sigma$, while it follows a square-root process when it is assumed that $\sigma_i(.) = \sigma_i\sqrt{x_{it}}$. From Equation (18.35) alone, we still cannot derive the time-series properties of the stochastic discount factor. Therefore, some additional assumptions about the interactions between the factors x_i and between the error terms ξ_i and ε^*_{t+1} need to be made.

From Equation (18.32) it is clear that an important component in determining the price of a discount bond at time t, is the covariance between the stochastic discount factor and the price at time $t + 1$. In addition, the interactions between the factors, as well as the statistical relationship between the error terms $\xi_{i,\,t+1}$ and ε^*_{t+1} are very important for the implications of the model. The studies that are mentioned above distinguish themselves from each other by making different assumptions about the dependence between factors, the number of factors and the assumptions on the error terms.

First, studies like Longstaff and Schwartz (1992), Chen and Scott (1993), Pearson and Sun (1994), Duffie and Kan (1996) and Duan and Simonato (1998), assume that the unobserved factors x_{it} are independent of each other. Other studies, like Jegadeesh and Pennacchi (1996), Gong and Remolona (1997), Balduzzi, Das, and Foresi (1998) and Dai and Singleton (2000) assume that there is a particular dependence between factors. Second, the number of factors K, is another feature that these studies use to distinguish themselves. Litterman and Scheinkman (1991) use factor analysis to determine the number of unobserved factors that are needed to describe the term structure of interest rates satisfactory. The number of yields that are available in the dataset limits the maximum number of factors. Most studies however, use models that contain two or three factors.

Finally, as shown in the previous section, the functional form of the volatility function is quite important for term-structure modelling. In affine-yield models this is determined by choosing the functional form and interaction between the error terms ε^*_{t+1} and $\xi_{i,\,t+1}$. Vasicek (1977) for example, assumes that there is one factor x without heteroscedasticity: $\sigma(.) = \sigma$ and $\varepsilon^*_{t+1} = \lambda\sigma\xi_{t+1}$. The constant λ is also known as the market price of risk. Another example is the multifactor CIR model (due to CIR, 1985) as investigated by, for example, Duan and Simonato (1998). Besides independence of the K unobservable factors, they assume a form of heteroscedasticity in the time-series process of the factors which is in line with CIR (1985): $\sigma_i(.) = \sigma_i\sqrt{x_{it}}$ and $\varepsilon^*_{t+1} = \sum_{i=1}^{K}\lambda_i\sigma_i\sqrt{x_{it}}$, where λ_i denotes the market price of risk for the i-th factor. Recently, Duarte (2004) extended this model by assuming that the market price of risk of factor i, depends on its own level: $\lambda_i = \lambda_i(x_i)$. His empirical results show an improvement of the empirical fit of the multifactor CIR model. All these examples show that different assumptions lead to a very diverse variety of affine-yield models.

When the number of maturities of interest rate data that are observed is larger than the number of factors, it is very unlikely that model (18.31) is capable of providing a perfect fit of the data. Therefore, in the empirical implementations of affine-yield models, random error terms are introduced. While these error terms capture any specification and measurement error, they are commonly referred to as measurement errors. Therefore, instead of Equation (18.31), the relationship:

$$y_t^{obs} = a_n(\theta) + b_n(\theta)x_t + v_t, \qquad (18.37)$$

is taken into consideration, where y_t^{obs} is the vector of observed yields and $v_t = y_t - y_t^{obs}$ is the vector of measurement errors. To be able to obtain estimates for the parameters, distributional assumptions about these measurement errors have to be made. These assumptions are an additional feature in which term-structure models are different from each other. Longstaff and Schwartz (1992) and Pearson and Sun (1994), for example, assume that there are as many factors as maturities. In this case there is no need to assume the presence of random error terms. Each factor represents the stochastic process of one maturity of the term structure. Others, like Chen and Scott (1993), assume that some of the maturities are observed without measurement error, while the remaining maturities are observed with error. The empirical results of studies within this last type are related to the choice of the maturities, which are observed without error. Finally there are studies, see for example Jegadeesh and Pennacchi (1996) and Duan and Simonato (1998), who assume that all maturities are observed with error.

The empirical results for affine term-structure models are mixed. Almost all studies find very low estimated variances of the measurement errors. This is a good sign for the empirical fit of the model because it indicates that the measurement errors are not that important. In addition, empirical results indicate a relatively good fit for the average yield curve. However, in a statistical sense, the affine-yield models are still rejected, which might be due to the extreme low sample variances of the observed (average) yield curve on US data. This lack of statistical performance of affine-yield models has led to a lot of adjustments to the "original" multifactor model with multiple independent factors (see, for example, Duffie & Kan, 1996; Dai & Singleton, 2000).

18.4.4. Recent Advances: The Term Structure and Macroeconomic Variables[8]

The term-structure literature developed more or less independently of the "regular" financial literature. From a finance perspective, the short rate is a fundamental building block for yields of other maturities, which are just risk-adjusted averages of expected future short rates. Hence, term-structure models in the "finance" literature typically boil down to regressions of interest rates on lagged interest rates.

From a macroeconomic perspective, the short-term interest rate is a policy instrument under the direct control of the central bank, which adjusts the rate to achieve its economic stabilization goals. Therefore macroeconomists run regressions of interest rates that include a variety of other variables like lagged inflation, output, unemployment, exchange rates and so forth (see Cochrane, 2001: 378). These regressions are interpreted as the Federal Reserve's policy-making rule for setting short rates as a function of macroeconomic conditions. This interpretation is particularly clear in the Taylor rule literature (see Taylor, 1999) and monetary Vector Autoregressive (VAR) literature (see Cochrane, 1994; Eichenbaum & Evans, 1999, for surveys). Recently, the term-structure literature realized that it should incorporate other explanatory variable than interest rates alone. To quote Cochrane (2001: 378): "Someone, it would seem, is missing important right-hand variables".

The criticism of finance models is most clear-cut when only the short interest rate is used as state variable. Multifactor models are subtler. If any variable forecasts future interest rates, then it becomes a state variable and it should be revealed by bond yields. Thus, bond yields should completely drive out any other macroeconomic state variables as interest rate forecasters. Recent studies show that they do not, which is an interesting observation.

There are several methods available to construct bond-yield factors and their loadings. In a statistical approach one would perform a factor analysis of yield changes and express the covariance matrix of yields in terms of a few factors that describe their common movement. Typically the first three principal components closely match simple empirical proxies for level (for example the long rate), slope (for example a long minus short rate) and curvature (for example a mid-maturity rate minus a short and a long-rate average). The trouble with this approach is that it is quite easy to reach a statistical representation of yields that implies an arbitrage opportunity, and you would not want to use such a characterization for economic understanding of yields for portfolio formation or derivative pricing (Cochrane, 2001: 356).

A second approach, which is popular among market and central bank practitioners, is fitting a dynamic three-factor model of level, slope and curvature (see Diebold & Li, 2005). However, these factors are unobserved, which allows for measurement error and the associated loadings have plausible economic restrictions (forward rates are always positive and the discount factor approaches zero as maturity increases).

Third, the model of choice in finance is a no-arbitrage dynamic latent factor model, similar to the model that was introduced in Section 18.4.3 above. The most common subclass of these models postulates flexible linear or affine forms for the latent factors and their loadings along with restrictions that rule out arbitrage strategies involving various bonds.

Several studies incorporate macroeconomic variables into a model for the term structure. Balduzzi, Bertola, and Foresi (1997) for example, consider a model based on the Federal Funds target rate. Piazzesi (2005) integrates a careful specification of high-frequency "jump" moves in the Federal Funds rate into an affine term-structure model. She documents that monetary policy shocks change the slope of the yield curve because they affect short rates more than long ones.

Ang and Piazzesi (2003) examine the structural impulse responses of the macro and latent factors that jointly drive yields in their models. They use the policy rule of Taylor (1999) to construct an affine term-structure model that includes macroeconomic variables. The Taylor rule states that movements in the short (instantaneous) interest rate could be explained by movements in observed macroeconomic variables f_t^o and a component which is not explained by these macroeconomic variables, the orthogonal shock v_t:

$$y_{1t} = c_0 + c_0 f_t^o + v_t. \tag{18.38}$$

The shock V_t may be interpreted as a monetary policy shock. As explained in the previous section, affine term-structure models use an equation very similar to this one (see

Equation (18.37) above). The main difference, however, between the short-rate dynamics in affine terms-structure models and the Taylor rule is that in the former models, interest rates are specified to be an affine function of the underlying unobserved (latent) factors f_t^u:

$$y_{1t} = \delta_0 + \delta_1 f_t^u, \tag{18.39}$$

where the unobserved factors themselves are following affine processes. Ang and Piazzesi (2003), combine both equations by writing:

$$y_{1t} = \delta_0 + \delta_{11} f_t^o + \delta_{12} f_t^u. \tag{18.40}$$

The errors $v_t = \delta_{12} f_t^u$ are thus interpreted as unobserved factors. For estimation tractability they only allow for unidirectional dynamics in their model. Macro variables help to determine yields, but not the reverse.

Ang and Piazzesi (2003) find that output shocks have a significant impact on intermediate yields and curvature, while inflation surprises have large effects on the level of the entire yield curve. They also find that better interest rate forecasts are obtained in an affine model in which macro factors are added to the usual latent factors. Dewachter, Lyrio, and Maes (2001), using Ang and Piazzesi's framework, also show that the misfit of the long end of the term structure can be quite substantial. They find large and highly persistent pricing errors that clearly suggest the existence of additional factors. Kozicki and Tinsley (2001; 2002) suggest that a missing factor may have a macroeconomic interpretation. Specifically, filtering the missing factor from the yield curve, they show that this factor may be related to the long-run inflation expectations of agents.

Berardi (2001) constructs a model that incorporates real interest rates and expected inflation rates. He shows that there are significant connections between interest rates, inflation and GDP growth and that the dynamics between these variables are highly interdependent. Diebold, Rudebusch, and Aruoba (2005) examine the correlations between three latent yield factors and macroeconomic variables. They find that the level factor is highly correlated with inflation and the slope factor is highly correlated with real activity. The curvature factor appears unrelated to any of the main macroeconomic variables. Rusebusch and Wu (2004) find similar results as Diebold, Rudebusch, and Aruoba (2005). Dewachter and Lyrio (2004) find that the standard "level" factor is highly correlated to long-run inflation expectations, the "slope" factor captures temporary business cycle conditions, while the "curvature" factor represents a clear independent monetary policy factor. In related work, Wu (2004) finds that most of the "slope" factor movement can be explained by exogenous monetary policy shocks, and the "level" factor movement is closely related to the technology shocks.

In contrast to the unidirectional dynamics in the model of Ang and Piazzesi (2003), Diebold Rudebusch, and Aruoba (2005) consider a general bidirectional characterization of the dynamic interactions and find that the causality from the macro-economy to yields is indeed significantly stronger than in the reverse direction but that interactions in both directions can be important. Ang, Dong, and Piazzesi (2005) impose no-arbitrage restrictions in addition to allowing for bidirectional macro-finance links. They find that the amount of yield variation that can be attributed to macro factors depends on whether or not the system allows for bidirectional linkages. When the interactions are constrained from macro- to yield-factors, the former can only explain a small portion of the variance of long yields. In contrast, the bidirectional system attributes over half of the variance of long yields to macro factors.

The literature that combines the term structure with macroeconomic variables is still very young, with many unresolved but promising issues to explore. Future research will, without a doubt, show how to deal with these issues.

18.5. Concluding Remarks

This chapter provides an overview of the research on the term structure of interest rates. We started from the general asset-pricing framework and showed that a model for the term structure is represented by the time-series behaviour of the stochastic discount factor. Furthermore an overview has been given of the most important topics in the term-structure literature, such as the expectation hypothesis, the modelling of short interest rates, affine-yields models. Finally, the recent trend of linking the "financial" and "macroeconomic" term-structure literature has been explored.

Research on the term structure of interest rates has been going on for decades and recently it has gained a renewed attention. The term-structure literature has only recently started to think whether the empirical successful discount factor processes of the asset-pricing literature can be connected back to macroeconomic events (Cochrane, 2001: 358). Moreover, the increase in available computer power enables researchers to estimate new, more complex and more accurate term-structure models. Interest-rate modelling will remain a topic for future research for some time to come.

Endnotes

1. In practice, even zero-coupon bonds with the same time to maturity might still have different yields due to differences in default risk, liquidity risk or tax rules. Here it is assumed that zero-coupon bonds do not posses any of these risks.
2. As explained above, in the case of US Treasury bonds a period is 6 months and c would then be half the conventionally quoted annual coupon rate.
3. "Correctly" in the sense that they reflect the stock and bond prices that are observed in the market.
4. This is only true in case of complete markets and arbitrage free pricing.
5. Although there is also a definition for the expectation hypothesis in terms of forward rates, it will not be treated here. For an explanation of forward rates and its applications, see for example Chapter 10 in Campbell, Lo, and MacKinlay (1997).
6. Although Dewachter (1996) estimates a regime-switching model for Germany
7. A function f is called affine in x if it can be written as $f(x) = \alpha + \beta x$, for some constants α and β.
8. See Diebold, Piazzesi, and Rudebusch (2005) for a short overview of where the macro-finance term structure literature is standing now and what are the challenges for future research.

References

Aït-Sahalia, Y. (1996a). Nonparametric pricing of interest rate derivative securities. *Econometrica*, *64*, 527–560.

Aït-Sahalia, Y. (1996b). Testing continuous-time models of the spot interest rate. *Review of Financial Studies*, *9*, 385–426.

Ang, A., & Bekaert, G. (2002a). Short rate nonlinearities and regime switches. *Journal of Economic Dynamics and Control*, *26*, 1243–1274.

Ang, A., & Bekaert, G. (2002b). Regime switches in interest rates. *Journal of Business and Economic Statistics*, *20*, 163–182.

Ang, A., Dong, S., & Piazzesi, M. (2005). *No-arbitrage Taylor rules*. Working paper University of Chicago.

Ang, A., & Piazzesi, M. (2003). A no-arbitrage vector autoregression of term structure dynamics with macroeconomic and latent variables. *Journal of Monetary Economics*, *50*, 745–787.

Balduzzi, P., Bertola, G., & Foresi, S. (1997). A model of target changes and the term structure of interest rates. *Journal of Monetary Economics*, *39*, 223–249.

Balduzzi, P., Das, S.R., & Foresi, S. (1998). The central tendency: A second factor in bond yields. *The Review of Economics and Statistics*, *80*, 62–72.

Bansal, R., & Zhou, H. (2002). Term structure of interest rates with regime shifts. *Journal of Finance*, *57*, 1997–2043.

Bekaert, G., & Hodrick, R.J. (2001). Expectations hypothesis tests. *Journal of Finance*, *56*, 1357–1394.

Bekaert, G., Hodrick, R.J., & Marshall, D.A. (2001). Peso problem explanations for term structure anomalies. *Journal of Monetary Economics*, *48*(2), 241–270.

Berardi, A. (2001). *How strong is the relation between the term structure, inflation and GDP?* Working Paper University of Verona.

Black, F., & Scholes, M. (1973). The pricing of options and corporate liabilities. *Journal of Political Economy*, *8*, 637–659.

Brennan, M.J., & Schwartz, E.S. (1977). Saving bonds, retractable bonds, and callable bonds. *Journal of Financial Economics*, *3*, 133–155.

Campbell, J.Y. (2000). Asset pricing at the millennium. *Journal of Finance*, *55*, 1515–1567.

Campbell, J.Y., & Cochrane, J.H. (1999). By force of habit: A consumption-based explanation of aggregate stock market behavior. *Journal of Political Economy*, *107*, 205–251.

Campbell, J.Y., Lo, A.W., & MacKinlay, A.C. (1997). *The econometrics of financial markets*. Princeton: Princeton University Press.

Campbell, J.Y., & Shiller, R.J. (1991). Yield spreads and interest rate movements: A bird's eye view. *Review of Economic Studies*, *58*, 495–514.

Chan, L.K.C., Karolyi, A., Longstaff, F., & Sanders, S. (1992). An empirical comparison of alternative models of the short-term interest rates. *Journal of Finance*, *47*, 1209–1227.

Chapman, D.A., & Pearson, N.D. (2000). Is the short rate drift actually nonlinear? *Journal of Finance*, *55*, 355–388.

Chen, R.R., & Scott, L. (1993). Maximum likelihood estimation for a multifactor equilibrium model of the term structure of interest rates. *Journal of Fixed Income*, *3*, 14–31.

Cochrane, J.H. (1994). Permanent and transitory components of GNP and stock prices. *Quarterly Journal of Economics*, *59*, 241–266.

Cochrane, J.H. (2001). *Asset pricing*. Princeton: Princeton University Press.

Constantinides, G.M., & Ingersoll, J.E. (1984). Optimal bond trading with personal taxes. *Journal of Financial Economics*, *13*, 299–335.

Cox, J., Ingersoll, J.E., & Ross, S. (1980). An analysis of variable rate loan contracts. *Journal of Finance*, *35*, 389–403.

Cox, J., Ingersoll, J.E., & Ross, S. (1985). A theory of the term structure of interest rates. *Econometrica*, *53*, 385–408.

Cox, J., & Ross, S. (1976). The valuation of options for alternative stochastic processes. *Journal of Financial Economics*, *3*, 145–166.

Dai, Q., & Singleton, K.J. (2000). Specification analysis of affine term structure models. *Journal of Finance*, *55*, 1943–1978.

Dai, Q., & Singleton, K.J. (2002). Expectation puzzles, time-varying risk premia, and dynamic models of term structure. *Journal of Financial Economics*, *63*, 415–441.

Diebold, F.X., & Li, C. (2005). Forecasting the term structure of government bond yields. Forthcoming *Journal of Econometrics*.

Diebold, F.X., Rudebusch, G.D., & Aruoba, S.B. (2005). The macroeconomy and the yield curve: A dynamic latent factor approach. Forthcoming *Journal of Eoconometrics*.

Diebold, F.X., Rudebusch, G.D., & Piazzesi, M. (2005). Modeling bond yields in finance and macroeconomics. Forthcoming *American Economic Review P&P*.

De Jong, F. (2000). Time series and cross-section information in affine term structure models. *Journal of Business and Economics Statistics*, *18*, 300–314.

De Jong, F., & Santa-Clara, P. (1999). The dynamics of the forward interest rate curve: A formulation with state variables. *Journal of Financial and Quantitative Analysis*, *34*, 131–157.

Dewachter, H. (1996). Modeling interest rate volatility: Regime switches and level links. *Weltwirtschaftliches Archiv*, *132*, 237–258.

Dewachter, H., & Lyrio, M. (2004). Macro factors and the term structure of interest rates. Forthcoming *Journal of Money, Credit and Banking*.

Dewachter, H., Lyrio, M., & Maes, K. (2001). A joint model for the term structure of interest rates and the macroeconomy. Forthcoming *Journal of Applied Econometrics*.

Dothan, U.L. (1978). On the term structure of interest rates. *Journal of Financial Economics*, *6*, 59–69.

Duan, J.C., & Simonato, J.G. (1998). Estimating and testing exponential-affine term structure models by Kalman Filter. *Review of Quantitative Finance and Accounting*, *13*, 111–135.

Duarte, J. (2004). Evaluating an alternative risk preference in affine term structure models. *Review of Financial Studies*, *17*, 379–404.

Duffee, G.R. (2002). Term premia and interest rate forecasts in affine models. *Journal of Finance*, *57*, 405–443.

Duffie, D., & Kan, R. (1996). A yield-factor model of interest rates. *Mathematical Finance*, *6*, 379–406.

Eichenbaum, C.L.M., & Evans, C. (1999). Monetary policy shocks: What have we learned and to What End? In: M. Woodford, & J. Taylor (Eds.), *Handbook of Macroeconomics* (pp. 65–148). Amsterdam: North-Holland.

Fama, E.F., & Bliss, R.R. (1987). The information in long-maturity forward-rates. *American Economic Review*, *77*, 680–692.

Fisher, I. (1896). Appreciation and interest. *Publications of the American Economic Association*, *11*, 21–29.

Gong, F.F., & Remolona, E.M. (1997). *A three-factor econometric model of the US term structure*. Staff Report Number 19, Federal Reserve Bank of New York.

Gray, S. (1996). Modeling the conditional distribution of interest rates as a regime-switching process. *Journal of Financial Economics*, *42*, 27–62.

Hamilton, J. (1994). *Time series analysis*. Princeton: Princeton University Press.

Harrison, M., & Kreps, D. (1979). Martingales and arbitrage in multiperiod security markets. *Journal of Economic Theory*, *20*, 381–408.

Hull, J., & White, A. (1990). Pricing interest rate derivative securities. *Review of Financial Studies*, *3*, 573–592.

Jegadeesh, N., & Pennacchi, G.G. (1996). The behavior of interest rates implied by the term structure of eurodollar futures. *Journal of Money, Credit and Banking, 28*, 428–451.

Koedijk, K.G., Nissen, F.G.J.A., Schotman, P.C., & Wolff, C.C.P. (1997). The dynamics of short term interest rate volatility reconsidered. *European Finance Review, 1*, 105–130.

Kozicki, S., & Tinsley, P.A. (2001). Shifting endpoints in the term structure of interest rates. *Journal of Monetary Economics, 47*, 613–652.

Kozicki, S., & Tinsley, P.A. (2002). Dynamic specifications in optimizing trend-deviation macro models. *Journal of Economic Dynamics and Control, 26*, 1585–1611.

Litterman, R., & Scheinkman, J. (1991). Common factors affecting bond returns. *Journal of Fixed Income, 1*, 54–61.

Longstaff, F.A. (1989). A nonlinear general equilibrium model of the term structure of interest rates. *Journal of Financial Economics, 23*, 195–224.

Longstaff, F.A., & Schwartz, E.S. (1992). Interest rate volatility and the term structure: A two-factor general equilibrium model. *Journal of Finance, 47*, 1259–1282.

Lubrano, M. (2000). *Baysian nonlinear modelings of the short term US interest rate: The help of nonparametric tools*. CORE discussion paper, CORE, Louvain-la-Neuve.

McCulloch, J.H., & Kwon, H.C. (1993). *US term structure data, 1947–1991*. Ohio State Working Paper 93–96, Ohio State University.

Merton, R.C. (1973). Theory of rational option pricing. *Bell Journal of Economics and Management Science, 4*, 141–183.

Newey, W.K., & West, K. (1987). A simple positive definite, heteroskedasticity and autocorrelation consistent covariance matrix. *econometrica, 55*, 703–708.

Pearson, N.D., & Sun, T.S. (1994). Exploiting the conditional density in estimating the term structure: An application to the Cox, Ingersoll, and Ross model. *Journal of Finance, 49*, 1279–1304.

Piazzesi, M. (2005). Bond yields and the federal reserve. *Journal of Political Economy, 111*, 311–344.

Pritsker, M. (1998). Nonparametric density estimation and tests of continuous time interest rate models. *Review of Financial Studies, 11*, 449–487.

Rusebusch, G.D., & Wu, T. (2004). *A macro-finance model of the term structure, monetary policy and the economy*. Working paper Federal Reserve Bank of San Francisco.

Schaefer, S., & Schwartz, E.S. (1984). A two-factor model of the term structure: An approximate analytical solution. *Journal of Financial and Quantitative Analysis, 19*, 413–424.

Shiller, R.J. (1990). The term structure of interest rates. In: B. Friedman, & F. Hahn (Eds.), *Handbook of monetary economics*. Amsterdam: Elsevier.

Sundaresan, S.M. (1984). Consumption and equilibrium interest rates in stochastic production Economies. *Journal of Finance, 39*, 77–92.

Taylor, J.B. (Ed.) (1999). *Monetary policy rules*. Chicago: University of Chicago Press.

Vasicek, O. (1977). An equilibrium characterization of the term structure. *Journal of Financial Economics, 5*, 177–188.

Wachter, J.A. (2005). A consumption-based model of the term structure of interest rates. Forthcoming *Journal of Financial Economics*.

White, H. (1980). A heteroskedasticity-consistent covariance matrix estimator and a direct test for heteroskedasticity. *Econometrica, 48*, 817–828.

Wu, T. (2004). Macro factors and the affine term structure of interest rates. Forthcoming *Journal of Money, Credit and Banking*.

Chapter 19

Incorporating Estimation Risk in Portfolio Choice

Jenke ter Horst, Frans de Roon and Bas Werker

19.1 Introduction

A general problem in portfolio selection is the fact that the necessary parameter values to compute efficient portfolios are usually unknown and have to be estimated. For instance, when implementing the mean–variance efficient portfolios introduced by Markowitz (1959), the mean returns and (co)variances are usually estimated from available data. This may lead to suboptimal portfolios. Since mean–variance efficient portfolio weights are very sensitive to the level of the expected returns (see, e.g., Chopra & Ziemba, 1993) and since it is well known that, unless the number of assets under consideration is very large, uncertainty in the estimated mean returns is higher than in the estimated (co)variances, it is especially the uncertainty in the mean returns that needs to be considered.

Previous papers have tried to come up with estimates of the mean returns that improve upon the sample average using, for instance, shrinkage or Stein estimators (Jobson, Korkie, & Ratti, 1979; Jorion, 1985; 1986; 1991). These estimators shrink the means toward a common value. Alternatively, Jorion (1991) uses the so-called capital asset pricing model (CAPM) estimators in which the means are assumed to be proportional to their beta relative to the market portfolio. A disadvantage of both shrinkage and CAPM-based estimators is that they presuppose a strong prior belief on expected returns, such as that there is a common value for the means or that expected returns can be fully explained by their market beta.

In this chapter, we take the uncertainty in mean returns as given and propose an adjustment in mean–variance efficient portfolio weights that incorporates this uncertainty or estimation risk. Several previous papers have analyzed this problem using a Bayesian perspective. Examples are Barry (1974), Klein and Bawa (1976), Brown (1979), Chen and Brown (1983), Alexander and Resnick (1985), and Balduzzi and Liu (2000). We take a classical decision theoretic point of view and consider the loss in expected utility when implementing a suboptimal portfolio. We show that investors can easily incorporate uncertainty in the mean returns by basing their mean–variance efficient portfolio on a

Advances in Corporate Finance and Asset Pricing
Edited by L. Renneboog
© 2006 Elsevier B.V. All rights reserved.
ISBN: 0-444-52723-0

pseudo risk aversion rather than on their actual risk aversion. The pseudo risk aversion is always higher than the actual risk aversion and the difference between the two depends on the number of assets under consideration, the sample size, and the efficient set constants. As is to be expected, the difference between the pseudo risk aversion and the actual risk aversion is increasing in the number of assets included in the portfolio and decreasing in the sample size. Our adjustment factor turns out to be different from the adjustment obtained in a Bayesian approach, in that it also takes into account the curvature of the mean–variance frontier, capturing the intuition that estimation risk is more serious a problem when errors in the expected returns are very costly in terms of volatility.

This chapter also presents two important extensions of the above-mentioned results. First, in case there are short sales constraints, the pseudo risk aversion can be obtained using a similar approach as in the standard case. In this case, the adjustment is based only on the assets for which the constraints are not binding. This implies that it is very well possible that a different set of assets appears in (optimal) portfolios with and without taking estimation risk into account. This effect indeed occurs in applications. Second, when returns are predictable from a set of observed instruments, our adjustment can take this into account and the pseudo risk aversion also depends on the values taken by the instruments. We find that the variability in mean–variance efficient portfolio weights over time is much reduced when estimation risk is accounted for.

We illustrate the effect of estimation risk for international asset portfolios based on either the G5 countries or on the G5 countries plus a number of emerging markets. The empirical problem we address is, therefore, similar to the one studied by Balduzzi and Liu (2000), who use a Bayesian approach. We show that the difference between the pseudo risk aversion and the actual risk aversion can be sizable even for investors that wish to invest in the G5 countries only. Using a sample of 25 years of monthly data, the difference in expected utility between the portfolio based on the actual risk aversion and the optimal pseudo risk aversion translates into an annual equivalent risk premium of at least 0.55% (depending on the risk aversion). This premium increases to 1.12% when only 5 years of monthly data are available and even up to 6.7% for a less risk averse investor. Comparing these premiums with those obtained from the previous Bayesian approaches, we find that the gains of our approach are, in utility terms, up to 10 times bigger. The effects of estimation risk are even more pronounced in the case where emerging markets are included as well. In that case, the difference between the actual and pseudo risk aversion increases dramatically with a corresponding strong effect on the optimal portfolio weights. This effect is a combined result of the increase in the number of assets and the higher uncertainty in the mean returns of emerging markets as reflected in the efficient set constants. The latter is the above-mentioned curvature effect. When short sales constraints are taken into account, the incorporation of estimation risk indeed has even more extreme effects. For instance, for the longest sample period available, a 5% Middle East investment does show up in the optimal adjusted portfolio, while it is absent when estimation risk is ignored. The utility gains from incorporating estimation risk are also evident in our out-of-sample results. The out-of-sample results even show more significant gains in terms of point estimates than the in-sample results. For instance, the 1.12% in-sample improvement for G5 investments only mentioned above turns out to be 2.16% in the out-of-sample analysis. When expected returns are predicted from a set of common instruments, estimation risk in the predictive regressions is taken into account. In that case, we find that there is less variability in the optimal portfolio weights because of the instruments that is commonly believed.

Our approach assumes that estimation risk in the (co)variances can be neglected. We present bootstrap simulations confirming this assumption, for all sample sizes and risk aversions that we consider. The fact that we use a bootstrap procedure also takes into account possible non-normalities in the data as well as time-varying covariances. As can be expected, the uncertainty in variances becomes more important as the risk aversion increases, but the magnitude of the loss in expected utility that results from this uncertainty remains small. It should be noted though that uncertainty in the covariances would become more important as the number of assets or asset classes under consideration increases. The issue of uncertainty in the covariance matrix, when the number of assets is large, is studied by Ledoit (1999), who gives an alternative variance estimator aimed at reducing this estimation risk. We do not consider the consequences of estimation risk on equilibrium pricing in this chapter. Results in that direction can be found in Brown (1979) and Coles, Loewenstein, and Suay (1995).

The plan of this chapter is as follows. Section 19.2 shows how estimation risk can be incorporated in mean–variance efficient portfolios by using a pseudo risk aversion coefficient. We consider the standard independent and identically distributed (i.i.d.) case as well as the extensions to short sales and predictability of expected returns. Section 19.3 describes the data and Sections 19.4–19.8 discuss the effect of estimation risk for international asset portfolios. This chapter ends with a summary and concluding remarks.

19.2 Incorporating Estimation Risk in Mean–Variance Efficient Portfolios

In this section we introduce our model and show how to construct portfolios that explicitly take estimation risk into account. In Section 19.2.1, we start with the standard *i.i.d.* case without restrictions on the portfolio holdings. In Section 19.2.2, we extend our results to the case where short positions are not allowed and in Section 19.2.3, we discuss estimation risk when there is return predictability.

19.2.1. Estimation Risk in the i.i.d. Case

Suppose that an investor has a menu of K different assets from which he chooses his portfolio. The returns on these assets are given by the K-vector R_t, and are assumed to be *i.i.d.* and normally distributed with mean vector μ and covariance matrix Σ. Since returns are normally distributed, the investor chooses his portfolio w to maximize:

$$w'\mu - \frac{1}{2} \gamma w'\Sigma w, \tag{19.1}$$

where $w'\iota = 1$, with ι, a K-vector of ones, and γ, the risk aversion of the investor. It is well known that the optimal portfolio for this investor is given by:

$$w^* = \gamma^{-1}\Sigma^{-1}(\mu - \eta\iota), \tag{19.2}$$

where η is the expected return on the zero-beta portfolio associated with w^* (see, e.g., Ingersoll, 1987).

In characterizing mean–variance efficient portfolios that satisfy Equation (19.2) it is useful to define the efficient set constants:

$$A = \iota'\Sigma^{-1}\iota, \tag{19.3a}$$

$$B = \iota'\Sigma^{-1}\mu, \tag{19.3b}$$

$$C = \mu'\Sigma^{-1}\mu. \tag{19.3c}$$

Using these constants it is straightforward to show that the zero-beta rate η can be written as a function of γ: $\eta = (B - \gamma)/A$ (this follows from premultiplying Equation (19.2) with ι and noting that $\iota'w^* = 1$).

In practice, the parameters μ and Σ are not known of course, but have to be estimated from the data. Denote the estimates of μ and Σ by $\hat{\mu}$ and $\hat{\Sigma}$, respectively. We assume that the uncertainty in $\hat{\Sigma}$ is small and can be neglected, and we focus on the estimation error in $\hat{\mu}$. Our simulation results in Section 19.7 shows that, for the problem at hand, this is a valid presumption. Based on the estimated mean returns $\hat{\mu}$, suppose that the investor chooses his mean–variance efficient portfolio analogous to Equation (19.2) as:

$$\hat{w}(\alpha) = \alpha^{-1}\Sigma^{-1}(\hat{\mu}-\rho\iota), \tag{19.4}$$

but with a possibly adjusted risk-aversion parameter α. We refer to this parameter α as the pseudo risk aversion. A naive investor would choose his portfolio by taking $\alpha = \gamma$. The zero-beta rate ρ depends on the pseudo risk aversion α and the estimated efficient set constants $\hat{A}$, $\hat{B}$, and $\hat{C}$ in the same way as η depends on γ, A, B, and C.[1]

Since the portfolio $\hat{w}(\alpha)$ depends on the estimated mean returns $\hat{\mu}$ rather than the true parameters μ, it will, in general, not be equal to the optimal portfolio w^* in Equation (19.2). Using the suboptimal portfolio $\hat{w}(\alpha)$ yields a loss in expected utility which, using Equation (19.1), is equal to:

$$L(\alpha) = \left(w^{*\prime}\mu - \hat{w}(\alpha)'\mu) - \frac{1}{2}\gamma(w^{*\prime}\Sigma w^* - \hat{w}(\alpha)'\Sigma\hat{w}(\alpha)\right), \tag{19.5}$$

and the expected loss equals:

$$\delta(\alpha) = E[L(\alpha)]. \tag{19.6}$$

In line with standard decision theory, we propose to choose the pseudo risk aversion α in such a way that the expected loss δ will be minimized, i.e.:

$$\alpha^* = \arg\min_{\{\alpha\}} \delta(\alpha) = \gamma\left(1 + \frac{A}{AC-B^2}\frac{K-1}{T}\right), \tag{19.7}$$

where the last equality is derived in ter Horst, de Roon, and Werker (2005). The optimal value α^* has an obvious interpretation. Since both A and $(AC - B^2)$ are always positive, the adjustment factor in Equation (19.7) is at least 1, and α^* is always larger than or equal to the actual risk aversion γ. The fact that the pseudo risk aversion exceeds the actual risk aversion reflects the higher uncertainty that is caused by using the estimated expected returns $\hat{\mu}$ rather than the true expected returns. Since this uncertainty induces a portfolio that is actually more risky than if the true parameters were known, the investor wants to adjust his portfolio for this by using a higher pseudo risk aversion and, therefore, a less risky portfolio. Basically, in using a higher pseudo risk aversion, the investor selects a portfolio that is closer to the global minimum variance (GMV) portfolio.

It is important to realize that $\delta(\alpha)$ measures the expected loss from using the risk aversion α and the corresponding portfolio weights based on estimated expected returns as compared with using the actual risk aversion γ and the corresponding portfolio weights based on the *true* expected returns. Clearly, the latter is infeasible since the true expected returns are unknown. A naive investor, using the risk aversion γ and estimated expected returns, would incur an expected loss of $\delta(\gamma)$. An investor using the pseudo risk aversion α^* incurs a loss of $\delta(\alpha^*)$ as compared to the ideal (infeasible) situation. The gain in expected loss from the use of the optimal risk aversion α^* as compared to the naive use of γ is thus measured by $g(\alpha^*)= \delta(\gamma) - \delta(\alpha^*)$. In ter Horst, de Roon, and Werker (2005) this quantity of interest is derived, as well as confidence intervals that go with it. The gain $g(\alpha^*)$ can also be interpreted in a different way. It is the (fixed) premium that an investor would be willing to pay when holding the optimal portfolio based on the risk aversion α^*, such that he would derive the same utility as from holding the portfolio based on γ.

The adjustment factor increases as the number of assets under consideration, K, increases. This reflects the fact that as the number of assets increases, the number of parameters in μ increases, implying a higher level of uncertainty. As the sample size T increases, the estimate $\hat{\mu}$ of μ becomes more precise and the adjustment factor decreases, as is to be expected. Finally, it is straightforward to show that the term $A/(AC - B^2)$ is proportional to the second derivative of the efficient portfolio's variance with respect to the expected portfolio return. Therefore, this term reflects the curvature of the mean–variance frontier. A high curvature implies that small changes in the expected return of efficient portfolios imply big changes in the corresponding volatility. Stated differently, a large value of $A/(AC - B^2)$ implies that estimation error in the expected returns can be very costly in volatility terms. The higher pseudo risk aversion α^* neutralizes this effect.

As noted in the introduction, several authors have studied the effects of estimation risk using a Bayesian approach (e.g., Barry, 1974; Klein & Bawa, 1976; Brown, 1979; Bawa, Brown, & Klein, 1979; Chen & Brown, 1983; Alexander & Resnick, 1985). In a Bayesian framework, these articles propose to use the so-called predictive distribution of returns. This predictive distribution is obtained as the posterior distribution given a (non-informative) prior and observed returns. In an *i.i.d.* setting, this predictive distribution uses the mean returns as expected returns and the covariance matrix must be multiplied with a factor depending on the number of assets in the problem and the sample size (see, e.g., Brown, 1979). Clearly, in a mean–variance setting, a factor of proportionality in the covariance matrix of returns cannot be, mathematically, distinguished from the same factor for the risk aversion. In that sense, the classical approach in this chapter and the Bayesian approach lead to similar answers. However, the adjustment factor obtained in a Bayesian approach with a non-informative prior is:

$$\gamma(1+1/T),\qquad(19.8)$$

as in Bawa, Brown, and Klein (1979). With a diffuse prior it also depends on the number of assets. Our adjustment factor is different in that it also takes into account the curvature of the mean–variance frontier, capturing the intuition that estimation risk is more important when errors in the expected returns are very costly in volatility terms. In addition, the next sections extend the analysis to the case where there are short sales constraints and to the case where expected returns are time-varying.

19.2.2. Including Short Sales Constraints

The previous section showed that investors that are unrestricted in their portfolio holdings can account for estimation risk in expected returns by choosing an efficient portfolio based on the pseudo risk aversion in Equation (19.7). When investors face short sales constraints, the portfolio problem becomes:

$$\max_{w}\ w'\mu-\frac{1}{2}\gamma w'\Sigma w,\qquad(19.9)$$

such that $w'\iota = 1$ and $w_i \geq 0, \forall i$.

In this case, the optimal portfolio is given by:

$$w^* = \gamma^{-1}\Sigma^{-1}(\mu-\eta\iota-\lambda),\qquad(19.10)$$

where λ is the vector of Kuhn–Tucker multipliers for the restrictions that the portfolio weights are non-negative. Denote by $R_t^{(\gamma)}$, the $K^{(\gamma)}$ -dimensional subset of the assets in R_t for which the short sales constraints are not binding. The superscript (γ) refers to this subset. It is straightforward to show that the mean–variance efficient portfolio in Equation (19.10) is equal to the mean–variance efficient portfolio without short sales constraints of the assets in $R_t^{(\gamma)}$ only (see, e.g., Markowitz, 1987). Thus, ordering the portfolio weights in w^* as $w^* = (w^{(\gamma)}{}'0'_{K-K^{(\gamma)}})$, such that the short sales constraints are not binding for the first $K^{(\gamma)}$ elements and binding for the last $K - K^{(\gamma)}$ elements, we get that:

$$w^* = \begin{bmatrix} w^{(\gamma)} \\ 0_{K-K^{(\gamma)}} \end{bmatrix},$$

$$w^{(\gamma)} = \gamma^{-1}\left(\Sigma^{(\gamma)}\right)^{-1}\left(\mu^{(\gamma)}-\eta\iota_{K^{(\gamma)}}\right).\qquad(19.11)$$

Following the ideas in Markowitz (1987) and DeRoon, Nijman, and Werker (2001), notice that for a given set of K asset returns R_t, there is only a finite number of subsets with $K^{(\gamma)}$ elements, $K^{(\gamma)} \in \{1, 2, .., K\}$. Let $G^{[j]}$ be the set of those values of γ for which the subset of assets for which the short sales constraints in the mean–variance efficient portfolios are not binding is the same, and denote the $K^{[j]}$-dimensional vector of returns for these assets as $R_t^{[j]}$, i.e., $R_t^{[j]} = R_t^{[\gamma]}$ if and only if $\gamma \in G^{[j]}$. Similarly, each variable or parameter that refers to the set $R_t^{[j]}$ will be denoted with a superscript $[j]$. Since for $\gamma \in G^{[j]}$ the short sales restricted mean–variance efficient frontier of R_t coincides with the unrestricted mean–variance frontier of $R_t^{[j]}$, the mean–variance frontier of R_t with short sales constraints consists of a finite number of parts of the unrestricted mean–variance frontiers of the subsets $R_t^{[j]}$.

To see how estimation risk can be incorporated in the optimal portfolio choice when there are short sales constraints, first of all note that, for a given segment of the frontier defined by $G^{[j]}$, the analysis in the unrestricted case still holds as long as both γ and α^* are an element of $G^{[j]}$. Alternatively, it may be the case that the portfolio that is adjusted for estimation risk is located on a different segment of the frontier. In this case, $\gamma \in G^{[j]}$, whereas the pseudo risk aversion calculated according to Equation (19.7), $\alpha \notin G^{[j]}$. Defining the transition point by $\alpha_t^{[j,j+1]}$ such that $\alpha_t^{[j,j+1]} \in G^{[j]}$ and $\alpha_t^{[j,j+1]} \in G^{[j+1]}$, the marginal decrease in the expected loss function δ is still positive for $\alpha = \alpha_t^{[j,j+1]}$. If the marginal decrease in $\delta^{[j]}$ is still positive for $\alpha = \alpha_t^{[j,j+1]}$ at the next segment, $G^{[j]}$, then we can simply go to the next segment defined by $G^{[j+1]}$, and continue until we find the α^* that minimizes the loss function, which is given by:

$$\alpha^* = \gamma\left(1 + \frac{K^{(\alpha^*)}-1}{T} \frac{A^{(\alpha^*)}}{B^{(\alpha^*)2}-A^{(\alpha^*)}C^{(\alpha^*)}}\right).$$

If the marginal decrease at the transition point α_t is positive for segment $G^{[j]}$ but negative for the next segment $G^{[j+1]}$ then it follows that the optimal α^* equals α_t. Thus the optimal value of the pseudo risk aversion is given by:

$$\alpha^* = \gamma\left(1 + \frac{K^{(\alpha^*)}-1}{T} \frac{A^{(\alpha^*)}}{B^{(\alpha^*)2}-A^{(\alpha^*)}C^{(\alpha^*)}}\right), \text{ if } \left.\frac{\partial\delta(\alpha)}{\partial\alpha}\right|_{\alpha = \alpha^*} = 0, \quad (19.12)$$

$$\alpha^* = \alpha_t^{[j,j+1]}, \text{ if } \left.\frac{\partial\delta^{[j]}(\alpha)}{\partial\alpha}\right|_{\alpha = \alpha_t^{[j,j+1]}} > 0 \text{ and } \left.\frac{\partial\delta^{[j+1]}(\alpha)}{\partial\alpha}\right|_{\alpha = \alpha_t^{[j,j+1]}} < 0.$$

Thus, when there are short sales constraints, the optimal value of the pseudo risk aversion α depends in the same way on the sample size T, the number of assets $K^{(\alpha)}$, and the efficient set constants as in the case where there are no constraints, except that $K^{(\alpha^*)}$, and the efficient set constants are now defined by the relevant subset of assets for which the short sales constraints are not binding.

19.2.3. Estimation Risk with Return Predictability

It is well known by now that stock returns can be predicted to some extent from common instruments such as the dividend yield and the short-term interest rate (see, e.g., Ferson & Harvey, 1999). We will assume that expected returns can be predicted from a set of instruments, but that the covariance matrix of the unexpected returns is constant, i.e., returns are conditionally homoskedastic. Suppose that stock return i can be predicted from a set of L_i instruments $z_{i,t-1}$, which may include a constant:

$$R_{i,t} = \beta_i' z_{i,t-1} + \varepsilon_{i,t}, \tag{19.13}$$

where β_i is a $L_i \times 1$ vector and where the error terms $\varepsilon_t = (\varepsilon_{1,t} \dots \varepsilon_{K,t})$, are assumed to be homoskedastic and normally distributed, $\varepsilon_t \sim N(0, \Omega_{\varepsilon\varepsilon})$. Conditionally on the instruments at time $(t-1)$, the optimal portfolio at time $t-1$ is then given by:

$$w_{t-1}^* = \gamma^{-1} \Omega_{\varepsilon\varepsilon}^{-1} (\mu_{t-1} - \eta_{t-1}\iota), \tag{19.14a}$$

$$\text{with } \mu_{t-1} = Z_{t-1}b, \tag{19.14b}$$

where b is a vector with length $\Sigma_{i=1}^K L_i$ containing all the vectors β_i, i.e. $b = (\beta_i', \dots, \beta_k')$ and Z_{t-1} is defined by:

$$Z_{t-1} = \begin{bmatrix} z_{1,t-1}' & 0 & \cdots & 0 \\ 0 & z_{2,t-1}' & \cdots & 0 \\ \vdots & & \ddots & \vdots \\ 0 & \cdots & 0 & z_{K,t-1}' \end{bmatrix}.$$

The zero-beta rate is now a time-varying function of the risk aversion γ:

$$\eta_{t-1} = \frac{B_{t-1} - \gamma}{A},$$

where $A = \iota' \Omega_{\varepsilon\varepsilon}^{-1} \iota$, $B_{t-1} = \mu_{t-1}' \Omega_{\varepsilon\varepsilon}^{-1} \iota$, and similarly, $C_{t-1} = \mu_{t-1}' \Omega_{\varepsilon\varepsilon}^{-1} \mu_{t-1}$.

As before, the parameters of interest are unknown to the investor and have to be estimated from the data. We assume again that the estimation error in the (co)variances is small and we neglect this uncertainty. We focus on the estimation error in expected returns, which is now caused by the fact that we have to estimate the regression coefficients b. We consider the standard least-squares estimator that we denote $\hat{b}$. Let the value of the instruments at time $t-1$ be given by a specific value $Z_{t-1} = Z_0$. Analogous to the unconditional case in Equation (19.4), suppose that the investor chooses his conditionally mean–variance efficient portfolio as:

$$\hat{w}(\alpha)_0 = \alpha^{-1} \Omega_{\varepsilon\varepsilon}^{-1} (Z_0 \hat{b} - \rho_0 \iota), \tag{19.15}$$

where, using obvious notation, the subscript 0 always indicates the value of the variables given that $z_{t-1} = z_0$. Since this portfolio depends on the estimated parameters $\hat{b}$ it will in general be suboptimal, and the loss in expected utility resulting from using $\hat{w}(\alpha)_0$, rather than the optimal portfolio w_0^*, is equal to:

$$L(\alpha)_0 = \left(w_0^{*'} \mu_0 - \hat{w}(\alpha)_0' \mu_0 \right) - \frac{1}{2} \gamma \left(w_0^{*'} \Omega_{\varepsilon\varepsilon} w_0^* - \hat{w}(\alpha)_0' \Omega_{\varepsilon\varepsilon} \hat{w}(\alpha)_0 \right), \tag{19.16}$$

with $\mu_0 = Z_0 b$. Likewise, the expected loss conditionally on $z_{t-1} = z_0$ equals:

$$\delta_0(\alpha) = E[L(\alpha)_0]. \tag{19.17}$$

In ter Horst, de Roon, and Werker (2005) it is shown that the value of α that minimizes δ_0 is:

$$\alpha_0^* = \gamma\left(1 + D_0 \frac{A}{AC_0 - B_0^2}\right), \tag{19.18}$$

with $D_0 = \text{trace} \, (Z_0' \Omega_{\varepsilon\varepsilon}^{-1} Z_0 \text{Var}\,[\hat{b}]) - \text{trace}(Z_0' \Omega_{\varepsilon\varepsilon}^{-1} \iota\iota' \Omega_{\varepsilon\varepsilon}^{-1} Z_0 \text{Var}\,[\hat{b}])/A$.

This solution α_0^* generalizes Equation (19.7) in a straightforward way. As expected returns depend on the specific value z_0 that z_{t-1} takes, we first of all have that the efficient set variables B_0 and C_0 also depend on the specific value of z_0. Apart from this, a second adjustment relative to the unconditional case has to be made through the term D_0, which depends on the inner product of z_0, weighted by the inverse of the covariance matrix $\Omega_{\varepsilon\varepsilon}$ and by the covariance matrix of $\hat{b}$. In the particular case where there is only one instrument which is a constant, i.e., $z_{i,t} = 1$, $\forall t$, Equation (19.18) reduces to the unconditional case in Equation (19.7), since in that case $\text{Var}\,[\hat{b}] = \Omega_{\varepsilon\varepsilon}/T$ and Z_0 is the identity matrix, implying that $\alpha_0^* = \alpha^*$. Again, the actual gain from using the risk aversion α^* instead of the naive approach of using the risk aversion γ is measured by $g(\alpha^*) = \delta_0(\gamma) - \delta_0(\alpha^*)$.

19.3. Data

We use a dataset that contains monthly returns on stock indices for the G5 countries as well as monthly returns on three emerging market indices. Returns are calculated as simple returns with dividends included. The data for the G5 countries are for the period January 1974 until December 1998 and for the emerging markets they are for the period January 1989 until December 1998. The G5 stock indices are the Morgan Stanley Capital Indices (MSCI) indices for the USA, France, Germany, Japan, and the UK. The emerging market indices are the indices for Latin America, Southeast Asia, and the Middle East/Europe.[2] These indices are from the Emerging Markets Data Base (EMDB) of the International Finance Corporation (IFC). The indices for the emerging markets are the IFC Investable indices and, therefore, they represent stock portfolios that are obtainable for US investors. All data are from Datastream. All returns are monthly unhedged US dollar returns.

Table 19.1 contains summary statistics for the returns on the G5 indices as well as the emerging market indices. These summary statistics present some common features of international stock returns. Monthly returns on the G5 indices are between 1% and 1.5% per month. The associated risk is around 7% for the non-US countries and somewhat lower for the US itself, which is due to the fact that all returns are based on indices denominated in dollars. The emerging markets are more volatile than the G5 countries, as can be seen from the standard deviations of the returns, which are always higher for the emerging markets than for the G5 countries. Due to the fact that we have emerging markets indices for regions rather than for individual countries, the standard deviations are not extremely high

Table 19.1: Summary statistics.

	Mean	Standard deviation	Correlation (G5)	Correlation (emerging countries)
G5 countries (January 1974 to December 1998)				
France	1.37	6.85	0.592	0.328
Germany	1.34	5.89	0.522	0.288
Japan	1.11	6.70	0.384	0.229
UK	1.49	7.22	0.584	0.253
US	1.25	4.49	0.466	0.328
Emerging markets (January 1989 to December 1998)				
Latin America	1.94	9.87	0.228	0.323
Asia	0.54	7.90	0.385	0.370
Middle East + Europe	0.85	9.38	0.243	0.313

Notes: The table contains summary statistics for monthly dollar denominated returns on the G5 countries and three emerging markets indices. Means and standard deviations are in percentages. The correlations are the average correlation of each country or region with the G5 countries and the average correlation with the emerging markets, excluding the correlation of each country or region with itself. The G5 indices are the MSCI indices and the emerging market indices are the IFC Investable indices.

though, never exceeding 10% per month. The variation in the mean returns also appears to be higher for the emerging markets, with a mean return of almost 2% for Latin America and only 0.5% for Asia.

Finally, Table 19.1 presents the average correlation of each index with the G5 countries and with the emerging markets, where the correlation of each index with itself is excluded from the average. Not surprisingly, the highest correlations are found between the G5 countries. The correlations between the emerging markets are about two-thirds of the correlations between the G5 countries, and the correlations between the emerging markets and the G5 countries are still lower.

19.4. Portfolios Based on the G5 Countries

In order to show the effects of estimation risk, Table 19.2 presents optimal portfolios for the G5 countries for three different sample periods and for different levels of the actual risk aversion γ. The first column of Panel A gives the mean–variance efficient portfolio for a risk-averse agent with $\gamma = 12$, based on the entire sample period of January 1974 until December 1998. This portfolio is located near the GMV portfolio and is, therefore, not very susceptible to estimation risk in the mean returns. This is also evident when comparing these portfolio weights with the ones in the second column, which are the ones based on the pseudo risk aversion α and thus incorporate estimation risk. The differences in optimal portfolio weights appear to be relatively small in this case.

The next columns of Panel A show similar portfolio weights for two shorter sample periods. The differences in the portfolio weights are most profound in the last and shortest

Table 19.2: Efficient portfolios of the G5 countries, incorporating estimation risk.

	January 1974 to December 1998		January 1989 to December 1998		January 1994 to December 1998	
	$w(\gamma)$	$w(\alpha)$	$w(\gamma)$	$w(\alpha)$	$w(\gamma)$	$w(\alpha)$
Panel A: Optimal portfolio weights, $\gamma = 12$						
France	−0.036	0.048	0.035	0.037	−0.056	−0.077
Germany	0.254	0.241	0.114	0.112	0.000	0.057
Japan	0.149	0.189	−0.223	−0.126	−0.399	−0.235
UK	0.032	−0.014	0.155	0.128	0.481	0.504
US	0.600	0.632	0.927	0.848	0.974	0.751
$A/(AC - B^2)$	361.40		16.41		7.56	

	January 1974 to December 1998			January 1989 to December 1998			January 1994 to December 1998		
	γ	α	*Bayes*	γ	α	*Bayes*	γ	α	*Bayes*
Panel B: Comparing different risk aversions									
Risk aversion	12.0	69.9	12.0	12.0	18.6	12.1	12.0	18.1	12.2
$E[r_t^p](\%)$	1.25	1.23	1.25	1.91	1.74	1.91	2.55	2.18	2.50
$g\ (\%)$	0.046		0.000	0.049		0.002	0.093		0.009
$[g_{0.025}; g_{0.975}]$	[0.013	0.048]		[0.019	0.088]		[0.036	0.170]	
Risk aversion	6.0	34.5	6.0	6.0	9.3	6.1	6.0	9.0	6.1
$E[r_t^p](\%)$	1.28	1.24	1.28	2.42	2.07	2.42	3.65	2.91	3.61
$g\ (\%)$	0.092		0.000	0.098		0.005	0.186		0.018
$[g_{0.025}; g_{0.975}]$	[0.026	0.097]		[0.038	0.177]		[0.072	0.341]	
Risk aversion	2.0	11.6	2.0	2.0	3.1	2.0	2.0	3.0	2.0
$E[r_t^p](\%)$	1.37	1.25	1.37	4.46	3.34	4.44	8.06	5.84	7.95
$g\ (\%)$	0.275		0.002	0.295		0.014	0.559		0.053
$[g_{0.025}; g_{0.975}]$	[0.077	0.290]		[0.112	0.530]		[0.217	1.022]	

Notes: The table presents the effects of estimation risk on optimal portfolios for different sample periods and different levels of risk aversion. Panel A shows mean–variance efficient portfolio weights for an agent with actual risk aversion $\gamma = 12$ for the three sample periods, with and without a correction for estimation risk. $w(\gamma)$ is the efficient portfolio based on the actual risk aversion and $w(\alpha)$ is the efficient portfolio based on the pseudo risk aversion. Panel B shows the differences between optimal portfolios for the three sample periods and for three different levels of the actual risk aversion γ. α is the pseudo risk aversion. $E[r_t^p]$ gives the estimated mean portfolio return on the portfolios with and without a correction for estimation risk. g gives the gain in utility from using the pseudo risk aversion. $[g_{0.025}; g_{0.975}]$ gives a 95% confidence interval associated with the estimated g. 'Bayes' refers to a portfolio adjustment based on a Bayesian approach, *cf.* Equation (19.8). All results are based on monthly dollar denominated returns on the MSCI indices for the G5 countries.

sample period, January 1994 until December 1998. The biggest impact of the estimation risk is on the weights for Japan and the US, where the adjustment for estimation risk amounts to 15% and 25% change, respectively.

Although the biggest adjustment in terms of portfolio weights occurs for the shortest sample period, Panel B of Table 19.2 shows that the difference between the actual and the pseudo risk aversion is actually the smallest for the shortest sample period. From Equation (19.7) this must be due to the differences in the efficient set constants for the different sample periods, since the effect of the sample size T itself must be such that the difference increases when the sample size decreases. Indeed, as can be seen from the last three lines of Panel A, the differences between the efficient set constants for the different sample periods is such that the change in the $A/(AC - B^2)$ term exceeds the change in T. This shows the relative importance of the curvature of the frontier for the adjustments that have to be made in the optimal portfolios in order to account for estimation risk.

Panel B of Table 19.2 also shows the difference in expected returns for the portfolios based on the actual risk aversion γ and the pseudo risk aversion α. Here we see that the differences in terms of expected return increase as the sample size decreases. The gain from using the pseudo risk aversion α^* instead of γ, $g(\alpha^*) = \delta_0(\gamma) - \delta_0(\alpha^*)$, increases as the sample period decreases and as the risk aversion decreases. For the longest sample period, which covers 25 years of monthly data, and a risk aversion $\gamma = 12$, the difference in utility translates into an equivalent risk premium of 0.046% per month, or about 55 basis points per year. For the shortest sample period and a risk aversion $\gamma = 2$, this increases to a sizable 0.559% per month, or 6.7% annually. This reflects the fact that uncertainty in the mean returns becomes more important for lower-risk aversions and for shorter sample periods. The values in square brackets show a 95% confidence interval for the estimate of $g(\alpha^*)$.[3] These confidence intervals show that we can estimate $g(\alpha^*)$ fairly precise.

Finally, Panel B of Table 19.2 also reports the portfolio returns and the gain $g(\alpha^*)$ when the correction is based on a Bayesian approach. The Bayesian approach is based on a non-informative prior and leads to choosing a portfolio based on $\gamma(1 + 1/T)$ rather than γ. Thus, there is only a correction for sample size and not for the number of assets or the curvature of the frontier. Here we see that the differences between the naive portfolio based on γ and the adjusted portfolio that results from the Bayesian approach are much smaller than the differences that result from using α. For the largest samples γ and $\gamma(1 + 1/T)$ are, of course, very close to each other. As the sample size is smaller the Bayesian correction becomes more important, but at best the gain that results from the Bayesian correction is about one-tenth of the gain from using the pseudo risk aversion α^* in $g(\alpha^*)$.[4]

In summary, the results show that there can be sizable adjustments in portfolio weights for estimation risk, especially for the shortest sample period. This is also reflected in the expected gain from using the pseudo risk aversion α^* which, for a true risk aversion γ of 2, can be as high as 6.7% per year for the most recent sample period of 5 years. The differences between the different samples are not simply due to the length of the sample period, but are also affected by the fact that the estimates of the efficient set constants are different for the different sample periods. As mean returns are especially important for investors with low-risk aversions, we find that the effects of estimation error increase when the risk aversion decreases.

19.5. Including Emerging Markets in International Portfolios

The previous section shows the relative importance of the combined effects of a decrease in sample size, the actual risk aversion, uncertainty in mean returns, and the curvature of the mean–variance frontier on the adjustments that have to be made in the optimal portfolios in order to account for estimation risk. From the summary statistics in Table 19.1 it follows that the uncertainty in the returns on emerging markets is higher than in the returns on the G5 countries. This confirms one of the stylized facts of emerging markets returns as described in, for instance, Harvey (1995), Bekaert and Harvey (1997), and DeRoon, Nijman, and Werker (2001), who show that both the variance of the returns, as well as the cross-sectional variability in the mean returns, is much higher for emerging markets than for developed markets. In addition, the sample period for which data for these markets are available is much shorter than for the G5 countries. Also, when looking at Equation (19.7), K increases from 5 to 8, which will have an added effect on the adjustment in the optimal portfolio as well. Therefore, when including emerging markets in the investment opportunity set, we may expect the effects of estimation risk to be even more pronounced than in case of the G5 countries only.

In terms of the expected gain using the pseudo risk aversion α^*, Panel B of Table 19.2 showed that for the G5 countries the expected gain is about four times higher for the period January 1989 until December 1998, than for the longer period January 1974 until December 1998. The emerging markets data are available since January 1989 only, implying that we should use this period for the G5 countries as a benchmark. From Table 19.3, for a risk aversion $\gamma = 12$, the expected gain increases from 0.049% per month for the G5 countries to 0.101% when the emerging markets are included as well, i.e., the expected gain is almost two times as high as for the G5 countries only. For the shortest sample period, the expected gain is about 50% higher when the emerging markets are included relative to the case of the G5 countries only. The resulting difference in utility translates into an equivalent premium of 0.77% per month, or about 9% per year for the shortest sample period, when the risk aversion is $\gamma = 2$.

As the first panel of Table 19.3 shows, both the actual and the pseudo risk aversion result in portfolios that have big short positions, especially for the short sample period. Therefore, Table 19.4 also shows the effects of estimation risk on the portfolios for the G5 countries and the emerging markets when there are short sales restrictions. When the 10-year period of January 1989 until December 1998 is used to calculate the optimal portfolio for a risk aversion $\gamma = 6$, use of the actual risk aversion yields a portfolio that only invests in the US, in Germany, and in Latin America. For all other countries the short sales constraints are binding. When estimation risk is taken into account, the optimal portfolio is located on a different segment of the mean–variance frontier, and now additional positions are taken in the UK and the Middle East as well, mainly at the expense of the position in the US market. For the shorter period January 1994 until December 1998, we even see that incorporating estimation risk shifts the portfolio from a 100% investment in the US to a portfolio that also invests in Germany and the UK. The finding that no position is taken in the emerging markets is in line with the result in DeRoon, Nijman, and Werker (2001) that there are no significant diversification benefits from emerging markets in recent periods when short sales constraints are taken into account.

Table 19.3: Estimation risk for the G5 countries plus emerging markets.

	January 1989 to December 1998		January 1994 to December 1998	
	$w(\gamma)$	$w(\alpha)$	$w(\gamma)$	$w(\alpha)$
Panel A: Optimal portfolio weights, $\gamma = 12$				
France	−0.055	−0.038	0.177	0.101
Germany	0.175	0.149	−0.006	0.042
Japan	−0.210	−0.093	−0.308	−0.194
UK	0.198	0.151	0.412	0.440
US	0.962	0.863	1.579	1.276
Latin America	0.103	0.063	−0.205	−0.175
Southeast Asia	−0.221	−0.157	−0.400	−0.315
Middle East	0.050	0.062	−0.250	−0.174

	January 1989 to December 1998		January 1994 to December 1998	
	γ	α	γ	α
Panel B: Comparing different risk aversions				
Risk aversion	12.0	20.5	12.0	16.3
$E[r_t^p](\%)$	2.12	1.83	4.45	3.73
$g\ (\%)$	0.101		0.129	
$[g_{0.025}; g_{0.975}]$	[0.042	0.138]	[0.062	0.194]
Risk aversion	6.0	0.3	6.0	8.2
$E[r_t^p](\%)$	2.80	2.22	7.14	5.71
$g\ (\%)$	0.202		0.258	
$[g_{0.025}; g_{0.975}]$	[0.084	0.276]	[0.124	0.388]
Risk aversion	2.0	3.4	2.0	2.7
$E[r_t^p](\%)$	5.55	3.83	17.92	13.60
$g\ (\%)$	0.605		0.773	
$[g_{0.025}; g_{0.975}]$	[0.252	0.827]	[0.373	1.165]

Notes: The table presents the effects of estimation risk on optimal portfolios for different sample periods and different levels of risk aversion. Panel A shows mean–variance efficient portfolio weights for an agent with actual risk aversion $\gamma = 12$ for the three sample periods, with and without a correction for estimation risk. $w(\gamma)$ is the efficient portfolio based on the actual risk aversion and $w(\alpha)$ is the efficient portfolio based on the pseudo risk aversion. Panel B shows the differences between optimal portfolios for the three sample periods and for three different levels of the actual risk aversion γ. $E[r_t^p]$ gives the estimated mean portfolio return on the portfolios with and without a correction for estimation risk. g gives the expected gain in utility from using the pseudo risk aversion. $[g_{0.025}; g_{0.975}]$ gives a 95% confidence interval associated with the estimated g. All results are based on monthly dollar denominated returns on the MSCI indices for the G5 countries and on the IFC Investable indices for the emerging markets.

Table 19.4: Estimation risk with short sales constraints.

	January 1989 to December 1998		January 1994 to December 1998	
	$w(\gamma)$	$w(\alpha)$	$w(\gamma)$	$w(\alpha)$
Panel A: Optimal portfolio weights, $\gamma = 6$				
France				
Germany	0.032	0.101		0.036
Japan				
UK		0.101		0.180
US	0.884	0.732	1.000	0.784
Latin America	0.084	0.013		
Southeast Asia				
Middle East		0.053		

	January 1989 to December 1998		January 1994 to December 1998	
	γ	α	γ	α
Panel B: Comparing different risk aversions.				
Risk aversion	12.0	45.2	12.0	25.0
$E[r_t^p](\%)$	1.58	1.51	1.85	1.72
$g\ (\%)$	0.102		0.072	
$[g_{0.025};\ g_{0.975}]$	[0.030	0.118]	[0.019	0.131]
Risk aversion	6.0	50.2	6.0	12.5
$E[r_t^p](\%)$	1.62	1.50	1.96	1.84
$g\ (\%)$	0.234		0.144	
$[g_{0.025};\ g_{0.975}]$	[0.059	0.238]	[0.038	0.261]
Risk aversion	2.0	50.2	2.0	71.9
$E[r_t^p](\%)$	1.67	1.50	1.96	1.64
$g\ (\%)$	0.699		0.388	
$[g_{0.025};\ g_{0.975}]$	[0.178	0.848]	[0.114	0.784]

Notes: The table presents the effects of estimation risk on optimal portfolios for different sample periods and different levels of risk aversion, taking into account short sales constraints. Panel A shows mean–variance efficient portfolio weights for an agent with actual risk aversion $\gamma = 6$ for the three sample periods, with and without a correction for estimation risk. $w(\gamma)$ is the efficient portfolio based on the actual risk aversion and $w(\alpha)$ is the efficient portfolio based on the pseudo risk aversion. Panel B shows the differences between optimal portfolios for the three sample periods and for three different levels of the actual risk aversion γ. $E[r_t^p]$ gives the estimated mean portfolio return on the portfolios with and without a correction for estimation risk. g gives the expected gain in utility from using the pseudo risk aversion. $[g_{0.025};\ g_{0.975}]$ gives a 95% confidence interval associated with the estimated g. All results are based on monthly dollar denominated returns on the MSCI indices for the G5 countries and on the IFC Investable indices for the emerging markets.

Although in terms of portfolio weights the effects of estimation risk are stronger when there are short sales constraints, the second panel of Table 19.4 shows that the effects on expected portfolio return and on the expected gain are much less pronounced than in Table 19.3. This finding is a result of the fact that the mean–variance frontier is limited and diversification benefits are smaller when there are short sales constraints.

19.6. Time-Varying Expected Returns

There is ample evidence available that stock returns can be predicted from common instruments such as the short-term interest rate, the default spread, and the dividend yield on the market portfolio (see, e.g., Ferson and Harvey, 1999). When implementing these predictabilities in forming efficient portfolios, a problem often encountered is that the optimal portfolio strategy shows a lot of variability in portfolio weights. Due to transaction costs, for instance, large variations in portfolio weights can be cumbersome. To the extent that the predictability in stock return is affected by estimation risk, the variability in portfolio weights may be diminished once estimation risk is explicitly accounted for in the optimal portfolio. The purpose of this section is to use our adjustment for estimation risk when implementing conditional portfolio strategies.

Section 19.2.3 shows how the pseudo risk aversion α^{*}_{t-1} should be optimally chosen in case returns are predictable from a set of instruments z_{t-1}. For the US, we use as instruments a constant; the short-term US risk-free interest rate at the beginning of the month measured by the 1-month TBill-rate; the US term spread, which is the spread between the yield on the 10-year US treasure note and the short-term US interest rate; the default spread, which is the yield spread between Moody's Baa and Aaa rated US bonds; and the spread between the lagged dividend yield on the US portfolio and the short-term US interest rate. For the other G5 countries (France, Germany, Japan, and the UK) we use a constant, the local dividend yield, the local risk-free rate (Eurocurrency based) and the interest rate spread versus the US interest rate. These instruments are similar to the ones used by DeSantis and Gerard (1997) and Ait-Sahalia and Brandt (2001), for instance,[5] and are often used in empirical studies to predict stock returns and are known to have some predictive power. Here, these instruments are used to predict returns on the G5 countries.

Following the set-up in Section 19.2.3, we assume that expected returns are a linear function of the instruments, whereas variances are constant over time. The parameter estimates in the predictive regressions are updated every month, using a moving window of 120 months.

Table 19.5 summarizes the results of the mean–variance efficient portfolio weights for the G5 countries when returns are predicted from the five instruments (including a constant) described above. The results in this table are based on the entire sample period, which contains 300 observations. The last column of Table 19.5 presents the R^2's of the predictive regressions of each of the five country returns on the instruments. The R^2 is always lower than 5%, and typically lower than the R^2's reported by, for instance, Ferson and Harvey (1999). However, they use US instruments to explain domestic stock portfolios, whereas we use both US and global (the dividend yield) instruments to explain country returns.

Table 19.5: Estimation risk for the G5 countries using conditioning information.

	$w(\gamma)$		$w(\alpha^*)$		ΔVar (%)	R^2 (%)
	Average	Standard deviation	Average	Standard deviation		
France	−0.15	0.53	−0.1	0.31	66	2.88
Germany	0.34	0.46	0.26	0.28	63	2.00
Japan	0.35	0.36	0.28	0.23	59	3.77
UK	−0.14	0.60	−0.09	0.35	66	1.90
US	0.59	0.60	0.64	0.35	66	5.35

Notes: The table presents the effects of estimation risk on optimal portfolios in case returns are predictable. The G5 country returns are predicted from a set country-specific instruments. For France, Germany, Japan, and the UK, the instruments used are a constant, the dividend yield on the local MSCI portfolio, the local short-term interest rate, and the change in the foreign exchange rate versus the US dollar. For the US, the instruments used are a constant, the short-term US interest rate, the US term spread, the US default spread, and the dividend yield on the MSCI US portfolio. The table gives the means and standard deviations of the optimal portfolio weights for the actual risk aversion $\gamma = 12$ and the pseudo risk aversion α. The parameter estimates in the predictable regression are updated every month using a moving window of 120 months. ΔVar gives the percentage reduction in the variance of the portfolio weights, due to using the pseudo risk aversion instead of the actual risk aversion. The last column gives the average R^2's of predictive regressions of the country returns on the instruments. The results are based on the sample period, January 1989 until December 1998, and the period January 1979 until December 1988 is used for the first predictive regression.

The first two columns show the mean and standard deviation of the unadjusted conditional mean–variance portfolio weights that are based on a risk aversion parameter $\gamma = 12$.[6] The standard deviations reflect the common finding that implementing conditioning information leads to large variations in the optimal portfolio weights. Even though the risk aversion is relatively high, implying that the portfolio should not be too sensitive to variation in expected returns, the standard deviation of the portfolio weights for the non-US countries is about 60%. Since the pseudo risk aversion α^* takes into account the estimation risk in the predictive regressions, accounting for estimation risk, may result in different and less variable portfolio weights. Indeed, the third and fourth columns of Table 19.5 show that the means and standard deviations of the adjusted conditional mean–variance portfolio weights are different from the unadjusted ones in the first two columns.

The adjusted mean portfolio weights for Japan and the US are less extreme than the unadjusted ones, and, more importantly, the standard deviations are about half the ones of the unadjusted weights. This is also shown by the fifth column, which shows the percentage reduction in the variance of the portfolio weights that results from taking estimation risk into account. Here we see that on average there is about 65% variance reduction in the weights. This suggests that the estimation risk in the predictive regressions is substantial and that accounting for this risk leads to conditional mean–variance portfolio weights that are much less variable than a straightforward implementation of the predictive regressions would suggest.

19.7. Out-of-Sample Results

The sample estimates in the previous sections indicate that there are clear benefits to investors from using the pseudo risk aversion α^* rather than their actual risk aversion γ, thereby accounting for estimation risk. In this section we want to analyze whether taking account of estimation risk also leads to better out-of-sample results. As a simple experiment we use a rolling estimation procedure in which we estimate the relevant parameters using either the past 60 or 120 months of data, and then use these to calculate the portfolio weights for the next month. For instance, the first panel of Table 19.6 shows summary results for mean–variance portfolios based on the G5 countries, where the parameters are estimated using the last 60 months of observations. Having an estimated efficient portfolio based on the last 60 months of observations we obtain a portfolio return for the next month. This procedure is repeated for the entire sample period, resulting in a total of 240 out-of-sample portfolio returns. Table 19.6 shows means and standard deviations for the returns of the portfolios that are based on either the actual risk aversion γ, or the pseudo risk aversion α, as well as the resulting out-of-sample estimate of the gain $g(\alpha^*)$. Notice that in this case the pseudo risk aversion will change each month because the estimated means and covariances will change each month.

For brevity, we do not report out-of-sample results for the Bayesian estimation risk correction (19.8). Given our sample sizes, those results would be virtually identical to the uncorrected case. Clearly, the Bayesian approach has the advantage that the same adjusted risk aversion can be used each month (as the Bayesian adaptation only depends on the sample size used and not on the curvature of the mean–variance frontier).

As Panel A of Table 19.6 indicates, in case of a 60-month estimation period, the out-of-sample performance of the G5 portfolio based on the pseudo risk aversion α dominates the performance of the portfolio that is based on the actual risk aversion γ. Taking estimation risk into account leads to portfolios that have higher mean returns and lower standard deviations for every level of the risk aversion chosen. Naturally, this translates into positive out-of-sample estimates of the gain g as well. The standard errors for g show that these gains are generally significant.

This picture changes slightly as we use a 120-month window to estimate the means and covariances, as Panel B of Table 19.6 shows. Again, the standard deviations of the out-of-sample portfolio returns are uniformly lower when using the pseudo-risk aversion, but in this case mean returns are also slightly lower. The combined effect in terms of the expected utility gain g is still positive, however, as the third line of Panel B shows, although the estimated gains are certainly lower than in the first panel and not significantly different from zero.

A similar picture emerges if we add the three emerging markets indices to the portfolio. In this case the number of assets in the portfolio is eight, and we use a 60-month window to estimate the means and covariances. Since the emerging markets indices are available from 1989 onwards only, this leaves 60 out-of-sample portfolio returns. Here we also see that the mean return of the portfolio that accounts for estimation risk is slightly lower than the mean return of the unadjusted portfolio, but this effect is more than offset by the decrease in portfolio variance as the estimates of the gain g convincingly show. The estimated gains are in all cases significantly different from zero, at least at 5% significance level. Finally, the last panel of Table 19.6 repeats this analysis taking into account short

Table 19.6: Out-of-sample results.

	$\gamma = 12$	α	$\gamma = 6$	a	$\gamma = 2$	α
Panel A: G5 countries, 60-month estimation window						
Mean (%)	1.25	1.28	1.18	1.23	0.87	1.04
Standard deviation (%)	4.38	4.10	5.25	4.33	11.54	6.42
g (%)	0.18 (0.08)		0.35 (0.15)		1.09 (0.42)	
Panel B: G5 countries, 120-month estimation window						
Mean (%)	1.50	1.49	1.53	1.51	1.65	1.59
Standard deviation (%)	4.29	4.12	4.79	4.21	8.36	5.15
g (%)	0.08 (0.06)		0.14 (0.11)		0.37 (0.33)	
Panel C: All countries, 60-month estimation window						
Mean (%)	1.60	1.59	1.64	1.61	1.79	1.70
Standard deviation (%)	4.67	3.84	7.21	4.80	19.83	11.36
g (%)	0.41 (0.22)		0.84 (0.44)		2.55 (1.36)	
Panel D: All countries, 60-month estimation window, n.s.s.						
Mean (%)	1.34	1.47	1.10	1.35	0.73	0.76
Standard deviation (%)	4.29	3.86	5.24	3.94	8.12	5.09
g (%)	0.34 (0.16)		0.61 (0.45)		0.43 (0.79)	

Notes: The table presents out-of-sample means and standard deviations for portfolios based on parameter estimates over the last 60 or 120 months. The parameter estimates are updated every month. Panels A and B show the results for portfolios of the G5 countries, based on the entire sample period January 1974 until December 1998. Panels C and D show the results for portfolios of both the G5 countries and the three emerging markets indices, based on the sample period January 1989 until December 1998. The estimated gains g are based on the mean portfolio returns and the standard deviation of the portfolio returns as reported in the first two lines of each panel, the standard errors of g are reported between parenthesis.

sales constraints as well. Again we find that the adjusted portfolios perform uniformly better out-of-sample than the unadjusted portfolios, although not always significantly so. Therefore, our out-of-sample experiment confirms the previous findings that investors gain when using the proposed adjustment for estimation risk.

19.8. Robustness Checks: Non-*i.i.d.* Returns

The analysis so far relied on two maintained assumptions. First, returns are assumed to be *i.i.d.* and, second, estimation risk in covariances is neglected. This section demonstrates that both assumptions are innocuous for the estimation risk problem studied in this chapter. In this section, we simulate a set of returns and analyze the loss in utility that occurs when calculating optimal portfolios based on either the true or the estimated means and (co)variances. Specifically, we use the sample of the G5 countries as the actual returns. From this we simulate a sample of T returns, using the bootstrap procedure from Politis and Romano (1994) with a smoothing parameter of 0.10 (implying that on average the mean length of the block taken from the sample is 10 observations).[7] The advantage of bootstrapping over Monte Carlo simulations is that we do not have to assume normality and retain the properties of returns that are present in the data such as skewness and time-varying volatility.[8] For each simulation we then calculate the loss in expected utility

$$L(\gamma;\hat{\mu}_T, \Sigma) = \{w^{*\prime}\mu - \hat{w}(\gamma;\hat{\mu}_T, \Sigma)'\mu\}$$
$$- \frac{1}{2}\gamma\{w^{*\prime}\Sigma w^* - \hat{w}(\gamma;\hat{\mu}_T, \Sigma)' \Sigma \hat{w}(\gamma;\hat{\mu}_T, \Sigma)\},$$

$$L(\gamma;\mu, \hat{\Sigma}_T) = \{w^{*\prime}\mu - \hat{w}(\gamma;\mu, \hat{\Sigma}_T)'\mu\}$$
$$- \frac{1}{2}\gamma\{w^{*\prime}\Sigma w^* - \hat{w}(\gamma;\mu, \hat{\Sigma}_T)' \Sigma \hat{w}(\gamma;\mu, \hat{\Sigma}_T)\},$$

$$L(\gamma;\hat{\mu}_T, \hat{\Sigma}_T) = \{w^{*\prime}\mu - \hat{w}(\gamma;\hat{\mu}_T, \hat{\Sigma}_T)'\mu\}$$
$$- \frac{1}{2}\gamma\{w^{*\prime}\Sigma w^* - \hat{w}(\gamma;\hat{\mu}_T, \hat{\Sigma}_T)' \Sigma \hat{w}(\gamma;\hat{\mu}_T, \hat{\Sigma}_T)\},$$

where w is calculated according to Equation (19.2), based on either the actual expected returns and (co)variances μ and Σ, resulting in the optimal portfolio w^* or based on the estimates $\hat{\mu}$, and $\hat{\Sigma}_T$, that are obtained from the T simulated returns.

Table 19.7 shows the averages of the losses in the expected utility over 10,000 simulations, which can be interpreted as the measure δ:

$$\delta(\gamma;\hat{\mu}_T, \Sigma) = E[L(\gamma;\hat{\mu}_T, \Sigma)],$$
$$\delta(\gamma;\mu, \hat{\Sigma}_T) = E[L(\gamma;\mu, \hat{\Sigma}_T)],$$
$$\delta(\gamma;\hat{\mu}_T, \hat{\Sigma}_T) = E[L(\gamma;\hat{\mu}_T, \hat{\Sigma}_T)],$$

These measures show the relative importance of estimation error in the expected returns and in the (co)variances of the returns. It is obvious from this Table 19.7 that estimation risk in expected returns is much more important than estimation risk in (co)variances. Since we use bootstrap simulations, the results in Table 19.7 do not rely on any normality or i.i.d. assumptions. For every risk aversion and sample size in Table 19.7, the expected loss that is due to uncertainty in the expected returns is at least six times as high as the loss that is due to uncertainty in the covariances. The third line of each panel in Table 19.7 shows the combined effect of estimation error in the means and the covariances. From these lines we see that there is also an interaction effect of the estimation errors, which results in a total expected loss that in most cases exceeds the sum of the individual effects of the estimation errors in the means and the covariances.

In terms of loss in expected utility, the uncertainty in expected returns becomes less important as the risk aversion increases, whereas the uncertainty in the covariances first decreases and then increases. Roughly speaking, this reflects the fact that, as the risk aversion increases, the interest is more in the variance of the portfolio return than in the expected portfolio return. As the risk aversion is 1, the effect of uncertainty in expected

Table 19.7: Simulation results for estimation errors in the expected returns and the (co)variances.

γ	1	2	5	10
$T = 60$				
$\delta(\gamma; \hat{\mu}, \Sigma)$ (%)	3.255	1.627	0.651	0.326
$\delta(\gamma; \mu, \hat{\Sigma})$ (%)	0.157	0.107	0.100	0.138
$\delta(\gamma; \hat{\mu}, \hat{\Sigma})$ (%)	5.237	2.622	1.077	0.797
$T = 120$				
$\delta(\gamma; \hat{\mu}, \Sigma)$ (%)	1.635	0.818	0.327	0.164
$\delta(\gamma; \mu, \hat{\Sigma})$ (%)	0.073	0.052	0.050	0.070
$\delta(\gamma; \hat{\mu}, \hat{\Sigma})$ (%)	2.179	1.093	0.453	0.338
$T = 300$				
$\delta(\gamma; \hat{\mu}, \Sigma)$ (%)	0.655	0.327	0.131	0.094
$\delta(\gamma; \mu, \hat{\Sigma})$ (%)	0.031	0.022	0.021	0.029
$\delta(\gamma; \hat{\mu}, \hat{\Sigma})$ (%)	0.762	0.382	0.159	0.119

Notes: The table shows the average difference in utility when the optimal portfolio is calculated from the actual expected returns and covariances, or from the estimated expected returns and covariances. Returns on five assets are simulated using bootstrapped returns from the G5 countries. The 10,000 samples with different lengths are simulated and the expected gains in utility $\delta(\gamma; \hat{\mu}, \Sigma)$, $\delta(\gamma; \mu, \hat{\Sigma})$, and $\delta(\gamma; \hat{\mu}, \hat{\Sigma})$ are calculated (in percentages).

returns is about 30 times larger than the effect of uncertainty in the covariances. As the risk aversion increases to 10, this ratio decreases to 3. This ratio appears to be somewhat independent of the sample size, although the magnitude of δ clearly does depend on the sample size. From the numbers in Table 19.5, the loss in expected utility appears to be a linear function of the sample size.

Clearly, the simulations show that the loss in expected utility from uncertainty in covariances is small. This justifies our approach, which focuses on the uncertainty in expected returns only. Although the relative importance of uncertainty in the expected returns compared with the uncertainty in the covariances decreases as the risk aversion increases, the loss in expected utility caused by uncertainty in the covariances appears to be small in all cases. It should be noted though that this result might not hold as the number of assets in the portfolio becomes very large (see, e.g., Ledoit, 1999).

19.9. Summary and Conclusions

This chapter proposes a new adjustment in mean–variance portfolio weights to incorporate estimation risk caused by uncertainty in expected security returns. Assuming that asset returns are homoskedastic and normally distributed, the adjustment amounts to using a pseudo risk aversion rather than the agent's actual risk aversion. This pseudo risk aversion is always higher than the actual risk aversion and the difference between the two depends on the number of assets under consideration, the sample size, and the efficient set constants. As is to be expected, the difference between the pseudo risk aversion and the actual risk aversion is increasing in the number of assets included in the portfolio and decreasing in the sample size. We extend the methodology to the case where short sales are prohibited and the case where mean returns are predictable. In the case where short sales are prohibited, the incorporation of estimation risk generally has significant effects. These results are also evident in our out-of-sample experiment. When returns are predictable from a set of observed instruments, the adjustment is also given and it depends on the values taken by the instruments.

Applying the adjustment to international portfolios, we show that the adjustments are non-trivial for the G5 country portfolios and that they are even more important when emerging markets are included and short sales are excluded. We also show that, in case of time-varying expected country returns, our adjustment induces a significantly smaller variability in portfolio weights.

Acknowledgment

Helpful comments of Olivier Ledoit, Bertrand Melenberg, and Theo Nijman are gratefully acknowledged.

Endnotes

1. The estimated parameters depend on $\hat{\mu}$ instead of: μ: $\hat{A} = A = \iota'\Sigma^{-1}\iota$, $\hat{B} = \iota'\Sigma^{-1}\iota\hat{\mu}$, and $\hat{C} = \hat{\mu}'\Sigma^{-1}\hat{\mu}$.
2. The emerging markets indices cover the following countries. For Latin America, the index includes Argentina, Brazil, Chile, Colombia, Peru, and Venezuela. For Southeast Asia, the index includes China, India, Indonesia, Korea, Malaysia, Pakistan, Philippines, Sri Lanka, Taiwan, and Thailand. Finally, for the Middle East/Europe the index includes Egypt, Israel, Jordan, Morocco, Czech Republic, Greece, Hungary, Poland, Russia, Slovenia, and Turkey.
3. The construction of the confidence intervals is shown in ter Horst, de Roon and Werker (2005).
4. The difference between $g(\alpha^*)$ and the gain that results from a Bayesian approach becomes smaller if we use a diffuse prior, in which case the Bayesian also takes into account the number of assets, but not the curvature of the frontier. In this case the difference varies between 10% and 90%. Results on the diffuse prior can be obtained from the authors upon request.
5. Except for the dividend yield, which in our case is the yield on the MSCI World index.
6. Results for other risk aversions are very similar and can be obtained from the authors upon request.
7. This bootstrap procedure is described, e.g., in Sullivan, Timmerman, and White (1999).
8. Indeed, although not reported, our tests suggest that the returns are not normally distributed. These tests may be obtained from the authors upon request.

References

Ait-Sahalia, Y., & Brandt, M. (2001). Variable selection for portfolio choice. *Journal of Finance, 56,* 1297–1351.

Alexander, G.J., & Resnick, B.G. (1985). More on estimation risk and simple rules for optimal portfolio selection. *Journal of Finance, 40,* 125–133.

Balduzzi, P., & Liu, L. (2000). *Parameter uncertainty and international investment.* Working paper, Boston College.

Barry, C.B. (1974). Portfolio analysis under uncertain means, variances, and covariances. *Journal of Finance, 29,* 515–522.

Bawa, V.S., Brown, S.J., & Klein, R.W. (1979). *Estimation risk and optimal portfolio choice.* Amsterdam: North-Holland.

Bekaert, G., & Harvey, C.R. (1997). Emerging equity market volatility. *Journal of Financial Economics, 43,* 29–77.

Brown, S.J. (1979). The effect of estimation risk on capital market equilibrium. *Journal of Financial and Quantitative Analysis, 14,* 215–220.

Chen, S., & Brown, S.J. (1983). Estimation risk and simple rules for optimal portfolio selection. *Journal of Finance, 38,* 1087–1093.

Chopra, V., & Ziemba, W.T. (1993). The effect of errors in means, variances, and covariances on optimal portfolio choice. *Journal of Portfolio Management, 19,* 6–11.

Coles, J.L., Loewenstein, U., & Suay, J. (1995). On equilibrium pricing under parameter uncertainty. *Journal of Financial and Quantitative Analysis, 30,* 347–364.

DeRoon, F.A., Nijman, T.E., & Werker, B.J.M. (2001). Testing for mean–variance spanning with short sales constraints and transaction costs: The case of emerging markets. *Journal of Finance, 56,* 723–744.

DeSantis, G., & Gerard, B. (1997). International asset pricing and portfolio diversification with time-varying risk. *Journal of Finance, 52,* 1881–1912.

Ferson, W.E., & Harvey, C.R. (1999). Conditioning variables and the cross section of stock returns. *Journal of Finance, 54,* 1325–1360.

Harvey, C.R. (1995). Predictable risk and returns in emerging markets. *Review of Financial Studies, 8,* 773–816.

ter Horst, J.R., de Roon, F.A., & Werker, B.J.M. (2005). *Technical appendix on estimation risk in portfolio choice.* Working paper, Tilburg University.

Ingersoll, J.E. (1987). *Theory of financial decision making.* Maryland: Rowman & Littlefield.

Jobson, J.D., Korkie, B., & Ratti, V. (1979). Improved estimation for Markowitz portfolios using James–Stein type estimators. *Proceedings of the American Statistical Association, Business and Economics Statistics Section,* 279–284.

Jorion, P. (1985). International portfolio diversification with estimation risk. *Journal of Business, 58,* 259–278.

Jorion, P. (1986). Bayes–Stein estimation for portfolio analysis. *Journal of Financial and Quantitative Analysis, 21,* 279–292.

Jorion, P. (1991). Bayesian and CAPM estimators of the means: Implications for portfolio selection. *Journal of Financial Economics,* 717–727.

Klein, R.W., & Bawa, V.S. (1976). The effect of estimation risk on optimal portfolio choice. *Journal of Financial Economics, 3,* 215–231.

Ledoit, O. (1999). *Improved estimation of the covariance matrix of stock returns with an application to portfolio selection.* Working paper, UCLA.

Markowitz, H.M. (1959). *Portfolio selection: Efficient diversification of investments.* New York: Wiley.

Markowitz, H.M. (1987). *Mean–variance analysis in portfolio choice and capital markets.* Cambridge: Basil Blackwell.

Politis, D., & Romano, J. (1994). The stationary bootstrap. *Journal of the American Statistical Society, 89,* 1303–1313.

Sullivan, R., Timmerman, A., & White, H. (1999). Data-snooping, technical trading rule performance and the bootstrap. *Journal of Finance, 54,* 1647–1692.

Chapter 20

A Risk Measure for Retail Investment Products[1]

Theo Nijman and Bas Werker

20.1. Introduction

Transparency of the market for retail investments has attracted a lot of attention in recent years because of four related developments. First of all, the range of investment products that are offered to retail investors has grown considerably. In many countries structured products that contain complicated derivatives are available in addition to mutual funds holding plain stock or bond portfolios. Good information about the cost loading and expected return of these products is scarce. At the same time, investment opportunities in funds of hedge funds are offered that are equally non-transparent. A second reason is that different, traditionally separated, retail markets are becoming more and more connected. Nowadays, many insurance, mortgage, and retirement products contain an element of investment choice. Sometimes such financial products are even offered under the name "savings products", while in fact they are risky speculative investments. A third reason is that in many countries individuals have to take more and more financial decisions. Decisions related to saving and investing for retirement in particular used to be taken collectively, but have been more and more individualized. A fourth reason for the enlarged attention for transparency in the retail market is the overwhelming evidence that many investors do not take well-informed investment decisions. As an example, in the Netherlands many retail investors borrowed money to invest in the stock market (through investments in the so-called "stock lease" products) shortly before the stock market crash in 2001–2003. Subsequently many of these investors not only lost their full investment, but also had to pay substantial sums of money to make up for the drop in value of their implicit stock portfolio — leaving many heavily indebted. Major court cases have signaled that many investors were not at all aware of the characteristics of their investments. Likewise, evidence on US investors in 401(k) plans has shown that many individuals hold undiversified portfolios in the same company that employs them (see Munnell & Sundén, 2004). Many papers in the behavioral finance literature illustrate the same point.

Advances in Corporate Finance and Asset Pricing
Edited by L. Renneboog
© 2006 Elsevier B.V. All rights reserved.
ISBN: 0-444-52723-0

This chapter proposes a risk measure for retail investment products. The risk measure will be based on the expected pay-off of the financial product in bad scenarios, in analogy to the well-known expected loss above Value at Risk (VaR) or expected shortfall. As of January 2006, most retail products with an investment component offered in the Netherlands will have to report their risk classification in the Financiële Bijsluiter (hereafter: financial information leaflet).[2] This risk indicator shall be based on a classification of financial products in risk categories (partly) on the basis of the risk measure described here. This chapter outlines the determination of the risk measure.

It should be evident that the risk measure proposed here does not contain complete information to take adequate investment decisions. Investment decisions for retail investors are much more complex than that. According to theory the optimal investment decision will depend on the characteristics of the full portfolio to which a product is to be added. The volatility of other assets or liabilities as well as correlations of returns on the product with these assets and liabilities can make a financial product more or less attractive. Moreover, the fiscal treatment of a product, including the possibility that this treatment will change in the future, and the possibility of default of the issuer of the product are important aspects to take into account. Such elements will be ignored in this chapter. The main advantage of a single-product risk measure is that it can be connected one-to-one to a financial product, while at the same time providing useful information to the investor. The challenge for regulators is not to make sure that all relevant information could be gathered by retail investor in some inaccessible way, but rather that a very important determinant of the investment decision is readily available and not misleading or ambiguous. This is the challenge for the risk measure to be proposed in this chapter.

The plan of this chapter is as follows. In Section 20.2, we briefly sketch the development of the Dutch legislation on required information for retail investors. In Section 20.3, we introduce the risk measure that is proposed, while Section 20.4 discusses the actual computational procedure. Section 20.5 is devoted to illustrative calculations for a number of financial products. Extensions to incorporate interest rate and inflation risk, which are not yet covered in the indicator that has been prescribed in the Netherlands, are discussed in Section 20.6. Section 20.7 concludes this chapter.

20.2. Information Requirements Towards Retail Investors in the Netherlands

In many retail markets, the expected return on an investment product seems to be the main component of the information communicated to potential investors. No doubt the expected return is easy to understand, but it can clearly also be very misleading. The risk associated with the investment product is an equally important input to the decision process. As discussed in the introduction (Section 20.1), we restrict ourselves in this chapter to the market risk of single-product investments and ignore other dimensions of risk.

In the Dutch retail market, at the turn of the century, many financial institutions had voluntarily classified a number of investment products in risk categories. These classifications appeared for investment products only, were issuer specific and, therefore, hard to compare and restricted to relatively straightforward products like mutual funds. The legislator and supervisor joint forces introduced, in July 2002, the obligation for many financial products to offer a financial information leaflet that describes risk, cost, and return aspects of the product in a coherent and uniform way.

The financial information leaflet has contributed to generating information that is comparable across products that are offered by different suppliers and has made the cost structure of products much more transparent. The leaflet also had a number of limitations. One of them is that it was a lengthy legally inspired document that was not very accessible for readers. At the same time, the risk information in the leaflet was based on a well-known but not very attractive risk measure: VaR.

VaR is a risk measure that is often used in the financial industry to manage short-term market risks. The $\alpha\%$-VaR is defined as the minimum amount such that with probability α the value of the asset or portfolio under consideration will drop below this amount. In short-term risk management, expected returns (which are dominated by risk for short horizons) are simply ignored. However, this is not applicable for the longer investment horizons that are typically relevant for retail investment products. The legislation has therefore prescribed that for a number of standard asset classes such as fixed income, diversified developed market equity portfolios, stocks in emerging markets specific assumptions on expected returns and volatilities are to be made. VaR focuses on the down-side of the distribution, unlike a risk measure like the volatility, which is symmetric. This seems a natural choice for a supervisor. The measure can also very easily be corrected for fixed and variable transaction costs.

The main drawback of VaR measures is that they are not coherent (see Section 20.3) since, intuitively, the pay-offs of scenarios that are more extreme than the threshold scenario do not play any role in the determination of the risk measure. If 10%-VaR is used, products with the same 10%-VaR will be classified as equally risky even if for one product this is the minimum pay-off while for the other products 1% and 5% quantiles of the distribution are much less attractive. Section 20.3 discusses risk measures in more detail and introduces the risk measure that is proposed.

20.3. Definition of the Risk Measure

A risk measure suitable for retail investment products should satisfy several (often conflicting) properties. First, the risk measure should be easily interpretable. The emerging behavioral finance literature provides persuasive evidence that retail investors often have problems understanding the fundamental concept of risk. As such, a risk measure should ideally be a one-dimensional quantity. This first requirement conflicts already strongly with financial theory that states that the complete pay-off distribution of a product is relevant for investment decision-making.[3] A second important problem is the relevant horizon over which the risk measure is calculated. For retail products the maturity is often several years and sometimes (e.g., plain investment funds) not specified a priori. However, financial theory teaches us that effective risk aversion of investors is not constant in maturity, for instance due to labor income. As such, a risk measure of a 3-year maturity product (calculated over a 3-year horizon) generally cannot be compared directly with a 20-year risk measure for (e.g.) retirement savings products. This problem is even aggravated by the fact that some products feature early exercise moments (possibly with additional costs). Finally, one must make sure that costs implicit or explicit in the financial product are fully taken into account.

From the point of view of the retail bank, the calculation and provision of the risk measure for all its products to all its customers should not be overly costly. This implies that the risk measure should be relatively easy to implement. At the same time, the algorithm for calculating the risk measure should be sufficiently simple as to prohibit multiple interpretations and, possibly, reverse engineering of products that have desirable properties from the perspective of the regulatory measure only.

The risk measure we propose tries to balance the above criteria. Concerning ease of implementation, we suggest to stick closely to the risk-management measure VaR. We give below a formal definition and explain why we prefer a different measure based on the expected shortfall. Intuitively, the difference between the two is that VaR only takes the probability of a loss into consideration, but not the size of the loss. With respect to costs implicit in investment products, we propose to take them fully into account and Section 20.5 explains how this is done is several situations. The horizon problem is fundamental to any risk measure and cannot be solved easily. We therefore propose to report the risk measure for several horizons.

This section details the risk measure we propose for retail products. In order to formally introduce the notions we will use, we follow the exposition in Acerbi and Tasche (2002). We start by defining the VaR. Let X denote the (random) pay-off of a given investment.

Definition 1: The VaR for the investment is defined as minus the α th quantile of the distribution of X. Formally:[4]

$$\text{VaR}(X) = -x_{(\alpha)}$$

$$x_{(\alpha)} = \min\{x \in \mathfrak{R} : P(X \le x) > \alpha\}.$$

Intuitively, the VaR may be defined as the largest loss that is possible with a probability of at most α. While the VaR measure has been popular for some time, it was severely criticized in the 1990s. One of the main points of critique is the observation that the VaR does not satisfy the conditions imposed in Artzner, Delbaen, Eber, & Heath, (1999) for so-called *coherent* risk measures. In particular, the VaR measure is not additive in an intuitive way. More precisely, VaR does not satisfy the condition that states that a portfolio of investments can never be more risky than the sum of the riskyness of each of its components. In other words, it is possible to construct (simple) portfolios for which the VaR is larger than the sum of the VaR of the individual components.

The risk measure that has since dominated the literature, and that does satisfy the coherency requirements, is expected shortfall (ES). The expected shortfall does not consider a single quantile in the left tail of the pay-off distribution, but it considers the complete tail. A formal definition is as follows:

Definition 2: The expected shortfall for the investment X is defined as the conditional expectation of X, given that it takes a value below its α th quantile. Formally:

$$ES(X) = -\bar{x}_{(\alpha)}$$

$$\bar{x}_{(\alpha)} = \frac{E\{XI(X \le x_{(\alpha)})\} + x_{(\alpha)}\{\alpha - P(X \le x_{(\alpha)})\}}{\alpha}.$$

Note that for continuously distributed X the latter expression simplifies to:[5]

$$\bar{x}_{(\alpha)} = \alpha^{-1}E\{XI(X \leq x_{(\alpha)})\}.$$

While Definition 2 is unambiguous, and thus leads to a risk measure that is difficult to manipulate, its disadvantage is the relatively cumbersome calculations needed even for simple products. This may be an undesirable feature for a risk measure that is designed for the retail market. In order to facilitate the calculations, we therefore use the following result in Acerbi and Tasche (2002).

Theorem 3: Under some weak regularity conditions, we have:

$$\bar{x}_{(\alpha)} = \alpha^{-1}\int_{0}^{\alpha} x_{(u)}du.$$

Proof: See Proposition 3.2 in Acerbi and Tasche (2002).

Investors possibly have a better understanding of the risks involved in a financial product if the possible pay-off in bad states of the world is described instead of possible losses. Therefore, we introduce the risk measure as the expected pay-off in bad states of the world. In the sequel of this chapter this measure will be denoted by the Dutch acronym Guise ("Gemiddelde uitbetaling in slechte eventualiteiten"). Theorem 3 expresses the Guise in terms of the left-tail quantiles, that is, in terms of the VaR for all levels below α. This is illustrated in Figure 20.1 for a financial product with an initial investment of 1000.

As is apparent from Figure 20.1, an exact calculation of the Guise requires integration over the quantile function of the pay-off distribution of the risky investment. This is an

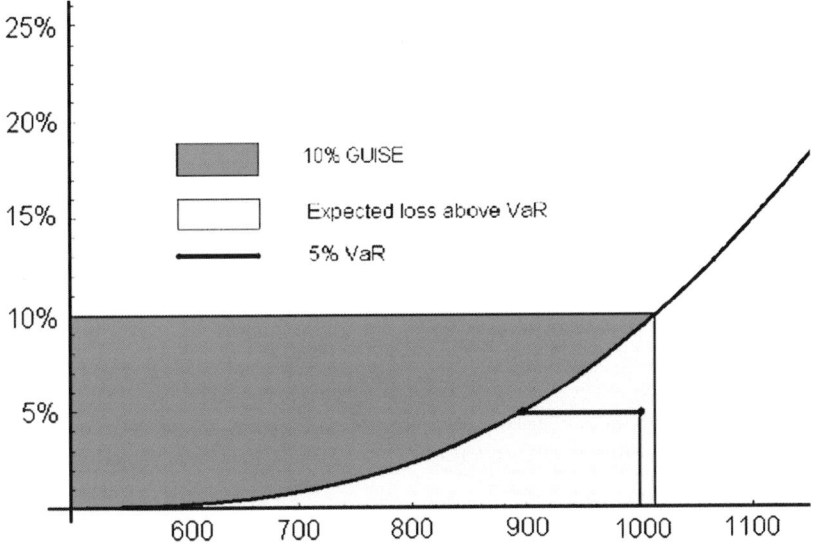

Figure 20.1: Illustration of the Guise, expected shortfall, and VaR for a product with 1000 initial investment.

appealing feature, as financial institutions have a large experience in calculating these quantiles in their VoR calculations. However, a full integration may be cumbersome in practice. Therefore, we propose to approximate the integral in Theorem 3 by a simple trapezium rule. The trapezium rule approximates the Guise, for $\alpha = 10\%$, as:

$$\bar{x}_{(0.10)} = 0.3125x_{(0.01)} + 0.4375x_{(0.05)} + 0.2500x_{(0.10)}.$$

This approximation to the Guise is illustrated in Figure 20.2.

It is clear that the calculation of the Guise crucially depends on the pay-off distribution of a given financial product. One therefore needs empirically acceptable assumptions for the distributions of the assets that underlie the given financial product. As far as stock-based products are concerned, we propose to use a normality assumption. Given the usually longer investment horizon for retail products, this is recognized in the literature as an acceptable approximation. In particular we ignore the documented stock predictability, skewness, and excess kurtosis effects. A further advantage of the normality assumption is that is consistent with the use of standard derivative pricing models like the Black–Scholes model for the valuation of possible (implicit) derivatives in a financial product.

Even given the normality assumption, one needs to decide on the appropriate expected return and volatility in order to calculate the Guise explicitly. It is well known that volatilies can be accurately estimated from high-frequency (say daily or weekly) asset returns. We therefore propose to estimate volatilities on the basis of returns over a relatively short horizon, say, 3 years. With respect to expected returns, the story is quite different. Under the Black–Scholes assumptions above, one easily shows that estimation uncertainty in expected return estimates is proportional to the square root of the time-span of data that is used to estimate these returns. In order to allow for regime changes and avoid

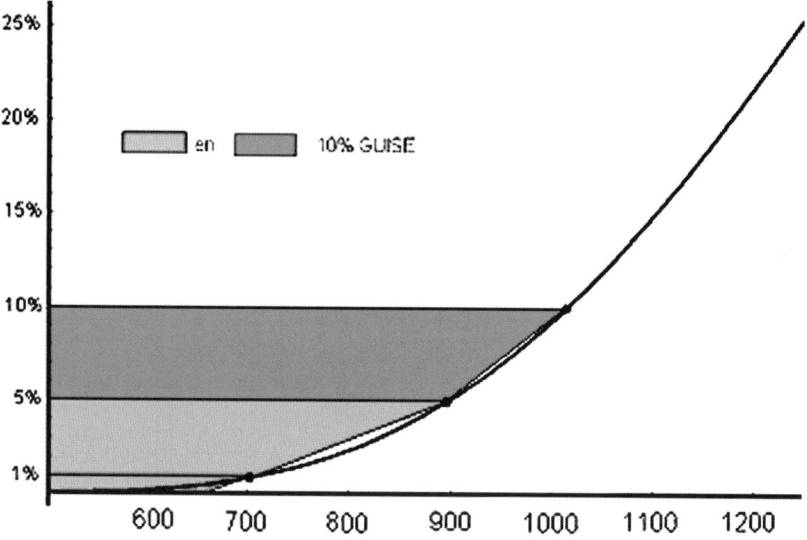

Figure 20.2: Illustration of the approximated Guise by two trapeziums.

data problems, we propose to limit the expected return estimates to data on the past 20 years. Individual assets can be selected which have shown very good performance over the past 20 years. In order to avoid selection biases where financial products would be based on such individual assets it seems natural to allocate all assets in broad asset classes like stocks and bonds, and to use expected return and volatility estimates for the asset class.

In case a financial product has a pay-off that depends on multiple underlyings, the distribution of the pay-off not only depends on the individual expected returns and volatilities, but also on their covariances. Fortunately, these covariances are easily estimated as well on relative short span of data. For coherency reasons we propose to base the covariance estimates on the same data span and frequency as the volatility estimates. It is well known that covariances are an intrinsically Gaussian concept. Many recent papers in finance literature are devoted to the use of copulas, which describe a general class of dependence functions between random variables. As a choice for a specific copula is intrinsically *ad hoc* and the best-known derivative pricing models are derived on the basis of normality assumption, we will not pursue this issue any further.

20.4. Calculation of the Risk Measure

The proof of the pudding is in the eating. Therefore we provide in this section the calculations needed to obtain the risk measure as defined in the previous section for various products. Note that, as soon as the distribution of the underlying assets of the retail product are known, it is always possible to simulate the distribution of the pay-offs of the product and, subsequently, obtain the risk measure. As the risk measure is based on standard quantiles of the distribution and the uncertainty in simulated quantiles is easily quantified, it is not difficult to come up with the number of simulations needed in order to get a reliable estimate of the risk measure. We will not discuss this in detail, nor do we discuss any of the many simulations techniques that may be useful in calculating the risk measure quickly. Instead, we provide analytical results for a few simple products.

20.4.1. Linear Products with Single Investment

The simplest retail product to consider is a product with an investment horizon of H years and an investment of initially $W_0 = 1000$ in an underlying asset that has an annualized expected (geometric) return of μ with a volatility σ. As this product does not contain any optionalities, we refer to it as a linear product.[6] The pay-off of this product can now be written as:

$$X = W_H = W_0 \exp\left(\sum_{t=1}^{H} R_t\right),$$

where $R_1, \ldots, R_H$ denote the (independent) returns on the underlying asset for the H subsequent years. Under the additional assumption that returns are normally distributed, we easily find:

$$x_{(\alpha)} = W_0 \exp\left(H\mu + z_{(\alpha)}\sigma\sqrt{H}\right),$$

where $z_{(\alpha)}$ denotes the α th quantile of the standard normal distribution. This readily leads to the risk measure for given parameters μ and σ, using the trapezium rule.

In general consumers of retail investment products incur costs. The Dutch regulatory authority requires financial institutions to provide risk indications after costs. It is therefore important to know how various types of costs affect the calculations above. Proportional one-time costs that are incurred at the initiation of the contract or when unwinding the product can easily be taken into account as effective reductions in the initial investment or pay-out. As an example, suppose a financial institution retains 5% of the investment of €1000 in the product, then one would simply have to use a net-of-cost initial investment of €950.

Costs that are incurred periodically are not much more difficult to take into account. They would simply lead to an effective reduction in the expected return μ. For example, in case the gross return on the underlying asset is in expectation 7% per annum, while the financial institution retains 0.5% costs per annum, one would need to use a net-of-cost expected return of 6.5% per annum.

20.4.2. Products with a Fixed Guarantee

Many retail investment products in the Netherlands and elsewhere nowadays provide a guaranteed minimum return. Such a minimum is usually guaranteed by an implicit or explicit put option in the product. On initiation of the contract, this put option is acquired and the costs involved are generally implicit.[7]

In order to calculate the risk measure, it is important to distinguish risk measures on a horizon that equals the maturity of the product (and, thus, of the underlying put option) and horizons that are strictly smaller. For a horizon equal to the maturity of the product, the calculations very much parallel those in Section 20.4.1 The put merely transforms the total return distribution as to guarantee the minimum level. For the sake of an example consider the case where the put guarantees a pay-off of at least 80% of the initial investment. Ignoring possible costs, this would mean that the pay-off of the product for given returns is determined by:

$$X = W_H = W_0 \exp\left(\max\left\{ \ln(0.8), \sum_{t=1}^{H} R_t \right\} \right).$$

Note the logarithmic transformation that is needed as the guarantee is specified as a fixed percentage of the initial investment. The resulting return distribution is thus effectively a truncated log-normal distribution for which exact quantiles are readily available.

The situation is more complicated in case the risk measure is needed for a horizon before maturity. Assuming that the contract stipulates that the financial institution will repay the market value of the put option in that case, this market value has to be assessed. For most retail products, which are based on an underlying stock market index, valuation with the classical Black–Scholes formula does not seem unreasonable. The value of the put option, in such a case, becomes a complicated but known and deterministic function of the value of the underlying investment. The corresponding quantiles can thus be easily calculated using the general result that the quantile of an increasing function of a random variable is the function of the quantile.[8]

20.4.3. Stock Lease Products

In the 1990s, stock lease products were extremely popular with retail investors in the Netherlands. Many perceived them as free lunches due to the high-average stock returns and low volatilities during this period. The stock market crash in 2000–2002 lead to many court cases where investors claimed not to have been informed about the risks in these products. Some of these cases have been settled recently by the so-called "Duisenberg solution", but others are still under legal investigation. In any case, this affair has strongly underlined the need for risk measures for retail products.

The calculations of the Guise for a stock lease product are very similar to those for regular stock products. The effective investment in the stock portfolio is higher due to the underlying loan, leading to a highly leveraged position and thus more risk. We assume a lump-sum initial investment. This investment is used to pay the interest rates on the loan underlying the stock portfolio. Clearly, retail rates are generally above the capital market rate and this has to be taken into account as well.

Some stock lease products as they have been offered to the public contained a guarantee to the extent that the value of the stock portfolio at the end of the investment period was at least equal to the loan. These products have a guaranteed non-negative pay-off at maturity. Risk measure calculations for such a product would be a simple combination of a regular stock lease product and a guarantee in the form of an appropriate put option.

20.4.4. Products with Periodic Investment

Many products in the retail market require (equal) monthly investments. While for single investments in linear products the pay-off distribution is exactly log-normal, this is no longer true for products with periodic investments. Formally, each of the individual payments into the product can be considered separately, which shows that the pay-off distribution is the sum of (dependent) log-normally distributed random variables. For these distributions, no analytic expressions for the quantiles are available. As a result, we propose to resort to a simple simulation algorithm to calculate the risk measure. It is clear that the accuracy of the simulated risk measure depends on the number of simulations with the usual square-root rule. Fortunately, standard statistical analysis leads to simple bounds on the (in)accuracy of simulation results. These can be used to calculate the appropriate number of simulations needed. As the quantiles we are interested in lie in the tails of the distribution, this number should not be underestimated. Moreover, in specific cases tailored simulation algorithms may provide an efficient alternative.

Insurance companies often offer products with periodic premium payments that are partly invested and are partly used to cover some insurance aspect. In that case one clearly would have to use the net invested periodic payments to calculate the risk measure. The risk measure will, consequently, be less favorable for a comparable product where payments are fully invested but without any insurance attached. It would then be up to the consumers to weigh the increased risk against the extra insurance.

20.5. Some Explicit Guise Calculations

We illustrate the calculation of the risk measure for four standard retail investment products. All the calculations in this section are exact in the sense that no simulations are required. For all products we consider an initial €1000 investment. The risk measure is provided on a 1- and 5-year horizon. As mentioned earlier, we fully take into account costs associated to these products. For the numerical examples in this section we take a 0.5% annual cost and 0.2% initial cost.

Four product types are considered: a standard mutual fund investment, the same investment but where part of the initial investment is used to obtain a put option that guarantees a 800 pay-off, a stock lease product, and a stock lease product with a guaranteed minimum pay-off that is equal to the loan amount. All products have a contractual 5-year maturity supposed. The derivatives are priced under the standard Black–Scholes assumptions.

Three different assumptions have been made on the underlying assets. We consider mixed stock-bond portfolios ("mix"), broadly diversified stock portfolios ("stock"), and emerging market portfolios ("emerging"). For the mixed portfolio we set the expected return of this portfolio to 8% and the volatility to 10%.[9] Concerning the stock index, we use a 10% expected return and a (modest) 15% volatility. The emerging markets products use the same equity premium, that is, 10% expected return, but with a 20% volatility.[10] The capital market interest rate is set at 4%, while the rate charged on the loan in the lease products is assumed to be 10%. The full investment is used to lease the underlying assets. Guises corresponding to $\alpha = 10\%$ are reported in Table 20.1.

Several interesting observations can be made from this table. Clearly, longer horizons tend to lead to a larger Guise through time diversification, that is a higher expected pay-off in the 10% worst states of the world. Note that this effect is not necessarily monotone as expected returns and volatilities have different short- and long-term effects. Moreover, the risk in the products with guarantee is lower than in the non-guaranteed products. The price to pay is clearly lower pay-offs in good states of the world as well, but those are not taken into account in the risk measure we propose. Lease products are far more risky than their non-lease counterparts. The leverage obtained by borrowing money to finance an initial stock portfolio is very large. Note also that the guarantee in the products as we devised them here only holds at maturity, that is, at a horizon of 5 years. The Guise measures before maturity can therefore

Table 20.1: Guise measure for various products on a 1- and 5-year horizon.

	1-year horizon			5-year horizon		
	Mix	Stock	Emerging	Mix	Stock	Emerging
Mutual Fund	882	819	744	940	831	657
Guarantee	888	849	814	937	855	800
Lease	−266	−407	−574	−134	−380	−770
G-lease	−161	−191	−219	2	0	0

The products are as described in the main text with G-lease referring to the lease product with a guarantee that the initial loan can be repaid by the final value of the underlying portfolio.

indeed lie below the guarantee. Note also that the Guise of a simple deposit will be above 1000 because of interest payments. The difference with the Guise of the investment products should make retail investors aware of the amount of investment risk incorporated in the product.

20.6. Products with Interest Rate or Inflation Risk

The risk measure Guise introduced above is applicable to any financial product whose pay-off depends on observable underlying financial quantities. The examples in Section 20.5, however, focus on stock related products. Many important financial products exhibit also a sensitivity to interest rate changes (with standard home mortgages as a prime example). Likewise, for long-term investments (e.g., that aim to generate retirement income), the risk measure should ideally also incorporate inflation risk since investors should be primarily interested in pay-offs in real terms. It is therefore important that the risk measure is able to handle interest rate and inflation risk as well. In the present section, we sketch how these can be taken into account.

Risk in interest-rate-sensitive products is caused by shifts in the underlying term structure. If various maturity sensitivities are present in a product, or the product uses derivatives, a term structure model is needed. Note that even standard home mortgages often have quite a number of (implicit) derivatives in them, like prepayment options. These would have to be valued in any appropriate risk measure. Any financially renowned term structure model can be used, but we would propose to stick to the standard Black model as this is consistent with duration analysis and thus familiar to financial, including the smaller ones. The cost of a more complex model for the issuing institutions would probably outweigh any benefits of an empirically more sound description of the term structure fluctuations. As VaR, also for simple interest sensitive securities, is often difficult to asses analytically, simulations have to be used to calculate risk measures in these cases. Financial institutions, however, should have no problem to do this as they are required to do similar calculations for their regulatory capital.

Investment products are widely used as building blocks of DC pension plans. Inflation risk in such very long-term investments is usually not addressed. Likewise, in recent years, many DB pension schemes have made the conditions under which pension rights will be indexed for price or wage changes much more explicit. Usually the indexation decision is related to the performance of the investment portfolio. The degree of inflation risk that remains is hard to judge for retail investors and can depend, for example, on the funding ratio of the scheme. Inflation exposure can be incorporated in the risk measure that is proposed in this chapter through additional assumptions on the distribution of future inflation rates and their correlation with changes in stock returns and nominal interest rates. An extensive literature is available that suggest models that could be selected as a starting point.

20.7. Concluding Remarks

We attempted in this chapter to use the main findings of extensive academic literature to build an accessible and relevant risk measure for retail investment products: the Guise.

The Guise is based on a number of simplifying assumptions and, like all other measures of risk, has its limitations. The Guise, in particular, does not address portfolio risk. Nevertheless we expect that such a risk measure can be very informative for retail investors. Extensive research has shown that many individual investors take investment decisions that are far from optimal and that broad groups of investors expect that simple risk measures will be very informative for them. The Dutch legislator and supervisor have (at the moment of writing this article) the intention to introduce a risk indicator, which classifies investment products in a number of categories ranging from low- to high-risk level. The risk assessment underlying this indicator is based on the Guise. Interest[11] and inflation risk are not yet incorporated in the risk indicator, but can be added in later revisions.

Endnotes

1. Piet Duffhues has an open eye for the practical implications of academic research during the many years that he devoted to Tilburg University. In his honor, we devote this chapter to a topic that is rather relevant for all retail investors and that attracted Piet's attention already many years ago.
2. *Financiële Bijsluiters* are information leaflets that have to be produced by financial institutions that offer so-called "complex" financial products. The layout and contents of these leaflets are bound by certain requirements set out by law. The purpose of the leaflets is twofold: first, to give potential investors a good understanding of the characteristics of the product (e.g., the costs, risks, obligations, etc.), and second, to facilitate comparisons to be made between different products.
3. More complicated still, as mentioned earlier, it is the joint distribution of the product under investigation with the existing assets in the investors portfolio that are relevant for the investment decision.
4. The minimum is not necessarily obtained for general pay-off distributions. More precisely, the minimum may not be attainable for distributions that have unconnected support. Such may be the case, for instance, for so-called click-funds. In those cases, we replace the minimum by the infimum in the definition.
5. Clearly, it is sufficient for this simplification that the α th quantile of the distribution is unique.
6. More precisely, we consider a linear product any investment product whose (geometric) return distribution is accurately described by a normal distribution.
7. It must be mentioned though that there also exist products where one may choose to have a fixed minimum pay-off and, if desired, some additional costs are explicitly taken into account.
8. For monotonically decreasing transformations (as is the case for put-option valuation) the required adaptation is trivial.
9. All expected returns and volatilities mentioned in this document are annualized parameters. Following Dutch regulatory rules, we consider assets to be log-normally distributed with a mean parameter equal to the given expected return minus half of the variance and variance equal to the volatility parameter squared.
10. These parameters correspond to the assumptions underlying the calculations for the pessimistic return in the current information leaflet.
11. Interest rate risk is, of course, indirectly reflected in fluctuations of bond prices.

References

Acerbi, C., & Tasche, D. (2002). *On the coherence of expected shortfall*. Working paper Technische Universitat Munchen.

Artzner, P., Delbaen, F., Eber, J.M., & Heath, D. (1999). Coherent measures of risk. *Mathematical Finance, 9*, 203–228.

Munnell, A.H., & Sundén A. (2004). *Coming up short, the challenge for 401(k) plans*. Washington, DC: The Brookings Press.

Chapter 21

Understanding and Exploiting Momentum in Stock Returns

Juan Carlos Rodriguez and Alessandro Sbuelz

21.1. Introduction

The existence of a predictable component in stock returns is well documented and the ensuing autocorrelation of holding-period returns does impact optimal portfolio choice by originating strategic-asset allocation. Positive (negative) autocorrelation is a clear-cut measure of momentum (mean reversion). Return autocorrelation has motivated well-known active portfolio-management strategies, like either 'buy winners/sell losers' to profit from momentum, or contrarian strategies to profit from mean reversion. These strategies are quite popular among practitioners and important in the academic assessment of the efficient markets hypothesis. However, although the asset-allocation literature has explored in depth the mean-reversion case, momentum has not received pairwise attention. The purpose of this chapter is to study the continuous-time asset-allocation problem of an investor who, given a finite time horizon, tries to exploit momentum. We focus on the characterization of her optimal demand for the risky stock. Since momentum implies a stochastic opportunity set for the investor (changes in momentum imply changes in the instantaneous conditional expected returns on the stock), we are not only interested in unveiling the active component of her speculative demand, but also in providing a thorough description of her hedging demand.

'Momentum-watching' investors are typically concerned with the latest levels of stock returns relative to some target or long-run level. Therefore, we introduce a model of stock price dynamics in which the state variable is observable, related to current performance as well as past performance of returns (it is a weighted average of up-to-date returns), and conducive to positive autocorrelation of holding-period returns. This is a novelty in the strategic-asset-allocation literature (so termed by Brennan, Lagnado, & Schwartz, 1997), which has never explicitly included weighted averages of past and current returns in the conditioning-information set. Our model is particularly well suited to study momentum in a complete-markets setting, which enables closed-form solutions and greatly facilitates the

Advances in Corporate Finance and Asset Pricing
Edited by L. Renneboog
© 2006 Elsevier B.V. All rights reserved.
ISBN: 0-444-52723-0

treatment of investor's intermediate consumption. Chiefly, given momentum-like departures from the efficient market hypothesis, our model is a neat extension of strategic-asset allocation to the study of how momentum impacts the speculative and hedging demands for the stock. We characterize a (weakly) efficient market as one in which the stock price is geometric Brownian motion (GBM).

In our closed-form analysis we isolate and discuss three clear effects of momentum on strategic-asset allocation: the speculative effect, the conditional-hedge effect, and the unconditional-hedge effect. Regarding the speculative demand, momentum induces a myopic but active strategy of buying winners/selling losers, in which the momentum parameter of the stock price dynamics neatly appears. The sign of the conditional hedging demand depends on whether the latest performance of returns has been either above (negative demand) or below (positive demand) the long-run expected return. By boosting the volatility of distant-future stock prices, momentum makes the unconditional hedging demand always negative.

In continuous-time partial equilibrium, Kim and Omberg (1996) and Wachter (2002) constitute the two reference closed-form analyses of optimal finite-horizon portfolio choice in the presence of drift-based predictability (see also Wachter & Sangvinatsos, 2005 and the references therein). They consider drift-based predictability by taking the market price of risk as the state variable. Wachter (2002) considers a complete markets special case of the Kim and Omberg (1996) economy to enable the treatment of intermediate consumption á la Cox and Huang (1989). Although there are clear similarities between our model and their reference models (they are discussed in Sections 21.7 and 21.8) we claim that our parameterization has important advantages. Chiefly, taking observable (current and past) returns as the state variable makes sure that momentum is introduced in a natural way (past winners/losers remain so) so that neat intuition accompanies the closed-form results we get. On these grounds, we escape a non-trivial pitfall of the existing theoretical literature on strategic-asset allocation. As Campbell and Viceira (2002) have pointed out (p. 127): 'While the theoretical literature has made considerable progress in recent years, the cases with known exact analytical solutions are still relatively few, and the solutions often have complicated forms that are hard to interpret ….' Following Wachter's (2002) solution techniques, our complete-markets model can easily handle the case of intermediate consumption.

Our work is organized as follows. Sections 21.2–21.4 review predictability of stock returns, its general impact on asset allocation, and its specific facet of momentum. Section 21.5 discusses our data-generating process and introduces the momentum state variable. Section 21.6 studies strategic-asset allocation in the presence of momentum and with utility from terminal wealth only. Section 21.7 relates our model to the Kim and Omberg (1996) setting. Section 21.8 treats the intermediate-consumption case. After the concluding section, an Appendix gathers the technical details.

21.2. Predictability of Stock Returns

Until the mid-1980s there was widespread consensus among financial economists that stock returns were unpredictable. Unpredictability was seen as a direct consequence of efficient markets. However, this consensus started to be eroded by the works of Fama and French (1988), and Poterba and Summers (1988), who found statistical evidence that past returns were helpful to predict future returns. Actually, they showed that equity returns tend to mean revert at long horizons.

Although the evidence provided by Fama and French (1988), and Poterba and Summers (1988) was rather weak, their research suggested a more general question: is it possible to find other variables, beyond past returns, that are useful to predict future returns? Efforts to answer this question gave rise to an explosion of research and to an entire new branch of financial literature.

A clear consequence of this new research is that, once additional variables are included into the analysis, the evidence of predictability looks much stronger than what Fama and French (1988), and Poterba and Summers (1988) have suggested. A surprisingly wide array of predictors has been found useful to forecast future returns. To cite just the most influential, they go from dividend-price ratios and earning-price ratios (Campbell & Shiller, 1988; Fama & French, 1988), changes in short-term interest rates (Fama & Schwert, 1977; Campbell, 1991), yield spreads (Keim & Stambaugh, 1986; Campbell, 1987), to the consumption-wealth ratio (Lettau & Ludvingson, 2001).

Nowadays the consensus seems to have changed to a wider acceptance of the idea that returns are actually predictable. Predictability has become a part of mainstream finance to such an extent that an authoritative textbook like Cochrane's (2001) devotes a chapter to it, calling it a new fact in finance. Schwert (2003) also provides an extensive account of predictability.

Given that predictability is in the data, financial economists have investigated how it affects the multiperiod asset-allocation decisions of a rational long-lived investor.

21.3. Predictability and Asset Allocation

In continuous-time finance, the benchmark of unpredictability of stock returns is represented by the GBM model. The GBM model of stock's instantaneous returns is:

$$\frac{dS_t}{S_t} = \mu \, dt + \sigma \, dZ_t, \tag{21.1}$$

where μ is the (constant) expected return, σ is the instantaneous volatility, and Z_t is a Wiener process. In Equation (21.1) there are no variables dated at time t that can be used to forecast returns between t and $t + dt$. In this sense we say that returns are unpredictable.

The GBM model of returns has dramatic consequences for asset allocation. Suppose that we have an investor who derives expected utility from her terminal wealth. Her value function is:

$$J(W, x, \tau) \equiv \sup_{\pi} E_t \left[\frac{W_{t+\tau}^{1-\gamma}}{1-\gamma} \right], \tag{21.2}$$

where W_t is her wealth at time t and τ is her constant relative risk aversion (CRRA) coefficient. Suppose that the investor knows that the correct dynamics of S_t is described by Equation (21.1). The investor can trade only on the stock (which can be understood in this context as the market portfolio) and a riskless bond. Therefore, her wealth evolves according to:

$$\frac{dW_t}{W_t} = r\,dt + \pi_t\left(\frac{dS_t}{S_t} - r\,dt\right) \tag{21.3}$$

where π_t is the fraction of her wealth allocated to the stock at time t and r is the riskless interest rate (assumed constant). This is a standard problem in which the investor chooses π to achieve (21.2) subject to (21.3). The ensuing optimal policy is:

$$\pi_t^* = \frac{1}{\gamma}\frac{\mu - r}{\sigma^2}. \tag{21.4}$$

In Equation (21.4) π^* is constant and independent of the investor's horizon. The model predicts that the investor will allocate a constant fraction of her wealth to the stock. Moreover, this constant fraction depends on the Sharpe ratio of the stock and on the investor's CRRA coefficient, but not on the investor's horizon. This has the odd implication that two investors with the same attitude towards risk should allocate the same proportion of their wealth to the stock, even if the first investor has a horizon of 1 week and the second investor has a horizon of 30 years. Such a prediction casts doubts about the usefulness of the model as a means to provide advise to real investors.

In the GBM model, expected return and instantaneous volatility are constant. The riskless rate is also assumed to be constant. The whole situation is summarized by saying that the investor faces a constant investment opportunity set. Merton (1971) was the first to explore the consequences on asset allocation of relaxing the assumption of a constant investment opportunity set. He showed that these consequences are far reaching. In particular, asset demands are no longer constant as a fraction of wealth and horizon effects may enter the picture.

Since predictability is a form of non-constant investment opportunity set (expected returns are time varying), we will illustrate Merton's seminal contribution in the context of predictability. We keep the focus on predictability by retaining the assumption that both the instantaneous volatility and the riskless rate are constant.

Suppose that the stock price is driven by the following dynamics:

$$\frac{dS_t}{S_t} = \mu(x_t)\,dt + \sigma\,dZ_t, \tag{21.5}$$

where x_t is a predictor that affects the conditional expected return $\mu(x_t)$. The predictor x_t evolves according to:

$$dx_t = \alpha(x_t)\,dt + \omega(x_t)\,dB_t, \tag{21.6}$$

with

$$E_t(dZ_t\,dB_t) = \rho\,dt \tag{21.7}$$

being the instantaneous correlation of the Wiener processes B_t and Z_t. The investor's problem is still one of achieving (21.2), but now there exists a variable x_t that is instrumental to predict future returns. Since x_t determines the state of the investment opportunity set and stock returns are correlated to changes in x_t, the investor is interested in hedging against unfavorable changes in the investment opportunity set. So, the optimal demand for the stock is:

$$\pi^* = \frac{1}{\gamma} \frac{\mu(x_t) - r}{\sigma^2} + \frac{J_{wx}}{-WJ_{ww}} \frac{\rho\omega(x_t)}{\sigma} \tag{21.8}$$

There are two new features in Equation (21.8) relative to the GBM case. First, the speculative demand depends now on the predictor observed at time t. This introduces the realistic possibility of market-timing strategies into the model. Market-timing strategies act through the conditional Sharpe ratio, which induces the investor to take a speculative position in the stock. Second, there is a new component, the intertemporal hedging demand, which is used to hedge against x driven stochastic changes in the investment opportunity set. A good (bad) opportunity set is welfare increasing (welfare decreasing) because it reduces (raises) the marginal utility of wealth, J_w, by improving (worsening) the conditional Sharpe ratio, that is, the conditional 'productivity' of wealth. It is to be noticed that, as long as the marginal utility of wealth is affected by x_t ($J_{wx} \neq 0$), the intertemporal hedging demand would be 0 only if x_t were deterministic ($\omega = 0$), or if x_t were uncorrelated to stock returns ($\rho = 0$).

Predictability has been studied in the asset-allocation literature mainly in the form of time-varying expected returns (see, for example, Campbell & Viceira, 1999; Barberis, 2000) and time-varying return volatilities (see Chacko & Viceira, 2005). The modern asset-allocation literature has tried to find a rationale to the known practitioner's advice that the allocation to stocks should increase with the investor's horizon, and, for this reason, it has concentrated on the study of mean-reverting returns.

Momentum represents a clear form of predictability of stock returns. Although momentum is a strong stylized fact of stock returns, it has been mostly disregarded by the strategic-asset-allocation literature — see Balvers and Mitchell (1997) for a discrete-time study of autocorrelated returns and optimal intertemporal portfolio choice. The next section is dedicated to reviewing how the phenomenon of momentum has been defined, measured, and understood in the existing literature.

21.4. Momentum

Campbell (2004) defines momentum to be the inclination of stock prices to keep on moving in the same direction for several months after an initial shock. Momentum gives rise to positive autocorrelation of certain holding-period returns. Price momentum occurs when the initial shock is a change in the price itself. Price momentum was found in aggregate US stock prices in the late-1980s (Conrad & Kaul, 1988; Lo & MacKinlay, 1988; Poterba & Summers, 1988), in individual US stock prices in the early 1990s (Jegadeesh & Titman, 1993), and in international markets later in the 1990s (Rouwenhorst, 1998; 1999). Different initial shocks yield other sorts of momentum. Post-earnings-announcement drift is momentum following a surprise earnings announcement (Ball & Brown, 1968; Bernard & Thomas, 1989; 1990), while earnings momentum is momentum following a revision in analysts' earnings forecasts (Chan, Jegadeesh, & Lakonishok, 1996).

Considerable evidence exists that momentum investment strategies produce excess returns. The work of Jegadeesh and Titman (1993), Chan, Jegadeesh, and Lakonishok (1996), Rouwenhorst (1998), Chan, Hameed, and Tong (2000), Grundy and Martin (2001), Jegadeesh and Titman (2001), Lewellen (2002), Patro and Wu (2004), and others reveals that a momentum strategy of sorting (portfolios of) stocks by previous returns and holding those with the best prior performance and shorting those with the worst prior performance generates positive excess returns. Momentum strategies typically work for a sorting period ranging from 1 month (or more commonly 3 months) to 12 months and a similar 1 (or 3) to 12 months holding period. Balvers and Wu (2004) shows that combination momentum-contrarian strategies, used to select from among several developed equity markets at a monthly frequency, outperform both pure momentum- and pure-contrarian strategies. A *caveat* is that profitable momentum strategies are hard to be implemented in extremely illiquid stocks (Korajczyk & Sadka, 2004).

Explaining momentum within a classical asset-pricing model is difficult. Such a model would explain momentum if stocks that have risen recently, or have had positive earnings surprises were to command high-average returns by exhibiting higher risk. Grundy and Martin (2001), Griffin, Ji, and Martin (2003) find that this is hardly the case. A well-known stylized fact like the leverage effect (the equity of a leveraged company becomes safer when it appreciates) is at odds with classical risk-based explanations of momentum.

Momentum is accommodated more easily within a behavioral asset-pricing model, where momentum is explained as the result of the interaction of imperfectly rational investors with rational arbitrageurs. Behavioral explanations of momentum are either stories of underreaction to relevant news for the future cash flows of a stock or stories of overreaction to fickle news.

Investors with limited ability to access and process information and overconfident investors who cherish their original views even in the face of relevant new information are the prime cause of underreaction (Daniel, Hirshleifer, & Subrahmanyam, 1998). Rational arbitrageurs do respond to fundamental news, but they trade gradually to unwind their positions profitably as, over time, the price adjusts fully to the news. Underreaction is consistent with the strong evidence for momentum in response to fundamental shocks such as earnings announcements or analysts' forecast revisions.

Overreaction is irrational exuberance in the face of indecisive or qualitative information (Daniel & Titman, 2004). Irrationality of this sort pushes prices away from the level that would be justified by fundamentals and can be exploited by rational arbitrageurs. Momentum ensues if irrational investors respond gradually to qualitative information, if they imitate each others' trades, or if they have a penchant for buying stocks that have performed well recently. 'Herding' is the term used to classify these behavior patterns. The herding hypothesis is consistent with evidence on flows into mutual funds (Sirri & Tufano, 1998). This evidence suggests that individual investors are attracted to funds, fund categories, and fund families that have performed well recently.

Irrational enthusiasts can trigger a stock market bubble if rational arbitrageurs find that riding positive short-term momentum is more profitable than selling off on the basis of poor long-term value. Brunnermeier and Nagel (2004) use this argument to show that hedge funds rode the technology bubble through the late-1990s even after technology stocks became recklessly overpriced.

The behavioral model of momentum implies that momentum should be stronger (i) when fundamental news is less obvious and harder to analyze (Zhang, 2004 finds stronger momentum in stocks that are hard to value, and Grinblatt & Moskowitz, 2004 in cases when news comes out slowly over several months); (ii) when other behavioral forces push in the same direction (Grinblatt & Moskowitz, 2004 find that tax-loss selling strengthens momentum in December and weakens it in January); and (iii) when rational investors face high transactions costs in their arbitrage trading (Johnson & Schwartz, 2000 find that momentum weakened in liquid markets such as the US and the UK).

In the next section we model momentum in continuous time as a weighted average of past and current returns on the stock that gravitates around the stock's unconditional expected return.

21.5. The Data-Generating Process

We make the following specification of stock's instantaneous returns:

$$\frac{dS_t}{S_t} = y_t dt + dy_t, \tag{21.9}$$

$$dy_t = -(1-\varphi)(y_t - \mu)\,dt + \sigma dz_t,\ 0 < \varphi < 1, \tag{21.10}$$

$$\mu > 0,\ \sigma > 0,$$

$$E\left[\frac{dS_t}{S_t}\right] = \mu dt\ (\text{unconditional expected return}),$$

$$\text{Var}\left[\frac{dS_t}{S_t}\right] = \sigma dt\ (\text{return's unconditional variance}),$$

where z_t is a Wiener process. The long-run expected return μ is above the constant interest rate r, $\mu > r > 0$ so that the unconditional Sharpe ratio $\frac{\mu - r}{\sigma}$ is positive. By construction, the momentum state variable is a weighted average of past stock returns[1]:

$$y_t = \int_0^t \exp(u-t)\frac{dS_u}{S_u},\quad dy_t = \frac{dS_t}{S_t} - y_t dt.$$

The pivotal role of the predictability parameter φ can be seen in this re-expression of the stock's instantaneous returns:

$$\frac{dS_t}{S_t} = (\mu + \varphi(y_t - \mu))\, dt + \sigma dz_t. \qquad (21.11)$$

If past performance has been above its long-run average ($y_t - \mu > 0$), stock returns are expected to be above their unconditional average $\left(E_t\left(\dfrac{dS_t}{S_t}\right) > \mu\right)$ GBM results from the case $\varphi \downarrow 0$, so that predictability drops out.

A further enhancement of our intuition of the model comes from analyzing the unconditional moments of discrete holding-period returns. Define $\Delta S_t = \log(S_{t+\tau}) - \log(S_t)$:

$$E(\Delta S_t) = \left(\mu - \frac{1}{2}\sigma^2\right)\tau,$$

$$\mathrm{Var}(\Delta S_t) = \frac{\sigma^2}{(1-\varphi)^2}\left[\tau + \frac{\varphi}{1-\varphi}\left(1 - \exp^{-(1-\varphi)\tau}\right)(\varphi - 2)\right],$$

$$\mathrm{Cov}(\Delta S_t, \Delta S_{t-\tau}) = \frac{\sigma^2}{(1-\varphi)^2}\left[\frac{\varphi}{1-\varphi}\left(1 - \exp^{-(1-\varphi)\tau}\right)^2\left(1 - \frac{\varphi}{2}\right)\right],$$

$$\rho_1(\Delta S_t, \Delta S_{t-\tau}) \equiv \frac{\mathrm{Cov}(\Delta S_t, \Delta S_{t-\tau})}{\mathrm{Var}(\Delta St)} = \frac{\dfrac{\varphi}{1-\varphi}\left(1 - \exp^{-(1-\varphi)\tau}\right)^2\left(1 - \dfrac{\varphi}{2}\right)}{\tau + \dfrac{\varphi}{1-\varphi}\left(1 - \exp^{-(1-\varphi)\tau}\right)(\varphi - 2)}.$$

The variance of the holding-period return grows without bound for all values of φ as the holding period goes to infinity, reflecting that the stock price is a non-stationary process. However, the variance's growth rate does depend on φ. The variance grows linearly with the horizon when $\varphi \downarrow 0$ (the stock return is a random walk with drift) and faster than linearly when $\varphi > 0$ (momentum). When $\varphi > 0$, the variance of the holding-period return is higher than the variance of the random walk case, for all finite τ. This latter property will have implications for long-term investors. When $\varphi > 0$, long-term investors will have fewer stocks in their portfolios, relative to the random walk case. This is because they will see stocks as increasing the risk of their portfolios when there is momentum.

The covariance and first autocorrelation of the holding-period return have the same sign as φ. When $\varphi > 0$, momentum generates positive autocorrelation. The closer is φ to 1, the more pronounced is momentum and the more intense is positive autocorrelation. It deserves to be re-stated that, in short-holding-period returns (e.g., daily, weekly, and monthly stock index returns), several studies report that there exist strong positive autocorrelations (see Conrad & Kaul, 1988; Lo & MacKinlay, 1988; Poterba & Summers, 1988). When $\varphi \downarrow 0$, autocorrelation disappears as predictability fades away to bear the case of random walk with drift.

21.5.1 Strategic-Asset Allocation

After the removal of its long-run average, the state variable becomes (we drop the time subscript t unless its presence is necessary),

$$x \equiv y - \mu.$$

The problem is to MAX the objective (21.2)

$$\text{s.t.} \quad \frac{dS}{S} = (\mu + \varphi x) \, dt \; \sigma dz, \; dx = -(1 - \varphi) \, x dt + \sigma dz. \tag{21.12}$$

Problem (21.12) involves solution steps that, although standard (see Kim & Omberg, 1996), shed much light on the structure of the optimal policy π^*. The Hamilton–Jacobi–Bellman (HJB) equation reads:

$$\sup_{\pi} E_t[dJ] = 0,$$

and the first-order conditions give:

$$\pi^* = \frac{J_w}{-WJ_{ww}} \frac{\mu - r + \varphi x}{\sigma^2} + \frac{J_{wx}}{-WJ_{ww}}, \tag{21.13}$$

so that the HJB equation evaluated at the optimal portfolio (21.13) becomes the partial differential equation

$$0 = -J_\tau + J_w W_r + J_x(-(1 - \varphi)x) - \frac{1}{2}J_{ww}(W\pi^*\sigma)^2 + \frac{1}{2}J_{xx}\sigma^2, \tag{21.14}$$

with boundary condition $J(W, x, 0) = \dfrac{W^{1-\gamma}}{1-\gamma}$.

The following trial solution for $J(W, x, \tau)$ implies that the horizon-end condition and the second-order condition for a maximum are satisfied:

$$J(W, x, \tau) = I(x, \tau)^\gamma \frac{W^{1-\gamma}}{1-\gamma}, \tag{21.15}$$

$$I(x, \tau) \equiv \exp\left(A_1(\tau)\frac{x^2}{2} + A_2(\tau)\, x + A_3(\tau)\right), \tag{21.16}$$

$$A_1(0) = A_2(0) = A_3(0). \tag{21.17}$$

Substitution of the trial solutions into the optimal portfolio gives

$$\pi^* = \frac{1}{\gamma}\frac{\mu - r}{\sigma^2} + \frac{1}{\gamma}\frac{\varphi x}{\sigma^2} + \frac{I_x}{I}, \tag{21.18}$$

where,

$$\frac{I_x}{I} = \frac{J_{wx}}{-WJ_{ww}} = A_1(\tau)\, x + A_2(\tau).$$

Therefore, we can decompose the overall optimal demand for stock into three portfolios:

$$\frac{1}{\gamma}\frac{\mu - r}{\sigma^2} = \text{myopic unconditional portfolio},$$

$$\frac{1}{\gamma}\frac{\varphi x}{\sigma^2} = \text{myopic active portfolio},$$

$$A_1(\tau)\, x = \text{conditional hedging portfolio},$$

$$A_2(\tau) = \text{unconditional hedging portfolio}.$$

The myopic unconditional portfolio is the well-known solution (21.4) of the GBM-investment problem with non-stochastic opportunity set. It can be interpreted in our context as a reference portfolio to which the investor will add short or long speculative positions on the stock depending on whether conditioning information implies negative or positive extra-expected returns ($x < 0$ and $x > 0$). The myopic active portfolio does nest momentum strategies: buy winners ($x > 0$) and sell losers ($x < 0$) to profit from momentum ($\varphi > 0$).

The hedging demand exploits the perfect positive correlation between stocks returns and the momentum innovation,

$$\frac{\mathrm{cov}\left(\dfrac{\mathrm{d}S}{S}, \mathrm{d}x\right)}{\sqrt{\mathrm{var}\left(\dfrac{\mathrm{d}S}{S}\right)\mathrm{var}(\mathrm{d}x)}} = 1,$$

to create positive (negative) returns when J_W is increased (decreased) by a negative (positive) shock on the investment opportunity set.

21.6. The Closed-form Solution

Substitution of the trial solution (21.15) and of the optimal portfolio (21.18) into the partial differential Equation (21.14) gives:

$$0 = -\frac{\gamma}{1-\gamma}\left(\frac{\mathrm{d}A_1}{\mathrm{d}\tau}\frac{x^2}{2} + \frac{\mathrm{d}A_2}{\mathrm{d}\tau}x + \frac{\mathrm{d}A_3}{\mathrm{d}\tau}\right)$$

$$+ r$$

$$+ \frac{\gamma}{1-\gamma}(A_1 x + A_2)\,(-(1-\varphi)x)$$

$$- \frac{1}{2}(-\gamma)\left(\frac{1}{\gamma}\,\frac{\mu - r + \varphi x}{\sigma^2} + A_1 x + A_2\right)^2 \sigma^2$$

$$+ \frac{1}{2}\,\frac{\gamma}{1-\gamma}\left(\gamma(A_1 x + A_2)^2 + A_1\right)\sigma^2.$$

The last equation is a quadratic equation for x. Since it must hold for any x and for any τ, its three coefficients must be 0, resulting in the system of first-order non-linear ordinary differential equations:

$$\frac{dA_1}{d\tau} = cA_1^2 + bA_1 + a, \tag{21.19}$$

$$\frac{dA_2}{d\tau} = cA_1 A_2 + \frac{b}{2}A_2 + fA_1 + af\frac{1}{\varphi}\,\frac{\gamma}{1-\gamma}, \tag{21.20}$$

$$\frac{dA_3}{d\tau} = \frac{c}{2}A_2^2 + \frac{c}{2}A_1 + fA_2 + f\frac{r}{\mu - r} + \frac{1}{2}af^2\left(\frac{1}{\varphi}\,\frac{\gamma}{1-\gamma}\right)^2, \tag{21.21}$$

$$a \equiv \frac{1-\gamma}{\gamma^2}\left(\frac{\varphi}{\sigma}\right)^2, \qquad b \equiv 2\left(-(1-\varphi) + \frac{1-\gamma}{\gamma}\varphi\right),$$

$$c \equiv \sigma^2, \qquad f \equiv \frac{1-\gamma}{\gamma}(\mu - r),$$

with the initial condition (21.17).

When $\gamma > 1$, the quantity q,

$$q \equiv b^2 - 4ac,$$

is always positive. Defining,

$$\eta \equiv q^{1/2},$$

the solutions to (21.19) and (21.20) are given by (see Appendix):

$$A_1(\tau) = \frac{2a(1 - \exp(-\eta\tau))}{2\eta - (b + \eta)(1 - \exp(-\eta\tau))},$$

$$A_2(\tau) = A_1(\tau) \left(\frac{1}{1-\varphi} + \frac{2}{\eta} \frac{\left(1 - \exp\left(-\frac{\eta}{2}\tau\right)\right)^2}{\left(1 - \exp\left(-\eta\tau\right)\right)} \right) f \frac{\gamma}{1-\gamma} \frac{1-\varphi}{\varphi}.$$

The solution to (21.21) does not enter the optimal policy (18) so that its study is not required to understand momentum-driven portfolio selection. When $\gamma > 1$, $A_1(\tau)$ is always negative because $a < 0$ and $2\eta - (b + \eta) > 0$. When $\gamma > 1$, $A_1(\tau)$ is negative because $\varphi \in (0, 1)$ and $f \frac{\gamma}{1-\gamma} < 0$. The clear-cut sign of $A_1(\tau)$ and $A_2(\tau)$ and the perfect positive correlation between stock returns and momentum innovations enable a neat interpretation of the hedging demand.

If the momentum variable is non-negative ($x \geq 0$), the hedging demand will be always negative. Indeed, a long-term investor desires negative (positive) returns in case of a positive (negative) shock in the momentum variable. This is because a positive (negative) shock in the momentum variable makes the investor better (worse) off by pushing down (up) the marginal utility of wealth, J_w, via an improvement of (damage to) the investment opportunity set.

If the momentum variable is moderately negative $\left(\frac{A_2(\tau)}{-A_1(\tau)} < x \leq 0 \right)$, the hedging demand will remain negative for the same argument above. If the momentum variable is sufficiently negative $\left(x < \frac{A_2(\tau)}{-A_1(\tau)} \right)$, the hedging demand becomes positive. This is because extreme values of x (even if negative) do imply good investment opportunities so that a positive (negative) shock in the momentum variable makes the investor worse (better) off by damaging (improving) the opportunity set.

For $\gamma = 5$, Figures 21.1–21.3 plot the myopic active portfolio and the hedging portfolio against the investor's horizon τ. The other parameters are: riskfree rate $r = 3\%$, unconditional risk premium $\mu - r = 7\%$, volatility $\sigma = 30\%$, momentum parameter $\varphi = 0.255$ (which implies a first autocorrelation of 1-year holding-period returns of $\rho_1 = 12\%$). The myopic unconditional portfolio is 15.56%.

In Figure 21.1, x is –20%, which implies that returns have been on average 20% below their long-run level of 10%. Since there is momentum, the investor expects further negative returns (losers remain so). This expectation induces a negative myopic active portfolio (a short position) equivalent to about 11% of wealth, and an overall negative hedging portfolio equivalent, for a very long-lived investor, to about 1.75% of wealth. In this case, the conditional component $A_1(\tau) x$ and the unconditional component $A_2(\tau)$ of the hedging demand work in opposite directions. The conditional component is positive, curbing the long position generated by the myopic active position, while the unconditional component is negative, curbing the short position generated by the long-run myopic position (the unconditional Sharpe ratio is positive in this example).

In Figure 21.2 returns have been on average at their long-run level, and so the myopic active portfolio is zero, while the hedging portfolio is negative reflecting only

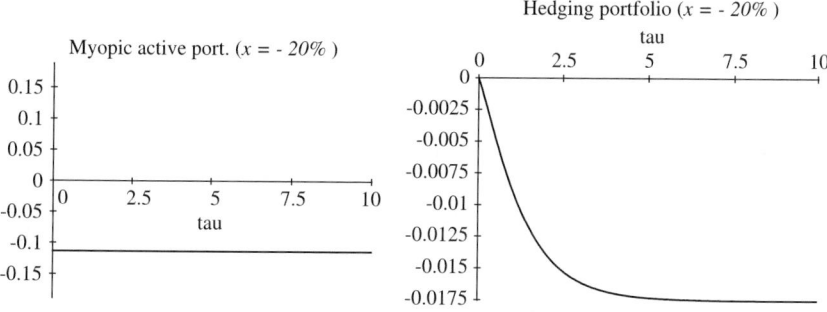

Figure 21.1: Myopic and Hedge portfolios with $x = -20\%$.

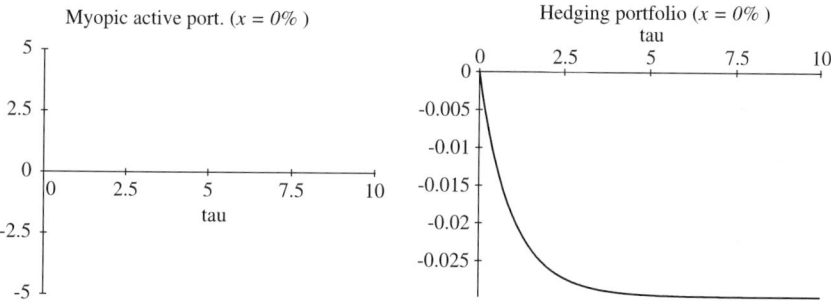

Figure 21.2: Myopic and hedge portfolios with $x = 0\%$.

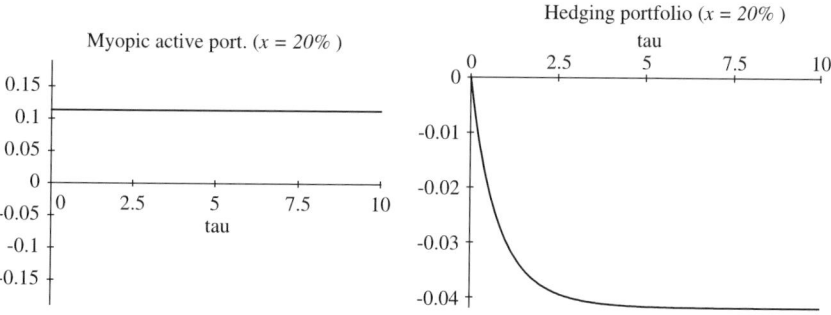

Figure 21.3: Myopic and hedge portfolios with $x = 20\%$.

the unconditional component of the hedging demand. Figure 21.3 shows the case in which returns have been on average 20% above their long-run level. In this case, the myopic active portfolio is positive (about 11% of wealth) as the investor expects winners to remain so. The hedging portfolio is strongly negative (about 4% of wealth of a very long-lived investor), because in this case the unconditional component and the long-run component of the hedging demand work in the same direction.

21.7. Recasting Kim and Omberg (1996)

Our setting recasts the Kim and Omberg (1996) model with a number of important restrictions. Their importance lies in that they are conducive to a state variable that is a clear signal for momentum (y_t is a weighted average of past and current returns on the stock) and to a neat interpretation of the resulting optimal policy (as discussed in the previous section). In Kim and Omberg (1996), the state variable is the market price of risk X, with dynamics,

$$dX = - \lambda_X(X - \bar{X})\, dt + \sigma_X\, dz_X. \tag{21.22}$$

The market price of risk enters the stock price dynamics in this fashion:

$$\frac{dS}{S} = (r + X\sigma)dt + \sigma dz. \tag{21.23}$$

Kim and Omberg (1996) fix the annualized instantaneous covariance $\frac{1}{dt}$ Cov(dz_x, dz) to be the parameter . Our assumption of market completeness implies

$$\rho_{mX} = 1.$$

The comparison of the two stock price dynamics (21.23) and (21.11) implies these three restrictions on the dynamics of the market price of risk,

$$\lambda_X = 1 - \varphi,\ \bar{X} = \frac{\mu - r}{\sigma},\ \sigma_X = \varphi,$$

together with the following relationship

$$X = \frac{\mu - r}{\sigma} + \frac{\varphi}{\sigma}\,(y - \mu).$$

21.8. Intermediate Consumption

Our complete-markets model allows the use of Cox-Huang (1989) martingale approach to solve the case with intermediate consumption, *c*, as in Wachter (2002). The problem is

$$J(W, x, \tau) = \sup_{\pi} E_t\left[\int_0^\tau \exp(-\rho s)\,\frac{c_{t+s}^{1-\gamma}}{1-\gamma}ds\right],$$

s.t.

$$\mathrm{d}w = W\left(r\,\mathrm{d}t + \pi\left(\frac{\mathrm{d}S}{S} - r\,\mathrm{d}t\right)\right) - c\,\mathrm{d}t,$$

$$\frac{\mathrm{d}S}{S} = (\mu + \varphi x)\,\mathrm{d}t + \sigma\,\mathrm{d}z,$$

$$\mathrm{d}x = -(1 - \varphi)\,x\,\mathrm{d}t + \sigma\,\mathrm{d}z.$$

This is the problem of an investor who still does market timing, but that at the same time consumes out of her wealth. The martingale approach to this problem states that, since the investor's wealth $W = W(Z, x, t)$ is a tradable asset, it must obey a no-arbitrage condition. In combination with a trial solution for $W(Z, x, t)$, such a condition generates a system of ordinary differential equations akin to that discussed in Section 21.3. For brevity we do not provide details of the solution method. These details can be found in Wachter (2002). The resulting optimal demand for the stock is:

$$\pi^* = \frac{1}{\gamma}\frac{\mu - r}{\sigma^2} + \frac{1}{\gamma}\frac{\varphi x}{\sigma^2} + \int_0^\tau \frac{I(x, s)}{\int_0^\tau I(x, v)\mathrm{d}v}\left[A_1(s)\,x + A_2(s)\right]\mathrm{d}s,$$

where $I(x, \tau)$ is as in the definition (21.16). The functions $A_i(\tau)$, $i = 1, 2, 3$ are the solutions of the terminal-wealth-case Equations (21.19)–(21.21). There is also no change in the speculative portfolios relative to the terminal-wealth case. In particular, active momentum strategies remain the same. The main difference between the two models is in the hedging portfolios, which are now a weighted average of the terminal-wealth-case hedging portfolios. Since $I(x, \tau)$ represents the value, scaled by today's consumption, of consumption in periods, the weights are the present values of future consumption at any time τ relative to the present value of the entire flow of consumption.

21.9 Conclusions

Active portfolio-management strategies suggest that, in the presence of autocorrelation of holding-period returns on the stock, the observation of current returns may induce changes in the composition of optimally chosen portfolios. In this chapter we present a model of stock price dynamics in which the state variable is a weighted average of current and past returns. Our choice of model allows us to study in closed form the asset-allocation consequences of momentum in a complete-markets setting, so to extend the literature on intertemporal portfolio selection with predictability to the analysis of complex momentum strategies adopted by rational investors who try to exploit existing departures from the efficient market hypothesis. We isolated and discussed three clear effects: the speculative effect, the conditional-hedge effect, and the unconditional-hedge effect.

A first natural extension of our model is to relax the assumption that the investor observes the long-run expected return, and to explore instead a situation in which she must estimate it using current information. Estimation risk may enhance the role of the hedging demand for the stock. A second natural extension is to relax the assumption of absence of model uncertainty. Model uncertainty and aversion to it are known to trigger an additional hedging-demand component that is not linked to Jw_x but to J_x instead (see for example Sbuelz & Trojani, 2004). This is likely to generate more interaction between the hedging demand and momentum-like predictability. Finally, we have studied the momentum case in isolation, disregarding the existence of mean reversion in long-holding-period returns on the stock. The interplay of both stylized facts in the asset-allocation decision of a rational investor is an issue that deserves investigation. The very recent work of Koijen, Rodriguez, and Sbuelz (2005) is the first to explicitly tackle the issue. This is the direction of our current research.

Endnotes

1. This model is introduced in Rodriguez (2005).

References

Ball, R., & Brown, P. (1968). An empirical evaluation of accounting income numbers. *Journal of Accounting Research, 6*, 159–178.

Balvers, R., & Mitchell, D. (1997). Autocorrelated returns and optimal intertemporal portfolio choice. *Management Science, 43*, 1537–1551.

Balvers, R.J., & Wu, Y. (2004). Momentum and mean reversion across national equity markets. Unpublished paper, College of Business West Virginia University and Rutgers Business School-Newark & New Brunswick Rutgers University.

Barberis, N. (2000). Investing for the long run when returns are predictable. *Journal of Finance, 55*, 225–264.

Bernard, V., & Thomas, J. (1989). Post-earnings announcement drift: Delayed price response or risk premium? *Journal of Accounting Research, 27* Supplement, 1–36.

Bernard, V., & Thomas, J. (1990). Evidence that stock prices do not fully reflect the implications of current earnings for future earnings. *Journal of Accounting and Economics, 13*, 305–340.

Brennan, M.J., Schwartz, E.S., & Lagnado, R. (1997). Strategic asset allocation. *Journal of Economic Dynamics and Control, 21*, 1377–1403.

Brunnermeier, M., & Nagel, S. (2004). Hedge funds and the technology bubble. *Journal of Finance, 59*, 2013–2040.

Campbell, J. (1987). Stock returns and the term structure. *Journal of Financial Economics, 18*, 373–399.

Campbell, J. (2004). *Understanding momentum*, Arrowstreet Capital, L.P., December Letter.

Campbell, J., & Viceira, L. (2002). *Strategic asset allocation*. New York: Oxford University Press.

Campbell, J.Y. (1991). A variance decomposition for stock returns. *Economic Journal, 101*, 157–179.

Campbell, J.Y., & Shiller, R.J. (1988). The dividend-price ratio and expectations of future dividends and discount factors. *Review of Financial Studies, 1*, 195–228.

Campbell, J.Y. & Viceira, L.M. (1999). Consumption and portfolio decisions when expected returns are time varying. *Quarterly Journal of Economics, 114,* 433–495.

Chacko, G., & Viceira, L.M. (2005). Dynamic consumption and portfolio choice with stochastic volatility in incomplete markets. Review of Financial Studies (Forthcoming).

Chan, L.K.C., Hameed, A., & Tong, W. (2000). Profitability of momentum strategies in the international equity markets. *Journal of Financial and Quantitative Analysis, 35,* 153–172.

Chan, L.K.C., Jegadeesh, N., & Lakonishok, J. (1996). Momentum strategies. *Journal of Finance, 51,* 1681–1713.

Cochrane, J. (2001). *Asset pricing.* Princeton: Princeton University Press.

Conrad, J., & Kaul, G. (1988). Time-variation in expected returns. *Journal of Business, 61,* 409–425.

Cox, J.C., & Huang, C.F. (1989). Optimum consumption and portfolio policies when asset prices follow a diffusion process. *Journal of Economic Theory, 49,* 33–83.

Daniel, K., Hirshleifer, D., & Subrahmanyam, A. (1998). Investor psychology and security market under- and over-reactions. *Journal of Finance, 53,* 1839–1885.

Daniel, K., & Titman, S. (2004). *Market reactions to tangible and intangible information.* Unpublished paper, Northwestern University and University of Texas.

Fama, E.F., & French, K. (1988). Dividend yields and expected stock returns. *Journal of Financial Economics, 22,* 3–27.

Fama, E.F., & Schwert, G.W. (1977). Asset returns and inflation. *Journal of Financial Economics, 5,* 115–146.

Griffin, J.M., Ji, X., & Martin, J.S. (2003). Momentum investing and business cycle risk: Evidence from pole to pole. *Journal of Finance, 58,* 2515–2547.

Grinblatt, M., & Moskowitz, T.J. (2004). Predicting stock price movements from past returns: The role of consistency and tax-loss selling. *Journal of Financial Economics, 71,* 541–579.

Grundy, B.D., & Martin, J.S. (2001). Understanding the nature of the risks and the source of the rewards to momentum investing. *Review of Financial Studies, 14,* 29–78.

Jegadeesh, N., & Titman, S. (1993). Returns to buying winners and selling losers: Implications for stock market efficiency. *Journal of Finance, 48,* 65–91.

Jegadeesh, N., & Titman, S. (2001). *Momentum.* Working paper, University of Illinois.

Johnson, W.B., & Schwartz Jr., W.C. (2000). *Evidence that capital markets learn from academic research: Earnings surprises and the persistence of post-announcement drift.* Unpublished Paper, University of Iowa.

Keim, D., & Stambaugh, R.F. (1986). Predicting returns in stock and bond markets. *Journal of Financial Economics, 17,* 357–390.

Kim, T.S., & Omberg, E. (1996). Dynamic nonmyopic portfolio behavior. *Review of Financial Studies, 9,* 141–161.

Koijen, R.S.J., Rodriguez, J.C., & Sbuelz, A. (2005). *Momentum and mean reversion in strategic asset allocation.* Working Paper, Tilburg University.

Korajczyk, R., & Sadka, R. (2004). Are momentum profits robust to trading costs? *Journal of Finance, 59,* 1039–1082.

Lettau, M., & Ludvigson, S. (2001). Consumption, aggregate wealth, and expected stock returns. *Journal of Finance, 56,* 815–849.

Lewellen, J. (2002). Momentum and autocorrelation in stock returns. *Review of Financial Studies, 15,* 533–563.

Lo, A.W., & MacKinlay, A.C. (1988). Stock market prices do not follow random walks: Evidence from a simple specification test. *Review of Financial Studies, 1,* 41–66.

Merton, R.C. (1971). Optimum consumption and portfolio rules in a continuous-time model. *Journal of Economic Theory, 41,* 867–887.

Patro, D.K., & Wu, Y. (2004). Predictability of short-horizon equity returns in international equity markets. *Journal of Empirical Finance, 11,* 553–584.

Poterba, J., & Summers, L.H. (1988). Mean reversion in stock returns: Evidence and implications. *Journal of Financial Economics, 22,* 27–60.

Rodriguez, J.C. (2005). *Hedging demand and stochastic volatility in dynamic economies.* Working Paper, Tilburg University.

Rouwenhorst, K.G. (1998). International momentum strategies. *Journal of Finance, 53,* 267–284.

Rouwenhorst, K.G. (1999). Local return factors and turnover in emerging stock markets. *Journal of Finance, 54,* 1439–1464.

Sbuelz, A., & Trojani, F. (2004). Equilibrium asset pricing with time varying pessimism. CentER Discussion Paper no. 2002-102, Tilburg University.

Schwert, G.W. (2003). Anomalies and market efficiency. In: G.M. Constantinides, M. Harris, & R.M. Stulz (Eds), *Handbook of the economics of finance: Financial markets and asset pricing,* (Vol. 1B, pp. 939–974). North Holland: Elsevier.

Sirri, E., & Tufano, P. (1998). Costly search and mutual fund flows. *Journal of Finance, 53,* 1589–1622.

Wachter, J. (2002). Portfolio and consumption decisions under mean-reverting returns: An exact solution for complete markets. *Journal of Financial and Quantitative Analysis, 37,* 63–91.

Wachter, J., & Sangvinatsos, A. (2005). Does the failure of the expectations hypothesis matter for long-term investors. *Journal of Finance, 60,* 179–230.

Zhang, X.F. (2004). Information uncertainty and stock returns. *Journal of Finance* (Forthcoming).

Appendix

Solution for A_1

The equation for A_1 is known as a Riccati equation and can be rewritten in integral form as:

$$\int_0^\tau \frac{dA_1}{cA_1^2 + bA_1 + a} = \tau.$$

We start from the differential form (19):

$$\frac{dA_1}{d\tau} = cA_1^2 + bA_1 + a,$$

Let's call $Y = \dfrac{1}{A_1}$. Note that Y also satisfies the following Riccati equation:

$$\frac{dY}{d\tau} + AY^2 + BY + C, \tag{21.24}$$

where $C = -c$, $B = -b$, and $A = -a$. It is a known result that if $u(\tau)$ is a solution the Riccati Equation (21.24), then the general solution of (21.24) is

$$Y(\tau) = u(\tau)\, \frac{1}{z(\tau)},$$

where $z(\tau)$ satisfies a linear ordinary differential equation. Notice that a constant solution of (21.24) is

$$u = \frac{-B + \sqrt{B^2 - 4AC}}{2A}.$$

Therefore, the general solution of () is $Y(\tau) = u + \dfrac{1}{z(\tau)}$, with:

$$\frac{dz}{d\tau} = -z\sqrt{q} - A,$$

where $q = B^2 - 4AC = b^2 - 4ac$.

This last equation must be solved with initial condition $z(0) = 0$ (this is implied by the condition that $A_1(0) = 0$):

$$z(\tau) = -\frac{A}{\sqrt{q}}\left(1 - \exp^{-\sqrt{q}\tau}\right).$$

The general solution of Y is

$$Y(\tau) = \frac{-B + \sqrt{q}}{2A} - \frac{\sqrt{q}}{A(1 - \exp^{-\sqrt{q}\tau})}. \tag{21.25}$$

Recall that $B = -b$ and $A = -a$, and that $A_1 = \dfrac{1}{Y}$. Plugging this information in the general solution (21.25) gives (after some additional algebraic manipulation):

$$A_1(\tau) = \frac{2a(1 - \exp^{-\sqrt{q}\tau})}{2\sqrt{q} - (b + \sqrt{q})\,(1 - \exp^{-\sqrt{q}\tau})}$$

$$= \frac{2a(1 - \exp(-\eta\tau))}{2\eta - (b + \eta)\,(1 - \exp(-\eta\tau))},$$

which is our stated expression for $A_1(\tau)$.

Solution for A_2

Given the restriction $\gamma > 1$, the closed form solution for $A_2(\tau)$ comes from knowing the closed forms for $A_1(\tau)$ and the auxiliary function $A_2^*(\tau)$. The auxiliary function $A_2^*(\tau)$ solves the following Cauchy problem,

$$\frac{dA_2^*}{d\tau} = cA_1 A_2^* + \frac{b}{2} A_2^* + fA_1,$$

$$A_2^*(0) = 0,$$

with analytical solution (see Kim & Omberg, 1996: 147–158):

$$A_2^*(\tau) = \frac{2}{\eta} \cdot A_1(\tau) \cdot f \cdot \frac{\left(1 - \exp\left(-\frac{\eta}{2}\tau\right)\right)^2}{(1 - \exp(-\eta\tau))}.$$

We formulate a trial solution for as a linear combination of $A_1(\tau)$ and $A_2^*(\tau)$:

$$(A_1(\tau)w = A_2^*(\tau))u,$$

By construction, such a trial solution substitution satisfies the initial condition $A_2(0) = 0$. Substitution of the trial solution into $A_2(\tau)$'s differential Equation (20) implies that the suitable values for the coefficients w and u are

$$w = f \cdot \frac{1}{1 - \varphi},$$

$$u = \frac{\gamma}{1 - \gamma} \frac{1 - \varphi}{\varphi},$$

which renders our stated expression for $A_2(\tau)$.

Chapter 22

Relating Risks to Asset Types: A New Challenge for Central Banks

Jacques Sijben

22.1. Introduction

Since the mid-1970s both in the academic world and in the environment of central banks the old debate between rules versus discretion in monetary policy has been revitalized. With the path breaking publication of Kydland and Prescott (1977) the concept of dynamic inconsistency of policymaking has been introduced, changing this debate dramatically. Based on theoretical and empirical research it has appeared clearly that a consistent, credible and transparent anti-inflation policy of an independent central bank will result in a better macroeconomic outcome than a time-inconsistent and discretionary policy.

In the 1980s and 1990s of the last century many central banks shifted to a new monetary policy regime, characterized by a pre-announcement of an anti-inflation strategy, giving priority to monetary stability and an anchoring of low and stable inflationary expectations (flexible inflation-targeting) (Bernanke, 2003b). According to this strategy, the central bank' interest rate is dependent on both the deviation of the inflation-target and the output gap (*Taylor rule*). The low-inflation era of the past two decades has seen significant improvements not only in economic growth and productivity, but also a substantial reduction in economic volatility. In this context Bernanke speaks about "the Great Moderation" (Bernanke, 2005).

Although this regime shift has been very successful, central banks have been faced with quite a new enemy on the battlefield: an increase of financial instability. Shortly, the successful monetary policy has not resulted in the peace dividend of a strengthening of the financial environment.

Since the beginning of the eighties a wave of deregulation and liberalization of financial markets, driven forcefully by the introduction of information and communication technology in the financial industry, has changed the financial world drastically. This new financial landscape can be characterized by a globalization of financial markets, a sharpening of international competitiveness between financial institutions, a blurring of these institutions and an increase both of liquidity and the availability of credit. It has appeared

Advances in Corporate Finance and Asset Pricing
Edited by L. Renneboog
© 2006 Elsevier B.V. All rights reserved.
ISBN: 0-444-52723-0

that the combination of a liberalized financial system and a less constrained and more elastic money-supply process (fiat money) may be a fertile soil for the arise of a boom–bust cycle in asset prices (Crockett, 2000). Economic history and in particular the 1920s of the last century has shown that in many instances strong money and credit growth has accompanied financial bubbles, whose subsequent bursting then endangered financial stability.

Inflation has been successfully contained for quite some time now at least in the major Organization for Co-operation and Economic Development (OECD) countries. But at the same time large cycles in a variety of asset prices can be observed which are accompanied by ample global liquidity. Researchers at the Bank for International Settlements (BIS) have labeled this environment as the *"paradox of central bank credibility"*. They hint at the possibility that due to central banks' success and gained reputation in fighting inflation, inflationary pressures would first show up in asset-price inflation and increase the vulnerability of financial systems (Trichet, 2005). However, it cannot be denied that the IT-enabled forces of globalization have also contributed to a lower inflation pressure through a reduction of the "pricing power" of the firms.

In this chapter attention will be given to the new challenge of central banks how to deal with financial imbalances and boom–bust cycles in asset prices in quite a new low-inflation environment and to reconcile monetary and financial stability. Recently Trichet expressed the importance of this challenge as follows, "The development of both the role of central banks in financial stability and thinking about appropriate responses to financial imbalances, such as excessive movements in asset prices, is one of the key challenges that central banks face today" (Trichet, 2004; 2005).

Section 22.2 deals with the current academic views about the interaction process between monetary and financial stability. In Section 22.3 attention will be given to the Wicksellian interest theory and the associated Austrian School, with representatives like Hayek and von Mises, because this analysis can give a theoretical foundation of the modern view that monetary stability is no guarantee for financial stability. In Section 22.4 the current academic debate about an ex-ante versus an ex-post intervention of the central bank to mitigate an asset bubble will be presented. Section 22.5 deals with the question whether a new financial "house bubble" has been arisen since the collapse of the stock market bubble in 2000. After the attention given in Section 22.6 to the importance of monetary uncertainties, Section 22.7 is emphasizing the crucial role of an early warning system in the monetary policy framework with regard to building-up financial imbalances. Section 22.8 presents a synthesis approach, conceptualizing the current debate regarding the role of asset prices and perceived financial imbalances in the formation of monetary policy by introducing financial imbalances as an additional intermediate target and modifying the central bank's loss function. In Section 22.9 some summarizing conclusions will be presented.

22.2. Monetary and Financial Stability

In the academic literature and economics profession three views have been put forward with regard to the interaction between monetary and financial stability.

The orthodox monetarist view or *Schwartz hypothesis* emphasizes that a consistent and predictable monetary policy guarantees financial stability (Schwartz, 1995). Schwartz concludes, "Monetary stability is a prerequisite of price stability, and price stability is a prerequisite of financial stability". She stresses that both inflation and deflation uncertainty leads to information problems, resulting in a misallocation of resources and inadequate investment decisions. The adherents of this view are driven by the bad experiences of the Great Depression in the 1930s of last century and identify a financial crisis with a sharp loss of confidence in the banking system, a bank-run and a contraction of the money supply. However this view has been in the meantime empirically rejected. Financial crises can occur also in times of relative consumer price stability, often undermining conditions for maintaining price stability. The Japanese stock market and property price boom in the late-1980s is a vivid example of this. Issing underlines this orthodox view, but he also points out, "Thus we must be aware that price stability is not a sufficient condition for financial stability" and further on, "... the choice of the monetary policy strategy has implications for financial stability" (Issing, 2003). In this context he refers to the 1920s and the 1990s in the last century in the USA and to the bubble period in Japan since the mid-1980s.

In this way Issing introduces the second or "new view" by emphasizing a relation with the analysis of Minsky, Zarnovitz and Kindleberger, according to which monetary stability is not a sufficient condition for financial and macroeconomic stability. In the spirit of the Austrian School (Section 22.3) these authors stress the important role of a boom–bust cycle in asset prices for macroeconomic development. According to this approach, endogenous cyclical forces, owing to both an excessive debt accumulation during the upswing of the business cycle and a speculative behavior of economic agents, will deteriorate the financial structure of households and firms. In these circumstances moods of optimism dominate financial markets, ample availability of credit exists, the external finance premium falls and asset prices increase, accelerating the upswing of the business cycle. However, after the top of the cycle and during the downturn of the business cycle, owing to a tightening of monetary policy, there exists a general loss of confidence and even a panic may arise, increasing financial instability (Kindleberger, 1978; Minsky, 1980; 1982).

The proponents of the third view rather focus on the importance of financial stability as a prerequisite of a successful monetary policy. They put forward that an unwinding of financial imbalances built-up during a bubble period might result ultimately in banking problems, a credit crunch, a loss of confidence with consumers, producers and investors and even in an economic stagnation. The recent experience in Japan during the nineties has shown very clearly that in an unstable financial environment, with non-performing bank loans and, according to Borio and Filardo (2004) "ugly" deflation, the effectiveness of both monetary and fiscal policy will disappear. Moreover in the current zero-interest rate scenario and a liquidity trap, the deflationary process in Japan increases the real rate of interest sharpening the downturn of the business cycle. In such an environment deflationary forces create a spiral of self-reinforcing disruptions in the economy (Robinson & Stone, 2005).

22.3. Wicksell and the Austrian School

The theoretical foundation of the "new view" according to which monetary stability is not a sufficient condition for financial stability goes back to the beginning of the last century. In his book "Money and the business cycle" Haberler (1932) emphasizes that the price level is a misleading guide for monetary policy. Under some circumstances a stable price level might generate false expectations, which together with an excessive credit expansion may lead to wrong investment decisions. An artificial low rate of interest of the central bank can result in a misallocation of resources and an overinvestment crisis. Haberler's view is based on the theoretical analysis of the Austrian School (Wicksell, 1936) which itself is an elaboration of Wicksell's natural interest rate concept.

Wicksell defined the "natural rate" as the rate of interest that equates saving with investment and that will fluctuate mainly according to changes in technology that affect the productivity of capital. He tried to provide a more rigorous foundation of the link between money growth and inflation. According to Wicksell's cumulative process theory, changes in the price level are caused by non-zero real rate gaps. If the loan and deposit rates set by banks are below the "natural rate", then there will be an excess demand for funds by firms to finance investment projects. Consequently, the creation of money by banks to absorb this excess demand will ultimately create excess money balances with households and in an effort to spend the excess cash prices begin to be driven upwards. According to Wicksell, the process of price inflation ceases when the market rate of interest is brought into equality with the "natural rate". Later the "natural rate" figured in theories of the business cycle that were developed during the interwar period. Even Friedman's long-run property of the "natural rate of unemployment" (1968) can be seen as a direct analogue of Wicksell's natural rate of interest (Amato, 2005).

After the burst of the stock market bubble in 1929, Hayek puts forward that during the 1920s, characterized by a strong rate of growth and low inflation, economists and policymakers believed that the economy has been faced with a new paradigm and that the business cycle was dead. However, after that collapse with a sharp downswing in the business cycle, there was the fear of deflation owing to a credit crunch in the banking sector. An aggressive monetary ease with a fall in the interest rate had to recover economic activity.

In the 1920s there was a lively debate, when some economists suggested that when rapid productivity growth, driven by the technologic revolution in the late 19th century, is bringing down the cost of production, overall price stability may be the wrong objective. Instead, average prices should be allowed to fall to pass productivity gains on the workers in the form of higher real incomes. In this context Borio and Filardo talk about "good deflations" which, "… would be those reflecting productivity improvements against the background of underlying or secular restraints on the growth of nominal demand" (Borio & Filardo, 2004). But just like in the last decade, monetary policy prevented prices from falling and profits surged. Then the mistaken belief that projects could continue to grow forcefully helped to inflate the late-1920s stock market bubble.

The best concept for understanding the forces at work is the Wicksellian "natural rate of interest". This idea, further developed by Austrian economists such as Hayek and von Mises, refers to the interest rate at which the supply of savings from households equals the demand for investment funds by firms. So when the central bank leaves the interest rate low for a too long period, creating a "natural rate gap", financial imbalances can be built-up in a masking way, giving rise to an overinvestment situation.

In retrospect, it is clear that the risk of *bad deflation*, when prices and output spiral downwards, in 2003 in the USA was exaggerated. Even so, it is hard to criticize the Fed's rate cuts in 2001–2003 to a 45-year low of 1%. Even if some of threatened deflation in

2003 was of the good sort, there was the risk of bad deflation after the bursting of the stock market bubble in 2000. At a time of weak growth, it was obvious that the Fed did not want to run the risk of any sort of deflation (Bernanke, 2002). The Fed was desperate not to repeat the mistakes of the Bank of Japan in the 1990s and to be faced with a liquidity trap and the zero rate bound. The experience of America in the 1930s and Japan over the last decade can be much more harmful than inflation. For falling prices increase real debt burdens, depress demand and so push prices even lower (Fisher's debt-deflation spiral).

Summarizing it can be concluded that in the current post-bubble era, two lessons can be drawn from the Austrian and Wicksellian School. First, fluctuations in the business cycle may be the result both of a central bank's one-sided policy of price stability and of accepting an excessive credit expansion of the banking sector. The second lesson refers to an overinvestment situation, with an associated bubble on financial markets, which will occur when the Wicksellian "natural rate gap" will last a too long period. In such a situation wrong and often irrational profit expectations together with a low-risk-adjusted discount rate, will feed a bubble economy and may sharpen the down turn of the business cycle when the bubble bursts.

22.4. The Academic Debate

In the past two decades it has appeared very clearly that in a low-inflation and high-growth environment, accompanied with an excessive mood of optimism of economic agents, financial instability can increase. In these circumstances psychologic behavior in finance drives the build-up of hidden financial imbalances during the boom of the business cycle, increasing the fragility of the macro economy. Then there is no fear of monetary tightening to cool down an overheated economy because of a stay away of inflation. Since the nineties of last century the masked overheated economy rather manifests itself in a strong rise of asset prices (*asset inflation*), while the traditional inflation (CPI (consumer price inflation)) remained low and stable.

However, the unsustainable dynamics of asset prices generated a surge in aggregate demand through the working of wealth and collateral effects, excessive credit expansion and Tobin's "Q", that might increase traditional inflation in the future. In this new environment the question comes about whether and how the central bank must respond to asset-price inflation to guarantee monetary and financial stability. It is well-known that monetary policymaking is always accompanied with macroeconomic uncertainty, leading, according to Brainard's view, to a prudential behavior in the implementation of monetary policy (Brainard, 1967).

In the recent past in the academic world two approaches have been put forward with regard to the question how to cope with asset prices in monetary policy. According to the *orthodox view* there is no need to change monetary policy by incorporating explicitly asset prices in the policy process. Bernanke and Gertler state that there is no need for an ex-ante intervention of the central bank, unless there exist clear signs of a rekindling of inflationary expectations (Bernanke & Gertler, 1999; 2001). It says that asset prices should be ignored beyond their impact on consumer price inflation via the regular transmission mechanism channel (wealth effects, etc.). These authors emphasize the great importance of the identification problem. This refers to the fact that it is impossible for policymakers to trace whether the movements of asset prices are dominated either by fundamentals or psychologic factors (emotion, herd behavior and sentiments of investors). Greenspan underlines this view and remarks, "Human psychology being what it is, bubbles tend to feed on themselves", and further on, "stock prices and equity premiums are then driven to unsustainable levels" (2002). In a speech, he argued that "we are unable to fully understand the process and interactions with asset prices" and that it was "very difficult to definitely identify a bubble until after the fact, that is, when its bursting confirmed its existence" (Greenspan, 2000). The Bernanke-Gertler's view is associated with the monetarist view of Schwartz cs. that monetary stability is a guarantee of financial stability. Although being a robust theory for most of times, this orthodox view has recently been repeatedly questioned for not being optimal in all circumstances.

The *"new view"* stresses the working of the masked endogenous cyclical forces, mentioned before, reflected by the build-up of financial imbalances during the upswing of the business cycle (Cecchetti, Genberg, Lipsky, & Whadwani, 2000; Borio & Lowe, 2002). These authors agree with the Wicksellian analysis and state that the potential problems will manifest themselves as soon as a bubble bursts. They hold the view that the current Taylor rule lacks a sufficient future orientation and is accommodating a bubble economy. The authors emphasize strongly a pre-emptive action of the central bank, *"a leaning against the wind policy"*, to prevent both an accumulation of financial imbalances in an early stage of the cycle and the potential negative macroeconomic outcomes (a loss of production and even deflation) in the post-bubble period (Bordo & Jeanne, 2002). The "leaning-against the wind principle" describes a tendency to cautiously raise interest rates even beyond the level necessary to maintain price stability over the short to medium run, when a potentially detrimental asset-price boom is identified. Proponents of this policy strategy have typically been very careful to mention the strong informational requirements concerning the characteristics of the asset bubble.

Next to the complexity of the identification problem, mentioned above, the central bank is faced also with the question whether bubbles can be pre-empted short of inducing a substantial contraction in economic activity, an outcome that the policymaker just would be seeking to avoid. This *"pricking-the-bubble"* strategy has its roots in the so-called "liquidationist" view of mainstream economists in the context of the heated debate over the stock market boom of the 1920s in the USA. However, this view is now widely rejected by today's profession, because the interest rate is just a too blunt instrument to allow the type of intervention that the "pricking" of the bubble would require. With regard to this dilemma, looking backwards, it can be stated that in the last decade the Federal Reserve has given priority to a policy-on-hold and switched to an aggressive monetary ease in 2001 to avoid the possible negative macroeconomic outcomes after the bubble had been burst in 2000. In this context recently Greenspan has put forward, "… our strategy of addressing the bubble's consequences rather than the bubble itself has been successful" (Greenspan, 2004). With this statement he was reacting to many critical remarks of economists and financial markets in the last few years that he was too late in July 1999 by tightening monetary policy to prevent the arise of an asset bubble in an early stage. These remarks had been made because Greenspan gave a warning signal already in December 1996, when he spoke about *"irrational exuberance"* on stock markets, but without any policy reaction.

22.5. A New Financial Bubble?

It cannot be denied that rising house prices, *a new financial bubble*, in the last few years have popped up the American economy forcefully after the stock market bubble burst in 2000. This boom in house prices has been driven by historically low interest rates and the portfolio switch of households from equities to property. The recent surge in house prices has been accompanied by an increase in household debt. Through the instrument of "refinancing mortgages", existing owners have increased their mortgages (*housing-equity withdrawal*) to turn capital gains into cash that they can spend.

This implies that housing booms tend to be more dangerous than stock market bubbles and are often followed by periods of prolonged economic weakness. By holding interest rates low for so long after equities crashed in 2000, the Fed helped to inflate house prices and tolerating a new bubble. This implies that since the mid-1990s the USA has become an "*asset-dependent economy*".

In the Annual Report 2005, the BIS worries about a different sort of risk: the rapid growth in debt in the US and the surge in house prices. Ironically, this is partly due to central banks' success in defeating inflation. Thanks to globalization and technology, which have helped to hold down inflation, central banks have recently not needed to raise interest rates by as much as in past cycles. According to the BIS, the combination of cheap money and a liberalized financial system may explain why there have been more booms and busts in credit and asset prices in the last few years. The BIS argues that policymakers need to modify their current policy framework in order to prevent the build-up of financial imbalances in the future (BIS, 2005). The risk is, according to the Economist "that in single-mindedly looking out for inflationary icebergs, a central bank will fail to spot the rocks that lie dead ahead" (2005).

This policy of "*benign neglect*", tolerating the build-up of financial imbalances, has been analyzed by Bordo and Jeanne based on an insurance perspective. These authors assume that the reduction of economic growth today through a pre-emptive action of the central bank is the insurance premium that has to be paid to prevent a strong contraction in economic activity and a potential financial crisis in the future. Analogous to the well-known reputation trade-off in the Barro-Gordon model, it can now be stated that the higher the priority given to a prevention of building-up financial imbalances, the greater the sacrifice in terms of a loss of real effects in the short run and vice versa. This refers to a new intertemporal trade-off between a moderate growth today with financial stability on the one hand and a higher rate of growth today with the risk of financial instability tomorrow on the other hand. The authors emphasize the role of a flexible inflation-targeting strategy augmented by judgmental and early discretionary actions based on relevant information variables, like asset prices. They focus on the endogenous character of financial instability, because an accommodative monetary policy will strengthen an asset bubble and can generate pro-cyclical effects during the downsizing of the business cycle.

It is obvious that asymmetric monetary policy actions during a boom–bust cycle may give rise to moral hazard behavior that lowers risk aversion during the upswing of the business cycle, enforcing the surge of asset prices. This phenomenon is called "Greenspan's put" (Miller cs., Weller, & Zhang, 2002).

Summarizing it can be concluded that the current debate boils down to the question of whether the reaction to asset prices should be limited to their impact on consumer price inflation via the regular transmission channels, or whether accounting for effects of a boom–bust cycle in asset prices may have on financial stability and thus price stability in the medium to long run — a central bank should occasionally consider to follow the "leaning-against the wind" principle.

22.6. Monetary Uncertainty

In the trade-off process between ex-ante versus ex-post intervention of the central bank, monetary uncertainties and the communication with financial markets play a crucial role.

In a speech at a conference of the Federal Reserve Bank of Kansas City on economic volatility, it appears that Greenspan is looking for a better model of the working of the economy to be able to react to asset prices in a more appropriate way. He remarks, "We do need to know more about the behavior of equity premiums and bubbles and their impact on economic activity. To date we have not been able to identify a policy that can effectively limit the size of bubbles without doing substantial damage in the process, though we or others might do so in the future" (Greenspan, 2002). A year later he introduces the concept of a "*risk-management approach*" in monetary policy, emphasizing a cost–benefit analysis with regard to the possible macroeconomic outcomes of alternative policy measures (Greenspan, 2003). He holds the view that policy rules are very simple, but cannot be used mechanically in an uncertain macroeconomic environment. This implies that formal economic models are no substitute for the judgment and evaluation of the current economic situation.

In a very recent speech Greenspan was emphasizing again the inevitably incomplete knowledge about key structural aspects of an ever-changing world economy and the sometimes asymmetric costs or benefits of particular outcomes (Greenspan, 2005). He puts forward; "The risk-management approach has gained greater attraction as a consequence of the step-up in globalization and the technologic change of the 1990s, which found us adjusting to events without the comfort of relevant history to guide us" (p. 3). And further on, "Our forecasts and hence policy are becoming increasingly driven by asset-price changes". Although the ratio of household net worth to disposable income fell with the collapse of equity prices in 2000, it has rebounded noticeably over the past couple of years reflecting the rise in prices of equities and houses (Section 22.5).

The behavior of financial markets plays also an important role in the debate about an ex-ante or an ex-post policy reaction on financial excesses. An early relatively small increase of the interest rate may be counterproductive by just increasing asset prices. For this policy action can rather strengthen investors' confidence with regard to the anti-inflation policy, enlarging the moods of optimism on financial markets. This could imply that a strong increase of the interest rate is necessary to prevent a further rise of the asset bubble. However in this situation the risk of "pricking-the-bubble" strategy may be enlarged, generating a real contraction with disappointed investors and a loss of the reputation of the central bank. This means that, according to Greenspan's "*balance-of-risk strategy*", the central bank must be very careful in controlling and managing financial imbalances.

It is quite obvious that an early surgical intervention of the central bank implies also a communication and transparency problem (Issing, 2005). For, analogous to the introduction of a sharp anti-inflation strategy after the mid-1970s, to eliminate the inflation psychology, now the public must clearly understand and be convinced that an ex-ante intervention through a rise of the interest rate is necessary, although inflation is low and stable. In the past few years, monetary authorities in Japan have been faced with such a communication problem, but just the reverse (Yamaguchi, 1999). Since the arise of a deflation process in 1998, the Bank of Japan had to convince the public that an anti-deflation strategy is beneficial for the macro economy and that the deflation-bias with a zero-interest rate has to be eliminated. Once deflationary expectations have taken hold, policies will be successful only to the extent that they manage to break expectations.

The rekindling of inflationary expectations and the associated reduction of the real interest rate to boost economic activity has also faced the central bank of Japan with a serious credibility problem. In these circumstances in game-theoretical terms a credibility problem exists, because the public assumes that the monetary ease will have only a temporary character and will be followed by a monetary tightening as soon as inflation starts to rise. In this context Krugman then defines the central bank's task as "to credible promise not be irresponsible" to eliminate the deflationary-bias (Krugman, 1998).

22.7. Indicators of Instability

In a new policy approach, based on the credit view, Borio and Lowe try to augment the current flexible inflation-targeting strategy with an early warning mechanism (Borio & Lowe, 2002; Borio & White, 2003). In this approach the simultaneous development of endogenous financial imbalances, that is, an excessive credit expansion, a strong increase of stock prices and real-estate prices and an overinvestment of firms, plays a very crucial role. In this way the authors try very early to trace ex-ante indicators of financial instability in the economy. The authors emphasize the risk of a reversal of asset prices and its potential consequences for the macro economy and financial stability. They hold the view that "prevention is better than cure", giving priority to an early intervention of policymakers above an ex-post intervention with possible high macroeconomic costs when the bubble bursts abruptly. The authors analyze which combination of these indicators gives the best reliable forecast of the arise of a financial crisis within a different policy horizon. These indicators will be used as information variables in the monetary policy-decision process as soon as they surpass a threshold, determined by an historic long-term average value. In this context they introduce a "credit-gap", an "asset-price gap" and the Wicksellian "investment-gap" as indicators of financial imbalances.

The theoretical roots of this new approach in monetary policy go back to the Austrian School and the credit view (balance-sheet channel and the financial accelerator) on the one side and to the financial instability hypothesis of Minsky and Kindleberger on the other side. According to this view there exists a strong interaction between credit expansion, asset prices and the investment activity of the firms. This interaction can generate major booms and busts in credit and asset prices, which can amplify business cycles and derail monetary policy objectives, including price stability.

Although this research is still in its infancy, in this way it must be possible to make statements cautiously about the dangers associated with the accumulation of financial imbalances (Borio & Lowe, 2002; Borio & White, 2003). It will be possible to take care of financial stability more explicitly in the monetary policy strategy than is the case at present. Cecchetti call this approach a *"leaning-against-the-bubble strategy"*, which, next to the current inflation-targeting model, incorporates also issues from the Keynesian-Minsky model and the Austrian School.

In the past few years Issing has put forward that the policy strategy of the ECB (European Central Bank) not only gives attention to inflation forecasting, but that the first pillar of this strategy incorporates also the importance of an early accumulation of financial imbalances in the policy-decision process (Issing, 2002). He emphasizes that to focus only on inflation is not sufficient to guarantee monetary stability in the medium term. In this context he concludes, "The policy stance would be like the one advocated by new regime proponents, which is a tightening in the build-up phase of a positive bubble and easing after imbalances start to unwind in abrupt downward corrections" (Issing, 2002). Trichet expresses this view very recently in the following way, "Maintaining price stability in times of financial crises is a very difficult task. It is thus reasonable that the monetary authority monitors carefully unusual asset-price developments at an early stage" and further on, "... allowing some short-term deviation from price stability in order to better ensure price stability over more extended horizons might be under very restrictive assumptions the optimal policy to follow" (Trichet, 2005: p. 8).

22.8. A Synthesis Approach

In a very recent publication Disyatat (2005) attempts, to conceptualize the academic debate regarding the role of asset prices and perceived financial imbalances in the formation of monetary policy. In line with arguments made by Borio and Lowe (2002; 2003), the measure of financial imbalances adopted by the authorities is assumed to be a weighted average of asset prices and household debt, reflecting primarily bank credit expansion. It is assumed that concerns about financial imbalances become material only once they have surpassed some arbitrary threshold, determined by the central bank. In practice the weight given to financial imbalances is likely to depend on the perceived costs of an implosion in the future. The central objective of the author is not to make a case for or against a greater incorporation of asset prices or financial imbalances in the monetary policy framework, but to highlight the underlying basis from which the answer to this question should be made.

In the ongoing debate on asset prices and monetary policy there is now a shift to the middle ground, how to operationally utilize and respond to the information content of asset prices and financial imbalances within the inflation targeting framework (Bean, 2003). However there is a need to adjust this framework to be able to judge the various arguments (Disyatat, 2005). Disyatat tries to derive the optimal policy response explicitly by a consideration of financial imbalances in the central bank's loss function, next to the standard output and inflation concerns. In this way it will be possible by a more proactive monetary policy to prevent the risks associated with an unwinding of these financial imbalances in the future. It can be realized both by lengthening the policy horizon and, according to Greenspan's view, a greater emphasis on "balance-of-risk" considerations in the policy-decision process. The focus will be on policymakers' judgment about how asset prices and the build-up of perceived financial imbalances can affect future output and inflation, and thus the optimal policy setting. This judgemental view is the theoretical counterpart of the Bernanke-Gertler's conclusion, mentioned before, and is also consistent with the results of Cecchetti of a leaning against a suspected asset-price bubble in a Taylor-type policy rule (Section 22.4).

A rapid build-up of financial imbalances is believed to be masking both underlying inflationary pressures, when the boom is expected to continue, and even deflationary pressures when a large reversal of asset prices is expected. Thus any conceivable policy action to cushion the expected impact of asset prices or financial imbalances on output and inflation in the future can be accommodated through judgmental factors in a way that is consistent with the flexible-inflation targeting framework (Disyatat, 2005). According to Bernanke's view, this policy strategy means "*constrained discretion*" within the inflation-targeting framework. Policy changes must be justified on the basis of how this extra model-information about asset-price movements or perceived financial imbalances affects conditional forecasts of inflation and output.

To better incorporate the risk posed by financial imbalances, Disyatat proposes to lengthen the policy horizon and to lay a greater emphasis on "balance-of-risk" considerations. These proposals are fundamentally a reflection of dissatisfaction with this aspect of available forecasting models rather than the framework of inflation targeting *per se*. They are intended more as a communication device for justifying a rebalancing of policy priorities in the short run towards concerns related to financial imbalances. The author remarks, "In the context of a Taylor rule, according to this model optimal policy implies a response to asset prices over and above that indicated by output and inflation gaps only in so far as they contain information that has marginal bearing on future movements in output and inflation" (Disyatat, 2005: 9).

The author's optimal interest rate setting equation implies that when financial imbalances are deemed severe enough, the interest rate responds explicitly to the degree of perceived misalignment with a positive coefficient. In this context he points out. "Moreover, the greater the weight attached to financial imbalances, the lower the weights on output and inflation. Therefore, a trade-off now exists between price and output stability on the one hand and financial imbalances on the other" (Disyatat, 2005: 19).

Disyatat also deals with the crucial question what to do when asset-price movements or developments in financial imbalances may contain the seeds of a future disturbance of the economy should their development be out of line with the fundamentals. In this context he remarks, "… growing imbalances, if left unchecked, could have adverse consequences for the goals of monetary policy if and when they implode" (Disyatat, 2005: 15). This means that the identification of the bubble is less important than in the academic debate mentioned before, but that a proactive policy has to be implemented to pre-emptively lower the probability of a disruption occurring in the first place. In this way a reduction of the risk of financial instability in the future may result (Sijben, 2004).

Disyatat's approach is a synthesis of the academic debate, because it is based on the view of the world where boom–bust cycles are not only strongly linked to financial imbalances, but also to the fact that the likelihood and severity of an implosion can be influenced by monetary policy. These two issues can be incorporated in monetary policy by both using financial imbalances today as an additional transmission channel in monetary policy and a modification of the central bank's loss function to explicitly include a concern for financial imbalances in addition to output and inflation. In this context the author points out, "financial imbalances become an additional intermediate target, which is traded-off against inflation and output forecasts" (Disyatat, 2005: 26).

22.9. Summarizing Conclusion

Based on the recent stimulating academic debate and the several views and expressions of policymakers, I hold the view that an appropriate monetary policy in an uncertain macroeconomic environment, with a strong "psychological behavior in finance", should not only be based on the forecasts with regard to inflation and output, but also on the risks surrounding these forecasts. As yet, the flexible inflation-targeting strategy presents a consistent policy framework with sufficient discretionary room for the judgmental issue with regard to the impact of financial imbalances on macroeconomic development. However, this implies according to Disyatat's synthesis approach a *pragmatic view*, emphasizing both a longer policy horizon than usual to include an asset-price cycle in the policy-decision process and a "balance-of-risk strategy" with regard to the most likely macroeconomic outcomes of the different policy actions. A lengthening of the policy horizon can lead to a better assessment of the "balance-of-risks" and an improvement of the communication with the public. Irrespective of how pre-emptive policy actions are motivated within a monetary policy framework, the practical implication is that greater tolerance will be accorded to departures of inflation from target. Therefore the central bank has to take into account an additional trade-off between price and output stability on the one side and financial imbalances on the other side, either implicitly in the transmission mechanism or explicitly, in Disyatat's sense, through a modification of its loss function.

This pragmatic approach implies that policymakers can react to macroeconomic risks associated with the build-up of financial imbalances, even if there is no threatening of monetary stability in the short run. In this way a hidden and masking overheating of the economy can be avoided in an early stage of the business cycle and the downward risks can be constrained. I agree with Bean's conclusion that, "A forward-looking inflation targeting central bank should bear in mind those longer-run consequences of asset-price bubbles and financial imbalances in the setting of current interest rates" (Bean, 2004). This conclusion implies that this author, just like Crockett, Trichet, Issing and other policymakers, are moving gradually in the direction of the new view that giving priority only to monetary stability is not a sufficient prerequisite to prevent financial and macroeconomic instability. However Bean emphasizes that this view requires a *"shift in the rhetoric of inflation fighter"* (Bean, 2003). That means that central banks will be faced with a communication problem. They have to present quite a new message to financial markets, which has to be explained in a transparent and credible way (Friedman, 2002). In the new view it is possible that in some circumstances an early intervention by increasing the rate of interest has to be implemented even when inflation in the short run is lower than the target.

It can be put forward that since the mid-1990s central banks have given more attention to the issues of transparency and communication in monetary policymaking, abandoning the tradition of monetary secrecy. This shift is associated very closely with both central banks' accountability and the lessons of the sixties and seventies that rational economic agents don't like to be fooled by the policymaker (Sijben, 1979).

Finally it can be concluded that a simultaneous anchoring of monetary and financial stability needs a sharp analytical analysis of the following two questions. First, to what extent are stock prices driven by non-fundamentals (equity-risk premium) and what is its interaction with the business cycle? Second, what are the macroeconomic costs in terms of a loss of output and employment of an unwinding or implosion of financial imbalances? This means that still a lot of research has to be done to give an adequate reaction on the old phenomenon of a boom–bust cycle in asset prices in quite a new international competitive financial environment, a world of "global finance" with a low and stable rate of inflation. However the task ahead should not be underestimated.

References

BIS (2005). Annual Report.

Amato, J. (2005). *The role of the natural rate of interest in monetary policy*. Working paper BIS.

Bernanke, B., & Gertler, M. (1999). *Monetary policy and asset price volatility*. Conference, Federal Reserve Bank of Kansas City.

Bernanke, B., & Gertler, M. (2001). Should central banks respond to movements in asset prices? *American Economic Review*, 91, 253–257.

Bernanke, B. (2002). *Asset-price "bubbles" and monetary policy*. Speech, New York.

Bernanke, B. (2003b). *A perspective on inflation targeting*. Speech, Washington, DC.

Bernanke, B. (2002). *Deflation: Making sure that "it" doesn't happen here*. Speech, Washington, DC.

Bernanke, B. (2005). *Reflections on monetary policy, 25 years after October 1979*. Conference, Review Federal Reserve Bank of St. Louis.

Bean, Ch. (2003). *Asset prices, financial imbalances and monetary policy: Are inflation targets enough?* Conference, Basel.

Bean, Ch. (2004). *Asset prices, monetary policy and financial stability: A central banker's view.* Conference, San Diego.

Bordo, M., & Jeanne O. (2002). *Monetary policy and asset prices: Does "Benign Neglect" make sense?* Working paper IMF.

Borio, C., & Lowe P. (2002). *Asset prices, financial and monetary stability: Exploring the nexus.* Working paper BIS.

Borio, C., & White, W. (2003). *Whether monetary and financial stability? The implications of evolving policy regimes.* Conference, Federal Reserve Bank of Kansas City.

Borio, C., & Lowe, P. (2003). *Securing sustainable price stability: Should credit comeback from the wilderness?* ECB-Workshop.

Borio, C., & Filardo, A. (2004). *Back to the future? Assessing the deflation record.* Working paper BIS.

Brainard, W. (1967). Uncertainty and the effectiveness of monetary policy. *American Economic Review*, 57, 411–425.

Cecchetti, S., Genberg, H., Lipsky, J., & Whadwani, S. (2000). *Asset prices and central bank policy.* Discussion paper CEPR.

Crockett, A. (2000). *In search of anchors for financial and monetary stability.* Speech SUERF-conference, Wenen.

Disyatat, P. (2005). *Inflation targeting, asset prices and financial imbalances: Conceptualizing the debate*. Working paper BIS.

Friedman, B. (2002). *The use and meaning of words in central banking: Inflation targeting, credibility and transparency*. Working paper NBER.

Greenspan, A. (2000). *Structural changes in the economy and financial markets*. Speech, New York.

Greenspan, A. (2002). *Economic volatility*. Speech, Conference, Federal Reserve Bank of Kansas City.

Greenspan, A. (2003). *Monetary policy and uncertainty*. Speech, Conference, Federal Reserve Bank of Kansas City.

Greenspan, A. (2004). *Risk and uncertainty in monetary policy*. Speech, San Diego.

Greenspan, A. (2005). *Reflections on central banking*. Speech, Conference, Federal Reserve Bank of Kansas City.

Haberler, G. (1932). Money and the business cycle. In: Q. Wright (Ed.), *Gold and monetary stabilization*. Chicago: University of Chicago Press.

Issing, O. (2002). *Monetary policy in a changing economic environment*. Conference, Federal Reserve Bank of Kansas City.

Issing, O. (2003). *Monetary and financial stability: Is there a trade-off?* Conference, Bazel.

Issing, O. (2005). *Communication, transparency, accountability; monetary policy in the twenty-first century*. Review Federal Reserve Bank of St. Louis.

Kindleberger, Ch. (1978). *Manias, panics and crashes: A history of financial crisis*. New York: Basic Books.

Krugman, P. (1998). It's baack! Japan's slump and the return of the liquidity trap. *Brookings Papers on Economic Activity*, 49, 137–206.

Kydland, F., & Prescott, E. (1977). Rules rather than discretion: The inconsistency of optimal plans. *Journal of Political Economy, 85,* 473–490.

Miller, M., Weller, P., & Zhang, L. (2002). Moral Hazard and the US-stock market: Analyzing the Greenspan Put. *Economic Journal*, 112, 171–186.

Minsky, H. (1980). Capitalist financial processes and the instability of capitalism. *Journal of Economic Issues* ,14, No. 2.

Minsky, H. (1982). *Can "It" happen again?* New York: ME Sharpe.

Robinson, T., & Stone, A. (2005). *Monetary policy, asset-price bubble and the zero lower bound*. Working paper NBER.

Schwartz, A. (1995). Why financial stability depends on price stability. *Economic Affairs Autumn*, 21–25.

Sijben, J. (1979). *Rational expectations and monetary policy*. Germantown, USA.

Sijben, J. (2004). *Monetary and financial stability: Revisited*. Farewell Speech, Tilburg University.

Trichet, J. (2004). *Monetary and financial stability in a non-inflationary environment*. Speech, Hamburg.

Trichet, J. (2005). *Asset price bubbles and monetary policy*. Speech, Singapore.

Wicksell, J. (1936) In: R. Kahn (Transl.), *Interest and prices* (1st ed.). London: Macmillan (Jena, Germany).

Yamaguchi, Y. (1999). *Asset prices and monetary policy: Japan's experience*. Conference, Federal Reserve Bank of Kansas City.

Author Index

Subject Index